CW01108823

The Church of Mary Tudor

The Church of Mary Tudor

Edited by
EAMON DUFFY and DAVID LOADES

ASHGATE

© The contributors, 2006

All rights reserved. No part of this publication may be reproduced, stored in a retrieval system, or transmitted in any form or by any means, electronic, mechanical, photocopying, recording or otherwise without the prior permission of the publisher.

Eamon Duffy and David Loades have asserted their moral right under the Copyright, Designs and Patents Act, 1988, to be identified as Editors of this Work.

Published by
Ashgate Publishing Limited
Gower House
Croft Road
Aldershot
Hants GU11 3HR
England

Ashgate Publishing Company
Suite 420
101 Cherry Street
Burlington
VT 05401-4405
USA

Ashgate website: http://www.ashgate.com

British Library Cataloguing in Publication Data
The church of Mary Tudor. – (Catholic Christendom, 1300–1700)
1. Mary, I, Queen of England, 1516–1558 – Religion 2. Pole, Reginald, 1500–1558 3. Catholic Church – England – History – 16th century 4. England – Church history – 16th century
I. Duffy, Eamon II. Loades, D.M.
274.2'06

Library of Congress Cataloging-in-Publication Data
The church of Mary Tudor / edited by Eamon Duffy and David Loades.
    p. cm – (Catholic Christendom, 1300–1700)
  Includes bibliographical references and index.
  ISBN 0-7546-3070-6 (alk. paper)
1. England – Church history – 16th century. 2. Catholic Church – England – History – 16th century. 3. Mary I, Queen of England, 1516–1558 – Religion. I. Duffy, Eamon. II. Loades, D. M. III. Series

    BX1492.C53 2005
    274.2'06–dc22

2004024643

ISBN 0 7546 3070 6

Typeset by Bournemouth Colour Press, Parkstone, Poole.
Printed and bound in Great Britain by TJ International.

Contents

List of Tables	vii
List of Contributors	viii
Series Editor's Preface	ix
Editors' Introduction	xi
List of Abbreviations	xxvi

Introduction: The Personal Religion of Mary I   1
David Loades

Part I: The Process

1. The Marian Episcopate   33
   David Loades

2. The English Universities, 1553–58   57
   Claire Cross

3. Westminster Abbey Restored   77
   C.S. Knighton

4. The Clergy, the Church Courts and the Marian Restoration in Norwich   124
   Ralph Houlbrooke

Part II: Cardinal Pole

5. The Success of Cardinal Pole's Final Legation   149
   Thomas F. Mayer

6. Cardinal Pole Preaching: St Andrew's Day 1557   176
   Eamon Duffy

7 Spanish Religious Influence in Marian England 201
   John Edwards

Part III: The Culture

8 The Marian Restoration and the Mass 227
   Lucy Wooding

9 The Theology and Spirituality of a Marian Bishop: the
   Pastoral and Polemical Sermons of Thomas Watson 258
   William Wizeman, SJ

10 Marking the Days: Henry Machyn's Manuscript and the
   Mid-Tudor Era 281
   Gary G. Gibbs

11 The Persecution in Kent 309
   Patrick Collinson

Index 334

List of Tables

3.1	Ordinations at London 1557–58 with reference to Westminster Abbey	86
5.1	Appeals by type of court and year	150
5.2	Appeals beginning with Pole's return in 1554 through 1555, by month	151
5.3	Appeals in 1557 by month	153
5.4	Appeals by diocese (raw numbers)	154
5.5	Appeals from York by year	160
5.6	Appeals from London by year, including those reserved but not filed	160

List of Contributors

Patrick Collinson, FBA is Regius Professor Emeritus of Modern History at the University of Cambridge.

Claire Cross is Professor Emerita of History at the University of York.

Eamon Duffy is President of Magdalene College, Cambridge, and Professor of the History of the Christian Religion at the University of Cambridge.

John Edwards, formerly Reader in Spanish History at the University of Birmingham, is now Research Fellow in Spanish at the University of Oxford.

Gary G. Gibbs is Associate Professor of History at Roanoake College, Virginia.

Ralph Houlbrooke is Professor of History at the University of Reading.

C.S. Knighton is Deputy Editor of the Catalogue of the Pepys Library at Magdalene College, Cambridge, and an editor for the National Archives.

David Loades is Emeritus Professor of the University of Wales, Honorary Research Professor at the University of Sheffield and Director of the British Academy John Foxe Project.

Thomas F. Mayer is Professor of History at Augustana College, Rock Island, Illinois.

William Wizeman, SJ is Assistant Professor of History at Fordham University, New York.

Lucy Wooding is Lecturer in History at King's College, London.

Series Editor's Preface

The still-usual emphasis on medieval (or Catholic) and Reformation (or Protestant) religious history has meant neglect of the middle ground, both chronological and ideological. As a result, continuities between the Middle Ages and early modern Europe have been overlooked in favour of emphasis on radical discontinuities. Further, especially in the later period, the identification of 'Reformation' with various kinds of Protestantism means that the vitality and creativity of the established Church, whether in its Roman or local manifestations, have been left out of account. In the last few years, an upsurge of interest in the history of traditional (or Catholic) religion makes these inadequacies in received scholarship even more glaring and in need of systematic correction. The series will attempt this by covering all varieties of religious behaviour, broadly interpreted, not just (or even especially) traditional institutional and doctrinal Church history. It will to the maximum degree possible be interdisciplinary, comparative and global, as well as non-confessional. The goal is to understand religion, primarily of the 'Catholic' variety, as a broadly human phenomenon, rather than as a privileged mode of access to superhuman realms, even implicitly.

The period covered, 1300–1700, embraces the moment which saw an almost complete transformation of the place of religion in the life of Europeans, whether considered as a system of beliefs, as an institution or as a set of social and cultural practices. In 1300, vast numbers of Europeans, from the Pope down, fully expected Jesus' return and the beginning of His reign on earth. By 1700, very few Europeans, of whatever level of education, would have subscribed to such chiliastic beliefs. Pierre Bayle's notorious sarcasms about signs and portents are not idiosyncratic. Likewise, in 1300 the vast majority of Europeans probably regarded the Pope as their spiritual head; the institution he headed was probably the most tightly integrated and effective bureaucracy in Europe. Most Europeans were at least nominally Christian, and the Pope had at least nominal knowledge of that fact. The papacy, as an institution, played a central role in high politics, and the clergy in general formed an integral part of most governments, whether central or local. By 1700, Europe was divided into a myriad different religious allegiances, and even those areas officially subordinate to the Pope were both more nominally Catholic in belief (despite colossal efforts at imposing uniformity) and also in allegiance than they had been 400 years earlier. The Pope had become only one political factor, and not one of the first rank. The clergy, for its part, had virtually disappeared from secular governments, as well as losing much of its local authority. The stage was set for the Enlightenment.

Thomas F. Mayer,
Augustana College

Editors' Introduction

The historiography of the Marian Church, like that of the reign as a whole, has been not so much chequered as stereotyped. In the long perspective of history, the most important thing about the Catholic restoration was that it was aborted by Mary's death without heirs of her body, in November 1558. It took about 20 years for the decisiveness of that outcome to become apparent, and much longer before Protestants ceased to worry about Catholic conspiracies, or Catholics to dream of a reversal of fortune.[1] For at least two centuries the historiography was straightforwardly polemical. To John Foxe, struggling in Elizabeth's reign to give the new Protestant establishment credibility, Mary had been the hapless and deluded victim of a sacerdotal conspiracy. To Nicholas Harpsfield she had been the model of a godly ruler, undermined and frustrated by the foul machinations of heretics.[2] Because the Protestant establishment eventually took root, myths of the pre- and non-Roman origins of British Christianity took root along with it, and because Pius V effectively declared war on Elizabeth in 1570, the Roman Church began to be associated, first with rebellion and assassination, and then with foreign invasion and the threat of 'arbitrary government'. By 1600 Protestantism had become an entrenched aspect of England's national identity, and the historiography of Mary's reign had settled into the pattern which it would retain almost to the present. To the majority who defended the establishment, Mary was at best the victim of Spanish manipulation, at worst a wicked tyrant who had tried to defy the 'manifest destiny' of a Protestant realm. To those who sought to justify her actions, on the other hand, she presented a hardly less formidable problem. How could so resolute a defender of God's truth have been so cruelly abandoned?

To say that she had thereafter a 'loser's press' is to state the obvious, but it is more important to notice how tenacious both traditions have been, long outlasting the conflicts which gave them real relevance. When the ninth and last of the old editions of John Foxe's *Acts and Monuments* was published in 1684, it was still a piece of occasional propaganda with

---

[1] See particularly John Bossy, *The English Catholic Community, 1570–1850* (London, 1975), 11–77.
[2] *Dialogi Sex contra Summi Pontificatus ... ab Alano Copo Anglo* [Nicholas Harpsfield] *editi*, 1566.

a contemporary political resonance; but the same could hardly be said of the bitter dispute between S.R. Maitland, the librarian of Lambeth, and the editors which accompanied the next major edition in 1837.[3] The polarity between John Strype and Charles Dodd in the early eighteenth century was hardly greater than that between John Lingard and J.A. Froude in the middle of the nineteenth, or that between Philip Hughes and Geoffrey Dickens in the middle of the twentieth. At the centre of these divisions lay and lies the Marian persecutions.

To John Foxe, the campaign to root out Protestantism by force and fire was the wicked murdering of the saints of God; to Nicholas Harpsfield or Robert Parsons, the infliction of just punishment for crimes against the law, English law as well as the law of the Church.[4] To the derivatives of Foxe which appeared at regular intervals in the eighteenth and early nineteenth centuries, the slaughter was the inevitable result of allowing foreign papists to run the country. For Geoffrey Dickens, the persecutions were the sign of a regime utterly out of touch with political reality, as well as with human decency, a sign of 'the madness of a system which could burn a virtuous human being for his inability to accept a metaphysical theory'.[5] To Philip Hughes, the majority of the victims were in any case radicals who would have been equally readily dispatched by any contemporary government, Catholic or Protestant. All these judgements were coloured by confessional allegiance, and until the early twentieth century conflicting interpretations were often linked to explicitly denominational agendas. Such sectarian contests are no longer considered a respectable use of history, but they have proved a remarkably resilient if sometimes subterranean influence on the historiography of the Reformation, and of the Marian episode in particular.

But if the Marian regime has always been most vulnerable to criticism on the strength of the burning of Protestants, negative judgements based on analogies with the queen's own unhappy life and personality have run those based on persecution a close second. Pollard's judgement on the ultimate 'sterility' of the regime and all its outcomes has proved if anything a more insidious historiographical influence, because less obviously religiously *parti pris*.[6] If the time has come to abandon

---

[3] Andrew Penny, 'John Foxe, Evangelicalism and the Oxford Movement', in D. Loades, ed., *John Foxe: An Historical Perspective* (Aldershot, 1999), 182–237.

[4] It has to be remembered that parliament in 1555 revived the early fifteenth-century statute *De Heretico Comburendo*, which had been repealed by Edward VI. This made heresy a statutory offence, and not simply an ecclesiastical one.

[5] A.G. Dickens, *The English Reformation* (London, 1964), 271.

[6] Expressed and elaborated in *The History of England from the Accession of Edward VI to the death of Elizabeth* (London, 1913).

denominational agendas, it is also essential that we attempt to appraise the policies and achievements of the 1550s without the benefit of hindsight. We know that Mary was to die young and childless in 1558, and that Elizabeth was to reign for 45 years. Neither eventuality could have been predicted in Marian England, yet we are prone to judge the policies of Mary's government, ecclesiastical and secular, as if she and her servants should or could have known that they had only five years to achieve their objectives. Recent scholarship, it is true, has changed the agenda in many ways. We no longer believe that the traditional Church was deeply and widely unpopular by 1547, or that significant numbers of people were simply waiting for Edward's council to sweep it away. Nor do we believe that Mary made herself so unpopular that the entire country greeted Elizabeth's accession with a huge sigh of relief. Measured against the upheavals and religious violence of Edward's reign, or the contradictions and uncertainties of religious policy in Elizabeth's early years, the Marian Church no longer looks so straightforwardly ineffectual.[7] And, as a flood of recent work on Foxe makes clear, not least Patrick Collinson's chapter in this book, it is no longer so obvious that John Foxe was always right about the popularity, the godliness or even the orthodox Protestantism of all his martyrs.[8] On the contrary, we know that persecution might be the product of local score-settling as well as of official policy, and that there was often grass-roots support for draconian measures against unpopular Protestant activists. Mary herself was hugely popular in 1553, not least because she stood for traditional religion; and there was considerable pastoral inventiveness in the restored Catholic Church, an impressive episcopate and an efficient ecclesiastical machine.

However, amid so much revision, certain historiographical landmarks have not moved, and that also needs to be recognized. The queen's marriage was unpopular at all levels of society; the persecution itself, whatever its local endorsements, was unprecedented in its scale and severity, and in many places seems to have been alienating even to Catholics and conformists. The event would prove that there was no lay party in the parliament of 1559 committed enough, or at any rate strong enough to prevent Elizabeth from abolishing the whole Marian achievement. What is now needed, therefore, is not so much a self-

---

[7] Cf. D. MacCulloch, *Tudor Church Militant: Edward VI and the Protestant Reformation* (London, 1999); and N. Jones, *The Birth of the Elizabethan Age: England in the 1560s* (Cambridge, Mass., 1993).

[8] See Chapter 11, this volume; also John King, 'Fiction and Fact in Foxe's Book of Martyrs', in D. Loades, ed., *John Foxe and the English Reformation* (Aldershot, 1997), 12–35.

conscious attempt to abandon old sectarian or historiographical agendas, as a fresh attempt to locate the events of 1553–58 in the cultural context to which they belong. The fairest comparison is not with the Elizabethan Church, which had such a long run, but with the Edwardian, which was of similar duration. Given its radical (and, in much of England, unpopular) nature, the Edwardian achievement was remarkable; but Mary overturned it in a matter of weeks.[9] Then, starting from a Henrician base, which was not always sympathetic, she reconstructed an orthodox Catholic Church in an even shorter space of time than Edward had, a success which should not be obscured by the fact that it was itself to prove short-lived. How deep-rooted that success would have proved is hard to say, for historians in the nature of things are mostly concerned with externals, and counterfactual speculation about how events could or should have been managed differently is of limited use as a historical tool. Whereof we cannot speak, thereof we must be silent. The Marian Church cared passionately about orthodoxy but, as with the Edwardian or Elizabethan regimes, we have little direct evidence for Mary's and Cardinal Pole's success in converting – or recovering – hearts and minds. What the mass of people believed remains and is likely to remain elusive. We are on surer ground in assessing what they were persuaded or constrained to accept, how they behaved, and the impact of politics and political culture on their behaviour.

But we are in any case coming to appreciate more fully the value of public behaviour as an indicator of political and religious success. Historians were once by and large dismissive of the apparently endless succession of Marian processions and pageants chronicled by Henry Machyn, seeing in them evidence of the superficial obsession of the Marian regime with the enforcement of mere externals, a sort of ritual fiddling while London burned. Henry Machyn, our main source for this London pageantry, was a conservative with a distaste for heretical notions, but hardly a doctrinal zealot – he chronicled 'godly' official religious events in the reigns of Edward and Elizabeth as well as those commanded by Mary,[10] 'never made an explicitly dogmatic or doctrinal statement' and, for all his conservatism, admitted scarcely a hint of disapproval into his descriptions of the quite different public face of Edwardian or Elizabethan worship. It would be hard to tell from his sparse and factual narrative whether or not he had any sympathy with

---

[9] D. Loades, *The Reign of Mary Tudor* (London, 1991), 96–128. E. Duffy, *The Stripping of the Altars* (New Haven, 1992), pp. 524–64.

[10] See Chapter 10. J.G. Nichols, ed. *The Diary of Henry Machyn* (Camden Society, 1848).

those who followed Thomas Wyatt, or suffered at Smithfield. Machyn was not a man to espouse lost causes, or to stick his head above the parapet. He was, in short, a very typical London citizen, and Professor Gibbs's study here should remind us that we are not looking at a country divided into predefined camps of Catholics and Protestants, no matter what proportions we assign to them, but rather at communities caught in unprecedented religious flux, concerned to obey the law, to protect their identity and to manage their lives in difficult times.[11]

Nevertheless, as Professor Gibbs's essay makes clear, Machyn's 'celebratory' response to such ceremonial Marian 'representations of the regime' should not be dismissed as superficial or unimportant. Machyn, far more than the defiant adherents of the tiny London Protestant underground congregations, was indeed a representative citizen, whose life was bound up with and articulated by the civic pageantry of London, a pageantry which in Mary's reign seems to have blended seamlessly back into the pageantry of the old Church. On the evidence of Machyn's chronicle, the Marian regime's concern to rebuild the ritual life of London was a mark of shrewd engagement with the concerns and tastes of the citizens of the capital, not of unreal distance from them. Communities, both urban and rural, were defined by their rituals, and to attack or reject those rituals was in Tudor England considered both revolutionary and anti-social. In Elizabeth's reign this kind of conservatism would appear unhelpful to theologically committed ideologues, Catholic and Protestant alike, because it both hindered the more drastic changes which reforming Protestants wished to make, and obscured the theological principles upon which recusant Catholic clergy sought to persuade the people to abandon a schismatic or heretical conformity. Under Mary, however, ceremonial reconstruction along traditional lines was probably one of the regime's strongest popular cards.

This collection of essays does not claim to be the comprehensive rewriting of the history of the Marian Church which some have called for, but it is a modest step in that direction. There is no single agenda, except that of trying to get the story right. The contributors do not necessarily agree with each other, or with the editors, and the essays cover what we hope are some of the most central concerns of the Marian Church from a number of different angles. Thus the centrality of the sacraments, and particularly of the Mass, to the devotional life and self-identity of the Church is the subject not only of Dr Wooding's study of Marian writing about the Eucharist, but of Dr Wizeman's examination

---

[11] Nichols, *The Diary of Henry Machyn*.

of the works of Thomas Watson: it looms large, too, in David Loades's account of the queen's personal faith. Careful readers of all three essays, however, will detect marked differences of emphasis and perception in exploring this common theme.[12]

Several of the essays reconsider, on the whole favourably, the objectives and competence of Cardinal Pole, whose English career, while escaping the obloquy that has surrounded the actions of the queen he so much revered, has by and large been damned with faint praise. Although he influenced the first year of the reign only indirectly, the priorities of Reginald Pole as cardinal legate and as Archbishop of Canterbury are central to any understanding of the Marian Church as a whole. Professor Mayer's essay represents a significant reappraisal of Pole's effectiveness as legate, based upon a careful examination of the processes which he controlled.[13] Pole may have been thought unworldly, both at the time and since, but his use of both judicial and administrative methods to achieve his ends were, Mayer argues, worthy of a skilled politician and of a committed and alert Counter-Reformation prelate. As Professor Cross shows, he was also the driving force behind the conversion of the universities, both of them heavily penetrated by Protestantism during the previous reign. According to her, his legatine visitations proved a 'watershed' in converting both centres, and especially Oxford, into the strongholds of Catholic learning which were to cause so much trouble to Elizabeth.[14] Pole's concern with the orthodoxy of the universities should not surprise: one of his central strategies, in fact, was the provision of adequate theological education for the clergy, as the foundation of a revived Catholic practice for the laity. Like Thomas More, whose writings supplied the Marian Church with much of its apologetic and polemical armoury, Pole was deeply distrustful of the explosion of religious debate which the reformation had stimulated, and which had led to drastic challenges to the teaching authority of the Church and to the standing of its clergy. Pole recognized the urgent need to instruct the laity in the Catholic faith, and his legatine synod took vigorous and imaginative steps to secure an educated preaching episcopate and parish clergy, and to provide a supply of orthodox printed catechetical and homilitic material for the use of priests unable to generate their own. But though he had a sophisticated humanist appreciation of the value of the Bible and of preaching, Pole condemned undirected Bible-reading and sermon-gadding, especially when the preachers were unauthorized, or worse, of questionable

---

[12] See Chapters 8, 9 and Introduction, this volume.
[13] See Chapter 5.
[14] See Chapter 2.

orthodoxy, and when, as he believed was often the case in London, the listeners were more interested in novelty or entertainment than in conversion of the heart. In line with the Council of Trent's teaching on the value of tradition, the restoration of the faith was for him and his coadjutors an endeavour in which sacramental discipline was deemed to be just as important as Bible-reading or preaching.[15] Sound belief was impossible without sound practice, because it was in humble and receptive participation in the Sacraments and sacramentals of the Church, and in obedience to her teaching, that true faith was embodied and manifest.

These reservations have been widely held by historians to have blinded Pole to the urgency of providing Catholic preaching and preachers, and of re-educating the Tudor laity in Catholic orthodoxy. He has been accused of nourishing a complacent conviction that all that was needed to reverse the Reformation was the reimposition of external cult. Eamon Duffy here re-examines this assumption. He argues that the belief that Pole distrusted and discouraged preaching is based on a misreading of his correspondence with Bartolomé Carranza. In fact, Pole believed preaching to be the principal duty of bishops and priests, and insisted on the centrality to his own strategy and that of the Church at large not only of regular and frequent preaching, but also of printed catechetical and polemical writings, which were essential to undo the havoc inflicted by a generation of Protestant preaching and pamphleteering. His own English sermons reveal a topicality and engagement with current events and controversies, and a polemical directness and clarity, startlingly at odds with the received historiography.[16]

The Marian Church thus had more features of strength than it has been generally given credit for. Thomas Watson was probably its ablest pastoral and theological writer, but he was by no means the only one. Pastoral and polemical concerns are here explored in Professor Duffy's analysis of Pole's St Andrew's Day sermon, Dr Wizeman's study of Watson's writings and Dr Wooding's exploration of the diversity of forms in which the Marian Church presented the centrality of the Eucharist. Dr Wizeman's demonstration that Watson made use of the decrees of Trent[17] and Dr John Edwards's exploration of the influence of Spanish theologians, above all Bartolomeo Carranza, on the Marian Church, anchor these English concerns firmly within the wider context of the early stages of the

---

[15] See Chapter 6, this volume; also Duffy, *Stripping of the Altars*, 543–54.
[16] Ibid. For a more traditional view of Pole's priorities, see Loades, *The Reign of Mary I*, 297–8.
[17] See Chapter 9.

European Counter Reformation.[18] As all these essays suggest, the conclusion drawn several years ago by Jennifer Loach, that the clergy of the Marian restoration took their responsibilities seriously in respect of a flock which had been without orthodox guidance for more than a generation, looks increasingly secure.[19] Whether they were as successful in converting the heretic or convincing the sceptic as they were in strengthening the faith of the sympathetic is a different and perhaps unanswerable question, but it is clear that the sympathetic were in a large majority.

Having said that, the extent both of Nicodemism, the merely external conformity of secretly convinced Protestants, and of more genuine changes of heart in a period of religious upheaval and flux, is unquantifiable, and Professor Houlbrooke's study of Norwich should warn us against making facile assumptions. Norwich was perhaps unusual in having its leading Edwardian preacher submit so decisively and apparently sincerely, but he was probably a more representative figure than the many more resolute resisters who feature in the pages of Foxe. As in other cities, Norwich's leading citizens conformed, more or less rapidly, in 1553 no less than in 1547 or 1559. On this evidence alone, one should no more conclude that such reversals reflected zealous Catholicism than that they were the mark of committed heresy.[20] Just as the events of 1553–54 appear to have tipped many waverers into conformity, and demoralized many more resolute Protestants with the conviction that their efforts had been inadequate in the sight of God, so the reversals of 1558–59 must have had a similar impact on many conservatives. Only the most zealous on both sides treated these setbacks as calls to labour more earnestly 'under the cross'. Loyalty to the Crown, and perhaps a certain fatalism, were to prove more decisive determinants of general behaviour than theological commitment or devotional conservatism. No one here has assessed the impact of either war or influenza upon the attitudes of ordinary people, but they form a background which should not be ignored. A generation accustomed (and taught) to interpret Divine favour by reading the signs of prosperity and adversity may well have begun to wonder about Mary and her policies. Staunch partisans like Miles Huggarde might attribute England's misfortunes in 1558 to the ingratitude of wicked heretics, but it is unlikely that the population at large saw it that way.[21] It was the

---

[18] See Chapter 7.

[19] J. Loach, 'The Marian Establishment and the Printing Press', *English Historical Review*, 101 (1986), 135–48.

[20] See Chapter 4. On Nicodemites in general, see Andrew Pettegree, 'Nicodemism and the English Reformation', in *Marian Protestantism: Six Studies* (Aldershot, 1996), 86–117.

[21] Miles Huggarde [Hogarde], *The Displayinge of the Protestauntes* (London, 1556).

queen who was unfortunate; a situation doubtless more likely to be attributed to her fondness for Spaniards than to her devotion to the Mass, but harvest failure, epidemic disease and the loss of Calais undoubtedly reduced morale in the summer of 1558. That, of course, was not the fault of the Church. However, a determined stand by a resolutely Catholic laity, both in the City and in parliament, could have changed the shape of the Elizabethan settlement drastically. It did not come, not because most were secret Protestants 'wishing for [their] Elizabeth', but in part at least because of the clouds of depression and uncertainty which accompanied Mary's death.

In November 1558 both committed Protestants and committed Roman Catholics were probably small minorities. Though most people were conservative, happy enough with the Marian Church's restoration of the old religion, they were not necessarily equally supportive of the hierarchy's firm but cautious papalism, and certainly less so of the regime's Spanish entanglements. In the event most proved fatalistic; willing to accommodate themselves to whatever the new queen and parliament might now decree. That, of course, was not the same thing as enthusiasm, and Elizabeth's council knew for years that it was skating on thin ice. That was why the queen was so reluctant to force issues, or to allow Protestant zealots to pursue those who celebrated clandestine Masses. The fact is that we do not know what most people thought of the state of the Church in November 1558; we only know what they did about it. In parliament only the attitude of Mary's bishops distinguished the defence of the Catholic establishment in 1559 from the defence of the Protestant establishment in 1553. And whatever the popularity of Mary's Catholic restoration, in the country at large, if we can count the Wyatt rebellion as even partly religious in inspiration, until 1569 there was actually more overt resistance to Mary than there was to Elizabeth.[22] Such ambivalences are perhaps to be expected among the laity: it is more surprising to discover an ambivalence, or at any rate flexibility, even at the highest levels of the Church. Although Mary's treatment of her leading episcopal opponents was both drastic and high

---

Sir Thomas Smith (admittedly a Protestant) wrote: 'God did so punish the realm with quartan agues, and with other long and new sicknesses, that in the last two years of the reign of Queen Mary, so many of her subjects were made away, what with the execution of sword and fire, what by sickness, that the third part of the men of England were consumed.' This sort of exaggeration, perpetuated by Foxe, passed into national mythology, but it was not altogether invented.

[22] M.R. Thorpe, 'Religion and the Rebellion of Sir Thomas Wyatt', *Church History*, 47, 4 (1978). The rebellion of 1569 (the 'Northern earls') was certainly religious in its inspiration, but was complicated by having two separate agendas, one papalist, one merely conservative.

profile, a surprising number of those bishops who had accepted the Edwardian settlement continued to serve her. These were men whose episcopal orders went back to before 1550 (no one consecrated under the new ordinal of that year was considered validly ordained), and most had conformed to the Protestant establishment reluctantly. Nevertheless they had so conformed, and it was not until the last two years of the reign that even a majority of the bench were men of the queen's own choosing. To what extent this blunted the efforts of Pole and Stephen Gardiner (himself, of course, compromised by his Henrician conformity) is hard to say. Many of these inherited Henrician and Edwardine conformists were administrators rather than spiritual leaders, and they were effective in that mode, but if anything up to 50 per cent of the episcopal team were effectively civil servants, so it would be surprising if the call to faith was not compromised.[23] By the end of the reign, however, the overhauled bench was a highly respectable body, committed to the Roman allegiance no less than to traditional theology, as their refusal to serve under Elizabeth would demonstrate. It had been an uphill task to achieve that degree of firmness and unanimity. Nevertheless, the transformation in less than five years of the Marian episcopate along lines laid down in the decrees of Pole's legatine synod was by any reckoning a notable achievement, one of the earliest and most effective renovations of a national episcopate anywhere in Counter-Reformation Europe.[24]

One of the least explored features of the Marian Church was Spanish influence. Despite the high profile of Philip and his entourage in general assessments of the reign, Dr John Edwards argues here that the presence of influential Spanish ecclesiastics was a far greater factor in the Marian religious restoration than has generally been appreciated. Not only were there numerous Spanish chaplains and confessors at court, but some of them, like Bartolomé Carranza, were men of distinction and real intellectual and strategic influence. A few were placed in university chairs or cathedral prebends, but most would have been unknown to the rank and file, whether clerical or lay.[25] It is consequently a mistake to suppose that the English court was untouched by the theology and intellectual priorities of the Counter Reformation. Whatever Pole's earlier reservations about the Tridentine decree on Justification, by the time of his legatine mission he had come to terms with it, and in theologians like Carranza, de Soto and Villagarcia he found congenial

---

[23] See Chapter 1, this volume.

[24] T.F. Mayer, *Reginald Pole: Prince and Prophet* (Yale, 2002). See also Duffy, *Stripping of the Altars*, 527–37.

[25] See Chapter 7.

friends and allies in the fight against ignorance and bewilderment, to say nothing of heresy. To most people, however, Spanish influence did not mean foreign prelates in senior ecclesiastical office, Dominican friars reviving Thomism in the universities or drafting Erasmian catechisms, or even preaching less than comprehensible sermons. Spain meant unpopular war and the contaminating presence of the servants and hangers-on of Philip's courtiers. However critical for the intellectual reconstruction of the Marian Church Spanish clerical participation may have been, this secular presence was a handicap, and was far more keenly felt. Tudor propaganda had long ago succeeded in branding the papacy as a foreign intruder, but that had not noticeably diminished enthusiasm for the 'Old Religion'. Indeed it was Protestantism which was the alien force, associated as it was with the German and Swiss theologians who had sought refuge in England under Edward. Under Mary the seed of a different perception was planted. Stephen Gardiner had seen the danger, which was the main reason why he had taken the risk of trying to restore the papal jurisdiction before Philip's arrival, a move which the emperor's agents successfully aborted, with Mary's help.[26] In the event the papacy returned in Philip's wake, and largely as a result of his efforts. This was good for Habsburg influence in Rome, but not necessarily in the best interests of those who were trying to undo the effects of a generation of Protestant and anti-papal propaganda in England. Ironically, Pole himself had exerted all his influence in an unsuccessful attempt to prevent the Spanish marriage, and its anticipated association of Catholicism with the Habsburgs. Whether opposition to the marriage was in any real sense a Protestant conspiracy scarcely matters. The government chose to present it in that light, and consequently gave its religious opponents the credit for fronting a movement of popular 'patriotism'. Too much should not be made of this shift in Mary's reign itself, but it did help in the long run to drive a wedge between the old religion (which was popular) and the papal/Spanish association (which was not). For most of his reign over England, Philip and Pope Paul IV were at daggers drawn, but that fact did nothing to disperse the mists of prejudice which were beginning to arise, and on which Elizabethan Protestant polemicists would capitalize. None of this might have mattered if Mary had not died when everything was going wrong, but as it was, the association of Spain with disaster helped to make Elizabeth's settlement (which in religious terms satisfied almost nobody except the queen) sufficiently acceptable to survive.

Most of the Spanish clergy who exerted influence over the course of

---

[26] J. Loach, *Parliament and the Crown in the Reign of Mary Tudor* (Oxford, 1986), 91–104.

the Marian restoration were friars, but the role of the religious life in Marian England is another problematic area. Mary in fact founded or re-established more religious communities than any other English monarch in history, but the handful of houses which resulted were of course a drop in the ocean by comparison with the vastly greater numbers dissolved in Henry's reign.[27] Pole, as is well known, was much preoccupied by the recovery of monastic property, but he told the courtiers, lawyers and alderman who listened to his St Andrew's Day sermon in 1557 that the restoration of the parishes was a more urgent priority than the rebuilding of monasteries. It is hard to disagree with him, but once again he has been criticized for pursuing his priorities. Famously, he declined an offer of assistance from Ignatius Loyola, but instead sought a Cassinese Benedictine presence, which in the event did not materialize. His Italian career in fact suggests that he highly valued both the older orders of monks and friars, and newer creations like the Theatines and Jesuits, but the place of the religious life in his order of priorities for the longer term of the Marian restoration remains an unanswered question.

In this context the fortunes of the one major house to be re-erected during the reign, the Abbey of Westminster, examined here by Dr Knighton, are instructive but perhaps not decisive.[28] Westminster was technically a new creation, but it carried much of the baggage of the old abbey, and the community included many of those who had been secularized between 1536 and 1540. Abbot Feckenham was a key figure in the Marian establishment, and his community was both large and vigorous, its vigour reflected in the surprising number of young novices it attracted, one of whom was to carry the English monastic tradition forward into the next century. Westminster Abbey played a conspicuous role in the ceremonial life of Marian London, but given the enormity of the task of restoration in the parishes, it should perhaps be viewed more as a symbol of the long-term intentions of the Marian Church than a key aspect of its immediate programme. Nevertheless, the queen took all her new foundations seriously enough to endow them (substantially in the case of Westminster) and to remember them in her will.[29] If the restored church had had more time to gather momentum they might well have

---

[27] Altogether six religious houses were established. Apart from the Benedictines at Westminster, there were Observant Franciscans at Greenwich, Carthusians at Sheen, Dominicans at St. Bartholomew's, Smithfield, Bridgettines at Syon and Dominicanesses at King's Langley. The knights of St John were also revived, both in England and Ireland. The total cost to the Crown was somewhat in excess of £3000 a year.

[28] See Chapter 3.

[29] The text of Mary's will is reproduced as Appendix III to D. Loades, *Mary Tudor: A Life* (Oxford, 1989), 370–83.

become important. In the event, it was the Jesuits, kept for whatever reasons at arm's length by Pole, rather than the older orders whom he favoured, who would make the major 'religious' contribution to the formation and perpetuation of recusant Catholicism.

This book is about Catholics, and not about Protestants, but given the priority which the queen particularly gave to the elimination of heresy, it is fitting that one of the essays should be specifically about the persecution. Kent was a county which saw more burnings than anywhere except London. It was a region with a long tradition of dissent, and Professor Collinson carefully scrapes away the whitewash liberally applied by John Foxe to reveal a very miscellaneous collection of victims.[30] It is clear that many of them were not the orthodox Edwardian Protestants which the martyrologist wished to present, and that he frequently massaged the evidence of their real beliefs. However, it does not necessarily follow, as Philip Hughes suggested, that most of these radicals would have been done away with by any sixteenth-century government. Edward's council had burned just two heretics in six years. In Kent alone the Marian authorities executed somewhere between 50 and 70 in a rather shorter time. Nor did anyone, not even Robert Persons, deny that these men and women had died for their religious beliefs. It is unlikely that contemporaries found such events as horrifying as we do, and it is therefore a mistake to project modern revulsion at the idea of torture and execution for sincerely held convictions into the sensibilities of Tudor England. Nevertheless, Professor Collinson suggests here that the 'black legend' of Bloody Mary was more than a matter of Elizabethan propagandist 'spin', and that enough of the men of Kent retained an indignant memory of the Marian burnings to ensure an enduring association between popery and tyranny, however the vicissitudes of dynastic politics had shaken out.

The paradox of the Marian Church thus remains, because in a sense both Foxe and his critics were right. A Church which had a broadly popular programme of worship and practice, and which was committed to education and evangelization, nevertheless carried out one of the most sustained persecutions seen anywhere in Europe, and succeeded in confusing its impeccable English credentials by association with Spain. It is quite legitimate to argue that the Marian Church was overthrown not because of any inherent weaknesses or strategic failures, but simply because the queen who was its great patron and protector died, and her successor was a very different woman. It is legitimate, but it is not necessarily true. We no longer believe that the restored Catholic Church

---

[30] See Chapter 11.

lacked serious evangelical purpose, or that it was heavily outgunned by Protestant polemic. However, the fact remains that it was overthrown with comparative ease in 1559 by a queen who may have known what she wanted, but who was feeling her way through what could have been a minefield of dissent.[31] In seeking to defend the Mass against the threat of the bill of uniformity, the bishops had significant support, and failed by a whisker. But seeking to defend the papacy against the bill of supremacy, they had almost none. For this the persecution may have been partly responsible, stirring up neighbour against neighbour and family members against each other more destructively than the Edwardine imposition of Protestant uniformity had done. A sour taste lingered in the communities which had been thus damaged, as Foxe's collection of stories testifies.

But persecution on its own would not have undermined the Church. More important, certainly at the gentry level, were the foreign political trappings and the ever-present threat to the holders of former ecclesiastical property, who rightly understood that Pole did not really hold them absolved of theft, no matter what the official dispensation might say. Political quarrels with the papacy in the last two years of the reign did not help either, ensuring (among other things) that there were far more episcopal vacancies at the time of Mary's death than there should have been.

No one ever did a more effective hatchet job upon a regime than John Foxe. The *Acts and Monuments* was never intended to be objective history in the modern sense. It was a savage polemic intended to demonize the Catholic Church, and particularly its clergy. Because of the eventual success of the Elizabethan settlement, Foxe's narratives came to seem the final verdict on the negative legacy of the Marian restoration for 200 years after he wrote. The positive legacy is less obvious, but equally real. Ironically, Mary's rebuilding of the episcopate may well have preserved it for the future of the Anglican Church. If Elizabeth had followed straight on from Edward, and the trajectory of reform reflected in the progressive radicalization of the Prayer Books of 1549 and 1552 had been continued, it is hard to see how the institution of episcopacy could have survived. More importantly, however, the theological and intellectual stiffening which Pole managed to give the Church laid the basis for the ideologically tough and resilient recusant movement in Elizabeth's reign, and thereby ensured the survival and disruptive presence of Counter-Reformation Catholicism in Elizabeth's Protestant kingdom.

---

[31] N. Jones, *Faith by Statute: Parliament and the Settlement of Religion, 1559* (London, 1982).

While most religious conservatives after 1558 drifted more or less reluctantly into Anglican conformity, committed Roman Catholics embraced a new identity, which the propaganda of their opponents and the hard choices of politics in an increasingly confessionalized Europe would project as detached from, and even hostile to, the national community. The struggle of Elizabethan and Jacobean Catholics to retain both their national and their religious identities, torn between allegiances at first openly hostile and enduringly deeply suspicious of each other, is one of the less likely legacies of the Marian Church. It is one which has taken on new and sharp resonances in a Britain in which religious identity and national and cultural allegiances are once again often perceived as being at odds. But that, as they say, is quite another story.

Eamon Duffy, Cambridge University, and
David Loades, University of Sheffield

List of Abbreviations

These selected abbreviations appear throughout this book, but many are particularly relevant to the Appendix in Chapter 3.

Acts	*Acts of the Dean and Chapter of Westminster, 1543–1609*, ed. C.S. Knighton (Westminster Abbey Record series i, ii, 1997–99)
AGS	Archivo General de Simancas
Anstruther	G. Anstruther, *The Seminary Priests: A Dictionary of the Secular Clergy of England and Wales, 1558–1850*, i, *Elizabethan, 1558–1603* (Ware and Ushaw, n.d. [1968])
APC	*Acts of the Privy Council of England*, new series, ed. J.R. Dasent (1890–1907)
Aveling	J.C.H. Aveling, 'Tudor Westminster, 1540–1559', and Appendix A, 'The Marian Westminster community', in *Ampleforth and its Origins: Essays on a living tradition by members of the Ampleforth community*, ed. J.P. McCann and C. Cary-Elwes (1952), 53–80, 271–85
Baskerville (1927)	G. Baskerville, 'The dispossessed religious of Gloucestershire', *Transactions of the Bristol and Gloucester Archaeological Society*, xlix (1927), 63–122
Baskerville (1933)	G. Baskerville, 'Married clergy and pensioned religious in Norwich diocese, 1555', *English Historical Review*, xlviii (1933), 43–64, 199–228
Bellenger	A. Bellenger, *English and Welsh Priests, 1558–1800* (Downside, 1984)
Biog. Hist. Caius	*Biographical History of Gonville and Caius College, 1349–1897*, ed. J. Venn et al. (Cambridge 1897–1978)
BL	British Library, London

ABBREVIATIONS

Bodleian	Bodleian Library, Oxford
Cal. Span	*Calendar of Letters, Despatches, and State Papers, relating to the negotiations between England and Spain, preserved in the Archives at Simancas and elsewhere*, ed. G.A. Bergenroth et al. (1862–1954)
Cal. Ven.	*Calendar of State Papers and Manuscripts, relating to English affairs, existing in the Archives and Collections of Venice and in other Libraries of Northern Italy*, ed. R. Brown et al. (1864–1940)
CERS	Church of England Record Society
Clark, 'St Albans'	J.G. Clark, 'Reformation and reaction at St Albans Abbey, 1530–58', *EHR*, cxv (2000), 297–328
coll.	collated
CPR	*Calendar of the Patent Rolls preserved in the Public Record Office*
CRS	Catholic Record Society
CRS, *Miscellanea*	CRS, *Miscellanea*, i (1905), ii (1906)
CRS, *Recusants*	*Recusants in the Exchequer Pipe Rolls, 1581–1592*, extr. H. Bowler, ed. T.J. McCann (CRS, lxxi, 1986)
CSPD	*Calendar of State Papers, Domestic Series*
CSPDM	*Calendar of State Papers, Domestic Series, of the Reign of Mary I, 1553–1558*, revised edition, ed. C.S. Knighton (1998)
CYS	Canterbury and York Society
DBM	Douai, Bibliothèque Municipale
DKR	*Reports of the Deputy Keeper of Public Records*
Douay Diaries	*The First and Second Diaries of the English College, Douay*, ed. T.F. Knox (1878)
Dugdale	W. Dugdale, *Monasticon Anglicanum*, ed. J. Caley, H. Ellis and B. Bandinel (1817–30)
EHR	*English Historical Review*
Emden	A.B. Emden, *A Biographical Register of the University of Oxford, A.D. 1501 to 1540* (Oxford 1974)
Excerpta Historica	[S.E. Bentley], *Excerpta Historica, or Illustrations of English History* (1831)
Fac. Off. Reg.	*Faculty Office Registers, 1534–1539: A Calendar of the first two Registers of the*

	Archbishop of Canterbury's Faculty Office, ed. D.S. Chambers (Oxford, 1966)
Foster	*Alumni Oxonienses: the Members of the University of Oxford*, ed. J. Foster (Oxford, 1891–92)
Foxe	John Foxe, *Acts and Monuments*, ed. S. Cattley and G. Townsend (1843–49)
Gasquet	F.A. Gasquet, *Henry VIII and the English Monasteries* (1888–89)
Grace Book Δ	*Grace Book Δ, containing the records of the University of Cambridge for the years 1542–1589*, ed. J. Venn (Cambridge, 1910)
Greatrex	J. Greatrex, *Biographical Register of the English Cathedral Priories of the Province of Canterbury, c. 1066–1540* (Oxford, 1997)
Guildhall	Guildhall Library, London
HBC	*Handbook of British Chronology* (3rd edn, 1986)
Hennessy	*Novum Repertorium Ecclesiasticum Parochiale Londinense*, compiled G. Hennessy (1898)
Hist. Parl 1558–1603	S.T. Bindoff, *The House of Commons, 1558–1603* (The History of Parliament, 1982)
HMC, *Salisbury MSS*	*Calendar of the Manuscripts of the Most Hon. the Marquess of Salisbury, K.G. etc. preserved at Hatfield House, Hertfordshire* (Historical Manuscripts Commission, 1883–)
Hodgett	*The State of the ex-Religious and former Chantry Priests in the Diocese of Lincoln 1547–1574, from returns in the Exchequer*, ed. G.A.J. Hodgett (Lincoln Record Society, liii, 1959)
House of Kings	*A House of Kings: The History of Westminster Abbey*, ed. E.F. Carpenter (1966)
inst.	instituted
Joseph, *Letter Book*	*The Letter Book of Robert Joseph, Monk-Scholar of Evesham and Gloucester College, Oxford, 1530-3*, ed. J.C.H. Aveling and W.A. Pantin (Oxford

	Historical Society, new series, xix, 1967 for 1964)
Knowles, *Rel. Orders*	M.D. Knowles, *The Religious Orders in England* (Cambridge, 1948–59)
Le Neve	J. Le Neve, *Fasti Ecclesiae Anglicanae, 1541–1857*, compiled J.M. Horn et al. (1969–)
Lond.	London
L & P (LP)	*Letters and Papers, Foreign and Domestic, of the Reign of Henry VIII*, ed. J.S. Brewer, J. Gairdner and R.H. Brodie (1862–1932) [cited in Appendix by entry number]
LPL	Lambeth Palace Library
Lunn	D.M. Lunn, *The English Benedictines, 1540-1688: From Reformation to Revolution* (1980)
Machyn	*The Diary of Henry Machyn, Citizen and Merchant-Taylor of London, from A.D. 1550 to A.D. 1563*, ed. J.G. Nichols (Camden Society, old series, xlii, 1848)
Marron	S. Marron, 'Dom Sigebert Buckley and his brethren', *Douai Magazine*, vii, no. 3 (1933), 130–38
Muller (1926)	J.A. Muller, *Stephen Gardiner and the Tudor Reaction* (1926)
Muller (1933)	*The Letters of Stephen Gardiner*, ed. J.A. Muller (Cambridge, 1933)
ODNB	*Oxford Dictionary of National Biography* (2004)
OHS	Oxford Historical Society
Ollard	S.L. Ollard, *Fasti Wyndesorienses: The Deans and Canons of Windsor* (Historical Monographs relating to St George's Chapel, Windsor Castle, [viii], Windsor, 1950)
OSB	Order of St Benedict
PCC	Parochial Church Council
Pantin	*Canterbury College: Documents and History*, ed. W.A. Pantin (Oxford Historical Society, new series, vi–viii, Canterbury College, xxx, 1947–85)
Pearce	E.H. Pearce, *The Monks of Westminster: Being a Register of the Brethren of the*

	Convent from the time of the Confessor to the Dissolution (Notes and Documents relating to Westminster Abbey, no. 5, Cambridge, 1916)
PRO	Public Record Office, London
Reg. Bath & Wells, 1518–1559	*The Registers of Thomas Wolsey, Bishop of Bath and Wells, 1518–1523, John Clerke Bishop of Bath and Wells, 1523–1541, William Knyght, Bishop of Bath and Wells, 1541–1547, and Gilbert Bourne, Bishop of Bath and Wells, 1554–1559*, ed. H. Maxwell Lyte (Somerset Record Society, lxi, 1940)
Reg. Bothe	*Registrum Carli Bothe, Episcopi Herefordensis, A.D. MDXVI–MDXXXV*, ed. A.T. Bannister (Canterbury and York Society, xxviii, 1921)
Reg. Gardiner & Poynet	*Registrum Stephani Gardiner et Johannis Poynet, Episcoporum Wintoniensium*, ed. H. Chitty and H.E. Malden (Canterbury and York Society, xxxvii, 1930)
Reg. Middle Temple	*Register of Admissions to the Honourable Society of the Middle Temple, from the Fifteenth Century to the year 1944*, compiled H.F. McGeagh and H.A.C. Sturgess (1949)
Reg. Bracy	Register of Bracy, Westminster City Archives
Reg. Parker	*Registrum Matthei Parker, Diocesis Cantuariensis, A.D. 1559–1575*, transcribed E.M. Thompson, ed. W.H. Frere (Canterbury and York Society, xxxv, xxxvi, xxxix, 1928–33)
Reg. Pole (arch.)	Lambeth Palace Library, Archiepiscopal register of Cardinal Pole
Reg. Whyte	*Registrum Johannis Whyte, Episcopi Wintoniensis, A.D. MDLVI–MDLIX*, ed. H. Chitty (Canterbury and York Society, xvi, 1914)
RHS	Royal Historical Society
RO	Record Office
RSTC	Revised Short Title Catalogue
Searle	'Lists of the Deans, Priors and Monks of

ABBREVIATIONS xxxi

	Christ Church Monastery', in *Christ Church, Canterbury*, ed. W.G. Searle (Cambridge Antiquarian Society Publications, octavo series xxxxiv, 1902), 153–96
SRS	Somerset Record Society
STP	*Sanctae Theologiae Professor*
TRHS	*Transactions of the Royal Historical Society*
VMA	Volumes of Miscellaneous Accounts, Canterbury
Wainewright	J.B. Wainewright, 'Queen Mary's religious foundations', *Downside Review*, new series, viii (1908), 125–46
WAM	Westminster Abbey Muniments
Watkin (1941)	A. Watkin, *Dean Cosyn and Wells Cathedral Miscellanea* (Somerset Record Society, lvi, 1941)
Watkin (1949)	A. Watkin, 'Glastonbury, 1538–9, as shown by its account rolls', *Downside Review*, new series, lxvii (1949), 437–50
WCA	Westminster City Archives
Wills Doc. Comm.	*Wills from Doctors' Commons: A selection from the wills of eminent persons proved in the Prerogative Court of Canterbury, 1495–1695*, ed. J.G. Nichols and J. Bruce (Camden Society, old series, lxxxiii, 1863)
Wright	*Three Chapters of Letters relating to the Suppression of Monasteries*, ed. T. Wright (Camden Society, old series, xxvi, 1843)
Zurich Letters	*The Zurich Letters, comprising the Correspondence of several English Bishops and others with some of the Helvetian Reformers, during the early part of the Reign of Queen Elizabeth*, i, ed. H. Robinson (Parker Society, Cambridge, 1842)

INTRODUCTION

The Personal Religion of Mary I

David Loades

Mary was a Catholic. The one thing that is, and always has been, clear about Henry VIII's elder daughter is that she was loyal to the old faith. However, it is less clear exactly what that allegiance involved at different times in her life, because the distinction between 'the old faith' as that term was employed at the time and Catholicism as it was being reformulated by the Council of Trent is only just becoming fully appreciated.[1] Traditionally the Catholic faith, as it had been presented to its lay practitioners, was a matter of sacramental participation and ritual rather than theology. By the early sixteenth century, however, there existed a literate laity which was theologically informed; mainly aristocrats, merchants and lawyers, of whom Sir Thomas More was the outstanding example. From the clerical point of view, such men were a mixed blessing because, although they might bring an informed intelligence to their faith, they were also prone to ask awkward questions. A layman, whether he was a king or a cottager (or a lawyer) was required to confess his sins to a priest, to receive the sacrament of the altar at least once a year and to follow the prescribed rites of passage for baptism, marriage and death. He was also encouraged to give alms to the Church and to the poor, according to his means, and to seek the intercession of a hierarchy of saints, headed by the Blessed Virgin. He was not expected to question the teaching of the Church, or challenge the authority of the clergy. The ordinary actions of piety were deemed sufficient for his soul's health, and were as much a part of the natural order as seed time and harvest. The clergy who provided these spiritual services were as necessary, if not always as unquestioned, as ploughmen and shepherds.[2]

The uncomfortable currents beneath this apparently placid surface came partly from the literate laity, and partly from disgruntled elements

---

[1] On this question see particularly E. Duffy, *The Stripping of the Altars* (1993), 527–37; and Lucy Wooding, *Rethinking Catholicism in Reformation England* (2000), 114–16.

[2] Peter Heath, *The English Parish Clergy on the Eve of the Reformation* (1969) demolishes many traditional myths about clerical behaviour.

among the clergy themselves. By insisting upon the necessity of the sacraments for salvation, and its own monopoly in providing them, the Church had become both rich and powerful. Not everyone thought that this was beneficial to its mission, and there had for centuries been voices raised proclaiming the doctrine of apostolic poverty, and urging the clergy to shed their temporal possessions and pretensions. These voices, which had been largely suppressed during the fifteenth century, were becoming distinctly audible again by 1510. The piety and anxiety of earlier generations had in the past created thousands of houses of prayer in England, controlling about a quarter of the landed wealth of the kingdom, and perfectly orthodox Christians were wondering whether this huge endowment was either necessary or justifiable. Clerical celibacy was a worthy ideal, but an uncomfortable one for a normal man. Were such vows either necessary or realistic for a priest working in an everyday community? These were issues to be addressed, and the Church as an institution was not doing very much about them. Clerical abuses were nothing new, and neither were the voices which drew attention to them and urged reform. John Colet began his celebrated convocation address of 1511 with the words

> Ye are come together today, fathers and right wise men, to enter Council; in the which, what ye do, and what matters ye will handle, yet we understand not. But we wish that once, remembering your name and profession, ye would mind the reformation of the church's matter. For it was never more need, and the state of the church did never desire more your endeavours. For the spouse of Christ, the church whom ye would should be without spot or wrinkle, is made foul and ill-favoured, as saith Esias; The faithful city is made an harlot. And as saith Hieremias; She hath done lechery with many lovers, whereby she hath conceived many seeds of wickedness, and daily bringeth forth very foul fruit …[3]

His words were not generally well received. In some quarters he was denounced as a heretic, but Colet in fact was voicing the concerns of the respectable community to which he belonged. It was because he cared so passionately for the Church that he wished the clergy to be worthy of their calling.[4] He was not a friar; but it was among the mendicants, who were the most effective preachers of the faith, that this kind of anxiety was most frequently voiced. Later a disproportionate number of them were to defect

---

[3] J.H. Lupton, *Life of John Colet* (1909), App. C, 293.

[4] Wooding, *Rethinking*, 34–5. For another contemporary expression of the same view, see Richard Whitford, *Werke for Householders* (1530). For the context and significance of Colet's convocation address, see Christopher Harper-Bill, 'Dean Colet's Convocation Sermon and the Pre-Reformation Church in England', *History*, 73, 1988, 191–210.

to the reformers.⁵ There were also among these questioning voices those who were absorbing the classical scholarship then being transmitted from Italy to the north. These were known as humanists, and their symbolic leader was the Dutch scholar Desiderius Erasmus. Not all the critics of contemporary abuses were so motivated, but many were, so that their learning became a matter of suspicion and hostility among defenders of the *status quo*. Even among the humanists there were differences of opinion; Erasmus, for instance, was much keener on vernacular scripture than was Thomas More; Erasmus was sceptical of the *opus dei* which provided the justification for monasticism; More and John Fisher not so. But they also had many ideas in common; particularly a strong belief in education, for laity and clergy alike, allowing pagan authors as well as Christian and encouraging the theological literacy of laymen. There was much emphasis upon moral probity, and women, particularly those of high rank, were encouraged to follow a similar programme. They were also sceptical about the more physical aspects of contemporary piety. There was an uncomfortable tendency, particulary among the poor and illiterate, to treat images as though they possessed a life and sanctity of their own; and Erasmus was scathing about the pious pretensions of that contemporary form of the package holiday, the pilgrimage.⁶ Humanism had seeped into England from about 1470 onward, being signalled by an interest in Greek at Oxford and Cambridge. Among its early patrons was the deeply pious Lady Margaret Beaufort, and she, it is now believed, had a strong influence on the education of her grandson, the young Prince Henry.⁷ Henry was the best educated young aristocrat of his generation, and his accession to the throne in 1509 was greeted with exultation by humanists all over Western Europe. Within weeks he had married the even more learned and similarly inclined Catherine of Aragon, the relict of his brother Arthur, who had been left stranded in England by the vagaries of Castilian politics.

Humanism thus became fashionable at court, and its future seemed to be assured. However, it was from the beginning a divisive tendency. Some clergy disliked it simply because they were averse to change, and too idle to meet a new intellectual challenge; others saw the education of the laity as subversive of their own position;⁸ but some also had more

---

⁵ On the role of the friars, particularly as preachers, see Susan Wabuda, *Preaching During the English Reformation* (2002), 107–46.

⁶ Erasmus wrote a satirical account of a pilgrimage to Walsingham. A.G. Dickens, *The English Reformation* (1964), 5.

⁷ M.K. Jones and M.G. Underwood, *The King's Mother; Lady Margaret Beaufort, Countess of Richmond and Derby* (1992), 202–31.

⁸ David Loades, 'Anticlericalism in the Church of England before 1558; an "eating cancer"?', in *Anticlericalism*, ed. Nigel Aston and Matthew Cragoe (2000), 1–18.

respectable doubts. It was very hard, for example, to draw a sensible line between acceptable practice and abuse in devotions to the saints. These cults were immensely popular, for the simple reason that saints, however virtuous, had been real people, and understood how real people felt. Christ, although in a sense a perfect man, was without sin, whereas the heroism of the saints lay precisely in overcoming that unfortunate feature of normal humanity. The orthodox teaching was that saints could only intercede, having no power of their own; but did it matter if that was not always understood? The piety of the simple needed such props. In fact there was little logic or consistency in popular devotion, which varied greatly from place to place. Christ was sometimes approached as a profoundly human friend, in a manner which would seem to remove the need for any form of intercession, and yet that was seldom the conclusion drawn.[9] The analogy with a human family was powerfully felt. God was the father, and the response to all prayer lay in his hands. The son was the human face of the father, but as he shared his power he was hardly an intercessor in the ordinary sense. The saints were the friends of Christ, and would intercede as human friends would do in a similar situation. The greatest intercessor of all, however, was the Virgin Mary, who was deemed not only to have all a woman's susceptibilities, but to share in a mysterious way in the influence which a human mother commonly exercised over her spouse and son. God was also unknowable, and his ways profoundly mysterious; even the learned had great difficulty in understanding his purposes.[10] Consequently it was a mistake to educate laymen to the point where they were able to ask questions to which there might be no answers, or at least no answers which could be formulated in words.

Unfortunately, while these disputes were simmering within the Church, the water was further muddied by Martin Luther. Luther was not a humanist but a traditionally trained theologian. Using St Paul and St Augustine as his starting points, he came to the conclusion that the abuses of the Church were the result, not of poor discipline, or even unworthy motivation, but of profound theological misunderstanding. God, he declared, had already decided upon whom he would bestow the grace of faith, and that was sufficient for the salvation of the recipient. Edifying and helpful as the offices of the Church might be, they were not

---

[9] On devotion to the humanity of Jesus, see Duffy, *Stripping of the Altars*, 232–8.

[10] John Standish later wrote 'Gods commands are unsearchable ... every foole can read and bable of the scripture, but only the Godly learned teachers can play the spiritual masons part in couching the lyvely stones in the spiritual building of Christes churche ...' *A discourse wherin is debated whether it be expedient that the scripture should be in English* (1555), sig. Eiv.

strictly necessary. At the same time Christianity was, and should be, a religion of the Word, and the Word was contained in the Bible. The accumulated traditions, laws and ceremonies of the Church were at best harmless and unnecessary accretions, and at worst a hindrance and an obstruction to true understanding. Threatened at its very heart by this marginalization of the sacraments, the Church in the person of Pope Leo X immediately proclaimed the defiant German a heretic in 1521. Within a decade a major schism had opened within the Western Church.[11]

Superficially, there were many similarities between Luther's teaching and the humanist critique. Both saw dangerous abuses in the practices of popular religion; both wished to open the Bible to the laity through education; both believed that the clergy had become too wealthy, and too often abused their calling. In fact the boundaries were symbolically drawn by a furious quarrel between Luther and Erasmus on the question of free will, but for about 20 years there was a great deal of confusion.[12] This played into the hands of conservatives, who were equally opposed to both, and enabled them to brand their Erasmian opponents as heretics when they were usually nothing of the kind. The Spanish *Alumbrados*, who were Erasmians with some mystical tendencies borrowed from the Brethren of the Common Life, were successfully branded as *Luteranos* by their enemies, and virtually wiped out by the Inquisition.

It was into this uncertain climate that Mary was born, and it provides the context of her upbringing. She was five when Luther was condemned, and just beginning to learn her letters. Because both her parents had received a first-rate humanist training, and were committed to its principles, Mary's academic education was taken seriously. Had Henry been the old-fashioned knight errant that he sometimes pretended to be, his daughter would have learned little beyond needlework and social graces; instead, she became a model for the offspring of ambitious courtiers. Catherine commissioned several treatises on the education of girls, not so much because she needed guidance as to make a point. In 1523 her fellow countryman Juan Luis Vives presented her with *De Institutione Foeminae Christianae*, writing in the preface 'Your dearest daughter Mary shall read these instructions of mine, and follow in living. Which she must needs do if she is to order herself after the example that she hath at home with her …'[13]

---

[11] Luther never considered himself to be a heretic, and blamed his condemnation on the politics of the Church. M. Brecht, *Martin Luther, his road to reformation, 1483–1521*, trans. J.L. Schaaf (Philadelphia, 1985).

[12] Erasmus attacked Luther in *De Libero Arbitrio* (1525), to which Luther replied with *De Servo Arbitrio*. See R.H. Bainton, *Erasmus of Christendom* (1969), 230–35.

[13] *Opera Omnia*, IV, 65–6. The reading programme was set out in another treatise, *De ratione studii puerilis*.

Vives did not suggest that Mary would grow up to have the intellectual capacity of a man, and measured his programme to a girl's supposed inferiority, but his ideas were radical by contemporary standards. A young girl needed protection, both against unsuitable literature and contaminating male company, because virginity was a virtue of the mind as well as the body. Nevertheless he prescribed a diet of scripture, the Latin fathers and certain acceptable pagan classics. Other advice tracts followed: two more from Vives himself, the *Rudimenta Grammatices* from Thomas Linacre and, perhaps most significantly, the *Christiani matrimonii institutio* from Erasmus. Catherine may have started to teach her daughter herself, but they were often apart and the queen had many calls on her time; so it was probably her chaplain, Henry Rowle, who had the first responsibility for this formidable task.[14] Vives himself spent some time in England, but seems not to have acted as a tutor in person.

Mary was not particularly precocious in her studies. The fragmentary stories of her early childhood which have survived refer to her being shown off by her father at court, being solemnly inspected by French envoys when a marriage negotiation was in prospect and toddling after Dominic Memmo, Henry's Venetian organist, with shrill cries of 'priest, priest'. The talents which attracted favourable comment were dancing and playing upon the virginals; if anyone was impressed by her scholarly aptitudes, they did not say so.[15] By the time that she was sent off to Ludlow at the age of nine, Mary could read and write fluently in English, had a good basic grasp of Latin and some French. Both Catherine and Henry were very careful to insist that she should be brought up as an English princess, so although she must have picked up something of her mother's native tongue (which she used with her Spanish servants) Mary never seems to have been formally instructed in the language.[16] The reading programme which Vives had prescribed was, of course, all in Latin. In 1525 the only English Bible was that of Wycliffe, which was both antique and illegal. Apart from being the recipient of frequent exhortations to piety, the content of Mary's

---

[14] Wages of the princess's household, 1 October 11 Henry VIII (1519) to i September 12 Henry VIII (1520). *Letters and Papers ... of the Reign of Henry VIII*, ed. S.R. Gardiner et al. (1862–1911), III, 970 and Addenda, 259.

[15] D. Loades, *Mary Tudor; a life* (1989), 31–4. What was mainly commented upon was her robust health.

[16] There is some uncertainty about Mary's facility in Spanish. In 1554 the Venetian Soranzo described her as fluent, but his successor Michieli says at one point that she was competent, at another that she understood it, but did not speak it. It is perhaps safest to conclude that she understood it sufficiently, but spoke it only hesitantly. In conversing with Philip she may well have used Latin, in which they were both fluent.

religious instruction can only be deduced. Catherine was a member of the third order of St Francis, and was held to be a model of orthodox practice. She gave alms generously in the traditional hand-to-mouth manner, and seems not to have been influenced by the more systematic approach advocated in *De subventione pauperum*, in spite of her regard for Vives.[17] When Henry went on hunting trips, the queen tended to visit the local shrines, and her assiduity in this respect was often commented upon. Catherine did not appoint her daughter's tutors, that was done by the king, but there were no disagreements between them in this respect. Mary's first steps in the faith were thus guided by people who are all known to have been zealous, orthodox and steeped in humanism. Virtually all the factual information we have about her very early years comes from the accounts of her cofferer, Richard Sydnor; and the only things which are relevant in this context are the small sums which were distributed in alms on the princess's personal instructions.[18] The accounts say nothing of the companionship of other children, of toys or even of play. The impression given is of an austere childhood, in an almost totally adult environment, and with few normal emotional outlets. On the other hand, no one described her as either lonely or unhappy, nor did she ever recall her childhood in such a way. Vives had said that '... a daughter should be handled without any cherishing. For cherishing marreth sons, but it utterly destroyeth daughters ...' It would appear that Henry and Catherine followed his advice assiduously.[19]

Mary departed for Thornbury in August 1525 to take up her first royal duties, and was accompanied by a household numbering over 300 persons, including the staff of her chapel. Her personal service was supervised by Margaret Pole, Countess of Salisbury, the mother of the future cardinal, and she was assigned a new schoolmaster in the person of Dr Richard Fetherstone.[20] Although an itinerary of her movements has been reconstructed, not very much is known of Mary's life during the four years which she spent in the Welsh Marches, and almost nothing of the progress of her studies.[21] Margaret Pole's instructions, which were specific in respect of Mary's diet, exercise and personal cleanliness, and careful to order that she should '... at due tymes ...

---

[17] Garrett Mattingly, *Catherine of Aragon* (1963), 134–5.

[18] For example, an unspecified sum given to the poor en route between Richmond and Ditton in December 1521. *Letters and Papers*, III, 2585.

[19] Foster Watson, ed., *Vives and the Renasence Education of Women* (New York, 1912), 133.

[20] Maria Dowling, *Humanism in the Age of Henry VIII*, (1986), 227. Vives seems to have approved of her new tutor, although he did not refer to him by name.

[21] W.R.B. Robinson, 'Princess Mary's itinerary in the Marches of Wales, 1525–7; a provisional record', *Historical Research*, 71, 1998, 233–52.

serve God from whom all grace and goodness proceedeth', were vague on the subject of schooling. She was to practise on the virginals, and work at her Latin and French, provided that she did not fatigue herself unduly.[22] Before she set off, Mary received an encouraging letter from her mother, and it is likely that they maintained a correspondence during the years when personal meetings were necessarily very rare; but the only writing of hers that survives from this period is a translation into English of a prayer by St Thomas Aquinas.[23] Fetherstone was a man with a good reputation as a scholar, and circumstantial evidence suggests that by the time that Mary returned to the Home Counties at the age of 13 she had a good command of both classical Latin and French; but of her devotional studies, if any, we know nothing at all.

By 1529 the process which was to turn a peaceful, and perhaps rather dull childhood into a turbulent and stressful adolescence was already under way. Henry had been trying to secure an annulment of his marriage since 1527, and the first crisis was reached with the failure of the Legatine Court in July 1529. Richard Fetherstone was one of the counsel assigned to advise Catherine, so he must have been either seconded from his place with Mary, or replaced. As soon as she discovered what was afoot, Mary sided with her mother. Whether this was simply the consequence of a natural empathy, or the result of the influence of Fetherstone and Margaret Pole, we do not know. It could have been a bit of both, and at first she was too young for it to matter much. However, as time went by without a solution, Mary's attitude became an embarrassment and an annoyance to her father. Catherine claimed that it was concern for Mary's legitimacy that motivated her fight for her marriage, but that was never the whole truth. If she had yielded to pressure and taken the veil, her daughter's legitimacy would not have been compromised, and her husband would have been free to marry again.[24] But the queen was bitterly offended by Henry's action, and had no intention of being co-operative. By 1533 both the court and the learned community had split right down the middle. On the king's side stood all those reformers who were having doubts (or more than doubts) about the Pope's role as the Vicar of Christ, and many humanists who thought that Henry's case was compelling. On the queen's side stood all those conservative clergy who detested the New

---

[22] BL, Cotton MS Vitellius C.i, f. 23.
[23] BL, Add. MS 17012; the prayer is written on a blank leaf at the end of a book of hours.
[24] The canon law of such a situation was not entirely clear, but since it would not have been in anyone's interest to obstruct such a move, it would almost certainly have had that effect.

Learning and thought that any doubts about the *status quo* were heresy; also such of the humanists as felt that the integrity of the Church was more important than its abuses. Among the latter were John Fisher, Thomas More and Richard Fetherstone.

The crunch came in the summer of 1533, when Mary was 17. Henry formally repudiated his first marriage, and relegated Catherine to the status of Princess Dowager of Wales. Her daughter was thus no longer princess and the king's heir, but simply the Lady Mary. Neither woman would accept this verdict, on the grounds that the king and parliament had acted *ultra vires*. Henry had dismissed Catherine from the court two years before, and the tension had been screwed up intolerably between that breakdown and the final judgement. Mary was the main sufferer from this, and she was quite seriously ill in March and April 1531. It is clear from the oblique references made to it, and from the large sums that Henry paid to his physicians, that this was a menstrual disorder of uncommon severity.[25] As Mary had turned 15 in February 1531, this is unlikely to have been the onset of puberty, but was rather a malfunction which was to recur regularly for the rest of her life. Whether it occurred naturally, or was brought on by the stress of her parents' marriage breakdown, we do not know. Henry had forbidden his wife and daughter to meet, but they clearly continued to correspond by means of trusted and discreet servants, and it seems likely that Catherine's influence was actually strengthened by this sharing of affliction. Until 1533, the king's attitude towards Mary remained in theory unchanged, but the mutual hatred that Eustace Chapuys, the imperial ambassador, reported between her and Anne Boleyn must have made her attendance at court a virtual impossibility.[26] Henry appointed Richard Wollman, formerly his own almoner and presumably a man of 'the king's party', to oversee Mary's continued studies, and it seems likely that Fetherstone did not return to her service after the Blackfriars court.[27] Apart from a fragile lifeline to her mother, Mary was now emotionally isolated, and it was at this time that she appears to have sought consolation in her devotions, or at least they begin to be mentioned for the first time. By 1533 Mary was becoming more important than her mother as a symbol of opposition to the king's proceedings, and in July rumours were circulating in Flanders of an impending rebellion in England in her interest, supported by the imperial fleet and the brother of the king of

---

[25] Loades, *Mary Tudor*, 61–2. There are many subsequent references to 'her usual malady'.
[26] *Calendar of State Papers, Spanish*, V, 12. (hereafter *Cal. Span.*). E.W. Ives, *Anne Boleyn* (1986), 247–8.
[27] Loades, *Mary Tudor*, 71.

Portugal. Mary seems to have done nothing to encourage these rumours, but then she did not have to. She was ill in March of that year, and again in June. At the end of that month the Venetian Marian Guistinian reported that 'some say' the king intended to make his daughter a nun; a reflection of her reputation for piety rather than any knowledge of Henry's mind.[28] The only good news was that, in spite of Anne Boleyn's best efforts, the lines of communication between Catherine and Mary remained open. However, another blow was pending. Provoked by her recalcitrance, which had become shrill and persistent, at the end of October Henry closed down her household altogether, and placed her, with a few personal servants, in the establishment then being created for the newly born Elizabeth.

The next three years were the most miserable of Mary's life, and planted iron in her soul. She now had neither a tutor nor a chapel of her own. She was not without friends, but they were perilous company. Fetherstone visited her, and reported to Eustace Chapuys that she was being threatened with prosecution for treason.[29] In 1534 Featherstone was himself imprisoned, and was to die on the scaffold in 1540. The issue was entirely political. Following her mother's example, Mary refused to accept any designation other than princess, or to recognize anyone but Catherine as queen. Chapuys described her as an heroic defender of the true Church, but what he meant was that she was a determined opponent of Henry's claim to ecclesiastical supremacy. Her position was very similar to that of John Fisher and Thomas More, both of whom suffered for treason in 1535. There was no other issue of doctrine or worship at this stage, and Henry still considered himself to be the model of a Catholic prince. The papacy was a corrupt and worldly institution, and he was the true defender of the faith. We have no idea what Mary thought about the papacy at this time, because she was only defending the Roman authority insofar as it was upholding her mother's cause. She did not hate either Anne Boleyn or Thomas Cranmer because they were heretics, but because they had conspired to destroy Catherine's marriage, and it was for the same reason that both women refused to accept the judgement of parliament. Catherine took a gloomy satisfaction in her daughter's martyrdom. 'The time has come,' she wrote, 'that Almighty God will prove you, and I am very glad of it, for I trust he doth handle you with a good love …'[30] The letters continued to pass to and fro, Catherine's sometimes scribbled in Spanish; and they both worked

---

[28] *Calendar of State Papers, Venetian*, IV, 928 (hereafter *Cal. Ven.*). On her illness, see Chapuys to the emperor, 28 June 1533, *Letters and Papers*, VI, 720.

[29] Dowling, *Humanism*, 55, 229.

[30] BL, Arundel MS 151, f. 194. *Letters and Papers*, VI, 1126.

themselves up into a state of moral and religious exaltation as they contemplated the unspeakable wickedness of the king's actions.

The third angle in this structure of defiance was Chapuys. Charles V was genuinely indignant over Henry's treatment of his aunt Catherine, and in a sense provoked the whole crisis by using his power in Italy to make sure that Clement VII did not yield to the king's importunities. However, he had no interest in diverting scarce resources from his struggles with Francis I and the Ottomans to overthrow the king of England. After 1533 his council urged him to accept the *fait accompli* because the queen's cause was a private matter, and Henry had made no hostile move against himself.[31] Charles, however, was a man of principle; he also had his own ideas about what was in his best interest. Catherine was becoming an embarrassment, but Mary's defiance might be useful, particularly if the English did rise in rebellion. He therefore allowed his ambassador to visit and encourage the beleaguered girl, and to upbraid Henry over his behaviour, secure in the knowledge that the king could not afford a complete breakdown of relations. Mary was almost pathetically grateful, and assured Chapuys that she regarded Charles as her one true friend, and her real father.[32]

This painful and difficult situation was brought to an end in 1536 by two dramatic events. In January Catherine died in the relatively comfortable seclusion of Kimbolton. There were the inevitable rumours of poison, but she probably died from a series of heart attacks. Mary, to her great distress, was not allowed to visit her mother in her last illness, and found her usual comfort in her devotions. If Henry expected his daughter's stance to be softened by the removal of its ostensible cause, then he was disappointed. However, in May Queen Anne Boleyn fell from grace and was executed on charges of treasonable adultery and incest. Mary had convinced herself that Anne was the sole cause of her father's grotesque aberrations, and hence of her own misfortunes. She therefore waited expectantly for an unconditional reconciliation. It did not come. Instead, during May and June she gradually became aware, through correspondence with Thomas Cromwell and conversations with Chapuys, that Henry was adamant in insisting upon her submission to his will as a condition of her restoration to favour.[33] For over a month extreme pressure was applied, and Chapuys became convinced that the king was serious when he threatened his daughter with execution. He

---

[31] Consulta of 31 May 1533. *Letters and Papers*, VI, 568.

[32] *Letters and Papers*, IX, 596. The proprietary interest which Charles began to show in Mary was much resented by Henry; Loades, *Mary Tudor*, 85–6.

[33] BL, Cotton MS Otho C.x, f. 278. *Letters and Papers*, X, 1022. Loades, *Mary Tudor*, 100–102.

joined his voice to Cromwell's in urging her to yield to save her life; and on 22 June she gave way. This surrender scarred her as deeply as the experiences of the previous three years. In later life she did not know whether to reproach herself for having rejected the opportunity of martyrdom, or to thank God for having preserved her to fight another day. At the time Chapuys represented her as smitten in conscience, and wholly dependent upon himself for consolation, but that was a self-interested view.[34] Contemporary evidence, including Mary's own letters, points in a different direction. Her household was restored, she was received at court and quickly developed a warm friendship with her new stepmother, Jane Seymour. She wrote to the emperor, and to Mary of Hungary, professing the genuineness of her conversion to her father's cause; and when rebellion broke out in the autumn – the Pilgrimage of Grace – she repudiated the actions taken in her name, and retained her father's favour.

It is difficult to know exactly where Mary stood in the last decade of Henry's reign. Her formal education had come to an end with the dissolution of her first household, and we get only occasional glimpses of how she survived during the dark years. When Marillac, the French ambassador, was making some pertinent enquiries in 1541, he spoke to a lady who claimed to have served Mary throughout that period, and who testified that her chief solace in painful and sleepless nights had been to read works of *litterae humaniores*.[35] Years later, in conversation with Pole's representative Henry Penning, she professed '… that she had always been a most obedient and affectionate daughter towards the apostolic see …', but she added '*interiormente*' – inwardly – suggesting that she had deliberately dissembled her submission.[36] However, that statement was made in very different circumstances, when it would have been difficult to say anything else. At the time there was no suggestion that she was anything other than a loyal and pious daughter. She was happy with the birth of her brother Edward, and mourned the death of her friend Jane Seymour. She disliked Catherine Howard, but that had nothing to do with either religion or politics, and became close to Catherine Parr. In learning, Catherine was an enthusiastic amateur, and Mary found herself acting as tutor. The queen's religious position was that which is usually described as 'evangelical'; orthodox on the sacraments, but supportive not only of the royal supremacy but also of the English Bible and experimental English liturgies. The evangelicals

---

[34] *Letters and Papers*, XI, 7.
[35] Marillac to Francis I, 12 October 1541, *Letters and Papers*, XVI, 1253. The enquiries concerned a possible marriage.
[36] *Cal. Ven.*, V, 429. 21 October 1554.

were hostile, not only to the papacy, but also to monasticism, the doctrine of purgatory and the use of images in worship. After the king's death it became clear from the publication of her *Prayers or meditations* and *The Lamentation of a Sinner* that Catherine had already embraced a Protestant position on justification, but that was not clear at the time.[37] The queen was, however, regarded with deep suspicion, not only by crypto-papists but also by conservatives like Thomas Wriothesley and Stephen Gardiner, who had followed the king on jurisdictional issues, but remained loyal to most aspects of traditional orthodoxy.[38]

Catherine's friendship with Mary consequently raises questions about the latter. Of her learning we have no direct evidence because she left nothing in writing to testify to it, and Lord Morley's dedication to her looked back to her childhood

> I do well remember that scant were ye come to twelve years of age but that ye were so ripe in the Latin tongue, that rare doth happen to the woman sex, that your grace could not only perfectly read write and construe Latin, but furthermore translate any hard thing of the Latin into our English tongue.[39]

In about 1545, Catherine persuaded Mary to undertake the translation of Erasmus's paraphrase on the Gospel of St John into English. She did not complete the work because of ill health, but her participation was well known, and when Nicholas Udall published *The First Tome or Volume of the Paraphrases of Erasmus* in 1548, he referred in the dedication to

> such a peerless flower of virginity as her grace is; who in the midst of courtly delights and amidst the enticements of worldly vanities hath by her own choice and election so virtuously and so fruitfully passed her tender youth, that to the public comfort and gladful rejoicing which at her birth she brought to all England she doth now also confer unto the same the inestimable benefit of furthering both us and our posterity in the knowledge of God's word, and to the more understanding of Christ's Gospel.[40]

All of which suggests that Mary fitted quite comfortably into the circle

---

[37] Susan E. James, *Katheryn Parr: the making of a Queen* (Aldershot, 1999), discusses the development of the Queen's religious position.

[38] For a discussion of Gardiner's alleged role in a conservative conspiracy against the queen, see G. Redworth, *In Defence of the Church Catholic; the life of Stephen Gardiner* (1990), 231–7.

[39] BL, Royal MS 17 C XVI. For a discussion of Morley's relations with Mary and his own religious position, see Richard Rex, 'Morley and the Papacy: Rome, Regime and Religion', in *Triumphs of English: Henry Parker, Lord Morley*, ed. Marie Axton and James P. Carley (2000), 87–106.

[40] Dowling, *Humanism*, 229.

around her father's last queen, and that there was nothing in either her intellectual tastes or devotional practice that set her apart as a rebel or a misfit. The explanation for this is probably that the core of her piety was the Mass, and in that she resembled Henry himself. Whatever else he may have doubted or discarded, and that included monastic vows and the doctrine of purgatory, the king remained committed to transubstantiation, as he demonstrated by his furious personal assault on the sacramentarian John Lambert.[41] His commitment may have been inconsistent with his desire to diminish that sacerdotal authority of which it was the foundation, but human beings are not logical, and it was the Mass which held Mary, Thomas Cranmer and the king together as the latter approached the end of his life.[42]

Unlike Cranmer, however, or Catherine Parr, Mary remained loyal to that commitment when Henry was no more than a memory. Charles V was puzzled and disappointed by her apparent spinelessness, and uncertain where she now stood in respect of 'the true faith'. In the eyes of Catholic Europe, she was Henry's only legitimate heir, and Charles waited expectantly for her to claim her inheritance in 1547. He deliberately did not respond to the salutations sent to him on behalf of King Edward VI; but Mary made no move.[43] Nothing which she had said or done since 1536 suggested that she doubted the authority of parliament or the king to determine the succession; or that she regarded her half-brother as anything other than his father's lawful heir. This was important, because if she had really retained her 'inward allegiance' to the papacy, she should have regarded Edward as a bastard, because his parents' marriage had been celebrated while his father was excommunicate, and the realm in schism. She may have simply kept her own counsel, believing that a challenge would have been merely suicidal in the circumstances; but of course she did not know that her chance would come again in 1553. As far as she knew, it was now or never in February 1547, and the death of the great schismatic might have seemed the obvious opportunity to put the situation right. However, not only did Mary not act, it is clear that no one in England was expecting her to act. No precautions were taken to frustrate such a bid, and all that Mary did was to complain that the Council had kept her in the dark for several days after her father's death.[44] The emperor soon realized that nothing was going to happen, and recognized the Protectorate government, distasteful as it was clearly going to be.

---

[41] J. Foxe, *Acts and Monuments* (1583), 1101–21.
[42] D. MacCulloch, *Thomas Cranmer* (1996), 353–5. According to Cranmer's own testimony, it was 1548 when he was converted to a Protestant view of the Eucharist.
[43] *Cal. Span.*, IX, 7, 15. Loades, *Mary Tudor*, 135–6.
[44] Ibid., 135.

Mary's opposition to the religious policies of her brother's governments is notorious, but requires careful examination. Her objection was to the replacement of the Mass by the Prayer Book Communion service. The Mass was in Latin and the Communion in English, but that was not the real issue. The issue was the abandonment of transubstantiation – the real and corporeal presence of Christ in the elements. None of this, however, arose immediately. For several months Mary remained in Catherine's household, where she had spent most of her time in the last two years of Henry's life, and then in the summer took seisin of the substantial independent estate which she had been granted under the terms of her father's will. With an income of nearly £4000 a year, she was now a magnate in her own right, with substantial patronage in her gift.[45] This was an entirely new situation, because although she had been consulted, and frequently nominated her own servants, they had actually been appointed and paid by the king. Such independence was timely from her point of view, because by the summer of 1547 it was clear that Protector Somerset was moving in a Protestant direction. The Royal Injunctions, and Cranmer's homily on justification were indicators of what was afoot, and provoked speedy protests from conservative bishops such as Stephen Gardiner.[46] Mary reacted rather similarly; she increased her devotional exercises, and her household began to be noted as a conservative stronghold. Her piety had not attracted much comment since 1536, except in the conventional context of praise, where it was mentioned in the same breath as her learning, virtue and modesty, and with the same emphasis. However, in June 1547 Chapuys's successor, François Van der Delft, commented specifically upon her firmness in 'the ancient faith', and reported that she was hearing as many as four Masses a day.[47] Shortly after, Mary wrote what appears to have been a formal letter of protest to Somerset about the direction of his policies. The letter does not survive, and its contents can only be reconstructed from the Protector's response, but they are highly significant. Her father, she claimed, had left the country in 'Godly order and quietness', which the Council were going about to disrupt with their innovations. Englishmen were now so divided that '... if we executors go not about to bring them to that stay that our late master left them, they will forsake all obedience'. Somerset, of course, denied the charge, and claimed that Henry had left an incomplete reformation. The only

---

[45] *Calendar of the Patent Rolls*, Edward VI, II, 20. The exact value was £3819 18s 6d.
[46] BL, Add. MS 28571, ff. 16–20. J.A. Muller, *The Letters of Stephen Gardiner* (1933), no. 126.
[47] Van der Delft to the emperor, 16 June 1547; *Cal. Span.*, IX, 100.

way to ensure the exclusion of popish authority was to exclude popish doctrine as well.[48] For the time being this dispute was no more than an irritation to the council, which had many more pressing matters to attend to; but by the end of 1548, when the legislation to introduce the First Prayer Book was already going through parliament, it began to be concerned. Mary was literally making an exhibition of herself, and in December Jehan Dubois, Van der Delft's secretary, wrote 'I understand that she was much welcomed in the north [she had just returned from Norfolk], and wherever she had power she caused the mass to be celebrated and the services of the church performed in the ancient manner …'[49]

A mild remonstration seems to have been attempted, but entirely without effect. By the beginning of 1549 Mary was gearing up for a fight, and when the new Prayer Book came into use on Whitsunday 1549, she had Mass celebrated with especial pomp in her chapel at Kenninghall.[50]

The emperor had already signalled his support through Van der Delft, and warned the English Council that he would not tolerate any pressure being put on his cousin to 'alter her religion'. Somerset should have told Charles to mind his own business, but he was in a weak position. Not only was he not the king, but with the French threatening hostilities over Boulogne, he could not afford to fall out with the emperor as well. His response was conciliatory, but pointed out that Mary was the king's subject, and could not be licensed to disobey his laws. Some private and limited dispensation might be possible, in view of her 'weakness', but no public permission.[51] Mary, however, was not disposed to hide her light under a bushel. On 16 June the Council wrote to her 'giving … advice to be conformable and obedient to the observation of his Majesty's laws [and] to give order that mass should no more be used in her house …' Mary responded on the 22nd, 'I have offended no law, unless it be a late law of your own making for the altering of matters of religion, which in my conscience is not worthy to have the name of law …'[52]

In effect, she had returned to her position of 1533. The Council and parliament had acted *ultra vires*; not, this time, because they had offended against the law of the universal Church, but because they had

---

[48] G. Burnet, *History of the Reformation* (1681), II, ii, 115.
[49] Loades, *Mary Tudor*, 143. The ambassador's knowledge of English geography was vague.
[50] *Acts of the Privy Council* (APC), II, 291.
[51] Emperor to Van der Delft, 25 January 1549; *Cal. Span.*, IX, 330.
[52] Mary to the council, 22 June 1549; J. Foxe, *Acts and Monuments* (1583), 1332.

broken her father's settlement. This was dangerous language because it impugned the council's authority to govern during a royal minority. Nor did it have much logic, because the laws to which she was appealing rested upon the same foundations as those to which she was objecting, that is the authority of statute. A rag of respectability was drawn around this argument by the claim that, since the royal supremacy was personal to the king, it could only be fully exercised when the king was an adult. When Edward came of age, Mary claimed, he would find her his obedient sister in this as in all other matters.[53]

Given the controversial nature of the reforms, and the disturbed state of the country in the summer of 1549, this was a perilous conflict. Some of her servants appeared in the ranks of the rebels in Devon, but it was conveniently assumed that they had acted without her knowledge and consent; and she made no move to support the dissidents when trouble broke out in her own backyard in Norfolk. The issues, however, were very limited. What Mary wanted was the freedom to celebrate the traditional rites of the Church, particularly the Mass, without interference. She took refuge in arguments of authority merely to defend that position. There was no intention to challenge the legitimacy of the government in any general way, or even to challenge the royal supremacy. The papal authority was not an issue, and there were no disputes over doctrine, except by implication. This dispute went through several phases between 1548 and 1552, and was never really resolved. It was only when Charles decided that the conflict was unproductive, and urged a compromise that Mary to some extent backed down. She accepted a less public and ostentatious display of traditional worship, and in return for this restraint, the Council diminished its campaign of harrassment. Neither side backed down completely, because by 1552 Edward's conscience was as offended with his sister's behaviour as hers was with his.[54] The stalemate was only ended by Edward's death, and it does not tell us as much about Mary's beliefs as might be supposed. Presumably her household kept all the traditional feasts and used the full range of sacraments, although we have no specific information to that effect. Her chaplains also seem to have preached, both within the household and outside, and were occasionally in trouble for so doing. But we have no idea what she thought about the doctrinal disputes which were exercising the fathers of the Church across Europe, or even whether she was aware of them. She probably continued her habit of reading the Latin fathers and the scriptures, although whether she

---
[53] Ibid.
[54] Edward to Mary, 24 January 1552. *Cal. Span.*, X, 209–12. Foxe, *Acts and Monuments*, 1338.

studied the latter in Latin, English or both, we do not know. English conservatives, both lay and clerical, looked up to her as an example, and her reputation as a 'good christian' spread across Catholic Europe,[55] but she seems to have had no network, and made no attempt to correspond with Catholic divines. In fact, in spite of her enthusiasm for the Mass, she was not ostensibly a Catholic at all, but what her father had made her – a conservative humanist with an extremely insular point of view.

Consequently, when the succession crisis of July 1553 brought her to the throne, most people thought they knew exactly what they were in for. She had publicly and stubbornly defended her father's settlement for nearly five years, and 'religion as King Henry left it' was what she stood for in the public mind. Her first pronouncement on the subject, the proclamation of 18 August, appeared to confirm no less.

> First, her majesty being presently by the only goodness of God settled in her just possession of the imperial crown of this realm and other dominions thereunto belonging, cannot now hide that which God and the world knoweth, how she and her father of famous memory, her grandfather and all her progenitours kings of this realm, with all their subjects have ever lived like Christian princes, both truly following themselves, and maintaining their subjects in Christ's true religion, and ended their lives therein ...[56]

However, in spite of including her father in this pantheon of virtue, the queen's intentions were not at all what they appeared to be. Her swift and unexpected triumph over the Duke of Northumberland had released a flood of pious exaltation. Her accession was a miracle, wrought by God for the specific purpose of restoring England to the true faith, and the true faith was not her father's settlement, but the faith in which her mother had lived and died.[57] Within a few weeks she had disclosed to her Council that she intended to restore the Church 'even to the Pope's authority'. It may be deduced that she had always, and for good reason, dissembled about the papacy, but we cannot be sure. If she had been mainly concerned about her own safety, she could have been less abrasive about her worship. She was persuaded to allow her brother to be buried with the Protestant rites to which he had been loyal; but against the advice both of her Council and of the imperial ambassadors, insisted on celebrating a requiem Mass as well, apparently oblivious of the fact that she could have offered his memory

---

[55] Rex, 'Morley and the Papacy', 97–8.

[56] J.L. Hughes and P.F. Larkin, *Tudor Royal Proclamations*, II (1969), 5–8. This form of words is taken from PRO, SP11/1/14.

[57] 'The Vita Mariae Reginae of Robert Wingfield of Brantham', ed. D. MacCulloch, *Camden Miscellany*, 28, 1984. This mood of exaltation was also reported in a number of the dispatches of the imperial ambassadors.

no more deadly insult.[58] Mary's state of mind over the next few months merits serious consideration, because her actions were a curious mixture of politic caution and impolitic zeal. On the one hand, as she pointed out to Francesco Commendone, restoring the true Church would take time because many bad laws would have to be repealed and nullified.[59] On the other hand she ignored, and encouraged her subjects to ignore, all those laws of the previous regime which offended her conscience. The queen's proceedings, as Stephen Gardiner pointed out to John Hales, were more to be regarded than the law. Her priorities were, first and foremost, the restoration of the Latin rite in all its richness, and particularly the Mass; and second the exclusion and punishment of all those clergy who had presumed to marry under the permissive law of 1549.

Once the Edwardian statutes were repealed, with effect from 20 December 1553, Mary used her authority as Supreme Head to press this programme hard, and one of the first instructions in the royal articles of March 1554 was that every bishop

> ... shall deprive or declare deprived, and amove according to their learning and discretion, all such persons from their benefices or ecclesiastical promotions, who contrary to the state of this order, and the laudable custom of the church, have married and used women as their wives ...[60]

The reason for this seems to have been a spin-off from her devotion to the sacraments. A married priest was polluted, and his sacraments consequently also polluted, although not necessarily invalid. In fact many married priests were not 'Protestants' in any other sense, so marriage was hardly an infallible test for heresy, but that hardly mattered to Mary. Indeed the thought that a sacrament might be both valid and polluted made it all the more obnoxious. She was also deeply concerned with chastity; partly as a result of having had it drummed into her by her mother, Vives and her tutors that this was a woman's crowning glory; partly because of an emotionally deprived adolescence in which her status was such that no man ventured to approach her; and partly, perhaps, because of her recurrent physical problems. However, beyond this distinctive preoccupation there is much less evidence of Mary's personal piety than might be supposed. She received innumerable dedications of works of Catholic devotion or polemic; but they tell us

---

[58] *Cal. Span.*, XI, 134. Loades, *Mary Tudor*, 193–4.
[59] *Cal. Ven.*, V, 785. Commendone was the secretary to the Cardinal of Imola, the nuncio in Brussels, and thus an indirect representative of Julius III.
[60] W.H. Frere and W.M. Kennedy, *Visitation Articles and Injunctions of the period of the Reformation* (1910), II, 326.

nothing beyond the fact that she was famously orthodox, and reputed to be remarkably learned for a woman.[61] Her own letters and official pronouncements say little more. We know that she was keen on 'good preaching' to undo the effects of 'evil preaching in times past'; and that she considered the punishment of heretics a duty which she owed to God. The comments of observers can take us a little further. Simon Renard, the imperial ambassador, was particularly close to Mary during the first year of her reign, and he reported at the end of October 1553, with regard to the negotiations for her marriage '… she said to me that she had wept over two hours that very day, praying to God to inspire her in her decision'.[62] This probably tells us more about her emotional state than her piety, but it is significant that prayer was her first resort in a crisis. Three days later Renard was able to report the queen's decision,

> On Sunday evening [29 October] the Queen sent for me, and I went to her. In the room where she spoke to me was the Holy Sacrament, and she told me that since I had presented your Majesty's letters to her she had not slept, but had continually wept and prayed God to inspire her with an answer to the question of marriage. … As the Holy Sacrament had been in her room, she had invoked it as her protector, guide and counsellor, and still prayed with all her heart that it would come to her help …[63]

The room in question was presumably her closet or private chapel, because it would have been unusual for any layperson, even a monarch, to keep the reserved sacrament in any other room, and confirms what earlier indications would suggest, that the sacrament of the altar was the focus of her spiritual life. The following year an anonymous Spaniard who had attended her wedding in Winchester Cathedral noted 'All the while, for an hour, she remained with her eyes fixed on the sacrament. She is a saintly woman. …'[64] By contrast, there are few references to other devotional practices. It would have been natural for her to have a particular regard for her namesake, but the evidence is very slight.[65] In conflict with her brother's council she had used the rosary as a 'badge' for her affinity; and Pole famously greeted her with the words of the

---

[61] Lord Morley's dedication, already referred to, was typical, although more specific than most. Miles Huggarde's *The Displaying of the Protestants* (1556) was simply dedicated to 'The most excellent and most vertuous Ladye …'

[62] *Cal. Span.*, XI, 319. Renard to the emperor, 28 October.

[63] Ibid., 327. Same to same, October 31.

[64] *Cal. Span.*, XIII, 7. Anonymous letter of July 1554.

[65] By contrast, Lord Morley's devotion to the Virgin is most conspicuous, and as he shared the queen's devotion to the sacrament, they may have been alike in that also; but there is no direct proof. *Triumphs of English*, 97–8, 253–69.

Hail Mary when he returned in November 1554, but that would have been a natural thing for him to have done in the circumstances, and not much can be read into it.

She was assiduous in her private devotions, and no doubt this would have involved many prayers to the Virgin and other saints, but she took no steps to restore any of the great Marian shrines, which might have been expected to feature among her first priorities. She dutifully kept all the major feasts of the Church, but there is no sign of favouritism there, either. Too much should not be made of silences, but her mother had been an assiduous pilgrim; many shrines had benefited from her generosity, and many people had commented upon the fact. The shrines had been destroyed in the 1530s, at a time when Pole and most religious conservatives believed that Henry had first become an enemy of the faith. They had gone down at the same time as the traditional noble families of Percy, Courtenay and Dacre. But whereas Mary restored the old nobility, she did not restore the shrines. St Thomas of Canterbury, St Cuthbert and Our Lady of Walsingham remained desolate. Neither did Mary ever undertake a pilgrimage as queen.

Pole's Legatine Synod discussed the possibility of a new and orthodox translation of the Bible, and that might have happened in due course, but no one in a position of authority suggested re-edifying the great shrines which had been such an important feature of English piety only a generation before.[66] The shrine of St Edward the Confessor at Westminster was indeed rebuilt, but that was undertaken by the monks, and owed nothing to Pole or the queen. Mary was well read in the scriptures but seems to have followed no particular saints, which was unusual, particularly in the middle of the sixteenth century. Nor do we have any idea of how her prime devotion to the sacrament was expressed in practice. In describing her daily routine in August 1554, Giacomo Soranzo merely wrote '... she rises at daybreak, when, after saying her prayers and hearing mass in private, she transacts business incessantly until after midnight ...'[67]

He was clearly more impressed by her application than by any unusual piety. The absence of specific comment about the queen's devotional practice, either then or later, suggests that it was regarded as normal. She confessed and received absolution whenever she felt the need, but received the host only at Easter. Several detailed descriptions of her wedding, for instance, do not suggest that she received it then, despite the special and sacramental nature of the occasion. The official account by the English heralds says

---

[66] J.P. Marmion, 'The London Synod of Cardinal Pole' (Keele University, MA, 1974).
[67] *Cal. Ven.*, V, 532.

> This done [the proclamation] the trumpets sounded, and thus both returned hand in hand, the sword being borne before them, to their traverse in the choir, the queen going always on the right hand, and there remained until mass was done; at which time wine and sops were hallowed and gave unto them ...[68]

Whatever hallowed sops may have been, they were not the host. To Mary the consecrated Host was literally the body of Christ, to be adored and invoked, but to be touched only rarely and after the most solemn preparation. This was not only perfectly orthodox, it was also the commonest form of orthodoxy. The only occasion upon which we are specifically told that she communicated was on her deathbed, when a temporary improvement in her condition was attributed to this 'sacred medecine'.[69] Giovanni Michieli, writing in May 1557, was slightly more enthusiastic than his predecessor, describing her as 'a real portrait ... of the true fear of God', and adding

> Few women in the world ... are known to be more assiduous in their prayers than she is, never chosing to suspend them for any impediment whatsoever, going at the canonical hours with her chaplains either to church in public or to her private chapel ... precisely like a nun and a religious.[70]

She kept all the fasts, he noted, and performed all Christian works. The records of her almsgiving remain, and show her to have been generous, but not especially so. It was of the Church as an institution that she felt it necessary to be particularly supportive, because of the hammering which it had suffered over the previous 20 years; but here again the signals are somewhat mixed. In spite of her enthusiasm for a settlement with the papacy, Mary played almost no part in the negotiations which produced it. This was probably because she recognized that a compromise over property was politically necessary, but the concessions offended her conscience. She was certainly opposed to the legislation which effectively gave the holders of former ecclesiastical land a legal title, but allowed herself to be overruled by Philip, who had conducted most of the negotiation.[71] In March 1555 Michieli reported that her conscience was still troubling her. She had set up a special committee of six councillors to decide what to do about the Church property still in

---

[68] *The Chronicle of Queen Jane*, ed. J.G. Nichols (Camden Society, 1850), App. XI, 169.

[69] Priuli, reporting on the deaths of the queen and the cardinal, ten days after the event, declared 'During their illness [they] confessed themselves repeatedly and communicated most devoutly, and two days before their end each received extreme unction, after which it seemed as though they rallied ...' *Cal. Ven.*, VI, 1286.

[70] Michieli's valedictory report, 13 May 1557. *Cal. Ven.*, VI, 884.

[71] Loades, *The Reign of Mary Tudor* (1991), 267–70.

the hands of the Crown. 'Her majesty,' he went on, 'wishes it to be entirely restored to those who were deprived of it ... although nothing is said of that which passed into the hands of private individuals, and constitutes the chief amount.'[72] Her committee probably advised against wholesale restoration, because only a relatively small amount was eventually given to pious uses, and the Crown went on selling former Church property, as it had done since 1536. Some episcopal estates, which were mostly in her hands through the attainder of the original grantees, were indeed restored; and many advowsons, which constituted a relatively cheap gesture.[73]

Altogether seven religious houses were restored, or more correctly refounded: the Benedictine monastery of Westminster, the Carthusian house at Shene, the Franciscan Observants at Greenwich and Southampton, the Black Friars in London and the nunneries of Sion and King's Langley. The total endowment, which came almost entirely from the Crown, amounted to some £3500 a year – about the income of one major peer.[74] Mary's attitude towards the regular religious is not entirely clear. Michieli reported that she had sent abroad for English friars of the orders of St Dominic and St Francis 'who, to escape past persecutions, withdrew beyond the seas ...', but it is not clear that any came.[75] She was allegedly delighted when 16 men in Benedictine habits presented themselves before her with a petition to return to the cloister, and swiftly granted their wish. However, she had taken no initiative herself, and it was in fact nearly two years before the Benedictine House of Westminster reappeared.[76] The general impression is that she was reactive rather than proactive and seems to have had no specific vision of monasteries or friaries as essential centres of spiritual regeneration. Westminster, with an endowment of about £2000 a year, was her only large foundation, and even that was not on a grand scale by past standards. The Hospital of the Savoy and the Preceptories of St John of Jerusalem, both in England and Ireland, were also re-established, along with a few colleges, of which Manchester is the best known. All these foundations would have had an intercessory function, but that was not

---

[72] Michieli to the Doge and Senate, 19 March 1555. *Cal. Ven.*, VI, 32.

[73] For such grants, see the *Calendar of the Patent Rolls*, Philip and Mary, IV, 399, 401, 420, 437, 439, 449, 450.

[74] This total is exclusive of the Hospital of St John (£1436) and the Savoy (about £250). Loades, *Reign of Mary*, 350–51.

[75] *Cal. Ven.*, VI, 32. As far as we know, all those who returned to the cloister in Mary's reign had remained in England. M.C. Knowles, *The Religious Orders in England*, III, (1959).

[76] It was November 1556 before the new monastery was given legal existence. *CPR*, III, 354. PRO, SP12/1/64.

their main purpose, and Mary did not establish any chantry or other institution for the primary purpose of praying for souls – her own or anyone else's. When she made her will in March 1558 she left significant bequests to all the houses of her foundation, asking them to pray for herself, her mother, her progenitors and, in due course, for her husband. But whereas her father, for all his reservations about purgatory, had requested the endowment of no fewer than 30 000 Masses for the repose of his soul, his pious and orthodox daughter did no such thing.[77]

Any assessment of Mary's religious foundations must take account of the context. By comparison with what had been lost, they were insignificant, but by comparison with the initiatives of other members of her family, they were generous. She gave less land to the Church than to the restored noble families, but far more than Elizabeth in a much longer reign. Henry VIII, in a sense, had given more still if his colleges and the new cathedrals are taken into account, but that would be a false perception because he was merely putting back part of what he had just confiscated. Mary's pious benefactions were substantial, both during her reign and at her death, but there is little sense of engagement. We simply do not know whether she rated the regular life highly, or merely regarded such houses as part of the proper equipment of a Catholic Church. Both Pole and More owed much of their spirituality to the Carthusians, but if any similar influence worked on the queen, we have no record of it.

Mary's will is, up to a point, a revealing document. Its opening formula is strictly traditional, bequeathing her soul to God, the Blessed Virgin and all the company of heaven.[78] Her first request was that £1000 be expended for the relief of poor prisoners, and the second that her mother's mortal remains should be brought from Peterborough, and interred next to her own burial place. There then followed gifts to all the seven religious houses, with a request for their prayers. Syon and Shene each received lands to the annual value of £100, plus £500 in cash; the Observants at Greenwich a similar lump sum of £500; the Black Friars at St Bartholomews 400 marks; the Observants at Southampton and the nuns at King's Langley each £200; and the Abbey of Westminster the same. The most generously treated was the hospital of the Savoy, whose endowment was more than doubled, to £500 per annum. However, these were not large sums, and they were widely scattered. For the sake of comparison, each university was to receive £500 for the support of poor students, Cardinal Pole £1000 to act as executor and her

---

[77] T. Rymer et al., *Foedera, Conventiones. litterae* etc. (1704–35), XV, 117.
[78] Loades, *Mary Tudor*, Appendix III, 370–83.

household servants a total of £3400.[79] The queen's continuing interest in education is significant. When she had felt inspired to give thanks to God for her victories over Northumberland and Sir Thomas Wyatt, she had made grants to Oxford University and to Trinity College, Cambridge.[80] Admittedly these were foundations with a religious purpose, but a more direct expression of piety might have been expected in the circumstances.

All the information which can be recovered about Mary's personal piety suggests two things: the intensity of her devotion to the sacrament of the altar, and the learned and reflective humanism in which she had been reared. Mary's emotions were engaged by the Mass and by the memory of her mother, but we have very little idea of what she thought about such controversial issues as justification by faith, purgatory or the priority of scripture. She felt strongly about the honour and respect due to the clergy – that was a consequence of her feelings about transubstantiation – and her strong views on clerical celibacy were partly a consequence of that. She deplored the English liturgy because it was not the Mass, but there are strong hints that she continued to read her Bible, and the English translation which her father had approved was never withdrawn. When her loyalty to the papacy was put to the test, it proved to be rather less strong than she claimed. When Paul IV and her husband went to war in 1556, she sided unhesitatingly with the latter, her earthly husband taking precedence over her spiritual father. In view of Paul's irascible and somewhat irrational conduct that is not surprising, but she risked excommunication, and that would have been a serious matter to her. She refused to accept Reginald Pole's recall to Rome in the following year,[81] and when Paul tried to nominate William Peto as a legate to succeed him, she refused to accept the appointment. It was believed in Rome that the English schism was to be renewed.[82] That did not happen, and Mary was never excommunicated, but relations with Rome were not at all cordial in the last 18 months of her life. Ironically, when she died in November 1558, the Pope's first reaction was one of relief at being rid of such an undutiful daughter.[83]

Mary's marriage to Philip put her in touch, probably for the first time, with the mainstream Catholicism of the Counter Reformation, but

---

[79] Ibid.
[80] Loades, *Mary Tudor*, 245.
[81] Sir Edward Carne to Philip and Mary, 10 April 1557. PRO SP69/10/586. Loades, *Reign of Mary*, 363–4.
[82] Navagero (Venetian ambassador in Rome) to the Doge and Senate, 14 August 1557. *Cal. Ven.*, VI, 1248.
[83] C.G. Bayne, *Anglo-Roman Relations, 1558–1565* (1935), 10.

it does not appear to have had much impact. Philip brought his own chaplains and confessors with him, men such as Alonso de Castro and Bartolomé Carranza, so that Mary must have been frequently in communication with them. She listened to their sermons, and no doubt talked to them in private, but it is not apparent that they had any influence on her actions. The king himself was a deeply pious man, but in the mode of his own country, and we do not know whether they normally shared their private devotions. In public, and particularly on important festivals, if Philip was in England, they attended Mass together; but if they shared their religious experiences, neither of them ever spoke of it to a third party. Philip, for all his orthodox zeal, had a much less emotional approach to his faith than Mary. Most particularly, he was prepared to regard heresy as a political problem, as his father had done in similar circumstances. However, Philip had been reared, and lived all his life in a climate of Catholic orthodoxy, whereas Mary's faith had, in her own eyes at least, been tested in the fire. As Soranzo wrote

> ... nor did she [during her brother's reign] chose by any act to assent to any other form of religion, her belief in that in which she was born being so strong that had the opportunity offered, she would have displayed it at the stake ...[84]

There had never been the slightest chance that she would have been called upon to make the supreme sacrifice at the hands of Protestant bigots, but that was her self-image, and the view which was widespread in Catholic Europe. Mary had shown more than a touch of hysteria on a number of occasions when under pressure. It had appeared in her reaction to the events of 1533–36, particularly in the insulting language which she deliberately used to her *bête noir*, Anne Boleyn. It had appeared in the summer of 1536, when the threat to her life had briefly been real, and it had appeared several times between 1549 and 1551; most notably when she had contemplated flight in the summer of 1550, and again when a delegation visiting her from the Council was sent on its way with her public insults ringing in their ears.[85] During her reign, Mary suffered a physical and emotional collapse after the failure of her pregnancy in the summer of 1555. She was also deeply disturbed by Philip's failure to return in 1556, and by his attempts to put pressure on her over his coronation. But she showed none of the hysterical uncertainty which had afflicted her in 1550, and neither her role as a persecutor nor her aversion to married clergy need be attributed to emotional reflexes.

---

[84] Soranzo's valedictory report, 18 August 1554. *Cal. Ven.*, V, 532.
[85] *APC*, III, 347.

In spite of the width of her reading and her exposure to the evangelical intellectuals around Catherine Parr, when it came to the point Mary was utterly unable to understand anyone who did not share her specific convictions. To her, heretics were people who had led her father astray, ruined her mother, plundered the Church and destroyed the godly peace of England. That they might be people with religious convictions as profound as her own, she never for a moment accepted. This attitude was partly the result of her own highly stressful experiences, and partly of the influence of seasoned politicians like Stephen Gardiner. Gardiner was convinced that heresy was a mere cloak for greed and political ambition, and the events of Edward's reign had provided some justification for such a view.[86] Moreover, Gardiner was a lawyer, not a theologian, and whereas he could find arguments to justify the Royal Supremacy, he could find none to attack such fundamentals as transubstantiation. By the time that he became Mary's Lord Chancellor he had become convinced that only the traditional doctrines of the Church and the authority of the clergy could protect the country from a criminal conspiracy.[87] Like Mary, although for rather different reasons, he did not take the beliefs of heretics seriously. During the first year of the reign they collaborated enthusiastically in sweeping the Protestants out of all their positions of power or influence, both apparently convinced that the destruction of their power base would reveal them for the time-serving frauds they really were. The failure of many of the leaders to recant under the pressure of deprivation and imprisonment was taken either as 'vainglory' or as a subtle political tactic to maintain a ground for counterattack. The fact that there were numerous Protestants of humble status was merely evidence of how easy it was to delude the 'common people'. Both Mary and Gardiner were convinced that once proper ecclesiastical jurisdiction had been restored, the 'sharp correction' of a few leaders would solve the problem.

Neither Philip nor Pole shared this optimistic view. The king had no more sympathy with heretics than Mary had, but he knew what they were, and did not expect them to be easily cowed. The cardinal's understanding was much more subtle, because he knew what the issues were and could see where the dissidents were coming from.[88] He did not disagree with persecution, but was uneasy, particularly over the execution of the ignorant. Once the fires had been lit in February 1555, it soon became apparent to everyone except Mary that English heresy

---

[86] Redworth, *In Defence of the Church Catholic*, 248–82.
[87] Ibid.
[88] For a full discussion of Pole's doctrinal position, see T.F. Mayer, *Reginald Pole, Prince and Prophet* (2001).

was a tough plant. It may have been small-scale, but it was prepared to meet conviction with conviction, and threats with defiance. By the summer of 1555 both Philip and Gardiner had decided that the burnings were a bad idea. The king did not intervene openly, but let it be known that he did not approve. What he may have said to Mary in private we do not know, but it did nothing to deflect her. Gardiner, in John Foxe's words, was 'utterly discouraged' and began arguing for a lower-key policy of sanctions.[89] However, Philip left England in August, and Gardiner died in November. From then on, the persecution was clearly driven by the Queen, dragging a reluctant Pole behind her.

'Touching the punishment of heretics,' she wrote in her only recorded pronouncement on the subject, 'methinketh it ought to be done without rashness, not leaving in the meantime to do justice to such as by learning would seem to deceive the simple, and the rest so to be used that the people might well perceive them not to be condemned without just occasion …'[90]

However, what might seem 'just occasion' to the Queen was not necessarily seen that way by her subjects. Eventually nearly 300 went to the stake, mostly labourers and artisans, and many of them women. As events turned out, this was a catastrophic mistake, and in spite of John Foxe's efforts to conceal the fact, it was Mary's own mistake.[91] So what turned this humane, well-read humanist Christian, who was so well loved by her servants, into the most ruthless persecutor in English history? That same commitment to the sacrament of the altar, which had caused her to defy her brother and celebrate four Masses a day with 'unusual splendour', also gave her a profound hatred for those who rejected it. It was not the denial of the papacy, or the English Bible or even justification by faith which was the crime against the Holy Ghost, but the rejection of transubstantiation. Over and over again, this was the issue which sent heretics to the stake, humble and learned alike. Of course it was also a key issue for the authority of the clergy, so it was easy for Foxe to make it appear that the priests were simply protecting their own intersts, but it was also the issue which touched Mary to the heart. To eradicate such a virus, which threatened the souls of all whom it infected, no measures were too extreme. To punish such heretics was not a policy, but a duty solemnly enjoined by God.

For all her humanist education, Mary was a woman whose convictions

---

[89] Foxe, *Acts and Monuments*, 1785.
[90] BL, Cotton MS Titus C.vii, f. 120.
[91] Foxe was concerned to demonize the Catholic clergy, and therefore consistently emphasized their role in the persecution instead of the queen's. Most of the bishops were very reluctant persecutors.

were stronger than her reason. When Thomas Cranmer was crumbling under the threat of burning in the winter of 1555–56 and busily recanting all he had ever stood for, the queen was unmoved. She hated Cranmer, both as an arch heretic and as the destroyer of her mother's marriage, and had reprieved him from a traitor's death specifically to face the fire. So in Foxe's words 'she would nothing relent' of her determination to execute him, although he had never relapsed and was not, apparently, obstinate.[92] It was publicly given out that his recantations were insincere, and therefore irrelevant. The Council even tried to suppress them, presumably on the queen's orders. Had Cranmer been allowed to live, and his recantation to stand, he would have been as utterly discredited as the Duke of Northumberland and his cause would have been severely damaged. As it was he died a martyr, and a nail in the coffin of Mary's historical reputation.

In a sense Mary was an enlightened Christian, well read in the Bible, the Latin fathers and not ignorant of pagan antiquity. From her childhood, her faith could have developed in several different ways, but it was steered in a conservative direction by loyalty to her mother. Most of the traditional teachings and practices of the Church were second nature to her, and how much she ever thought about them we do not know. She found a congenial soulmate in Reginald Pole, one of the most subtle and learned churchmen of his generation, and a man whose true convictions still defy lucid reconstruction.[93] However, her belief in the sacrament of the altar was a different matter altogether. This was a profound faith which could not be compromised, either in adversity or prosperity. All the emotional frustrations of her life were channelled into the devotion of the Lord's body, and it made her both holy and perilous. As a monarch her priorities for the Church lay in the restoration of the sacraments, in education and in the re-establishment of parochial discipline, as her tutors had taught her long ago. Her programme failed partly because she died too soon, but the strength and nature of her personal faith also brought failure of another kind. She was quite incapable of treating heresy – and particularly sacramental heresy – as a political problem. Her bishops and Pole's commissioners hammered away incessantly on a single theme: '… after the words of consecration spoken, what remaineth in the bread and wine?' The answers brought death to scores of men and women. Mary could have found another way, and neither Pole nor Philip would have objected, but she would not do so because to her the denial of the corporeal presence was an unspeakable blasphemy. That also made its contribution to the rejection of her cherished ideals, and left her with the sobriquet 'Bloody Mary'.

---

[92] *Acts and Monuments*, 1884.
[93] Mayer, *Reginald Pole*.

Part I

The Process

CHAPTER ONE

The Marian Episcopate

David Loades

When Mary was recognized as queen, towards the end of July 1553, two bishoprics were vacant by the course of nature. John Scory of Rochester had been translated to Chichester in May 1552, and not replaced; and Arthur Bulkeley of Bangor had died on 14 March.[1] There was also confusion in the north east of England because the ancient Prince Bishopric of Durham had been abolished by statute in March 1553. In theory it had been replaced with two new dioceses, one in Durham and the other in Newcastle upon Tyne. However, neither of these had been filled; the temporalities had consequently never been granted, and the administration of the old see simply carried on as though nothing had happened.[2] Nevertheless, the queen was faced with 23 bishops, one of whom, John Hooper, held two sees, and all of whom had subscribed, willingly or unwillingly, to the Edwardian settlement.

Of these, four were swiftly deprived as having been unlawfully intruded into their sees. The reason for this was that their predecessors had been removed by royal commissions which the queen chose to regard as illegal. They had not in fact been illegal because they had operated under the terms of the Henrician Acts of Supremacy; and since Mary was doing the same in reversing their decisions, there was little logic in her position. Her lawyers knew this perfectly well, and found (or invented) procedural defects in order to justify her actions.[3] George Day of Chichester, John Veysey of Exeter, Edmund Bonner of London and Stephen Gardiner of Winchester were all restored to their episcopal functions at once, without even waiting for the formal nullification of their deprivations. As a result John Scory of Chichester, Miles Coverdale of Exeter, Nicholas Ridley of London and John Ponet of Winchester found that they had never held those sees, and that all the legal dispositions which they had made during their incumbencies, including

---

[1] *The Handbook of British Chronology*, ed. E.B. Fryde, D.E. Greeway, S. Porter and I. Roy (Royal Historical Society, 1986) [*HBC*], pp. 267, 292.

[2] D. Loades, 'The Dissolution of the Diocese of Durham, 1553–4', in D. Marcombe (ed.), *The Last Principality* (1987), pp. 101–17.

[3] Felicity Heal, *Of Prelates and Princes* (1980), pp. 151–3.

routine matters like the renewal of leases, were null and void. The consequent legal disputes went on for years.[4] Cuthbert Tunstall was similarly recognized at once as Bishop of Durham, in spite of the fact that he had been deprived, and his see abolished. This caused a modicum of embarrassment, because when parliament was asked to repeal the statute of abolition in November 1553, it declined to do so, in spite of the fact that Tunstall was sitting in the House of Lords as bishop at the time.[5] Mary therefore resorted to the dubious expedient of re-erecting the ancient see by Letters Patent in January 1554; and parliament was finally persuaded to tidy up the anomalies in April.[6] For some reason Nicholas Heath, who had been deprived of Worcester in 1551, was not restored at once, and his supplanter, John Hooper, was not described as intruded. Hooper was deprived as a result of the visitation of March 1554, and Heath was then reinstated.

The queen's purpose, of course, was to get rid of Protestant bishops as quickly as possible. Thomas Cranmer was effectively deprived by his conviction for high treason in November 1553, although it took another two and a half years to unravel his canonical status.[7] Robert Farrer of St Davids also seems to have been regarded as deprived before the end of that year, although the formal proceedings are obscure. Others, such as John Hooper of Worcester and Gloucester and John Taylor of Lincoln, were put out of action by imprisonment. Although Mary officially abandoned the title of Supreme Head in December 1553, when the traditional rites of the Catholic Church were restored, in fact she continued to exercise the power in the service of her own policy. In March 1554 royal visitations were conducted, as a result of which a further five bishops were deprived, and one resigned.[8] Where a bishop had married, even if he was not a particularly zealous Protestant, that was the reason usually given, as was done with Robert Holgate of York, who subsequently (and unsuccessfully) sought reinstatement. The less obliging could be removed for doctrinal reasons, as was done with Hooper. By June 1554, 13 Edwardian bishops had been excluded by one means or another; of these six had been consecrated in accordance with the new Ordinal introduced in 1550, and their episcopal status was

---

[4] See, for example, N.L. Jones, 'A bill confirming Bishop Bonner's deprivation and reinstating Bishop Ridley as the legal bishop of London, from the parliament of 1559', *Journal of Ecclesiastical History*, 33, (1982), 580–85.

[5] J. Loach, *Parliament and the Crown in the Reign of Mary Tudor* (1986), 80–81.

[6] *CPR, Mary*, I, 378. Heal, *Of Prelates and Princes*, 153–4.

[7] As Cranmer had been confirmed in office by Clement VII in 1533, he could only be removed by a direct exercise of papal authority, not by a legate. Diarmaid MacCulloch, *Thomas Cranmer* (1996), 554–605.

[8] *HBC*, 227–84.

therefore disallowed as well.⁹ Six Catholics had been restored. Three of these, Bonner, Heath and Day, had been consecrated and appointed under the royal supremacy; while the remaining three, Tunstall, Veysey and Gardiner, went back before 1533. At this stage it did not make any difference. Of the thirteen who were deprived four, Cranmer, Ridley, Hooper and Farrer were subsequently burned at the stake for heresy; a further four, Barlow, Scory, Coverdale and Ponet, escaped into exile; while five, Bird, Bush, Harley, Taylor and Holgate, remained obscurely in England.¹⁰ Harley continued with some clandestine Protestant activity, while Holgate tried to ingratiate himself with the regime. All five were dead by the end of the reign. Only Ponet died in exile, the other three returning in 1559, two of them to episcopal office.¹¹

Even the most perfunctory calculation, however, will reveal that this leaves a substantial number of conformists. Of the twenty-three men who were actually in possession of a see in July 1553, no fewer than ten accommodated themselves to the Catholic restoration and retained their positions; although in the case of Thomas Goodrich, who died in May 1554, his departure may have been opportune. Given that both Northumberland and Mary were concerned to weed out the uncooperative as well as the downright hostile, this is a surprising statistic. Only one Marian bishop, Anthony Kitchin of Llandaff, was prepared to be similarly accommodating in 1559.¹² Apart from Kitchin and Thomas Thirlby, by then of Ely, the remaining seven of these conformists all died during the reign, the last being Robert King of Oxford, who departed in December 1557. Thirlby was not prepared to flex his conscience a second time, and was duly deprived in July 1559. Of those converts who lived to see the development of persecution after February 1555, only Thirlby and John Salcot of Salisbury were much involved. There was little heresy in Oxfordshire or Cumberland, and even less in Henry Man's diocese of Sodor and Man, or Robert Parfew's two patches – St Asaph and Hereford. There was some persecution in Peterborough, and one high-profile burning in Cardiff, but Foxe does not particularly castigate either John Chambers or Kitchin, although the former was

---

9 The degradation of John Hooper, as described by John Foxe, makes this clear. *Acts and Monuments* (1583), p. 1508.

10 See the lives of these bishops, as presented by the *Oxford Dictionary of National Biography* (*ODNB*). On Holgate, see A.G. Dickens, 'The marriage and character of Archbishop Holgate', *English Historical Review*, 52, 1937, 428–42; also, Dickens, *Robert Holgate, Archbishop of York and President of the King's Council in the North* (St Anthony's Hall Publications, 8, 1955). Holgate's petition to the queen is PRO, SP11/6, no. 84. This was published and annotated by Dickens in the *EHR* (56, 1941, 450–59).

11 Barlow became Bishop of Chichester, and Scory of Hereford.

12 *HBC*, 294.

safely dead by the time that he wrote.[13] Thirlby and Salcot did not escape condemnation. Neither was in a front-line diocese, the former having moved from Norwich to Ely in July 1554, but both were involved in the interrogation of heretics, which Foxe regarded as particularly obnoxious hypocrisy in view of their personal histories. In Thirlby's favour at least it may be said that he had never been at ease with the Protestant establishment, and that his conformity in 1553/4 was not only genuine, but probably a considerable relief.[14]

So between conformists and restored Henricians, Mary had more than half her bench. She was without an archbishop until June 1555, when Nicholas Heath was translated to York from Worcester; but that function was performed until January 1555 by Stephen Gardiner, both Lord Chancellor and Bishop of Winchester; and thereafter by Reginald Pole, first as Cardinal Legate and then (after March 1556) as Archbishop of Canterbury.[15] However, there were thirteen other sees to be filled, either as a result of deprivation or natural vacancy, and in the absence of either Pope or Metropolitan, the queen had no option but to fill them herself. During 1554 she provided eleven bishops on her own authority, eight of these before Pole returned to England and was permitted to exercise his jurisdiction, and all before he in fact began to do so. There was, however, a hidden agenda here. Although Pole was not permitted to exercise his legatine authority in England until 10 November 1554 – and even that was technically illegal because his attainder could not be repealed until parliament met on the 12th – he had in fact been confirming the queen's appointments since the beginning of the year.[16] Unlike the Henrician restorations, therefore,

---

[13] In recounting the story of Rawlins White, the fisherman who was burned at Cardiff, Foxe says '… this hys kepyng, whether it were by the Bishops meanes, because he would rid hys handes of hym, or through the favour of hys keeper, was not so severe and extreme, but that [if he had so listed] he might have escaped oftentymes'. When Kitchin was finally compelled to condemn his victim, he proceeded with prayer 'which commonly the popish persecutors were not wont to do …' *Acts and Monuments* (1583), 1557. Chambers died in February 1556.

[14] T.F. Shirley, *Thomas Thirlby; Tudor Bishop* (1964), gives the fullest account of his career and attitude.

[15] D. Loades, *The Reign of Mary Tudor* (1991), 96–128, 262–303. See further, Glyn Redworth, *In Defence of the Church Catholic: The Life of Stephen Gardiner* (1990), and Thomas F. Mayer, *Reginald Pole, Prince and Prophet* (2000).

[16] According to one report (*Calendar of State Papers, Venetian*, V, 453) the first list of appointments was submitted to Pole as early as 24 February, that is before the deprivations. The date of Pole's confirmation is 18 March, just three days after the relevant commission. Bourne, Morgan, Brooks, Parfew, White, Cotes and Griffin were reconciled by proxy on 19 March. After their confirmation, Pole wrote to all the new bishops, urging them to 'bring back to a recognition of the true faith and the unity and obedience of the

who still had to make their peace with the Pope, these new appointments were men who, from the first, were regarded as reconciled. At the time when the papal jurisdiction was restored, therefore, Mary's episcopal bench consisted of a strange mixture of men. The five of the six who had been restored and were still alive were technically schismatics rather than heretics, because, like the queen herself, they had accepted the Henrician Supremacy but rejected the Protestant Church of Edward. Needless to say, none of them showed the slightest reluctance to accept a return to the papal jurisdiction. The ten survivors, however, should have been regarded as heretics, because they had accepted, and enforced, the Prayer Books and the Forty-two Articles. With the exception of Goodrich, they were all conservatives, and their survival under Edward is probably more remarkable than their conformity under Mary.[17] Goodrich, however, had been a noted reformer, suspected of heresy as early as 1540. He had been one of the compilers of the Book of Common Prayer, and had sat on the commission which deprived Gardiner. In 1549 the radical Hooper had regarded him as an ally. He was Lord Chancellor at the time of Edward's death, and had accepted the succession of Jane Grey. As a result, in August 1553 he was one of those listed for arrest and trial for high treason.[18] However, the queen personally struck his name from the list; he submitted and did homage, losing only the Great Seal. Thereafter he simply conformed, and his true feelings are unknown. He was never formally reconciled or faced scrutiny by Cardinal Pole, because he died on 10 May 1554.

Robert Aldrich of Carlisle was simply a survivor. He had had an orthodox, but not particularly distinguished career, culminating in the provostship of Eton College, before being appointed to the northern see in 1537. He had been a promoter of the Act of Six Articles, and had opposed all the Edwardian changes while they were under discussion, accepting them only when they became law.

His degrees were in arts and divinity, so he should probably be

---

Holy Roman Church all those of the said kingdom who have departed from the catholic faith, and the obedience of the same church.' A similar procedure was followed with the other appointments made later in the year. Pole's legatine register; microfilm in Lambeth Palace library; original Douai MS 922 fols. 3 et seq., in the municipal archive.

[17] For a discussion of the conformist pressures applied under Edward, see D. MacCulloch, *Tudor Church Militant; Edward VI and the Protestant Reformation* (1999).

[18] As late as 19 July Goodrich was still signing letters as a member of Jane's council. By the following day he had changed sides, and not later than the 26th he signed (along with Cranmer and the courtier Amyas Paulet) a set of articles 'wherein the queens pleasure is to be known'. *The Chronicle of Queen Jane*, ed. J.G. Nichols (Camden Society, 48, 1848), 91, 109. *Calendar of State Papers, Domestic, Mary*, ed. C.S. Knighton (1998), no. 5.

counted as a theologian, but he seems to have written nothing of note.[19] By contrast Richard Sampson of Coventry and Lichfield was a civil lawyer who had begun his career as a diplomat in Wolsey's household. He had been appointed to Chichester in 1536, but by 1540 was a sworn enemy of Thomas Cromwell. Following the latter's fall, in 1543, he was translated to Coventry and Lichfield and served a term as President of the Council in the Marches. He was more a civil servant than an ecclesiastic, and simply subscribed to each change in turn. Like Goodrich, he died unreconciled, in September 1554.[20] Thomas Thirlby was also a lawyer and diplomat, although rather younger. Cranmer had been his first patron, and he had become Dean of the Chapel Royal in 1534. He was the first (and only) bishop of Westminster, and sufficiently opposed to the Reformation to vote against the Act of Uniformity in 1549. However, he enforced it when it was law, and was sufficiently out of the country to avoid most of the domestic crises. He was resident with the emperor when Henry died, and again when Edward died.[21] At that time he was bishop of Norwich, and simply submitted on his return, which seems to have been accepted without question. He was translated to Ely in July 1554, and subsequently reconciled.

Robert King of Oxford was a more obvious conservative, having started his career as a Cistercian monk at Rewley. He was elected abbot of Thame in 1530, and of Oseney in 1537; from whence he made a seamless transition to become the first bishop of Oseney and Thame in 1541, and to move with the see to Oxford four years later. His record under Edward VI is obscure, and he presumably did as he was told. If anything, he was a theologian, but left no mark as such.[22] John Chambers of Peterborough was rather similar. First monk and then abbot there, he surrendered his house in 1539 in return for the large pension of £266, and stepped sideways into the new see in 1541. He was described as 'a safe and conformable person', and seems to have floated with the tide, in whatever direction it was set.[23] John Capon, or Salcot, was another ex-monk; this time a Benedictine, who was abbot of St Benet, Hume in Norfolk as early as 1517. He was favoured by Wolsey and was a promoter of the king's divorce; so his nomination to Bangor in 1533 can hardly have been a surprise. Translated to Salisbury in

---

[19] ODNB. Nothing is recorded under his name in the *Revised Short Title Catalogue*.
[20] ODNB.
[21] Shirley, *Thomas Thirlby*. D. MacCulloch, 'A reformation in the balance; power struggles in the diocese of Norwich, 1533–1553', in *Counties and Communities: Essays on East Anglian History*, ed. C. Rawcliffe, R. Virgoe and R. Wilson (1996), 97–114.
[22] ODNB.
[23] Ibid.

1539, he supported the Six Articles, and kept a low profile during the upheavals of Edward's reign. Like the other ex-monks, he was clearly a conservative, but not one who was prepared to stand up and be counted.[24] The bishop of Sodor, the appropriately named Henry Man, had been a Carthusian of Shene, although not in the heroic mould. Most of his career was spent at Oxford, where he graduated DD in 1539. He became dean of Chester in 1541, and was consecrated to his see in 1546, but his career there is obscure, and it seems likely that he never left London.

Anthony Kitchin was yet another monk, who was officially at Westminster and then at Eynesham as abbot from 1530, but seems to have spent most of his time in Oxford, where he graduated DD in 1538, at the advanced age of 61. He supported the divorce, and surrendered Eynesham without a fuss in 1539. In 1545 he was appointed to Llandaff, and took up residence there. Like the others, he voted against the Edwardian changes, but accepted them. Uniquely, he survived to do the same again in 1559, dying in possession in 1563, at the age of 85. The last of this particular group was Robert Parfew, or Warton. He was also a monk, this time a Cluniac, and Abbot of Bermondsey; a post which he continued to hold *in commendam* with the see of St Asaph from 1536 until 1538, when the house was suppressed. He then appears to have moved to Denbigh, where he managed to evade all the conformist pressures of 1547–53. So successful was he that Mary translated him to Hereford in March 1554 to replace the deprived John Harley.[25]

Of the 16 bishops whom Mary either resurrected or accepted, Tunstall, Veysey, Salcot and Kitchin were all of very advanced age. Tunstall had been a man of distinction, both in the Church and the royal service, but by 1553 his restoration owed more to nostalgia and the queen's sense of justice than it did to his usefulness. When the persecution began, he distanced himself from it as far as possible, and was not responsible for any deaths. Foxe tells the story of Tunstall warning his chancellor to have no man's blood on his hands, and described him as 'no great bloody persecutor'.[26] Gardiner, Bonner, Thirlby and Goodrich were also men with distinguished records of service, and of an age to be more active. Goodrich's early death makes it pointless to speculate about how useful he might have been, but Gardiner and Bonner were among the foremost executors of Mary's Catholic policies, and earned the dubious distinction of being pilloried

---

[24] Ibid.
[25] Ibid.
[26] *Acts and Monuments* (1583), 2102.

as persecutors. In neither case was this evil reputation entirely deserved. Gardiner was a 'strategic persecutor', who believed that a few high-profile executions would be sufficient to cure the heresy problem. He lived long enough to become disillusioned with this policy, and died in November 1555; so he was not responsible for the indiscriminate executions of Mary's later years.[27] Bonner was responsible, in a sense, and was demonized by Foxe in consequence; but this was largely because he was in London, which was the main battlefield. He was a rough diamond; an administrator and diplomat rather than a pastor or theologian, and was driven on against his better judgement by the Privy Council.[28] Thirlby was involved in the trials of Hooper, Rogers and Taylor, and in the degradation of Cranmer, but that was more because of his status, and because he could hardly refuse, than because he desired it. Even Foxe admits that he participated very reluctantly in the proceedings against his former patron.[29] Of the other survivors, Heath, Salcot, Kitchin and King were all involved in trials and inquisitions to some extent, but only King was noted as a persecutor, and the reluctance of Heath is manifest in a number of stories. Sampson, Goodrich and Veysey died before the end of 1554, and most of those who survived into the era of restored papal jurisdiction simply did their duty; Aldrich, Thirlby, Chambers, Salcot, Man, Kitchin, Tunstall and Parfew – these were hardly men with the zeal of the Counter Reformation burning within them, and neither was Robert King, for all that was said of him. Gardiner, Bonner, Heath and Day were the only ones who can be said to have shown much in the way of enthusiasm or commitment, and it was upon the shoulders of Mary's own appointees that the burden of promoting the Catholic cause was mainly to fall.

Eleven new bishops were appointed during 1554. Of these one, Nicholas Heath, was a restoration and has already been counted; a second was the translation of Robert Parfew from St Asaph to Hereford. The other nine were new recruits to the bench. None of these had been 'civil servants', and their background was uniformly academic and ecclesiastical. Although he had been a fellow of All Souls College, Oxford, in 1531, Gilbert Bourne's career had enjoyed no great distinction; but he had stood by his patron, Edmund Bonner, when the latter was in trouble in 1549. He had himself conformed, but had enjoyed no preferment in the Edwardian Church. On Mary's accession the most telling point in his favour was probably that he was the nephew

---

[27] Redworth, *In Defence of the Church Catholic*, 311–29.
[28] G. Alexander, 'Bonner and the Marian persecutions', *History*, 60, 1975, 374–92.
[29] *Acts and Monuments* (1583), 1881–3.

of Sir John Bourne, the Principal Secretary.[30] In August 1553 he preached the notorious sermon commending Bonner's restoration which caused a riot at Paul's Cross.[31] This was no doubt an additional mark in his favour, and he replaced William Barlow at Bath and Wells in April 1554. He played a leading role in the disputation against the reformers which took place at Oxford in the same month, and was a zealous promoter of the traditional order. He sat on several heresy commissions, but was usually noted as a moderate influence, and seems to have had little appetite for persecution. He refused conformity in 1559, and was placed under house arrest, where he died ten years later.[32] He was an honourable and respectable figure, but a man of no great ability. James Brooks, who was appointed to Gloucester at the same time, was a man of similar background, but greater achievement. He had proceeded DD at Oxford in 1546, become master of Balliol in the following year and vice-chancellor in 1552. This indicates that he had not been a notorious non-conformist at that point; but he had been chaplain and almoner to Stephen Gardiner, and it was probably the latter's favour which gained him his promotion. He was also favoured by Cardinal Pole, and in 1555 served as Papal Commissary for the trials of Cranmer, Ridley and Latimer.[33] In spite of John Foxe's attempts to make him appear ridiculous and maladroit, he was clearly a man of ability and an energetic diocesan. Like Bourne, he refused conformity in 1559 and was deprived, but he died in the following year.

John Holyman was the oldest of the new recruits, being 59 when he was promoted to Bristol in November. He was also the only one to have been a regular, although his profession at Reading seems to have been little more than nominal, as he spent virtually all his time in Oxford. He was a fellow of New College as early as 1512, and thereafter collected four degrees in arts, civil law and divinity, culminating in a DD in 1531.[34] He was noted as a zealous anti-Lutheran, and an opponent of the king's 'proceedings'. This probably accounts for his lack of preferment, but he was reasonably discreet and did not suffer further for his opinions. During Edward's reign he was in virtual retirement, and made only the minimum gestures of conformity. The reason for his promotion is obscure. As bishop he took part in the proceedings against several heretics, but never in a principal role, and seems to have been a

---

[30] ODNB.
[31] *The Diary of Henry Machyn*, ed. J.G. Nichols (Camden Society, 1848), p. 41. *Acts and Monuments* (1583), p. 1409.
[32] ODNB.
[33] *Acts and Monuments* (1583), 1757–68.
[34] ODNB.

reluctant persecutor. George Cotes, appointed to Chester on the deprivation of John Bird in April 1554, was another man of sound academic background, but no great distinction. He had been fellow at both Balliol and Magdalen Colleges, Oxford, and University Proctor in 1531. He proceeded DD in 1536, and had held a couple of rectories before moving to Chester in 1544 as canon and archdeacon. His views on the divisive issues of the day are not recorded, which presumably means that he simply conformed. However, he must have convinced the Council of his sound conservatism, and it was a fairly obvious move to translate him from archdeacon to bishop.[35] He died in December 1555, without having made much impact one way or another. His diocese was not troubled with heresy, and he seems to have played no part in the proceedings. The new bishop of Lincoln, John White, was a man of a very different stamp. He also had a respectable academic background, having been a fellow of New College, Oxford, in 1527, and Warden of Winchester in 1541. His views on the Henrician controversies are not known, but after 1547 he emerged as a strong opponent of change. By 1551 his recalcitrance had led to his imprisonment in the Tower of London, from whence he was transferred to Cranmer's custody after a few weeks. He submitted in 1552 and was appointed to a prebend at Lichfield, but his views had not changed and he crossed swords famously with John Philpot, the zealously Protestant archdeacon of Winchester.[36] He was therefore an obvious man to promote Mary's policies, and was already campaigning vigorously for the restoration of the property of the Church before he was named to the bench in March. Thereafter he was a prominent activist, and a keen heresy hunter who presided at Ridley's trial and preached at Gardiner's funeral.[37] He was one of the bishops who consecrated Pole to Canterbury in March 1556, and was translated to Winchester in July. He preached at Mary's funeral in November 1558 in a manner which earned him a rebuke from Elizabeth's Council, and was a leading member of the 'Catholic team' in the disputation of the following March. His apparent truculence on that occasion earned him a second spell in the Tower, and he was one of the first to be deprived for refusing the oath of supremacy in June 1559.[38] He died in the following January. Along with Bonner and Brooks, he was one of the most forceful and uncompromising advocates of Catholic orthodoxy.

John Hopton was unusual in that he had started out as a Dominican

---

[35] Ibid.
[36] *Acts and Monuments* (1583), 1794–6.
[37] Ibid., 1764.
[38] Ibid., 2123–5.

friar, and had been prior of the Oxford house of that order. He had taken a theological doctorate at Bologna some time before 1529, and incorporated it at Oxford in that year. He proceeded DD in his own university in 1542, and held various minor preferments without leaving the university. Again, his views on the Henrician controversies are not known, but were presumably not overtly hostile to the king. In 1548 he entered Mary's newly independent household as chaplain, and became her warm supporter in her conflicts with Edward's Council. He was repeatedly in trouble, and briefly arrested, for a loyalty which the new queen was to remember with gratitude in 1553.[39] He was provided to Norwich in October 1554, and became very active in the persecution that followed. However, Norwich was a diocese in which there was a lot of resistance to the Marian restoration, and it may have been his notorious chancellor, Michael Dunning, who was mainly responsible for the 31 burnings which took place between the summer of 1555 and the autumn of 1558.[40] Hopton's death in August of that year spared him any need to answer for his (or Dunning's) actions.

Ralph Baynes was a Cambridge man who had taken an MA at St John's College in 1521, having been ordained to the priesthood about two years earlier. He became a prominent Hebrew scholar, and held the chair in that language at the university of Paris. He was clearly a man of strong conservative views, and may well have wished to avoid the pressures operating in the English Church between 1535 and 1553. He was appointed to Coventry and Lichfield in November 1554, and played an active part in the persecution of Protestants in Coventry, as well as assisting at the trials of Hooper, Rogers and Taylor.[41] He was also one of the Catholic disputants in April 1559. Deprived in June, he died in the following November. The remaining two men in this group are relatively obscure figures. Maurice Griffin, or Griffiths had taken a BD in Oxford in 1528, and been archdeacon of Rochester since 1537. This means that he must have served under Ridley, Ponet and Scory, all of whom were strong Protestants, without upsetting them sufficiently to lose his job. Nevertheless he was promoted to fill the vacant bishopric in April 1554; perhaps for no better reason than that he was conformable, and on the spot. He avoided the Elizabethan settlement by dying three days after Mary.[42] Henry Morgan also had a low profile. He was an Oxford man,

---

[39] ODNB, PRO SP10/8, no. 30; D. Loades, *Mary Tudor: A Life* (1989), 157–70.
[40] *Acts and Monuments*; Philip Hughes, *The Reformation in England*, II (1953), 262–4; D. Loades, *The Oxford Martyrs* (1970), 12.
[41] Foxe blames him particularly for his pursuit of Robert Glover and his brother. *Acts and Monuments* (1583), 1709–13.
[42] HBC, 268.

but a civil lawyer, having taken a DCL in 1525, and entered Doctors Commons three years later. He was ordained about 1529, and held various minor preferments, but was too obscure to have left any record of his views. He became a canon of Exeter in 1548 and of Hereford in 1551, so presumably he was not a notorious opponent of reform. Why he was named to St David's in April 1554 to replace the deprived Robert Farrer is not clear. He seems to have been a satisfactory incumbent but, beyond the fact that Farrer was burned in his diocese, he had little connection with the persecution. He retired to Oxford on Elizabeth's accession, and died (horribly, according to Foxe) in December 1559, without having either submitted or been deprived.[43]

During the period in which the Pope's authority was acknowledged, that is from January 1555 to May 1559, nine further bishops were consecrated, and two nominated but not consecrated.[44] Of these by far the most important and distinguished was the Cardinal Legate, Reginald Pole himself. Pole was of the royal blood, being the son of Margaret, countess of Salisbury, and grandson of George, duke of Clarence, the younger brother of Edward IV. He had been educated generously by Henry VIII, but quarrelled bitterly with his patron over the latter's divorce in 1533, and retreated to Italy. Famous both because of his learning and his princely status, he there became cardinal and bishop of Viterbo. Henry had taken his revenge upon Pole's family, and the division between them was unbridgeable; so it is ironic that their views on the need for ecclesiastical reform were in many ways similar. Both were humanists, believing strongly in the merits of education and in the value of scriptural translation. Both were in two minds about the doctrine of justification. But whereas Pole placed great emphasis upon Christian unity and the role of the Pope in preserving it, Henry rejected the latter entirely.[45] As soon as the news of Mary's accession reached Italy Pole sought, and obtained, the post of Cardinal Legate to England, with a brief to end the schism. For a variety of political reasons, he was prevented from discharging that duty openly, or from coming to England, until November 1554; although, as we have seen, he had been confirming episcopal appointments since the spring. Pole was not

---

[43] *Acts and Monuments* (1583), 2099; '... Morgan, Byshop of St. Davids, who sitting uppon the condemnation of the blessed Martyr bysh. Farrar, and uniustly usurping his rowm, not long after was stricken by Gods hand, after such a strange sort that hys meate would not go down, but ryse & prycke up again ...' In fact there was an interval of four and a half years between Farrer's execution and Morgan's death.

[44] The two nominated but not confirmed were Thomas Reynolds to Hereford and Francis Mallett to Salisbury. William Peto had been papally provided to Salisbury in 1543, but Mary ignored this no less than her predecessors.

[45] Mayer, *Reginald Pole*.

entirely happy with the terms of the reconciliation, which were finally embodied in the Statute of Repeal of January 1555, but knew that he had to make them work.[46] The emphasis of his mission was upon the restoration of order and obedience in the English Church, and for that reason he was strongly in favour of rehabilitating the dignity, wealth and authority of the episcopate.

Mary wished to appoint Pole to Canterbury at once, regarding the see as vacant by Cranmer's attainder; but he was reluctant. Cranmer had been papally confirmed in 1533, and therefore technically only the Pope could remove him from office. This was a view which the queen accepted, and it was therefore only after Cranmer's degradation and execution in March 1556 that he was consecrated and installed.[47] For a little over a year he was both legate and archbishop; and then in April 1557 Pope Paul IV cancelled his legacy, and recalled him to Rome. Mary refused to allow him to go, or to accept his nominated replacement, William Peto. Peto himself declined the position, on the valid grounds that he was too old and lacked the relevant experience. Pole remained as archbishop until he died a few hours after Mary. He was therefore in theory responsible for the whole persecution that took place under his jurisdiction, either as legate or archbishop, and in practice for the remaining episcopal appointments of the reign. Although he had a lively dislike of heresy, Pole was not a persecutor by conviction, and intervened on more than one occasion to save individuals from the stake. He recognized his duty in this respect, and did not flinch from it. He was more than a little out of sympathy with the ways in which Catholic reform was developing in most of Europe, clinging to the humanist values in which he had been trained, and to the priority of education.[48] The bishops who were appointed under his jurisdiction reflect those priorities clearly.

There were four new consecrations in 1555. Richard Pate followed Nicholas Heath at Worcester, some time between June and September; James Turberville followed the deceased John Veysey at Exeter in September, after a vacancy of more than a year; Thomas Goldwell took over St Asaph from Robert Parfew after a similar interval in the same month; and William Glyn filled the long-vacant see of Bangor.[49] Pate was

---

[46] He objected strongly to the implication in the statute that a papal dispensation was insufficient to secure the lands. This reflected an understanding on the part of English lawyers that no Pope could bind his successors.

[47] *HBC*, 234. Until that point Pole had been only in deacon's orders; he therefore had to be ordained priest before he could be consecrated.

[48] Mayer, *Reginald Pole*; D. Loades, 'The Piety of the Catholic restoration in England, 1553–1558', in *Humanism and Reform in Britain and the Continent: essays presented to Professor J.K. Cameron* (Studies in Church History, subsidia, 1991).

[49] *HBC*, 292.

a conservative of long-standing credentials, and a good deal more cosmopolitan than most of his colleagues. He had taken a BA at Corpus Christi College, Oxford in 1523, and had then proceeded MA in Paris before being appointed archdeacon of Worcester in 1526, and of Lincoln two years later. It is doubtful whether either of his benefices saw much of him at this stage, because he entered the royal service as a diplomat and was sent to the court of Charles V, where he resided from 1533 to 1536. Out of sympathy with Henry's policies, he had declined to return.[50] Paul III provided him to the see of Worcester in 1541, vacant in theory by the death of Gasparo Contarini, and as bishop of Worcester he had sat in the opening sessions of the Council of Trent in 1547, where he would have been well known to Pole, who was one of the presiding legates. He remained in exile during Edward's reign, and was therefore one of the few unsullied Catholics available for promotion. He returned to exile after a brief imprisonment in 1559, and died at Louvain (Leuven, Belgium) in 1565.[51] Turberville had taken his MA as a Fellow of New College in 1520, and had then gone abroad, but it is not known where. He returned with a DD, which he incorporated at Oxford in 1532, and was rector of Hartfield in Sussex by 1541, but little else is known of him over the next 20 years, or why he should have been thought worthy of promotion. He features occasionally in Foxe's martyr narratives, but there was only one burning in Devon, in 1558. Deprived in 1559, he returned to obscurity, and seems to have died about 1570. Thomas Goldwell had taken his degrees in Oxford, culminating in a BD in 1534, when he was described unsympathetically as 'more eminent in mathematics and astronomy than in divinity'.[52] He probably studied for a while in Padua, and had joined Pole's household in 1535; so the reason for his advancement is not far to seek. He had joined the Theatine order in 1550, and served as an emissary for both Pole and the Pope. He was consecrated to St Asaph in September 1555, and was named to Oxford in November 1558, a few days before the queen's death. In 1559 he returned to exile, becoming Theatine superior in Naples in 1561. As such he attended the final sessions of the Council of Trent, and was attainted in 1562.[53] In 1580 he became a pensioner of Philip II and died, the last survivor of the Marian bench, in 1585. William Glyn was a scholar of some distinction. He had taken his MA as a fellow of Queen's

---

[50] ODNB; for some of Pate's activities in connection with Pole, see T.F. Mayer, *The Correspondence of Reginald Pole ... 1518–1546* (2002).
[51] ODNB.
[52] Ibid. Jonathan Woolfson, *Padua and the Tudors: English Students in Italy, 1485–1603* (1998), 239–40.
[53] ODNB.

College, Cambridge in 1530, and proceeded DD in 1544. In the latter year he was also appointed to the Lady Margaret chair of Divinity, a position which he lost in 1549 because of his opposition to the government's religious policy. As he received the rectorship of St Martin's, Ludgate in 1551 he was presumably not regarded as incorrigible, but he had done enough to establish his bona fides with Mary, and was also a chaplain to Bishop Thirlby. As a native Welsh speaker and a scholar in that tongue, he was an unusually appropriate appointment to Bangor.[54] He died before Mary, in May 1558, and the see was again vacant on her death.

There were just two appointments, apart from Pole, in 1556 – Cuthbert Scott to Chester in July and Owen Oglethorpe to Carlisle in August. Scott was a Cambridge man, who took his MA as a fellow of Christ's in 1538. He proceeded DD in 1547 and became a canon of York, but earned no further preferment during Edward's reign, presumably because of lack of sympathy with public policy. He became master of Christ's in 1553 and took a second DD from Oxford in 1554. He served as vice-chancellor of Cambridge in both 1554 and 1556, before being nominated to Chester. In that see he was out of the way of the persecution, but seems to have gained a reputation for Catholic zeal, as he served a term in the Fleet after his deprivation.[55] He was allowed to retire to Louvain in 1563, and died there in the following year. Oglethorpe was also an academic; a fellow of Magdalen College, Oxford in 1526, and DD there ten years later. He was president of Magdalen from 1535 to 1552, and vice-chancellor in 1551, before being forced out by Protestant pressure. He was certainly a man of Catholic sympathies, but hardly a strenuous defender of the faith. Nevertheless he was reinstated at Magdalen by Mary, and became dean of Windsor in the same year. He was also one of the Oxford men chosen to dispute against Cranmer and his colleagues in April 1554, having a good reputation as a technical theologian. He crowned Elizabeth in 1559, but declined to accept her religious settlement, and died on 31 December in the same year.[56]

Finally, there were three appointments in 1557: Thomas Watson to Lincoln and David Pole to Peterborough in August, and John Christopherson to Chichester in November. Pole, who was no relation to the cardinal, was a civil lawyer who had taken a DCL from All Souls, Oxford in 1528. He had become archdeacon of Shropshire by 1536, but went abroad soon after, and was Reginald's vicar general by 1542, when

---

[54] *HBC, ODNB*.
[55] *Acts and Monuments* (1583), 2102.
[56] *ODNB*.

he was attainted. He returned to England with the cardinal, and sat on the commissions which tried Cranmer, Latimer and Ridley.[57] This level of favour is probably sufficient to explain his advancement. Like his colleagues, he refused conformity in 1559, and appears to have remained quietly in England until his death in 1568. Watson, by contrast, was one of the most distinguished members of the Marian bench, whose career is examined separately elsewhere. He was a humanist scholar who had become a fellow of St John's, Cambridge in 1535, at the age of 22. He was chaplain to Gardiner from 1545 to 1553, and served two spells in prison, in 1547–48 and 1550. Immediately after Mary's accession he was appointed master of S John's, and took his DD in 1554. A noted preacher, he was also dean of Durham from 1553 to 1557, one of the Oxford disputants in 1554, and a visitor of Cambridge University in the latter year.[58] After his deprivation in 1559 he remained in prison for 25 years, until his death in 1584. Christopherson was also a Cambridge man of the younger generation and a celebrated Greek scholar, who was in turn fellow of Peterhouse, St John's and Trinity between 1541 and 1546. He retreated to Louvain in 1547 to avoid the taint of heresy, and was thus marked for preferment on Mary's accession. He was immediately appointed master of Trinity and confessor to the queen, becoming dean of Norwich in the following year. As a bishop he was a notorious persecutor. He was responsible for some 27 deaths during his relatively brief incumbency, although, as with Hopton, this may have resulted more from the nature of his diocese than from his personal wish. However, he was imprisoned immediately after Elizabeth's accession for violently anti-Protestant preaching, and died before the end of the year.

A total of 35 men served the restored Catholic Church as bishops. Of these, seven had made their careers originally in the administrative or diplomatic service of the Crown, and of them, six had been rewarded with sees while actively engaged in such service: Tunstall, Goodrich, Thirlby, Veysey, Bonner and Gardiner. Only Richard Pate was appointed later, and for a quite different reason. Six were ex-religious, although apart from John Hopton these were men of reasonably flexible conscience, and it is not clear that their former status had much effect upon their views. Three others, David Pole, Morgan and Sampson, had been trained principally in the civil law. The remaining 19 were all in some sense academic theologians, and apart from Bourne – and of course Reginald Pole – none had any particular advantage from family connections. Although most are reported to have been effective

---

[57] Ibid. Mayer, *Reginald Pole*, 257.
[58] *Acts and Monuments* (1583), 1428–58.

preachers, only a small minority presented any evidence of their rhetorical or polemical skill in the form of published books. Twenty-two left no surviving or recorded work in print, and four published nothing after 1553. Of those whose works did reach the public during Mary's reign, Gardiner hardly counts, since the edition of *De Vera Obedientia* which appeared in the autumn of 1553 was edited by a Protestant in order to demonstrate the inconsistencies in his position.[59] Reginald Pole was a prolific writer, particularly of letters, but a very reluctant publisher, and the only thing which was actually printed during his incumbency was a copy of a letter to Bonner on the subject of confessionals.[60] John Christopherson's only offering was effective in its way, but scarcely pastoral. After the Wyatt rebellion in 1554 he published *An Exhortation to all menne to take heed and beware of rebellion*, which expounded the official view that the rebellion had been a heretical conspiracy.[61]

Only five of Mary's bishops took the fight to the Protestants in any positive way. James Brooks published one of his Paul's Cross sermons in 1553, which went through two further editions in the next year. John White in the same year issued an attack upon the Eucharistic doctrine of Peter Martyr, which also went to a second edition in 1554; but since it was written in Latin verse it probably did not have a wide readership outside the ranks of the clergy.[62] Cuthbert Tunstall, who had published several works before 1540, qualifies here only by virtue of Thomas Paynell's translation of a collection of his Latin prayers, which appeared in 1558.[63] The two bishops who did publish significantly were Edmund Bonner and Thomas Watson. The latter issued two works, *Holsome and catholique doctryne* and *Two notable sermons*, both in several editions.[64] These were distinguished works of controversial theology, but since they are discussed in detail elsewhere in this collection, little needs to be said about them here. Bonner produced four separate items. Two of these were formal: a declaration concerning the intended reconciliation of the Church in February 1554, and an exhortation to the clergy to promote a decree for the defence of the realm in 1558. The other two were among the most important promotional efforts of the reign.

An honest godly instruction ... for bringinge up of children (1556)

---

[59] RSTC, 11585–87.
[60] RSTC 20085.5. *The true copy of the transcript or wrytinge of late sent to the bishop of London by the Lord Cardinal Pole concerning the due use of the confessionals* (1557). On Pole as a writer, see T.F. Mayer, *Reginald Pole*.
[61] RSTC, 5207
[62] RSTC, 3838–3839.3.
[63] RSTC, 24321.
[64] RSTC, 25112–14, 25115–15.5. See also below, 258–80.

was a catechism with suitable guidance for its use. It was modelled upon several similar works which had been issued since 1535 by both Henrician and Edwardian governments, and was much needed since no one under the age of 30 had actually been brought up in a fully Catholic Church.[65] By far the most important, however, was *A profitable and necessary doctrine with certaine Homilies*. The homilies were actually issued separately, and were modelled unashamedly on Cranmer's efforts of 1547. Both parts went through numerous editions, and together they form the most effective instruments of Catholic evangelization to appear in print during the restoration.[66] The Marian Church's use of the printing press is a controversial subject, and it is now believed to have been both larger in scale and more effective in content than was once believed, but among the bishops only Bonner and Watson can be said to have led from the front.[67] Somewhat ironically, after the Elizabethan settlement they were consigned to oblivion, because the new generation of Catholic writers and polemicists who emerged in the 1560s had a quite different style, if not a different purpose. Only Pole and Tunstall had an afterlife in the recusant period, and that was both limited and ambiguous. The only piece to appear on the Catholic side of the debate was *A treatise of justification, found among the writings of Cardinal Pole*, which was issued at Louvain in 1569 and was intended to demonstrate that the cardinal had not been, as some claimed, a heretic on that issue.[68] The other two works to appear were *The seditious and blasphemous oration of Cardinal Pole intytled the defence of ecclesiastical unytye* (1560), which is self-explanatory, and *A letter written by Cuthbert Tunstall ... unto R. Pole* in the same year.[69] Tunstall had only been dead a few months, having refused to accept the oath of supremacy a second time, and been deprived. This tract was a posthumous swipe at his memory, drawing attention to the fact that he had once been a keen advocate of the royal authority.

Mary appointed her bishops partly for their record of conservative opinions, and partly for their learning. Very few of them on appointment were actually Catholics in the full sense – but then neither

---

[65] This was a point which was made frequently by those accused of heresy during Mary's reign, but it did not receive much sympathy. *RSTC*, 3281.

[66] J. Loach, 'The Marian Establishment and the Printing Press', *English Historical Review*, 100, 1986, 138–51. Eamon Duffy, *Stripping of the Altars* (1992), 529. *RSTC*, 3281.5–3285.10.

[67] E.J. Baskerville, *A Chronological Bibliography of Propaganda and Polemic Published in English between 1553 and 1558* (American Philosophical Society, 1979). See also below.

[68] *RSTC*, 20088.

[69] *RSTC*, 20087

was she. In spite of their mixed antecedents, as a bench they served the Church well, and in 1558 virtually all those still in post were fully committed to the Church universal, as well as to the customs and rituals of the Old Religion. They failed, however, to convince the secular elite, and when they made their stand against the Royal Supremacy in the parliament of 1559, they found that they were officers without an army.[70] They did better than their Edwardian predecessors, whose own ranks had divided more or less evenly in 1553, but they were no more successful in retaining the *status quo*. This meant, of course, that Mary's Church died with her. The convocations supported their leaders far more resolutely in 1559 than they had in 1553, but the outcome was the same; and eventually fewer clergy were deprived for refusing the Elizabethan oath than had lost their benefices for marriage or heresy in the previous reign.[71] The main reason for this was not religious conviction, or the lack of it, but loyalty to the Crown. The majority accepted 'the Queen's proceedings' in both cases; so we must conclude that the country was only slightly more Catholic in 1559 than it had been Protestant in 1553. Protestant bishops such as John Hooper flagellated themselves after Mary's accession for not having taken the opportunities which God had given them. Their Catholic successors did not, apparently, do the same, or feel that Elizabeth's decisions were in any way a reflection upon their diligence or effectiveness.

If they were satisfied with their ministry, they had some justification. Not all of them were diligent preachers, but many were, sharing Mary's conviction that it was high time that good preaching corrected the effects of the 'evil preaching' in which many of the Protestant clergy had been active.[72] Surviving administrative records suggest diligence in visitation and in the conduct of ordinations, with much emphasis upon discipline and good order. On the other hand, there were areas of disagreement. Perhaps the most important of these was the attitude to heresy. No bishop wished to, or could afford to, tolerate that kind of dissent, but only a minority were keen or active persecutors. With one or two exceptions the most enthusiastic heresy hunters were deans, archdeacons and lay officials rather than bishops.[73] No bishop could refuse to serve on

---

[70] N.J. Jones, *Faith by Statute: Parliament and the Settlement of Religion, 1559* (1982). For Nicholas Heath's cogent speech against the Supremacy Bill in the House of Lords, see T.E. Hartley, *Proceedings in the Parliaments of Elizabeth I, 1559–1581* (1983), 12–17.

[71] Rather fewer than 200 were deprived for refusing the oath. Between 1553 and 1555 the diocese of Norwich alone saw 243 deprivations.

[72] A memorandum containing the queen's thoughts on the subject of preaching remains in British Library, Harleian MS 444, fol. 27.

[73] *Acts and Monuments* (1583), *passim*.

a royal or legatine commission if appointed to it; but reading between the lines of the *Acts and Monuments* (to say nothing of less biased sources) makes it clear that many of them were deeply uneasy with this service. It was the queen who was the driving force, not out of any natural cruelty, but from an implacable sense of duty. Another area of uncertainty was the use of the English Bible. There was nothing intrinsically heretical about vernacular scripture, and many good Catholics, including Reginald Pole, believed that, if properly handled, the English Bible could be a very useful tool in the hands of Catholic evangelists.[74] Apart from Pole himself, only Hopton, Pate, Goldwell, David Pole and Baynes had been partly educated, or had spent significant time, abroad. The majority of Mary's bishops had been educated, as she had herself, in an insular humanist tradition. This sprang from continental roots, particularly from the influence of Erasmus, but was largely untouched by the more rigorous and intolerant aspects of Catholic reform which had arisen since the 1530s.[75] Strenuous voices were raised in England, notably that of John Standish, denouncing the English Bible as an heretical device, full of wicked errors; but it was never banned. It seems that bishops exercised their discretion in this respect. In the diocese of Exeter such Bibles were called in, but elsewhere they were put away in cupboards, or even left *in situ*. It is highly unlikely that they continued in open use, but no bishop issued any order for their destruction.[76]

In spite of the fact that she used her own authority extensively to restore the Mass and other aspects of the traditional faith, Mary believed firmly in the autonomy of ecclesiastical jurisdiction. The repeal in December 1553 of the various statutes which had constituted the Edwardian settlement did away with the appointment of bishops by Letters Patent, and restored the *conge d'elire*. The latter was a mere fiction, because the queen proceeded to appoint bishops no less surely than her father and brother had done, but it had some symbolic significance.[77] Mary did not repeat the Edwardian experiment of issuing

---

[74] Mayer, *Reginald Pole*; The *Cambridge History of the Bible* (1969), 492–505 examines the positive attitude of Erasmus to vernacular scripture. The prohibition in England was local, and not absolute.

[75] Lucy Wooding, *Rethinking Catholicism in Reformation England* (2000) and Eamon Duffy, *The Stripping of the Altars* (1992) represent two different views of this situation.

[76] John Standish, *Discourse wherein it is debated whether it be expedient that the Scripture should be in English* (STC, 23207). Less a debate than a diatribe against translation. The parish of Morebath dutifully packed up its English Bible and sent it to Exeter, which must have been in response to an instruction, possibly verbal since no record of such an order survives. E. Duffy, *The Voices of Morebath* (2001), 162.

[77] The *congé d'élire* was a formal permission for the chapter of an episcopal cathedral

new commissions to her bishops, because she accepted that their jurisdiction was 'ordinary'; that is, that it derived from their consecration rather than their appointment. For a similar reason, ecclesiastical administrators returned to the use of pontifical years to date official documents, rather than the regnal years of the king.[78] It was thus emphasized that the courts were the bishops', and that the law which they administered was the law of the Church.

However, it required more than a few adjustments of this nature to restore to the bishops the prestige and *gravitas* which they had once enjoyed. In the past, important sees were often filled by men who had held, or were holding, senior offices of state. Gardiner had been the king's secretary, Tunstall Lord Privy Seal. Although often of humble birth, such men were at ease with the peers of the realm. To this the large revenues and extensive *manred* of their sees made a major contribution. Even second-rate sees such as Carlisle or Rochester conferred upon their holders the substance and status of lords. However, ruthless pressure in the latter part of Henry's reign, and even more during Edward's, had stripped almost every see of valuable lands. In an extreme case, like Bath and Wells, the annual income had been reduced from £1844 to £480 between 1535 and 1550.[79] To this process, the Protestant conviction that bishops should be pastors and leaders rather than rulers, had contributed significantly. Apart from Goodrich as Lord Chancellor, no bishop had held a major lay office under Edward. The advancement of learned preachers like Ridley and Hooper to the bench during the same reign tended in the same direction. By the summer of 1553 the English bishops were royal servants of the second rank, and more akin in their wealth and social status to the major gentry than to the peerage. Only in their automatic membership of the House of Lords did the traditional situation linger on.

This tendency Mary was determined to reverse. Throughout her reign she consistently returned lands and revenues to her bishops whenever possible. She also forgave them debts to the Crown, usually for first-fruits and tenths, and in the first year of her reign this generosity cost her about £10 000. Henry Morgan, appointed to St Davids (never a rich see) was exonerated of nearly £1000; James Brookes of Gloucester £500.[80] The most extreme example of such favour was shown to Bonner

---

to elect a new bishop; it was always accompanied by a royal nomination. The process of election was therefore a sham, but preserved an appearance of ecclesiastical independence.

[78] Loades, 'Bishops of the Restored Catholic Church'.

[79] Heal, *Prelates and Princes*, 133.

[80] PRO, SP11/1, no. 2, 'Account of the arrears of the tenths and subsidies of the clergy due by divers bishops at and before Christmas last', 20 July 1553. *Calendar of the Patent Rolls, Mary*, I, 112 (8 May 1554).

of London, who was not only permitted to recover his previous estate by virtue of invalidating Ridley's grants as an intruder, but was also given further lands worth nearly £500 a year.[81] In addition he was discharged of debts worth £552. Apart from London, actual grants of new land were rare, but recoveries were considerable. When first-fruits and tenths were returned to the Church in 1555, the £25 000 per annum was used almost entirely to pay monastic pensions, and the bishops benefited hardly at all. More to the point were the grants of almost 500 advowsons, still in the hands of the Crown following the dissolution of the religious houses which had formerly held them. Altogether seven bishops received such grants, York being the main beneficiary with 195.[82] These added little directly to the bishops' incomes, but substantially to their patronage, and hence their power. This was particularly the case when the appointments were cathedral prebends. Both Heath and Tunstall secured control of their cathedral chapters by such means.

In one respect, however, Mary followed her brother rather than ancient practice. Of the bishops she appointed, as distinct from those she restored, none held significant secular preferments. The Lord Chancellorship was held successively by Gardiner of Winchester and Heath of York, both of whom (and particularly Gardiner) were prelates of the old style. Mary's own choice almost invariably fell upon scholars and academics, rather than lawyers or diplomats. Four bishops and one dean served on a Privy Council which numbered at its largest nearly 40, and all of them she had inherited in one way or another.[83] Although Pole enjoyed a unique influence, he was never a councillor in the ordinary sense, and it is a mistake to suppose that the queen was dominated by a clerical cabal. Great as was her respect for the priesthood, she did not turn to the clergy for advice outside their proper sphere. Only Gardiner provides the exception which proves the rule.

Consequently, there was a degree of inconsistency about Mary's use of the episcopate. Both Gardiner and Pole, who were her chief advisers in ecclesiastical matters, placed great emphasis upon discipline and ritual as being the best ways to restore the Catholic Church to its former glory, and those priorities were regularly followed, as an inspection of the injunctions issued during the reign will demonstrate. The strength of the men whom she appointed to the bench, however, lay in their theological scholarship, a skill which only Thomas Watson is known to have deployed effectively. An emphasis upon discipline

---

[81] *Calendar of the Patent Rolls, Mary*, I, 119 (3 March 1554).
[82] *Calendar of the Patent Rolls, Mary*, IV, 399, 401, 402, 420, 437, 449, 450.
[83] Loades, *Reign of Mary Tudor*, 404–11.

does not necessarily mean that evangelism was neglected, and the balance no doubt shifted from see to see and bishop to bishop. Clerical education, for example, was an equal priority for Pole, and greatly influenced his dealings with the universities.[84] However, a man has only so much time, and so much energy, and bringing demoralized clergy and confused congregations up to the mark left little time for theological niceties. In spite of the immense amount of time which was spent in interrogating Protestant leaders such as John Philpot, many heresy trials simply boiled down to a denial of transubstantiation, followed by conviction and execution. None of Mary's bishops showed the pastoral application of a John Hooper, but that was hardly their fault.

It is often argued that Mary's Church simply had too little time. There was time to reconstitute a Catholic Church, but not to defeat a determined Protestant minority. Most important of all, there was no time to convert a conservative mass, which thought of itself as Catholic, into an aware and obedient Church focussed on Rome. Moreover, it took too long to shape an episcopate ripe for that purpose. Too many of the bishops whom she inherited simply submitted and stayed on; old men were restored, who should have been dismissed to an honourable retirement. It was not until after the visitation of March 1554 that Mary was able even to begin the task of bringing the bench up to date with suitable men. Although she made good appointments, it was not until the second half of the reign, after her failed pregnancy had damaged the long-term prospects of her regime, that a majority of her bishops had the kind of zeal and commitment which was needed. Both Mary and Pole believed that the English bishops had to be the key agents in the task of restoration.[85] This was partly a pragmatic and partly a principled position, but it also helps to explain their shared lack of enthusiasm for the religious orders, particularly the Jesuits.[86] This was probably a mistake. With the benefit of hindsight we can see that the task of Catholic evangelism needed all the help it could get. However, it was more straightforward, and more orthodox, to rely upon the bishops. Like any other bench, they were a mixed bunch. Some were too old for the job; some were mere survivors. Most had respectable intellectual credentials, and very few were distracted by secular tasks. A few were distinguished by learning or zeal, and almost all were sufficiently committed as to refuse further compromise. This

---

[84] Mayer, *Reginald Pole*, 293, 295.
[85] Loades, *Reign of Mary*, 262–303.
[86] T.F. Mayer, 'A test of wills: Cardinal Pole, Ignatius Loyola and the Jesuits in England', in T.M. McCoog, ed., *The Reckoned Expense* (1996), 21–37.

meant that Elizabeth was able to do in 1559 what Mary had felt herself unable to do – make a clean sweep and start a new task with a new team.

CHAPTER TWO

The English Universities, 1553–58

Claire Cross

On 20 August 1553, scarcely more than a month after she had wrested the throne from the supporters of the Protestant Lady Jane Grey, Mary Tudor, 'knowing it our bounden duty to Almighty God, by whose only goodness we acknowledge ourselves called and placed in the royal estate of this realm', sent virtually identical letters to Oxford and Cambridge. Having set out her intention 'to travail by all the ways we may that, his glory and holy will being truly declared to all our subjects, He may of all sorts in their several vocations be reverently feared, served and obeyed', the queen informed the heads of houses, the regent masters and the undergraduates that she

> thought good for a beginning to wish that the examples hereof may first begin in our universities where young men and all sorts of students, joining godly conversations with their studies in learning, may after as well by their doings as by their preachings instruct and confirm the rest of our subjects both in the knowledge and fear of Almighty God, in the due obedience toward us, our laws, and all others their superiors, and in their charitable demeanours towards all men.[1]

These directions mirror exactly Mary's priorities and those of her ecclesiastical advisers. Protestantism could not be rooted out and the Catholic Church brought back until she had restored her two universities to the condition in which they had been before her father had engineered the break with Rome. Catholics in the summer of 1553 faced a task the magnitude of which they may not have fully recognized. England had been separated from Rome for more than a generation; Protestantism, which had penetrated Oxford and Cambridge at first clandestinely then more openly between 1520 and 1547, had been the

---

[1] J. Lamb, ed., *A Collection of Letters, Statutes, and other Documents, from the Ms. Library of Corpus Christi College Cambridge, illustrative of the History of the University of Cambridge, during the Period of the Reformation, from A.D. MD to A.D. MDLXXII* (London, 1838), 165–6; PRO, SP 11/1/201; the spelling of quotations has been modernized throughout.

only authorized form of Christianity for the previous six years. Consequently, both because of their ancient role as seminaries for the clergy and their more recent function as training grounds for servants of the state, the Crown now needed the universities to re-establish the reputation they had enjoyed in the first quarter of the sixteenth century as champions of Catholic orthodoxy.

The English universities had become enured to state intervention decades before the accession of Mary Tudor, indeed in certain circumstances they had positively welcomed it. In the 1520s the senior members of Oxford thought no hyperbole too lavish to confer upon Wolsey when he was proposing to endow a college on a more magnificent scale than the university had ever known, and most considered it entirely acceptable that the cardinal should subsequently have striven to control the heterodox beliefs of some of the fellows he had imported from Cambridge to staff his new foundation. Under pressure from Henry VIII, early in 1530 the theologians of both Cambridge and Oxford had eventually conceded that a man might not wed his brother's widow, and so lent their weight to proceedings which eventually led to the king's repudiation of Catherine of Aragon. The first wholesale attempt to regulate the religious opinions of the two universities, however, came only in 1534 when both Oxford and Cambridge formally rejected the Pope's supremacy, and senior and junior members alike swore an oath renouncing papal obedience and recognizing the marriage of Henry VIII and Anne Boleyn.[2]

Then in the autumn of 1535 Cromwell's commissioners descended upon both universities. In the course of their visitation they effectively linked humanism with religious reform by issuing injunctions which, among much else, outlawed the teaching of canon law, substituted lectures on the text of the New Testament for the *Sentences* of Peter Lombard and instituted in the larger colleges public lectures in Latin and Greek. They had set Duns Scotus in Bocardo, Richard Layton boasted to Cromwell, and banished scholasticism from Oxford for ever. The commissioners, though, appreciated that the universities could not be transformed overnight. In the heads of colleges at Cambridge they observed 'great pertinacity to their old blindness'; only when with time they had been replaced by the younger sort 'of much towardness' would learning flourish as it ought. At Oxford, too, some heads feared dispossession, and Dr London, the warden of New College, in his anxiety to retain his office, denied being a defender of 'papistical

---

[2] W.T. Mitchell, ed., *Epistolae Academicae 1508–1596* (Oxford Historical Society, New Series XXVI, 1980), nos 125, 153, 194; *L & P. Henry VIII*, IV, no. 6247; VII, no. 891; Lamb, *A Collection of Letters* ... , 37–9.

purgatory'. On the fall of Cromwell, the chancellor of Cambridge and the high steward of Oxford, the conservatives in the universities, gained a respite. In 1540 Thomas Barnes, one of the earliest scholars to disseminate Lutheran ideas in Cambridge, paid for his beliefs with his life, and in the religious reaction of Henry VIII's last years a number of young Protestant scholars considered it politic to seek refuge on the Continent. The capture of power by the Protestants on the accession of Edward VI, however, returned the initiative to the supporters of change in the universities.[3]

In 1547 Stephen Gardiner, bishop of Winchester and chancellor of Cambridge, who had striven to control criticism of surviving Catholic ceremonies in the university after Cromwell's fall, was sent to the Tower and replaced as chancellor by Protector Somerset, who relaxed all controls upon Protestant discussion both in the universities and in the nation at large. With the old king dead, Cranmer, as Archbishop of Canterbury, now had the freedom to follow his Protestant sympathies, inviting continental Protestant theologians to aid him in his task. Because the Interim had made it impossible for Zwinglian and Calvinist clergy to minister within the empire, a number of extremely influential divines took refuge in England at this time, among the first being Peter Martyr. In March 1548 the government required Dr Richard Smith, the regius professor of divinity, to surrender his Oxford chair in order that Martyr might be installed in his place. Subsequently advanced to a canonry at Christ Church, the Italian scholar at once embarked on a course of Protestant evangelism, lecturing first on St Paul's epistles to the Corinthians and then, early in 1549, elaborating a Protestant interpretation of the sacrament of the altar, which so incensed the leader of the conservatives, Richard Smith, that he challenged him to a public debate. This controversy coincided with fresh state intervention into the affairs of the university.[4]

The second Tudor visitation of the universities, intended like the first to cultivate true doctrine, root out superstition and encourage good learning, occurred in the late spring of 1549. At Oxford the visitors, led by Henry Holbeach, bishop of Lincoln, and Richard Cox, dean of Christ Church, endorsed Martyr's interpretation of the Eucharist as a service of thanksgiving rather than a propitiatory sacrifice in which the bread and wine became the very body and blood of Christ. Having rooted out all

---

[3] *L & P. Henry VIII*, IX, nos 350, 615, 616, 661, 664, 666; *L & P. Henry VIII, Addenda*, no. 1085; H. Robinson, ed., *Original Letters relative to the English Reformation*, I (Parker Society; Cambridge, 1846), nos 21, 104–20, 149.

[4] C.H. Smyth, *Cranmer and the Reformation under Edward VI* (London, 1926), 108–25.

traces of popery from the colleges they went on to promulgate new injunctions enforcing conformity and regulating the public lectures.[5]

At Cambridge, where a much more detailed account of the visitation has survived, the visitors led by Nicholas Ridley, bishop of Rochester, opened the proceedings in King's College chapel on 6 May, where all those present took an oath against the Bishop of Rome. In addition to scrutinizing the affairs of every college – at Clare expelling the master, Rowland Swinburn, and one of the fellows and pulling down six altars in Jesus chapel – the visitors also superintended a formal disputation on Corpus Christi day on the propositions that the Scriptures did not sanction transubstantiation nor allow the re-enactment of Christ's last supper as an oblation, but only as a ceremony of commemoration and thanksgiving. The university received similar statutes to those assigned to Oxford.[6]

Isolated among religious conservatives in Oxford, Peter Martyr had for some time been trying to attract to England the doyen of Rhineland reformers, Martin Bucer. With reluctance Bucer eventually conceded that the Interim had brought his ministry in Strasbourg to an end, and in the spring of 1549 he and Paul Fagius set out for England. Almost immediately on their arrival Bucer was appointed to the divinity chair in Cambridge and Fagius to a readership in Hebrew, and the university received the two men with the greatest honour when they reached the town in the autumn of 1549. In the 16 months of life remaining to him Bucer exercised an extraordinary influence not only within the Cambridge theology faculty, but also among the Divines in Cranmer's circle engaged in compiling the second Edwardian Prayer Book. Matthew Parker, Edwin Sandys and Edmund Grindal, respectively the masters of Corpus, St Catharine's and Pembroke, all deferred to this patriarch among the continental reformers.[7]

Bucer seems to have been blessed with a more pacific temperament than Martyr, who went out of his way to court controversy, though there can be little doubt that he encountered more open opposition in Oxford than Bucer in Cambridge. Even after the promulgation of the new statutes, some Oxford students in 1550 attempted to stage a fresh disputation on transubstantiation and to get Dr William Chedsey, 'a great papist', to moderate the proceedings. Within Christ Church itself,

---

[5] J. Foxe, *The Acts and Monuments*, ed. J. Pratt, with an introduction by J. Stoughton (London, 1887), VI, 298–305; S. Gibson, ed., *Statuta Antiqua Universitatis Oxoniensis* (Oxford, 1931), 355–60.

[6] Lamb, *A Collection of Letters* ..., 109–21, 122–50; PRO SP 10/7/10, 11; Foxe, *Acts and Monuments*, VI, 305–36.

[7] Smyth, *Cranmer and the Reformation*, 155–77.

however, Martyr was beginning to build up a party of supporters led by the dean Richard Cox, Henry Sidall the sub-dean, James Curtop, Thomas Barnard, Robert Banks, Christopher Goodman and William Whittingham. A group of young Swiss disciples, who included Heinrich Bullinger's adopted son Rodolph Gualter, John ab Ulmis and his two cousins, Andrew Croariensis, Augustine Bernher and his nephew, Alexander Schmutz, John Rodolph Stumphius and Christopher Froschover, joined Martyr in Oxford and at once added their weight to the cause. Having spent the latter part of Henry VIII's reign in Switzerland Bishop Hooper took a particular interest in these students while his friend, John Parkhurst, kept in contact with Martyr even after he had left Merton for Gloucestershire to take up his living at Cleeve. Though a member of Corpus, Parkhurst's pupil John Jewel associated himself closely with the Christ Church circle. In Oxford between 1547 and 1553 these pockets of committed Protestantism seem to have been confined largely to Christ Church, Magdalen and Corpus: at Cambridge in the same period, though concentrated most in St John's, Protestantism appears to have been more generally distributed among colleges. Cambridge moved yet further in the direction of reform in June 1553 by making assent to the Forty-two Articles obligatory upon all members of the university proceeding to the degrees of DD, BD, and MA. The requirement can have had little effect at the time, since it came within a month of Edward VI's death, but it set an ominous precedent for the future.[8]

Already marked as corrupted by heresy, Cambridge brought yet further unwelcome attention upon itself on the failure of the attempt to divert the succession from the Catholic Mary Tudor to the Protestant Lady Jane Grey on the death of Edward VI in July 1553. Marching from London to confront Mary in East Anglia, Northumberland, the university's chancellor, halted in Cambridge on 15 July and commanded the vice-chancellor, Edwin Sandys, to preach the following day in favour of Queen Jane and the Protestant party. Yet even before the sermon could be dispatched to London for publication the duke realized the hopelessness of his cause and proclaimed Mary queen. A congregation of the Regent House immediately forced Sandys to resign, replacing him as vice-chancellor with a safe conservative and former adversary of Bucer, Dr John Young; but short though the episode had been it had the

---

[8] J. Strype, *Cranmer* (London, 1694), 251–2; Smyth, *Cranmer and the Reformation*, 133–8; J.E.A. Dawson, 'The Early Career of Christopher Goodman and his Place in the Development of English Protestant Thought', Durham PhD thesis, 1978, 63–98; J.B. Mullinger, *The University of Cambridge from the Royal Injunctions of 1535 to the Accession of Charles the First*, II (Cambridge, 1884), 145–6.

effect of branding Protestant intellectuals as potential if not actual traitors to the new Tudor regime. On the defeat of the political coup the government reappointed Stephen Gardiner as chancellor, and sent Sandys and other leading Protestant ministers, who with varying degrees of reluctance had countenanced Northumberland's attempt to deprive Mary of her inheritance, to join him in the Tower. In Oxford, with a conservative chancellor and vice-chancellor in the persons of Sir John Mason and Richard Marshall, the new Catholic government attracted positive co-operation from the university's administration. So within only weeks of her accession Mary had the means to embark on a purge of higher education.[9]

The speed with which the state turned to the reformation of the universities indicates the key role it intended they should play in the restoration of Catholicism. Mary's letter of 20 August, expressing the belief that the disorders in the universities had been brought about by 'the sensual minds and rash determinations of a few men', abrogated the Edwardian statutes and commanded Sir John Mason as chancellor of Oxford and Stephen Gardiner as chancellor of Cambridge to reinstate the ancient statutes of the university and the colleges and to see that for the future they be kept inviolate and strictly observed. With the queen herself setting the example priests began celebrating Mass in both Oxford and Cambridge in the early autumn of 1553.[10]

The government directed its attention first to the foreign Protestants who, with no right of residence in England, could be expelled forthwith. Having placed Martyr under house arrest in Christ Church soon after Mary came to the throne, it subsequently permitted him to depart, but not before he had seen the Mass once more being performed in the college chapels and had remarked despairingly that his labours of the previous five years seemed to have been totally in vain. With his friend Giulio Terenziano he arrived in Strasbourg on 29 October. Their master gone, the young Swiss students quickly made their way back to the Continent. Around the same time John Immanuel Tremellius, Fagius's successor in the Hebrew readership, left Cambridge for the Rhineland – which may also have been the destination of Peter Bizzari, a fellow of St John's since 1549.[11]

---

[9] Mullinger, *Cambridge*, II, 147–8.
[10] PRO SP 11/1 ff. 20–21; J. Strype, *Ecclesiastical Memorials* (London, 1721), III, 52–3; A. Wood, *History and Antiquities of the University of Oxford*, ed. J. Gutch, II (London, 1796), 117–22.
[11] A. Wood, *History and Antiquities of the University of Oxford*, II, 117–22; H. Robinson, *Original Letters relative to the English Reformation*, II (Parker Society; Cambridge, 1847) no. 237; G.C. Gorham, *Gleanings of a Few Scattered Ears during the*

The English converts to Protestantism at the two universities faced a much bleaker choice, either to embrace Catholicism or flee. At Christ Church Richard Marshall, who had supplanted Richard Cox as dean in mid-September, exerted such pressure on Martyr's former supporters among the canons and theology students that most resolved to withdraw from the college and its associated Broadgates Hall. In addition to Cox, Theodore Newton, John Pullain, Thomas Randolph, Thomas Spencer and William Whittingham sought refuge on the Continent within the next few months. The other chief centre of Protestantism in Oxford, Magdalen, suffered a similar fate, with Thomas Bentham, Thomas Bickley, Laurence Humphrey, Hugh Kirk, Peter Morwin, John Mullins, Luke Purefoy, Michael Reniger and Arthur Saule seeking refuge abroad. Christopher Goodman from Brasenose, William Cole and John Jewel from Corpus Christi, Richard Tremayne from Exeter, possibly Thomas Allen from Lincoln, Thomas Huick and John Parkhurst from Merton and Augustine Bradbridge from New College followed their lead. A minimum of 50, possibly as many as 60, of the Marian exiles had graduated from Oxford.[12]

Cambridge contributed an even larger number to the exodus. St John's College produced the most refugees, with the master Thomas Lever, William Ireland, Roger Kelke, Thomas Lakin, the brothers John and Ralph Lever, and James and Leonard Pilkington, Robert Swift, Percival Wiburne, Thomas Wilson and possibly others migrating to Switzerland or Germany. Walter Austin, Anthony Gilby, Richard Rogers and Thomas Wattes withdrew from Christ's, Thomas Jeffreys from Clare Hall, William Birch and perhaps John Orphinstrange from Corpus Christi, Edmund Chapman from Gonville Hall, Sir John Cheke, Nicholas Carvell, Robert Cole and Thomas Wilson from King's, Edmund Grindal, Thomas Horton, Robert Hutton, Anthony Mayhewe and Thomas Sampson from Pembroke, Robert Beaumont from Peterhouse, John Pelham and possibly others from Queens', Edwin Sandys, Edward Frensham and James Taylor from St Catharine's, Thomas Acworth, John Banks, Matthew Carew, Henry Cockcroft, Thomas Donnell, John Jeffrey and John Pedder from Trinity and Christopher Southouse from Trinity Hall. Taking into account a further ten or so scholars whose college membership has been lost, this

---

Period of the Reformation in England (London, 1857), 261–2, 280–83, 286–7; Smyth, *Cranmer and the Reformation under Edward VI*, 161; *ODNB*, (Bizzari).

[12] J.E.A. Dawson, 'The Early Career of Christopher Goodman ...', 17–21; J. Loach, 'Reformation Controversies' in J. McConica, ed., *The Collegiate University: The History of the University of Oxford*, III (Oxford, 1986), 380; the analysis of Oxford exiles has been compiled from C.H. Garrett, *The Marian Exiles* (Cambridge, 1938).

constituted a total of some 76 exiles from Cambridge, of whom at least 23 were resident fellows.[13]

In February 1554 Martyr in Strasbourg sent news to Bullinger that in the previous few days English youths from both Oxford and Cambridge had come over in great numbers, 'whom many godly merchants are bringing up to learning, that, should it please God to restore religion to its former state in that kingdom, they may be of some benefit to the church of England'. By October 1554 members of the newly formed English Church in Zurich were 'beseeching God, for his mercy's sake, to assuage his wrath, to give us repenting hearts, and patient continuance to our brethren at home, with pity to behold his vineyard there miserably spoiled and trodden under foot; and to call us home, after his fatherly chastisement, eftsoons fruitfully to work in the same'.[14]

With Mary established on the throne for little more than a year these scholars had no means of knowing how short or how long their exile from their native land might be, or indeed whether they would ever be permitted to return to rebuild a Protestant Church. Their departure indisputably advanced the government's design for re-establishing Catholicism in the universities, since with the hard core of resistance dissipated the conservatives could now seize the initiative. In many respects the queen's advisers had correctly diagnosed a rift between the generations, some of the junior members inclining to the new religion, with their seniors in many cases eager to revert to the old order. At Cambridge Gardiner resumed the mastership of Trinity Hall which he had lost at the beginning of Edward's reign to Dr Mowse. On Thomas Lever's flight he secured the appointment of Thomas Watson as Master of St John's, while the enforcement of clerical celibacy with the reimposition of the old statutes facilitated the deprivation of Ainsworth at Peterhouse and Sandys at St Catharine's, succeeded respectively by Andrew Perne and Edmund Cosyn. Laurence Moptyd became master of Corpus from which Matthew Parker withdrew early in the reign, and at Pembroke John Young supplanted Nicholas Ridley. At Queens' Dr Glyn ousted Dr Mey, and at Christ's Cuthbert Scott replaced Richard Wilkes. With Cheke in the Tower Richard Atkinson acquired the provostship of King's and on the removal of Dr Bill John Christopherson the mastership of Trinity. Consequently within only six months of Mary's accession all but three of the colleges, Gonville, Jesus and Magdalene, had fallen under the influence of new, conformable heads.[15]

---

[13] This analysis is based on Garrett, *The Marian Exiles* and H.C. Porter, *Reformation and Reaction in Tudor Cambridge* (Cambridge, 1958), 74–98.

[14] H. Robinson, *Original Letters*, II, 514; E. Arber, ed., *A Brief Discourse of the Troubles at Frankfort, 1554–1558 A.D.* (London, 1908), 33.

[15] Mullinger, *Cambridge*, II, 150–51; Strype, *Ecclesiastical Memorials*, III, 52–3.

Once the Protestant radicals had been expelled from Christ Church, Magdalen and Corpus Oxford required fewer changes among the senior members than Cambridge. In addition to the appointment of Marshall as dean of Christ Church in the room of Cox, on Haddon's ejection Oglethorpe returned as president of Magdalen, and at Corpus Morwen and Chedsey enthusiastically led the conservative dons in restoring Catholic practice. Richard Smith and Hugh Weston, who had withdrawn from the university when Protestantism had been at its height, returned in triumph, Smith to the regius chair he had had to vacate for Martyr. As early as October 1553 in a sermon at Paul's Cross Weston preached in commendation of purgatory and prayers for the dead. By March 1554 the central government felt sufficiently confident of the university's orthodoxy to stage in Oxford the most important religious show trial of the reign.[16]

Because of his involvement in Northumberland's attempt to exclude Mary from the throne Cranmer had been found guilty of treason against the state at the Guildhall in November 1553, and he could have been executed without delay, but the queen stayed her hand that he might answer for the even greater crime of treason against God. By royal warrant in the spring of 1554 she sent Cranmer, together with Nicholas Ridley and Hugh Latimer, from the Tower to Oxford 'so as their erroneous opinions being by the word of God justly and truly convinced, the residue of our subjects may be thereby the better established in the true catholic faith'. On 14 April they appeared at a convocation of the university in St Mary's church in the presence of a delegation of Catholics from Cambridge, which included the vice-chancellor, Dr Young, Dr Glyn, Dr Seaton, Dr Watson, Dr Sedgewick and Dr Atkinson, and the mayor and aldermen of Oxford to dispute with the Oxford theologians Dr Weston, Dr Tresham, Dr Cole, Dr Oglethorpe, Dr Pie, Mr Harpsfield and Mr Feckenham on three central tenets of the faith:

1. Whether the natural body of Christ be really in the Sacrament, after the words spoken by the priest, or no.
2. Whether in the Sacrament, after the words of consecration, any other substance do remain than the substance of the body and blood of Christ.
3. Whether in the mass be a sacrifice propitiatory for the sins of the quick and the dead.[17]

---

[16] A. Wood, *History and Antiquities of the University of Oxford*, II, 118–22; C.E. Mallet, *A History of the University of Oxford*, II (London, 1924), 94–7.

[17] D.M. Loades, *The Oxford Martyrs* (London, 1970), 119–21, 129; Foxe, *Acts and Monuments*, VI, 439, 531–2.

Even before the formal debate began Foxe records that the notaries, Mr Say and Mr White, went to the colleges to collect subscriptions in support of the articles. With the dice thus loaded heavily against them, on Monday 16 April Cranmer attempted to confute the propositions, the following day Ridley had his turn, and Latimer came last on 18 April. Though the proceedings took the form of an academic disputation and were conducted in Latin, Watson, the prolocutor, had key exchanges translated into English, and on occasions deliberately incited the townspeople, encouraging them to shout Ridley down and proclaim 'Verity hath the victory. Verity hath the victory.' On their refusal to recognize the truth of the propositions at the end of the week Watson solemnly condemned the three Protestant leaders as heretics, and then posted to London to make his report to the government. Ridley believed that the council intended to stage a similar disputation at Cambridge with the imprisoned John Rogers, Edward Crome and John Bradford as the chief antagonists, but this never happened, perhaps because of the recalcitrance of the parties concerned. Resenting the fact that at Oxford the issues had been decided before the debate had even begun, in May 1554 Rogers, Crome and Bradford, together with Robert Ferrar, Rowland Taylor, John Hooper and others, wrote an open letter refusing to dispute anywhere except in the presence of the queen, the council or parliament.[18]

It cannot have been coincidental that Oxford received a major royal grant immediately upon the successful conclusion of the disputation. Considering that it pertained 'to her royal office to raise up the academy in which the orthodox faith overthrown by heretics cannot enter and be defended, the truth in controversy extracted, nor justice administered', on 2 May 1554 Mary bestowed upon the university, 'so afflicted by the wrongs of the times that ... its public schools ... are laid waste and converted into private gardens, its public treasury plundered, its ornaments carried off and its revenues reduced almost to nothing' the rectories of South Petherwyn in Cornwall, Syston in Leicestershire and Holme Cultram in Cumberland, together worth a little more than £132 a year. This gift tripled the university's income and made possible an extensive restoration of the schools in the Marian period. In June 1554 the university council informed the queen that through her actions their studies had been raised up by the revival of ancient discipline, and that once again the worship of God, pure doctrine and good letters were being set forth.[19]

---

[18] Loades, *The Oxford Martyrs*, 133–7; Foxe, *Acts and Monuments*, VI, 439–520.

[19] *CPR Philip and Mary*, I, 165–6; PRO, SP 11/4/no. 15; I.G. Philip, 'Queen Mary Tudor's Benefaction to the University', *Bodleian Library Record*, V (1954), 27–37.

Although Mary had good cause to favour Oxford over Cambridge, in actuality – perhaps because in Gardiner Cambridge possessed an orthodox and a very active chancellor – both universities benefited from royal bounty. In the summer of 1554 as a thank-offering for the defeat of the rebellions by Northumberland and Wyatt, the queen made a substantial endowment, much on the lines of a chantry foundation, to Trinity College, Cambridge, to support twenty scholars, ten choristers and a master, four chaplains, thirteen poor scholars and two sizars.[20]

All these stages in the restoration of Catholicism in the country in general and in the universities in particular took place before the arrival of the papal legate and the Archbishop of Canterbury elect, Reginald Pole, detained on the continent by the Emperor Charles V until the solemnization of Mary's marriage to Philip of Spain. Then in a sombre ceremony before the queen and the prince and the two Houses of Parliament on 30 November 1554 the cardinal absolved the queen's subjects from 20 years of schism and reconciled the nation to Rome. In response as an expression of gratitude parliament revived the medieval heresy laws. Mary dissolved this third parliament of her reign on 16 January 1555; less than three weeks later on 4 February the first Protestant, John Rogers, a Cambridge graduate, went to his death at Smithfield. Yet again the queen felt it necessary to demand a further demonstration of Catholic orthodoxy from the universities.[21]

During the trials of Cranmer, Latimer and Ridley the government had directed most of its attention to Oxford, but it could not ignore the fact that Cambridge graduates were providing the backbone of resistance among the Protestants remaining in England, and as its chancellor Gardiner strove to procure the university's absolute conformity. In March 1555 he ordered the vice-chancellor to see that

> in all your elections and giving of voices to any graces and admissions to all degrees none shall be admitted to give voice or receive degree, but such only as have openly in the congregation house detested particularly and by articles the heresies lately spread in this realm and professed by articles the catholic doctrine now received and subscribed the same with their hands.[22]

On 26 July 1555 he received a confession of faith signed by some 130 regent and non-regent members of the university which emphasized the importance of good works, expressed a belief in the real presence of

---

[20] D.M. Loades, *The Reign of Mary Tudor* (London, 1979), 159; Mullinger, *Cambridge*, II, 165.
[21] D.M. Loades, 'The Enforcement of Reaction, 1553–1558', *Journal of Ecclesiastical History*, XVI (1965), 54–66.
[22] J.A. Muller, *Letters of Stephen Gardiner*, 475–6.

Christ in the sacrament of the altar, confessed the inerrancy of the Catholic Church, allowed the veneration of saints and relics, affirmed a belief in purgatory and in the indissolubility of vows and quite specifically rejected the doctrines of Zwingli, Oecolampadius, Luther, Calvin, Bucer and all other heretics.[23]

Since March 1554 Cranmer, Latimer and Ridley had remained in different prisons in Oxford as the government possessed no powers to inflict the death penalty for heresy until new legislation had gone through parliament. With the passing of the law '*de heretico comburendo*' the three convicted heretics anticipated an early end, but in the event the government took no action until the autumn. Then in September the papal delegate, James Brooks, bishop of Gloucester, began a formal investigation into the circumstances in which Cranmer, a *legatus natus*, had rejected papal authority. Unlike Cranmer, Ridley and Latimer had not accepted their bishoprics from Rome and no obstacles now stood in the way of their execution. On 30 September 1555 they appeared in the divinity schools before the bishops of Lincoln, Gloucester and Bristol, who examined them yet again on the opinions they had defended at the Oxford disputation. Both refused either to recognize the supremacy of the Pope or to recant their heretical opinions. The next day, having summoned the university officers, the heads of houses, the local gentry in Oxford for the Quarter Sessions as well as the mass of the people to St Mary's, the three bishops denounced Latimer and Ridley as heretics, degraded them from their priestly orders and handed them over to the secular arm. On 16 October before the burning Dr Smith tried to instil into his auditory the differences between true and false martyrdom. Then before the commissioners, Lord Williams of Tame, the vice-chancellor, the mayor and many others from the university and the town Ridley and Latimer died in the flames 'in the ditch over against Balliol College'.[24]

The sentencing of Cranmer, delayed by the legal necessity of consultation with Rome, provided the government with yet more opportunities for propagating Catholicism in the university. Isolated after the deaths of Ridley and Latimer, Cranmer, through the intervention of his sister, spent the Christmas period outside prison in the custody of the dean of Christ Church, and the canons of the house – led by Henry Sidall and the new regius professor of theology, the Spanish friar, John de Garcina – made persistent efforts to secure his conversion. Their persuasions seemed at first to have been in vain, but, on his return to Bocardo when news of his condemnation in Rome

---

[23] Lamb, *A Collection of Letters* ... , 170–75.
[24] Loades, *The Oxford Martyrs*, 167–91; Foxe, *Acts and Monuments*, VII, 518–51.

reached Oxford, Cranmer began to waver. Reluctant to withstand his monarch any longer, he signed his first retraction recognizing the Pope as head of the Church in so far as the laws of the realm would allow. He followed this with a whole series of recantations, each more unqualified than the last, and at Candlemas attended Mass. Dismissing these submissions as insincere, Bishop Thirlby of Ely and Bishop Bonner of London proceeded to pronounce the papal sentence against Cranmer in the choir of Christ Church on 14 February 1556 and divested him of his orders. In late February he signed yet another retractation which Garcina and Sidall published in London in a fruitless attempt to gain a reprieve. Then for the second time in the reign on 21 March 1556 Lord Williams, representatives of the university, the mayor and aldermen and a great concourse of people gathered in St Mary's to witness the punishment of a heretic. In his sermon Dr Cole sought to justify the severity of the penalty, explaining that despite his repentance the queen had determined that Cranmer deserved to die both on account of his heretical activities in the past and his dissolution of her parents' marriage, and in reparation for the death of Bishop Fisher, for which the burning of Ridley, Hooper and Ferrar had not sufficed. He nevertheless commended the former archbishop for his conversion and promised that Masses would be offered for his soul. Despite Cranmer's dramatic renunciation of his recantations at the eleventh hour and his death as a professing Protestant, Catholics could still see his execution as a definitive stage in the eradication of heresy in Oxford. On Maundy Thursday, 2 April 1556, a much less celebrated Protestant, John Hullier, a one-time scholar of Eton and King's, was burned on Jesus Green at Cambridge.[25]

By the autumn of 1556 both Oxford and Cambridge had come under the direct control of the chief promoter of Catholic orthodoxy in England, Reginald Pole. On the death of Stephen Gardiner in November 1555 Cambridge had chosen the cardinal as its new chancellor. A little under a year later Sir John Mason resigned as chancellor of Oxford to enable the university to elect Pole in his place. High among the archbishop's priorities for the renewal of Catholicism was Catholic education. The legatine synod which he summoned to meet in Westminster from December 1555 to January 1556, in addition to passing decrees for the restoration of Roman authority, law and ceremonies and the removal of abuses among the clergy, stressed the importance of education and re-education, and resolved that all English

---

[25] Loades, *The Oxford Martyrs*, 192–223; D. MacCulloch, *Thomas Cranmer: A Life* (New Haven and London, 1996), 554–605; Foxe, *Acts and Monuments*, VIII, 44–90, 378–80.

cathedrals should establish seminaries to prepare boys for the priesthood. The diocese of York among others hastened to comply, the statutes of its new school in 1557 having as their main object the hope that 'in the church militant shepherds may everywhere be preferred who with the sword of the spirit ... may be able to drive away and put to flight the rapacious wolves, that is devilish men ill understanding the catholic faith, from the sheepfolds of the sheep intrusted to them ...' In due time the most gifted students from these cathedral schools would have been expected to progress to Catholic universities. Yet, despite all the efforts of Gardiner and Mason, Pole in 1556 considered Oxford and Cambridge had still not attained the goal of unequivocal Catholic orthodoxy.[26]

In the summer of 1556 the cardinal decided upon a legatine visitation of Oxford, issuing to his commissioners James Brooks, the bishop of Gloucester, Nicholas Ormanet, the papal datary and Pole's secretary, Robert Morwen, president of Corpus Christi, Dr Cole and Dr Wright 30 articles designed to expose novelties introduced into the university in the time of schism, to remove all traces of heresy and remedy any inadequacies of teaching in either the university or the colleges. On 20 July the visitors reached Oxford where they addressed the university formally in St Mary's. They then proceeded to each college in turn where they punished any scholars still in possession of Protestant books, before going on to burn English Bibles and other Protestant literature in the market place and, as a further deterrent against heresy, to exhume the bones of Martyr's first wife from Christ Church Cathedral and cast them on a dung hill. In November Pole sent down new statutes governing all aspects of university life, which yet again censured any teaching which might reflect adversely upon Catholic faith and customs, and exhorted all members of the university to cleave to good doctrine, and live honest and pious lives.[27]

Later in 1556 the cardinal commissioned a similar visitation of Cambridge. The registrary there, John Mere, kept a unique journal of the event which reveals the lengths to which Pole would go to impose Catholicism upon the university. On 9 December 1556 the vice-chancellor received a citation from the cardinal for the visitation, and at

---

[26] Strype, *Ecclesiastical Memorials*, III, 288–9; Bodl. Archives Reg. 18 f. 163v; R.H. Pogson, 'The Legacy of the Schism: Confusion, Continuity and Change in the Marian Clergy', in J. Loach and R. Tittler, eds, *The Mid-Tudor Polity c. 1540–1560* (London, 1980), 116–36; A.F. Leach, *Early Yorkshire Schools*, Yorkshire Archaeological Society, Record Series, XXVII (1899), xxxv.

[27] Bodl. Twyne Ms. VII, ff. 155–7; S. Gibson, *Statuta Antigua* ... , 363–75; A. Wood, *History and Antiquities of the University of Oxford*, II, 130–34.

once ordered the heads of houses and others to appear in Great St Mary's on 11 January. On 10 January John Christopherson, bishop of Chichester and master of Trinity, Thomas Watson, bishop of Lincoln, Nicholas Ormanet and others arrived at Trinity College where they heard Mass. The next day the visitation proper began. After orations at Trinity the chief members of the university attended a mass of the Holy Ghost at King's before gathering in Great St Mary's where Mr Peacock preached, 'inveighing against heresies and heretics, as Bilney, Latimer, Cranmer, Ridley etc', after which the registrary read the cardinal's commission. In the afternoon the commissioners adjourned to the schools and called in the university statutes for examination. The next two days they gave over to a public condemnation of Bucer for heresy. After this on 14 January they proceeded to a visitation of the individual colleges, starting with King's. They made a point of being present at Mass in almost the colleges they inspected. On 15 January in Great St Mary's the congregation of the university formally repudiated the doctrines of Bucer and Fagius, and the visitors took public possession of a new commission from Pole to enquire into heresy. At most of the colleges they discovered little out of the way, though at Christ's they found one Tomlinson with prohibited books and committed him to the Tolbooth. On 29 January they warned the vice-chancellor, the heads of the colleges and representatives of the Cambridge town parishes to supply in writing particulars of all their books. On Sunday 31 January the university heard a sermon on the significance of Candlemas, and the bishop of Lincoln preached against Bucer. At the beginning of February cartloads of books from both the town and the university began to be brought in, many of which the visitors condemned and on 6 February caused to be burned in the market place alongside the remains of Bucer and Fagius.

The following day they rehallowed Great St Mary's where the heretics had been given Christian burial. For several more days the commissioners persisted in their search for suspect books and authorized another bonfire on Market Hill. Very significantly on 13 February the datary, Pole's secretary, took the registrary aside and told him that complaints had been made about him for heresy and for maintaining heretics beyond the sea. The interrogations came to an end on 16 February. The visitors returned the university's muniments to the vice-chancellor and after Mass before the assembled university presided over a formal reading of the new statutes, which, in addition to re-ordering the teaching of the university as at Oxford and giving new prominence to the heads of houses, made special provision for the preservation of the Catholic faith.[28]

---

[28] Lamb, *A Collection of Letters* ... , 184–236; Mullinger, *Cambridge*, II, 157.

By the spring of 1557 Pole could realistically presume that his officers had extirpated all outward signs of heresy from both universities. Yet with his new statutes he was attempting to reconstruct as well as purge, reverting to the tradition of Christian humanism, free from all taint of heresy, which Fisher had done so much to advance in Cambridge and Wolsey and Sir Thomas More in Oxford in the first quarter of the century. Some of the laity as well as the clergy shared his concerns, and the two universities once again began to attract benefactions from the Catholic faithful. In 1555 a friend of More, Sir Thomas Pope, who had gained his wealth through a successful career in the Chancery, acquired the abandoned buildings of the former Durham College in order to set up in Oxford a new foundation, dedicated to the Holy Trinity, of 12 fellows and 12 scholars, to honour and glorify God, serve the nation and promote the orthodox faith and the Christian religion. With the same end in view as the cardinal, he went on to insist that all the senior members of the college should be ordained priests within four years of taking their master's degree.[29]

Sir Thomas White, a Merchant Taylor and former Lord Mayor of London, also obtained a licence in 1555 to establish St John's College on the site of the former St Bernard's College in Oxford, though it did not accept its first students until 1557. Planned on a considerably more ambitious scale than Trinity, the college shared the same ideological purpose to further 'the increase of the orthodox faith and of the Christian profession in so far as it is weakened by the damage of time and the malice of men', and especially to advance the study of theology 'much afflicted of late, as we see with sorrow and grief.' White followed Pole in requiring all fellows to proceed to the priesthood within three years of completing their degrees.[30]

In addition to the queen's donation to Trinity, Cambridge also gained a further substantial lay benefaction at this time. In 1557 Dr John Caius, a graduate of both Cambridge and Padua and a fellow of the College of Physicians in London, refounded Gonville Hall as Gonville and Caius College. Another supporter of the old religion, in his own person Caius embodied the Catholic humanism so characteristic of the age. He designed himself gates of humility, virtue and honour for the college in the classical style, and, like White in Oxford, he also assumed the direction of his foundation in its early years. Yet further linking Catholic renewal with educational provision in her will made early in 1558, Mary

---

[29] *CPR Philip and Mary*, II, 90–91; J. McConica, 'The Rise of the Undergraduate College', in *The History of the University of Oxford*, III, 42–5.

[30] *CPR Philip and Mary*, II, 322–3; J. McConica, 'The Rise of the Undergraduate College', 45–8.

left £500 each to both universities 'to be distributed and given amongst the ... poor scholars from time to time as they shall think expedient for their relief and comfort, and specially to such as intend by God's grace to be religious persons and priests'.[31]

The legatine visitations of Oxford and Cambridge together with the promulgation of the new statutes marked a watershed in the history of the two universities in the Marian period. From the spring of 1557 both the queen and the cardinal could take pride in the success of their campaign for the eradication of heresy; neither, it seems, realized that they had so little time to implant Catholic reform. As Cranmer had introduced Protestants from overseas into the academic posts, so in a similar fashion Pole recruited foreign Catholic scholars. His secretary, the papal datary Ormanet, took an active part in the legatine visitations of both universities, though otherwise the cardinal largely directed the incomers to Oxford. Two Spanish Dominican friars incorporated there in the autumn of 1555, John de Villagarcia and Peter de Soto, previously confessor to the Emperor Charles V, the one following the other in the regius chair of theology. A third Spanish Dominican, Bartolomé Carranza, may have spent some time in the university where a fourth Spaniard, Frater Antony Rescius, certainly taught and disputed before he proceeded to the degree of bachelor of divinity in 1558. Having employed Spanish friars to reverse the effects of Martyr's teaching, Pole, perhaps to avoid unsettling more conservative Catholics, deliberately chose not to expose either of the universities to the innovatory teaching methods of the Jesuits which proved to be so attractive to English students later in the century.[32]

As with the strength of committed Protestantism in the universities at the end of Edward VI's reign, the extent of Catholic reconversion only became apparent with the change of government on the queen's death on 17 November 1558. Elizabeth and her advisers moved as quickly as

---

[31] J.P.C. Roach, 'The University of Cambridge in the Sixteenth Century', in *Victoria County History: Cambridge and the Isle of Ely*, III (London, 1959), 179–81; D. Loades, *Mary Tudor: A Life* (Oxford, 1989), 372–3; D. Loades, 'The Spirituality of the Restored Catholic Church (1553–1558) in the Context of the Counter Reformation', in T.M. McCoog, ed., *The Reckoned Expense: Edmund Campion and the Early English Jesuits* (Woodbridge, 1996), 3–19.

[32] J. Loach, 'Reformation Controversies', in *The History of the University of Oxford*, III, 378–9; A. Wood, *History and Antiquities of the University of Oxford*, II, 122–9; J.H. Crehan, 'St Ignatius and Cardinal Pole', *Archivum Historicum Societatis Iesu*, XXV (1956), 72–98; T.M. McCoog, 'Ignatius Loyola and Reginald Pole: A Reconsideration', *Journal of Ecclesiastical History*, XLVII (1996), 257–73: M. Questier, 'Clerical Recruitment, Conversion and Rome c. 1580–1620', in C. Cross, ed., *Patronage and Recruitment in the Tudor and Early Stuart Church* (Borthwick Studies in History 2, York, 1996), 77–8.

Mary had done in the summer of 1553 to overturn the religious settlement, and by the close of 1558 the Protestant exiles were preparing to return. When he reached England Jewel was appalled by the magnitude of the reaction, writing to his Zurich hosts that only two persons in the whole of Oxford shared his and Bullinger's beliefs, while Parkhouse pronounced the university 'a den of thieves, and of those who hate the light'.[33]

In striking contrast with what had happened in the reigns of Henry VIII and Edward VI, in 1559 the Catholic bishops mounted an organized and informed resistance, in both the House of Lords and convocation, to the government's proposal to repudiate papal authority and re-establish an independent Protestant Church. Despite their efforts, after Easter parliament succeeded in passing the Acts of Supremacy and Uniformity and so set in place laws which permitted a new purge of the universities. Before the end of 1559 royal commissioners visited Oxford and Cambridge charged with the task of enforcing the oath of supremacy, removing popish abuses and restoring the Edwardian statutes.[34]

There can be little doubt that the change in religion affected Oxford more than Cambridge. Even before the royal commissioners arrived in Oxford the heads of two houses, Wright of Balliol and Henshaw of Lincoln, relinquished their offices. The visitors deprived four more, Reynolds of Merton, Marshall of Christ Church, Slythurst of Trinity and Chedsey of Corpus Christi, for refusing the oath of supremacy while the founder of St John's ejected Belysyre later in the year for alleged financial impropriety. Within two years of the passing of the Elizabethan settlement only one Marian head of house remained in office: in their places the government secured the appointment of the former exiles Thomas Sampson at Christ Church and Lawrence Humphrey at Magdalen.[35]

At Oxford the royal visitation also precipitated an exodus of Catholics to the Continent on an even greater scale than the Protestant migration in the previous reign. New College under Whyte proved a particular centre of opposition. Nicholas Sanders, Thomas Stapleton and John Fowler went into exile in 1560 and as late as 1561 24 senior members, a third of the fellowship, refused the oath of supremacy.

---

[33] P. Williams, 'Elizabethan Oxford: State, Church and University 1558–1603', in McConica, ed. *History of the University of Oxford*, III, 405; *Zurich Letters*, I, 11–12, 29, 33.

[34] N.L. Jones, 'Elizabeth's First Year: The Conception and Birth of the Elizabethan Political World', in C. Haigh, ed., *The Reign of Elizabeth I* (London, 1984), 27–53.

[35] P. Williams, 'Elizabethan Oxford ... ', 406–7.

Corpus Christi exhibited a similar resolution until the government procured the election of William Cole as head of the house in 1568. Early in the reign William Allen, John Hemming and John Herniman left Oriel for the sake of religion. William Tresham, David de la Hyde and Anthony and Robert Dawkes led the Catholic party at Merton. In 1569 Edmund Campion felt it politic to withdraw from St John's, and a further 12 recusant senior members lost their fellowships between 1567 and 1574. Exeter continued a strongly conservative college under the patronage of the Catholic Sir John Petre until late in the 1570s, and Catholicism also lingered in Balliol even after the resignation of Robert Parsons in 1574. After their departure from England a considerable number of these scholars congregated around William Allen at Douai, setting up an English college in exile which for decades to come provided a congenial alternative for English students seeking a university education free from Protestant constraints.[36]

Disruption at Cambridge was on a somewhat smaller scale. Two Edwardian heads of houses, William Bill of Trinity and William Mey of Queens', regained their offices before the arrival in September 1559 of the royal commissioners who, in addition to Matthew Parker, included the exiles Anthony Cook, William Bill, Robert Horn and James Pilkington. Cosyn retired as master of St Catharine's in favour of John Mey and on William Taylor's departure for the Continent Cecil's nominee, Edward Hawford, replaced him at Christ's. The commissioners removed George Bullock from the mastership of St John's, installing the exile James Pilkington in his stead. At Pembroke Edmund Grindal succeeded John Young and at Trinity Hall and Jesus William Mowse and John Redman respectively made way for Henry Harvey and Edward Gascoigne. The exile Roger Kelke supplanted Richard Carr at Magdalene. Thomas Bailey abandoned the mastership of Clare first for the Catholic university of Louvain and later to collaborate with Allen at Douai. Both John Seton and his fellow logician John Saunderson found the university too Protestant for their tastes after 1559. Having been forced out of his professorship for endorsing Catholic ceremonies, Saunderson spent the last years of his life in Douai and Rheims. With the large number of Marian exiles reinstated in their former colleges the government seems to have felt it less urgent at Cambridge to investigate the behaviour of suspect senior members of the university. Dr Caius continued as master of Caius, Andrew Perne remained master of Peterhouse and Philip Baker stayed on as provost of King's, the latter secretly preserving copes and crucifixes against the day

---

[36] Ibid., 407–13; J. McConica, 'The Catholic Experience in Tudor Oxford', in T.M. McCoog, ed., *The Reckoned Expense*, 39–63.

when Catholicism might return once more. Their predilections, however, counted for little against the fervent Protestantism of the new generation of Cambridge regent masters.[37]

Mary ruled England for a scant five years, Elizabeth for almost 45. The shortness of her reign constituted the primary reason for Mary's failure to secure a permanent restoration of Catholic scholarship at Oxford and Cambridge. The form of humanism fostered by Pole might well have put down lasting roots in the universities had the queen secured a Catholic succession. At Cambridge as well as at Oxford by the end of the Marian period the younger students were beginning to respond to the allure of Catholic humanism. Perhaps the most celebrated of these graduates, Edmund Campion, left St John's College in Oxford in 1569 to enter first the Catholic priesthood at Douai and soon after the Jesuit order. Passionately believing that his country could be won back to Catholicism by rational argument, on his dispatch a decade later on the mission for the conversion of England he aspired to demonstrate publicly before the Privy Council and learned men of the two universities 'the faith of our catholic church by proofs invincible, scriptures, councils, fathers, histories, natural and moral reasons …' In 1558 it would not have been unrealistic to have expected that Oxford and Cambridge might have produced many more scholars of Campion's calibre. More than any other single factor, time frustrated the plans of Mary and Pole for Catholic higher education in England.[38]

---

[37] Lamb, *A Collection of Letters* … , xxxvii–xxxix; Mullinger, *Cambridge*, III, 171–82; D.R. Leader, *A History of the University of Cambridge*, I (Cambridge, 1988), 350–51.

[38] A.O. Meyer, *England and the Catholic church under Elizabeth* (London, 1915), 92–121: P. McGrath, *Papists and Puritans under Elizabeth I* (London, 1967), 168–9.

CHAPTER THREE

Westminster Abbey Restored*

C.S. Knighton

Surviving monuments of Marian Catholicism are few. By far the most notable is to be found at the nerve-centre of the consecrated English monarchy, the shrine of Edward the Confessor in Westminster Abbey. In its present form the shrine is owed to the last abbot of Westminster, John Feckenham, who presided over the Benedictine community restored there at the instigation of Queen Mary. Although the revival lasted less than three years, from late 1556 to the summer of 1559, it has had enduring and in some ways surprising consequences. In the first place, it is cherished by the modern English Benedictine congregation, and particularly by Ampleforth Abbey, which claims direct descent from the last survivor of Marian Westminster. This association was powerfully marked on 25 March 1976 when, on the day of his installation as archbishop of Westminster, Dom Basil Hume came with the Ampleforth community, of which he had been abbot, to sing vespers in Westminster Abbey.[1] In this connection the Marian foundation is essential, because it is generally accepted that the ancient abbey of Westminster, along with all other religious houses *de facto* dissolved by Henry VIII and Edward VI, had been rendered canonically extinct by the bull *Praeclara charissimi* of Paul IV, dated 21 June 1555.[2] Consequently the Marian

---

* I am indebted to the dean and chapter of Westminster for permission to consult and use their archive. I am grateful to Dr R. Mortimer, keeper of the muniments of Westminster Abbey, and Miss C. Reynolds, assistant keeper, for their help and guidance over many years. Miss B.F. Harvey very kindly read a draft of this paper, to its advantage. Dr P. Cunich has been good enough to share his extensive data on the ex-religious.

[1] Cf. E.F. Carpenter and D. Gentleman, *Westminster Abbey* (1987), 69. The Ampleforth monks again sang vespers in Westminster Abbey on 23 October 2002 as part of the celebration of the 200th anniversary of the community's settlement in Yorkshire.

[2] So dated in Cardinal Pole's legatine register: Douai, Bibliothèque Municipale [hereafter DBM], MS 922, tome iv, ff. 44v–47v (microfilm at Lambeth Palace Library [hereafter LPL]). Text printed in *Documenta ad legationem Cardinalis Poli spectantia*, ed. J.F. Moyes, F.A. Gasquet and D. Fleming (Rome 1896), 18–23 gives 'Duodecimo Kal. Julii', that is 20 June, but this is a reading of 'undecimo': I am grateful to Professor T.F. Mayer for confirming that Archivio Segreto Vaticano, Reg. Vat. 1850, ff. 34–7, from which the *Documenta* text was taken, reads (f. 37) as Douai (f. 47v). All subsequent texts and comments derive the incorrect date from Gasquet's transcript, first published in *The*

abbey was a new foundation, not a continuation of the old. The bull of 1555 has, as will appear, other implications for the status of Westminster in Mary's reign, and perhaps beyond. The story of the Marian abbey itself has been told several times,[3] and the abbey muniments have already yielded most that they can tell. The present concern is chiefly with the constitutional aspects of the refoundation. Biographical details of the monastic community are presented in an appendix which builds on the pioneering work of Dom Hugh Aveling.

The restored Westminster Abbey and the Marian religious foundations generally have not received much attention or praise save from Catholic historians.[4] There has been a feeling that the available effort and expense was directed to reviving flawed institutions of the past rather than harnessing forward-looking aspects of the Counter Reformation. The Westminster monks have even been criticized for being inadequately youthful; though in fairness the community inevitably contained a good many men of middle age or more[5] There were young men there, too, but they had no time to develop whatever

---

Tablet, lxxxvi, no. 2890 (28 September 1895), 499–500, 502–3, viz.: W.H. Frere, *The Marian Reaction in its relation to the English clergy: a study of the historical registers* (Church Historical Society, xviii, 1896), 223–32; A.S. Barnes, *The Popes and the Ordinal* (1896), 125–9. Cf. M.D. Knowles, *The Religious Orders in England* (Cambridge 1948–59), iii, 423, 426; D.M. Lunn, *The English Benedictines 1540–1688; from Reformation to Revolution* (1988), 3 and nn. 7, 8 (on p. 8); D.M. Loades, *The Reign of Mary Tudor: Politics, Government and Religion in England 1553–8* (2nd edn, 1991), 299.

[3] A.P. Stanley, *Historical Memorials of Westminster Abbey* (5th edn, 1882), 400–406. J.B. Wainewright, 'Queen Mary's religious foundations', *Downside Review*, new ser. viii (1908), 125–46, esp. 133–7. E.H. Pearce, *The Monks of Westminster* (Notes and Documents relating to Westminster Abbey, no. 5, Cambridge 1916), 214–17. S. Marron, 'Dom Sigebert Buckley and his brethren', *Douai Magazine*, vii, no. 3 (1933), 130–38. H.F. Westlake, *Westminster Abbey* (1923), i, 223–40. J.C.H. Aveling, 'Tudor Westminster, 1540–1559', and Appendix A, 'The Marian community', in *Ampleforth and its Origins*, ed. J.P. McCann and C. Cary-Elwes (1952), 53–80, 271–85. Knowles, *Rel. Orders*, iii, 424–38, 442–3. A. Tindal Hart, in *A House of Kings*, ed. E.F. Carpenter (1966), 122–9. J.I. Tellechea Idigoras, *Fray Bartolomé Carranza y Cardenal Pole: un Navarro en la Restauración Católica de Inglaterra* (Pamplona 1977), 64–7. Lunn, *Engl. Benedictines*, 2–6. P. Cunich, 'Benedictine monks at the University of Oxford and the dissolution of the monasteries', in *Benedictines in Oxford*, ed. H. Wansbrough and A. Marett-Crosby (1997), 155–81, esp. 178–80. *Idem*, in *Monks of England: the Benedictines in England from Augustine to the present day*, ed. D. Rees (1997), 164–6. C.S. Knighton, 'Brother Goodluck and St Philip's left foot – both survivors in Queen Mary's monastery', *The Westminster Abbey Chorister*, iii, no. 10 (1998/9), 39–40.

[4] A recent judgement is that Mary 'did not resurrect the regular clergy as a significant aspect of the religious or political life of the country': D.M. Loades, *Tudor Government: Structures of Authority in the Sixteenth Century* (Oxford 1997), 200.

[5] R.H. Pogson, 'Cardinal Pole: papal legate to England in Mary Tudor's reign' (Cambridge PhD dissertation, 1972), 336–7.

might have been an appropriate monachism for England in the second half of the sixteenth century. Nor was Westminster an ideal location for spiritual regeneration.[6] It was, however, the obvious showcase for the queen's purpose. Local considerations were not overlooked: Cardinal Pole was concerned that the refounding of the abbey should not lead to pastoral neglect in surrounding parishes.[7] There is no reason to suppose that the people of Westminster or the former diocese felt any grievance; the only recorded parochial connection with Westminster Abbey when it was a cathedral (1540–56) is a dispensation for the faithful to avoid attendance there.[8] Knowles saw the choice of Westminster for the principal monastic refoundation chiefly as an economic consideration; the Crown would be able to endow it by dissolving the secular chapter recently filled with its own loyal appointees.[9] It may also be significant that (as Professor Loades has noted) the queen gave new statutes to Durham Cathedral in 1555 and so signalled her intention to retain its secular chapter; there may even have been general reluctance to embark on the extra complication of restoring any of the pre-Reformation cathedral priories.[10] Westminster was still technically a cathedral in 1556, but that status was only a fiction devised in 1552 to validate the continued existence of the church and its chapter after the diocese (created in 1540) had been dissolved.[11] With effect from 1550 to 1556 Westminster Abbey was the second cathedral of the diocese of London, but that role could conveniently be dropped when the abbey was restored. The bishop of London had no need of a secondary chapter such as existed at Bath and Coventry before the dissolution. Westminster was, importantly, alive and intact, but unencumbered by diocesan and parochial responsibilities. It was the only greater church in this condition, and therefore the only suitable recipient for a major monastic transplant.

When the decision was made to perform this operation remains

---

[6] For Westminster Abbey in its local context see esp. A.G. Rosser, *Medieval Westminster, 1200–1540* (Oxford 1989), 255–63; B.F. Harvey, *Living and Dying in England, 1100–1540: the Monastic Experience* (Oxford 1993), 2–6, and both works *passim*. See also F. Kisby, 'Courtiers in the community: the musicians of the royal household chapel in early Tudor Westminster', in *The Reign of Henry VII*, ed. B. Thompson (Harlaxton Medieval Studies, v, Stamford 1995), 229–55.

[7] Pogson, 'Cardinal Pole', 335.

[8] *Acts of the Dean and Chapter of Westminster, 1543–1609*, ed. C.S. Knighton (Westminster Abbey Record Ser. i–ii, 1997–99) [hereafter *Acts*], i, 18 and n. 57.

[9] Knowles, *Rel. Orders*, iii, 424. Married or otherwise unacceptable canons were ejected in March 1554 and replaced by Marian loyalists: *Acts*, i, 85 n. 299.

[10] Loades, *Tudor Government*, 181.

[11] 5 & 6 Edward VI, Original Act no. 36.

unknown. It is unlikely to have been before the general agreement on monastic lands in December 1554.¹² The first prompting was the appearance at court, reported on 19 March 1555, of the dean of St Paul's, John Feckenham, and 15 others, habited as Benedictines. The queen is said to have appointed Lord Chancellor Gardiner and three other councillors to see how this prospective community could be accommodated.¹³ Westminster had been selected for the community by 14 April when Sir John Mason reported that the incumbent dean and chapter had 'laid sore law' to prevent their church being made into an abbey – Dr Henry Cole in particular maintaining that the monks had 'none institution of Christe'. Mason knew, however, that the only choice for the secular chapter was 'whether they will depart with their wills or against their wills.¹⁴ It might be thought that the issuing of *Praeclara* in June 1555 would have impeded any monastic revival then in prospect. Actually, by legitimizing the Henrician cathedral foundations (Westminster among them), Paul IV's bull opened the way for Mary to dissolve the secular chapter of Westminster and re-use its revenues for the endowment of the new abbey. Henry VIII's structure was made canonically secure before it could be dismantled. Mary was not averse to taking short-cuts to achieve her aims;¹⁵ but she must have wanted the new

---

12 1 & 2 Philip & Mary c. 8.

13 *Calendar of State Papers and Manuscripts, relating to English affairs, existing in the Archives and Collections of Venice and in other Libraries of Northern Italy*, ed. R. Brown et al. (1864–1940) [hereafter *Cal. Ven.*], vi, I, no. 32 (27). Knowles, *Rel. Orders*, iii, 424. Feckenham (for whom see below, 86), had been in trouble with the Privy Council in November 1554 after a sermon at Paul's Cross which advocated total restoration of monastic property: *The Diary of Henry Machyn, Citizen and Merchant-Taylor of London, from A.D. 1550 to A.D. 1563*, ed. J.G. Nichols (Camden Soc. xlii, 1848), 76. *Acts of the Privy Council of England*, new ser., ed. J.R. Dasent (1890–1907) [hereafter *APC*], v, 85. *Calendar of Letters, Despatches, and State Papers, relating to the negotiations between England and Spain, preserved in the Archives at Simancas and elsewhere*, ed. G.A. Bergenroth et al. (1862–1954) [hereafter *Cal. Span.*], xiii, 108. Cf. Loades, *Reign of Mary*, 268; S.J. Loach, *Parliament and the Crown in the Reign of Mary Tudor* (Oxford 1986), 108. Feckenham was in favour again by spring 1556 when he examined several state prisoners: *Calendar of State Papers, Domestic Series, of the Reign of Mary I, 1553–1558*, ed. C.S. Knighton (1998) [hereafter *CSPDM*], nos 338, 400, 424. PRO, SP 46/162, ff. 174, 176. *Cal. Ven.* vi, I, no. 477 (p. 439) refers to the dean of Westminster in this capacity, identified by the editor as Feckenham, but perhaps this is correctly the dean of Westminster (Hugh Weston), who also examined prisoners (cf. *CSPDM*, nos 390, 391, 432).

14 G. Burnet, *The History of the Reformation of the Church of England*, ed. N. Pocock (Oxford 1865), vi, 379–80 (Mason to Peter Vannes, 14 April 1555).

15 Cf. D.M. Loades, 'The dissolution of the diocese of Durham, 1553–54', in *The Last Principality: Politics, Religion and Society in the Bishopric of Durham, 1494–1660*, ed. D. Marcombe (Studies in Regional and Local History, no. 1, Nottingham 1987), 109.

Westminster Abbey to have unimpeachable title in canon as well as English law. The countdown to the actual refoundation begins with a letter, provisionally assigned to February 1556, from Pole to the president of the Benedictine congregation of Monte Cassino, of which the cardinal was protector. Westminster was not named, but Pole expressed the hope that representatives of the Cassinese congregation would assist the restoration of the monastery about to be effected.[16] Pole may have avoided employing Jesuits in England for personal reasons, because they were not part of the indigenous religious structure he meant to restore, or simply because they were not gentlemen; but he certainly wanted the revived English Benedictines to follow the reformed Italian model. In fact the Cassinese visitors never appeared, so the revival proceeded without them[17] The spring of 1556 was not, however, a good moment. In March the queen and her government were confronted by what appeared to be a major security crisis.[18] This proved to be a mare's nest, but it may (along with other preocccupations such as the trial and execution of Cranmer) account in some part for the delay of the Westminster Abbey project. Not until 7 September were letters patent issued for the dissolution of the secular chapter and its replacement with a monastery.[19] The cardinal legate, not the Crown, was to be the agent of the foundation. On 15 September he gave his authority for the dean and chapter to surrender, and he notified the king and queen of this act.[20] Three days later the receiver-general of Westminster, John Moulton, who was at his country house at Batsford, Gloucestershire, saddled his horse and returned to deal with the financial realities of the changeover.[21] On arrival he was joined by the auditor, and they drew up valours and other documents.[22] On 23 September Pole was authorized to grant pensions to the outgoing secular chapter.[23] He duly notified them that they would receive payments from

---

[16] *Cal. Ven.* vi, I, no. 403 (352); *The Correspondence of Reginald Pole*, ed. T.F. Mayer Vol. 3 (2004), 254, no. 1436. Knowles, *Rel. Orders*, iii, 425 and n. 1.

[17] T.F. Mayer, *Reginald Pole, Prince and Prophet* (Cambridge, 2000), 106, 188–9, 283–4. Idem, 'A test of wills: Cardinal Pole, Ignatius Loyola, and the Jesuits in England', in *The Reckoned Expense: Edmund Campion and the Early English Jesuits*, ed. T.M. McCoog (Woodbridge, 1996), 21–37, esp. 31–2, 35. Cf. McCoog, 'Ignatius Loyola and Reginald Pole: a reconsideration', *Journal of Ecclesiastical History*, xlvii (1996), 268–72.

[18] D.M. Loades, *Two Tudor Conspiracies* (Cambridge, 1965), 149.

[19] *Calendar of the Patent Rolls preserved in the Public Record Office* [hereafter CPR], 1555–7, 546; printed in W. Dugdale, *Monasticon Anglicanum*, ed. J. Caley, H. Ellis and B. Bandinel (1817–30), i, 324.

[20] DBM, MS 922 (legatine reg.), tome vi, ff. 110v-111. Dugdale, *Monasticon*, i, 323–4, prints the letter to the dean and chapter only.

[21] Westminster Abbey Muniments [hereafter WAM] 37662, f. 12.

[22] WAM 37710–12, 37716–17, 37718, ff. 2v, 3.

[23] *CPR*, 1555–7, 547.

the new abbey until other preferment was found for them.[24] There seems to have been no suggestion that any of the secular chapter might wish to enter religion, and none did. On 25 September the bishop of London gave formal consent to the dissolving of what was still his cathedral church.[25] The dean and chapter, having held their last meeting on the 24th, resigned on the 26th.[26] The departure of the canons was reported by the Venetian envoy Michieli on the 28th; he expected that the monks would make their entry on the following day, Michaelmas.[27]

The abbot and convent would be financially accountable from that day. The first record of one of the monks in receipt of funds is on 7 November 1556. The only known activity of these weeks is the distribution of alms on five Sundays ending at All Saints (so beginning 4 October).[28] The patent of endowment passed the Great Seal on 10 November.[29] There is no official record of the formal inauguration. Michieli reports that on 20 November (Friday) the monks, 16 in all, were put in possession by the Lord Chancellor and Pole's datary Niccolò Ormanetto.[30] Charles Wriothesley gives the 21st as the day on which Feckenham and 14 more 'receaved the habitt', the queen having given them all such (ex-Westminster) lands as remained in her hands.[31] Henry Machyn distinguishes three events: on the 21st Feckenham and 14 monks were 'shorne in'; on the next day (Sunday) there was a procession 'after the old fassyon' with the monks in their habits preceded by vergers with silver rods; a week later, Sunday 29th, the abbot was blessed in the presence of the cardinal, the Lord Chancellor celebrating the Mass.[32] In

---

[24] DBM, MS 922 (legatine reg.), tome vi, ff. 121v–122 (25 September).

[25] WAM 12972 (original instrument). Guildhall Library, London, MS 9531/12, f. 407 (register entry).

[26] *Acts*, i, 99. WAM Register Book III, f. 307; date of resignation from this source wrongly given as 27th in Westlake, *Westminster Abbey*, i, 222, followed by Knowles, *Rel. Orders*, iii, 425.

[27] *Cal. Ven.* vi, I, no. 634 (p. 651). Knowles, *Rel. Orders*, iii, 425 n. 2, with misplaced 'same to same', mistakenly attributes this report as from Pole to the Cassinese president.

[28] WAM 37708, 37662, f. 12v.

[29] WAM LXXXVI (original instrument); illustrated in T. Cocke, *900 Years: The Restorations of Westminster Abbey* (1995), facing p. 40. Francis Yaxley, a clerk of the signet, was paid £2 for writing it: WAM 37662, f. 12v. WAM 6484F is an office copy. CPR, 1555–7, 348–54.

[30] *Cal. Ven.* vi, II, no. 723 (p. 809).

[31] *A Chronicle of England during the reigns of the Tudors, from A.D. 1485 to 1559, by Charles Wriothesley, Windsor Herald*, ed. W.D. Hamilton, ii (Camden Soc., new ser. xx, 1877), 136.

[32] Machyn, *Diary*, 118–19, 119–20. Stanley, *Hist. Memorials* (p. 401) wrongly identifies the celebrant as the former Lord Chancellor, Gardiner. E.T. Bradley's article on Feckenham for the 1st edition of the *DNB* says the abbot was consecrated by the legate on 30 November; this date was followed in A.B. Emden, *A Biographical Register of the*

what was clearly a separate occasion, on Monday 30 November the cardinal was again present in the abbey, along with the court (though the queen was ill); 26 monks were then counted with the abbot.³³ This was the commemoration of the reconciliation with Rome in 1554, which the legatine synod of 1555–56 had ordered to be kept annually.³⁴ Yet another procession took place on 6 December, when inmates of the Westminster sanctuary were paraded – among them a scholar of Westminster School, John Elles, who had killed a stallholder in Westminster Hall on 5 November.³⁵ By 20 December the queen was well enough to travel by water to Westminster to hear vespers sung by the monks, who now numbered 28. They were said to be all of 40 years or more, and to have renounced incomes of between 500 and 1500 crowns; all this comes from Michieli, who accompanied the queen and the cardinal in the royal barge.³⁶ Clearly the community had already expanded from the 14 or 16 who had been installed at the end of November; it would seem that as yet they were all veterans of the pre-1540 monasteries.

A solitary paper in the Abbey muniments (WAM 9327) is the source for the core of the Marian community at Westminster.³⁷ It may be summarized thus:

> *The names of the bretheren of Westmonasterie.* Abbot. Prior and 20 others (surnames only). *The names of those that shalbe religius and be now in comons.* 14 names (in one case forename and surname, the rest surname only). *The names of my lorde abbat men.* Marshal, gentleman usher, 2 of the chamber, caterer, usher of the hall, 2 butlers, 2 cooks, 2 skullions, porter, poor man, sub-almoner (all named except skullions). *The names of the common servantes.* 2

University of Oxford, A.D. 1501 to 1540 (Oxford 1974), 201, perhaps by confusion with the event next mentioned. Knowles (*Rel. Orders*, iii, 425) says consecration was by Bonner (bishop of London) on 'Saturday, the 29th' (an impossible date). It is likely that the blessing was performed by whoever celebrated *coram cardinale*, the interpretation given in my article on Feckenham for the *ODNB*.

33 *Cal. Ven.* ii, II, no. 743 (p. 836) (Michieli's despatch of 1 December).
34 Ibid. vi, I, no. 305 (p. 275). *The Anglican Canons 1529–1947*, ed. G. Bray (Church of England Record Soc. vi, 1998), 74–7.
35 Machyn, *Diary*, 121. Identification from inquisition in London Metropolitan Archives, Acc. 591/1. The stallholder, John Obett, chased away some inquisitive boys by throwing a stone. Elles returned it, fatally injuring his attacker, for which he was adjudged guilty of murder. Stanley (*Historical Memorials*, pp. 401–2), writing before the discovery of the inquisition evidence, saw the incident as a heroic model for Westminster boys in their fights with 'skies' (local toughs).
36 *Cal. Ven.* vi, II, no. 771 (p. 879), no. 884 (p. 1082).
37 Printed in Pearce, *Monks*, 214–15. Aveling, 'Marian community' (pp. 271–7) prints the names in the first two sections as headings for his biographical register.

tailors, butler, bellringer, porter, servant to sub-cellarer, cellarer's man, servant to archdeacon, servant to prior, keeper of granary, 2 barbers, servant to one of the named monks [thought to be a quondam abbot], shoemaker, 2 cooks, an old man to clean vessels, slaughterman, bellringer; (12 named). *The chappell men and childerne that be in commons.* 2 names. 6 choristers, 3 embroiderers, 2 gardeners. Chanter and 2 other names [precentor and 2 secular clerks].

The list is undated. Though it may reasonably be assumed to illustrate an early stage in the development of the community, there are difficulties in fitting it in with the other meagre documentary evidence.[38]

At some date also unstated four former monks of Glastonbury, John Phagan, John Neott, William Adelwold and William Kentwyne (three of whom can be identified as *Mr Phagan, Mr Newte* and *Mr Adthelwolde* in WAM 9327) petitioned the Lord Chamberlain for the restoration of their house, alleging a promise from the queen and the pleasure expressed by the cardinal for such a project. The petitioners called themselves 'now monks here in Westminster', and said that their abbot had procured a book of particulars and, by virtue of a warrant from the lord treasurer, many repairs had already been done. They asked no more than a gift of the site of their abbey, and the residue (unspecified) of the property at the accustomed rent, intending to live there as religious until their number could be augmented by the charity of other benefactors.[39] It has naturally been assumed that this document dates from the early days of the refoundation at Westminster, when a more general restoration of monasticism was expected.[40] It is just possible that 'here in Westmynster' has only geographical meaning, and that the petition dates from the appearance of the monks led by Feckenham (considered abbot designate) at court in March 1555. This might explain why Kentwyne, alone of the petitioners, is not in the WAM 9327 list. But if the address to the Lord Chamberlain is strictly interpreted, the petition is much later. The chamberlainship was vacant from the death of Sir John Gage on 18 April 1556 until the appointment of Sir Edward Hastings, who is so styled from 15 December 1557. Hastings was further advanced to a barony on 19 January 1558. The monks' petition

---

[38] Aveling (p. 271), for reasons to be further considered below, suggests March–September 1557.

[39] BL, Harleian MS 3881, f. 38v (17th-century copy); printed in Dugdale, *Monasticon*, i, 9. Another (?lost) MS printed by Burnet, *Hist. Reformation*, v, 461–3.

[40] Wainewright ('Mary's religious foundations', 133) suggested 1557. The date of 21 November 1556 given in *VCH Somerset*, ii, 96 is impossibly precise, and must have simply been taken from the date of the community's inauguration as given by Machyn (above, n. 32). For another intended restoration see J.G. Clark, 'Reformation and reaction at St Albans Abbey, 1530–58', *English Historical Review*, cxv (2000), 320–21.

is addressed 'your lordship', which does not rule out a knightly holder of the chamberlainship, but would more precisely indicate a peer. Interestingly Burnet printed a text of the petition 'ex. MS. nob. illustr. com. de Huntingdon'. Hastings was the brother of the incumbent earl; he was also well known to favour the religious revival, and in his will of 1556 he made a bequest to the Observant Franciscans of Greenwich.[41] The Glastonbury petition therefore dates either some six months before the restoration of Westminster; or, more probably, no earlier than December 1557. Assuming the latter, it would represent not a failed attempt to establish a community at Glastonbury subsumed into the eventual foundation at Westminster, but an offshoot from the already operational Westminster house. It may, of course, reflect some tensions in that community from which the ex-Glastonbury men hoped to escape. Nevertheless it implies that further Benedictine revival was envisaged in more than six months after the last hope Pole had expressed on the subject.[42]

The other chief prosographical source is the London ordination register (Guildhall Library MS 9535/1), which contains six entries that record the presentation of Westminster monks for orders; five of the candidates can be identified with names in the WAM 9327 list, and a further ten names are supplied of men 'de mon. Westm'' who are ordained. Some further entries, relating to secular clerks ordained to the title of Westminster Abbey, need to be distinguished from the ordinations of religious. By comparing the ordination lists with the WAM list, some approximation can be made of the date of the latter. The WAM list has 'Mr Este' as prior; this must, as Aveling noted, date the document after 13 March 1557, when William Easte as subprior presented ordinands, and before 15 October following, by which time he was dead.[43] Aveling was cautious about the title given for Easte in the ordination register, but it is written twice, in differing ways (*supprioris, viceprioris*). It will be seen from Table 3.1 that of those who received

---

[41] S.T. Bindoff, *The House of Commons, 1509–1558* (The History of Parliament, 1982), ii, 181 (Gage), 315–17 (Hastings). Hastings occurs as Lord Chamberlain in the Privy Council register from 15 December 1557: *APC*, vi, 216.

[42] On 28 May 1557 Pole anticipated that one of the two Canterbury monasteries would soon be restored: *Cal. Ven.* vi, II, no. 904 (p. 1119). St Augustine's is thought to have been a more likely site than the cathedral: M. Sparks, in *St Augustine's Abbey, Canterbury*, ed. R.D.H. Gem (1997), 148.

[43] Aveling, 'Marian community', 271–2, from ordination registered 13 March 1557 [Guildhall, MS 9531/1, f. 59v], and 16th-century note in martyrology of Faversham Abbey, now Bodleian Library, Oxford, MS Jones 9, f. 135: 'Id. Octobris. Apud Westmonasterium sancti Petri apostoli depositio dompni Wilelmi Est prioris [*three other names*] anno domini MVcLVIJ'. As Aveling observed, this is 'rather enigmatic'.

86   THE CHURCH OF MARY TUDOR

Table 3.1 Ordinations at London 1557–58 with reference to
Westminster Abbey

	1557					1558			
	Mar 13	Apr 3	Apr 16	Sep 19	Dec 18	Mar 5	Mar 12	Apr 9	Jun 4
(51) *Fyscher*	MS	D	P						
(36) Anderson+	MS	D							P
(47) Brampston	M								
(48) Presse	M								
(49) Founteney	M								
(50) Egers	M								
(32) Prince+	M								
(33) Johnson+	MS	D							
(34) Grundye+		MS	D						
(35) Wayte+	MS	D		P*					
(52) Athee		M							
(53) Ferne		M							
(46) Ebden		MS			D				P
(55) *Clerke*		D	P						
(56) *Mynyvere*				M	S	D	P		
(44) Feckenham W.					MS		D		P
(43) Seaberte					MS	D			P
(45) Gardyner					MS	D			P
(57) *Hunte*							M	S	D

Roman type: Westminster monks.
Italic type: seculars ordained to title of Westminster Abbey (in one case* a former monk ordained as a secular to another title).
+ listed in WAM 9327.
M minor orders; S subdeacon; D deacon; P priest.
Numbers as Aveling, appendix, 271–9, and extended below, pp. 106–23.
Source: Guildhall Library, MS 9535/1, ff. 59v–62v, 63v, 65, 66–67v, 69v, 71–71v, 72v, 74.

minor orders on 13 March 1557, four (Anderson, Grundye, Johnson and Wayte) proceeded to the subdiaconate on the same day, and to the diaconate on 3 April; of the five who go no further in orders, only one (Prince) is named in WAM 9327, and so definitely was in the community when Easte became prior. One would expect Prince and the remaining four (Brampston, Presse, Founteney and Egers) to have appeared in the ordination lists of 3 or 16 April. A new group of names appears on 3

April (Athee, Ferne, Ebden), who are not in WAM 9327. On this basis it can be argued that the WAM list shows the composition of the community between the two ordinations, 13 March and 3 April 1557. Against this is the record that annuities were granted to Brampston, Prince and *Laurence* Fountenaye (Founetayne) on 3 December 1558. By his own later statement Brampston is known to have stayed for only a year.[44] It may not therefore be certain that those who cannot be followed through the ordination 'dropped away one by one' as Aveling (p. 279) suggested. He also noted (p. 278) that the presentation of Ebden, Seaberte, W. Feckenham and Gardyner as professed monks on 18 December 1557 implied that these men should have been in the novitiate for at least a year, yet none is listed in WAM 9327. It may be supposed that the new Westminster community allowed some flexibility in these matters. WAM 9327 remains of uncertain date, and may well be incomplete. The probability is that it shows the community as it was around Lady Day (25 March) 1557.

Aveling (p. 279) distinguished ten names in the ordination register as possible 'seminarians'; he thought they might be the result of the legatine synod's decree for educating diocesan clergy.[45] A reference from Horne's attack on Feckenham is tentatively cited in support;[46] but it is doubtful if it refers to anything more than the generality of those in the abbot's charge. One of the names may be wholly discounted: Fairchilde appears alongside the Westminster ordinands in the register, but is clearly not one of them.[47] Of Aveling's other nine, three (Egers, Founteney, Presse) were presented for at least some of their orders by the abbey's official, and two (Athee, Ferne) are described as 'mon. Westm'' – which may mean only 'of Westminster Abbey' in some unspecific way, but which on the analogy of other entries less tersely abbreviated most probably

---

[44] WAM 33198E, m. 5d; 37929, f. 1v; 37932, ff. 1v–2. Founteney is *Martin* in the ordination register. Brampston's testimony is PRO, SP 12/188, no. 46; cf. below, 108. The 1557–58 ordination data, though only a brief sample, may usefully be compared with the much more ample evidence from the previous community. Clearly the Marian novitiate was less structured (and did not even have its own master), but we still see monks moving forward in cohorts through the London ordination process: cf. B.F. Harvey, 'A novice's life at Westminster Abbey in the century before the dissolution', in *The Religious Orders in Pre-Reformation England*, ed. J.G. Clarke (Woodbridge, 2002), 51–73, esp. 62–4. I am grateful to Miss Harvey for sending me a copy of her essay.

[45] Bray, *Anglican Canons*, 126–9.

[46] T. Stapleton, *A Counterblast to M. Hornes vayne blaste against M. Fekenham* (Louvain 1567), f. 476v: 'There was never none so blind or ignorantly brought up in your cures, belonging to the Abbey of Westminster, but that did wel perceive ... ' [that clergy could not speak with tongues]. There is a similar usage on ff. 478v–479.

[47] Guildhall, MS 9535/1, ff. 66, 66v, 67v, 69v, 71v; in the last instance, ordained priest to the title of the Savoy Hospital.

extends in translation to 'monk of Westminster'. This leaves four out of the ten who are never more than recipients of the abbey's title to orders (Clerke, Fyscher, Hunte, Mynyvere). By definition these cannot be monks (whose title was and is holy poverty). It cannot even be supposed that they were in some expectation of livings in the abbey's gift; in fact none of them was thus preferred. Two of the four did, however, have their grants of title recorded in the abbey's register.[48] The function of title, and its distinction from presentation (to orders), are matters still imperfectly understood. The large probability is that a fee was payable for this sponsorship, though no evidence of this has yet been produced.[49] It is of interest to find monastic titles reappearing in Mary's reign;[50] but the individuals can be confidently removed from the roll of the monastic community, and there is no need to suppose that Marian Westminster housed a group of secular novices. The ordination data, albeit sparse, offers interesting comparison with the much more amply documented pre-dissolution practice.

Three further names are found in the Abbey muniments (Figge, Maldon, Style). Figge might just be *Mr Legge* in WAM 9327. Style appears in the Westminster records in 1570 when there was a dispute over his pension payments. Pearce (p. 192) placed him as an addendum to his register of the monks down to 1540. The pension in question, however, was from the abbot and convent, not the Crown, and that alone sets him in the Marian ranks. When he took up residence at Gonville and Caius College, Cambridge, in 1562 at the age of 40, he was described as a former fellow of Trinity and then (*postea*) monk of Westminster.[51] Trinity was founded six years after the original monastery was dissolved.

Other names come from external sources. White is known only from

---

[48] WAM Register Book IV, ff. 23, 25 (Mynyvere, 2 December 1557), Hunte (2 February 1558); in both cases this occurs between minor orders and the subdiaconate. Another clerk (Edward Pype) received the abbey's title (ibid., f. 51v) but does not appear in the ordination lists. Hunte and Pype were both Oxford MAs (1542): Emden, *Biog. Reg. 1501–40*, 305, 470.

[49] See particularly R.N. Swanson, 'Titles to orders in medieval episcopal registers', in *Studies in Medieval History presented to R.H.C. Davis*, ed. H. Mayr-Harting and R.I. Moore (1985), 233–45, esp. 234, 236 (on monastic titles), 239–42 (on distinction between title and presentation). Cf. M. Bowker, *The Secular Clergy in the Diocese of Lincoln, 1495–1520* (Cambridge, 1968), 61–4; M.C. Cross, 'Ordinations in the diocese of York 1500–1630', in *Patronage and Recruitment in the Tudor and Early Stuart Church*, ed. Cross (York, 1996), 6–7, 17.

[50] The London register also records a title given by Syon Abbey: Guildhall, MS 9535/1, f. 74.

[51] Gonville and Caius College, Cambridge, Matriculation Book TUT/01/01, f. 6. For the pension dispute and other biographical details see below, 118.

the obituary notice in Bodleian MS Jones 9. Kentwyne is presumed to belong to the community by virtue of his signature to the Glastonbury petition; his inclusion is proved if the petition is accepted as dated 1557 or 1558.[52] Bucknall was included by Aveling on the strength of an entry in the Winchester episcopal register of his having vacated a benefice *propter ingressum religionis* in 1556; similar entries occur for Cooke, Eden and Figge in the same register, and their certain or probable identification with Westminster monks makes that of Bucknall the more plausible. The same cannot be said of Thomas Twysden, *alias* Bede, a former monk of Battle, whose membership of the Westminster community has recently been proposed.[53] One further group of names must be mentioned. In one of the general histories of Westminster Abbey there is printed (without source) a list of monks 're-admitted' and another of monks 'professed by Abbot Feckenham'.[54] One name in the first list (Austin Ringwoode) and all seven in the second (George Gervaise, Mark Lambert, Anthony Martin, John Mervin, Austin St John, Gregory Sayer and Maurice Scott) appear in no other account of the Marian community. It is not hard to see why. Gervaise was born in 1569 and professed in 1608. Anthony Martin was born in 1565 and professed (as Athanasius) in 1594. Gregory Sayer, born Robert in 1560 and professed in 1602, is a prominent figure. Maurice Scott must surely be William, born 1578 and professed as Maurus in 1605.[55] All these

---

[52] See above, 117. Pearce (*Monks*, 216) thought Kentwyne might be *Kyngeswoode* of WAM 9327.

[53] Cunich, in Wansbrough and Marett-Crosby, *Benedictines in Oxford*, 312 n. 73, from information supplied by Professor S.M. Jack (and which Professor Jack kindly passed to me), of a pardon granted to Twysden by the legate on 12 March 1557 and confirmed by his vicar-general on 20 May following, in which Twysden is described as a professed monk of the Order of St Benedict: Pierrepont Morgan Library, New York, MS MA 1254, f. 47 (original instrument); LPL, Reg. Pole (Archiepiscopal register), ff. 25–6. However, since Twysden is licensed to retain secular dress and hold a cure until houses of religion are restored (*donec regularia loca restaurata fuerint ... in honesta toga clerici secularis remanere, et alicui beneficio ecclesiastico curato ... deservire*) he cannot at the time of the pardon have been a monk of the already established Westminster community, and there is no evidence that he joined it thereafter. Professor Jack, Dr Cunich and I have agreed on this point. For Twysden see Emden, *Biog. Reg. 1501–40*, 36; date of pardon there impossibly dated 1 March 1559, following L.F. Salzman, 'Sussex religious at the dissolution', *Sussex Archaeological Collections*, xcii (1954), 31–2, in faulty reading of the Lambeth MS.

[54] H.J. Feasey, *Westminster Abbey historically described* (1899), 44. I am indebted to Dr Cunich for bringing this to my attention.

[55] A. Bellenger, *English and Welsh Priests 1558–1800* (Downside 1984), 63 (Gervaise), 86 (Martin), 105 (Sayer, Scott). G. Anstruther, *The Seminary Priests: A Dictionary of the Secular Clergy of England and Wales 1558–1850*, i, *Elizabethan 1558–1603* (Ware and Ushaw [1968]), 220 (Martin), 302–3 (Sayer). J. Gillow, *A Literary*

names must definitely belong to later generations; how they came to be listed among Feckenham's monks is a small mystery, but not one that need concern us here.

Discounting Twysden and the names from Feasey, and not allowing for any possible aliases among the names in WAM 9327, there are 52 men we can place in Marian Westminster. Of these, 16 may with some assurance be identified with former religious; varying degrees of possibility allow 26 in all. Of these, three were from old Westminster, five from Glastonbury; from all the Benedictine houses there were 14 (perhaps 22). There were two Cistercians and, perhaps, two Austin canons. Ten (perhaps 12) had been students at Oxford in their previous monastic lives (and five of these had belonged to the circle of Robert Joseph of Evesham). Six (perhaps 14) had subsequently held parochial livings or minor posts in cathedrals; three had been higher clergy. The 13 who received orders while in the Marian community were, by contrast, young men (with the exception of Copynger). Three (perhaps four) would begin new careers at Oxford or (in one case) Cambridge in the early years of Elizabeth's reign. Two became minor canons in the restored Protestant Church, and one served as a lay choirman. Eight (perhaps nine) can be found as recusant priests, in prisons or exile; one of them (Brampston) left a complete account of his career, which would have ended in martyrdom but for the coronation of James I. One (Style) can be followed to the moment of death in a Belgian monastery, after a remarkable life passed in permanent blindness. And another (Figge) would carry about with him the foot of an apostle from an English reliquary until it could be delivered to the safe-keeping of the former king of England.[56]

Not all the 52 can have been present in the house simultaneously. It seems unlikely that a projected target of 40 was ever reached; the complement of 26 or 28 achieved by the end of 1556 had not advanced beyond 30 by August 1557 if the attendance of the funeral of Anne of Cleves is reliably reported.[57] This may be compared with an average of 48 professed monks (not including the abbot and prior) who were to be found at Westminster between 1378 and 1529.[58] Recruitment to Marian

and Biographical History ... of the English Catholics from the breach with Rome to the present time (1885–1903), v, 481–2 (Sayer), 486 (Scott). E.J. Mahoney, *The Theological Position of Gregory Sayrus, O.S.B., 1560–1602* (Ware, 1922).

[56] Calculations and data from appendix below, 106–23. Cf. Aveling, 'Tudor Westminster', 60–2 and Knowles, Rel. *Orders*, iii, 426–7, 442.

[57] [S.E. Bentley], *Excerpta Historica, or Illustrations of English History* (1831), 307 [from College of Arms, MS I.15, ff. 232–242v].

[58] Harvey, *Living and Dying*, 73–4.

Westminster seems modest when set against the possibility that up to 1000 English Benedictines may have been still living in 1553, perhaps 1600 to 1800 from all the contemplative orders (reducing somewhat by the time Westminster was established).[59] But even such a man as Robert Joseph, who by temperament and associations might have been expected to return to the cloister, preferred to remain a country parson.[60]

A statement by Peter Heylyn that the Marian community did not have the resources to support more than 14 monks is clearly derived from the numbers at the inauguration.[61] There are nevertheless indications that the house was inadequately funded. Full analysis of its finances is impossible because the evidence is fragmentary – disappointingly so by comparison with the impressive archive of the old abbey and its secular successor. At the outset the gross revenue of Mary's foundation was calculated at £2129 0s 1½d per annum.[62] Three years later, at the end of the revival, the figure was put at £2118 2s 3½d, this time remembering to add 70 quarters of wheat and one boar.[63] A first estimate of annual expenditure allowed £147 for the clothing (including summer and winter linen) of a monastic community of 40, abbot included, and £1344 for the diet of the monks, their servants and 'suche as shall resorte unto them'; but the abbey also had to support six lay choirmen, eight boy choristers and their master, 40 scholars and their two masters, 12 almsmen and a host of other lay officers and servants – virtually the whole of the 1540 cathedral establishment save the dean and canons. With miscellaneous running expenses, the estimate rose to £2519 11s 9½d per annum.[64] Even so, no provision was made for other costs shown in a bill of actual payments made at the abbot's entry. Out of a notional £1000 revenue calculated at Michaelmas 1556, a total of £969 19s 3½d was immediately swallowed up in pensions to the former secular chapter (£144 15s), the wages of the residual collegiate body and tenths to the Crown payable through the bishop of London (£294 6s 0½d). Emergency repairs to the church, the cloisters and the water conduit, the expenses of the endowment charter

---

[59] On the basis of figures kindly supplied by Dr Cunich from his 'Monastic database for England and Wales in the sixteenth century',www.hku.uk/history/cunich/monastl.html; Dr Cunich stresses that these calculations, though based on verified statistical data, are approximations only.

[60] *The Letter Book of Robert Joseph, Monk-Scholar of Evesham and Gloucester College, Oxford, 1530–3*, ed. J.C.H. Aveling and W.A. Pantin (Oxford Historical Society, new ser. xix, 1967 for 1964), p. xvi.

[61] P. Heylyn, *Ecclesia Restaurata, or the History of the Reformation of the Church of England*, ed. J.C. Robertson (Cambridge, 1849), ii, 189.

[62] WAM 37711.

[63] WAM 33198*.

[64] WAM 37716 (my addition; MS sum £2273 11s 9½d, deleted).

(£50) and other charges put the abbot out of pocket by £156 12s 7½d before (apparently) he or his monks were clothed or fed; and a further £100 was earmarked for the household implements of the departing secular clergy.[65] Another paper drawn up at Michaelmas 1556 shows income of £1992 11s 3d set against expenses of £1729 1s 6½d (including £301 12s 9d already paid to the abbey). But this calculation on its own admission makes no provision for the tenths of £294 6s 0½d, or £144 15s which was payable to members of the deposed secular chapter, and which the abbot and convent would have to tell their predecessors they could not yet pay. In addition £26 13s 4d had to be found for a set of vestments ordered by Dean Weston, which the unpaid embroiderer was, reasonably enough, about to repossess. A special extra was £13 6s 8d to gild the rood (implying that a bare carved image had already been restored).[66]

A solitary obedientiary roll survives for the restored abbey: Richard Eden accounted as cellarer for the year to Michaelmas 1557.[67] A total income of £1655 2s was paid over by the receiver-general at various dates.[68] A principal outlay remained the pensions of the former chapter (£99 2s 6d), though this would diminish as they received compensatory benefices. The other members of the collegiate body (clerks, almsmen, scholars, choristers and servants) would be a continuing part of the monastic institution. Together with the pensions to vicars of appropriated churches, and casual rewards, the wage bill for secular clerks and laypersons was £319 10s 11d. Almost as much (£277 17s 4d) went on cattle, veal and lambs. Other victuals, repairs and miscellaneous household charges brought the cellarer's outlay to £2059 6s 0½d, which, after deductions of £26 8s 8d for sums charged to the accounts of the receiver-general and the last collegiate treasurer,[69] represents excess spending of £377 15s 4½d. However, £569 16s 7d had been recycled into the domestic economy by payments to the abbot and other monks, and so the cellarer's roll may be judged to show the house clear by £192 1s 2½d.

Overall financial management remained in the hands of the lay receiver-general. John Moulton occupied this post through successive

---

[65] WAM 37717.

[66] WAM 37712. For progressive restoration of roods see E. Duffy, *The Stripping of the Altars: Traditional Religion in England, c. 1400–c. 1580* (1992), 556–7.

[67] WAM 18961. The MS is an actual roll, and therefore a reversion to monastic practice in distinction to the codical format of the collegiate accounts.

[68] WAM 18960 gives another partial list of these transfers.

[69] £25 15s 8d from the receiver and 13s from Canon Henry Cole, correctly said to be recorded in their respective accounts, viz. WAM 33198C, m. 8; 37714, f. 6v. These sums are charged in Eden's account of income, and appear to relate to actual payments, so it is not clear why he is allowed discharge of them.

regimes at Westminster from the reign of Henry VIII to that of Elizabeth. His only surviving full year's view of account for the restored abbey (for the year audited at November 1558, with some later adjustments) shows arrears of £757 9s 5d on the previous year's account and receipts of £2065 10s 11d, producing a liability of £2822 11s 4½d. Against this were set his own payments and allowances, and a total of £1756 12 8½d paid over to the monastic officers between 10 February 1558 and 1 February 1559.[70] This represents a modest increase in internal revenue against that recorded in the cellarer's roll for the year to Michaelmas 1557. After the departure of the monks, Moulton was himself responsible for paying the continuing body of scholars, clerks, choristers and other laymen.[71]

The abbot and convent were not as inclined to grant such very long leases as their secular predecessors had done: of 86 leases registered (and by no means the likely total made) during the restoration, the average term for country properties (17 grants) was 24.9 years; for urban tenements (69 grants) it was 37.6 years. The urban figure may be distorted because longer terms were common when properties were leased in groups. These figures compare with 54 years average for the country and 49 years average for urban leases in the time of the first collegiate church, 1542–56.[72] Nor were any special favours shown to courtiers and other grandees. The abbot and convent did, however, retain some useful friends as stewards and legal counsel, including Sir William Cordell, speaker of the House of Commons (1558), Sir Thomas Parry, treasurer of the household, and the lawyer Edmund Plowden.[73] The abbot maintained a separate establishment at Chiswick. Writing from there on 21 September 1557 or 1558 he complained that he had been obliged to send away his masons, and without immediate payment of £10 from the receiver he would have to do the same with his joiners.[74] In general the inadequacy of the abbey's endowment, especially as

---

[70] WAM 33198D.

[71] WAM 33198D*.

[72] Calculation of monastic lease terms from WAM Register Book IV. Equivalent data from Register III (covering the first collegiate church) in C.S. Knighton, 'Economics and economies of a royal peculiar: Westminster Abbey 1540–1640', in *Princes and Paupers in the English Church, 1500–1800*, ed. M.R. O'Day and F.M. Heal (Leicester, 1981), 54.

[73] WAM Register Book IV, ff. 2 (annuity of £4 to Cordell, not yet knighted, as counsel, 1 January 1557), 72v (patent to Parry as high steward, with £10 fee, 7 March 1559); other appointments on ff. 1v, 2v, 20, 21v, 23. An annuity of £4 to Plowden as counsel is not registered, but the original patent is extant at Plowden Hall, Shropshire: G. de C. Parmiter, *Edmund Plowden: An Elizabethan Recusant Lawyer* (Catholic Record Society monograph ser. 4, 1987), 45 and n. 6.

[74] WAM 37788A.

encumbered with payments to members of the previous regime, and its own unaggressive estate policy, restricted income when expenditure was particularly high.

It is not always possible to distinguish the expenses of the restored abbey from those of the preceding secular chapter; the restoration of the apparatus of Catholic worship was a process continuous through both regimes from 1553 to 1558. A sacrist's bill for a massive outlay of £689 8s 4d includes £220 spent on copes and other fabrics, £38 for setting up the rood with the images of Mary and John, and among a total of £54 5s 4d on plate, £4 for a copper and gilt crosier.[75] It is possible that this last item was for a boy bishop; the custom was widely revived in Mary's reign (though discouraged in 1554 to avoid ribaldry at the time of the reconciliation with Rome) and one London church bought its boy a new mitre and other equipment.[76] The boy bishop is well documented in pre-Reformation Westminster Abbey, and survived in secularized form in the school play.[77] But most likely the crosier bought in Mary's reign was for the new abbot, and the accompanying expenses must therefore date from the year of the refoundation. Use of the crosier was no longer a special privilege of the abbots of exempt houses, though it remained a mark of high status. Use of all seven items of *pontificalia* is held to be implicit in a grant to Westminster of 1192, although curiously neither in that grant nor in those which confirmed it is the crosier specified.[78] It is nevertheless evident that the abbots of Westminster had used the staff from at least the early 12th century.[79] Its assumption by Feckenham without specific regrant would therefore have been an important indication of the new abbey's claims to the

---

[75] WAM 37727.

[76] R. Hutton, *The Rise and Fall of Merry England: The Ritual Year 1400–1700* (Oxford, 1996), 97–8.

[77] L.E. Tanner, *Westminster School: A History* (1934), 9–10, 56–7.

[78] M.C. Knowles, *The Monastic Order in England* (Cambridge, 1940), 711–12. *Westminster Abbey Charters, 1066–c.1214*, ed. E. Mason (London Record Society, xxv, 1988), 86, 88 (nos 173–5, 180). Cf. Mason, *Westminster Abbey and its People, c.1050–c.1216* (Woodbridge, 1996), 54, 61–2, 68, 125, 126; Mason's listing of pontificalia invariably conflates dalmatic and tunicle.

[79] Westminster Abbey, tomb of Abbot Gilbert (1121). Cf. *Customary of the Benedictine Monasteries of Saint Augustine, Canterbury, and Saint Peter, Westminster*, ed. E.M. Thompson, ii (Henry Bradshaw Society, xxviii, 1904), 5 (ll. 28–9); *The History of Westminster Abbey, by John Flete*, ed. J.A. Robinson (Notes and Documents relating to Westminster Abbey, no. 2, Cambridge, 1909), 126 (ll. 12–14), 135 (ll. 20–21). Miss Harvey kindly drew my attention to an illumination in the Litlington Missal (Westminster Abbey, MS 37), f. 144, which shows a prelate, presumably an abbot of Westminster, standing with an elaborate crosier. There is a modest specimen in the abbey museum.

rights of the old.⁸⁰ A more substantial legacy of the monastic revival was the present deanery. This had been the abbot's lodging until 1540; between then and 1550 it was the bishop's house. On the dissolution of the diocese of Westminster it became home to successive Lords Wentworth. The second baron offered to exchange part of it with the dean and chapter in 1554, but it was not until 1557 that the whole property was restored to the church.⁸¹

Above all, there was the shrine. Despoiled by Henry VIII, it was nevertheless not destroyed, and (crucially) the Confessor's body was not ejected. He was, after all, an English king before he was a Roman saint. Machyn reported that the shrine was about to be restored (20 March 1557) and had so been (19 April) on the occasion of a visit by the Grand Duke of Muscovy.⁸² It was long supposed that the wooden superstructure of classical design was made at the time of Feckenham's reconstruction.⁸³ In 1958, however, J.G. O'Neilly examined the structure in detail; his conclusions, presented in association with L.E. Tanner (librarian and keeper of the muniments of Westminster Abbey), were that the shrine had been totally dismantled in the 1530s and rebuilt from the ground 20 years later. It was argued that the wooden canopy was workmanship of such high quality that it could not have been executed within the five months between Feckenham's appointment and April 1557. On stylistic grounds the canopy was thought to date from the 1520s, perhaps associated with work on the chapel of Henry VII.⁸⁴ It need hardly be said that historical circumstances preclude the possibility of reconstruction between 1530 and the accession of Mary. No archival evidence has been found to test O'Neilly's conclusions, which have not

---

⁸⁰ Feckenham wore the mitre from the day of his blessing: Machyn, *Diary*, 119–20. At the parliament service of 1559 he was 'robed pontifically': *Cal. Ven.* vii, no. 15 (p. 23).

⁸¹ *The Abbot's House at Westminster*, ed. J.A. Robinson (Notes and Documents relating to Westminster Abbey, no. 4, Cambridge 1911), 13–14. *Acts*, i, 86. Cf. Loach, *Parliament and Crown*, 114.

⁸² Machyn, *Diary*, 130, 132. Stanley (*Hist. Memorials*, 402) confuses the issue by misquoting a reference to the *screen* ('scrynne' in the source) being set up on 5 January 1557, from *The Chronicle of the Grey Friars of London*, ed. J.G. Nichols (Camden Society, liii, 1852), 94. Cf. J.H.T. Perkins, *Westminster Abbey: Its Worship and Ornaments* (Alcuin Club Collections, xxxiii, xxxiv, xxxviii, 1938–52), ii, 79–87.

⁸³ For example, Royal Commission on Historical Monuments, *An Inventory of the Historical Monuments in London*, i, *Westminster Abbey* (1924), 28–9; Stanley, *Hist. Memorials*, 402; Perkins, *Westminster Abbey*, ii, 84–5.

⁸⁴ J.G. O'Neilly and L.E. Tanner, 'The shrine of St Edward the Confessor', *Archaeologia*, c (1966), 129–54. Summary in Tanner, *Recollections of a Westminster Antiquary* (1969), 181–5. O'Neilly later discussed the dating of the canopy with John Harvey, who thought it unlikely to be after 1536: WAM, Dykes Bower Papers, Box 3, O'Neilly to S.E. Dykes Bower (surveyor of the fabric of Westminster Abbey), 23 March 1965.

passed into general circulation.⁸⁵ I am not competent to evaluate the stylistic argument. The timescale issue is only significant if it is assumed that reconstruction of the shrine did not begin until the abbey was refounded. But since there was a sustained process of restoring furniture and ornament through the collegiate and monastic regimes of Marian Westminster, there seems no reason why the remaking of the shrine may not have been in hand for three and a half years. One possibility is that Nicholas Bellin of Modena, who in Edward VI's reign had worked on a tomb for Henry VIII at Westminster, might have been re-employed in a project for which Mary had more enthusiasm.⁸⁶ The canopy date may eventually be known from dendrochronology. Even if it is shown certainly to be an earlier construction, Feckenham must still take credit for the completion of the shrine in its present form. It has proved a more enduring part of the abbey's furniture than the Stone of Destiny.

Also rehabilitated in the Marian abbey was Anne of Cleves, who died a Catholic, and for whom the queen decreed a royal funeral.⁸⁷ This began on 4 August 1557 with the abbot and convent, and the lay choir, escorting the cortège through the streets. On the following day the requiem was sung by the prior, and the abbot preached.⁸⁸ On 22 August it was reported that the monks had surreptitiously removed the banners and hangings in the choir.⁸⁹ The College of Arms complained, but

---

⁸⁵ P. Tudor-Craig (Lady Wedgwood), in *Westminster Abbey* (New Bell's Cathedral Guides, 1986), 117–18, still credits Feckenham with the canopy; so also Lunn, *Engl. Benedictines*, 4. B. Nilson, *The Cathedral Shrines of Medieval England* (Woodbridge, 1998), 229–31, 240–41 shows convincingly that the revenue of St Edward's shrine dwindled to insignificance by 1530, in keeping with the national trend.

⁸⁶ L.E. Tanner, 'The shrine of Westminster Abbey and Nicholas de Modena' (unpublished paper; copies in WAM, Dykes Bower Papers, Box 3, dated 1954, and WAM 64299, dated 1956). Tanner's evidence of Modena's continuing presence in Westminster, though not his suggestion of work on the shrine, is taken up in M. Biddle, 'Nicholas Bellin of Modena. An Italian artificer of the courts of Francis I and Henry VIII', *Journal of the British Archaeological Association*, 3rd ser. xxix (1966), 106–21. Modena occupied what was called the 'tomb house': *Returns of Aliens dwelling in the City and Suburbs of London, from the reign of Henry VIII to that of James I*, ed. R.E.G. and E.F. Kirk (Huguenot Society of London Publications, x, 1900–08), i, 106. *APC*, iii, 347, 380. Cf. *Acts*, i, 53 and n. 172 (but disregarding the laborious and totally wrong editorial explanation), 65. For the never-completed tomb see principally A. Higgins, 'On the work of Florentine sculptors in England in the early part of the sixteenth century; with special reference to the tombs of Cardinal Wolsey and King Henry VIII', *Archaeological Journal*, li (1984), 128–220, 367–70, esp. 165–6. For a connection with the shrine see P.G. Lindley, *Gothic to Renaissance: Essays on Sculpture in England* (Stamford, 1995), 57 n. 46.

⁸⁷ *APC*, vi, 128.

⁸⁸ Bentley, *Excerpta Historica*, 303–13. Summary in M. Saaler, *Anne of Cleves* (1995), 113–14.

⁸⁹ Machyn, *Diary*, 148.

Feckenham and the sacrist, Dom Hugh Phillips, were able to persuade the cardinal and others of the Privy Council that the church of Westminster was traditionally entitled to these furnishings.[89] The queen's funeral in the following year must have been an especially dread occasion for the refounded community.[90] But as yet there was no liturgical change, and none of the debate which had delayed the funeral of Edward VI. On that occasion Mary had wanted a requiem for her brother, an idea as distasteful to most Catholics as it was to all Protestants. It was chiefly the advice of the imperial ambassadors, endorsed by the emperor, which persuaded the queen to allow the king a Protestant burial.[91] The reasoning had been political, not ecumenical; but there would be a reciprocal courtesy, for Charles V himself died while England remained Catholic, and was mourned with traditional rites in the abbey. The service, on Christmas Eve 1558, was switched from St Paul's to Westminster so that Queen Mary's hearse could be re-used in the interests of economy.[92] It was to a still monastic church that Elizabeth I came for her coronation on 15 January 1559.[93] For the last

---

[89] WAM 6327 (listing councillors who heard the case), 6398, 6399 (submissions by Phillips and Feckenham, 7 and 20 February 1560, when the successor dean and chapter was involved in a similar dispute with the heralds).

[90] For the ceremonial see PRO, SP 12/1, no. 32 (*Calendar of State Papers, Domestic Series ... 1547–1580*, ed. R. Lemon (1856) [hereafter *CSPD 1547–80*], 117); for the attendance, PRO, LC 2/4(2). Summary by P.G. Lindley in *The Funeral Effigies of Westminster Abbey*, ed. A.E. Harvey and R. Mortimer (Woodbridge, 1994), 55–7. The sermon (on Eccles. 4:2) by John White, Bishop of Lincoln, is in BL, Sloane MS 1578, and Cotton MS Vespasian D.18, ff. 94–107 (old foliation), 92–105 (new foliation); printed in J. Strype, *Ecclesiastical Memorials* (Oxford, 1822), iii, II, 536–50. White was immediately arrested for seditious speaking: *APC*, vii, 45. *The Zurich Letters*, i, ed. H. Robinson (Parker Society, Cambridge, 1842), 7. Feckenham has been wrongly identified as the preacher (*ODNB*, 1st edn, and Knowles, *Rel. Orders* iii, 423), seemingly because the Cotton text, without author or date, follows in the same hand as that of a parliamentary speech by Feckenham. The Sloane MS is ascribed to White and dated 13 December; this has been taken as the date of delivery: *DNB*, 1st edn (White). Emden, *Biog. Reg. 1501–40*, 633. J.M. Stone, *The History of Mary I, Queen of England* (1901), 472. C. Erickson, *Bloody Mary* (1978), 483–4. It is however clear from the SP account that the ceremonies extended (as was customary) over two days, with the actual requiem, and therefore White's sermon, on 14 December, as D.M. Loades, *Mary Tudor: A Life* (Oxford, 1989), 313.

[91] *Cal. Span.* xi, 117–19, 122, 134–5.

[92] PRO, SP 12/1, no. 38 (*CSPD 1547–80*, 117) (Winchester to Cecil, 19 December). For the ceremony see College of Arms, MS I.15, f. 285v; PRO, SP 12/1, nos 41, 42 (*CSPD 1547–80*, 117, 118).

[93] The principal sources for the ceremony are printed and discussed in C.G. Bayne, 'The coronation of Queen Elizabeth', *English Historical Review*, xxii (1907), 650–73. A correction to the Venetian calendar's text is given in G.L. Ross, 'Il Schifanoya's account of the coronation of Queen Elizabeth', *English Historical Review*, xxiii (1908), 533–4. W.P. Haugaard, 'The coronation of Elizabeth I', *Journal of Ecclesiastical History*, xix.2 (1968),

time an abbot of Westminster took his traditional part in the ritual. Feckenham's assisting role was the more prominent because the consecrator was the relatively obscure Owen Oglethorpe, bishop of Carlisle.[94] Ten days after the coronation the queen returned to the abbey for the service which customarily preceded the state opening of parliament. According to the Venetian ambassador, the traditional votive mass of the Holy Ghost was omitted, Mass having been sung earlier, and without the elevation. Most famously, when the queen arrived she dismissed the taper-bearing monks with a snub.[95] It has been ingeniously suggested that she had no real objection to the tapers (having already accepted incense), but merely wished to proceed through the church accompanied by her chapel choir singing the English litany.[96] This may demand too much of the queen's liturgical logic. The tone of the occasion would in any case be more decisively set from the pulpit by Richard Cox, who launched into a denunciation of the monastic life. Since he had been driven from the deanery of Westminster at Mary's accession, he can have had no misgivings about condemning those whose guests he now was.

The abbey was the setting for the religious disputation staged in the

---

161–70 discusses and disposes of much of the controversy which followed Bayne's article, though is not followed in D.R. Starkey, *Elizabeth: Apprenticeship* (2001), 273–6 and nn. on pp. 359–60. In N. Williams, *Elizabeth I, Queen of* England (1967), 58, the dean and chapter of Westminster make an anachronistic appearance. Cf. also R.D. Bowers, 'The chapel royal, the first Edwardian prayer book, and Elizabeth's settlement of religion, 1559', *Historical Journal*, 43 (2000), 328; D.E. Hoak, 'A Tudor Deborah? The coronation of Elizabeth I, parliament, and the problem of female rule', in *John Foxe and his World*, ed. J. King and C. Highley (Aldershot, 2001), 73–91; idem, 'The coronations of Edward VI, Mary I, and Elizabeth I, and the transformation of the Tudor monarchy', in *Westminster Abbey Reformed*, ed. C.S. Knighton and R. Mortimer (Aldershot, 2003), 114–52.

[94] One point of dispute has been the celebrant of the coronation Mass. The fullest account (PRO, SP 15/9, no. 9, printed in Bayne, 'Coronation', 666–71), says (p. 670) 'the Bishop began the Masse'; although other bishops have featured, this must refer to Oglethorpe's continuing role. College of Arms, MS WY, p. 197 (Bayne, 671) says 'the masse began by the Deane', agreeing with the Venetian report ('*la Messa ... cantata dal decano della sua capella*': Ross, 'Il Schifanoya's account, 533). Haugaard (pp. 163–4) considered that an 'unlettered English reporter' might have mistaken 'the vested dean' for a bishop, but a herald would not have thought a bishop was a dean; he concluded that the celebrant was the dean of the chapel royal, George Carew. The 'English reporter' may in fact have been Anthony Anthony, surveyor of the ordnance (from whose MSS the SP 15 text derives); he was certainly literate, but no liturgiologist. It is just possible that Feckenham celebrated, and was mistaken for a bishop because of his *pontificalia*, and as 'dean' because of his local precedence. But Haugaard's interpretation remains the more convincing, for the further reason that celebration by a prelate would have added to ceremonial which the queen wished to minimize.

[95] *Cal. Ven.* vii, no. 15 (p. 23).

[96] W.P. Haugaard, *Elizabeth and the English Reformation* (Cambridge 1968), 82.

parliamentary recess at Easter.[97] When parliament reassembled (the Catholic party having been induced to spike its own guns at the abbey disputation) the Marian religious houses were quickly suppressed. Feckenham fought his corner in the House of Lords; he was derided for suggesting that Christ and the Apostles exemplified the monastic life.[98] A suppression bill was introduced in the Commons on 24 April, and received assent on 8 May.[99] Special protection was given to those who had received leases of monastic property since 1 October 1558: in particular, one George Basford, a Westminster Abbey tenant in St Martin-le-Grand, London.[100] Those religious who within 40 days of the passage of the act swore the oath prescribed in the uniformity statute (1 Eliz. I c. 1, sect. 9) would be assigned pensions, but not others. During May friends and foes predicted the imminent demise of the Marian houses.[101] On 6 June it was reported that an offer by Philip II's envoy to

---

[97] Count Feria, Philip II's special envoy, reported on 30 March that the event would be 'in parliament': *Calendar of Letters and State Papers relating to English affairs, preserved principally in the archives of Simancas*, ed, M.A.S. Hume (1892–99), i, 45. It has been wrongly located in Westminster Hall: G.R. Elton, *England under the Tudors* (1955), 272; P. Collinson, in *Andrew Perne Quatercentenary Studies*, ed. Collinson, D. McKitterick and E. Leedham-Green (Cambridge Bibliographical Society monograph no. 11, 1991), 7. For all sources, which make it clear the abbey was used, see Haugaard, *Elizabeth and the English Reformation*, 101 n. 3. The event is wrongly placed in Holy Week: N.L. Jones, 'Elizabeth's first year: the conception and birth of the Elizabethan political world', in *The Reign of Elizabeth I*, ed. C.A. Haigh (Basingstoke 1984), 42, though only because Holy Week and Easter week are thought to be the same (cf. p. 41). For the record, the disputation sat from Easter Friday (31 March) to Low Monday (3 April): Haugaard, 102–3. J.E. Neale, *Elizabeth I and her Parliaments, 1559–1581* (1958), 72.

[98] Robinson, *Zurich Letters*, i, 20 (Jewel to Martyr, 13 April). A later speech by Feckenham in the Lords is in *Proceedings in the Parliaments of Elizabeth I*, ed. T.E. Hartley (Leicester 1981–95), i, 27–32.

[99] *Journals of the House of Commons*, i, 60, 61. *Journals of the House of Lords*, i, 579. Statute 1 Eliz. I c. 24, printed in *Statutes of the Realm*, iv, I, 397–400, and (with minor omissions) in *Select Statutes and other Constitutional Documents illustrative of the reigns of Elizabeth and James I*, ed. G.W. Prothero (4th edn, Oxford 1913), 37–8. Cf. E.J. Davis, 'An unpublished manuscript of the Lords' Journals for April and May 1559', *English Historical Review*, xxviii (1913), 541; P. Hughes, *The Reformation in England* (1950–54), iii, 21 and n. 2; Neale, *Elizabeth and her Parliaments*, 73–4; G.R. Elton, *The Parliament of England, 1559–1581* (Cambridge 1986), 44 and n. 10.

[100] 1 Eliz. I c. 24, sects 14, 15. Basford's lease is actually dated 20 September: WAM Register Book IV, ff. 73–74v.

[101] *Cal. Ven.* vii, no. 71 (p. 84) (Venetian ambassador, 10 May). Robinson, *Zurich Letters*, i, 30 (Parkhurst to Bullinger, 21 May). *Calendar of State Papers, Foreign Series, of the reign of Elizabeth*, ed. J.J. Stevenson et al. (1863–1950), i, 288 (Edmund Allen, 28 May, saying most of the monks of Westminster had already changed their coats; this report was originally ascribed to Alexander Nowell, but corrected in the photographic reprint of the calendar).

take all the religious to Flanders had been accepted by the government, then restricted to those who were survivors of the previous dissolutions. It was further said that Feckenham had been offered a deal whereby he and his community could remain as long as they swore an oath and conformed to the liturgical practice of the London churches.[102] If the latter proposal had really been made, it can only have been in the confidence that it would be refused. A story that Feckenham was offered the primacy has been discredited as an eighteenth-century interpolation.[103] On 17 June the deadline for the oath-taking expired.[104] Two days later the Westminster receiver wrote that he expected to see the house dissolved any day.[105] Once again he would ride up from Gloucestershire to superintend the transfer of power.[106] He arrived on the 22nd, when he signed what is the last surviving document of the abbey's routine administration.[107]

If there was a formal surrender, no record of it remains. Accounts were settled on and up to various dates between 23 June and 10 July.[108] The Venetian envoy believed that by 27 June the monks had been deprived of their revenues, and Midsummer Day (24 June) can be reckoned as the terminal date of the monastic regime.[109] The only solid details come from a warrant of 18 July whereby Sir Richard Sackville, Sir Walter Mildmay and Peter Osborne, commissioners for a survey of religious houses lately dissolved (all of them old augmentations hands) direct the receiver of Westminster to pay £713 8s 7½d to the former abbot, including £347 14s 7d for the fees of inferior ministers, almsmen and servants of Westminster Abbey for the quarter ending at Midsummer, and other expenses for 14 days thereafter [that is to 8 July], as agreed by Feckenham, the receiver

---

[102] *Cal. Ven.* vii, no. 78 (p. 95).

[103] Haugaard, *Elizabeth and the English Reformation*, 34 and n. 3.

[104] Not 29 June (as Knowles, *Rel. Orders*, iii, 434), or 24 June (as Perkins, *Westminster Abbey*, iii, 88).

[105] WAM 33199 (Moulton to Bowland, 19 June), printed in Pearce, *Monks*, 216–17, and Westlake, *Westminster Abbey*, i, 232.

[106] WAM 33198E, f. 6.

[107] WAM 37882.

[108] WAM 6497, referring to other papers not located.

[109] *Cal. Ven.* vii, 82 (p. 105). Knowles (*Rel. Orders*, iii, 434) gives 10 July as the date on which the abbey 'ceased to exist as a legal entity'; this date is used by Tindal Hart in Carpenter, *House of Kings*, 129, and by Lunn, *English Benedictines*, 4. This would seem to derive from the first (but not earliest) of the dates mentioned in WAM 6497 for settling accounts. The terminal date 12 July is given by R. Widmore, *An History of the Church of St Peter, Westminster, commonly called Westminster Abbey* (1751), 138, followed in *DNB*, 1st edn (Feckenham), and in Perkins, *Westminster Abbey*, iii, 888; this date cannot be traced to an archival source. The diarists report the departure of monks in July: Machyn, 204 (2 July); Wriothesley, ii, 145–6 (day unspecified).

Moulton and the auditor Humphrey Bowland on 10 July, and £309 10s 8½d for goods bought and sums borrowed, as by another agreement of the same parties on 30 June. Feckenham is also to allow the departing monks their personal effects, valued at £40 17s, and to pay them such sums as belong to their 'portions' as may remain after the debts have been settled. All the church ornaments were to be inventoried; those which by the following Easter were in legal use were to be kept in the abbey for future purposes; those which were *illegal* by the same time, Feckenham was allowed to appropriate.[110] Payment of the £347 14s 7d, which Moulton had been authorized to set against the revenues due at Michaelmas, is duly recorded (with some small variations in the pence and fractions), along with a further £1161 17s 1½d.[111] The inventory was made on 22 July, and lists 28 copes, six sets of vestments, five chalices, and other items, to the value of £234 13s 4d.[112] Some plate had already been pledged by Feckenham against the possibility of its being needed for future liturgical use.[113] Quite possibly other treasures were quietly removed before the stocktaking began. While much had been achieved in restoring the ornaments of worship, the 1559 inventory is painfully slim by comparison with those of 1540.[114] Some copes were retained by Feckenham, who rashly passed them to the dean and chapter in 1563. It has been suggested that these may have included the residue of vestments given by Henry VII as part of his massive chantry benefaction.[115] No such fabrics could have escaped seizure in 1553,[116] but it is not impossible that Mary might have returned some of her grandfather's vestments had they been in her hands. If so, their fate was to be made into a canopy below which Elizabeth would process to the parliament service of 1571.[117]

---

[110] WAM 6497.

[111] WAM 37930; 33198E, m. 9d. The sum of £347 14s 7d has been misrepresented as a personal pension to Feckenham: Emden, *Biog. Reg. 1501–40*, 201, following (as to the sum) *DNB*, 1st edn (Feckenham), itself from Historical Manuscripts Commission, *Fourth Report* (1874), 178. The end source is WAM 6497.

[112] WAM 9489.

[113] WAM 9490 (13 July). Perkins, *Westminster Abbey*, iii, 91.

[114] M.E.C. Walcott, 'The inventories of Westminster Abbey at the dissolution', *Transactions of the London and Middlesex Archaeological Society*, iv (1873), 313–64. Sources given in C.S. Knighton, 'King's College', in Knighton and Mortimer, *Westminster Abbey Reformed*, xxx n. 10.

[115] WAM 9491A, B. Perkins, *Westminster Abbey*, iii, 92 (references confused). L. Monnas, 'New documents for the vestments of Henry VII at Stonyhurst College', *The Burlington Magazine*, cxxxi (1989), 346.

[116] *Acts*, i, 108.

[117] Ibid. ii, 50. Other copes were made into cushions: WAM 33631, f. 5. Mary had lent copes to the abbey at her coronation: WAM 37713, f. 1v.

In its secular jurisdiction the Marian abbot and convent claimed to have recovered the rights of their predecessors. An instrument directed to their tenants of Steventon, Berkshire, rehearsed letters patent of September 1557 by which the Crown restored to the abbot and convent all amercements of tenants, goods and chattels of outlaws, convicts and felons *de se*, and return of writs, and also granted their tenants freedom from tolls and market dues throughout the realm, furthermore prohibiting the unlicensed incursion of royal officers and purveyors into the abbey's liberties; all and much else notwithstanding the taking away of such rights by statute of 27 Henry VIII.[118] There is no such patent on the roll or in the abbey muniments, though its existence seems to be proved from Feckenham's later allusion. Defending the abbey's sanctuary in 1558, he spoke of a 'charter' by which the queen granted him 'by generall woordes all liberties priviledges and fraunchises ... as my predecessors ... enjoyed'.[119] As Professor Loades has demonstrated, the restoration of the monastery did not in itself affect the legal position of the Westminster sanctuary, which now had its basis in a statute of 1540. But Feckenham's prominent assertion of what he believed to be the abbey's immemorial privileges made it an issue, and one which unfortunately associated the Counter Reformation with a thieves' kitchen. There was little sympathy for the institution of sanctuary even among Mary's councillors, and Feckenham undoubtedly hastened the abolition of what he sought to revive.[120]

By contrast, Westminster's ecclesiastical franchise is a live issue, where the dead hand of Marian Catholicism may yet be detected. The Confessor's abbey had since 1222 enjoyed unchallenged exemption from diocesan and provincial authority.[121] By virtue of the dispensations act, 25 Henry VIII c. 21, Westminster and all other exempt houses came under the Crown's control.[122] The abbot and convent thereafter

---

[118] WAM 7344 (office copy, without day of month). Refers to 27 Henry VIII c. 24, the franchises act, whose chief target was the palatinate of Durham: G.R. Elton, *The Tudor Constitution* (Cambridge 1960), 32–3, 37–9. Loades, *Tudor Government*, 213–16. S.E. Lehmberg, *The Reformation Parliament, 1529–1536* (Cambridge 1970), 222–3. C.J. Kitching, 'The Durham palatinate and the courts of Westminster under the Tudors', in Marcombe, *Last Principality*, 49–50.

[119] Bodleian Library, Rawlinson MS D. 68, f. 5v.

[120] D.M. Loades, 'The sanctuary', in Knighton and Mortimer, *Westminster Abbey Reformed*, xxx.

[121] WAM 12473. Earlier bulls of exemption are in Mason, *Westminster Abbey Charters*, 85–6 (no. 172), 87–8 (no. 179). Cf. M.C. Knowles, 'The growth of exemption', *Downside Review*, new ser. xxxi (1932), 201–31, 396–436, esp. 425–30, and *Monastic Order*, 579–91. For parallels with secular foundations cf. J.H. Denton, *English Royal Free Chapels, 1100–1300: A constitutional study* (Manchester 1970), 16, 17, 91, 134.

[122] Elton, *Tudor Constitution*, 354.

described themselves as *regie majestati immediate subjecti*.[123] This status naturally ceased in 1540 with the dissolution of the monastery and the creation of a diocese with the abbey church as its cathedral.[124] The period of the first collegiate church therefore forms a hiatus in the transition of Westminster from *eigenkloster* to royal peculiar. The intermission is as awkward for Erastians as the break in monastic observance is for those who prefer that tradition. Westminster Abbey had separate peculiar jurisdiction in St Martin-le-Grand, by virtue of the appropriation of the free chapel there as part of the Henry VII benefaction.[125] During the time of the bishopric, the dean and chapter kept no court of their own in Westminster, but from at least 1549 they resumed jurisdiction in St Martin's.[126] From March 1555 the dean and chapter further claimed in Westminster itself an exempt jurisdiction *ad Romanam curiam nullo medio pertinente*.[127] This assertion undoubtedly rested on the second Marian statute of repeal (1 & 2 Philip & Mary c. 8) which became law in January 1555, abrogating the whole body of Henrician and Edwardine anti-papal legislation, including the 1533 dispensations act.[128] The papal franchises were thereby again recognized in English law. But the repeal statute also incorporated the legate's dispensation of 24 December 1554 which had (subject to papal approval, duly given in the bull *Praeclara* of June 1555) respectively validated the cathedral foundations of the time of the schism. Westminster thus stood exempt by one provision of the second statute of repeal, and by another it was a lawful cathedral: an obvious nonsense, since no cathedral church can be other than subject to its own bishop, however much some medieval chapters may have striven to the contrary. Moreover, by the letters patent which dissolved the diocese of Westminster in 1550, and a confirming statute of 1552, Westminster Abbey lay in the diocese of London.[129] In fact neither Edward VI nor Mary took notice of this, and made appointments to the Westminster chapter without reference to the bishop of London.[130]

---

123 Cambridge University Library, Ely Diocesan Records, G/1/7, f. 105v.
124 Cf. parallel of Ely in 1109, when the see was created in the former exempt abbey: Knowles, *Monastic Order*, 586–7.
125 *CPR, 1494–1509*, 304, 378. *Calendar of Close Rolls preserved in the Public Record Office, 1500–9*, no. 389 (xx) (p. 150). B.F. Harvey, *Westminster Abbey and its Estates in the Middle Ages* (Oxford 1977), 408.
126 WAM 13242. Westminster City Archives [hereafter WCA], Reg. Wyks, ff. 63–75. *Acts*, i, 48.
127 WCA, Reg. Bracy, f. 72.
128 Cf. Loach, *Parliament and Crown*, 107–15.
129 *CPR, 1549–51*, 171–2. 5 & 6 Edward VI, Original Act no. 36.
130 *Acts*, i, p. xx and n. 22.

Abolition of the secular chapter in 1556 did not wholly eliminate this anomaly. The abbot and convent claimed an exemption in exactly the same form as their collegiate predecessors had done.[130] The bishop of London (or his officials) nevertheless continued to regard Westminster Abbey as being within that diocese.[131] It could be argued that the dissolution of the dean and chapter did not affect the bishop's rights in the *locus*. Alternatively, the elimination of the last element of the Henrician foundation might have removed the contradictory effects of 1 & 2 Philip & Mary c. 8, and the pre-1540 exemption could be held to have re-emerged at this point. Nothing in the legatine or royal instruments of 1556 addresses the issue of exemption. Pole's licence of 15 September did no more than permit the dean and chapter to resign their goods to the Crown so that the abbey might be endowed. Exemption might be held implicit in the intention (as stated in the letters patent of 7 September) to return Westminster to the state *in quo ante erat*; but there was uncertainty if the abbey was being restored (*restauretur*) or newly established (*de novo erigatur*).[132] A solitary entry in Pole's archiepiscopal register does, however, acknowledge the abbey's exempt style, and this must carry more weight than Westminster's own claims, or the bishop of London's usage to the contrary.[133] The Elizabethan act of supremacy (1 Eliz. I c. 1) restored the Henrician dispensations act, and thereby papal exemptions became again subject to the Crown. Westminster's present independence is deemed to rest on this point.[134] Some difficulty remains, in that the cathedral foundation of 1540, as confirmed by *Praeclara*, had destroyed the exemption, and it is not clear that the revival of the 1533 statute by Elizabeth could in this respect defeat the patent of 1540. It would be helpful for the present church to have absolute assurance that the Marian abbey was exempt, since only then would its jurisdiction have passed to the Crown in 1559. If Westminster had been in the diocese of London on the day Queen Mary was alive and dead, the Elizabethan act (referring to places exempt) would not have touched it. Lawrence Tanner was able to make the 1222 legatine award and the 1560 letters patent of the second collegiate church effective before a

---

[130] WCA, Reg. Bracy, f. 93 (from 1 December 1556).

[131] WAM 6488 (tax return of 27 April 1558). Guildhall, MS 9531/1, ff. 63v, 66, 67v (ordination register).

[132] PRO, C 66/916, mm. 35–6 (*CPR, 1555–7*, 546), printed in Dugdale, *Monasticon*, i, 324.

[133] LPL, Reg. Pole (archiepiscopal), f. 75 (institution to vicarage of Shoreham, 13 January 1558).

[134] Sir Reginald Pullen, receiver-general of Westminster Abbey, in Carpenter, *House of Kings*, 453.

20th-century tribunal.[135] But even Cardinal Langton's instrument must have been nullified by Paul IV's bull, and it is very doubtful if it is reactivated (as Tanner claimed it was) by the Elizabethan patent. A more persuasive argument might rest in long and continual user, since it would seem that since 1556, and probably since 1550, the Church of Westminster has been in practice exempt.[136] It has been occasionally noted that, without the Marian abbey to dissolve, Elizabeth might not have created the present collegiate church.[137] Queen Mary, therefore, may not only have saved episcopacy for the Church of England;[138] she may have ensured that Westminster Abbey would remain outside the jurisdiction of the Anglican episcopate.

---

[135] Tanner, *Recollections*, 112–22. Cf. A. Fox in Carpenter, *House of Kings*, 373–4. The issue was the status of the chapel in the new Church House, Westminster. The foundation charter of the present collegiate church, 21 May 1560, is WAM LXXXVI (original instrument\). WAM 6484G is an office copy. *CPR, 1558–60*, 397–403. Printed in *First Report of Her Majesty's Commissioners appointed to inquire into ... cathedral and collegiate churches* (1854), appendix, 78–80 (with omissions).

[136] In 1879 Coleridge CJ was much impressed by the fact that the dukes of Norfolk had kept the Fitzalan chapel clear of Anglicans, and indeed anyone else, for many centuries ('a stronger assertion of an absolute right of property ... can hardly be conceived'): M.T. Ellis, *Arundel Priory, 1380–1980: The College of the Holy Trinity* (1981), 95–6.

[137] Cocke, *900 Years*, 122. *Acts*, i, p. xx. A scheme of the 1570s would have replaced the deaneries of Westminster and Windsor with a bishopric of the royal household: PRO, SP 12/107, no. 42 (*CSPD 1547–80*), 517. Elton, *Parliament of England*, 277 n. 2, 279.

[138] As suggested in D.M. Loades, *Politics, Censorship and the English Reformation* (1991), 197.

Appendix: Biographical survey of members of the Marian community at Westminster

This extends and, where necessary, corrects the details given by Dom Hugh Aveling in McCann and Cary-Elwes, *Ampleforth and its Origins*, 271–9. Aveling numbered the individuals according to the sources from which their names were derived: 1–32 from WAM 9327, 37–42 from miscellaneous sources, 43–7 from the London ordination registers (monks), [48–57] from the same (supposed seminarians); no numbers were assigned by Aveling, but his sequence is here continued.

The following list is arranged in alphabetical order, and includes Aveling's numeration as now extended. Entries headed wholly in square brackets are those from Aveling's final category, who cannot now be counted among the monastic community. Names elsewhere suggested but rejected in the present chapter are not included.

Adthelstane [WAM 9327. Aveling, 273, no. 7]
Thomas Athelston (Adelston, Adthelstone, Athelstone, Ethelstan), OSB Glastonbury Abbey, junior monk in 1525, senior monk and cellarer at dissolution [PRO, SC 6/Hen VIII/3118, mm. 17, 26–8 (*ex inf*. Dr P. Cunich)]; priest by 1525 [*Reg. Bath & Wells 1518–59*, 86]. Student of Gloucester College, Oxford 1525 x 1535, BD adm. 3 Nov. 1535 after nine years' study [Emden, 16]. At dissolution of Glastonbury (22 x 28 Sep. 1539) all three BDs there reported to be 'but meanly learned' [*LP*, xiv, II, 205, 232. Wright, 256]. Correspondent of Robert Joseph: *Letter Book*: recipient of 4 letters and mentioned in 5 others; biographical note (p. 274) wrongly identifies him as signatory to petition for restoration of Glastonbury temp. Mary (*recte* next).

Adthelwolde [WAM 9327. Aveling, 275, no. 17]
William Adelwold (Athelwold, Athelwood), OSB Glastonbury Abbey, junior monk in 1526, priest by 1532/3, senior monk and refectorer at dissolution 22 x 28 Sep. 1539 [PRO, SC 6/Hen VIII/3118, mm. 17, 19 (*ex. inf*. Dr P. Cunich); *LP*, xiv, II, 206, 232 (for date of dissolution only)]. Signatory to petition for restoration of Glastonbury temp. Mary [BL, Harleian MS 3881, f. 38v].

Andersone [WAM 9327. Aveling, 277, 278, no. 36]
Anthony Anderson *alias* Esteneye, of York diocese, ordained (Lond.) all minor orders and subdeacon 13 Mar. 1557, presented by sub-prior of Westminster Abbey; deacon 3 Apr., as of Westminster Abbey; priest 4 Jun. 1558, presented by sub-prior [Guildhall MS 9535/1, ff. 59v, 60, 62v, 74]. Aveling's tentative suggestion that he conformed and became

vicar of Stepney [coll. 25 Feb. 1587: Hennessy, 411] seems unlikely; this man's career is established in *ODNB* as a native of Lancashire who became vicar of Medbourne, Leics, 1573, and also of Dengie, Essex, sworn gentleman of the chapel royal 12 Oct. 1591, subdean 26 Jul. 1592, died 10 Oct. 1593 [*The Old Cheque-Book or Book of Remembrance of the Chapel Royal from 1561 to 1744*, ed. E.F. Rimbault (Camden Soc., new ser. iii, 1872), 5, 33, 196 and *passim*. D. Baldwin, *The Chapel Royal, Ancient and Modern* (1990), 85–6]. The 'puritanic character' of his published writings (STC 566–72) does not disprove a monastic upbringing, but makes the identification the less persuasive.

Athee, Arthur [Aveling, 279, no. 52]
Of Canterbury diocese, ordained (Lond.) all minor orders 3 Apr. 1557, as of Westminster Abbey [Guildhall MS 9535/1, ff. 61v, 62].

Possibly student of Christ Church, Oxford, BA 1 Jul. 1560, MA 1564, B&DCL 1574, fellow of Merton College 1562, principal of St Albans Hall 1569–81, public orator 1572–82, MP 1572 x 1604, secretary to the earl of Leicester from 1574, knighted 11 May 1603, died 2 Dec. 1604 [Foster, i, 44. G. Ungerer, *A Spaniard in Elizabethan England: The Correspondence of Antonio Pérez's Exile* (Colleción Tamesis, xxvii, liv, 1974–76), ii, 255–8. *Hist. Parl. 1558–1603*, i, 363–4. S.L. Adams, 'Papers of Robert Dudley, earl of Leicester. II. The Atye-Cotton collection', *Archives*, xx (1993), 131–44, esp. 132–3. *Household Accounts and Disbursements of Robert Dudley, Earl of Leicester, 1558–1561, 1584–1586*, ed. S.L. Adams (Camden Society, 5th ser. vi, 1995), *passim*, esp. p. 462. Sir A. Atye's will is PRO, PROB 11/105, ff. 47v–48. [I am indebted to Dr Adams for sending me a copy of his *Archives* paper, and for discussing the possibility that Sir Arthur Atye was the Westminster monk Arthur Athee, first suggested by Wainewright (p. 136). We conclude there is no case proven, and there is difficulty accommodating the date of Atye's BA with a monastic career even if abandoned in 1557.]

Aulton [WAM 9327. Aveling, 274, no. 12]
Possibly Thomas Alton, OSB Winchester Cathedral priory 1528 to surrender 14 Nov. 1539 [Greatrex, 664–5, but there suggested as possible *alias* of Figge, *q.v.*]. Cannot be Andrew Alton of Hyde [as Marron, 132], who died by 1544 [Emden, 7].

Bayli [WAM 9327. Aveling, 274, no. 11]
Stephen Bayly (Bailie, Baylye), OSB St Albans Abbey at dissolution 1539 (pension) [*LP*, xv, 1032 (p. 547)]. Probably scholar of Gloucester College, Oxford, BD supp. June 1539. Dispensed to hold benefice with

change of habit 12 Dec. 1539; dispensed to hold additional benefice 1 May 1548 [*Fac. Off. Reg*, 202, 310]. Vicar of Redbourn, Herts, vac. Dec. 1556. Rector of Little Bardfield, Essex, adm. 2 May 1548, vac. Feb. 1556. Rector of Knapton, Norfolk, adm. 10 June 1553, res. *propter ingressum religionis* 1556 [Emden, 34. Baskerville (1933), 209]. Buried at St Albans (*as monachus*) 1 Feb. 1559 [Herts RO, D/90/1/1 (microfilm 89); *The Parish Register of St Albans Abbey 1558–1689*, transcr. W. Briggs (Harpenden 1897), 177]. Mentioned in WAM 18961, 37718. Cf. Clark, 'St Albans', 321.

Bowcer [WAM 9327. Aveling, 275, no. 15]
Thomas Bowser (Bochar, Boughier), born *c*. 1509, OSB Canterbury Cathedral priory, tonsure 15 May 1527, professed 2 Mar. 1528 [Searle, 195]. Scholar of Canterbury College, Oxford, occ. 1538 [Pantin, *Cant. Coll.* iii, 153]. Epistoler on new foundation of Canterbury Cathedral 1541 [*LP*, xv, 452]. Minor canon there, occ. 19 Aug. 1560 [*Reg. Parker*, ii, 632, 635]. [Emden, 64–5. Greatrex, 97]. Occ. (as Thomas Bowser, monk and sacristan), apparently serving St Margaret's church, in WAM 33198D, m. 5, 33198D* (1558), and therefore the identity with the Thomas Bowser of Canterbury, doubtful to Aveling, seems much more likely.

Brampston, Thomas [Aveling, 279, no. 47]
(Bramestone, Bramston, Braunston). Born *c*. 1541. King's School, Canterbury under John Twyne [cf. C.E. Woodruff and H.J. Cape, *Schola Regia Cantuariensis* (1908), 70 n.]. Ordained (Lond.) to all minor orders 13 Mar. 1557, presented by sub-prior of Westminster Abbey [Guildhall MS 9535/1, ff. 59v, 60]. Annuity of £4 granted by abbot and convent 3 Dec. 1558 [WAM 33198E, m. 5d; 37929, f. 1v; 37932, f. 1v]. By his own testimony he left Westminster after a year in the novitiate. A year at Eltham, Kent, in house of one Roper. St John's College, Oxford; BA June 1562, fellow 1566–69 (though he claimed to have no degree in the schools). Served Abbot Feckenham in the Tower two years. Ten years as schoolmaster in the house of Sir Thomas Tresham, until prohibited from teaching Catholic faith by statute 'about' 18th year of Elizabeth [*recte* 23 Eliz. I c. 1, sect. 5]. Deacon 6 Dec. 1584, priest (Cardinal of Guise at Rheims) 6 Apr. 1585. To England 1586. Arrested and sent to Marshalsea. Convicted for heresy 17 July 1587 as *clericus* of St George's parish, Southwark [CRS, *Recusants*, 26]. Banished and went to Douai 1601. Returned to England 1603, arrested 24 May and imprisoned in Newgate. Execution remitted at request of earl of Northumberland at time of James I's coronation. Banished again, and died at Douai 23 Dec. 1606 [PRO, SP 12/188, no. 46 (*CSPD 1581–90*, 323), examination 30 Apr. 1588, printed Anstruther, i, 47–8 (with letter

to ?Tresham, 24 July 1603). Bellenger, 42. *Douay Diaries*, 203, 205, 208, 263. Wainewright, 135–6].

Bramsgrove [WAM 9327. Aveling, 276, no. 25]
Perhaps John Bromsgrove, OSB Evesham Abbey at dissolution 27 Jan. 1540, pension £6 13s 4d, still in receipt 1556 [*LP*, xv, 118 (p. 38), 1032 (p. 550). Dugdale, ii, 9 note *c* (from PRO, E 164/31, f. 43). Emden, 74 (where distinguished from one this name, rector of Pendock, Worcs, who died 1545, thereby eliminating a suggestion by Aveling. Aveling gives name as Thomas, which does not apply to either man)].

Bucknall, Francis [Aveling, 278, no. 41]
OSA Christchurch Priory, Hants, reader in theology there at surrender 28 Nov. 1539; pension occ. 1540 x 1545 [*LP*, xv, 139; xvi, 91 (p. 27); xx, I, 557 (p. 265/f. 41); xxi, I, 643 (p. 319/f. 49)]. Vicar of Sopley, Hants, by virtue of grant *pro hac vice* from Christchurch 13 Mar. 1540 [*Reg. Gardiner & Poynet*, 121]. Res. *propter ingressum religionis* 1556 [*Reg. Whyte*, 19]. Supposition that he joined Westminster from circumstances of resignation of living, coincident with entry in Winchester register for Cooke (*q.v.*) also of Christchurch.

[**Clerke, Thomas** (Aveling, 279, no. 54]
Of Bath and Wells diocese, ordained (Lond.) deacon and priest to title of Westminster Abbey 3 and 16 Apr. 1557 [Guildhall MS 9535/1, ff. 62v, 63v]; therefore not a monk.

Cley [WAM 9327. Aveling, 276, no. 31]
Just possibly Peter Freeston *alias* Claye (Claie, Clee, Freston, Freyston, Frixstonne), OSB Crowland Abbey, pension granted 4 Dec. 1539 [*LP*, xiv, II, 631]. Dispensed for change of habit 7 Feb. 1540 [*Fac. Off. Reg.*, 208]. Still in receipt of pension, and curate of Friskney, Lincs, 1554 [Hodgett, 108]. Vicar of Wrangle, Lincs, pres. 17 July 1557; died in possession 1561 [*CPR 1557–8*, 249. Hodgett, 129]. Tenure of living 1557–61 makes identity with Westminster monk unlikely, though it would fix the WAM 9327 list before July 1557.

Cooke [WAM 9327. Aveling, 275–6, no. 21]
Probably Thomas Cook, OSA Christchurch Priory, Hants at surrender 28 Nov. 1539; pension occ. 1540 [*LP*, xv, 139, 1032 (p. 549/f. 160)]. Dugdale, vi, I, 306]. Rector of St Maurice, Winchester, coll. 11 Aug. 1554, res. *per ingressum religionis* by 22 Dec. 1556 [*Reg. Gardiner & Poynet*, 140. *Reg. Whyte*, 18]. Witness to will of former nun in Winchester, and legatee of a secular clerk [Gasquet, ii, 477]. Imprisoned in Winchester gaol; sent to ?London by archbishop's order 16 Mar. 1572 [?1572/3] in Marshalsea 1579; died by 1580 [J. Strype, *Annals of the*

Reformation (Oxford 1824), ii, II, 660. CRS, *Miscellanea*, i, 60, 70]. Perhaps also 'Cook' who added obits of Catholics in Winchester gaol, and of some ex-religious, to a printed psalter of 1528, now Exeter College, Oxford 171.G.8.

Copynger *alias* **Gardyner, William** [Aveling, 278, no. 45]
Born (Copinger) 1523 or 1524, of Old Fish St, London. Relative of (or adopted as such by) Stephen Gardiner, Bishop of Winchester, who supported his education from age ten. Winchester College, adm. scholar 1535 (age 12). New College, Oxford, adm. scholar 23 Mar. 1537, fellow 23 Mar. 1541, vac. 1542 [T.F. Kirby, *Winchester Scholars* (1888), 119. Emden, 136 (giving nothing further)]. BCL 1541 [Wainewright, 135, unsupported]. In Bishop Gardiner's service from *c*. 1544, and with him in Tower from 1549 and at his trial 1551; had yearly wage of £4 and reward of 53s. At Michaelmas 1550 had £10 and reversion of bailiwick of Wargrave by death of bishop's brother William. Legacy from bishop 1555 [Foxe, vi, 192–4. *Wills Doc. Comm.*, 45. Muller (1926), 290, 271 n. 1, 373 n. 29, 391 n. 36]. Mentioned in epitaph by John Morwen for Bishop Gardiner (*quem sanguine junctum*) 1555 [T. Hearne, *A Collection of Curious Discourses* (1774), ii, 419]. Ordained (Lond.) acolyte and subdeacon 18 Dec. 1557, presented as professed monk by cellarer of Westminster Abbey; deacon (Copynger *alias* Gardyner), as of Westminster Abbey, 5 Mar. 1558; priest (same *alias*) 4 June 1558, presented by sub-prior [Guildhall MS 9535/1, ff. 67, 67v, 69v, 74].

Coventri [WAM 9327. Aveling, 274, no. 10]
Several ex-monks of this name are noted by Aveling, but no identification is ventured. For some see *Fac. Off. Reg.*, 76, 131, 150, 208.

Possibly Thomas Coventry (Coventree, Coventrie), OSB Evesham Abbey and scholar of Gloucester College, Oxford, occ. 1530 x 1539; pension £10 at surrender 27 Jan. 1540 [*LP*, xv, 118 (p. 37)]. BD supp. 1541 after 13 years' study [Emden, 143]. Wrote to Thomas Cromwell shortly before dissolution of Evesham, from which he had an exhibition; having studied Hebrew, Greek and Latin the better to refute papistical sophistry (for which he cited Richard Morison as witness), asked favour for further study [*LP*, xiv, II, 437]. Correspondent of Robert Joseph [*Letter Book*: recipient of six letters and mentioned *passim*; biographical note p. 273].

Edon [WAM 9327. Aveling, 272–3, no. 3]
Richard Edon *alias* Hayles (Eddon, Hailes), OCist Hailes Abbey, Glos, by 1531 to dissolution 1 Dec. 1539 [*LP*, xiv, II, 771 (p. 291); xv, 1032 (p. 551)]. St Bernard's College, Oxford 1531/2 x 1538. BD adm. 31 May

1538 [Emden, 277]. Living at Wells with £5 pension 1552/3 [Baskerville (1927), 89, 113]. Perhaps vicar choral of Wells Cathedral [*ex inf*. Dom A. Watkin to Aveling, and so to Knowles, *Rel. Orders*, iii, 427]. Canon of Winchester, pres. by Crown 1 May 1554, inst. and installed 21 June, vac. *per ingressum religionis* by 25 Nov. 1556 [*CPR 1553–4*, 383. *Reg. Gardiner & Poynet*, 139. *Reg. White*, 19. Le Neve, iii, 100.] Rector of Calstock, Cornwall, pres. by Crown 8 May 1554, inst. 19 June 1554, res. by 26 Oct. 1556 [*CPR 1553–4*, 150; *1555–7*, 506. Emden. Cf. A.L. Rowse, *Tudor Cornwall* (1941), 309]. Canon of Wells and prebendary of Combe III, coll. 24 May 1556, vac. 1556 [as for Winchester] by 25 Nov. 1556 [Le Neve, v. 31]. Vicar of North Petherton, Som., pres by Crown 1 June 1554, inst. 24 Aug. 1554, vac. by 1557 [*CPR 1553–4*, 151. *Reg. Bath & Wells 1518–59*, 132. Emden. Vicar of Dunkeswell, Devon, vac. by Nov. 1555 [Emden]. *Perhaps* vicar of Burnham, Bucks, pres. by Crown 20 Dec. 1553 [*CPR 1553–4*, 357]. Present at Gardiner's funeral in Winchester Cathedral Feb. 1556 [Muller (1933), 502].

Cellarer of Westminster Abbey from refoundation: account for year to Michaelmas 1557 [WAM 18961; voucher for same WAM 18960]; final settlement with receiver-general 27 Nov. 1557 [WAM 37756]. Many receipts with his signature; last as cellarer dated 3 Nov. 1557 [WAM 37746] and 13 November [WAM 37739, 37765]. Prior from 22 or 23 November 1557 [WAM 37763]. Archdeacon from 22 Apr. 1558; last act 13 Apr. 1559 [WCA, Reg. Bracy, ff. 114v, 150v]. He and Hugh Phillips (*q.v.*) still charged for tenements in Westminster 1562/3 [WAM 38142, f. 2].

Returned to Oxford after 1559; pension of £7 from Sir Thomas White. Signatory to foundation deeds of Gloucester Hall 13 Apr. 1560; head of that house 1561–63; last occurs there 9 Apr. 1565 [W.H. Stevenson and H.E. Salter, *The Early History of St John's College, Oxford* (OHS, n.s., i, 1939), 38, 45, 340, 435. M. Foster, 'Thomas Allen (1540–1632), Gloucester Hall and the survival of Catholicism in post-Reformation Oxford', *Oxoniensia*, xlvi (1981), 106 & nn. 40, 41 (suggestion that Richard was son of Thomas Eden, clerk of Star Chamber, doubtful). Gave works of St Augustine in seven volumes to St John's [Emden].

Egers, John [Aveling, 279, no. 50]
Ordained (Lond.) to all minor orders 13 Mar. 1557, presented by sub-prior of Westminster Abbey [Guildhall MS 9535/1, ff. 59v, 60].

Este, Prior [WAM 9327. Aveling, 271–2, no. 2]
William East (Erste, Este), OSB St Albans Abbey by 1534, pension £8 at dissolution 5 Dec. 1539, occ. Feb. 1556 [*LP*, xv, 1032 (p. 547). *DKR 8th Report*, 39]. Oxford, BD supp. Sep. 1538 after nine years' study,

adm. 3 June 1539. Ordained priest (Lincoln) 28 Feb. 1534 [Emden, 193]. Dispensed to hold benefice and change habit 12 Dec. 1539; granted right to wear grey almuce of canon at his pleasure 2 May 1545 (as DD) [*Fac. Off. Reg.*, 202, 257]. Archdeacon of St Albans, app. 8 Mar. 1544; retained when archdeaconry transferred to diocese of London 1 Apr. 1550; res. by 26 Feb. 1557 [*LP*, xix, I, 1036 (p. 643). Le Neve, i, 14. Cf. Clark, 'St Albans', 321]. Little trace of his administration survives [R. Peters, *Oculus Episcopi* (Manchester 1963), 2]. Canon of Windsor (as chaplain to queen), pres. 5 Mar. 1554, vac. by 11 Jan. 1557 [*CPR 1553–4*, 242; *1555–7*, 452. Ollard, 60]. Rector of St Mary Magdalene, Milk St, London, occ. 5 July 1554 [Hennessy, 268]. Rector of St Albans, vac. Feb. 1557 [Emden].

Sub-prior of Westminster Abbey, occ. 13 Mar. 1557 (presenting candidates for orders in St Paul's Cathedral) [Guildhall MS 9535/1, ff. 59v, 60]. Sang Lady mass at funeral of Anne of Cleves in Westminster Abbey 4 Aug. 1557 [*Excerpta Historica*, 311]. Died by Sep. 1557 [Bodleian MS Jones 9, f. 135].

[Farechilde, William, BA (Aveling, 279, no. 57)]
(Fachyld, Fayerchild, Fayerchilde). Suggestion that he is among the 'seminarians' appears to rest on Guildhall MS 9535/1, f. 69v, where his name follows two of those bracketed as monks of Westminster, when all were made deacons 5 Mar. 1558. Farechilde's name is followed by 'London dioc. Ad titulum' (no more); it is doubtful if this is connected with the preceding entries; the two previous names were those of undoubted monks, who by definition could not be ordained to the title of their house. Farechilde's previous orders were not recorded alongside Westminster names, and his priesthood was to the title of the Savoy hospital [*ibid.*, ff. 66, 66v, 67v, 71v].

Feckenham *alias* **Howman, John, abbot** [WAM 9327. Aveling, 280–83, (no. 1]
(Fecknam, Homan, Whoman). Son of Humphrey and Florence Homan of Beanhall, Feckenham, Worcs. OSB Evesham Abbey, ?by 1520. Probably ordained priest (Worcester) Sep. 1530 [Joseph, *Letter Book*, 107]. Scholar of Gloucester College, Oxford from *c*. 1530 to 1540. BD, supp. Oct. 1538 and 11 years' study, adm. 11 June 1539. Pension £10 at dissolution 27 Jan. 1540 [*LP*, xv, 118 (p. 37)]. Vicar of Feckenham, Worcs, adm. 27 Jan. 1540, still 1545. Dispensed to hold another benefice 3 Apr. 1545 [*Fac. Off. Reg.*, 255]. Rector of Solihill, Warwicks, adm. 17 Mar. 1545, vac. 1554. Canon of St Paul's and prebendary of Kentish Town *alias* Cantlers, coll. 25 Jan. 1554, res. by 22 Nov. 1556. Dean of St Paul's, el. 10 Mar. 1554, conf. 17 Mar., until installation as abbot of Westminster 21 Nov. 1556; successor el. 11 Dec. [Le Neve, i,

5, 25. Wainewright (p. 133) wrongly says he vacated deanery Jan. 1556]. Canon of Canterbury, pres. 20 June 1554 but ineffective as another presentation to same vacancy 21 Nov. 1554 [*CPR 1553–4*, 330; *1554–5*, 35. Le Neve, iii, 24]. Rector of Finchley, Middx, adm. 26 June 1554, vac. Nov. 1556. Rector of Great Greenford, Middx, adm. 24 Sept. 1554, vac. Dec. 1556. Chaplain to Bonner, Bishop of London 1548–49. Chaplain and confessor to Mary I.

Abbot of Westminster, installed 21 Nov. 1556, blessed 29 Nov., to dissolution July 1559 [see above]. Imprisoned in the Tower 20 May 1560 [PRO, SP 12/18, no. 3 (*CSPD 1547–80*, 179). Machyn, 225. Date incorrectly given as 20 Mar. in *House of Kings*, 129 (misquoting Machyn) and 22 May in Knowles, *Rel. Orders*, iii, 434 (perhaps by reference to letter from John Jewel to Peter Martyr, 22 May, referring to the imprisonment: *Zurich Letters*, i, 79). Died in captivity at Wisbech 16 Oct. 1584 and buried there.

[F.A. Gasquet, 'Abbot Feckenham and Bath', *Downside Review*, xxv (1906), 242–60. A.H. Sweet, 'John de Feckenham and the Marian reaction', in *Persecution and Liberty: Essays in honour of George Lincoln Burr* (New York 1931; no editor credited), 255–69. Joseph, *Letter Book*: recipient of 12 letters and mentioned *passim*; biographical note pp. 274–5. Emden, 201–2. P. Tudor, 'John de Feckenham and Tudor religious controversies', in *The Cloister and the World: Essays in medieval history in honour of Barbara Harvey*, ed. W.J. Blair and B. Golding (Oxford 1996), 302–22. C.S. Knighton in *ODNB*].

Feckenham *alias* **Wyborne, William** [Aveling, 278, no. 44]
(Wiborne). Ordained (Lond.) to all minor orders and subdeacon 18 Dec. 1557, presented as professed monk by cellarer of Westminster Abbey; deacon Mar. 1558; priest (Feckenham *alias* Wyborne) 4 June 1558, presented by sub-prior [Guildhall MS 9535/1, ff. 67, 67v, 71v, 74]. Convicted for recusancy 27 June and 20 Dec. 1581. In the Fleet gaol in London 1586 for assisting recusant priests. Imprisoned in Newgate 7 Oct. 1556 [CRS, *Miscellanea*, ii, 267. CRS, *Recusants*, 60. PRO, SP 12/195, no. 34 (*CSPD 1581–90*, 360)].

One Henry Fecknam, otherwise Wyborne, gent., was among Middlesex recusants 1592 [HMC, *Salisbury MSS*, iv. 256].

Ferne, John [Aveling, 279, no. 53]
Of Canterbury diocese, ordained (Lond.) to all minor orders 3 Apr. 1557, as of Westminster Abbey [Guildhall MS 9535/1, f. 61v].

Figge, Thomas [Aveling, 277, no. 37]
(Figg). Born *c*. 1509, OSB Winchester Cathedral priory. Minor orders (Winchester) 11 Apr. 1528, not yet professed [Greatrex, 693–4, where

suggested as possible *alias* of either Thomas Eston, student at Oxford on new foundation of Winchester Cathedral, designated 14 Nov. 1539, or of Thomas Alton, monk 1528 x 1539: ibid., pp. 664–5, 690]. Minor canon on new foundation of Winchester Cathedral 28 Apr. 1541 [*Documents relating to the Foundation of the Chapter of Winchester*, ed. G.W. Kitchin and F.T. Madge (Hampshire Record Soc., i, 1889), 55]. Occ. at enthronement of bishop 1551, and installation of dean 1554 [*Reg. Gardiner & Poynet*, 98, 189]. Occ. at marriage of king and queen 25 July 1554 [Bogan, as below]. Rector of Stoke Bishop, Hants, coll. 1 Dec. 1553, res. *propter ingressum religionis* by 8 Dec. 1556 [*Reg. Gardiner & Poynet*, 136. *Reg. Whyte*, 18]. Assisted at Bishop Gardiner's funeral in Winchester Cathedral 27 and 28 Feb. 1556 [Muller (1933), 513, 515].

Steward and sub-cellarer of Westminster Abbey 1556/7 [WAM 37927, f. 1v; 37929, f. 3; also named in WAM 18961, 37718; not in 9327 unless 'Legge' (as Aveling suggested) or 'Aulton' (cf. Greatrex above)]. Fled to continent to escape persecution; occ. in Belgium 8 Feb. 1570 [AGS, Stado Leg. 583, cited Knowles, *Rel. Orders*, iii, 443 n. 3]. On outbreak of Dutch revolt moved to France, where occ. 1582 [PRO, SP 15/27, no. 124 (*CSPD Addenda 1580–1625*, 124)]. Returned to Bruges 1585. Chaplain to Anne, Lady Hungerford, in Ghent. Had come into possession of left foot of St Philip the Apostle, secreted from Henrician plunder of Winchester Cathedral [AGS, E 593, deposition of 3 Sept. 1585 in connexion with intended gift of the relic to the abbot of St Andrew's, Bruges, printed in P. Bogan, 'Dom Thomas Figge and the foot of St Philip, *Winchester Cathedral Record*, lxi (1992), 22–6].

Filde [WAM 9327. Aveling, 275, no. 18]
Possibly Thomas Fylde *alias* Hemyngford (Felde, Field, Fielde), OSB Ramsey Abbey, Hunts, pension £5 at dissolution 22 Nov. 1539; still in receipt 1554 when curate of Hemingford Abbots, unmarried [*LP*, xiv, II, 565. Hodgett, pp. xv, 26, 32, 35, 94]. Association with Hugh Phillips (*q.v.*) makes this identification plausible.

Another possibility Edmund Fyld (Feld), BA Oxford, and deputy principal of St Alban Hall in Sept. 1557. Schoolmaster of Evesham Abbey occ. 1530–31. Curate of St Laurence, Evesham, 1535 [Emden, 223; Joseph, *Letter Book*: recipient of three letters, and mentioned *passim*; biographical note p. 275]. Aveling did not consider this possibility.

Foster [WAM 9327. Aveling, 273, no. 5]
Probably John Foster (Forster), OSB Westminster Abbey, novice 1513/14. Ordained priest (Lond.) 16 Feb. 1516. Gloucester College,

Oxford, scholar occ. 1532, senior at 17 Dec. 1537 [Pearce, 184–5. Emden, 211. Joseph, *Letter Book*, 265]. Signed surrender of Westminster Abbey 16 Jan. 1540 [PRO, E 322/260 (*LP*, xv, 69)]. Pension £8, still in receipt Feb. 1556 [*LP*, xvi, 745 (pp. 354, 355). PRO, E 164/31, f. 6v (cited by Emden)]. Assumed to be Marian monk because named next to Goodlooke (*q.v.*) in WAM 9327 [Pearce, 216, followed by Aveling].

Founteney, Martin [Aveling, 279, no. 49]
Of London diocese, ordained (Lond.) all minor orders 13 Mar. 1557, presented by sub-prior of Westminster Abbey [Guildhall MS 9535/1, ff. 59v, 60].

Laurence Founetayne (Fountayne, Founteyn) granted annuity of £4 by abbot and convent 3 Dec. 1558 (as were Brampston and Prince, *qq.v.*) [WAM 33198E, m. 5d; 37929, f. 1v; 37932, f. 1v].

Frevell [WAM 9327. Aveling, 273–4, no. 9]
George Frevell (Frebel, Frewell), born *c.* 1508. OSB Canterbury Cathedral priory, tonsure 25 May 1527, professed 2 Mar. 1528 [Searle, 195]. Sub-chaplain to prior, and scholar of Canterbury College, Oxford, age *c.* 30 and 'wytty' *c.* 1538 [PRO, SP 1/116, f. 45 (*LP*, xii, I, 437). Pantin, *Cant. Coll.* iii, 153]. Still sub-chaplain to prior at dissolution, when nominated student on new foundation of Canterbury Cathedral with £3 reward, 4 Apr. 1540 [PRO, E 315/245, f. 79 (*LP*, xv, 452(1)). Dugdale, i, 112]. Paid £10 as Oxford student in 1541/2 [Canterbury Cathedral Library, receiver's account 1541/2, f. 11]. [Emden, 216. Greatrex, 162]. *Perhaps alias* of Guylyn, Gwyllyn (etc.), student at Oxford on Canterbury Cathedral foundation *c.* 1541, 1542/3 (occurrences not coincident with Frevell's) [Canterbury Cath. Lib., DE 164(ii); VMA 40, f. 3. *The Cantuarian*, xxvii, no. 1 (Dec. 1956), 42 (for 1541 list); xxiii, no. 3 (July 1949), 248 (for 1542/3 list); xlix, no. 2 (Apr. 1985), 111 (synopsis)]. Oxford, BA adm. Feb. 1542, MA inc. 7 Apr. 1544. Rector of Goodnestone, Kent, comp. 25 Feb. 1551 [Emden, 252]. *Frevell* epistoler of Canterbury Cathedral occ. 1553/4, vac. Michaelmas 1556; listed as minor canon 18 May 1556. In 1555/6 paid 12d for writing legends of St Thomas [LPL, Reg. Pole (arch.), f. 32v; Estate Documents 93, ff. 2v, 65. Canterbury Cath. Lib., VMA 49, f. 54v. *Ex inform.* Dr R.D. Bowers, to whom I am indebted for the reference to the St Thomas legends which he used in *A History of Canterbury Cathedral*, ed. P. Collinson, N.L. Ramsay and M. Sparks (Oxford 1995), 431 and n. 104].

As monk of Westminster, sub-chaplain to abbot; letter from him as such to one of the rent collectors, dated Chiswick 14 Nov. *s.a.*, probably 1557 [WAM 37796]. Receipt from him 25 Oct. 1557 [WAM 37735].

Archdeacon, occ. 4 Dec. 1556 to 12 Mar. x 22 Apr. 1558 (when succeeded by Edon, *q.v.*) [WCA, Reg. Bracy, ff. 93, 94v, 114].

Perhaps to Douai, whence 'D. Frevill' left 1 Feb. 1586 [*Douay Diaries*, 209].

A Frevell (Frewell, etc.) occ. as minor canon of Westminster Abbey from 1560/1 [WAM 33617, ff. 3, 6v, 7 (no forename)], called *William* in 1561/2 [WAM 33619, f. 2] and *Edmund* from 1562/3 to death 1566/7 [WAM 33629, f. 2v; 38953, f. 3]. These may all be one man; it is not likely that the ex-monk George had two further *aliases*. The George Gwyllym identification is also doubtful because it would mean study for the arts degree began *c.* 1538; monastic students did a time in that faculty without graduating, proceeding direct to BD [Joseph, *Letter Book*, p. xx].

[**Fysher, Richard** (Aveling, 279, no. 51)]
Of London diocese, ordained (Lond.) all minor orders and subdeacon 13 Mar. 1557, deacon 3 Apr. 1557, priest 1557; all major orders to title of Westminster Abbey [Guildhall MS 9535/1, ff. 59v, 60, 61v, 62v, 63v]. Therefore not a monk.

Goodlooke [WAM 9327. Aveling, 273, no. 6]
John Allen *alias* Goodluck (Alyn, Goodlock, Goodluck), OSB Westminster Abbey, novice 1519/20; ordained (Lond.) subdeacon 25 May 1521, deacon 21 Sept. 1521, priest 19 Dec. 1523. Student at Oxford 1531 x 1533 [Pearce, 187. Emden, 241]. Signed surrender of Westminster Abbey 16 Jan. 1540 [PRO, E 322/260 (*LP*, xv, 69)]. Pension £2 on 11 Apr. 1541 [PRO, E 315/235, ff. 85v–86 (*LP*, xvi, 1500, p. 718)]. Epistoler in 1540/1 [PRO, LR 2/111, ff. 56v, 59v, 62v, 65v, 68v, 71v, 74v]. Gospeller occ. 1541 x 1556 [WAM 6478, f. 4; 37709; 37714]. Bequest from William Britten, canon of Westminster (d. 1552) [PRO, PROB 11/35, f. 157]. Minor canon in second collegiate church of Westminster from 1560 (Alyn *alias* Goodluck) to death 1571 [WAM 33617, ff. 3, 6v, 7; 33631, f. 3]. Will dated 31 Jan. 1571, proved 9 May following; bequests to choristers and scholars, and four other minor canons; left Bibles in English and Latin, and works of St Ambrose [WCA, Reg. Elsam, f. 53]. The only cleric who certainly belonged to all four regimes at Westminster between 1540 and 1560.

Distinguish from John Alen, OSB Westminster Abbey, priest 1532; not documented after 1535 [Pearce, 189].

Grundye, Roger [Aveling, 279, no. 34]
Of Chester diocese, ordained (Lond.) all minor orders and subdeacon 13 Mar. 1557, presented by sub-prior of Westminster Abbey; deacon 3 Apr. 1557, as of Westminster Abbey [Guildhall MS 9535/1, ff. 59v, 60, 62v].

[**Hunt, Ralph, MA** (Aveling, 279, no. 56)]
(Hunte). Of Bath and Wells diocese. Oxford, BA adm. 17 Feb. 1539, MA inc. 27 Mar. 1542. Hart Hall, scholar occ. 1533/4 [Emden, 305]. Presented by abbot and convent of Westminster to all bishops of England for all orders not yet received, with title of Westminster Abbey, 2 Feb. 1558 [WAM Reg. IV, f. 25]. Ordained (Lond.) all minor orders 12 Mar. 1558; subdeacon 9 Apr. 1558 to title of Westminster Abbey; deacon 4 June 1558 to same [Guildhall MS 9535/1, ff. 71, 72v, 74]. Therefore not a monk. Nevertheless perhaps associate of Langdon and Phillips (*qq.v*) and arrested with them 20 Apr. 1561 [PRO, SP 12/16, no. 65 (*CSPD 1547–80*, 175). CRS, *Miscellanea*, i, 50].

Johnson, Robert [Aveling, 2777, no. 33]
Of Norwich diocese, ordained (Lond.) all minor orders and subdeacon 13 Mar. 1557, presented by sub-prior of Westminster Abbey; deacon 3 Apr. 1557, as of Westminster Abbey [Guildhall MS 9535/1, ff. 60, 62v].

Kentwyne William [Aveling, 277, no. 38]
OSB Glastonbury Abbey, ordained (Bath & Wells) priest 19 Sep. 1523 [*Reg. Bath & Wells 1518–59*, 86 n. 1]. At visitation July 1538 complained of tediousness of services etc. [Watkin (1941), 142]. Of middling seniority 1538/9 [PRO, SC 6/Hen VIII/3118, m. 17; *ex inf*. Dr P. Cunich]. Presumably to surrender 22 x 28 Sept. 1539 [*LP*, xiv, II, 206, 232]. Signed petition for restoration of Glastonbury temp. Mary [BL, Harleian MS 3881, f. 38v]. Pearce (p. 216) suggests possibly 'Kyngeswoode' [see below] in WAM 9327.

Kyngeswoode [WAM 9327. Aveling, 276, no. 30]
See previous entry. Cannot be Thomas Kyngeswoode, OSB Gloucester Abbey (as Marron, 132), who was canon of Gloucester Cathedral till death 1559 [Emden, 335 (date of death wrongly given 1549). Le Neve, viii, 50, 51].

Langdon [WAM 9327. Aveling, 275, no. 20]
Thomas Langdon *alias* Odian (Longdone), born *c*. 1513. OSB Canterbury Cathedral priory, tonsure 12 May 1533, professed 21 Mar. 1534 [Searle, 196. Greatrex, 218]. Canterbury College, Oxford, scholar *c*. 1538, age 25, 'good man' [PRO, SP 1/116, f. 45 (*LP*, xii, I, 437. Pantin, *Cant. Coll*. iii, 154; Aveling (p. 275) misattributes Thomas Langdon's age and character to *John* Langdon in same list; John was age 58, 'symple' (Pantin, 152)]. Thomas replaced in pension list of 4 Apr. 1540 [PRO, E 315/245, f. 79 (*LP*, xv, 452)].

As 'Mr Longdone, monk of Westm'' was left 5s in will of former dean of Westminster, Hugh Weston (d. 1558) [PRO, PROB 11/42B, f. 56]. Reported by John Coxe 14 and 17 Apr. 1561 that Thomas Langdon, late monk of Westminster, had asked him to procure copy of sermon by [Thomas] Watson [Marian Bishop of Lincoln], and that Langdon and John Ramridge [a Marian canon of Westminster] had said mass in the house of one Stubbes in Broad Sanctuary; subsequent order for Hunt, Langdon and Phillips to be sent for from Canterbury. Indicted before Essex assizes 5 June 1561; escaped to Flanders [PRO, SP 12/16, nos 49(i, ii), 65 (*CSPD 1547–80*, 173, 175. CRS, *Miscellanea*, i, 43, 50, 51–2. *CSP Rome*, i, 66]. Presumably the 'Langham', ex-monk of Westminster, reported in Belgium 8 Feb. 1570 [AGS, Stad. Leg. 583, cited Knowles, *Rel. Orders*, 443 n. 3, *ex. inf.* Aveling]. Probably writer of letter of devotional guidance to Mrs Brydeman, no date [PRO, SP 11/11, no. 68 (*CSPD Mary*, no. 968)].

Previous identification with *John* Langdon, OSB Canterbury Cathedral priory, born *c.* 1470, BD Oxford [Emden, 339–40. Greatrex, 218] appears to rest on Aveling's confusion of details in the Canterbury College list [noted above]. John was in any case surely too old to have been the fugitive of 1561 x 1570.

Legge [WAM 9327. Aveling, 275, no. 19]
Unidentified, unless meaning Figge, *q.v.*

Lowell [WAM 9327. Aveling, 276, no. 24]
Thomas Lovewell, OSB Westminster Abbey, ordained (Lond.) acolyte 24 Sept. 1519, deacon 24 Mar. 1520, priest 19 Dec. 1523. Student at Oxford 1525 x 36 [Pearce, 186. Emden, 336. Joseph, *Letter Book*: recipient of three letters, and mentioned *ter*; biographical note p. 279]. Signed surrender of Westminster Abbey 16 Jan. 1540 [PRO, E 322/260 (*LP*, xv, 69)]. Minor canon on new foundation of Westminster Cathedral, occ. 1541 x 1542 [BL, Add. MS 40061, f. 3v. PRO, LR 2/111, ff. 56, 59, 62, 65, 71. WAM 6478, f. 3v].

Lucie [WAM 9327. Aveling, 276, no. 23]
Not otherwise known.

Maldon, Reginald [Aveling, 278, no. 32]
Occ. as monk of Westminster 1556 [WAM 37718, f. 6v].

Discount Roger Maldon, OSB Bury St Edmunds Abbey; pension £6 13s 4d at dissolution 4 Nov. 1539 [*LP*, xiv, II, 462]. Aveling's suggestion; but the Bury monk is identified as vicar of Moulton, Suff., 1547, buried in neighbouring village of Kentford 1564 [G. Baskerville, 'Married clergy and pensioned religious in Norwich diocese, 1555' *EHR*, xlviii (1933), 223. B.G. Blackwood, *Tudor and Stuart Suffolk* (Lancaster 2001), 311].

Marshall, George [WAM 9327 (the only man there given a forename). Aveling, 276–7, no. 29]
Possibly George Marshall *alias* London, OSB Ramsey Abbey, Hunts; pension £5 at dissolution 22 Nov. 1539; still in receipt 1555 when living at 'Cokeley, Suffolk' [*recte* Cockley Cley, Norfolk]; unmarried, and good Catholic [*LP*, xiv, II, 565. Hodgett, 26, 32, 34. Baskerville (1933), 219–20 (there identified as rector of 'Cookley' and of Long Stanton St Michael, Cambs, 1535–57; but conflicts with statement in text that pensioner had no other living). But cf. Emden, 380, giving George Marshall (not a monk), BA Camb. 1531/2, rector of Cockley Cley, adm. 18 July 1554].

Treasurer of Westminster Abbey, occ. as signatory to receipt 1 Feb. 1559 [WAM 33204]. Payment to him as late treasurer of £677 11s 1½d by receiver-general 1560 [WAM 37927, f. 1v; 37929, f. 3].

Distinguish from George London, OSB Evesham Abbey, BD Oxford [Emden, 359. Joseph, *Letter Book*, 279 and *passim*].

Mathewe, Thomas *alias* **Ebden** [Aveling, 278, no. 46]
Of London diocese, ordained (Lond.) all minor orders and subdeacon 3 Apr. 1557 (Ebden), as of Westminster Abbey; deacon 18 dec. 1557 (Mathewe), presented as professed monk by cellarer of Westminster Abbey; priest 4 June 1557 (Mathewe *alias* Ebden), presented by sub-prior [Guildhall MS 9535/1, ff. 61v, 62, 67v, 74].

[**Mynyvere, Thomas** (Aveling, 279, no. 55)]
(Minyver, Mynever). Of Hereford diocese, ordained (Lond.) all minor orders 19 Sep. 1557 [Guildhall MS 9535/1, ff. 66, 66v]. Letters dimissory from Pole 12 Oct. 1557 [Reg. Pole (arch.), f. 57v]. Presented by abbot and convent of Westminster to bishop of London for all orders not yet received, with title of Westminster Abbey, 2 Dec. 1557 [WAM Reg. IV, f. 23]. Subdeacon 18 Dec. 1557, deacon 5 Mar. 1558, priest 12 Mar. 1558, all to title of Westminster Abbey [Guildhall MS 9535/1, ff. 67v, 69v, 71v]. Therefore not a monk. Reported as recusant priest in Herefordshire 1564, 1577 [*Camden Miscellany IX* (Camden Soc., new ser. liii, 1895), 19. PRO, SP 12/118, no. 7(1) (*CSPD 1547–80*, 564)].

Newte [WAM 9327. Aveling, 273, no. 8]
John Newte (Neot, Neote, Neott, Noett, Nootte, Notte, Nowot), OSB Glastonbury Abbey; scholar of Gloucester College, Oxford, occ. 1525 × 1539; BD adm. 3 Nov. 1535. At visitation July 1538 was criticized for his long absences at Oxford, and deficiency as preacher. Hosteler and 3rd prior at dissolution 22 × 28 Sept. 1539, when reported (as one of the three BDs 'but meanly learned' [*LP*, xiv, II, 206, 232. Wright, 256. Watkin (1941), 160, 161, 162. Watkin (1949), 450. Emden, 414.

Joseph, *Letter Book*: recipient of 11 letters, and mentioned *passim*; biographical note p. 280; BD *supplicat* printed p. 259]. Signed petition for restoration of Glastonbury temp. Mary [BL, Harleian MS 3881, f. 38v].

Sub-prior of Westminster Abbey, occ. 4 June 1558, presenting ordinands in St Paul's Cathedral [Guildhall MS 9535/1, f. 74].

Phagan [WAM 9327. Aveling, 276, no. 28]
John Phagan *alias* Piddesley (Phagon), OSB Glastonbury Abbey, occ. 1525; scholar of Gloucester College, Oxford, occ. 1530 [Emden, 447]. Probably junior priest 1525 [*Reg. Bath & Wells 1518–59*, 58]. At visitation July 1538 complained of lack of books in library [Watkin (1941), 162–3]. Archdeacon 1538/9. Pension £4 at dissolution, still in receipt 1553 [PRO, SC 6/Hen VIII/3115, m. 29; LR 6/104/1, m. 5 (*ex inf.* Dr P. Cunich). Watkin (1949), 449]. Signed petition for restoration of Glastonbury temp. Mary [BL, Harleian MS 3881, f. 38v].

Phillips [WAM 9327. Aveling, 274, no. 13]
Probably Hugh Phelype (Phillipe), OSB Ramsey Abbey, Hunts; pension £6 at dissolution 22 Nov. 1539. Chantry priest at Fenstanton, Hunts, occ. 1548; additional pension of £4 from chantry, occ. 1551; also rector of Grafham, Hunts, worth £16 [PRO, E 315/245, f. 64. *LP*, xiv, II, 565. Hodgett, 17, 26–7, 32–3, 35, 94].

Hugh Phillips (Phillippes, Phillyppes) as monk of Westminster occ. 1556/7 [WAM 18961]. Sexton at funeral of Anne of Cleves, Aug. 1557 [WAM 6398]. Cellarer by 18 Dec. 1557, presenting ordinands in St Paul's Cathedral [Guildhall MS 9535/1, ff. 67, 67v]. Many accounts and vouchers holograph or signed by [WAM 37786, 387797–9, 37810, 37813–14, 37822, 37828, 37839–42, 37913]. Also occ. WAM 37978, ff. 6v/9v. Order for Phillips, with Hunt and Langdon (*qq.v.*), to be sent from Canterbury *c.* Apr. 1561 [PRO, SP 12/16, no. 65 (*CSPD 1547–80*, 175). CRS, *Miscellanea*, i, 50]. Phillips still charged with Westminster tenement next to Richard Edon (*q.v.*) 1562/3 [WAM 38142, f. 2]. Presumably the Hugh Phillips, prisoner in the Gatehouse, who petitioned the dean of Westminster 30 June *s.a.*, asking for more of his household goods to be allowed him than the bailiff had delivered ('but a lyttell olde apparrell which will doo mee small pleasure to releyve my necessytye that I am dryven untoo through my long imprysonment') [WAM 38529 (signature not similar to that of WAM 6398, but both differ from those used by Phillips as cellarer, e.g. WAM 37797, 37798]. On 7 Feb. 1568 signed a deposition concerning the abbey's claim to funeral furnishings of Anne of Cleves (on occasion of the dean and chapter making similar claim) [WAM 6398]. On Easter Sunday [22 Apr.] 1576 said Mass in house of John Pinchin of Westminster, attorney, late of the Middle Temple; sent with others for trial 29 May [BL, Lansdowne MS 23, ff. 123, 123v. For Pinchin see *Reg. Middle Temple*, i, 20; CRS, *Miscellanea*, ii, 206; HMC, *Salisbury MSS*, iv. 267].

Presse, Thomas [Aveling, 279, no. 48]
Of London diocese, ordained (Lond.) to all minor orders 13 Mar. 1557, presented by sub-prior of Westminster Abbey [Guildhall MS 9535/1, ff. 59v, 60].
Possibly Thomas Price, priest, imprisoned in King's Bench 27 Apr. 1561 [Wainewright, 136–7, but not followed by Aveling].

Prince [WAM 9327. Aveling, 279, no. 32]
Edward Prince (Prynce), of Bristol diocese, ordained (Lond.) to all minor orders 13 Mar. 1557, presented by sub-prior of Westminster Abbey [Guildhall MS 9535/1, ff. 59v, 60]. Annuity of £4 granted by abbot and convent 3 Dec. 1558 [WAM 33198E, m. 5d; 37929, f. 1v; 37932, f. 2]. Lay vicar in the second collegiate church 1560–61 [WAM 33617, ff. 3, 3v; 37931, f. 3v; 37983, f. 2; 37984, f. 2v; 37978, f. 5v]. Annuity redeemed by dean and chapter for £3 in 1560/1 [WAM 33619, f. 4].

Redborne [WAM 9327. Aveling, 273, no. 4]
John Redborn died as monk of Westminster by Sep. 1557 [Bodleian MS Jones 9, f. 135]. Also distinguished in WAM 9327 by having a servant.
Probably (because of that servant) John Redborne (Radborn), OCist, abbot of Dore, blessed 24 Mar. 1529 [*Reg. Bothe*, 208]; pension occ. 1536 x 1553 [Dugdale, v, 533; also occ. in subsidy list, *LP*, xvi, app., 1]. There are suggestions that some of the Dore community remained together after the surrender of 1536, but Abbot Redborne is not mentioned [D. and A. Mathew, 'The survival of the dissolved monasteries in Wales', *Dublin Review*, clxxxiv (Jan.–June 1929), 70–81]. Knowles (*Rel. Orders*, iii, 426–7) accepted probability of identification.

Sebarte, Robert [Aveling, 278, no. 43].
Sigebert Buckley (Seaberrte), born Staffordshire *c.* 1517. Ordained (Lond.) to all minor orders and subdeacon 18 Dec. 1557, presented as professed monk by cellarer of Westminster Abbey; deacon 5 Mar. 1558; priest 4 June 1558, presented by sub-prior [Guildhall MS 9535/1, ff. 67, 67v, 69v, 74]. Imprisoned in Marshalsea 13 Sep. 1582. Convicted for recusancy 11 Mar. 1583 and 18 Feb. 1585 [CRS, *Recusants*, 30]. Still in Marshalsea 1586; further imprisoned Wisbech 1588–99, Framlingham 1599–1603; then Gatehouse, Westminster, where 21 Nov. 1607 he professed Robert Sadler and Edward Mayhew, from which act the Westminster succession is derived. Died at 'Cisson' near 'Wendham' [?Waxham], Norfolk, 22 Feb. 1610, buried at 'Pontshall' [?Portnall in Egham], Surrey [E.C. Butler, 'The Westminster succession', *Downside*

Review, xxiv (1905), 291–8 (with pedigree of succession at p. 295). Wainewright, 134. S. Marron, 'Dom Sigebert Buckley and his brethren', *Douai Magazine*, vii (1933), 130–8. R.H. Connolly, 'The Buckley affair', *Downside Review*, xlix (1931), 49–74 (printing all documents relating to transmission of community). *Memorials of Father Augustine Baker*, ed. P.J. McCann and R.H. Connolly (CRS, xxxiii, 1933) (incl. Buckley's recollections of life in Marian Westminster pp. 181–2). Knowles, *Rel. Orders*, iii, 443, 446–55. Lunn, 92–5 and *passim*].

Selbe [WAM 9327. Aveling, 276, no. 26]
Unidentified, unless meaning 'Sebarte' (above).

Strotforde [WAM 9327. Aveling, 276, no. 22]
Perhaps John Stretforthe, OSB Evesham Abbey to surrender 27 Jan. 1540, pension occ. 1540 x 1555 [*LP*, xv, 118 (p. 38). Dugdale, ii, 9 note c]. Not in Joseph, *Letter Book*.

Style, Henry [Aveling, 277, no. 40]
(Stile, Stils). Born Enfield, Middlesex, *c.* 1522. Trinity College, Cambridge, fellow before becoming monk of Westminster. Perhaps scholar of attached grammar school on foundation of Trinity 1546 [Trinity College, Senior Bursar's Muniments, Box 29, C.II.a, f. 2; but inconsistent with given age]. BA 1550/1, MA 1554 [*Grace Book Δ*, 69, 71, 94]. Received 4 marks in will of John Redman, master of Trinity and canon of Westminster (d. 1551) [PRO, PROB 11/40, f. 21v]. Gonville and Caius College, Cambridge, adm. 12 Feb. 1562, age 40 [*Biog. Hist. Caius*, i, 48, from Matriculation Book TUT/01/01, f. 6]. As an unnamed blind priest, received half of yearly pension from dean and chapter of Westminster 1560 (£6 13s 4d) [WAM 33617, f. 7]. This annuity was by chapter order 17 June 1570 redeemed for payment of £20 [*Acts*, ii, 45. WAM 33629, f. 6v; 33630, f. 17; 38495. Pearce (p. 192), citing this last reference, placed Style at the end of the pre-1540 monks, impossible in view of details now known]. To Douai by 18 May 1579 [*Douay Diaries*, 153]. Long resident at St Ghislain in Hainault, whose abbot Hazart paid tribute to his long suffering; from this source it is known he was blind from birth [Baron (F.A.F.T.) de Reiffenberg, *Monuments pour servir à l'histoire des provinces de Namur, de Hainault et de Luxembourg* (Brussels 1844–74), viii, 799–800].

Ulborne [WAM 9327. Aveling, 276, no. 27]
Replaced 'Slyngsbe' in WAM 9327; otherwise no record.

Vowell [WAM 9327. Aveling, 275, no. 14]
William Vowell, dies by Sep. 1558 [Bodleian MS Jones 9, f. 135] [Aveling suggested identity with man now given in Emden (pp. 211–12)

as William Fowell *alias* Fawell, BA Oxford 1519, possibly rector of Newton St Cyres, Devon 1548; died by Nov. 1557; no mention of monastic career].

Wayte, Richard [Aveling, 279, no. 35]
Of Coventry and Lichfield diocese, ordained (Lond.) to all minor orders and subdeacon 13 Mar. 1557, presented by sub-prior of Westminster Abbey; deacon 3 Apr. 1557, as of Westminster Abbey; priest 19 Sept. 1557 to title of £5 given by John Payton of Knolton [Guildhall MS 9535/1, ff. 59v, 60, 62v, 67].

White, Thomas [Aveling, 277, no. 39]
Died as monk of Westminster by Sep. 1557 [Bodleian MS Jones 9, f. 135].

Possibilities include T.W. *alias* Spalding, OSB, prior of Spalding, Lincs, pension occ. 1540 x 1553 [not in Hodgett]; T.W., OCist, Newenham, Devon; T.W., OSB Glastonbury Abbey [Dugdale, i, 9].

Wooseter [WAM 9327. Aveling, 275, no. 10]
Unidentified. Many names deriving from Worcester are noted by Aveling, but none is proposed; one possibility is Thomas Rusburye *alias* Worceyter, OSB Reading Abbey, dispensed to wear habit below secular dress 31 Oct. 1537 [*Fac. Off. Reg*, 110]

CHAPTER FOUR

The Clergy, the Church Courts and the Marian Restoration in Norwich

Ralph Houlbrooke

Norwich, second city of Tudor England, occupies a remarkably small space in general accounts of the Marian restoration. It witnessed the trials and burning of a number of heretics but only two Norwich people were executed. A far smaller proportion of the city's population suffered at the stake than in London. In her recent study of Tudor Norwich, principally based on a magnificent set of sixteenth-century mayor's court books, Professor Muriel McClendon attributed the city's relative freedom from persecution above all to its lay magistrates' determination to maintain internal unity, minimize the interference of external authorities in the city's affairs and practise a *de facto* toleration.[1] The mayor's court was concerned about threats to order posed by seditious words and religious quarrels. This account will draw on Professor MacClendon's work but concentrate on the role of the clergy and the Church courts, to whom belonged the prime responsibility for implementing and enforcing changes in worship and religious observance. The Norwich Church court records are far from complete. The act books of the consistory court cover only the period to October 1555, but transcriptions of acts in several Norwich heresy processes remain among John Foxe's papers. Much additional personal testimony is to be found in his justly famous *Acts and Monuments* and in *Aetiologia Roberti Watsoni* (1556), written by one of Norwich's leading Protestants.[2]

A striking aspect of the Marian interlude in Norwich is the capitulation or flight of her leading Protestant clergy. There was a substantial cluster of evangelical ministers active in and around the city during Edward's reign. Three of them stand out. The ex-Carmelite Dr

---

[1] M. McClendon, *The Quiet Reformation: Magistrates and the Emergence of Protestantism in Tudor Norwich* (Stanford, 1999), 183–90.

[2] Norfolk Record Office (NRO), DN/ACT 7/8; British Library (BL), Harley MS 421, ff. 140–217; J. Foxe, *Acts and Monuments*, ed. J. Pratt (8 vols, London, 1877); R. Watson, *Aetiologia Roberti Watsoni Angli, in qua explicatur, quare deprehensus annum unum et menses pene quatuor, propter Evangelium incarceratus fuit* ... (Emden, 1556).

John Barret, reader in theology at Norwich Cathedral, was presented by the Crown to the rectory of St Michael at Pleas in 1550.³ Robert Watson became a sort of lay minister of considerable theological learning. Resident in Norwich from *c.* 1528, he criticized a sermon by the conservative bishop William Rugge in 1539. Extraordinarily, Watson was presented by the Crown to a prebend in Norwich Cathedral in May 1549 even though a layman and twice married, but had resigned it by 26 September 1551. A 'preacher in those days of good Estimacion', he was chosen by Robert Kett's rebels to be one of their 'captains'.⁴ Thomas Rose was the most notorious of the three. Active during the 1530s, especially in Suffolk, he had had to flee abroad twice before arriving in the city in 1547. In December that year he was described as preaching at St Andrew's. Rose was presented to the benefice of West Ham in 1552.⁵ Of these three leading evangelicals, Barret and especially Rose aroused among the Norwich laity hostile and sometimes violent reactions which were reported to the mayor's court.⁶

At least five other men may be counted among the Norwich evangelicals of Edward's reign. John Salisbury, a former Benedictine monk suspected of heresy while studying at Oxford in the 1520s, had been dean of the cathedral since 1539. Henry King STP was appointed to a prebend there *c.* 1548.⁷ Of much lower status than these two were three parochial clergy whose radical activism got them into trouble. Thomas Coniers, priest of St Martin-at-Palace, was involved in September 1547 in the unauthorized removal of images from churches. In 1549 he conducted services in English at the request of the rebels led by Kett. William Stampe, rector of St Augustine's, helped break down the altar in his church in May 1549, and in 1551 conducted services with his cope turned inside out. Andrew Colby may have helped remove the altar from the church of St Michael Ber Street in 1549; at Christmas 1550, now at St Martin-at-Palace, he admitted to Communion a man from the more conservative St Stephen's parish, and in 1552 he refused

---

³ *ODNB, L & P Henry VIII*, ix. 76; NRO, DCN 29/3, f. 113r.

⁴ G.R. Elton, *Policy and Police: the Enforcement of the Reformation in the Age of Thomas Cromwell* (Cambridge, 1972), 138–9; NRO, Mayor's Court Book (MCB) 1534–40, f. 152; *CPR Edward VI, II, 1548–49*, 178; *IV, 1550–53*, 53; N. Sotherton, *The Commoyson in Norfolk 1549*, ed. S. Yaxley (Dereham, 1987), 7.

⁵ Foxe, *Acts and Monuments*, viii, 581–4; McClendon, *Quiet Reformation*, 117–18; *CPR Edward VI, IV, 1550–53*, 48.

⁶ McClendon, *Quiet Reformation*, 75–6, 118, 120, 133–4.

⁷ *ODNB*, l.191; J. Le Neve, *Fasti Ecclesiae Anglicanae 1541–1857, VII: Ely, Norwich, Westminster and Worcester Dioceses*, comp. J.M. Horn (London, 1992), 59; NRO, MCB 1540–9, 403–4; McClendon, *Quiet Reformation*, 116–17. The identity of the 'Doctor Parker' who criticized a sermon by King remains a mystery.

to observe the fast on the eve of the feast of St John the Baptist. St Andrew's, the Norwich parish where Protestantism was strongest, was served by Thomas Johnson. His removal in 1554 suggests that he should be counted among the Edwardian evangelicals, but he appears to have avoided controversy during Edward's reign.[8]

Some evangelical clergy beneficed outside Norwich were probably familiar figures in the city during Edward's reign. The future archbishop Matthew Parker, a native of the city, tried to dissuade Kett's followers from further rebellious actions in 1549. Gilbert Berkeley, the Elizabethan bishop of Bath and Wells, may have been the Gilbert Bartley who was incumbent of the lesser part of the rectory of Attleborough about 13 miles from Norwich and curate of St Peter Mancroft, the foremost church in the city after the cathedral. A third minister who visited Norwich was the ex-Carthusian Peter Wattes, rector of Winterton. He was probably the Peter Wattys or Wattes, late of Norwich and other places, chaplain of the earls of Oxford and Sussex, who was given a general pardon in July 1547.[9]

Edward VI's death on 6 July 1553 cut short the process of gathering subscriptions to the recently issued Forty-two Articles, already signed by many of the Norwich clergy. On 16 August, a month after Mary Tudor's triumph, the Privy Council dispatched an order prohibiting any preaching whatsoever within the diocese without the queen's special licence. Thomas Thirlby, bishop of Norwich since 1550, had rarely visited his diocese, but his chancellor John Fuller had brought much-needed vigour and efficiency to its administration. Thirlby was unusual among Edwardian episcopal appointees in his lack of evangelical credentials, and both men readily implemented Mary's policies.[10]

On 18 August the queen issued her famous proclamation willing all her subjects to live together in charity and disavowing any intention of compelling them to adopt Catholicism until such time as further order might be taken by common consent. It was probably this proclamation that one Norwich man, John Hallybred, was held to have disobeyed by

---

[8] NRO, NMCB 1540–9, 402–3; DN/ACT 6/7a, ff. 156v, 161v; DN/ACT 6/7b, f. 102v; DN/ACT 7/8, f. 177v; ANW 1/1 (unfoliated), returns to spring 1551 inquisition; F.W. Russell, *Kett's Rebellion in Norfolk* (London, 1859), 37–8; McClendon, *Quiet Reformation*, 116, 140–42.

[9] Russell, *Kett's Rebellion in Norfolk*, 62–6; G.R. Baskerville, 'Married Clergy and Pensioned Religious in Norwich Diocese, 1555, *EHR*, xlviii (1933), 53, 56; NRO, DN/DEP 5/5A, ff. 2–4; DN/DEP 6/5B, f. 169; *CPR, Edward VI, II, 1548–49*, 145.

[10] NRO, DN/SUN 3, ff. 13v–16v; *Acts of the Privy Council of England*, ed. J.R. Dasent (London, 1890–1907), iv, 321; T.F. Shirley, *Thomas Thirlby, Tudor Bishop* (London, 1964); R. Houlbrooke, *Church Courts and the People during the English Reformation 1520–1570* (Oxford, 1979), 42, 71, 79, 147.

'lewd talk' seemingly about Church services. The mayor and aldermen sent Hallybred to London some time before 31 October. The Privy Council returned him to Norwich with instructions to the mayor to have him make public acknowledgement of his offence. In the record of consistory court proceedings the first sign of impending change came on 23 September 1553 with a warning to Dominus Peter Valensem not to minister to the French and other travellers staying in Norwich.[11]

Mary's first parliament repealed the religious legislation of Edward's reign and restored the celebration of mass with effect from 20 December. On 10 January, the mayor's court bound over Thomas Johnson of St Andrew's in the sum of £20 for his good abearing towards the queen and her people. It was to the house in St Andrew's parish of his friend Thomas Beamonde, draper, that Robert Watson returned from London on 25 January. He was evidently a marked man from the moment of his arrival. On 1 February, before a substantial number of aldermen, he admitted that though he had attended matins and evensong in St Andrew's parish church, he had not come to Mass. Nor did he intend to do so, because his presence at Mass was against his conscience. He was committed to the gaol. He made his will on 10 February, appointing Thomas Beamonde one of his executors. He left his wife Elizabeth his house in the parish of St Martin-at-Palace. On 17 February the Privy Council instructed the mayor and aldermen to deliver him to the bishop's chancellor, to be kept incommunicado until he might be 'otherwise ordered' by the law. According to Watson's later account he was sent up to the Privy Council, but returned to Norwich after Stephen Gardiner had failed to win his submission.[12]

It is from the mayor's court book that we learn of the momentous acceptance of the Marian restoration by John Barret, Norwich's longest-serving evangelical minister. The precise reasons for his decision remain obscure. It was sufficiently prompt to enable him to avoid any formal abjuration. Indeed, his change of heart appeared genuine enough to warrant his being authorized to preach. He was nevertheless subject to surveillance. On 15 March the Duke of Norfolk wrote about Barret to the mayor and other leading Norwich men. He had received conflicting

---

[11] *Tudor Royal Proclamations*, ed. P.L. Hughes and J.F. Larkin (3 vols, New Haven and London, 1964–69), ii. 5–8; NRO, MCB 1549–55, 284, 291, 294; DN/ACT 7/8, f. 15r; McClendon, *Quiet Reformation*, 157–8. Professor McClendon believes that Hallybred was John Hallibread *alias* Stokes, prebendary of Norwich Cathedral. He was not, however, described as a priest, and during Edward's reign there had been at least one other John Halybred or Halybrede in Norwich, a minor office holder: see *An Index to Norwich City Officers 1453–1835*, ed. T. Hawes (Norfolk Record Society, lii, 1986), 75.

[12] NRO, MCB 1549–55, 310, 319; PRO, PCC will Chaynay, f. 247; *Acts of the Privy Council*, iv. 394; Watson, *Aetiologia*, ff. 7v–9r.

reports as to whether or not Barret had preached in accordance with the queen's commission and come to divine service. If he had not done so, Norfolk was greatly surprised that they had not told him during his recent visit to the city. He commanded them in the queen's name to advise Barret to have proper regard to himself and the discharge of his duty, and to imprison him if he failed. The mayor and his colleagues answered Norfolk's letter on 23 March, two days after receiving it. Barret had preached once in the Green Yard next to the cathedral, Norwich's main preaching site, but ill health prevented his preaching there as often as he had done in the past. Every Sunday and holy day he had declared God's word in his parish church, where he had also performed divine service and ministered according to statute. As the leading theologian in Norwich and probably the best-known and longest-serving preacher there, Barret was in an especially exposed position. By the same token, his speedy defection almost certainly had a devastating effect on the morale of the city's Protestants.[13]

Thomas Rose was eventually to be arrested in London. He had, however, kept his connection with Norwich. He was one of the already mentioned subscribers of the Forty-two Articles. In January 1554 Richard Sotherton, grocer and member of a well-known family in the city, was bound over by the mayor's court in the sum of £20 to appear to answer concerning certain words spoken in his house by a servant of Thomas Roose, almost certainly the evangelical minister, against Stephen Gardiner.[14]

Royal injunctions issued in March 1554 ordered among other things the removal of preachers and teachers who propagated evil corrupt doctrine, and the deprivation of all the married clergy. The proceedings against the married clergy of Norwich diocese began on 13 March. At least 15 clergy of Norwich and its cathedral were deprived or suspended. They included John Salisbury, Henry King, William Stampe and Andrew Colby. Stampe and Colby subsequently disappear from the record, though Stampe eventually returned to claim his old benefice after Elizabeth's accession. Gilbert Bartley lost his benefice at Attleborough, and (if he was indeed the same as Gilbert Berkeley) fled abroad. The injunctions allowed widowers and priests who made an open profession of chastity with the consent of their women to be restored to the ministry, though not in the same place. John Salisbury was one of those to benefit from relatively speedy restoration. Some Norwich men, however, including Andrew Colby, were among the several seculars who declared their unwillingness to be parted from their wives. (The ex-

---

[13] NRO, MCB 1549–55, 332–4.
[14] NRO, DN/SUN 3, f. 15v; MCB 1549–55, 314.

religious were given no choice, and automatically divorced.) Several men who admitted still living with their partners were assigned penance from 14 November 1554 onwards. Peter Wattes confessed on 12 January 1555 that he had continued to come to Norwich to frequent the company of Margaret Willoughby since their separation, and that he had known her carnally – though not, he insisted, on the occasion specified by his accusers. His offence was especially serious because he was an ex-religious. He had to perform penance in the cathedral, and was warned to shave off his beard with all speed. In April, Margaret, who confessed that she had had a child by Wattes, was told to do penance in the church of St Martin-at-Palace.[15]

Few proceedings against Norwich layfolk were recorded in the consistory court in 1554. Richard Greye of St Clement's parish had failed to receive the Eucharist the previous Easter. William Sedon of St Martin-at-Palace (until recently scene of Andrew Colby's ministry) had not been confessed before his Easter Communion. Both men were enjoined to make their confession and receive the sacrament; Greye was in addition ordered to abstain from meat for a day. Sedon was probably the grammar school usher of the same name. The schoolmaster, Mr Henry Birde, was subsequently to be a victim of persecution. Were these really the only cases in Norwich of failure in religious observance during the first months after the Marian restoration of the Mass? It seems more likely that the archdeaconry court, whose Marian records no longer survive, was the main agency involved in the work of enforcement. If so, however, it is difficult to explain why these particular cases should have reached the consistory court. Religion was involved in a few cases investigated by Norwich lay magistrates during 1554 and already described by Professor McClendon. A carpenter who claimed to have taken part in Wyatt's rebellion (possibly a stranger to the city) had allegedly expressed his determination never to hear Mass again. A Norwich man called William Mason was pilloried in May for devising unfitting songs against the Mass.[16]

---

[15] *Documentary Annals of the Reformed Church of England, 1546–1716*, ed. E. Cardwell (Oxford, 1844), i, 123–4; NRO, DN/ACT 7/8, ff. 71r–75r, 89v, 91r, 100, 116r, 168v, 174r, 183, 238v–239r; Baskerville, 'Married Clergy and Pensioned Religious', 49, 52, 53, 56; Le Neve, *Fasti VII*, comp. Horn, 42, 55; F. Blomefield and C. Parkin, *An Essay towards a Topographical History of the County of Norfolk* (2nd edn, London, 1805–10), iii, 618; J.F. Williams, 'The Married Clergy of the Marian Period', *Norfolk Archaeology*, xxxii (1961), 85–95; C.H. Garrett, *The Marian Exiles: a Study in the Origins of Elizabethan Puritanism* (Cambridge, 1938), 87; *DNB*, l, 191.

[16] NRO, DN/ACT 7/8, ff. 116, 123v; MCB 1549–55, p. 339; Foxe, *Acts and Monuments*, viii, appendix no. vi (unpaginated, from edition of 1563, 1677–79, 1681); McClendon, *Quiet Reformation*, 161–3, 164–5.

On 28 October 1554, following Thirlby's translation to Ely, John Hopton was consecrated bishop of Norwich, shortly before the restoration of papal supremacy and the medieval heresy statutes by Mary's third parliament. Hopton had been Mary's chaplain during the previous reign. He brought to Norwich a strong personal commitment to the task of Catholic restoration, shared by his chancellor, Michael Dunning.[17]

Measures to monitor and where necessary enforce in the parish churches of Norwich a process of restoration which should by now have been well under way began on 10 December 1554. Thomas Bemond, one of the churchwardens of St Andrew's, doubtless Robert Watson's friend Thomas Beamonde, was warned to provide ornaments and other necessaries with all speed. The same day Thomas Johnson, curate there, was given a week's notice to cease his ministry in the parish. The following 4 February, Bemond, this time in company with his colleague John Sutterton, was warned under threat of excommunication to obliterate the passages from scripture written on the walls and elsewhere in St Andrew's. Sutterton, or a man of that name, received the same warning in respect of St Clement's. Proceedings had begun with the parish where Protestant sentiment had long been strongest. The churchwardens of 17 other parishes were summoned to appear on 6 February. Those of five of the parishes in question failed to do so, incurring excommunication. (They included Colby's parish of St Martin at the Palace Gates, and Barret's St Michael at Pleas.) Five of the remainder (including the adjacent wealthy parishes of St Stephen's and St Peter Mancroft) reported that they had all things necessary for Catholic worship. The seven others lacked one or more essential item: among the few actually specified were a holy water stoup, a crucifix and books. In several cases it is not clear whether or not texts were painted on the church walls. Some churches, however, which had the full complement of books and ornaments (including St Stephen's and St Peter Mancroft) still had such texts on their walls, while others that lacked some necessaries had never had them.[18]

Decisive action against the most prominent Norwich Protestants took place in 1555. On 15 January Henry King (an ex-religious already compulsorily divorced) failed to appear in the consistory court to answer certain articles concerning the health of his soul. His name nevertheless disappears from the act book after a further non-appearance on 4 February. His institution to the rectory of Winterton in

---

[17] *ODNB*; C.H. and T. Cooper, *Athenae Cantabrigienses* (3 vols, Cambridge, 1858–1913), i, 203; Foxe, *Acts and Monuments*, vii, 372.
[18] NRO, DN/ACT 7/8, ff. 177v, 199r, 203r–204r.

succession to the deprived Peter Wattes points to his subsequent conformity, though his former wife Elizabeth Hill and her daughter were the principal beneficiaries of the will he made in October 1557.[19]

Much more important was the case of Robert Watson. After a year in prison, he was at last permitted to write to his old friend John Barret. He had known what Barret had thought about transubstantiation for 20 years, Watson told him in his letter of 20 February 1555: if Barret had finally accepted that doctrine which he had so long rejected, Watson undertook to embrace it if it agreed with the scriptures or the writings of the fathers. In his answer, dated 22 March, Barret insisted that salvation was only to be found in the Catholic Church. Pure doctrine was to be sought in a tradition going back to the Apostles' time, and what the Catholic Church had believed and taught. The authority of the Church was to be preferred to the opinions of the most learned Protestants. Watson in his rejoinder of 28 March appealed to the authority of Christ, the Prophets, the Apostles and the most ancient fathers. He took his stand on the words of Lactantius: '*Sola catholica Ecclesia est, quae verum Dei cultum retinet.*' The religion that Barret had professed for over five years had been in many respects contradictory to that of the Church that he now claimed to be Catholic. If he really regretted his defection, then Barret should now render public account, and bring back to the path of truth those whom he had misled. Watson repeatedly expressed his surprise at Barret's change of opinion. Barret had felt revulsion against the doctrine of transubstantiation for over 20 years, and for five had openly opposed it. (Watson later described his old friend as having adhered to Luther for over 15 years and then, having repudiated Luther, joined 'us' – clearly those who held reformed Eucharistic beliefs.) He had, Watson concluded, conformed through fear. The following day Barret joined the rest of Watson's friends in seeking his release. Watson also engaged in argument about the real presence with John Christopherson, since April 1554 dean of Norwich in succession to John Salisbury. Eventually, however, Christopherson refused to continue their discussions. Instead, Watson was now presented with an unequivocal statement of the doctrine of transubstantiation for his subscription. After three refusals he was told that all was up with him unless he signed. He did so, but with a careful qualification: he assented to the words of the statement in so far as they rested on the Word of God and in the sense in which they were understood by the Catholic Church and the holy fathers.[20]

---

[19] NRO, DN/ACT 7/8, ff. 191v, 196v; NCC wills Hustinges, ff. 245v–246v; Blomefield, *Norfolk*, iii, 666.

[20] Watson, *Aetiologia*, ff. 10r–30r, 37v–52r.

After a further five weeks, on a rumour of the queen's grave danger or even death in childbirth, Watson was, according to his own account, summoned before Bishop Hopton and dismissed. This would have been in the late spring of 1555. Enemies of the Gospel, seeing him on the streets, were angry that a heretic should have escaped without penance. On the sixth day, hearing that worse would be in store for him if the queen had a happy outcome, he left for Cambridge to see his son. Six miles out he encountered John Young, 'a fierce enemy of Christ', on his way to preach in Norwich, but passed by, hiding his face. (Young was presumably the erstwhile critic of Martin Bucer who was appointed regius professor of divinity in 1555.) When Young saw Watson's subscription he was furious, but nevertheless read it in the church of St Peter Mancroft the following Monday, insisting that the statement Watson had subscribed did indeed agree with the Word of God and the sense of the fathers and the Catholic Church, but completely demolished the doctrine he had previously taught. Watson fled abroad. His *Aetiologia*, basis for the above account of his imprisonment and release, completed in November 1555, was published at Emden in 1556. Seemingly designed for an audience of learned exiles, it is most unlikely to have had much impact in Norwich. He had died by 30 June 1559, when his will was proved.[21]

Thomas Rose, unlike Watson, was arrested in London – where he had been conducting a clandestine ministry – on 1 January 1555, but sent to Norwich after preliminary examination. Two records of the subsequent proceedings survive: the official acts of court and Rose's own much fuller account, published by John Foxe. According to Rose, he was first informally examined by Bishop Hopton on 5 June. Rose claimed to have preached doctrine authorized by Henry VIII and Edward VI, and to have kept silent since the change in the law. He would obey all laws set forth 'for the establishment of Christ's true religion … according to the faith and doctrine of the holy patriarchs and prophets, Jesus Christ, and his holy apostles, with the faithful fathers of Christ's primitive church'. On 7 June, examined within the Lady Chapel of Norwich Cathedral by the chancellor, presumably Michael Dunning, who took the leading role, as well as Hopton, Rose, according to his own account, accepted that auricular confession was permissible under certain circumstances, but insisted that compulsory detailed confession once a year was not of God, and was without scriptural foundation. He admitted that he had preached that the 'real, natural, and substantial presence of Christ' was

---

[21] Ibid., ff. 52v–56r; *DNB*, lxiii, 379; D. Loades, *Mary Tudor: A Life* (Oxford, 1989), 248–51; A. Pettegree, *Marian Protestantism: Six Studies* (Aldershot, 1996), 16, 32, 169, 186–7; PCC will Chaynay, f. 247.

not in the sacrament of the altar. When Christ had said 'This is my body', he had spoken figuratively, as in other places in scripture. Rose appealed to Justin Martyr (*c.* 100–*c.* 165), 'one of the ancientest writers that ever wrote upon the sacraments', in support of his assertion that bread and wine remained in them. According to the acts of court, Rose accepted the necessity of at least annual confession to a 'ghostly father', but admitted that he had preached, at the cross in the Green Yard in Norwich, that the true and natural body and blood of Christ were not present in the Eucharist. He would defend what he had taught as long as he lived. Between this and his next examination, Rose had further discussions with John Barret and two unnamed chaplains of Hopton. All these agreed, relying on what they took to be St Augustine's support for transubstantiation. This did not entail, the chaplains protested, the 'gross doctrine' of the presence of 'flesh, blood, bones, hair, nails'. Christ's ' "visible, palpable, or circumscriptable body" ' was always at the Father's right hand. In the sacrament it was invisible, and could neither be felt, seen nor occupy any place, but was there by the omnipotency of God's Word. Rose saw an opportunity here. During his final appearance before Hopton, he rehearsed what the chaplains had said:

> ... and so I granted a presence, but not as they supposed. For only I said, that Christ, after the words pronounced, is present in the lawful use and right distribution of his holy supper; which thing I never denied, or any godly man that ever I heard of.

He had never intended this to be a recantation, he later insisted. But Hopton was about to set off on visitation; fearing that Mary had miscarried in childbirth, and apprehensive of 'some stir' if Rose were burned, the diocesan authorities were glad to be rid of him 'so that by any colourable means for their own discharge it might be'.[22]

According to the act book, Rose utterly renounced his error, saying 'That I from the botompe of my hart do confesse that aftre the wordes of consecrac[i]on spoken by the m[in]istre that in the blyssed Sacrament of thaltar Christ the secunde person is really p[rese]nt.' The confession is subscribed with his name. The exceptional and (surprising) vagueness of the formula, together with the use of the word 'minister' rather than 'priest' give Rose's account some credibility. A tacit concession had been made in order to win the subscription of the man who had been Norwich's most controversial evangelical preacher. It is nevertheless difficult to avoid the conclusion

---

[22] This and preceding quotes, Foxe, *Acts and Monuments*, viii, 584–9; NRO, DN/ACT 7/8, f. 263r.

that Rose had been emasculated by this appearance of public recantation. He soon fled overseas.[23]

Peter Wattes subscribed a far fuller and more precise confession when he appeared before Hopton in his palace on 1 September. The ceremonies used within the Church of England were good; he allowed and would observe them. He specifically mentioned holy bread and holy water (whose meaning he explained), palms, ashes and creeping to and following the cross. Invocation and prayer to saints were laudable; he endorsed the doctrine written by St Jerome against Vigilantius as declared by Hopton, and allowed all other ceremonies used in the Catholic Church. He allowed praying for the dead and all other prayers used in the mass. In the sacrament of the altar after the words of consecration there remained only the natural and real body of Christ and no substance of bread or wine; by the omnipotence of God's Word the bread and wine were transubstantiated into the body and blood of Jesus Christ. Finally, he agreed that the Pope was by the Word of God supreme head of Christ's Church on earth; he would both privately and openly publish this doctrine. Wattes's capitulation could scarcely have been more explicit.[24]

The flight or surrender of Norwich's leading Protestant clergy makes more understandable the relative paucity of instances of recorded lay nonconformity in the city during Mary's reign. In the first such case to reach the consistory court after the restoration of the heresy statutes, Robert Carvell, probably a worsted weaver of St Margaret's parish, was charged with bearing an unhallowed candle on Candlemas Day (2 February) 1555, his wife Matilda with carrying no candle at all. Allegedly they would not hold up their hands at the elevation of the Sacrament. Both were ordered to purge themselves of suspicion of the offence with five hands – a middling number which indicates that the alleged delicts were not considered exceptionally grave. Apparently more serious than Carvell's case was that of William Pykeringe, barber, who on 14 October 1555 was interrogated about his opinions concerning the ceremonies of the Church and the sacrament of the Eucharist. He thought and believed as the Church taught, he answered, and he believed that the body and blood of Christ were present after the consecration. During the metropolitical visitation of 1556, on 1 May, a Robert Barwyk of Norwich appeared before Michael Dunning after failing to receive the sacrament of the altar for two or three years. Somewhat surprisingly, he escaped with a warning to prepare himself to receive it at once.[25]

---

[23] Ibid, f. 267r; Foxe, *Acts and Monuments*, viii, 590.
[24] NRO, DN/ACT 7/8, f. 293v.
[25] Ibid., ff. 204r, 321v; NRO, NCC will Goldingham 201; DN/ORR 1(b), f. 14r.

The most intense phase of persecution in Norwich occurred between February and July 1557, when no fewer than five heretics were condemned to death there. Three of them, however – William Carman of Hingham, Richard Crashfield of Wymondham and Simon Miller of Middleton near King's Lynn – came from outside the city. Simon Miller, unlike Carman and Crashfield, was condemned because of his actions in Norwich. A merchant, according to Foxe's account, he went among people just coming out of a church service and asked them 'where he might go to have the communion'. He seems to have imagined that a clandestine celebration of the Protestant rite would be taking place in the city, though there is no other evidence of such a service. His bold enquiry caused great surprise, and an unnamed Catholic took him before Michael Dunning. During his examination, his confession of faith was noticed, poking out of his shoe; he affirmed it and was imprisoned. He was condemned in May for his insistence that the body of Christ was in the sacrament of the altar by faith alone.[26]

Two Norwich women went to the stake in 1557. The signification of the condemnation of Elizabeth, wife of John Cooper or Cowpre, pewterer, of St Andrew's parish, is dated 9 May, and she was burned together with Simon Miller about 13 July. Cicely Ormes, wife of Edmund Ormes, worsted weaver of St Lawrence's parish, was arrested at the execution of Miller and Cooper, condemned on 23 July and burned two months later. There were similarities between the two women's patterns of behaviour. Foxe wrote that both had 'recanted' earlier. Ormes 'did for a twelvemonth before she was taken, recant'. No record of any previous judicial recantation by either woman survives. Both repudiated their previous recantation or conformity in the most dramatic and public fashion. Elizabeth Cooper came into St Andrew's church in service time in order to do so, provoking her immediate arrest. At the execution of Miller and Cooper, Cicely Ormes announced that she would 'pledge them of the same cup that they drank on'. She had already had a letter prepared to give to the chancellor, 'to let him know that she repented her recantation from the bottom of her heart', but she was arrested before she could show it. The sentence against Cooper recorded her sorrow at having received the sacrament of the altar the previous Easter, as well as her denial of the presence of the true and natural body of Christ in the sacrament after the consecration. Ormes went to the stake insisting that she believed herself to be saved by the death and passion of Christ, not by her own action in offering herself to death for the Lord's cause.[27]

---

[26] PRO, C 85/141/27, 28, 30; Foxe, *Acts and Monuments*, viii, 380–81; BL, Harley MS 421, ff. 155v–156r.
[27] PRO, C 85/141/30, 33; Foxe, *Acts and Monuments*, viii, 380–81, 427–9; BL, Harley MS 421, ff. 152r–153r; *Norwich City Officers*, ed. Hawes, 114.

Another inhabitant of Norwich, Thomas Wolman, grocer, of St Andrew's parish allegedly declared that William Carman (burned in March 1557) died well 'for that he ded affirme and saye that he ded beleve that Christ was not p[rese]nt in the Sacrament of thaltar'. Wolman had also said to one George Redman 'that the sacrament shall be his god and not myn'. Wolman was charged with the above words as well as with disbelief in papal supremacy, with believing and affirming that holy bread, holy water, ashes, palms and other ceremonies were not good and laudable means of encouraging devotion, and with believing and affirming that the true and natural body of Christ was not present after the words of consecration spoken by the priest. Wolman solemnly abjured his heresies, and confessed that the sacrament of the altar after the words of consecration contained Christ's natural and real body and no substance of bread and wine. Of all the Norwich layfolk who were in trouble on account of religion during Mary's reign, Wolman enjoyed the highest social status. More Norwich mayors came from the ranks of the grocers than from any other occupation during the period 1547–1603. A man of the same name had been common councillor for Wymer great ward from 1537 to 1542, and again from 1546 to 1551. Wolman had made his will on 4 June 1553, including a very strong statement of his belief that he would have remission of his sins and resurrection of his body and soul by Christ's merits and the virtue of his passion and resurrection. Among pious bequests totalling over £16, mainly to the sick, the poor and prisoners, was one of 20 shillings towards the fabric of St Andrew's church. The will was proved on 15 April 1559.[28]

John Foxe mentioned a few residents of Norwich of whose persecution no other record survives. One, 'father Moore of Norwich worsted wever', was put in the stocks with a paper on his head. William Hammon, shoemaker, who would not observe the ceremonies of the Church or believe in the sacrament of the altar, had to leave the city with his wife. Henry Birde, husband of Alice, daughter of Joan Morrant, widow, 'a very nurse to al good people', was also driven out 'to seke the hyding of his heade in straunge places'. Later on, Foxe again mentioned 'a scholemaister at Norwich, maister Henry Bird before touched'. Joan had been the wife of William, a grocer (died *c.* 1544). The will she made in September 1558 (proved in February 1559) is prefaced with a firm

---

[28] BL, Harley MS 421, f. 151r, 154r–v; *Norwich City Officers*, ed. Hawes, xviii, 168; *Depositions taken before the Mayor & Aldermen of Norwich, 1549–1667; Extracts from the Court Books of the City of Norwich, 1666–1668*, ed. W. Rye (Norwich, 1905), 26 (debtor of Thomas Wolman's implied that he was a false knave and a rich man), 36, 37; NRO, NCC will Colman, ff. 160r–161v.

declaration of her belief in her salvation through Christ's death and merits. She left 20 shillings to be distributed among the neediest poor of Stoke by Nayland (Suffolk), and further bequests to her brother's children James, Anne and Margery Abbes. A James Abbes of Stoke by Nayland had been among the first Protestants to be burnt in the diocese in 1555. She named Henry Birde one of her two executors. Either Birde's withdrawal from Norwich was of short duration or not seen as a serious hindrance to his administration of his mother-in-law's estate. Foxe's description of Joan, together with her will, allow us to glimpse the Marian Protestant underground in Norwich. Birde had become divinity lecturer in Norwich Cathedral by 1568. John Parkhurst, first Elizabethan bishop of Norwich, named him one of his executors.[29]

Foremost among those who enforced Marian policies in Norwich were John Hopton and his chancellor Michael Dunning. In Foxe's opinion they were unequalled 'for straitness and cruel tormenting the bodies of the saints', for which he especially blamed Dunning. Their aim was nevertheless to bring about the conformity, rather than the deaths, of those accused of heresy. Each burning represented the failure of their efforts at persuasion. Foxe's detailed accounts of the examinations of heretics by Hopton and Dunning show their readiness to argue with heretics, sometimes patiently and at length. Dunning, far from being a searching inquisitor, sometimes showed himself prepared to accept minimal outward conformity. Faced with Cicely Ormes, Dunning offered her, according to Foxe's own account, 'if she would go to the church and keep her tongue, she should be at liberty, and believe as she would'. He was 'loth to condemn her, considering that she was an ignorant, unlearned, and foolish woman'.[30]

Miles Spenser served as chancellor alongside Dunning. Originally appointed by Bishop Nykke (died 1535), he was retained in office by Nykke's successors, even though they introduced appointees of their own, perhaps because he had a patent for life. Last dean of the secular college of St Mary in the Fields in Norwich, Spenser purchased the college on its dissolution. His wealth, experience and influence, especially over the consistory court staff, made Spenser one of the most powerful churchmen in the city. Despite his natural conservatism, he readily conformed to every successive change in religious policy. In 1553

---

[29] Foxe, *Acts and Monuments*, vii, 328; viii, appendix no. vi (unpaginated, from edition of 1563, pp. 1677–9, 1681); NRO, NCC wills Hyll, ff. 181–3, Veysye, ff. 316v–319v ; DCN 47/1, ff. 395–6; *The Letter Book of John Parkhurst Bishop of Norwich*, ed. R.A. Houlbrooke (Norfolk Record Society, xliii, 1974 and 1975), 53, 214–15.

[30] Foxe, *Acts and Monuments*, vii, 328, 372; viii, 146, 398–400, 427–8.

he headed the list of subscribers to the Forty-two Articles. He presided over proceedings against heretics in Suffolk, but in Norwich his role seems to have been a comparatively restricted one. Thomas Wolman came before him in 1557, and according to Foxe he was one of those who drove William Hammon out of Norwich.[31]

Dunning's sentence against Elizabeth Cooper records that he condemned her *'cum consilio et Judicio Jurisperitorum et sacrarum litterarum professorum'*. One of these experts is likely to have been Thomas Briges or Briggs STB, who was present at the sentence passed against Roger Coo of Long Melford, shearman, in August 1555. Briggs was probably the 'Dr Brydges' who 'sat in judgement' on Cicely Ormes, and who engaged in an argument with Richard Crashfield about the proper interpretation of some passages of scripture. As rector of Eccles by Wilby, Norfolk, Briggs reportedly continued to celebrate Mass and other services according to the Use of Sarum after the introduction of the first Book of Common Prayer in 1549. Eccles lies almost next to Kenninghall, the Lady Mary's principal East Anglian residence under Edward VI. Briggs left a close to Kenninghall vicarage in his very conservative will, made in August 1558 and proved the following January, as well as bequests of vestments or money to the churches of Wicklewood, Crownthorpe, Hethel and Eccles. He named Bishop Hopton one of his two executors. A colleague to whom, in Foxe's account, 'Brydges' turned for help after abortive attempts to convince Richard Crashfield was 'Dr Pore'. 'Pore' may well have been John Pory, vicar of St Stephen's church in Norwich, who gained his doctorate in divinity and was elected master of Corpus Christi College in Cambridge in 1557, the year of Crashfield's execution.[32]

The star performer in Hopton's team of persuaders was, however, John Barret, who, after his still mysterious decision to conform, became an active participant in efforts to win over his Protestant former colleagues. Barret compiled a collection of passages from leading Protestant writers on a wide range of Christian doctrines, including those whose interpretation lay at the heart of Reformation disputes, endeavouring to show where those writers were in agreement with the dogmas of the Church and the truly Catholic and more ancient fathers.

---

[31] R.A. Houlbrooke, 'Church Courts and People in the Diocese of Norwich, 1519–1570' (University of Oxford DPhil thesis, 1970), 102–4; Blomefield, *Norfolk*, iv, 171, 182–3; NRO, DN/SUN 3, f. 13v; BL, MS Harley 421, f. 151; Foxe, *Acts and Monuments*, viii, 493–6 and appendix vi (unpaginated).

[32] BL, MS Harley 421, f. 152v; Foxe, *Acts and Monuments*, viii, 398–400, 428; Blomefield, *Norfolk*, i, 410; NRO, DN/ACT 7/8, ff. 264, 293r; C/S 3, 1549; NCC wills Ingold ff. 296r–297v; *DNB*, xlvi, 200–201.

Calvin is the most frequently cited author, followed by Bullinger and Musculus: the overwhelming majority of the passages come from the works of reformed theologians. Robert Watson believed that Barret held a reformed conception of the Eucharist during Edward's reign. It is unclear exactly when his collection was assembled. The fruit of extensive study, it presumably took a long time to compile. Whatever its original purpose, indirect evidence that this unusual enterprise was used to support arguments to win over reformed Protestants is to be found in Rose's account of his arguments with two of Hopton's chaplains. They undertook to confirm their doctrine of the Eucharistic presence 'with Martin Luther, Melancthon, Bucer and Calvin'. The most significant names on this list are the last two. Rose afterwards talked with Barret, whom he found 'of the same judgment in that behalf'. It is likely that the two chaplains took their cue from Barret rather than the other way round. 'Father Rose, you may be a worthy instrument in God's church', said Hopton after Rose's seeming submission, no doubt in the ill-founded hope that Rose would follow Barret's example. The bishop valued Barret's efforts sufficiently highly to collate him to a prebend in Norwich Cathedral in 1558.[33]

John Christopherson, dean of Norwich Cathedral 1554–57, argued about the real presence with Robert Watson, according to the latter's account, and was the first witness to sign Watson's qualified acceptance of transubstantiation. One other cathedral clergyman, Thomas Tedman STP, attracted unfavourable Protestant comment through his exposition of Catholic doctrine. As early as November 1553, a grocer's servant remarked that 'doctor Tedenham', after lying in his den for seven years had now preached, 'and for his prechyng had like to have been pullyd out of the pulpyt'. Robert Watson made a hostile reference to Tedman's account of the Mass as a propitiatory sacrifice available for the dead as well as the living. Tedman was present at Thomas Rose's confession of the real presence. His very full and interesting will, written with his own hand and dated 12 August 1557, begins with a thoroughly conservative preamble, and contains very large charitable legacies as well as substantial bequests (including a rich variety of vestments) to the cathedral and his own church of Acle. Tedman also made an impressively lavish, and in the Marian

---

[33] Cambridge, Corpus Christi College, MS 124, 'Iohannis Barret collectanea quaedam in communes locos digesta ex eruditioribus celebrioribusque Germanorum protestantium scriptoribus, quibus non modo pie et orthodoxe in dogmatibus ecclesiasticis sentire sed et cum vere catholicis ac antiquioribus sanctis patribus consentire visi sunt'; Foxe, *Acts and Monuments*, viii, 587–8, 589; *CPR Philip and Mary, III, 1555–57*, 359; Blomefield, *Norfolk*, iii, 663.

context exceptional, investment in the intercessory masses whose efficacy he had defended.³⁴

Besides those whose active participation in the work of exposition and persuasion is well documented, there were in Norwich other men of reliable orthodoxy whose role remains more shadowy. One of the pensioned clergy of the diocese judged 'honest and Catholic' men in 1555 was Edmund Harcocke BD, ex-prior of the Norwich Dominicans, who had been in trouble in 1535 for seeming to challenge the royal supremacy. Licensed to preach by Queen Mary, the former Black Friar became in 1556 rector of St Michael in Coslany.³⁵ Altogether, Hopton's efforts in Norwich were supported by a team of preachers and theologians who in numbers, expertise and commitment to their cause probably matched their Edwardian predecessors, and almost certainly surpassed the men present in Norwich during the first few years of Elizabeth's reign.

The clergy bore the chief responsibility for preaching and persuasion. The Church courts, however, key elements in the machinery of enforcement, were largely run by laymen, who served as proctors, scribes and registrars. The volume of business dealt with by the central administration of the vast diocese of Norwich helped make the fortunes of the men who ran it. Some of them became prominent in the government of the city itself. William Mingay, Alexander Mather and John Atkyns were all notaries involved in diocesan administration who also served as aldermen. Mingay (1554–55) and Atkyns (1548–49) were sheriffs. Mingay was mayor in 1561–62, and Mather sat as MP for Norwich in Edward's second parliament and Mary's third. All three took part in proceedings against religious nonconformists. Mather warned Watson that all would be up with him unless he subscribed the doctrine of transubstantiation, and witnessed his subscription. He made a strongly conservative will in 1555. Both Mather and Mingay named their 'singular good friend' Miles Spenser overseer of their wills; Mather referred to him as his 'master'.³⁶

Besides the aldermen professionally involved in the work of the consistory court, two others were singled out as persecutors by Foxe or

---

³⁴ ODNB; Watson, Aetiologia, ff. 36v–50v, 52r; NRO, MCB 1549–55, 295; DN/ACT 7/8, ff. 267r, 305; NCC wills Hustinges, ff. 153r–160v.

³⁵ Baskerville, 'Married Clergy and Pensioned Religious', 219; McClendon, *Quiet Reformation*, 80–81, for Harcocke's troubles under Henry VIII.

³⁶ Houlbrooke, 'Church Courts and People', 108, 110; *Norwich City Officers*, ed. Hawes, 6, 100, 107; *The History of Parliament. The House of Commons 1509–1558*, ed. S.T. Bindoff (3 vols, London, 1982), ii, 587–8; NRO, DN/ACT 7/8, ff. 291r, 293r; NCC wills Marten, ff. 187–9; PRO, PCC wills 25 Mellershe; Watson, Aetiologia, ff. 13v–14r, 51r, 52r; Foxe, *Acts and Monuments*, viii, 146 and appendix vi (unpaginated).

Watson: Thomas Codde and Thomas Marsham. Watson characterized Codde and Marsham as enemies of the Gospel who did their best to find him at the time of his flight from Norwich in 1555. Foxe named Marsham as one of those who called for the arrest of Elizabeth Cooper. Codde, who served for 20 years as an alderman, is perhaps best remembered for the fact that Kett's rebellion broke out during his first mayoralty. Elected one of the rebels' governors, Codde made ineffectual efforts to curb their activities. The experience probably marked him deeply, and may have strengthened his dislike of anything that smacked of nonconformity or subversion. Codde's conservatism was, however, seemingly notorious even before the rebellion, for a cordwainer called Peter Lynage got into trouble for allegedly describing him as a popish knave on the very day of his election as mayor. Marsham finally became mayor in 1554, when he was a candidate for the fourth time, and was the first named witness of the formal examination and abjuration of Thomas Rose in June 1555. Both Codde and Marsham made strongly conservative wills before they were carried off by the great epidemic of 1558–59. Two more obscure figures mentioned by Foxe were 'one Bacon' of St Andrew's parish, who called for Elizabeth Cooper's arrest, and 'maister Head', one of William Hammon's persecutors. Bacon may have been John, councillor for Wymer great ward. Head was probably Richard Head or Hedde, sheriff in 1560 and alderman for St Stephen's ward, 1562–68, a benefactor of St Stephen's parish, where some consistory court lawyers and notaries lived.[37]

In at least one case involvement in the arrests and executions of heretics was allegedly distasteful to the individual concerned. It was Thomas Sotherton's misfortune to be sheriff in 1556–57. Foxe claimed that he was forced against his conscience to arrest Elizabeth Cooper by the remonstrations of Marsham and Bacon. He was loath to do so because they had once been servants in the same house, 'and the more for the gospel's sake'. When William Carman was burned, the first heretic to be executed during Sotherton's shrievalty, the writ *de heretico comburendo* was, exceptionally, copied into the mayor's court book. Did an unwilling Sotherton demand this unusual registration? On 20 March, after the execution, a note was written in the book that Sotherton had delivered into court a Bible, a testament and three psalters of Carman that remained in the old council house. Carman had

---

[37] Watson, *Aetiologia*, f. 55v; Foxe, *Acts and Monuments*, viii, 381, 777 and appendix vi (unpaginated); *Norwich City Officers*, ed. Hawes, 8, 40, 80, 103; Sotherton, *Commoyson*, 7–11, 19–20; McClendon, *Quiet Reformation*, 140; NRO, DN/ACT 7/8, ff. 265r, 267r; NCC wills Colman, f. 431, Hustinges, f. 150, Ponder, f. 54; Blomefield, *Norfolk*, iv. 164.

presumably had them with him at the time of his arrest. The diocesan authorities would no doubt have held that any such materials should be delivered to them. Sotherton may have been trying to ensure their survival.[38]

Religious developments in Norwich, and particularly nonconformity or discord, attracted the attention of local magnates and gentry throughout the Reformation. The local gentleman most closely connected with the city was John Corbet Esq. of Sprowston, son of a Norwich brazier, but himself a successful lawyer who became steward of the sheriff's court (1540–47), recorder (1547–50) and a burgess for the city in Mary's third parliament. An extensive purchaser of Church lands, including his own seat at Sprowston, Corbet nevertheless provided for Masses for his own and his parents' souls in a will dated 26 December 1558, over a month after Elizabeth's accession. He was a dependant of the notoriously conservative third duke of Norfolk. Corbet had been responsible for the arrest of Dorothy, John Bale's wife, during her visit to the city in 1545, and in 1557, according to Foxe, he personally arrested Cicely Ormes after she had pledged Miller and Cooper at their execution. Another gentleman present with Corbet at Rose's recantation in June 1555 was Sir John Shelton, a loyal supporter of Mary, who as sheriff of Norfolk and Suffolk in 1555 had allegedly treated Rowland Taylor with needless brutality at his execution.[39]

Two other more important laymen sought to win Rose over, according to his account. Neither appears in the official record of proceedings. Henry Radcliffe, second earl of Sussex, was the foremost magnate in Norfolk between the death of the third duke of Norfolk in August 1554 and his own death in February 1557. As Lord Fitzwater, Radcliffe had in 1539 interceded with Thomas Cromwell on behalf of Robert Watson after investigating the latter's confrontation with Bishop Rugge. Later in Henry's reign, by then earl of Sussex, Radcliffe had sheltered Rose and his wife and child in his house at Attleborough until this support for a heretic was 'blazed abroad'. Peter Wattes was possibly chaplain to Sussex around that time. Sussex's will, made only just over a month after Rose's submission, includes a very strong affirmation of faith in the remission of his sins and his everlasting happiness through

---

[38] Foxe, *Acts and Monuments*, viii, 381; NRO, MCB 1555–62, 138, 140. There is no evidence that Sotherton searched Carman's house (which was presumably not in Norwich), or that any of the judicial process against Carman prior to his delivery to the secular arm was conducted in municipal courts, pace T.S. Freeman, review of McClendon, *Quiet Reformation*, in *Journal of Ecclesiastical History*, 51:2 (2000), 420.

[39] *House of Commons 1509–1558*, i, 698–9; iii, 312; NRO, DN/ACT 7/8, f. 267r; McClendon, *Quiet Reformation*, 85; Foxe, *Acts and Monuments*, vi, 699–700; viii, 428.

the passion of Jesus Christ. A crucial supporter of Mary's bid for the throne, and overall commander of her forces, Sussex also sought to protect the princess Elizabeth and wept openly at her imprisonment in the Tower. Sussex may have been, like Elizabeth herself, a Nicodemite who hid evangelical convictions behind strict outward obedience to lawful authority. Norfolk's relative freedom from persecution during Sussex's dominance could have been due in some measure to his moderating influence. The other layman who sought to persuade Rose was Sir William Woodhouse of Hickling, veteran sailor and by now justice of the peace, who served successive Tudor monarchs with equal loyalty. Greatly favouring Thomas Rose, Woodhouse took him into his own house during Hopton's absence on visitation. Having told Hopton that he would not be Rose's gaoler, Woodhouse allowed him to 'visit friends' and thus escape.[40]

A striking feature of the Marian restoration in Norwich was the submission of the foremost Protestants active in the city during Edward's reign. This was by any reckoning a notable success for the diocesan authorities. The character and extent of the submission made varied from man to man. John Barret's surprisingly prompt and still mysterious acceptance of the restoration almost certainly demoralized the other leading Protestants. His vigorous efforts to win them over possibly helped to weaken the resistance of both Watson and Rose, despite their understandable later desire to play down the influence of his arguments. From a Catholic standpoint, Watson's and Rose's subscriptions were hardly satisfactory. Their shortcomings were nevertheless far outweighed by the appearance of a bloodless triumph for the authorities. Martyrdoms had been avoided, and the influence of the two men had probably been neutralized far more effectively than if they had been sent to the stake.

The submission or flight of the city's foremost Protestants may help to explain the paucity of known acts of resistance or defiance among the lay population. There is no evidence, as there is from Colchester, of clandestine Protestant services or of open mockery of the Catholic clergy in the streets. No reports reached Foxe's hands that substantial numbers of Norwich people were presented in the Church courts for absence from Communion or refusal to observe ceremonies. This relative passivity could simply have been due to the smallness and weakness of

---

[40] ODNB; Elton, *Policy and Police*, 138–9; Foxe, *Acts and Monuments*, viii, 583, 588, 589; *CPR Edward VI, II, 1548–49*, 145; PRO, PCC will 33 Wrastley; *The Chronicle of Queen Jane and of two years of Queen Mary*, ed. J.G. Nichols (Camden Society, old series, xlviii, 1849), 71; *House of Commons 1509–1558*, iii, 653–5; Pettegree, *Marian Protestantism*, chapter 4, 'Nicodemism and the English Reformation', 86–117.

the Protestant minority in Norwich. Numerous entries in the mayor's court books for Edward VI's reign nevertheless testify to a lively clash of opinions and to some open popular hostility towards images and vestments. Surviving evidence points to a strong evangelical presence in the parish of St Andrew's. Protestantism appears to have gained adherents among the important occupational groups of the grocers and worsted weavers. Elaine Sheppard's analysis of Norwich wills shows that in 1552–53 the majority of the city's testators employed the statement of faith in Christ's merits favoured by evangelicals. Thereafter this proportion fell to 40 per cent in 1554 and 25 per cent in 1558.

During the years 1554–58 only 35 per cent employed a 'traditional' preamble: the return to Catholic formulae was much more pronounced in London than it was in Norwich. Few testators provided for intercessory prayers and votive lights, once popular forms of pious bequest. When all allowances have been made for the difficulty of interpreting will formulae, these Norwich figures seem to indicate the continued existence of a substantial minority of testators who leant towards Protestantism rather than restored Catholicism.[41]

The low profile adopted by Norwich's Protestants was no doubt due above all to a fear of persecution. The city was the seat of diocesan administration, under the eye of the bishop and his chancellors. In a detailed criticism of Professor McClendon's analysis, Dr Thomas Freeman has argued that the city's lay magistrates were exceptionally zealous persecutors. Thomas Codde and Thomas Marsham were indeed regarded by Robert Watson as 'enemies of the gospel'. The ruling class was almost certainly more conservative than the city's population as a whole. Of the 13 aldermen who made wills during Mary's reign, eight – nearly two-thirds – committed their souls to the holy company of heaven and/or provided for Masses. It is possible that the religious conservatism of men like Codde had been strengthened by the traumatic experience of Kett's rebellion and the rebels' gestures of support for the Edwardian Reformation. Rose's explanation of his own release reveals a continuing official fear of the disruptive potential of popular heretical sympathies.[42] But Dr Freeman seems to overlook the fact that other aldermen implicated in persecution were members of the consistory court staff,

---

[41] M. Byford, 'The Birth of a Protestant Town: the Process of Reformation in Tudor Colchester, 1530–80', in P. Collinson and J. Craig (eds), *The Reformation in English Towns 1500–1640* (Basingstoke, 1998), 29–36; McClendon, *Quiet Reformation*, 111–51; E.M. Sheppard, 'The Reformation and the Citizens of Norwich', *Norfolk Archaeology*, 38 (1981), 53–4, 56; S. Brigden, *London and the Reformation* (Oxford, 1989), 629.

[42] Freeman, review of McClendon, 419–21; McClendon, *Quiet Reformation*, 265; Foxe, *Acts and Monuments*, viii, 589.

men whose institutional loyalties were divided between the city and the diocesan hierarchy. Known participants in persecution made up only a small minority of the aldermen. At least one, Thomas Sotherton, did his duty as sheriff reluctantly. Professor McClendon is right to emphasize how few victims the Marian persecution claimed in England's second city. This may have been above all because the great majority of Norwich's evangelicals adopted a Nicodemite strategy due to their fear of persecution in a deeply divided city. It seems highly likely, however, that they were also strongly influenced by the capitulation or flight of all the city's leading Protestant ministers and the active collaboration in the Marian restoration of the longest-serving Norwich evangelical, John Barret.

By the time of the Elizabethan settlement, many of the men who had played key parts in Norwich's Marian restoration were either dead or had left the city for good. John Barret remained, and continued to hold his prebend in Norwich Cathedral until his death in 1563. Along with other clergy he subscribed acceptance of the royal supremacy, the Book of Common Prayer and the royal injunctions during the royal visitation of 1559. He later confirmed and amplified this subscription.[43]

Barret's will is dated 9 March 1563. He trusted to have remission of his 'most grevous and innumerable' sins and final salvation by God's mercy and grace and the merits of the blessed Passion of Christ. He desired all Christians both in heaven and in earth to pray for his soul. 'And by this Testament,' he continued, 'I declare and confesse that I beleve as the holie Catholike Church doth beleve and teache & hath euer beleved and taught.' He provided for ten sermons to be preached in Norwich and the nearby villages of Hethersett, Cantley and Thorpe, and made bequests to the poor. He left 40s to Mr Kemp to pray for him. (This may well have been John Kempe, the Norwich Common Hall priest from 1541 until 1555, and again, briefly, at the beginning of Elizabeth's reign. An ex-religious, he had been dismissed for marriage.) To the library of Norwich Cathedral Barret gave books that had cost him and Robert Talbot, his immediate predecessor as prebendary, £20. A schedule annexed to the will lists some 50 of these books. Works of the fathers, amounting to more than a third of the items on the list, make up by far the largest category. There are also a number by medieval theologians and commentators. The most interesting titles are, however, those of recent books by Roman Catholic controversialists: John Fisher, Martin Perez de Ayala, Alfonso de Castro, Johann Gropper, Stanislaus Hosius, Conrad Kling, Wilhelm Lindanus and Ruard Tapper.

---

[43] Corpus Christi College, MS 114B, 837.

The inclusion of these works, and the absence of even a single Protestant treatise, is an especially striking feature of the list. Barret named as his executors the Norwich aldermen Augustine Stywarde and Thomas Parker, brother of the archbishop, and the 'right worshipful Mr doctor Spencer' as his supervisor.[44]

Barret's will expresses his personal sense of belonging to a transcendent and enduring Catholic Church. While accepting in turn the Edwardian, the Marian and the Elizabethan settlements, he had also sought to maintain some sense of his own consistency and to identify and hang on to essential Christian doctrines. His exhaustive investigation of the extent to which the leading reformed theologians might be judged truly orthodox probably helped provide his personal bridge from Edwardian Protestantism to Marian Catholicism, as well as arguments to persuade his erstwhile colleagues to follow him. He had to subscribe his acceptance of the main elements of the Elizabethan settlement, including Communion in both kinds, and acknowledge that the royal injunctions tended to godliness and the abolition of superstition. Yet he kept his faith in prayers for the dead, and probably tried to hang on to as much of the religion he had professed under Mary as he could. What mattered above all was to identify and uphold the essential core of Christian faith. Through all the changes he experienced, Barret probably also maintained his belief in bonds of friendship capable of surviving transient divisions. One of his deepest convictions was no doubt encapsulated in a sentence in a manuscript book of his: '*Non in magna scientia, sed in recta fide atque charitate Christianorum pietas consistit.*'[45]

---

[44] NRO, NCC wills Knightes, ff. 119v–122r; McClendon, *Quiet Reformation*, 197, 200; Baskerville, 'Married Clergy and Pensioned Religious', 53; NRO, DN/ACT 7/8, f. 73r.

[45] Corpus Christi College, MS 428, f. 205.

Part II
Cardinal Pole

CHAPTER FIVE

The Success of Cardinal Pole's Final Legation

Thomas F. Mayer

I wish to assert a counter-intuitive proposition, as much for me as for anyone else: Cardinal Pole's final legation, unlike any of his earlier papal missions, succeeded.[1] Defence of this heresy rests in part on a change in perspective, from outcomes to processes, from winners in the long term to winners in the shorter haul, losers in common parlance. Apart from talk of tortoises and hares, such a change in perspective builds on my earlier polemical demand that we abandon the equation between mid-sixteenth-century Catholicism and incompetence.[2] Beyond

---

[1] For the prevailing interpretation, which I endorsed to some degree in *Reginald Pole, prince and prophet* (Cambridge: Cambridge University Press, 2000), 252-4, see R. H. Pogson, 'Cardinal Pole – papal legate to England in Mary Tudor's reign' (PhD thesis, Cambridge University, 1972), 230. Some of this material appeared in a pair of articles, 'Reginald Pole and the priorities of government in Mary Tudor's church', *Historical Journal*, 18 (1975), 3–20 and 'Revival and reform in Mary Tudor's church: a question of money', in *The English reformation revised*, ed. Christopher Haigh (Cambridge: Cambridge University Press, 1987), 139–56. All of these need to be handled carefully on any point of detail. My thanks to the following: the staff of Somerset Record Office (SRO), especially for producing a volume clearly marked NFFP; Gloucestershire RO (GRO), especially Mrs J.V. Thorpe; Herefordshire RO (HRO), especially Sue Hubbard and Elizabeth Semper O'Keefe; Bristol RO (BRO); Lichfield RO (LRO); Borthwick Institute, University of York (BI), especially Christopher Webb; Lincolnshire Record Office (LincsRO); London Metropolitan Archives (LMA); Public Record Office (PRO); Hampshire RO (HaRO); Canterbury Cathedral Archives (CCA), especially Cressida Annesley and Mark Bateson; West Sussex RO (WSRO), especially Peter Wilkinson, who in addition to providing much other help, also agreed to release a volume marked 'Do not produce'; Norfolk RO (NRO) and its director John Alban; Bill Sheils; Tom Freeman; Donald Logan; Melanie Barber at Lambeth Palace Library (LPL); Alexandra Walsham; and for financial assistance the Renaissance Society of America and the Augustana Faculty Research Committee.

[2] Yet another example of this unwarranted assumption is in D.M. Smith, 'The York institution act books: diocesan registration in the sixteenth century', *Archives*, 13 (1977–78), 171–9, at 178 where he writes of 'Marian registrational inefficiencies' in for example Nicholas Heath's register, but cf. the earlier Inst.AB.2, part 2 for some much more impressive messes in its early folios. Let it be made clear at the outset that, as in my biography, Pole is a collective enterprise, and talk of 'his' legation is only a convenience in

Table 5.1 Appeals by type of court and year

Arches	Legatine court of audience	Canterbury audience	Unknown
1554	11*	1†	
1555	40	39‡	
1556	20	58§	3
1557	40	73	2
1558	14	11	3
Totals	125	182	8
Grand total 315			

Notes: In Tables 5.1 and 5.2 appeals in the legatine register are counted twice if the original case was appealed to either Arches or the legate, but only once if they originated in the PCC.

Totals do not include 24 cases appealed directly to the Pope from the PCC. The difficulties of reading the microfilms of the act books from the consistory court of London means that types of cases have not been identified, and that in addition some inhibitions may have been missed.

Sources: SRO, D/D/Ca, 28; GRO, GDR 7B and 11–13; BRO, EP/J/1/2 and 3; HRO, HD4/1, box 3; LRO, B/C/2/5, unfoliated; BI, Cons. AB 20 and 21 and Chanc. AB.8; BMD, 922, vols 5 and 6; LincRO, Cj 7; CCA, DCb, Y.2.17 and 19; LMA, DL/C/6 and 607–10; PRO, C85/207 nos 11, 13–22 and 66, and /27 nos 11–19 and 21–2 and PROB 29/9; LPL, Charta miscellanea 52; HaRO, 21M65C2/4; NRO, DN/ACT 7/8; Strype (as in note 7); Wiltshire and Swindon Record Office, D1/39/1/1; Henry Gee, *The Elizabethan clergy and the settlement of religion, 1558–1564* (Oxford, 1898), p. 21.
*London and Norwich only.
†Suspensive appeal to Rome from York.
‡All from York, including one suspensive appeal to Rome; total also includes two cases appealed to Julius III alone.
§Includes one case from York appealed to '*pape pauli moderni*'.

historiographical realignment, demonstrating the truth of my opening assertion entails both an interim report on a project designed to identify all Englishmen, especially clergy, and women who approached Pole for absolution and dispensation, part of the fourth volume of an edition of his correspondence, as well as a more nearly completed effort to document the impact of Pole's legation on the ecclesiastical courts in England. One of the backbones of the argument for Pole's failure has been that only a very small number of cases were appealed to him and

place of constantly speaking of Pole's legatine staff. For my purposes, it matters little how much Pole was directly involved, much more that a group of experts, including of course the legate, took matters securely in hand.

Table 5.2 Appeals beginning with Pole's return in 1554 through 1555, by month

	Arches	Legatine court (or Pope)
1554		
November	2	–
December	1	1 (suspensive appeal from York)
1555		
January	1	2
February	4	4
March	5	1
April	–	8
May	7	1
June	7	2
July	7	7
August	1	2
September	–	1
October	1	–
November	3	8
December	2	3

only slowly. Both propositions fail. Added to the statistics derived from Pole's legatine register, now in Douai, an exhaustive study of diocesan and many other lower court records demonstrates that an impressive number of people thought it worth asking Pole's help sorting out their religious lives, coming to him in his capacities both as legate and as archbishop, that they did so with dispatch and that they continued to do so right down to the end of the reign, despite the apparent end of his legation in mid-1557. This demonstration will lead to some consideration of the persons Pole chose to assist him as *legatus natus* (as archbishop, traditional head of the *ecclesia anglicana*) and in his emergency role as local stand-in for the Pope, legate *a latere* with extraordinary powers.

Consideration of the volume of appeals must take into account four points. One, we know that the legatine register is defective, but given that none of the appeals found in local records appear among the 22 entered in it must mean that a separate register or registers of the legatine court of audience have been lost.[3] Two, the care with which

---

[3] Since describing Bibliothèque municipale de Douai, MS 922 in *The Correspondence of Reginald Pole*, 5 vols, St Andrews Studies in Reformation History (Aldershot: Ashgate Publishing, 2002–) (hereafter *CRP*), 1, 21–30, I have turned up more than two dozen

court records were kept varied widely, suggesting that entire cases, perhaps large numbers of them, might have been missed. The consistory and chancery courts in York set the standard for precision, with not too far behind the prerogative court of Canterbury, the Canterbury diocesan courts (albeit with a much smaller volume of business from a much smaller diocese than York) and London a fairly distant fourth. In York the notaries recorded virtually every detail of all actions, including the complete form for the appointment of a proctor in each and every case, entirely formulaic as it was; whereas at Bath and Wells by contrast the absolute minimum of information was taken down, and at Hereford, although the thoroughness of the record inspires some confidence, any individual notation is usually telegraphic. Three, and more important, the records are fragmentary for most of these courts: for consistory courts there is virtually nothing before 1556 at Bath and Wells and Bristol, although really not before 1557 in the second place; also the case in Coventry and Lichfield commencing late in that year. Lincoln by contrast ends in April 1556, Winchester has two volumes of office cases and one of instance (which produced a grand total of one inhibition from the legatine court of audience), Gloucester is fairly well but not completely covered, London has a gap from 14 November 1556 to 6 March 1557, there is nothing at all in Worcester, and Chichester is little better with only a few folios of a very miscellaneous act book for the sede vacante after Bishop Christopherson; and, incredibly enough, the act book of the prerogative court of Canterbury covering 1553 and 1554 is missing.[4] York and Hereford are the only places with continuous runs of material and perhaps not by coincidence they are one and three in the league table, with London just slipping past Hereford for number two. These three lead the rest of the pack by a wide margin, with more than two-thirds of the total (see Table 5.4); York alone accounts for almost 44 per cent of appeals. Even at Hereford there is one peculiar void from October 1555 to May 1556.[5] The counter case to these two is Canterbury, where a complete record of the 'officiality' court from 1552 to 1559 produces only a single appeal to Arches and two other instances in which an appeal was apparently contemplated but ultimately rejected.[6] More cases may appear in other kinds of records

---

dispensations in local sources not to be found in it, half of them from periods covered by the register.

[4] A few odds and ends of Ely consistory court materials are scattered through Cambridge University Library, EDR G/1/7 and 8.

[5] HRO, HD4/1, box 3, unfoliated.

[6] CCA, DCb Y.2.17, f. 190r a case of 2 July 1555, and f. 246r another of 28 July 1556.

Table 5.3 Appeals in 1557 by month

	Arches	Legatine court
January	1	2
February	4	7
March	2	12
April	2	2
May	2	11
June	1	4
July	10	11
August	2	1
September	–	1
October	3	2
November	2	2*
December	2	–

*Plus one case cited in Gee, p. 21 without particulars of time, except that it had been further appealed to the Pope before 1 Eliz. I c. 1 was passed.

besides those of the courts themselves. For example, the records of the metropolitical visitation of Lincoln in 1556 contain two, although there are none among the *comperta* for Salisbury in the previous year, or in Nicholas Harpsfield's very searching visitation of Canterbury diocese in 1557 or in 1556.[7]

The state of the records has a final unfortunate consequence, making it difficult if not impossible to identify the kind of case or follow its course, a problem possibly compounded by the loss of the sentence books some of these courts may have kept; but their complete disappearance makes me wonder whether they ever existed in the first place. Worse is the virtually complete loss of deposition books, leaving us with little idea of the particulars of any individual action. (Naturally, Bristol has the only extensive deposition book, but the related act book is extremely slight; Canterbury has another slimmer one; Peterborough and Exeter have only a deposition book each.)[8] This makes it impossible to detect patterns in cases that might help to account for which kinds,

---

[7] John Strype, *Ecclesiastical memorials relating chiefly to religion, and its reformation, under the reigns of King Henry VIII, King Edward VI, and Queen Mary*, 3 vols (Oxford: Clarendon Press, 1816), 3:2, 402 and 403; Wiltshire and Swindon RO, D1/43/2; and L.E. Whatmore, ed., *Archdeacon Harpsfield's visitation, 1557*, 2 vols (Catholic Record Society, 1946–50), 45–6, *passim*.

[8] Northamptonshire RO, Diocesan records, Miscellaneous book 4.

Table 5.4 Appeals by diocese (raw numbers)

	Current number		Pogson's
Bangor	1	[0/1]	–
Bath and Wells	13	[8/5]	9
Bristol	7	[5/1/1]	–
Canterbury	5	[1/3/1]	–
Chester	4	[0/4]	–
Coventry & Lichfield	5	[5/0]	–
Ely	2	[0/2]	–
Exeter	1	[0/1]	–
Gloucester	13	[13/0]	6
Hereford	35	[24/10/1]	8
Lincoln	15	[9/8]	–
London	44	[26/10/6]	–
Norwich	10	[10/0]	–
St Asaph	5	[4/1]	–
St Davids	2	[0/2]	–
Salisbury	13	[11/1/1]	–
Winchester	3	[1/2]	–
Worcester	0	–	–
York	112	[0/112]	20
Diocese unknown	25**	[5/19/1]	–
Total	**315**	**[122/182/11]**	**43**

First number in square brackets is appeals to Arches, second legatine court of audience, third Canterbury audience or unknown.
NB: Except for York (see Table 5.5), the numbers are too low to show any meaningful pattern by year. Twenty-four appeals direct to the Pope from PCC not included.
*Including 14 from the PCC, all to legatine court.

lodged by what types of persons, were likely to be appealed. It can be said that an appeal was very unlikely in office cases; I have found only eight.[9] Third, since it appears that York Chancery was in some sense superior to its consistory court (although both were courts of first instance and divided such business between them, with no further appeal possible within the archdiocese) and yet appeals went direct from consistory to Pole, then there might be appeals elsewhere that circumvent the highest diocesan court.[10] I have tested this theory in four

---

[9] I have not gone through two large volumes of such cases at Hereford.
[10] W.J. Sheils, *Ecclesiastical cause papers at York: files transmitted on appeal*

diocesan courts – the Exchequer in York, those of the archdeacons of Lincoln and Canterbury, and of the commissary of the archdeacon of Lewes in Chichester diocese – as well as in the handful of surviving acts arising from the *sede vacante* jurisdiction of deans and chapters and of the keeper of spiritualities of Chichester, and in all cases found nothing.[11] The first four of these might not have been a very helpful experiment, since Exchequer dealt solely with testamentary matters which were also increasingly important to the archdeacons. Comparatively little such business came to Pole, a total of only 15 appeals, and when it did at least some of the time he was just as happy to get rid of it.[12] Then again, by the seventeenth century, appeals went direct to Arches from a number of archdeacons' courts.[13]

Just which courts other than those of archdeacons might have sent cases to Pole remains to be worked out, since the structure of jurisdiction varied from one diocese to another and it is not yet known how many other cases there were like York, with two essentially parallel courts at the top of the hierarchy.[14] The situation was certainly similar in Lincoln and Canterbury where litigants also had a choice of appellate courts; except that in Canterbury, in addition to the twin courts of Arches (originally the consistory) and audience, there was yet a third court, recently dubbed the 'officiality', but in the documents consistory.[15]

1500–1883, vol. 9, Borthwick texts and calendars (York: Borthwick Institute of Historical Research, 1983), pp. i and iv–v. I base my supposition about their relative positions on the apparent removal of an almost record-length case from Consistory to Chancery, brought against Marmaduke Atkynson as rector of Baynton and Thornton, begun 14 February 1555 (BI, Cons. AB 20, ff. 250r, 252r, 274r, 288r etc.), removed to Chancery in December 1555 or January 1556 (BI, Chanc. AB 8, ff. 7v, 10r etc). Cf. M.D. Slatter, 'The records of the court of Arches', *Journal of ecclesiastical history*, 4 (1953), 139–53 at 145, who says appeals lay to Chancery in York.

[11] BI, Exch. AB 1 and 2; LincRO, Cij 1–3, the last of which is six folios long; CCA, Y.4.6 and Y.2.23; and WSRO, Ep/I/10/10 and Ep2/9/1.

[12] *CRP*, no. 1949b.

[13] Melanie Barber, ed., *Process books of the court of arches: supplementary list for use with the microfiche and the printed index* ([London]: [Lambeth Palace Library], 1981), 82–6.

[14] Ronald A. Marchant, *The church under the law: justice, administration and discipline in the diocese of York 1560–1640* (Cambridge: Cambridge University Press, 1969), 14 and Ralph Houlbrooke, *Church courts and the people during the English Reformation* (Oxford: Oxford University Press, 1979), 27.

[15] Margaret Bowker, *The Henrician reformation: the diocese of Lincoln under John Longland 1521–1547* (Cambridge: Cambridge University Press, 1981); CCA, DCB Y.2.19 diocesan officiality of the archbishop according to F. Donald Logan, 'Canterbury', in *The records of the medieval ecclesiastical courts, part 2, England*, ed. Charles Donahue, Comparative studies in continental and Anglo-American legal history (Berlin: Duncker & Humblot, 1994), 40 and 94ff.

Its records at least survive, while almost all those for Arches and audience do not.[16] We do know the names of these courts' presiding officers before, after and during Pole's tenure, and that a handful of cases went to audience instead of Arches, suggesting that the two remained distinct, but little beyond this.[17] The existence of these three courts, plus the two at York, immediately raises the question of the process of appeal. The act in restraint of appeals (24 Henry VIII c. 12, para. 3) stipulated that the old course of appeals from archdeacons to the courts of either Arches or archiepiscopal audience was to hold, with final recourse to the metropolitan; but 25 Henry VIII c. 19 redirected appeals from Arches to Chancery and eventually to the court of delegates.[18] The mid-century *Reformatio legum ecclesiasticarum*, section 54, para. 11 is vaguer. Appeals were to go in sequence from lower authorities to bishops, archbishops, the Crown and thence to a provincial synod or panel of bishops.[19] The general consensus of the few but fortunately very learned persons who have worked in this area recently is that Arches retained its jurisdiction, but I have yet to demonstrate this. My only test hole came up dry, that is, there were no appeals from Coventry and Lichfield in 1546 (the only year for which records survive in the couple of decades before Mary's reign) despite the fact that all the later appeals thence went to Arches.[20] Thus there is no

---

[16] Irene Josephine Churchill, *Canterbury administration: the administrative machinery of the archbishopric of Canterbury illustrated from original records*, 2 vols (London: SPCK, 1933), 1, 490 for audience and Slatter, 'Arches', 139. See also Thomas Oughton, *Ordo judiciorum; sive, Methodus procedendi in negotiis et litibus in foro ecclesiastico-civili Britannico et Hibernico: Ubi, quæ mendis olim cum innumeris edita fuêre, castigatè nunc et dilucidè digesta, juxta normam ordinis judiciarii, exhibentur, ac notis et observationibus illustrantur. Per Thomam Oughton* (Londini: Impensis authoris, 1738), xv. To the very slim corpus of Arches material for the sixteenth century, thus far consisting of one muniment book covering 1554–65 (Lambeth Palace Library, Film 163), and a few scraps taken from old bindings (BL, Add. MS 38651) can be added a complete register of its proceedings for the years 1568–69 which I discovered in the Hereford RO, filed as Appeals to Arches. Lambeth has recently acquired an early 17th-century register for audience (MS 3711), which at least confirms that its procedures were then virtually identical to those followed earlier in other ecclesiastical courts. I am grateful to Melanie Barber for bringing this to my attention.

[17] For example, see the appointment of the official (probably) of the court of audience sede vacante [1553] (CCA, DCc Reg U3, f. 11r); William Mowse as vicar general and auditor of audience and dean and official of Arches 20 May 1559 (CCA, DCc, Reg U2, ff. 2v–3v); and Henry Harvey's commission as auditor of the court of audience of Canterbury 20 Dec 1553 (CCA, DCc, Reg N, f. 1r–v).

[18] Cf. Slatter, 'Arches', 145.

[19] Gerald Bray, ed., *Tudor church reform: the Henrician canons of 1535 and the Reformatio legum ecclesiasticarum* (Woodbridge: Boydell Press, 2000), 705.

[20] LRO, B/C/2/5, unfoliated.

reasonable way to determine why a case went to audience rather than Arches.[21] Irene Churchill summarized the earlier situation between Arches and audience by making audience, derived from the archbishop's legatine authority and arising from his household, 'in some respects' superior to Arches and certainly the more flexible of the two – much as seems to have been true of Pole's legatine judiciary.[22]

In both cases, whether as legate or as archbishop, Pole thought he retained a good deal of residual authority, as of course did the king despite the elaboration of fixed royal courts, the parallel Churchill used. This further complicates matters, since cases appealed to the legatine court of audience could have a further appeal direct to Pole, who appointed deputies to hear them, originally a single auditor but later two.[23] It would be unsurprising had the two courts been amalgamated at least in practice, since certainly at York and London, and apparently most other places as well, the drive to rationalize and centralize ecclesiastical jurisdiction was if anything gaining momentum during Mary's reign.[24] The personnel of most of these diocesan courts from the top down were nearly always the same, for example either John Dakyn or John Rokeby usually exercising the highest posts in York regardless of court, and the same proctors in all of them, so it can have made little difference to litigants which court they used. The most impressive evidence at a slightly lower level of this consolidation and rationalization is the fact that at least by mid-1558 the presiding officer in the archdeacon of Canterbury's court sat as the archbishop's official, not the archdeacon's, despite the relatively much greater power of the archdeacon in Canterbury than in most dioceses and the very high profile of the current holder, Nicholas Harpsfield, one of the main cogs in the whole of Pole's judicial apparatus.[25] They would appear to have agreed sufficiently about the urgency of reconstruction not to worry much about jurisdictional niceties.

---

[21] Cf. the situation for Lincoln, Bowker, *Lincoln under Longland*, 55.

[22] Churchill, *Canterbury administration*, 1, p. 499.

[23] The earliest appeal known was granted on 30 June 1556, redirected from Thomas Stemp, legatine auditor, to William Cooke, keeper of the PCC (LPL, Charta miscellanea 52), but delegation to Cooke in particular or to any single judge was an anomaly. The next appeal known in July went to the usual panel of two auditors (BMD, MS 922, 6, ff. 47v–48r).

[24] Marchant, *Church under the law*, p. 13. Stephen Lander, 'Church courts and the reformation in the diocese of Chichester, 1500–58', in *Continuity and change: personnel and administration of the Church of England, 1500–1642*, ed. Felicity Heal and Rosemary O'Day (Leicester: Leicester University Press, 1976), 218–35; 219–23 for the distinctiveness of Sherburne's reforms in Chichester. It appears that their reversal in the 1550s ran against the national pattern.

[25] CCA, DCB Y.2.23, f. 1r. The official in question, Robert Collins, had held the office since at least 13 February 1554 (CCA, DCB Y.4.6, f. 2r).

The ultimate test of any appeal is its effect on a case, and here the records are almost entirely silent, confirming Ralph Houlbrooke's observation that it can be very difficult to discern simply whether an appeal was prosecuted.[26] I have found a handful of cases in which anything changed because of an appeal, and about a half-dozen which reached judgement.[27] One of these is also about the only one in which we know the costs involved, and they were large.[28] Otherwise, there are very few cases in which it is possible to follow their course at all easily right through, appeal or no appeal, except at Canterbury, where the notaries developed the apparently idiosyncratic but extremely useful habit of recording the entire case under the original entry. Even here, I cannot demonstrate the impact of a single appeal. The situation is even less satisfactory in the case of inhibitions, again since any successful one will have left no further impact, given the loss of all the central records. Here I have only one case where an inhibition can be demonstrated to have done its job. Once more the final outcome seems not to have been recorded, although it is known in a parallel suit, for what this is worth.[29]

To the statistics. In order not to belabour the shortcomings of previous work, I shall simply observe that instead of 43 cases, the new total is 315 (see Table 5.1), from many of the same sources used before, although the sometimes vague references in the earlier study make certainty elusive.[30] In terms of raw numbers, the appeals divide in proportions of almost two to

---

[26] Houlbrooke, *Church courts*, 43.

[27] It may be that another search looking more carefully for the later course of these suits would turn up a few more resolutions, but I was and am primarily interested in the volume of appeals.

[28] A suit between Walter Green and Thomas Richardes picked up in the records on 2 October 1556 (BRO, EP/J/1/2, p. 19); 23 October [1556] appeal lodged (BRO, EP/J/1/2, pp. 50 and 56). Not until 22 July 1558 was Richard Adens, Green's proctor in the appeal to Arches, paid £9 6s 4d for expenses, plus costs of the appeal which resulted in Green's condemnation. He paid Richards £9 5s 4d on 4 August (BRO, EP/J/1/3, p. 76). Green was also sued by the bishop of Gloucester, also in Arches. *CRP*, no. 2029a. The other case case brought at least near to judgement was in the PCC, appeal lodged 3 December 1555 in Dartnoll v. Bardolf and Bardolf, fees assessed 27 January 1557, but it is not certain this ended the matter (PRO, PROB 29/9, ff. 80r and 186r). For cases brought to judgement, see BI, Cons. AB 20, ff. 235v etc; 294v; 416r; Chanc. AB 8, ff. 78v and 197v.

[29] LincRO, Cj 7, f. 95v [day missing] April 1555 inhibition from legatine court (Pole's full style given), probably in John Morison v. Helen Palmer of Winthorpe; f. 95v another inhibition, once [?incorrectly] dated 6 April in John Hardy v. 'said Helena [Palmer]', judgement for Hardy from legatine court read in 19 July 1555 and Palmer cited to appear (f. 125r); 8 August 1555 office case promoted by Morison v. 'dominus' John Hardy and Helen Palmer, continued 10 August (f. 131v), 17 August Morison absolved and Palmer excommunicated (f. 132r–v).

[30] Pogson, 'Cardinal Pole', 230. Beyond the large discrepancy in our numbers, and the fact that he included only York, Bath and Wells, Gloucester, Worcester (which

one between the legatine court of audience and Arches. In terms of time, business zooms up in both courts already in 1555, with the number of cases almost equal between them: 40 and 39. The sharp initial rise suggests that word got out quite quickly and that, while there may have been no reservoir of unfulfilled religious vocations, there was pent-up demand for papal justice, as there may also have been for the Arches variety. There are three cases just in advance of Pole's return, but I confess I did not think to look at the rest of the reign to this point, except in London where the annual total for 1555 is almost double that for 1554, 13 against seven (see Table 5.6). It is hardly surprising that there should be demand, given the highly evolved systems in both courts, but that any appeals went to either place as early as they did is impressive testimony to the depth of the desire for ecclesiastical justice at the highest level. A suspensive appeal to the Pope from York shows just how much was known about the state of play already at the end of 1554.[31] That in this case and several others the York lawyers had to invent a style for Pole, sometimes apparently borrowing from that for the Archbishop of York as legatus natus of his province, further suggests that here at least appellants were not content to wait for word from the centre before approaching the legate.[32] Another number, a sample of appeals reserved but not usually prosecuted, may indicate that the lure of papal justice was even stronger, if reservation was more than a formality. In London (see Table 5.6), while 44 appeals were lodged, 24 were reserved (a few later filed), but in the Prerogative Court of Canterbury (PCC) the balance is different, with 31 appeals reserved in the period between 29 January 1555 and 9 July 1557, during which time 23 were prosecuted, including three of those reserved.

---

produced no cases) and Hereford, Pogson did not distinguish between appeals to Pole as archbishop and as legate. Although he noted the problem of terminology for the various courts to which appeals were lodged, he went on to assert somewhat disconcertingly that 'Pole's small group of lawyers was likely to deal with the problem ultimately if it proved difficult, whatever the wording' (229 n. 3).

[31] BI, Cons. AB 20, f. 208r.

[32] On 1 February 1555 Pole was addressed both as '*sanctisssimum in Christo patrem et dominum nostrum papam eius nominis tertius* [sic] *eiusque audienciam apostolicam vel legatum suum in hoc regno Anglie directe*' (BI, Cons. AB 20, f. 241v) and as the Pope's 'delegate' in England. For the form of an appeal to the archbishop of York, see, for example BI, Cons. AB 21, f. 87r. Since there were apparently no appeals from York to Arches, there may have been no other model than legatus natus ready to hand. The role of the lawyers in generating and managing business requires further attention, although it can be said that it appears not to make very much difference to whether an appeal was filed or who the proctor in charge of it was. In places like York with relatively large numbers of proctors, business appears pretty equally spread among them as it does in smaller places like Bath and Wells, where there might be only two or three proctors practising at the same time.

Table 5.5 Appeals from York by year

1554	1
1555	27
1556	41
1557	38
1558	5
Total	112

Table 5.6 Appeals from London by year, including those reserved but not filed

	Arches	Other*	Appeal reserved†
1554 (all year)	7	3 (D & C of Canterbury)	7
1555	13	–	7
1556	3	3	2
1557	8	1	3
1558	4	3	2
Total	35	9	24

*Canterbury audience, legatine audience, unknown, unless otherwise stated.
†Usually to Arches

After the first dramatic increase, as Table 5.2 shows the numbers are pretty steady right through 1555 up to the usual December lull. Appeals to the legate in the next year increase by two-thirds to 58, while declining by half in Arches to 20. Both hit their peak in 1557. The spike is steeper in Arches, where the number precisely doubles to its previous high of 40. In the legatine court, the number rises by almost another third to 73, all but six of those before the end of July. Both decline precipitously in 1558 down to 11 or possibly 12 to the legate and 14 to Arches, the final two in November. That business in both courts falls off well before the end of the regime (see Table 5.3) and that there were still 17 appeals to the Pope in 1558, a dozen of them from the PCC, reinforces my reservations about one of the two principal explanations for Pole's failure, insufficient time.[33] But what to make of those appeals to the legate in the second half of 1557 and 1558, especially two in October 1557 from York which earlier had been exceptionally *au*

---

[33] Pogson, 'Cardinal Pole', 223, 232, 248, 257 and 353.

courant (see Table 5.5)? Obviously there was a period of adjustment there at the end as at the beginning, eager to get started, reluctant to stop: from the last appeal to Pole to the first to Paul IV took from 30 October 1557 to 22 January 1558.[34]

Still, why should there have been *any* appeals to a then powerless figure? The answer seems plain: some lawyers, including some on Pole's legatine staff, and perhaps more importantly some litigants, were no more persuaded than I am that Pole's legation was ever decisively and finally revoked.[35] After all, no less a person than Cardinal Farnese in May 1557 confidently reported to his agent in Philip's court in Brussels that Pole's legation would be restored.[36] It might appear that the question was settled by Paul's answer on 14 July to Mary and the bishops' strong protest against the removal of Pole's powers that England should indeed have a legate, but it was not proper (*non convenire*) to reappoint a man whose powers had just been revoked.[37] And Paul does seem to have treated the matter as settled, no further discussion being recorded in the consistorial acts, although there might well have been in those of the congregation of the Inquisition, which probably do not survive. For present purposes, it matters less what happened in Rome than how the English responded, and at least some of them acted as if the Pope had never issued either his decree or its confirmation. The most substantial evidence for this proposition comes from nine significavits to Chancery beginning 1 June 1557 to the end of the reign filed on behalf of Pole as legate a latere.[38] One of the acts in December 1557 for the restoration of the Hospitallers bears Pole's legatine seal.[39] These, combined with all those appeals after April 1557 (see Table 5.3), appear to make a compelling case, and in canon law Pole's powers would have remained in effect while he appealed their revocation. Even if he did not formally appeal, it certainly appears that the lawyers in England elected to act as if he had.[40]

---

[34] BI, Cons. AB 21, ff. 291r–323r.

[35] Mayer, *Pole*, 309–20.

[36] Annibale Caro, *Delle lettere del commendatore Annibal Caro scritte a nome del cardinale Alessandro Farnese*, 4 vols (Milan: Società tipografrica de' classici italiani, 1807), 3, 167.

[37] Archivio segreto vaticano (ASV), Archivio concistoriale, Acta vicecancellarii, 8, f. 87r.

[38] PRO, C85/207 and 27. The PRO catalogue says C 85/207 came from York province, and /27 is supposed to be Canterbury province but I see no difference in provenance and only one case in /207 came from York. The first document from Pole in /207 is for a case in Exeter diocese. Eight of the nine documents are from /207, nos 15 to 22, and the last is /27 no. 16. A significavit was a warrant to Chancery requesting a writ *de excommunicato capiendo*.

[39] CRP, no. 2130.

[40] I owe this suggestion to Andrew Hegarty.

There remain several difficulties. First, two of the copies of those significavits in Pole's archiepiscopal register omit his direct legatine powers.[41] Second, five other significavits from the same period treat Pole as archbishop and *legatus natus* only.[42] Third, only one more appeal to the legate was lodged after June 1557 in the PCC, which one might have expected to be exceptionally well-informed.[43] Then again, this may not be all that significant, given the steady stream of appeals to the Pope from this court, 24 in total, even when Pole certainly still had legatine powers. Pole himself scrupulously ceased to use, or at least claim, his powers. This did not prevent him from demanding in increasingly strident terms that the Pope return them, culminating in a special mission in early 1558, the instructions for which are extremely pointed on this head.[44] If he did actually retain them, the decline in business becomes that much harder to explain, although it further undermines lack of time as the problem. It may simply be that the backlog had been cleared by mid-1557, and it does seem that local circumstances, the changing of the judicial guard, in several places had an impact, and it may also be that the tailing off was cyclical and related to the economic downturn in 1557.[45] This last hypothesis could be tested by comparision to the volume of business in secular courts.

Even leaving aside the question of when Pole's legation ended, interpreting the numbers will not be easy. For one thing, a good deal of caution will be required. Martin Ingram has recently made two important points. First, the volume of business in the commissary court of London saw 'violent fluctuations' in business in the late fifteenth and early sixteenth centuries, so any short-term movement will need careful handling if it is to prove significant. Second, Ingram warns us that 'the pattern of church courts' activities was affected by numerous administrative and other internal factors, so changing levels of activity cannot be taken as an index of public attitudes'.[46] More serious yet, constructing a baseline presents large difficulties. I could skip the issue by offering the immediate reaction of one of the best-informed students

---

[41] PRO, C 85/27, nos 18 and 20; LPL, Pole's register, ff. 26r–v and 30v–31r. That the significavits appear in this register rather than the legatine is of no particular significance, since there is a good deal of other legatine business found in it.

[42] C/85/27, nos 15 and 19–22.

[43] PRO, PROB 29/9, f. 289r.

[44] Mayer, *Pole*, 316–20.

[45] I am grateful to Richard Rex for the first of these suggestions and to Steve Gunn for the second.

[46] Martin Ingram, 'Regulating sex in pre-Reformation London', in G.W. Bernard and S.J. Gunn, eds, *Authority and consent in Tudor England: essays presented to C.S.L. Davies* (Aldershot: Ashgate, 2002), 79–95, at 85–6.

of Arches when I recited its numbers – 'That's a lot!' – or by deferring to Houlbrooke's slightly contrary impression that appeals to it were 'fairly common'.[47] Here at least it may prove possible to get some crude comparisons for at least one or two dioceses, especially Hereford and Norwich, but probably not York, whose records are complete and from which not a single case went to Arches during Mary's reign. For the legatine court the situation is probably completely hopeless. I have elsewhere observed that in terms of physical space occupied, not necessarily numbers of cases, Pole's legatine register is not particularly impressive by comparison with somewhat later ones kept by several legates to France.[48] The nearest in time to Pole's, Carlo Carafa's, apparently does not survive. Comparison to legates in Paul III's reign would not help much, since Paul, unlike Julius III, kept his personal representatives on short leashes in order not to cut into business to Rome. It would be possible to dig out appeals direct to the Pope, even though the calendar of papal letters for Britain has not got past the 1510s. The difficulty here is that the numbers are likely to be much smaller than for appeals to Pole because of the vastly greater expense and difficulty of prosecuting an appeal in Rome.[49] Cardinal Wolsey's experience might tell us something, but only a fragment of his legatine register survives.[50] Even were all this not the case, we need a situation of a legate even vaguely parallel to Pole's in England – a place that changed religious colours as often as England and yet had such an unrestricted opportunity to restore itself to papal obedience – and there is only one other such, Augsburg, perhaps significantly under the care of one of Pole's allies, its prince-bishop Otto Truchsess von Waldburg.

If a real statistical analysis or a more profound study of the mechanics of appeals will both probably permanently elude us, it still seems safe to observe baldly that a very large number of cases came to Pole in one or the other of his capacities, first and foremost as legate. Certain persons in England, most of them lay, eagerly availed themselves of the legal opportunity afforded by his broad faculties. Is this number in any way representative? We have no way of knowing. The situation is a little easier when we turn to a rapid survey of the clergy who approached Pole as legate for absolution and dispensation. We know immediately that

---

[47] Houlbrooke, *Church courts*, 43.
[48] *CRP*, 1, 22.
[49] I can confirm this claim based on an impressionistic survey of episcopal registers from the late 1520s to the end of Mary's reign which contain only a small handful of appeals to the Pope. LincRO, Epis. Regs 26 and 27, for example, contain for the 1520s seven papal dispensations and ten from Wolsey as legate a latere.
[50] More bulls are scattered around the episcopal registers, but not enough to help and almost all for pluralism.

those who asked indulgence for pluralism, the largest group, are anything but representative. They belong to the clerical elite, if not necessarily to its upper ranks. Of a total of approximately 834 clergy who came to Pole, 232 or nearly 28 per cent fall into this category.[51] Interestingly enough, this number comes close to the best estimates for the percentage of pluralists at several other periods in the fifteenth and sixteenth centuries, which seems to mean that these men, however unrepresentative of the clergy as a whole, represent its pluralist minority well.[52]

Pluralism and its regulation had bedevilled the Church since at least the Fourth Lateran Council in 1215. Beginning then with Innocent III, the popes had tried to exert close control over priests with multiple benefices, and England had caused special trouble. Later in the century both Pole's lodestars in his Westminster synod (1555), the legates Otto and Ottobono, had laid down stringent regulations. For Otto, any cleric who took a second benefice without dispensation had to resign it immediately. He allegedly required bodyguards to protect him from outraged pluralists. Ottobono went even further, putting in place a machinery of enforcement involving ordinaries and the two metropolitans, and demanding inquiry whether a priest had a dispensation before he could receive his second benefice. A lie

---

[51] The total is approximate because of uncertainties over men with the same name. It also does not include bishops or the members of Canterbury Cathedral at its visitation in 1556. A further 21 dispensations either exhibited or demanded during the visitation of Salisbury in 1555 (Wiltshire and Swindon RO, DI/43/2, unfoliated) cannot safely be added to the total since none of them identify the source of the dispensation, and Pole readily accepted those from the Faculty Office, as well, of course, as from the Pope or his legates.

[52] Margaret Bowker, *The secular clergy in the diocese of Lincoln 1495–1520* (Cambridge: Cambridge University Press, 1968), 73 found approximately 25 per cent non-resident pluralists and concluded in her later study that it is difficult to say whether the rate had increased, but the number she arrived at, 28.6 per cent, is almost identical to that in my sample. Bowker, *Lincoln under Longland*, 42–3. Most other figures fall between 25 and 30 per cent. In a slightly earlier period, Peter Heath found no more than 25 per cent non-residents as a result of holding multiple benefices. *The English parish clergy on the eve of the reformation* (London and Toronto: Routledge and Kegan Paul and University of Toronto, 1969), 57. In Kent in 1550–52 at least 23 per cent of incumbents were pluralists and at least 19 per cent non-resident. Michael Zell, 'The personnel of the clergy in Kent, in the Reformation period', *English Historical Review*, 89 (1974), 513–33, at 531. In the early years of Matthew Parker's episcopate, pluralism in Canterbury diocese shot up from 17 per cent to 45 per cent as a function of deprivations. J.I. Daeley, 'Pluralism in the diocese of Canterbury during the administration of Matthew Parker, 1559–1575', *Journal of Ecclesiastical History*, 18 (1967), 33–49, at 41–2. Something similar may have happened in the early years of Pole's tenure. The most recent study, Tim Cooper, *The last generation of English Catholic clergy: parish priest in the diocese of Coventry and Lichfield in the early sixteenth century*, ed. Christopher Harper-Bill, Studies in the history of medieval religion (Woodbridge: Boydell Press, 1999), 62–72, finds substantially lower numbers of non-resident pluralists. See also the valuable comparative table on 62.

on this score brought automatic deprivation. At the end of the thirteenth century, Archbishop Peckham tried to moderate these draconian measures, laying down that anyone then holding two benefices without dispensation could keep the second, but anyone who failed to get a papal dispensation in the future would lose both livings. John XXII laid down the 'definitive' medieval canon law (*Execrabilis*, 1317). A priest could hold only one benefice with cure of souls, and had to choose which of two he held within a month of gaining the second. If he did not, he lost both. Again, England got special treatment, but also more effective enforcement. The bull *Consueta* established that any clergy with two compatible benefices had to notify their ordinary within a month (six months for England, because the problem was so widespread) after a diocesan synod announced the new regulation, sending up both their names and, perhaps more important, their value. Diocesans then had a month to compile a list which they sent up to the metropolitans who forwarded it to Rome. This procedure was followed scrupulously by Archbishop Langham, but apparently never again.[53] The Council of Trent's decree of 1547, just after Pole gave up the presidency, returned to Innocent III's harsh assertion that holding multiple benefices meant ipso facto deprivation.[54] On his own, Pole probably inclined to the rigorous line; at least his datary Niccolò Ormanetto reports him as having conceded grudgingly that he would grant dispensations for pluralism during the protracted negotiations over regularizing the status of the ex-monastic property leading to 1 & 2 Philip and Mary, c. 8.[55] In the sequel, just as Pole was forced to bend most of the way on the score of the 'possessioners' of ex-monastic property, so he proved much more generous in practice, ignoring this provision (as he had other inconveniences thrown up by the Council).

The procedure might be clear, how well it was followed less so; but there could be no missing that the popes meant to control pluralism, even if by the late fifteenth century their interest seems to have been more financial than pastoral, and the situation only got worse in England under the new Faculty Office established in 1534.[56] As usual, there is an immediate problem on the score of clerical finance when

---

[53] A. Hamilton Thompson, 'Pluralism in the medieval church; with notes on pluralists in the diocese of Lincoln, 1366', *Reports and papers of the associated architectural societies*, 33 (1915), 35–73, at 43–72.

[54] R. Naz, ed., *Dictionnaire de droit canonique* (Paris: Letouzey et Ané, 1935–), 2, col. 1059.

[55] CRP, no. 1047. Unfortunately the multiple enclosures Ormanetto sent, detailing almost moment by moment Pole's stance in the negotiations, have been lost. Cf. the detailed summary of the act's provisions in Felix Makower, *The constitutional history and constitution of the church of England* (New York: Burt Franklin, n.d.).

[56] D.S. Chambers, *Faculty Office registers 1534–1549* (Oxford: Clarendon Press, 1966), 58.

moving into Pole's legation. From at least Urban V's bull *Horribilis* of 1363, the popes had tried to limit the total income from multiple benefices even in the case of the more exalted (and supposedly learned) clergy who had always received more lenient treatment, officially by Innocent III's *Cum ex eo*, allowing and even encouraging non-residence for study. Urban's limits were generous, even if I have yet to establish exactly what currency he was using.[57] By Clement VII's day, the limits had virtually been removed to judge from one dispensation allowing petitioners to hold two benefices worth together not more than 3000 ducats.[58] The act of 1529 was much less accommodating. In future, any cleric holding more than one benefice worth over £8 per annum had his first holding thereby invalidated along with his dispensation. Of course, there were multiple loopholes for present holders (who could keep four benefices), chaplains of bishops, nobles and so on.[59] Thomas Cranmer seems to have adhered fairly closely to the law, and Pole usually accepted his dispensations at face value, thereby implicitly accepting the statute, for what this is worth.[60]

What neither it nor Cranmer nor anyone else before Pole did, as far as I know, was say anything about the distance allowable between multiple benefices. Cranmer issued more than one egregious dispensation for benefices 50 or more miles apart, including some on opposite sides of the country where learning or other distinction seems not to have been involved. As Donald Chambers well said, dispensations for pluralism were one of the financial mainstays of the Faculty Office, and no one wished to muzzle that particular cash cow.[61] Pole, however much he may have made out of these dispensations (and unfortunately we know almost nothing about his legation's finances), did inquire carefully both about value and distance. I have yet to establish by exactly what warrant he did so, but in addition to a possible extension of the principle set out in *Consueta*, it was almost certainly a regulation of the papal chancery which was only poorly understood in the sixteenth century. Printed sets of these or commentaries on them for most of the sixteenth-century popes from Julius II on are known, but I have not yet been able to consult the most immediately applicable ones for Julius III

---

[57] Hamilton Thompson, 'Pluralism', 69.

[58] LincRO, Epis. Reg. 26, ff. 239r–v, 13 February 1533. The figure of 3000 might be wrong, since it is very difficult to read, but the limit was certainly in the thousands.

[59] 21 Henry VIII c. 13, paras ix–xii; *Statutes of the realm*, 9 vols in 10 vols ([London], 1810–22), 3, 292–6 (293–4).

[60] Chambers, *Faculty Office*, xxxvii. Contrariwise, the Elizabethan authorities rejected at least one of Pole's dispensations. Devon Record Office, Chanter 20, f. 69r.

[61] Given Chambers's conclusion just cited, it may be that the cases I have come across have something peculiar about them not yet discovered.

and Paul IV.⁶² Nevertheless, Pierre Rebuffi's extensive contemporary commentary on their immediate predecessor Paul III's *regulae*, no. 22 stresses the importance of petitioners giving a true '*Annuum valorum ... secundum communem aestimationem*', which is the same formula Pole used, and when discussing no. 55 Rebuffi emphasized that the two livings had to be '*contiguae & propinquae*' and not worth '*insimul ultra 24 florenos auri de camera*', which translates into Pole's £8 standard.⁶³ The only thing missing is a maximum distance; Pole once used the figure of 12 miles in the abstract.⁶⁴ Interestingly enough, such dispensations from Paul III as I have checked note only value, as do most of those from earlier popes thus far found, and most of these did not actually give the values.⁶⁵ Pole certainly customized the usual justifications for dispensations for pluralism – petitioner's nobility and education – instead spelling out that he acted because of a shortage of clergy. There is no indication that Pole ever refused a petition on grounds of value or distance, but there is very good evidence that a number of supplicants thought he might. Although work on the values submitted is still at an early stage, that for distance shows a substantial proportion of clergy lying through their teeth. Of 176 benefices where mileage is reported,

---

⁶² Quintiliano Mandosio, *In regulas Cancellariae Apostolicae sanctissimi D. nostri Iulii tertii pontificis maximi commentaria: alter propriam cuiusq[ue] regulae materiam breuiter ostendit: alter uerò omnia in commentarijs memoratu digna ordine complectitur* (Venice: Michele Tramezini, 1554) and *Regulae omnes, ordinationes, et constitutiones Cancellariae S.D.N.D. Pauli diuina prouidentia papae IIII.* (Paris: Magdaleine Boursette, widow of François Regnault, 1555). For the immediately preceding situation, including a few ordinances governing the application of canons on pluralism, see Michael Tangl, *Die päpstlichen Kanzleiordnungen von 1200–1500* (Innsbruck: Wagner, 1894).

⁶³ Pierre Rebuffi, *Praxis beneficiorum* (Lyon: Heirs of Guillaume Rovilli, 1599), pp. 356–7 and 393–4. For the exchange rate between pound sterling and papal gold florin (increasingly becoming a money of account already in Rebuffi's day) see my 'Cardinal Pole's Finances: The Property of a Reformer', in Thomas F. Mayer, *Cardinal Pole in European Context: A Via Media in the Reformation* (Aldershot: Ashgate Publishing, 2000), no. XV, 3. Although Rebuffi, a well-known French law professor, never actually practised in Rome, he held the position of auditor with the rank of protonotary of the Roman Rota and was an acknowledged expert on the law of benefices. Howell A. Lloyd, 'Constitutional Thought in Sixteenth-century France: The Case of Pierre Rebuffi', *French History*, 8:3 (1994), 259–75, at 261 and 269–72.

⁶⁴ *CRP*, no. 1830.

⁶⁵ A bull of plurality for Richard Tollett of 12 April 1511 noted the value of two benefices (Devon Record Office, Exeter Diocesan Records, Chanter 13, ff. 43r–v); three bulls for Richard Norton in Chanter 13, ff. 136v–138v, say nary a word; a bull of 1481 (DRO, EDR, Chanter 13, ff. 139v–142) mentions value, but fails to give one, and the same holds for another of 1 Apr 1505 allowing John Rise to hold a total of three benefices with cure of souls (DRO, EDR, Chanter 13, ff. 142v–143r. Ergo, there seems to have been no consistent papal practice and consequently no clear precedent for Pole beyond the *regulae*. See also ASV, Registrum vaticanum 1691, ff. 149r (1545) and 212v (1547) and *passim*.

the average distance alleged is 5.4 miles, while the actual number in the case of a slightly smaller sample of benefices for which the distance can be determined (165) is almost twice that, 10.4 miles.[66] Only 29 distances were exact or very nearly so, but 13 were even closer than alleged and 34 were within 1 mile of what was claimed. Backing these 76 scrupulous clergy out of the total would, of course, make the fibbers look even worse. Is this a case of a 'medieval' attitude to numbers, where armies in the 20 miles just means 'a very long way'? This facet of 'the pluralist mentality' could use further study.

The whole phenomenon of pluralism could stand to be handled with a little more care, as Michael Zell pointed out back in 1974. He suggested a distinction between 'official' pluralists, men like Richard Thornden, suffragan bishop of Dover who resided on none of his many benefices and, more important at the moment, 'resident' pluralists whose benefices were close enough together (Zell suggests 10 miles) that they could be served by the same man without undue loss of spiritual provision.[67] I hasten to add my own call for greater care in the study of pluralism and non-residence, precisely on the matter of distance. I had thought one of my champion pluralists, Thomas Gilby, could not possibly have served both his Lincolnshire benefices, All Saints, Thornton le Moor and Saltfleetby St Clements, which were more than 28 miles apart in a county notorious for its bad roads. Then I read his will. The pattern of bequests seemed to favour Thornton le Moor, except that Gilby asked to be buried in the second place and one of his executors came from nearby; but much more interesting, he left legacies not only to each parish but also to a network of surrounding parishes (South Kelsey, Holton le Moor, Owersby in the first case, all three Theddlethorpes in the second). He was also of reasonably exalted social standing, being related to the leading family in Theddlethorpe All Saints, as well as a client (perhaps a chaplain) of one of the most powerful families in Lincolnshire, the Askews, by whose patronage he received his first benefice, and in the house of Sir Francis, whose principal residence was at South Kelsey, he was cared for in his final illness.[68] Gilby left the residue of his estate to a man who may have been a relative of one of the richest men in Lincolnshire and who was to distribute it on good works, exactly as Pole's synod had suggested.[69] Most interesting of all, this

---

[66] My thanks to my student Courtney Berry for her extremely careful work on these statistics.

[67] Zell, 'Kent clergy', 532.

[68] LincRO, Epis. Reg. 27, f. 57v.

[69] His estate was worth about £24. LincRO, LCC Wills 1557, iii, ff. 88v–89v. W.H. Frere and W.M. Kennedy, eds, *Visitation articles & injunctions of the period of the*

executor lived in Utterby, north of Louth, and together with Gilby's bequest for repair of the stone bridge between Owersby and Thornton, this tells us the route he used between his two benefices.[70] How he served them I cannot say, but that he must have to at least some degree seems borne out by his carefully planned legacies.[71]

Gilby got his second benefice (at Saltfleetby) on 8 June 1554, after holding the first since 1534.[72] He should have sought a dispensation before adding the second, but like nearly all the dispensations Pole issued, this one came after the fact, by more than two years.[73] Prospective dispensations were demanded in only 10 per cent of the 63 cases for which full data about admission and supplication are presently known. The average time between institution and dispensation is 18 months and the median 15.5 months. On the more positive side, 15 per cent of dispensations were issued within one month of institution and 94 per cent within a year. Thus as with many other things procedural, lack of regard for the law governing benefices was beginning to change by the end of Pole's legation. A pair of cases from perhaps the blackest hole of the southern English dioceses, Chichester, emphasizes the point. In them two clergy followed the law in seeking dispensation before being admitted to their second benefice. In the second case, acting on Pole's orders the keeper of spiritualities duly investigated both the allegations in the petition for dispensation and also the candidate's fitness.[74] The first man was later reported as a notorious recusant who had preached under Mary and later supported the exile and polemicist Thomas Stapleton as well as owned Nicholas Sander's *Rock of the church*.[75] The second, if less distinguished, was a client of another prominent recusant, Sir Richard Lewkenor.[76] In this case, Pole and the keeper of spiritualities

---

reformation, 3 vols (London: Alcuin Club, 1910), 3, 403 and cf. Eamon Duffy, *The stripping of the altars. Traditional religion in England c. 1400–c. 1580* (New Haven: Yale University Press, 1992), 552.

[70] The bridge no longer survives, replaced by a concrete structure, probably in the middle of the last century. Except for Theddlethorpe All Saints, much the same is true of all the churches associated with Gilby, especially Saltfleetby St Clements, now a failed restaurant.

[71] They do not include any horses, so Gilby may have borrowed his transport. Other Lincolnshire clergy, George Lilborne, for example, willed several horses, making it relatively easy for him to serve his two benefices, Maltby le Marsh and Mavis Enderby, about a dozen miles apart (*CRP*, no. 1232).

[72] LincRO, Epis. reg. 27, f. 57v.
[73] *CRP*, no. 1603.
[74] *CRP*, nos 1631 and 1836.
[75] *VCH, Sussex*, 2, ed. William Page (London: Constable and Co., 1902), 25 and 26.
[76] WSRO, Ep/I/1/6, f. 80v and *VCH, Sussex*, 24.

chose well. Two instances may not seem much, but it has to be remembered that on the score of pluralism, Pole faced a problem dating back centuries against which no one else had made much headway, and this case and several others reflect a tightening of the regulations his own legatine synod had laid down that allegations were to be checked only at episcopal visitations, not prior to admission to a benefice.[77] Another case from Exeter suggests a similarly heightened scrupulosity, as it highlights the rather cumbersome procedure involved at the same time as it underscores that loss of records may have a great deal to do with making Pole's administration appear more slipshod than it was. An office case was lodged there in 1557 against the rector of Ashcombe, Devon, which turned on how far it was from Uplyme. A number of witnesses had to be called to establish the fact (most agreeing that it was at least 20 miles distant), but the outcome is unknown.[78]

The keeper of spiritualities in question in Chichester was Richard Brisley, who was assigned to clean up the mess following the virtual collapse of Bishop Sherborne's streamlined administrative machinery.[79] Part of the problem apparently lay in its very efficiency, leading Pole, for example, to make heavy use elsewhere of William Pye, and thereby cause him to neglect his duties in Chichester as dean of the cathedral, for which Mary had singled him out.[80] From late 1554 a turnaround began. Brisley, archdeacon of Lewes since 1551, by becoming resident from Michaelmas 1554 reversed the usual absence of both the archdeacons of Lewes and Chichester.[81] It was he who conducted the legatine visitation

---

[77] CRP, no. 1824 and possibly 1898.

[78] Devon Record Office, Chanter 855, f. 129v.

[79] This is not the view of Brisley put forward by Lander, 'Church courts', 233–4, who compares him very negatively to his predecessor John Worthiall. It does appear that Brisley's penchant for sitting in Chichester made business more inconvenient for those living in the eastern half of the diocese, but it is not true that his court met there exclusively and any conclusions are dangerous given the extreme thinness of the records. Lander is almost certainly wrong that Brisley failed to go after clerical non-residence, if these two cases are any indication.

[80] W.D. Peckham, ed., *The acts of the dean and chapter of the cathedral church of Chichester 1545–1642*, vol. 58, Sussex Record Society (1959), nos 523 and 525–6. For Pye's role in Pole's financial machinery, see CRP nos 1829, 1833 and 1945, this last as collector in Hereford. However much Pole might be blamed for keeping Pye away from Chichester, Pye was a very high flyer, who held numerous cathedral posts among his many benefices.

[81] WSRO, Ep/I/1/6, f. 82r; Lander, 'Church courts', 218; Peckham, nos 536 and 547; and WSRO, Ep. II/9/1, ff. 91v and 107r. Alban Langdale, archdeacon of Chichester, continued to be non-resident. John Le Neve, *Chichester diocese*, ed. J.M. Horn, vol. 2, Fasti ecclesiae anglicanae 1541–1857 (London: Institute of Historical Research, 1971), 15. It is a drawback of Le Neve that it does not indicate when an office-holder exercised his office in person.

first of the cathedral clergy in April 1556 and then in June of the diocese.[82] But Brisley was only one of many. Another of my favourite cases is William Dalbie, whom Pole appointed vicar general and keeper of spiritualities of Hereford in 1557.[83] Dalbie was a lawyer. Like many such, his career was originally launched in London shortly after taking his DCL in 1552.[84] His first high-profile assignment saw him share with William Cooke the *sede vacante* administration of the Canterbury deaneries of Shoreham, Croydon, Bocking, Risborough Pagham et al. [*sic*], at a time when he was already a very active proctor in the consistory court of London.[85] A little later he deputized for the vicar general of Canterbury diocese, Henry Harvey, and again for the dean of St Paul's, John Harpsfield, in December 1555.[86] On the strength of this success, Dalbie became vicar general, commissary and official principal of Bristol by August 1556.[87] He sat in court there until he resigned its jurisdiction on 9 June 1559, and in Hereford at least through the end of 1558, although he occasionally had to employ deputies.[88] It cannot have been easy to combine these two posts. Pole could have employed one or the other of the men whom Dalbie used as deputies, perhaps especially the career pluralist Richard Sparcheforde in Hereford, but chose not to.[89] He wanted Dalbie, and Dalbie wanted Pole. He was cited as having 'fled' to appear before royal commissioners in September 1559 and disappears from his benefices by 1560.[90] John Foxe's assignment of three

---

[82] WSRO, Ep. I/10/10, at end, marked no. 72, ff. I–II, and R. Garraway Rice and W.H. Godfrey, eds, *Transcripts of Sussex wills*, vols 41, 42, 43, 45, Sussex Record Society (1935–41), 3, 156.

[83] *CRP*, no. 2104. Brisley may have acted together with Thomas Packard. *CRP*, no. 2190.

[84] G.D. Squibb, *Doctors' Commons: a history of the college of advocates and doctors of law* (Oxford: Clarendon Press, 1977), 151; A.B. Emden, *A biographical register of the university of Oxford A.D. 1501 to 1540* (Oxford: Clarendon Press, 1974), 158, and Joseph Foster, ed., *Alumni oxonienses: the members of the university of Oxford, 1500–1714* (Neudeln: Krause, 1968), 1, 367 give only the first degree, which is also the only one documented as of 11 December 1552 when Dalbie acted as archdeacon of London (Guildhall, 9535/1, f. 12r).

[85] CCA, DCc, Reg U3, ff. 13v–14r and LMA, DL/C/607, unfoliated.

[86] LMA, DL/C/607, unfoliated. See also LMA, DC/L/331, f. 180r for his deputization in a probate case.

[87] BRO, EP/J/1/2, 8 and *Calendar of patent rolls, Philip and Mary*, 4 vols (London: HMSO, 1936–39), 4, 247.

[88] BRO, EP/J/1/3, p. 42 and *passim* and Martha C. Skeeters, *Community and clergy: Bristol and the Reformation, c.1530–c.1570* (Oxford: Clarendon Press, 1993), 199; for Hereford see HRO, HD4/1, box 3, unfoliated.

[89] For him see *CRP*, vol. 4 *sub nomine*.

[90] Skeeters, *Bristol*, 199 and *Emden to 1540*, 158. He seems very unlikely to be the William Dalbie who died in 1583 (PRO, PROB 11/82, f. 291r).

martyrs in Bristol to his account (and perhaps against Bishop Holyman's wishes) reinforces the supposition of more than a strictly legal tie between Dalbie and Pole.[91]

This pattern repeats itself elsewhere where Pole carefully chose *sede vacante* keepers of spiritualities and vicars general, for example John Williams at Gloucester.[92] The very active Williams, archdeacon from 1552 to 1559, was also vicar general (and chancellor) from 1547 whom Pole continued in office during the sede vacante following Bishop Brooke's death. Like his opposite number at Bristol, Williams left office at the end of the Marian regime. Williams shares with Dalbie the distinction of appearing among Foxe's persecutors, albeit with a higher profile. Foxe says that he died during John Jewel's visitation of the western dioceses after refusing to meet Jewel and thereby implicitly rejecting his authority. To judge from Jewel's itinerary, this must have been in August 1559, but Williams had already disappeared by February from consistory court records.[93] But perhaps the best illustration of how well Pole chose and how well he was served is William Geffrey at Salisbury. His career closely parallels those of Pole's other vicars general, Dalbie's especially closely since they were at one time probably colleagues at Hereford. Geffrey came into his own in the wake of Pole's visitation of Salisbury in 1556. Masses of office cases resulted, far more than are known from any other diocese (a precise count has yet to be made). Foxe may have exaggerated only a little when he claimed that

---

[91] John Foxe, *Actes and monuments of these latter and perillous days* (London: John Day, 1563; *STC*, no. 11222), 1736. Dalbie was reduced to a footnote in the 1583 edition. I owe both references to Dr Freeman. The *Old DNB* entry on Holyman (9, 1109) says that he refused to attend the executions. Skeeters, *Bristol*, 126–7 makes the number of Dalbie's victims between four and eight.

[92] The mechanics by which keepers were selected are treated in Churchill, *Canterbury administration*, 1, 161–207. In some cases, as at Salisbury, a composition demanded that the dean and chapter nominate three candidates and Pole choose one; it is printed in ibid., 2, 55–9 and cf. *CRP*, no. 2274. In other places he could act out of his archiepiscopal powers without reference to the cathedral clergy.

[93] GRO, GDR 2A, 4 and 21; GDR 11, 14 and 101; GDR 14, 75ff. and GDR 15, for example, 23ff. and 48; GDR 15, 61; HRO, HD4/1, box 3, unfoliated; and John Foxe, *Actes and monuments* (1583), 2105. Foxe based himself on a second-hand account of 1579 from the dean of Gloucester which still survives among Foxe's papers (BL, Harleian MS 425, ff. 136r–v). I owe information about this tale to Thomas Freeman. The dates for Jewel's visitation and Williams's rejection of it are in C.G. Bayne, 'The visitation of the province of Canterbury, 1559', *English Historical Review*, 29 (1913), 634–51, at 638 and 640, also drawing in part on the dean of Gloucester. The Gloucester consistory court records become quite sloppy in 1559, often failing to record the presiding judge's name, and some cases were even allegedly heard before a rural dean. *Emden to 1540* says Williams died in 1558, but aside from calling Foxe's account 'unreliable' presents no evidence for the date.

Geffrey intended to 'conduct an inquisition' on 90 persons the day he died.[94] It was only natural that Pole would choose Geffrey as his *sede vacante* vicar general in 1557.[95] All these instances suggest a hypothesis about the relations between Pole's legation and the regular ecclesiastical judicial apparatus in England as it may partly account for a geographical anomaly in the statistics. Two dioceses, Williams's Gloucester and Norwich, sent no cases at all to the legate, but ten and thirteen respectively to Arches, and Salisbury a tiny proportion relative to the total number of cases brought. The competence of the official in charge and the confidence Pole reposed in him may explain the situation in Gloucester and Salisbury, although the obvious counter-example to this theory is Dakyn at York, or Williams and Geffrey may have been more than usually overbearing and intimidated those appearing before them from appealing to Pole as legate. A zealous Marian official may also explain the absence of appeals from Norwich, where Michael Dunning was commissioned one of two vicars general by Bishop Hopton on 29 October 1554 and probably immediately began to preside over the consistory court, certainly from November 1554 to the end of the record in late 1555 and probably into late summer 1557, shortly before he removed to Lincoln to take up first a prebend and then the archdeaconry of Bedford.[96] Like Dalbie, Williams and Geffrey, Dunning had several executions for heresy to his credit, and Foxe labelled him the second cruellest persecutor after Nicholas Harpsfield.[97] It is also true that the

---

[94] *The first (second-) volume of the Ecclesiasticall History* (London: John Day, 1570; RSTC, no. 11223), 2256 for Geffrey's cruelty, 2299 for the intended inquisition. Foxe's date for Geffrey's death is out by only one day, but the number of Geffrey's intended victims cannot be easily confirmed.

[95] *CRP*, no. 2273.

[96] NRO, DN/12/18, ff. 84v–55r. The other vicar general was Miles Spenser who held office from 1531 to 1570, but he never appears in the surviving record of the consistory court during Mary's reign and Dunning supplanted him in the other functions of a vicar general – except for a very few occasions – beginning 8 November 1554 until 14 August 1557, that is, almost exactly the period covered by Pole's legation. See Houlbrooke, *Church courts*, p. 24, for Spenser's tenure, allowing the possibility that it may have had 'one short break' in it. See NRO, DN/ACT 7/8, unfoliated and DN/REG/12/18, ff. 92r–179r (institutions to benefices) and DN/ORR/1 (a), ff. 74r, 81v, 84r, 86v (ordinations, for the last time in June 1557). Spenser took over from Dunning instituting to benefices from 1 Sept 1557 (NRO, DN/REG/12/18, f. 179r), became the custodian during the sede vacante and sat in the consistory court again by 1560 when the records resume (DN/ACT 8/9). For Dunning's move to Lincoln see R.E.G. Cole, ed., *Chapter acts of the cathedral church of St Mary of Lincoln A.D. 1547–1559* (Lincoln Record Society, 15, 1920), 145, 148, 157. He died in either late 1558 or early 1559 (ibid., 162n).

[97] John Foxe, *Actes and monuments* (1563; RSTC, no. 11222), 1706, 1602, 1618 and 1655 for his role in five executions. In the 1583 edition, Foxe added that Dunning had died in Lincolnshire of a sudden fit while Mary was still alive and adjusted his total of

bishop of Norwich had powers peculiar to himself which may have cut down on appeals, especially those of uniting benefices, elsewhere reserved to the Pope and hence to Pole.[98] Whatever the situation in Norwich, the existence of men such as Brisley, Dalbie, Williams, Geffrey and Dunning makes even more galling the continuing truth of Peter Heath's observation in 1969 that '[a] much more intimate knowledge of the ecclesiastical administrators of Tudor England than we have at present is badly needed.'[99]

Out of a population of some millions came 315 appeals, 232 pluralists against perhaps 10 000 or 15 000 clergy.[100] The bloody-minded may remain unimpressed, but the merely sceptical may be more receptive to the conclusion that by 1558 a good deal had been done and an administrative and legal framework put in place that would have allowed a good deal more, to say nothing of the progress of Christian instruction and restoration of Catholic ceremonial described by Eamon Duffy, together with reserves of traditional piety and practice emphasized by Christopher Haigh and David Loades, among others, or the Marians' success in grasping the value of the printing press brought out by Jennifer Loach and recently underscored by Alexandra Walsham.[101] That England did not remain a Catholic country must be

---

'murders' to three, including one not listed in 1563. Foxe, *Actes and monuments* (1583; RSTC no. 11225), 2009, 2005, 2023. I owe these references to David Loades. Muriel C. McClendon, *The quiet reformation: magistrates and the emergence of protestantism in Tudor Norwich* (Stanford University Press, 1999), p. 175 assigns only two deaths to Dunning and makes him reluctant to proceed. Foxe, however, had spent 18 months in Norwich and was exceptionally well-informed about the diocese, as Dr Freeman tells me.

[98] T.F. Barton, ed., *The registrum vagum of Anthony Harrison*, Norfolk Record Society, 32–3 (1963–64), 32, 56, one of a whole section of such unifications in the register. Hopton frequently exercised the same power, for example NRO, DN/REG/12/18, f. 107r.

[99] Heath, *The English parish clergy on the eve of the reformation*, (1969), 61.

[100] If nothing else, all this should put paid to the silly story of Pole too abstractedly daydreaming of Italy to conduct business: the document on which it rests cannot be located, its author is not otherwise known; I almost suspect an invention. My very best thanks to Cressida Annesley for repeated efforts to track down the reference, CCA, Y 14: 2 and 3, 49, John Edward to the dean of Canterbury on Pole's behalf, that Pogson ('Cardinal Pole', 116) cited to support the tale.

[101] Duffy, *Altars*; Christopher Haigh, *English reformations. Religion, politics and society under the Tudors* (Oxford: Clarendon Press, 1993), especially chapters 11 and 12; David Loades, 'The piety of the Catholic restoration in England, 1553–8', in *Politics, censorship and the English reformation*, ed. David Loades (London and New York: Pinter Publishers, 1991), 200–212; Jennifer Loach, 'The Marian establishment and the printing press', *English Historical Review*, 109 (1986), 135–48; Alexandra Walsham, '"Domme preachers"? Post-reformation English catholicism and the culture of print', *Past and Present*, 168 (2000), 72–123.

accounted much more of an accident than we have been readily prepared to admit.

CHAPTER SIX

Cardinal Pole Preaching: St Andrew's Day 1557

Eamon Duffy

In the spring of 1558 the Spanish ambassador in London, Count Feria, put on record a series of judgements about Reginald Pole which have coloured perceptions of the cardinal, and of the effectiveness of the Marian restoration of Catholicism, ever since. To Feria it seemed that Pole was sleep-walking through his task of re-Catholicizing England. He was a 'dead man', whose fatal listlessness could be stirred to ardour only by news from the Italy he manifestly pined for. Radically deficient in the zeal necessary for the reconversion of England, he was the wrong man in the wrong place at the wrong time. 'The Cardinal,' Feria wrote, 'is a good man, but very lukewarm: and I do not believe the lukewarm go to Paradise, even if they are called moderates.'[1]

Some of these remarks were addressed to King Philip II of Spain, but the occasion of this latter oft-quoted judgement was a letter to the Jesuit activist, Pedro Ribadeneira, briefly based in London, in which Feria attempted to explain (and exculpate) his own failure to persuade Pole and Queen Mary to establish the Society in England. Such apparently inexplicable resistance to a Jesuit presence, Feria thought, must spring from the cardinal's lack of zeal or insight, and could only be the mark of a secret son of the Church of Laodicea, condemned in the Book of Revelation as being 'neither hot nor cold', a symbol of the spiritually half-hearted, whom the apocalyptic Christ had threatened to 'spew out of [his] mouth'.[2]

Given Pole's friendship with Ignatius and his financial support for new Jesuit enterprises in Italy, it does not seem very likely that he would indefinitely have declined Jesuit help in England. But had he done so he would have been by no means the only Counter-Reformation bishop with reservations about the unqualified value of the Jesuit order. In the mid-1550s the Society was pastorally still something of an unknown

---

[1] Royall Tyler (ed.), *Calendar of Letters, Despatches and State papers relating to the negotiations between England and Spain*, xiii, London, 1954, 366, 370.

[2] Revelation 3: 15–16.

quantity, whose independence of episcopal control and extra-parochial base of operations ran counter to some of the most fundamental emphases of the reform party at Trent. Even two generations later, and in territory in which, as in Marian England, the Church was fighting to reclaim hearts and minds after a period of Protestant dominance, so successful a Counter-Reformation activist as Archbishop Matthew Hovius of Mechelen would fight tooth and nail to prevent an able seminarian from joining the Jesuit order.[3]

Two recent studies of Pole's relationship with the Society have helped clarify the complex of reasons which may have informed his caution.[4] Nevertheless, Pole's rejection of the Jesuits (if that is what it amounted to) has continued to be linked to his supposed lukewarmness, and has been consistently read by historians as one aspect of a general disinclination on his part towards the more adventurous expressions of the Counter-Reformation spirit, indicating a fatal lack of imagination which would have doomed the Marian restoration even if death had not brought it to an abrupt end. The seminal work here has been that of Rex Pogson, whose invaluable study of Pole's legatine mission exhaustively documented both the difficulties confronting Pole and the careful solidity of his administrative and financial reconstruction. However, Pogson stressed also Pole's supposed lack of imagination. The cardinal, Pogson thought, 'possessed valuable gifts for leadership of a Church in peaceful times', but 'nothing more': he recoiled from the extraordinary measures which the reign of Mary demanded. Above all, Pogson insisted, the cardinal distrusted preaching: 'right to the end of the mission he took the line that preaching was useless for the time being, for people were corrupted by the schism and so listened with avarice in their hearts and were untouched by God's Word'. In this, Pole could not entirely be excused simply as a man of his times: others saw what had to be done, even if he did not, and so he 'differed crucially' from advisers as various as Queen Mary, King Philip and Pope Julius III, on the 'urgency to be attached to the organisation of vigorous widespread preaching'. For Pole, preaching would become valuable only when the people had been 'compelled to realise the truth by a terror of the law'. In June 1558, just a few months before his death, Pogson claimed, Pole wrote to his Dominican friend and former collaborator Bartolomé

---

[3] Craig Harline and Eddy Put, *A Bishop's Tale: Matthew Hovius among his flock in Seventeenth Century Flanders*, New Haven and London, 2000, 178–94.

[4] Thomas M. McCoog, 'Ignatius Loyola and Reginald Pole: a Reconsideration', *Journal of Ecclesiastical History*, 17 (1996), 257–73, Thomas Mayer, 'A test of wills: Pole, Loyola and the Jesuits in England', in T.M. McCoog, (ed.), *The Reckoned Expense: Edmund Campion and the early English Jesuits* (Woodbridge, 1996), 21–8.

Carranza, recently appointed archbishop of Toledo and Primate of Spain, a letter in which he spelled out these fundamental reservations about the value of preaching, declaring that 'I think it is better to check the preaching of the Word rather than to proclaim it, unless the discipline of the Church has been fully restored.'[5]

Pogson's line has been closely followed in most subsequent writing about Pole, even by historians who have consciously striven to do justice to the cardinal and his methods. For David Loades, Pole and his colleagues 'were not slack or inept, but they were committed to a long-term policy which ignored certain important features of the immediate situation', above all 'the desperate need for spiritual leadership of a high calibre'. Pole drew back from the Jesuits who might have provided such leadership because he 'simply did not want men with the fire of the counter-reformation in their bellies'. He belonged to an 'older generation' (though Pole was in fact nine years younger than St Ignatius) which 'saw the future in terms of the past', he valued right behaviour above right belief and feared sermons as 'liable to be controversial'. The cardinal was thus 'unenthusiastic about preaching', 'seldom preached himself', and when he did 'his main theme was exhortation to gratitude and obedience'.[6] Christopher Haigh, who makes a vigorous case for the effectiveness of Pole's efforts, nevertheless agreed that 'Pole regarded energetic evangelism as unnecessary and inappropriate', and cited the letter to Carranza in support of this judgement.[7] For Diarmaid MacCulloch, Pole and his collaborators 'showed themselves weak in understanding the need to communicate a dynamic message, having embarked on the negative work of dismantling Protestantism and tidying up after it'. Pole distrusted 'preaching campaigns', which he associated 'with brilliant former associates like Peter Martyr or Bernard Ochino, who had betrayed the Church by turning Protestant'.[8] For the Jesuit historian Thomas McCoog, also, Pole's bitter experience as leader of the Italian *Spirituali*, and the damaging apostasy of evangelists like Martyr and Ochino, led him to renounce his earlier enthusiasm for preaching as an indispensable instrument of reform, and this disillusion was the root cause of his rejection of the Jesuits, who were above all else preachers. Predictably, McCoog backed up his argument about Pole's

---

[5] Rex H. Pogson, 'Reginald Pole and the Priorities of Government in Mary Tudor's Church', *Historical Journal*, xviii (1975), 3–20, quotations at 19, 18, 13, 16, in that order.

[6] David Loades, *The Reign of Mary Tudor*, 2nd edn, London, 1991, 272, 276, 293.

[7] Christopher Haigh, *English Reformations*, Oxford 1993, 224.

[8] Diarmaid MacCulloch, *The Later Reformation in England, 1547–1603*, 2nd edn, London, 2001, 20.

distrust of preaching by recycling Pogson's 'quotation' from Pole's letter to Carranza.[9]

In fact, all these judgements rest on a catastrophic misreading of what Pole himself actually said. Rex Pogson was an admirable historian, but his Latin evidently left something to be desired. He misunderstood Pole's letter to Carranza, which offers a far more specific, nuanced and subtle estimation of the value of preaching – and of controversial writing – than Pole has been given credit for. Pogson's mistranslation has been unquestioningly reproduced by almost everyone writing about Pole since 1975, and has decisively shaped recent estimates of the cardinal's outlook and intentions.[10] A more accurate reading of the letter to Carranza is thus the place to begin a reconsideration not only of Pole's attitude to preaching, but of his openness to the newer energies of the Counter Reformation more generally.

Pole's letter to Carranza, written on 20 June 1558,[11] is a highly defensive document. Detractors had evidently told Carranza that Pole, almost permanently at court and preoccupied with affairs of state, was neglecting both his diocese of Canterbury and also the 13 London parishes which fell under his peculiar jurisdiction. Carranza duly passed these accusations on to Pole, and his motives in doing so may not have been entirely spiritual. Phillip II and his advisers had cause to be worried about Pole's acknowledged influence over the queen, as inimical to Spanish interests, and Carranza may have had his royal master's concern in mind in urging Pole to leave the court and attend to his episcopal responsibilities. At any rate, his criticisms touched Pole on a raw nerve, for episcopal responsibility was a high priority with him. The momentous sixth session of the Council of Trent had produced a trenchant decree on the necessity of episcopal and canonical residence, and this Tridentine insistence had been forcefully reiterated in the third decree of Pole's own legatine synod.[12] In this matter the Marian Church practised what it preached: the Marian bench of bishops was dominated not by lawyers and diplomats, but by theologians and pastors, whose ministries were strikingly characterized by punctilious attention to the religious concerns of their own dioceses.[13]

---

[9] McCoog, 269–70.

[10] An exception is Tom Mayer's recent biography of Pole, for which see below note 21.

[11] *Epistolarum Reginaldi Poli*, ed. Angelo Maria Quirini, Brescia, 1744–57, vol. v, 69–76. For a recent discussion of the Pole-Carranza correspondence, which appeared too late to be considered here, see Dermot Fenlon, 'Pole, Carranza and the pulpit', in John Edwards and Ronald Truman (eds), *Reforming Catholicism in the England of Mary Tudor* (Aldershot, 2005), 81–97.

[12] N.P. Tanner (ed.), *Decrees of the Ecumenical Councils*, London and Washington 1990, vol. II, 681–3; Gerald Bray (ed.), *The Anglican Canons 1529–1947* (Church of England Record Society, vol. 6, 1998), 94–101. Bray's edition is now the most convenient text of the decrees of Pole's legatine synod, providing a parallel Latin/English text.

[13] See David Loades, Chapter 1 this volume.

Stung by these insinuations of neglect, therefore, Pole vigorously defended his record. He was indeed often absent from his diocese and at court (the letter was written from Richmond), but the times demanded this, for his advice was needed not only on religious affairs but also on matters of state. Pole nevertheless was content to be judged by his record: let those who thought he was not doing his job properly consider the woeful state of the country and of the Church in the very recent past, down to the previous year, and compare it with the present, when the 'face of religion' [*facies Religionis*] was at last beginning to recover its pristine form [*quo iam pristinam formam recipere incipit*]. Above all, he was bound to assist Queen Mary. He had often petitioned her to be allowed to go back to look after his diocese, but she and her counsellors considered his presence vital for the good of Church and state, and he could not refuse Mary, as she held the helm of state in stormy waters. She was the nursing mother to whom God had committed the care of the Church in England, the woman to whom indeed the English Church owed everything [*cui tanquam matri, et secundum Deum conservatrici obedientiae Ecclesiae in hoc Regno, omnia ipsa debet Ecclesia* …]. Thus he could be of most use not only to the country but even to the Church, by being present at court. For the foreseeable future much of his time would be absorbed by the task of sorting out the Church's finances after the depredations of earlier reigns, now happily reversed by the piety of the king and queen. But on the outcome of those efforts to restore the Church's possessions, and hence provision for its ministers, the pastoral effectiveness of the clergy and the restoration of proper Church discipline depended. In the light of the many demands on his time, he was, he said, only too well aware of his own inadequate performance as a pastor, which he daily lamented. He knew that Carranza's informants took a cynical view of these protestations, however, since they argued that even if his responsibilities for the English Church as a whole took him away from Canterbury, he could at least look after his London parishes better than in fact he did, since he was near them while at court. And indeed he knew the urgency of London's need, which he was eager to help even more than Canterbury.

It was at this point in the letter that Pogson imagined that Pole had told Cararanza that it was better to 'check' preaching than to advance it, 'unless the discipline of the Church has been fully restored', and that the people should be 'compelled to realise the truth by a terror of the law'.[14] The second claim seemed strange in a man who notoriously

---

[14] Pogson misread '*obesse*' as a transitive verb, with '*verbum*' as its object, rather than as intransitive, in an accusative and infinitive construction in which '*verbum*' is in fact the subject. Thus the sentence '*sed nisi vel ante sit, vel simul constituta Ecclesiastica disciplina,*

shrank from strong-arm techniques, the first was even more improbable: Pole was deeply imbued with Pauline theology, and would have been horrified by the mere thought of 'checking' or hindering the Word of God. And in fact he said nothing of the sort. What he actually wrote to Carranza was very different. Many people thought that what London needed most was the medicine of more and more preaching. But in truth, Pole told Carranza

> From ample daily experience I learn how corrupt and diseased is the state of that body, [the city of London], [and] I find that wherever the Word most abounds, men least profit from it, when it is misused: we see this to be nowhere more so than in London. Of course I don't on that account deny the necessity of preaching the Word, but I do say that the Word can be more of a hindrance than a help, unless it is proceeded or at the same time accompanied by the establishment of Church discipline, because carnal men turn [preaching] into an empty ear-tickling entertainment, rather than a health-giving discipline and food for the soul.[15]

> Ego vero qui quotidie magis experientia disco, qui sit infecti atque infirmi hujus corporis status, hoc reperio, ubi major est verbi copia, ibi minus homines proficere, ea abutentes; quod nusquam magis videmus accidere, quam Londini; nec tamen nego necessarium esse verbi praedicationem, sed nisi vel ante sit, vel simul constituta Ecclesiastica disciplina, dico potius obesse verbum, quam prodesse, quia hoc carnales homines ad inanem aurium delectationem, non ad salutarem animi disciplinam, et alimentum transferunt.

He then quoted Ezekiel 33: 31–2 – 'they sit before thee as my people, and they hear thy words, but they will not do them: for with their mouth they show much love, but their heart goeth after their covetousness. And lo, thou art unto them as one that hath a pleasant voice.' And so it is in London – despite the preaching of the Word, people neglect the celebration of divine worship, except when compelled by the fear of the law, and the Church's discipline is almost wholly ignored. So in Pole's

---

dico potius obesse verbum, quam prodesse' means literally 'I say that the Word may hinder more than help, unless it is proceeded or accompanied by the establishment of Church discipline'. Pogson however translated this as 'I think that it is better to check the preaching of the Word than to proclaim it, unless the discipline of the Church has been fully restored', wrecking the careful balance of what Pole has to say about the timing of the restoration of discipline. Pogson also misunderstood Pole's complaint that Londoners are unresponsive to preaching and only go to church when they are made to do so, '*nisi terrore legum impellerenter, nec sacris ac divinis officiis interessent*', as a general *prescription* for reconversion – that they *should* be 'compelled to realize the truth by a terror of the law'. Once again, Pole's thought has been coarsened and distorted by a misreading of what he actually wrote.

[15] *Epistolarum Reginaldi Poli*, v, 72–3. I am indebted to the superior Latinity of my colleague Dr Richard Rex for help with Pole's sometimes elusive Latin prose.

opinion at this particular point in time it is in the people's interests that more effort be put into sorting out discipline than into preaching. But we need to give full weight to his use of the word '*simul*' – preaching and discipline must go together and at the same time, and Pole adds that in fact discipline itself cannot be established rightly unless there is preaching [*Quare si in iis constituendis atque confirmandis, quae ad disciplinam pertinent, maior opera, quam in praedicando verbo ponatur, id certe huic populo utilius esse ad tempus video, quanquam hoc sine verbo recte fieri non potest*].

But in any case, he insisted, there is no question of the people of London lacking preaching. The 'good bishop of London' has made this a priority, and there is preaching in many places in the city, and in particular every Sunday at St Paul's Cross, to which great assemblies of people come. Pole himself has provided for frequent preaching in the parishes under his direct care, appointing pious and learned men to do this work, and his chancellor, Henry Cole, is also tireless in parochial reform and reconstruction. So contrary to these accusations, Pole was fulfilling his duty as a pastor, even if he had to do it by proxy. Indeed he claimed that he felt easier in his mind about London than about the other parts of the Church under his care, because, as he had shown Carranza, London had plenty of preaching [*verbi copia*]. But if it was still thought that the shepherd's own voice was essential, then Pole's sheep were not deprived of that, either: he himself preaches often, both in his Metropolitan church, and in many other parts of his diocese, he has preached twice in London itself, and with God's help he intends to go on preaching.

Moreover, he has tackled the problem of warning, instructing and correcting his people not simply by the *spoken* word, but by the use of the press. In this task he has good collaborators, men who have advised him that orthodox and wholesome printed works in English were an urgent need, because, they tell him, heretic writings had played a bigger part in corrupting the people even than the spoken word. That was why, as Carranza well knew, the bishops at the legatine synod had insisted on the need for doctrinal and devotional instruction, above all on truths which had been contradicted by the heretics, and that was why they had called for the preparation of a set of English homilies by pious and learned men. Among these he singles out the bishop of Lincoln, Thomas Watson,[16] and, rather more surprisingly, the queen's secretary, John

---

[16] Pole was evidently referring to Watson's collection of sermons on the sacraments, one of the most effective publications of the Marian Restoration: *Holsome and Catholyke doctryne concerning the seven Sacramentes of Chrystes Church, expedient to be knoen to all men, set forth in maner of short e Sermons to bee made to the people* ..., London, 1558, RSTC 25122.

Boxall:[17] some of their writings, Pole declared, were already in print, and some were in the press. Carranza's own excellent catechism was at this very moment being translated out of Spanish for use in England [*tuo ... docto et pio Catechismo ... qui nunc in nostram linguam vertitur*].[18]

There were now, therefore, so many suitable writings of this kind that Pole himself might well be excused from adding to them. In fact, however, he had been persuaded to publish some of the things he had written on controverted questions, and he would do so after they had been vetted by friends and advisers, including Carranza himself. Pole offered all this as proof that he was far from neglecting the pastoral duties in which, as primates of their respective Churches, he and Carranza were joined in a single responsibility. But Carranza was fortunate to minister in a Spain in which, blessedly and almost uniquely, no one had been led astray by corrupt teachers, and Satan had not been able to find a chink through which he could insinuate the poison of heresy. Pole added drily that he hoped that in offering welcome advice and admonition in the future, Carranza would draw on his own pastoral experience rather than on book learning. The implication was that Toledo did not offer the sort of difficulties that Pole had to contend with in England, where the going was tougher and the pastoral challenges far greater.[19]

This is a remarkable utterance, as near as Pole ever got to a comprehensive rationale and defence of the whole teaching programme of the Marian restoration, and in effect a retrospective, composed a matter of months before that restoration came to an abrupt end with his own and Mary's deaths. Its importance in assessing the relationship between Pole and Carranza has been recognized by Spanish historians, but in England it has been either ignored, or disastrously misunderstood.[20] Of all those who have used it, only Pole's recent biographer, Thomas Mayer, has grasped that far from providing evidence of Pole's distrust of preaching, the letter establishes that, in Mayer's words, 'preaching was important to [Pole], and he put effort into it'.[21]

The letter to Carranza is a very rich source for Pole's understanding

---

17 Pole is quite explicit about the writer in question's role as royal secretary, so Boxall is certainly the person referred to in the printed text of Pole's letter as 'Brexallus', though so far as I am aware Boxall published no homilitic material under his own name.

18 For Carranza's catechism, see John Edwards, Chapter 7 this volume.

19 *Epistolarum Reginaldi Poli*, v, 74–5.

20 It was published *in extenso* in Tellechea Idigoras, *Fray Bartolome Carranza y el Cardenal Pole: Un navarro en la retauracion catolica de Inglaterra (1554–1558)*, Pamplona, 1977, 191–6.

21 Thomas F. Mayer, *Reginald Pole, Prince and Prophet*, Cambridge, 2000, 250.

of the Marian enterprise, not least for what it reveals about his own reverence for Mary as 'established by God as the maintainer of obedience to the Church in this realm' [*secundum Deum conservatrici obedientiae Ecclesiae in hoc regno*], a strikingly full-blooded expression from so zealous an opponent of the royal supremacy as Pole.[22] Equally emphatically, Pole here asserts a coherent preaching and teaching strategy by the Marian Church, appealing both to the actual provision of such teaching, and to the programmatic legislation of the legatine synod, whose emphases on episcopal residence and visitation, instruction, preaching and publishing is carefully echoed and at several points quoted directly in his letter.[23]

Moreover, Pole claims that this strategy had been effectively implemented and was working, as he contrasts the woeful state of English religion in the recent past with the present time in which 'it is just beginning to recover its pure form'. That sense that some sort of corner had been turned by the summer of 1558, however, was certainly not born of complacency. Pole's letter is throughout informed by a sense of the daunting scale of the tasks and dangers confronting the regime, and of the extent to which the Reformation had 'deformed' the religious sense of the people. Pole is often accused of seriously underestimating the extent and strength of the Protestant penetration of English lay religious culture, of imagining that 'the breach with Rome had been the work of a tiny faction' and of lacking 'an informed overall judgement of the schism's impact'.[24] There is no sign in the letter of any such lack of awareness, though he was admittedly playing up his own difficulties as a form of self-defence. For our purposes, however, perhaps the most striking features of the letter are the careful balance of what Pole has to say in it about preaching, and the specific reference of what he does say, not to preaching in general, but to preaching in the city of London, which he thinks and says is a special and desperate case.

It should not surprise us that Pole defends so vigorously his record on preaching. Preaching and teaching dominate three of the first four decrees of his legatine synod, signalling the high priority he placed on them from the outset of his mission. The first decree indeed invented a ground-breaking propagandist technique, normally associated with the Protestant regimes which succeeded Mary. The decree provided for an annual procession and thanksgiving Mass on St Andrew's Day (30

---

[22] *Epistolarum Reginaldi Poli*, v, 71.

[23] For example, Bray, *Anglican Canons*, 104, Synodal decree 4, on the preparation of homilies by '*piis et doctiis viris*', and the same formula in *Epistolarum*, v, 74.

[24] Rex Pogson, 'The Legacy of the Schism', in J. Loach and R. Tittler (eds), *The Mid-Tudor Polity c. 1540–1560*, London, 1980, 122.

November), the anniversary of the reconciliation of England with the papacy, in the course of which 'a sermon shall be preached to the people in which the reason for this solemnity shall be explained'. The synod directed that where there was no qualified preacher, an official homily on the subject should be read out by the parish priest, and John Harpsfield duly produced such a model sermon for St Paul's in 1556, which was published for wider use on the instructions of Bishop Bonner.[25] Historians have recently recognized the importance and effectiveness of *Protestant* anniversary celebrations, and the role which 'bonfires and bells', with their accompanying sermons commemorating events like Queen Elizabeth's accession or James's deliverance from the Gunpowder Plot, played in consolidating Protestantism within popular culture.[26] It has not, I think, been noted that the invention of this innovatory technique is Pole's, and its introduction certainly does not suggest a timid reluctance to use preaching for propagandist purposes.

The synod's second decree introduced tight control of the press to eliminate heretical books, prohibited heretical preaching, emphasized the need for orthodox teaching above all on the principal Reformation targets of papal primacy and the seven sacraments, and, since Trent had not yet produced a compact formulation on the sacraments as a whole, the synod provided clergy with a brief but comprehensive summary of Catholic sacramental teaching, derived from the Council of Florence. That sacramental teaching was given symbolic endorsement in new provisions for the public reservation of the Blessed Sacrament in a tabernacle on the high altar of every church. The third decree was devoted to enforcing clerical residence, but decree four explained that the point of all this was to ensure the proper discharge of their pastoral duties by the clergy, from the bishop down, and that 'the pastoral office ... chiefly consists in the preaching of the divine word'. This was above all the bishop's task: he must preach often in person, and he must ensure that all parish priests 'feed the people committed to them with the wholesome food of preaching', at least on Sundays and other feast days. They must also catechize, taking special care to admonish and if necessary threaten laypeople who had been seduced into heresy, and they must be specially vigilant against anyone 'unauthorised by the apostolic see, or by the catholic bishop of his diocese', who dares 'usurp the office of a preacher'. Finally, the decree ordered the preparation of

---

[25] Bray, *Anglican Canons*, 75–7; John Harpsfield, *A Notable and learned Sermon made upon Saint Andrewes daye last past 1556 in the cathedral churche of St Paule in London ... set forth by the bishop of London*, London, 1556 (RSTC 12795).

[26] David Cressy, *Bonfires and Bells: National Memory and the Protestant Calendar in Elizabethan and Stuart England*, London, 1989.

English homilies for use 'by such curates as are not capable of preaching'.[27]

All this, it must be emphasized, was Pole's own agenda, not some alien programme thrust upon him by others more committed to preaching than he was himself, and all these concerns are revisited in the letter to Carranza. That letter makes it clear that Pole did not distrust preaching as such; he distrusted heretical preaching by self-appointed evangelists who operated without proper authority. He thought preaching to be the principal duty of all pastors, but he insisted that it should be orthodox and programmatic, focussed on fundamentals of the Christian life like the nature and use of the sacraments and the unity of the Church. He thought it the special responsibility of the bishops to preach themselves, to choose parish clergy able to preach, to determine and to police the content of parochial preaching, and to provide model sermons for the inept or uneducated clergy to read. Far from discouraging preaching, he was active in securing all that. As we shall see, however, he was also convinced that there were special problems in London, corrupted by years of Protestant polemics, preached and printed, in which sermons had become sources of dissension rather than of consolidation in the Christian life. Preaching in such an environment was prone to become separated from the sacramental life of the Church, the practice of charity and penitential asceticism. In such a culture of contestation the proper reception of the Word of God, a matter of humble openness rather than fractious judgement, was a rarity, and audiences were liable to become opinionated and hardened against the life of grace. So he thought the restoration of a Catholic pattern of sacramental practice, including regular use of the sacrament of penance, a vital and compelling context for preaching. But he did not on that score think preaching should be outlawed or discouraged, for he recognized that sermons and catechizing were needed to explain and underpin the restoration of sacramental discipline. He commended the record of Bonner and his own record in the provision of pastoral preaching in London parishes, as well as the set-piece official (and controversial) weekly sermons at Paul's Cross.

Pole himself, it will have been noted, told Carranza that he preached 'often' [*saepius*]. We badly need an edition of Pole's English sermons, of which a mere handful survive, several only as fragments.[28] His most recent biographer has pointed out, however, that in terms of frequency

---

[27] Bray, *Anglican Canons*, 101–5.
[28] They are catalogued by Tom Mayer in 'A Reluctant author: Cardinal Pole and his Manuscripts', *Transactions of the American Philosophical Society*, 89, Part 4 (1999), 68–74.

Pole's record as a preacher compares favourably with that of his successor at Canterbury, Matthew Parker.[29] Pole's style has been disparaged,[30] but in fact his vernacular sermons display a keen sensitivity to audience and occasion, and a literary skill displayed not so much in fine language (he was almost certainly happier writing in Latin or Italian) as in a remarkable ability to develop key ideas by an almost musical technique of variations on recurring texts and topics, sustained through the length of a sermon.

One sermon in particular allows us to test the thinking about preaching expressed in the synodal decrees and the letter to Carranza against Pole's actual practice. This was the sermon he preached at Whitehall on St Andrew's Day 1557, the third anniversary of the nation's reconciliation with Rome.[31] In this major set-piece utterance before the queen, the court, the legal profession and the mayor and aldermen of London, Pole confronted head-on the problem of London, the nature of the city's apostasy, its continuing role as a centre of dissent and his own vision of the best means of restoring it. Preached just over six months before his letter to Carranza, the St Andrew's Day sermon deals in greater detail with issues touched on in that letter. Between them, the two documents offer a striking corrective to much of the conventional wisdom about the limitations of Pole's pastoral vision.[32]

---

[29] Mayer, *Reginald Pole*, 250.

[30] J.W. Blench, *Preaching in England in the late fifteenth and sixteenth centuries*, Oxford, 1964, 164–5.

[31] The manuscript, once among the Foxe manuscripts, appears to be lost, and the sermon survives only in a long but still incomplete edition by John Strype, *Ecclesiastical Memorials Relating Chiefly to Religion and its Reformation under the Reigns of King Henry VIII, King Edward VI and Queen Mary*, Oxford 1816, vol. III pt 2, 482–510; Mayer, *Cardinal Pole and his Manuscripts*, 70, 72. I differ from Professor Mayer, however, over the precise time of the sermon's delivery. Henry Machyn does not in fact link Pole's sermon to Sir Thomas Tresham's installation as prior of the Order of St John, as Professor Mayer suggests, though both occurred at Whitehall on the same day, and Pole was indeed present for the installation ceremony, during a Mass and procession at Westminster Abbey in the morning, at which Abbot Feckenham presided. According to Machyn, Pole's sermon was preached in the Chapel Royal in the afternoon: cf. John Gough Nichols (ed.), *The Diary of Henry Machyn*, Camden Society, 1848, 159. There can be no doubt that Strype's text was this sermon preached by Pole in the afternoon of 30 November 1557: the deliberate and rather artificial reference to St Andrew is inexplicable otherwise (Strype, III pt 2, 501) and, together with Pole's remark that 'three years and mo' had passed since the reconciliation (498), pinpoints the date, since it cannot have been preached earlier than 30 November 1557, and Pole was dead by 30 November 1558. It does not seem likely that the cardinal preached twice on the same day, given the great length of the surviving sermon.

[32] It has been surprisingly neglected: it was summarized at length by Philip Hughes, who recognized that it was 'the nearest thing we possess to a public review of the quality

Pole's St Andrew's Day sermon was the culmination of a day of extraordinary Catholic triumphalism in London. That morning (a Tuesday) the procession, Mass and 'godly sermon' stipulated in the first synodal decree had been duly held at St Paul's, with a priest from every parish in London participating. Later that day, the queen and the cardinal rode from St James's to Whitehall, for a display of Catholic chivalry at which Sir Thomas Tresham was installed as prior of the newly revived Order of St John, and four Knights of Rhodes were made. The ceremony was attended by all the bishops, and by the judges and sergeants of the law, and it took place in the context of a solemn Mass and procession at Westminster Abbey at which Abbot Feckenham presided in his mitre. After dinner the court and the legal profession moved to the Chapel Royal, where they were joined by the Lord Mayor and all the aldermen of London, who had presumably attended the Mass and sermon at St Paul's that morning. There, in the presence of the legal profession, the city governors and 'many Lordes and knyghtes, and lades and gentyllmen', Pole preached.[33] He is often accused of being out of touch with the English scene, insufficiently aware of the extent of the impact of the Reformation, his antennae for English affairs and English sensibilities dulled by years of residence in Italy. His sermon that day however, suggests quite another picture. It forcefully targets some of the different constituencies who made up his audience, and it intervenes tellingly in the affairs of the city, in particular the fraught issue of the city hospitals and their confessional significance. Pole tackles head-on some of the thorniest problems confronting the regime in London, above all the city's continuing sympathy for Protestantism, or at any rate for the victims of the Marian regime's campaign of repression.

In the course of his sermon Pole observes that St Andrew had seen Jesus walking by the Sea of Galilee, an incident from the Gospel prescribed for St Andrew's Day, Matthew chapter four verses 18–22.[34] The sequence (hymn between the readings at Mass) for the day, however, specifically identifies Andrew as a preacher of repentance, and perhaps following this clue, Pole took as his text a passage in Matthew chapter three, in which John the Baptist urges the people of Judaea to 'bring forth fruits meet for repentance', and warns that trees that fail to bear

---

of the Marian Restoration', and it has been quarried by many writers about the Marian restoration and about Pole, but Hughes's insight was not developed by him and has been pursued by nobody else; cf. Philip Hughes, *The Reformation in England*, vol. 2, London 1951, 246–53.

[33] Nichols, *The Diary of Henry Machyn*, 159.

[34] F.E. Warren (ed.), *The Sarum Missal in English*, London, 1913, pt 2, 246–9; Strype, *Ecclesiastical Memorials*, 501.

such fruit will be cut down and cast into the fire. In a city which had witnessed many recent burnings, it was a pointed and uncomfortable choice of text. The opening of the sermon is missing, but in it Pole had evidently identified as one of the chief sins of Reformation England the dissolution of the monasteries and the theft of monastic property, 'whereby ... was overtoorned the welthe of the realme, and of the prynce also himselfe'. Pole hastens to reassure his audience, of lordes, gentlemen and city fathers that they are not required as the fruit of their repentance to rebuild the monasteries, 'which I knowe you be not able to do'. Rather, 'yf you were able, and had such a gay mynde to restore the ruynes of the chyrches', they should help their parish churches, which 'have byn sufferede to fawle downe of themselves maynye, and yn lyke maner spoyled as the monasteryes were'. With his eye on the judges and the city magistrates, he presented such restoration as an act of common prudence, for respect and care for the churches was part of the maintenance of civic society, 'the whyche you maye yn no wyse fayle to doo, excepte you wyll have your people wax brutyshe and wylde, and your commonwealthe wythout foundacyon'.[35]

Though Pole thus absolved his audience from the obligation to restore monastic property, he did not leave the matter there. As the letter to Carranza was to make clear, he was much preoccupied with the Church's finances, and he reminded his hearers that they held monastic property by the concession of the Church, their indulgent Mother, and not by right. The recent appetite for Church property which had impoverished and weakened religion was, he thought, an infantile disorder, and those affected by it were like a greedy child gobbling an over-large apple given by his mother, which she 'perceyvinge him to feade too much of, and knowynge yt sholde doo him hurte ... would have him give her a lytyll pece therof'. They should attend to the requests of their loving mother Church, famished as she was for sustenance, when they had far more than was good for them, or else, like an angry father intervening in a mother–child stand-off, Christ would come and take the apple away altogether, and cast it 'out of the wyndowe'. The Church herself would not constrain her children in this matter, but Pole hoped that in a little while, 'you by [Christ's] grace waxinge a lytyll stronger, youre appetite shalbe retourned to his natural course. As I have harde that some have begonne veray well al readye ...'[36]

Pole now turned to the fraught issue of charity and poor-relief. He was preaching at a time of desperate social hardship and recurrent dearth and

---

[35] Strype, *Ecclesiastical Memorials*, 482.
[36] Ibid., 483.

disease. The city had responded to this mid-century crisis by founding or recasting its five hospitals – St Bartholomew's, St Thomas's, Bethlem, Christ's Hospital and Bridewell – as centres for poor-relief and social discipline. These measures had been supported across the religious spectrum of Reformation London: Thomas White, founder of Trinity College Oxford and an ardent Catholic, was involved, as was that archetypical establishment conformist, the former Lord Mayor and MP Sir Martin Bowes, reviled by John Stow for his prominent role in the dismantling and sale of pre-Reformation monuments, and a pillar of the Edwardine Chantry Commission for London, yet whose personal religious views were conservative, and who 'of his benevolence and good wille, paid for the gilding and painting of the rood, Mary and John' in his parish church in 1557.[37] But the pace in Edward's reign had been set by Reformation activists like the printer and chronicler Richard Grafton, while Bishop Ridley and other Protestant clergy had urged the use of former Church property for poor-relief and especially the establishment of hospitals which would be 'truly religious houses', and Christ's Hospital had been established as a reception centre for foundling children in the premises of the former Greyfriars. The Franciscans, led by William Peto, were to make determined but unsuccessful efforts to recover their house, if necessary at the cost of dissolving the hospital, early in Mary's reign. The imposition of moral discipline on the erring poor confined in Bridewell, moreover, cut across the jurisdiction of Bonner's restored Church courts. So to many people the future of the Edwardine social initiatives in London looked uncertain, and the city hospitals were in danger of becoming confessional footballs, in a quarrel in which Protestants occupied the high moral ground with an apparent monopoly on charity. As a character in a dialogue on the hospital question by Grafton's servant John Howes asked, 'Could not the Pope's clergy and Bridewell be friends?'[38]

Pole now intervened directly in this highly charged debate, to demonstrate that Protestants had no monopoly on concern for the poor. Indeed, the citizens must make use of their ill-gotten Church wealth to 'enlarge your hande more to the helpe of the poore'. Christ would judge men not by empty professions, but by what they did for the needy.

---

[37] C.S. Schen, *Charity and Lay Piety in Reformation London 1500–1620* (Aldershot, 2002), 31, 80. My thanks to Dr Peter Marshall for this reference, and for helpful discussion of Bowes's religious position.

[38] Paul Slack, 'Social policy and the Constraints of Government 1547–1558', in Jennifer Loach and Robert Tittler (eds), *The Mid Tudor Polity c. 1540–1560*, London, 1980, esp. 108–13; Susan Brigden, *London and the Reformation*, Oxford 1989, 620–23.

Almsgiving went along with prayer and penance as 'special means to injoie the goodnes of God', and England compared wretchedly with Catholic Italy, 'where is more almes gyven to monasteryes and poore folkes in one monthe, than yn this realme in a hole yeare'. There were fewer than ten hospitals and religious houses to relieve the poor in London: as Pole could personally testify, there were, by contrast, hundreds in Milan, Bologna and Rome. The reason for this was plain: in Catholicism, unlike Protestantism, charity as well as faith was required for salvation. In a characteristically careful formulation, avoiding any crude notion of justification by works, Pole insisted that 'the doctryne of the chyrche ys the doctryne of the mercye and almes of God. Whyche mercye is receyved more wyth comforte: but of them that use mercye, and gyve almes to other, that ys the veraye waye to enjoye all the grace and benefyts of God graunted to the chyrche.' They, who had specially offended in stealing from the Church, must above all bring forth this fruit of repentance, charity to the poor.[39]

Having thus neatly stolen the reformers' clothes on the question of poor-relief, Pole pressed home his argument. Robbing the poor was just part of the sin of the Reformation in stripping the Church of her property. They had also stripped their priests, and, in the process, the Christ whom the clergy represented. In this the English 'have gone further than any schismaticall natyon hath done, that ever I redde of', 'dyshonouringe [God's] prystes, wythdrawinge from them that shoulde be theyr lyvinge, by the appoyntment of God'. Contempt of priests was excused by complaints of the unedifying lives of the clergy, but they should be honoured for what they taught, whatever their lives, and the people should pray for good clergy, especially that they might be spared the priests they deserved, men who instead of opposing sin and error 'wyll conforme themselves to your desyres'. The clergy were their spiritual fathers, and the mercy of God would be withheld from any who rejected their authority. That was why the special mark of a heretic was hatred of priests, 'that are onlye the stay and lett, that theyr pernycyouse attempts take none effect'.[40]

The mention of the curse of a docile clergy who would not challenge the errors and vices of their people introduces a section of the sermon in which Pole considers the fruits of schism, and the way in which the rejection of papal authority had led inexorably to the undermining of morality and godly order, as well as the utter rejection of the sacraments. Heresy was a calamity in society, for 'there ys no kynd of men so pernycyouse to the commonwelthe ... no theves, no murtherers, no

---

[39] Strype, *Ecclesiastical Memorials*, 484.
[40] Ibid., 486.

advouterers, nor no kynd of treason to be compared to theyrs', since true religion was the foundation of the commonwealth, and heresy overthrew that foundation.[41] Pole was speaking to judges and city worthies, and could take it for granted that most of them were likely enough to be opposed to religious radicalism. Equally clearly, he was aware that most of those sitting before him had acquiesced in, and in many cases directly benefited from, the Reformation, and that even the many alienated by the drastic Protestantism of Edward's reign might be more ambivalent about the demerits of the Henrician schism. And so he pressed on them the necessity of communion with Rome, and the inexorable momentum of the Reformation towards extremes once that communion had been broken. To the worst excesses of the reform, when the priesthood, the laws of the Church and the sacrament 'were cast awaye, and troden underfoote', he told them, 'you cam not sodenlye', for at first 'you toke nothynge from the chyrche, but the pre-emynence and prerogative of the supreme hed, whiche you toke from the highest pryste, and gave yt to the Kynge: all the sacraments standynge and remaynynge wyth streight lawes, that they sholde not be violated, but reverentlye kept'. But all in vain: though the sacraments were maintained under Henry despite his 'straunge tytle', yet the realm received no grace from them, being in schism. They had been like a withered branch, cut off from the vine, or like the Philistines when they stole the Ark of the Covenant from the Israelites, receiving only cursing and disease from the presence of God among them. And the English had sinned more deeply than the Philistines. In the Ark of the Covenant had been the rod of Aaron, symbolizing priestly authority, and the miraculous manna, symbolizing the Mass. These the Philistines had left unharmed, but under Edward England had rejected both.[42]

Pole here was deploying standard arguments familiar from many of the official publications of the Marian restoration.[43] He now mounted a critique of the Henrician schism and its consequences linked directly to the publication of the folio edition of the English *Workes* of Thomas More earlier that year.[44] More and Fisher had long been iconic figures for Pole: their executions had precipitated him into open opposition to

---

[41] Ibid., 487.

[42] Ibid., 488–9.

[43] For a similar account of the disastrous consequences of the breach with Rome, for example, see Henry Pendleton's homily on the authority of the Church in *Homelies sette forth by the right reverend father in God, Edmunde Byshop of London*, London 1555, RSTC 3285.7, fols 41v–42r.

[44] *The Workes of Sir Thomas More Knyght, sometyme Lorde Chancellour of England, wrytten by him in the Englysh tonge*, ed. William Rastell, London, 1557, RSTC 18076.

Henry and his Reformation, and they loom large in his first major publication, the treatise *Pro Ecclesiasticae Unitatis defensione*, addressed to Henry VIII in 1536.[45] In the sermon, the theme first explored by Pole in *De Unitate*, that More and Fisher were miraculous witnesses and sacrifical victims raised up for the salvation of England as it stood poised on the edge of schism, is elaborated and focussed: they are invoked specifically as witness not merely to England, but to London in particular. England, Pole declared, had been greatly blessed from her first reception of the Gospel, and in Catholic times had brought forth 'nobyl fruytes to the honore of him that planted you', till at last, by their own fault, their branch had been cut off and would have withered entirely if the schism had not been ended. 'What countrye hathe ever had the lyke grace?'[46] And London had special cause for gratitude, not merely in being the first part of the realm to be reconciled, but for 'having more dyligent labour bestowede upon you, to make you a grounde to bryng furthe all fruyte of sanctitie and justice, wyth more frequent rayne of preachynge and teaching than all the realme besyde'. Instead of bearing good fruit, however, it seemed that London had produced nothing but thorns. In a gruesome and daring joke, Pole allows that this may be an optical illusion. It is true that 'a greater multytude of thes brambles and bryars were cast in the fyre hear among you, than yn any place besyde', but they may have grown elsewhere, since London was the epicentre of the Marian campaign against heresy. So, many of those burned there for heresy were not native Londoners, which 'maye gyve occasyon that you have the worse name wythoute your deserte'.[47]

Be that as it might, God had raised up for Londoners marvellous witnesses, whose miraculous example should have preserved them 'when the realme was fawlinge from the unytie of the churche'. Of these witnesses the greatest was Thomas More, 'a cytesyn of yours', assaulted on all sides on this very question of the unity of Christendom, and like other laypeople bound by bonds of family affections and obligation, concern for which might have plucked him from the unity of the Church. Pole illustrated his account of More with a vivid anecdote he had received from the rich London–Lucca merchant Antonio Bonvisi, one of More's oldest and closest friends, godfather to his son John and

---

[45] Discussed in Mayer, *Reginald Pole*, 13–61; there is an excellent annotated French translation by Noelle-Marie Egretier, *Reginald Pole, Defence de l'Unite del l'Eglise*, Paris 1967. I have not seen J.G. Dwyer's English version, *Pole's Defense of the Unity of the Church*, Westminster, Md, 1965.
[46] Strype, *Ecclesiastical Memorials*, 489.
[47] Ibid., 490.

purchaser of his house in Bishopsgate. Bonvisi had been a key member of the More circle and of Catholic resistance to the Reformation after More's death, and had been banished from England as a consequence. He had sheltered Pole's future archdeacon and More's biographer, Nicholas Harpsfield, together with members of the More family, in his house in Louvain, and before Pole's arrival in England Bonvisi had acted for him as a go-between with Mary.[48] A translation of an ardently affectionate letter to Bonvisi from More formed the penultimate item in the 1557 folio edition of More's English *Workes*,[49] and Pole clearly expected his audience to recognize him, introducing him as a familiar city figure 'whom I thinke you all knowe'.[50] He tells how when Bonvisi at the outset of the Henrician Reformation had asked More's opinion about papal primacy, More had answered at first that he thought it a matter of secondary importance, 'rather inventyd of men for a polytical ordre, and for the more quyetnes of the ecclesiasticall bodye, than by the verye ordynance of Cryste'. Regretting this hasty judgement, however, he told Bonvisi that he would study more and deliver a considered opinion. In due course he returned to the subject, declaring 'Alas! Mr Bonvyse, whither was I fawlinge, when I made you that answer of the prymacye of the chyrche? I assure you, that opinione alone was ynough to make me fawle from the rest, for that holdyth up all.'[51]

Alongside More, an example to the laity of constancy to the Pope and hence to the unity of the Church, Pole set as an example to the clergy John Fisher, whom Henry VIII himself had recognized as the most learned clerk in Christendom. The pairing was of course another Marian convention, given its most spectacular expression at the execution of Cranmer by Pole's chancellor, Henry Cole, who declared that as the death of Northumberland would atone for More's death, so those of the heretical bishops Ferrar, Cranmer, Ridley and Latimer would atone for Fisher's.[52] Pole now put a personal mark on this conventional pairing, recalling how on his first return from study in Italy, Henry had quizzed him about the learned men he had met, boasting that there was none to compare with Fisher: yet when his conscience was challenged by Fisher, he had him beheaded. This beheading was symbolic, Pole declared, a sign of the cutting off of the realm from the true head of the Church, the

---

[48] Archivio Segreto Vaticano Bolognetti 94, fols 29r–v, 63v–70r, 73v–77r: references from Dr Thomas Mayer via Dr Thomas Freeman, to both of whom many thanks.
[49] *Workes of Sir Thomas Moore*, 1455–7.
[50] Strype, *Ecclesiastical Memorials*, 491.
[51] Ibid., 493.
[52] Nicholas Harpsfield, *Bishop Cranmer's Recantacyons*, London 1877–84, 96–7: my thanks to Tom Freeman for reminding me of this reference.

Pope. London had received further witnesses in the deaths of the martyred priests and religious 'oute of those religiouse howses that were most reformed' – from the London Charterhouse, from Syon, from the Observant Franciscans. 'And why was all this, but for your staye? And but for your example?' And here Pole picks up the ruling metaphor of the sermon again: despite such examples, they had fallen, and tasted the bitterness of the fruit 'receyved by the swervynge from the unytie of the churche. Whiche at the fyrste semed verey sweete, as dyd the apple to our fyrst mother, eaten agaynst the commandement.'[53]

All that had happened when royal authority was pressing men into schism. Yet even now, when the authority of the king and queen was on the side of Catholicism, and 'the favour of heaven and earth agree together', still the city harboured Protestants. So Pole turned to examine London's continuing infidelity. As his letter to Carranza would make clear, he was under no illusions about the resistance of many in the city to the restoration of Catholicism. Early in his legation he had been jeered as he passed through Cheapside with the queen, blessing the people, and he was well aware of the continuing support for arrested heretics in the city.[54] Who then was to blame, 'whome shall I fyrst accuse?'

Pole's first attempt at an answer to his own question was the suggestion that the Reformation was a youth movement:[55] he considered first as 'one great cause' the attractions Protestantism exercised over the London apprentices and other 'yowthe brought up yn a contrarye trade', ignorant of the true faith and prejudiced against it by the polemic of the Protestants, 'and herein I have great compassyon of the youthe'. But the real blame, he thought, lay with those who had charge of the young, and who tolerated such youthful rebellion, and failed 'to bringe the youthe to followe the same [religion], that your fathers afore have followed'. Disorder and error would never cease 'untyll the fathers and masters cease to suffer any alteracyon yn his sonne or servant touching religion'. And there is now nothing to prevent every man in the city enforcing true religion in his own house, 'and so I truste they do'. Yet Pole knew, he told them, that whenever heretics were carried through the city to execution, each one was comforted and encouraged to die 'in his perverse opinions', and they were much cherished in prison. The city's alibi was that it was the young who were responsible for all this, and

---

[53] Strype, *Ecclesiastical Memorials*, 494.

[54] John Gough Nichols (ed.), *Narratives of the Days of Reformation*, Camden Society, 1859, 209–10 (Autobiography of Thomas Mountayne).

[55] On which topic see Susan Brigden, 'Youth and the English Reformation', *Past and Present*, 95 (May 1982), 37–67.

that more time was needed to reform them. Pole was unimpressed: three years had passed since the reconciliation, 'this beinge a thinge not to be suffered one houre'.[56]

But for Pole the key to London's sympathy for the heretics lay in the debate about real and pretended martyrdom. More's English writings were the main quarry for the Marian Church's arguments against the martyr status of condemned heretics, the 'pseudo-martyr' debate. As we have seen, Pole's sermon is certainly shaped by the recent publication of those works, and there are striking parallels between his presentation of More and Fisher and that of his archdeacon, Nicholas Harpsfield's life of More, written in the same year to accompany the *English Workes*.[57] It was entirely natural therefore that Pole should raise the 'pseudo-martyr' issue.[58] But given the numbers of Protestants burned for heresy in the city, he could hardly have avoided it, and there had been a much-publicized burning of three city heretics at Smithfield, only a fortnight before. One of those burned then, Richard Gibson, was a very prominent Londoner, whose grandfather had been Lord Mayor, and whose father was bailiff of Southwark.[59] Even so conservative a London commentator as Henry Machyn displayed an unusual interest in the circumstances of Gibson's burning, almost certainly because of his distinguished city connections, and sympathy for such a sufferer was bound to be widespread.[60] Pole therefore tackled this issue head-on. He told the listening aldermen that the cause of Protestantism in London was being nourished by the citizens' mistaken admiration for the courage and constancy of the heretics in death, courage which seemed to confirm the truth of their teaching, especially in the eyes of those who knew no better. 'Thys, men say, ys a greate stoppe, and a great blocke yn theyr way that have none other lernyng than theyrs, to let them to come to the ancyent doctryne, as I thynke yt be indeed.' But this was a terrible error: what heretics displayed was not holy courage in defence

---

[56] Strype, *Ecclesiastical Memorials*, 498

[57] E. Vaughan Hitchcock (ed.), *The Life and Death of Sir Thomas Moore ... written in the tyme of Queene Marie by Nicholas Harpsfield*, Early English Text Society, 1932, 209–13,

[58] Anne Dillon, *The Construction of Catholicism in the English Catholic Community 1535–1603*, Aldershot, 2002, 18–71; Brad Gregory, *Salvation at Stake: Christian Martyrdom in Early Modern Europe*, Cambridge, Mass., 1999, 315–41.

[59] *Diary of Henry Machyn*, 157–8.

[60] Machyn's account makes it clear that the execution of Gibson was postponed for a day as the result of an intervention by Abbot Feckenham, perhaps to buy time to persuade Gibson to recant: it is likely that the regime was anxious about the fallout from the execution of a member of a leading city family. I am indebted to Dr Tom Freeman for comment on this point.

of the truth, but a 'develysche pertynacye'. Stubborness in death for one's own opinion was not martyrdom. True martyrs like More and Fisher had died for the ancient faith, inherited from their fathers, not for some concocted gospel, pieced together from books and citations of the ancient fathers 'that were not harde of in our fathers dayes'. A faithful man is known, 'not by the faythe he hath found of himselfe, or taken of the fathers so fur off, not allegyng his next father, but by the fayth of his next father, contynuyng the same untyll he come to his fyrst father'. Nor was his cause vindicated by an apparent lack of fear at his death, for rash courage might be a sign of error rather than truth. Christ at his death, the paradigm of all martyrdom, had not displayed the arrogant defiance which characterized the heretics burned in London, but had showed more 'heavynes and doloure at his dying houre' than the thieves with whom he was crucified. It was the wicked thief on Calvary who showed no fear, 'and so doe these heretykes at their deathe lyke the blasphemer, whatsoever theyr wordes be yn honour of Chryste'.[61]

Pole drew all this together in the final section of his sermon, in which he considered how the true Christian may see and follow Christ, as Andrew did in Galilee, to which his answer is by humble openness to the grace of God in the Church, and by participation in the sacraments and in the life of charity. That day had been a day of ceremonial, and accordingly he focussed in this final section on ceremonies as a concrete expression of the state of mind needed for salvation. The good Christian follows the commandments of Christ, and of Christ's spouse, the Church. For a great while the Church's commandments have been despised, especially her ceremonies, which are always the first target of the heretics. But 'of the observation of ceremonyes, begynneth the verye educatyon of the chylderne of God': it is the *'pedagogium in Christum'* of which Paul speaks. Heretics despise such things, and their dismissal of them seemed plausible: 'yt semed nothing here amongst you to take awaye holy water, holy breade, candells, ashes, and palme'. But from little things great consequences flow, and 'what yt came to, you sawe, and all felt yt' – the breakdown of all order, the triumph of heresy and the loss of the sacraments. Obedience in the small things commanded by the Church is the sign of submission to the will of God. 'What lesse thinge woulde there be commanded, than to forbeare the eating of an apple', but Eve's apple had been a poisoned fruit which killed the whole of humanity.

Pole made it crystal clear that he was talking here about inner dispositions, not external ceremony. Without the Spirit of God, neither

---

61 Strype, *Ecclesiastical Memorials*, 499–501.

ceremonies 'whiche the heretykes doe rejecte, nor yet the Scripture whereunto they so cleve' are of any use. It is not that ceremonies bring salvation, but that contempt of ceremonies brings damnation. The 'thinge that gyveth us the veraye light, ys none of them both; but they are most apt to receive light, that are the more obedyent'. So obedience in ceremonies is the mark of the *'parvuli'*, the little ones to whom (unlike the assertive youth of Reformation London) belongs the kingdom. Many think there is 'no better nor spedyer waye ... for to come to the knowledge of God and his lawe, then by reading of books, wherein they be sore deceyved', though 'so yt be done in its place, and with right order and circumstance, [reading] helpeth muche'. But the light of God is not got by reading: where have the prophets enjoined on anyone the reading of scripture? It is the works of mercy, joined with fasting, prayer and true repentance, expressed in the sacrament of penance, 'that makyth all in this waye to come to light'. At Judgement Day it will be by the measure of our acts of mercy that we will be weighed. What a terror to this realm this should be, he warned them, where there is so little charity, so little mercy, so little repentance, where they not only do no mercy but 'have taken away the fruyte of the almes that was gyven by other'. Never had a country been shown such mercy, restored from schism, but in no other country has there been such excess, 'bothe on your bodies and yn your houses' and yet 'the churches remaynynge bare, robbyd and spoyled'.[62]

If they want quietness of mind, therefore, and seek the highway to paradise, they must 'utterly leave your own wyll'. They must abandon the vain and presumptuous itch for 'more knowledge than God hath lymyted unto us', which is the mark of the Reformation, the sin which misled Eve and brought poisoned fruit into the world; and they must forsake the carnal pleasure of the body, resting instead in the joy of the heavenly manna, the body of Christ in the Mass, the food which quietens all our cravings of body and spirit. Then they will have fulfilled the prophetic injunction to keep a true holy day, and can return to their houses rejoicing.[63]

In some ways Pole's St Andrew's Day sermon is conventional enough. Most of his theological and polemical arguments can be paralleled from his own writings or in those of other apologists for the Marian Church. What is striking about it, however, is Pole's tough and specific analysis of the problems confronting the Church in London, his stark confrontation of lay resistance to the burnings, his understanding of the role of youth culture in that resistance, and the subtlety, clarity and force

---

[62] Ibid., 506–8.
[63] Ibid., 508–9.

of the Catholic account of salvation he opposes to the Protestant Gospel. There is nothing vague or generalized about this preaching, and there is considerable rhetorical resourcefulness in the way in which he rings the changes on the unifying theme of good and bad 'fruits'. Pole displayed here, too, an acute sense of his audience and their interests: this is emphatically a London sermon. Church property, poor-relief in the city, turbulent apprentices and the campaign against heresy were all topical in 1557: and Pole confronts them all. In this he is strikingly and unexpectedly in tune with another very different London polemicist. Pole is not normally thought of as a populist writer or preacher, but most of these issues had been addressed by the artisan polemicist Myles Hogarde a year before, in his savagely effective *The Displayinge of the Protestantes*, and there are striking similarities between Hogarde's and Pole's handling, especially on the pseudo-martyr issue.[64] In one respect at least, however, Pole goes beyond Hogarde. Pole understood perfectly well that papal supremacy was a difficult doctrine to sell after a generation of schism, and he mobilized the history of More, Fisher and the other London martyrs skilfully to highlight and support it. Hogarde too had recalled the witness of the English martyrs of Henry's reign, but in his brief recital More was not singled out for special attention. The much more prominent place given to More in Pole's sermon, and the deployment of theological arguments first aired in More's polemical writings against heresy and of the extended anecdote credited to Bonvisi, both given new prominence by More's recently published English *Workes*, indicate Pole's own long-standing personal regard for More; but also, in its link to the publication of the English *Workes*, a cohesion and direction in the developing Marian restoration that has yet to be fully explored.[65]

Finally, Pole's stern discussion of the continuing hold of Protestantism in the city, and his subtle and balanced dissection of the problematic place of knowledge and reading in faith, and of the corresponding need for the disposition of a humble learner, underlie his qualified endorsement of the value of preaching in London, an exaggerated and negative estimate of which has exercised and misled readers (or rather *non*-readers) of the letter to Carranza. Debate will no doubt continue

---

[64] Myles Hogarde, *The displaying of the Protestantes*, 2nd edn, London, 1556, RSTC 13558, ff. 44–51 (campaign against heresy and pseudo-martyrs); 93v–95v (turbulent apprentices and the Protestant young); 110–112v (monasteries, Church property and charity to the poor).

[65] It is often claimed that the publication of More's English *Workes* was exclusively a More/Roper family venture entirely independent of direct involvement by Pole: I do not think this view can be sustained in view of Pole's handling of More here.

about the merits or otherwise of Pole's strategy for the restoration of Catholicism in Marian England. But the St Andrew's Day sermon and the letter to Carranza between them surely establish that he was guilty neither of inattention to preaching, nor of lack of realism about the challenges confronting the Marian Church.

CHAPTER SEVEN

Spanish Religious Influence in Marian England

John Edwards

When Prince Philip of Spain landed at Southampton, on 20 July 1554, his controversially large entourage inevitably included a significant contingent of Catholic clergy, in addition to the singers and instrumentalists of his *Capilla Real* (Royal Chapel). The task of some of these secular priests and religious was to minister to the spiritual needs of the prince, but foremost in the minds of the Spanish clergy themselves, and of their lay compatriots, was the restoration of the English Church to obedience to Rome, and the revival and strengthening of Catholic religious life in the kingdom of which Philip was very soon to be King Consort. Whatever his doubts about the marriage, these churchmen seem to have had none. The initial arrivals in Mary's realm included, apart from the royal chaplains, Don Pedro de Castro, bishop of Cuenca, Dr Bartolomé Torres, who was later bishop of the Canary Islands, and the formidable Don Fernando de Valdés, archbishop of Seville and Inquisitor-General of Spain. Also on board various ships in Philip's fleet were friars who would have a rather longer-term impact on religious affairs in Mary's England. Notable among them were two Observant Franciscans, Fray Alfonso de Castro and Fray Bernardo de Fresneda, and two Dominicans, Fray Juan de Villagarcía and Fray Bartolomé Carranza de Miranda, to be joined in May 1555 by Fray Pedro de Soto.[1] Until recently, it has largely been assumed by British scholars of Mary Tudor's reign that the Spanish churchmen who came to England with Philip played a marginal, or even a non-existent, part in religious developments between 1554 and the queen's death. Since Philip's Spanish household is largely absent from the standard sources consulted by Tudor historians, that notorious plague of historical researchers, the 'documentary illusion' (that if something is not documented it did not happen) has led smoothly to the assumption that

---

[1] José Ignacio Tellechea Idígoras, 'Bartolomé Carranza y la restauración católica inglesa (1554–1558)', in Tellechea, *Fray Bartolomé Carranze y el cardenal Pole. Un navarro en la restauración católica de Inglaterra (1554–1558)* (Pamplona: Diputación Foral de Navarra, 1977), 27, 29.

whatever did happen in Mary's Church was a purely insular affair, and to be understood largely without reference to the Continent. In the specific case of these Spanish Franciscans and Dominicans, David Loades's comment in his standard survey of Mary's reign is typical:

> With the exception of Juan de Villagarcía and Pedro de Soto, who were appointed to the chairs of divinity and Hebrew at Oxford, no Spanish clerics were promoted in the English Church, or appeared in any official capacity outside the court.[2]

In Loades's life of Mary Tudor, Villagarcía and de Soto make a unique intervention in the context of the final attempts to reconcile Archbishop Thomas Cranmer to the Roman Church, and, given the character of the English sources already referred to, it is perhaps inevitable that none of Philip's Spanish ecclesiastical advisers appears in Loades's anthology of chronicles on the subject of the Tudor queens.[3] It is natural that, in Diarmaid MacCulloch's magisterial biography of Cranmer, Villagarcía and de Soto should be mentioned, once again in the context of the archbishop's last days in Oxford, but no picture emerges of their overall role in the English ecclesiastical scene during Mary's reign.[4] Eamon Duffy, who has rightly stated that 'a convincing account of the religious history of Mary's reign has yet to be written', openly acknowledges the influence on the English Church in this period of what would much later come to be known by many as the 'Counter Reformation'.[5] Lucy Wooding, on the other hand, in her study of Catholic writers and thinkers in Tudor England, stresses the native, insular character of English Catholicism in the period, not as a nostalgic return to an imagined 'traditional' past but as an organic development of currents of Catholic reform already evident in the reign of Henry VIII. She writes, 'If we evaluate the Marian Church in the light of its own declared objectives, we begin to get a more accurate appreciation of its potential for religious renewal. Rather than import foreign ideas, or even foreign religious orders, there was an attempt to build upon an existing religious ideology.'[6]

In this assessment, Philip of Spain's ecclesiastical advisers have no place, but the same cannot be said of the work of William Wizeman,

---

[2] David Loades, *The Reign of Mary Tudor. Politics, Government and Religion in England, 1553–58*, 2nd edn (London: Longman, 1991), 297.

[3] Loades, *Mary Tudor. A life* (Oxford: Blackwell, 1989), 325–6; Loades, *The Chronicles of the Tudor Queens* (Stroud: Sutton Publishing, 2002).

[4] Diarmaid MacCulloch, *Thomas Cranmer. A Life* (New Haven and London: Yale University Press, 1996), 581–2, 586–9, 595–6, 600, 603.

[5] Eamon Duffy, *The Stripping of the Altars. Traditional religion in England, 1400–1580* (New Haven and London: Yale University Press, 1992), 524, 564.

[6] Lucy E.C. Wooding, *Rethinking Catholicism in Reformation England* (Oxford: Clarendon Press, 2000), 150.

who stresses the common features between English Catholic writers of the Marian period and their Spanish contemporaries, some of whom were present in England between 1554 and 1558.[7] How, though, can these 'invisible men' be brought back to life in their original context?

As things stand, the main route to an understanding of the role of Spanish churchmen in the attempted restoration of Roman Catholicism in England is through the voluminous records of the subsequent trial (1559–76), by the Spanish and Roman Inquisitions in turn, of Fray Bartolomé Carranza. These records, which have been edited, over a period of years, by José Ignacio Tellechea Idígoras, contain much testimony, from Carranza's clerical and lay companions in Philip's household, and even from the king himself, concerning Spanish activities in Marian England in general, and ecclesiastical matters in particular. Eight volumes of documents from the trial of Carranza, who from 1558 until his death in 1576 was archbishop of Toledo, have been published by Tellechea, from the archives of the Real Academia de la Historia in Madrid, while further documentation, concerning the transfer of the trial from Spain to Rome in 1567 and the subsequent proceedings and sentence, is in the British Library.[8] In accordance with Inquisition procedure, the archbishop drew up a fixed list of 100 questions, which were to be put to those witnesses who were prepared to speak in his defence: 23 of them (nos 42–64) were concerned with his time in England.[9] Carranza's troubles with the Inquisition began after his return to Spain, but they arose from his time in England, and in particular from his authorship of 'Commentaries on the Christian Catechism' (*Comentarios sobre el Catechismo christiano*) which were published in Antwerp in 1558, but explicitly intended for the English clergy as well as those on the Continent.[10] Philip's insistence on Carranza's appointment to the primatial see of Spain, the richest in the Western Church after Rome, brought his many Spanish enemies into action against him, accusing him of expressing Protestant sentiments in his 'Catechism'. Traditionally, diocesan bishops, as those who remained ultimately responsible for the orthodoxy of the faithful in their care – even after the introduction, in the

---

[7] William Wizeman, 'The Pope, the saints and the dead: uniformity of doctrine in Carranza's *Catechismo* and the printed works of the Marian theologians', in John Edwards and Ronald Truman, eds, *Reforming Catholicism in the England of Henry Tudor: The Achievement of Friar Bartolomé Carranza* (Aldershot, Ashgate, 2005), 115–137.

[8] Tellechea, ed., *Fray Bartolomé Carranza: documentos historicos*, 7 vols (Madrid: Real Academia de la Historia, 1962–94); BL, Additional MS 8690, and Egerton MS 599.

[9] Tellechea, 'Fray Bartolomé Carranza: a Spanish Dominican in the England of Mary Tudor', in Edwards and Truman, eds, *Reforming Catholicism*.

[10] Bartolomé Carranza de Miranda, *Comentarios sobre el Catechismo christiano*, ed. Tellechea, 2 vols (Madrid: Biblioteca de Autores Cristianos, 1972) [first edition, Antwerp: Martín Nucio, 1558].

thirteenth century, of specialized tribunals of inquisitors – were themselves exempt from inquisitorial action. But Fernando de Valdés, who had for a short time been with Carranza in England, made representations to Rome and, in January 1559, Pope Paul IV empowered inquisitors, for a limited period of two years, to act against bishops who were suspected of heresy. Paul was able to act under the terms of the brief of Innocent VIII, issued on 25 September 1487 to Tomas de Torquemada, as Inquisitor-General.[11] Valdés received the relevant brief on 8 April 1559, and found that it contained a catch, from the point of view of his Spanish tribunals. This was that the Pope required all such cases to be referred directly to Rome, as ordered by Innocent VIII's brief. Nevertheless, the Spanish Inquisitor-General quickly went into action, and on 6 May 1559 a prosecutor (*procurador fiscal*) drew up an indictment against Carranza, accusing him of having preached, written and taught as doctrine numerous 'Lutheran heresies'. On 26 June, the king reluctantly agreed to inquisitorial action against his protégé, and on 6 August (the Feast of the Transfiguration of Jesus) Carranza was summoned to Valladolid, though overtly by the Crown rather than the Inquisition. The archbishop responded, but only slowly, and thus it was on 16 August that one of his Dominican brothers, who had been a colleague at the University of Alcalá de Henares, warned him that the Inquisition planned to arrest him. On 20 August, at Torrelaguna, just north of Madrid, he met another Dominican, his companion in England and former Oxford professor, Fray Pedro de Soto, who also had come down from Valladolid to warn him of what was in store. But, without his knowledge, Inquisition officials had been lying in wait in Torrelaguna for the last four days. The arrest took place early on Tuesday 22 August. In truly 'Pythonesque' fashion, the Inquisitor Diego Ramirez, and Rodrigo de Castro, who was a member of the Supreme Council of the General Inquisition (*La Suprema*), backed up by ten part-time lay inquisitorial officials, or 'familiars' (*familiares*), demanded entry to his bedroom in the name of the Holy Office. Carranza protested his exemption, but was shown Paul IV's brief to Valdés, and, with the town under strict curfew, the archbishop was spirited away to Valladolid, where he arrived in the early hours of 28 August and was placed under house arrest. Thus began an ordeal which was to end in Rome nearly 17 years later, when the 73-year-old prisoner was made to abjure 16 supposedly heretical doctrinal propositions, given religious penances and released into the care of his Dominican brothers at Santa Maria sopra Minerva. There he died, at three in the morning on 2 May 1576, the Feast of St Athanasius, being

---

[11] Gonzalo Martinez Díez, *Bulario de la Inquisición española hasta la muerte de Fernando el Católico* (Madrid: Editorial Complutense, 1998), 208.

buried in the Dominican basilica, with an epitaph written by the then Pope, Gregory XIII.[12] What, though, emerges from his trial concerning his activities, and those of his Spanish clerical companions, in the England of Mary Tudor?

Whatever the correctness of the new king-consort's welcome – from his bride, from the English aristocracy and from pro-Catholic churchmen, including Bishop Stephen Gardiner of Winchester – it was not long before some of his retinue came to blows with members of the English public, including taverners and landlords, especially in London and Westminster. Long-standing political, dynastic and economic ties, dating back at least to the time of Henry III, seem to have been easily forgotten in an outburst of xenophobia which long predates the activities of the modern British tabloid press. English and Spanish accounts both suggest that some of Philip's Spaniards were not averse to becoming involved in violence against their reluctant hosts, and this was the uneasy climate in which the Spanish friars began their work in the 'sceptred isle'.[13] Bartolomé Carranza had been given a specific task in the restoration of Catholicism in England. He had been granted a licence by his superior in Castile, Fray Alonso de Hontiveros, to bring with him two Dominican brothers of his choice: they were Fray Pedro de Soto and Fray Juan de Villagarcía. In addition, the Dominican General had appointed Carranza as his vicar and commissary general, with the task of re-establishing the English Province of the Order. He was placed in charge of all the dissolved English houses of the Order of Preachers, with powers to absolve lapsed friars who wished to return to their vocation, to re-establish and reorganize the economic structure of the Province if circumstances required it and to draft in reinforcements of friars from other provinces, if this proved to be necessary in the early stages. Carranza himself suggested that Flanders might be a suitable recruiting ground for this purpose, perhaps because of cultural affinity, or because Flemish friars were already accustomed to confronting reformed Christians on their home territory. Carranza and his fellow Dominicans took up residence in the formerly Benedictine cloisters of Westminster Abbey, at the very centre of English government.

The religious, among the Spanish ecclesiastical contingent, had been advised before their arrival that, in view of recent developments in England, it might not be wise for them to wear their habits in public. In

---

[12] Tellechea, Introduction to Carranza, *Comentarios*, i, 42–8; Henry Kamen, *The Spanish Inquisition. An historical revision* (London: Weidenfeld and Nicolson, 1997), 160–63.

[13] Kamen, *Philip of Spain* (New Haven and London: Yale University Press, 1997), 56–8; Loades, *Mary Tudor*, 229.

the event, they resolved to do so only when moving between their living quarters and church, and this decision was quickly vindicated by the hostility and disorder which affected Spanish clergy as much as their lay compatriots.[14] According to one Spanish diplomatic document, written in the early days, the friars were subjected to particular abuse in the streets: 'for the English are so bad, and fear God so little, that they handle the friars shamefully, and the poor men do not dare to leave their quarters'.[15] Although this situation evidently changed, at least to some extent, as their later travels round the country demonstrate, it should be remembered that all the work of these Spanish clerics took place in a prevailing climate of mutual prejudice, ignorance and misunderstanding. Anti-Spanish feeling among the English may have been born, in some cases, of hostility to Catholicism, and to Spain as its representative, and perhaps more generally of a not unreasonable fear among all social classes that Mary's marriage to Philip would subjugate England to Habsburg interests. It is important to realize, though, that these feelings had their equivalents on the Spanish side. Spaniards who arrived with Philip in 1554, their minds filled with the chivalric romances which the mighty Miguel de Cervantes was later to satirize so cruelly in Don Quixote, saw England as the archetypal island of chivalry. The initial delight of these Arthurian enthusiasts at seeing the 'Round Table', supposedly preserved at Winchester, was soon dampened, first by the apparently ceaseless rain and then, metaphorically, by the hostile attitude shown towards them by many English people. Yet the Spaniards had their own grudges against the English, a 'Black Legend' to match the one which Protestants were developing at this time to characterize Spanish cruelty in Europe and the New World. From this point of view, on the record of Henry VIII and Edward VI's reigns, the English were seen as a barbarous and heretical nation, which had grossly ill-treated Mary Tudor's mother, Catherine of Aragon, the youngest daughter of the 'Catholic Monarchs', Ferdinand and Isabella, as well as dissolving monasteries and convents and persecuting those who remained loyal to the old faith, notably John Fisher and Thomas More.[16]

Despite this conflictive background, Philip was concerned to learn as much as he could about England, and certainly did not confine himself to Arthurian romances. In Geoffrey Parker's words, 'He learned a lot about the governance of England, both during his two years of residence and while absent (for he insisted on being consulted on a wide range of issues).' Indeed, 'his personal experience convinced the king that he was

---

14 Tellechea, 'Carranza y la restauración', 27–8.
15 *Calendar of State Papers, Spanish*, xiii, 33.
16 Kamen, *Philip of Spain*, 59; Loades, *Mary Tudor*, 250–51.

the world's foremost expert on English affairs'.¹⁷ This last was a farfetched claim but, nevertheless, such comments give some credence to the refrain of witnesses in Carranza's Inquisition trials, that the archbishop had the ear not only of the king but also of the queen, in matters spiritual. Many questions remain to be answered about the nature and the level of communication between the Spaniards and the English in political and religious matters, but at least some of the truth may be discovered from an examination of certain aspects of the former's attested work in England between 1554 and 1558. During his lengthy trial, Carranza constantly asserted (as a Catholic prelate on trial accused of Lutheranism might have been expected to do) that his twin aims in England were the restoration of Catholicism and the repression of Lutheran heresy.¹⁸ Included among these tasks were the re-establishment of religious orders, the building up of Catholic teaching in the universities of Oxford and Cambridge, and the restoration of traditional liturgical practice. Over everything, though, loomed the question of heresy.

There seems to be little dispute that at least 280 English men and women were burned as Protestant heretics during the period of the Spanish friars' residence in the kingdom. What if any, though, was the role in all this violence of Philip and his personal entourage, and especially of its ecclesiastical members? It is probably fair to say that this repression, which, mainly thanks to John Foxe's massive and committed record in his *Acts and Monuments*, has earned Mary the epithet 'Bloody', is generally ascribed to native rather than foreign inspiration. Thus Jasper Ridley, in his popular biography of Mary, largely absolves the Spaniards of responsibility for the burnings. He refers to 'Philip's efforts to persuade his wife to abandon her persecuting religious policy' and notes a well-known sermon preached at Court by Alfonso de Castro, on 10 February 1555, just after the burning of John Rogers, Lawrence Saunders and Bishop John Hooper. Apparently, Castro did indeed state, on this occasion, that bishops were directed in Scripture, for example in Paul's Epistles to Timothy, to be gentle and kind to erring Christians, and not to have them handed over to the 'secular arm' for burning. Tellechea adds that the trial and death of Rogers also led the imperial ambassador, Simon Renard, to intervene with Philip to the same effect.¹⁹ Carranza's attitude to the question, which is much better

---

17 Geoffrey Parker, 'The place of Tudor England in the Messianic vision of Philip II of Spain', in *Transactions of the Royal Historical Society*, sixth series, 12 (2002), 182, 184–6.
18 Tellechea, 'Carranza y la restauración', 30.
19 Jasper Ridley, *Bloody Mary's martyrs. The true story of England's terror* (London: Constable, 2001), 73; Tellechea, 'Carranza y la restauración', 49.

documented than Castro's, merits close examination. It appears, from his own testimony and that of other witnesses in his Inquisition trial, that Carranza was generally in favour of the violent repression of Protestants and their views. Thus he is recorded as having supported, indeed as having gone from London to Hampton Court to urge upon Philip and Mary, the trial and subsequent burning of Thomas Flower, a former monk and priest who had gone to St Margaret's Church, Westminster, on Easter Sunday 1555, and stabbed a Dominican while he was administering Holy Communion. It also appears, from his later trial, that Carranza was subject to death threats during his remaining time in England. According to Cristóbal Becerra, a chaplain from Toledo Cathedral who was with him in England, this was because of his activities against Protestants.[20] Nevertheless, Loades's impression from the English sources is that the Spanish friars, even including Carranza, were marginal to discussions of heresy at Mary's court. Thus de Soto and Villagarcía's failure with Cranmer was to be ascribed not so much to naivety on their part as to ignorance of the government's political strategy in the case.[21] The evidence in Carranza's trial suggests, though, that Spanish involvement in the English heresy trials was very much more direct and intimate than that.

In Carranza's case, activity on behalf of the Inquisition had begun many years before. It cannot be denied that the Dominican had considerable experience of dissident religious views, and of their repression, within the Catholic Church in Spain. Even before it was conquered by Ferdinand in 1512, the kingdom of Navarre, in which he was born of lesser noble (*hidalgo*) parents at Miranda de Arga, had seen considerable inquisitorial activity, which was directed against Jewish Christian (*converso*) refugees from neighbouring Castile and Aragon. By 1530, when he was Regent of Studies in the Dominican college of San Gregorio in Valladolid, Carranza was acting as a consultant (*consultor*) to the Inquisitors of the town. He came to the notice of the Vatican in 1539, on a visit to Rome during which he was awarded, by his Order, its distinguished degree of Master of Theology. But it was in the service of the Emperor Charles V, during the first two sessions of the Council of Trent (1545–46 and 1551–52) that he was licensed to read, and censor, a wide range of Protestant, or supposedly Protestant, works, consigning many of them to the flames, in the approved manner of the Spanish Inquisition.[22] While his fellow friars seem not to have been so directly

---

[20] Tellechea, 'Carranza y la restauración', 50–53.
[21] Loades, 'The English Church during the reign of Mary', in Edwards and Truman, eds, *Reforming Catholicism*, 33–48.
[22] Carranza, *Comentarios*, i, 11–16 (introduction).

involved with the Holy Office, there is thus no doubt of Carranza's preparedness to use violence in the defence of the Catholic faith. It is also clear that the Navarrese Dominican continued in England his work on book censorship, and actively supported English measures to remove vernacular Bibles from churches and to control the book trade.[23]

The purging and reorganization of the universities of Oxford and Cambridge was another part of the efforts made by Mary's government to control intellectual life. Until recently, it has been hard to discern Spanish hands in the visitations of the two universities which took place in Mary's reign. Now, though, Andrew Hegarty has investigated the matter thoroughly, and has concluded that Pedro de Soto and Juan de Villagarcía, as postholders at Oxford, were not the only Spaniards to become involved in this process.[24] Virtually all the evidence comes from Spanish sources, but it is no less significant for that. Carranza's longstanding friend, Cardinal Reginald Pole, included the universities in his effort to reconcile England to Rome, which began as soon as he arrived in the country, in November 1554. They had been specifically included in the powers granted to Pole, as legate, by Pope Julius III, in a bull dated 8 March 1554. There is no documentary evidence of direct Spanish involvement in the affairs of the University of Cambridge in this period, but things were very different in Oxford. There, two Dominicans in particular, Pedro de Soto and Juan de Villagarcía, were to play a prominent part, which went well beyond the trial of Archbishop Cranmer. When he arrived in England in May 1555, apparently at the request of Pole and very probably with the support of Carranza, de Soto, a former confessor to the Emperor Charles V, had occupied for the previous six years the chair of theology in the new Catholic university of Dillingen, founded by the archbishop of Augsburg. There, he had engaged in active controversy with Protestants, notable among them the main architect of the Reformed Church order in Württemberg, Johannes Brenz.[25] According to the Venetian ambassador in London, Giovanni Michieli, Pole, who had been with him in Germany before finally being summoned to England, greatly respected de Soto's judgment.[26] The

---

[23] Tellechea, 'Carranza; a Spanish Dominican', in Edwards and Truman, eds, *Reforming Catholicism*, 21–32.

[24] Andrew Hegarty, 'Bartolomé Carranza and the English universities', in Edwards and Truman, eds, *Reforming Catholicism*, 153–72. This section owes much to Dr Hegarty's researches.

[25] Thomas F. Mayer, *Reginald Pole: prince and prophet* (Cambridge: Cambridge University Press, 2000), 207–8, 211; G. Scott Dixon, 'The princely Reformation in Germany', in *The Reformation World*, ed. Andrew Pettegree (London: Routledge, 2000), 152, 157, 159.

[26] *Calendar of State Papers: Venice, 1555–56*, 60–63 (letter of Giovanni Michieli to the doge and Senate, 6 May 1555).

Cardinal Legate quickly seized on the Spanish Dominican as the ideal man to restore scholastic theology to the university, by means of a course on the Sentences of Peter Lombard. The device adopted was to abstract, and divert, the revenues of the Regius Chair of Hebrew, whose current holder, Richard Bruerne, apparently had few takers. The subsequent position is somewhat confused, but Bruerne eventually, in 1557, became a canon of St George's Chapel, Windsor, while de Soto was listed as 'professor of Hebrew' in the dean's register at Christ Church, between October 1555 and August 1556, after which his position was presumably formalized, as befitted the distinguished theologian that he was.[27] Like Carranza, de Soto was honoured by the Order of Preachers with its own degree of Master of Theology, and on 14 November 1555 he was incorporated as Doctor of Divinity at Oxford.[28] Pedro de Soto's Dominican companion, Juan de Villagarcía, had been a pupil of Carranza, at San Gregorio in Valladolid, and, as his master's protégé, had worked with him in the English court since July 1554. By his own account, he went to Oxford in October 1555, and thus became involved with Latimer, Ridley and Cranmer, during their last days. Villagarcía incorporated as Bachelor of Divinity on 14 November 1555 and shortly afterwards became a Reader in Theology at Magdalen College, though he appears to have lived in Lincoln College. He was to remain in that post until 1557, having additionally become Regius Professor of Theology, in 1556. He took an Oxford Doctorate of Divinity on 11 July 1558.[29]

Andrew Hegarty has now shed much light on the formal visitations of Oxford and Cambridge Universities, which took place, under a legatine commission from Pole, in 1556. The Oxford visitation began on about 20 July of that year, and there is some controversy over whether there was Spanish representation in the team. During his Inquisition trial, Carranza claimed to have heard viva voce the welcoming address to the Visitors, delivered by Nicholas Sanders of New College.[30] Even so, the future archbishop appears nowhere in the Oxford records, though

---

[27] V.D. Carro, *El maestro Pedro de Soto, OP*, 2 vols (Salamanca: Convento de San Esteban, 1931–50), i, 246–7.

[28] *Historiadores del Convento de San Esteban de Salamanca*, ed. J. Cuervo, 3 vols (Salamanca: Convento de San Esteban, 1914–15), iii, 597; Oxford University Archive, NEP/supra/Reg. 1/fol. 155v.

[29] Hegarty, 'Carranza and the English universities', citing Oxford University Archive [OUA] NEP/supra/Reg. 1, fols 155r, 176r; Magdalen College Archives, MS 730a, Vice-President's Register 1, 25, 29; Tellechea, ed., *Documentos*, ii, pt 2, 51–3; G.D. Duncan, 'Public lectures and professorial chairs', in *The Collegiate University* [*History of the University of Oxford*, iii], ed. James McConica (Oxford: Clarendon Press, 1986), 353.

[30] Tellechea, *Documentos*, v, 230.

Villagarcía later testified that he had spent a fortnight (*quinze dias*) in the city, and thus evidence of his activity has to be gleaned largely from his own testimony, during his trial.³¹ Most notably, Carranza later claimed to have been instrumental in the exhumation of the remains, in Christ Church Cathedral, of the wife of Peter Martyr Vermigli, on the grounds not only that she had been a heretic, but that her proximity to the shrine of St Frideswide constituted desecration.³² Although he seems never to have visited Cambridge personally, Carranza claimed also to have been involved in the exhumation and burning of the remains of Martin Bucer, a former member of his own Dominican Order.³³ Nevertheless, it seems clear that the main Spanish influence in the Marian universities came not through Spaniards' participation in the legatine visitations, but through Pedro de Soto and Juan de Villagarcía's brief attempt to restore scholastic theology to Oxford.

More public, and probably more extensive, was Spanish involvement in the official restoration of the Catholic liturgy, after 30 November 1554. In this case, too, Carranza was prominent. On Corpus Christi Day 1555, a liturgical procession took place at Kingston upon Thames.³⁴ The evidence for what happened comes, once again, from statements made later to the Inquisition. The procession of the Blessed Sacrament, in a monstrance and under a canopy, seems to have been largely, or wholly, a Spanish affair. Philip and Mary, who were at nearby Hampton Court Palace, did not attend, though some of their English subjects did. Large white candles were carried by various Spanish noblemen and knights, including Philip's secretary, Pedro de Hoyos, while other prominent participants were the king's Portuguese favourite, Ruy Gomez de Silva, later prince of Eboli, and the Spanish royal quartermaster-general, Don Alonso de Aguilar. The Eucharistic Host was carried by a chaplain of the royal chapel (*Capilla de los Reyes*) in Toledo Cathedral, Cristobal Becerra, and it appears that all the arrangements were made by Fray Bartolomé Carranza.³⁵ Probably as a result of the depredations of the last years of Henry VIII, as well as the reign of Edward VI, it proved essential to use Spanish liturgical objects, as well as Philip's Hispano-Burgundian Chapel Royal (*Capilla Real*), whose musical and liturgical order for the day has survived, in a revision

---

31 Tellechea, *Documentos*, ii, pt 2, 514.

32 A. Wood, *The History and Antiquities of the University of Oxford*, ed. J. Gutch, 2 vols in 3 (Oxford: Clarendon Press, 1792–96), ii, 133–4.

33 Tellechea, 'Carranza y la restauración', 96.

34 For a fuller account of the Kingston procession, and its context, see Edwards, 'Corpus Christi at Kingston upon Thames: Bartolomé Carranza and the Eucharist in Marian England', in Edwards and Truman, eds, *Reforming Catholicism*, 139–52.

35 Tellechea, *Documentos*, iii, 55–6.

of 1559, by one Aguirre, a royal chaplain.³⁶ Before the arrival in England of Philip and his entourage, attempts had been made to revive the Corpus Christi liturgy, including the procession of the sacrament, but there had been strong opposition to a procession held in London, on Corpus Christi 1554, and a participating priest had been stabbed. Kingston may well have been regarded as a more secure environment than teeming London, though Pole organized a similar procession in Canterbury, on the same day.³⁷ In any case, it was decided, by leading Spanish and also English churchmen, that the experiment might be repeated in the following year. Thus, on Corpus Christi 1556, Bishop Edmund Bonner himself carried the sacrament in procession at Fulham, though the most adventurous effort took place on the Sunday in the Octave, when a procession was held in the politically and symbolically significant setting of Whitehall. Thus Edward's Protestant bastion was re-occupied by the Lord in the Eucharistic bread, and, on this occasion, the Host was carried by Carranza himself.³⁸ According to Becerra's account:

> In the second procession which was held in London, the expenditure of the said procession was at the charge of the Most Reverend [Archbishop] of Toledo [Carranza] and of this witness [Becerra]. And he saw many English people who with great haste and excitement came to see the said procession. And when the said Most Reverend [Archbishop] raised the Most Holy Sacrament in his hands, [this witness] saw many English people kneeling on their knees, weeping, and giving thanks to God because they were seeing such a good thing, and calling down blessings on those who had been the cause of it.³⁹

There are no further records, between then and 1558, of the specific involvement of Carranza and his fellow Spanish churchmen in the revival of the Corpus Christi liturgy, and the whole 'restoration' experiment was, of course, short-lived. Nevertheless, it is evident that the effort to promote the Mass, both as a focus of Christian devotion and as a means of identifying heretics, was actively, and often jointly, undertaken by English and Spanish churchmen. As always, given the nature of the surviving evidence, Carranza's activity appears prominently. In advance of the Kingston Corpus procession, on the first

---

³⁶ Bernardette Nelson, 'Ritual and ceremony in the Spanish Royal Chapel, c.1559–c.1561', *Early Music History*, 10 (2000), 105–200, at 141–2.

³⁷ Mayer, *Reginald Pole*, 299.

³⁸ MacCulloch, *Tudor Church Militant. Edward VI and the Protestant Reformation* (London: Allen Lane, The Penguin Press, 1999), 82–3.

³⁹ Tellechea, 'Carranza y la restauración', 67. This and subsequent translations are by this writer.

Tuesday of Lent, 1555, the future archbishop preached a sermon to Philip and the Court, in the Chapel Royal, on the proper reception of the Most Holy Sacrament of the Altar, as a result of which he was asked, by the duke of Medinaceli, to commit his words to writing, which he duly did, as a 'Short treatise on the Mass', which attempts to see the liturgy from the point of view of a member of the congregation rather than a minister of the sanctuary.[40]

Carranza evidently recalled his Corpus Christi experiences in England, when he wrote his Catechism. In the sixth chapter of his commentary on the Sacrament of Holy Communion, he states:

> After tyrants and heretics began shamelessly to abuse this most Holy Sacrament, the Church became more determined in venerating it. For this reason it was ordained, three hundred years ago, that on the first Thursday after Trinity there should be celebrated, with much solemnity, the festival of this Most Holy Sacrament, with its Octave. This is done generally among Catholics, and in the greater part of the Church it is customary to make solemn processions, with fiestas and honest rejoicings, carrying the Most Holy Sacrament, with much reverence, publicly through the streets. This custom is very holy and religious, and should be observed much more at this time than in the past, because the shamelessness of the heretics against revering this Sacrament is greater than ever. Thus it is proper that Catholics should insist more on the public veneration of this Sacrament, as long as the prelates and justices ensure that, in these public acts, nothing improper takes place.[41]

Carranza introduces his treatment of the Sacrament of the Altar by outlining three aspects of Catholic doctrine on its nature. The first of these, which might, though he does not say so, provide common ground with Luther, is the Real Presence of Christ:

> because this Sacrament, which is administered at the altar, contains, really and truly, the true Body and the true Blood of Jesus Christ, under those figures of material bread and wine which we see with our bodily eyes; and the Body of Jesus Christ contained beneath them is the same, in substance, which was born of the Virgin Mary, His Mother, and the same that suffered for our redemption on the Cross, and rose again on the third day, and after forty days ascended to the heavens, and is now at the right hand of God the Father.

But Carranza, unsurprisingly, is not satisfied with this, and goes on to reaffirm the doctrine of transubstantiation:

---

[40] Tellechea, 'Un tratadito de Bartolomé Carranza sobre la Misa', *Archivio Italiano per la Storia della Pietà*, xi (1998), 145–79.
[41] Carranza, *Comentarios*, ii, 229–30, for this and following extract.

> For this reason, this Sacrament is more excellent and offers more advantages than all the others, of the Old and New Testaments. Because all the other Sacraments retain the matter in which they are consecrated, without changing their substance by means of that consecration [...] Only in this Sacrament is the matter changed substantially. Before the consecration, it was the substance of bread and wine: after the consecration, it is the substantial flesh and blood of Jesus Christ.

Yet it should not be assumed from this that Carranza was merely interested in reiterating theological formulae. In this introductory passage, he immediately goes on to put such statements in a wider perspective, by stressing the mystery inherent in this sacrament:

> The tongue of Man may speak this truth, which Faith teaches by means of this ineffable Sacrament, and may adore with humility, because to presume to speak of, or to understand, the mysteries which God encloses there, would be a mad presumption. It is enough to know that God wished to declare Himself in this Mystery.[42]

In the context of the religious conflicts of the mid-sixteenth century, in England and on the Continent, this seems a daring assertion, and, indeed, its author was to suffer severely for it, but it provides a clue to Carranza's fundamental approach to Christian doctrine and practice. Interestingly, in the discussion which follows, he refers to this Sacrament as the 'Holy Communion', 'Eucharist', 'Viaticum', 'Sacrifice', 'Memorial' and 'Lord's Supper', but not by its popular name, 'Mass'.[43] This is not, of course, to suggest – despite what his Spanish enemies were later to say – that Carranza had explicitly or deliberately espoused any of the reformers' main teachings, but it does raise questions about the ideas that he and his Spanish ecclesiastical contemporaries had in their minds when they landed in England in July 1554. It was not only Pole, let alone the rest of the English bishops, who had ideas for the running of the restored (Roman) Catholic Church in Mary's kingdom. Those among the ecclesiastical contingent in Philip's entourage who stayed to work in England had, of course, already been involved, over several decades, in religious upheavals, whether in Spain itself or in other parts of Charles V's empire; and many of them, including Carranza and Alfonso de Castro, had also participated in the debates at Trent.[44] Many

---

[42] Ibid., 203; also preceding extract.

[43] Ibid., 207–8.

[44] For religious currents in the Spain of Charles V and Philip II, see Lu Ann Homza, *Religious authority in the Spanish Renaissance* (Baltimore and London: The Johns Hopkins University Press, 2000); for Spanish participation in the first two sessions of the Council of Trent, see Bernardino Llorca, 'Participación de España en el Concilio de

of these men had taught and preached in Spain, in the 1520s–50s, and in many cases they had published extensively. The question is: Did Carranza and his companions have some kind of blueprint in mind for the future life of the English Church?

Those Spanish churchmen who had particular contact with Carranza before his arrival in England include 'Maestro' Juan de Ávila, Diego de Valtanas and Luis de Granada, while other writers of the period included Martin de Frias, Juan de Bautista and Juan Bernal Diaz de Luco, who was commonly known as 'Dr Bernal'. All these authors were clerics, and they all wrote what might be described as 'reforming' treatises about the Church. Frias and Dr Bernal were both ecclesiastical judges who worked for the bishop of Salamanca, while Valtanas and Juan de Ávila also worked in the Leonese region of western Spain. There is evidence that these men read each other's works, and Dr Bernal and Carranza were both personally present in the sessions at Trent, up to 1552. They all wrote in Spanish, though Carranza also published works in Latin. Lu Ann Homza has justly observed of these authors that:

> They used identical vocabulary, from *reformacion* ('reformation') to *ocio* ('leisure' or 'idleness'), or their Latin equivalents, and they cited the same authorities, from Chrysostom to John 21: 15–17.[45] There is no doubt that they conceived of themselves as attempting to reform their religious and even social environments, for their self-consciousness about their objectives was remarkably high.[46]

Carranza was not, however, alone among them in coming into conflict with the Inquisition. A case in point is that of Juan de Ávila (*c.* 1499–1569), born of Jewish convert stock in Almodovar del Campo (Ciudad Real), who studied at the University of Alcalá de Henares, and then became an evangelistic preacher in Andalusia, in southern Spain. He was denounced to the Seville Inquisition in 1532 for supposedly preaching heretical doctrine, and, although he was released in the following year, he naturally remained under suspicion thereafter. The views he was accused of espousing, in 1532, suggest a mixture of

---

Trento', in *Historia de la Iglesia en España*, ed. Ricardo Garcia-Villoslada, iii, pt 1 (Madrid: Biblioteca de Autores Cristianos, 1980), 387–452.

[45] 'When they had finished breakfast, Jesus said to Simon Peter: "Do you love me more than these?" He said to Him: "Yes, Lord, You know that I love You". He said to him: "Feed my lambs". A second time He said to him: "Simon, son of John, do you love me?" He said to Him: "Yes, Lord, You know that I love You". He said to him: "Tend my sheep". He said to him the third time: "Simon, son of John, do you love me?" Peter was grieved because He said to him the third time "Do you love me?" And he said to Him: "Lord, You know everything, You know that I love you! Jesus said to him: "Feed my sheep".' (All Biblical quotations are from the *Revised Standard Version*.)

[46] Homza, *Religious authority*, 118.

Erasmian and Lutheran ideas, as well as native Spanish illuminism (*alumbradismo*), and a statement that those burned in Inquisition trials were martyrs, which cannot have endeared him to the Holy Office. While still preaching and teaching in Andalusia, he met the Dominican Fray Luis de Granada, who introduced him to Carranza. Despite his earlier contretemps with the inquisitors, Maestro Juan succeeded in founding a new university at Baeza, in upper Andalusia, for the training of priests, and no action was taken by the Inquisition against him and his staff until the 1550s. His 1556 treatise, *Christian advice and rules on David's verse* 'Audi, filia' [Psalms 44/45:11–12], on which he had worked for 20 years, was placed, three years later, on Valdés's 'Index of forbidden books'. Maestro Juan was arrested by the Inquisition in 1559, and spent the remaining ten years of his life amending '*Audi, filia*' in a vain attempt to placate Valdés and his henchmen.[47]

Nevertheless, like Carranza, he was never paraded in an *auto de fe*. The same applied to Diego de Valtanas (1488–1568), a member, with Carranza, of the Dominican Order, who was also threatened by the Spanish Inquisition, in 1555. He was a friend of Maestro Juan de Ávila and Luis de Granada, and the cause of his trouble was his publication in Seville, in that year, of a systematic *Doctrina cristiana*. Such was the stir caused by this work that Fray Diego felt constrained to publish, in 1556, an *Apologia*, which claimed to treat of 'certain moral matters about which there is debate'.[48] The fourth of this quartet, all of whom found themselves in the sights of the Spanish Inquisition at one time or another, was Fray Luis de Granada (1504–88), who joined the Dominican Order in 1525 and became a pupil of Carranza. Born in Granada, Fray Luis divided his career between his native Andalusia and Portugal, where he became Dominican Provincial. His writings aroused controversy in Spain, and three of them, including *Guía de Pecadores* ('Guide for sinners'), were placed on the 1559 Index. This was the company that Carranza kept, before his visit to England. All of them had strong views on what the Church should teach, and how it should be organized, and it was natural that Carranza, when presented with an opportunity to take part in a new start, in Philip's new kingdom, should have been influenced by this thinking.

Like his spiritual companions at home, Carranza began from the

---

[47] Ángel Alcalá, *Literatura y ciencia ante la Inquisición española* (Madrid: Ediciones del Laberinto, 2001), 50–51; Maestro Juan de Ávila, *Avisos y reglas cristianas sobre aquel verso de David. Audi, filia*, ed. Luis Salas Balust (Barcelona: Juan Flors Editor, 1963). See also a summary of his biography in Helen Rawlings, *Church, Religion and Society in Early Modern Spain* (Basingstoke: Palgrave, 2002), 153.

[48] Alcalá, *Literatura y ciencia*, 53; Homza, *Religious authority*, 117, 121.

basic assumption that the Catholic Church, subject to the authority of the bishop of Rome as Christ's vicar, was the only true Church. It is, of course, true that those who are declared heretics by the Church's leaders normally believe that they are entirely orthodox, and, in the context of the sixteenth-century debates, all protagonists claimed to have the authority of Scripture and the Early, or 'Primitive' Church behind them. Yet, in the cases of these Spanish reformers, despite the intervention of inquisitors against them, it is clear that there was no intention on the part of any of them to overthrow the doctrine and organization of the Roman Church. Rather, their aim was to make the old system work better, though it is equally clear that even those who remained in Spain throughout their lives were strongly influenced by the spiritual and ecclesiological controversies of their day. All this is made plain by the teaching included in Carranza's Catechism, and may be confirmed by the writings of his Spanish contemporaries. The complete identification of Carranza, and his clerical compatriots in England, with Queen Mary's intense focus on the Mass as the centre and touchstone of Catholic devotion and conformity has already been indicated, and it greatly facilitated co-operation between these Spaniards and English Church leaders, most notable among them Cardinal Pole and Bishops Gardiner and Bonner. Nevertheless, in reaffirming the traditional sacramental system of the Church, Carranza inevitably engaged with reformed theology and ecclesiology, just as he shared in the often quite radical critiques of current practice that both he and some of his Spanish contemporaries had produced during the two decades before 1554.[49]

A case in point is Carranza's treatment of the subject which lay at the heart of Luther's split with Rome, the doctrine of Justification. In his 1558 Catechism, in the prologue to his discussion of the Ten Commandments, Carranza places himself firmly in the Catholic tradition of active Post-Lapsarian co-operation between Man and God in the process of salvation. His starting point in this discussion is the text, so fiercely debated in sixteenth-century Europe, from the Epistle of James: 'So faith by itself, if it has no works, is dead' [2:17], and he goes on to state that 'faith is the principal rule by which we have to order our lives', the Ten Commandments being a primary guide to the proper means of doing so.[50]

---

[49] The traditional Catholic nature of the work of these Spanish writers and teachers has been rightly affirmed by José C. Nieto in his lengthy and comprehensive study, *El Renacimiento y la otra España. Visión cultural socioespiritual* (Geneva: Librairie Droz, 1997) [Travaux d'Humanisme et Renaissance, no. cccxv], pp. 280–300. Nieto characterizes Juan de Ávila, Valtanas, Carranza, Luis de Granada, and also Ignatius of Loyola and Francisco Borja, as 'Roman Catholic Evangelicals'.

[50] Carranza, *Comentarios*, i, 433–4.

Carranza's approach here is a good illustration of David Bagchi's observation 'that justification by grace through faith was a highly traditional teaching which no-one in the sixteenth century could actually deny'.[51] Nevertheless, while it cannot be denied that the 'double' view of Justification, involving both faith and works, was held by these Spaniards, and clearly separated them from opponents such as Luther and Calvin, their writing can at times, as inquisitors thought, have a distinctly 'Lutheran' feel to it. For example, in his 'Guide for sinners', which was indeed condemned by Archbishop Valdés, Luis de Granada issues this instruction to the reader:

> Above all, fix your eyes on that unique and singular example of love that Christ found for us; He who loved us so strongly, so sweetly, so graciously, so perseveringly, and so without His own self-interest *or our deserving* [my italics], that you [the sinner], strengthened by ... so noble an example, and obligated by so great a benefit [*beneficio*] should dispose yourself, according to your possibilities, to love your neighbour in this way, so that in this way [Fray Luis's repetition] you may fulfil that commandment which the Lord laid upon you as he left this world: 'This is my commandment, that you love one another, as I have loved you.'[52]

In fact, though, Fray Luis was no '*Luterano*', to use the Spanish inquisitors' blanket term, but rather positioned himself, at least partly, in the Netherlandish tradition of the Devotio Moderna, which had such a strong influence on fifteenth- and sixteenth-century Spanish piety.[53] His spiritual companion, Maestro Juan de Ávila, published a translation of the *Imitation of Christ*, in Cordoba in 1536.[54] Luis de Granada, in any case, made his disagreement with Luther on the subject of Justification perfectly plain in the 'Guide'. While he recognizes that Luther, in rejecting the meritorious effect of works, was attempting to avoid the kind of 'Pharisaism' that was roundly condemned by Jesus, he feels that the result is unbalanced: 'But the Lutherans, now, ... understanding this trap [Pharisaism], in order to escape from one extreme landed in another, which was to despise all exernal virtues,

---

[51] David Bagchi, 'Luther's Catholic opponents', in *The Reformation World*, ed. Andrew Pettegree (London and New York: Routledge, 2000), 106. See also Nieto, *El Renacimiento*, 290–91.

[52] Fray Luis de Granada, *Guia de pecadores*, ed. Matias Martinez Burgos (Madrid: Clasicos Castellanos, 1929), 217–18.

[53] For the influence in Spain of this movement, on Cardinal Francisco Jiménez de Cisneros among others, see J.N. Hillgarth, *The Spanish Kingdoms, 1250–1516*, ii, *1410–1516. Castilian Hegemony* (Oxford: Clarendon Press, 1978), 409–10, and Erika Rummel, *Jiménez de Cisneros. On the threshold of Spain's Golden Age* (Tempe, Arizona: Arizona Center for Medieval and Renaissance Studies, 1999), 18, 42.

[54] Alcalá, *Literatura y ciencia*, 50.

falling, as they say, into the danger of Scylla to escape that of Charybdis.'[55]

Carranza, too, rejected Luther's views on Justification, and also opposed the Protestant idea of the Church on earth as consisting only of the gathered Elect, justified by faith alone. In his commentary on the ninth article of the Apostles' Creed ('I believe in one, holy, Catholic and Apostolic Church, the communion of saints'), Carranza distinguishes between the Church Triumphant, 'that fortunate assembly of souls who reign in heaven with Christ ... without fear of losing the state which they possess', and the Church Militant, on earth, which still struggles against the World, the Flesh and the Devil. He accepts that the Church on earth does indeed contain the 'Elect', being members who have already been chosen by God, but rejects the conclusion drawn from this by the reformers, stating that: 'The greatest temptation which Christians have had, and have at present, is to [claim to] know where the true Church is, because the heretics [that is Protestants] claim that their church is the true one.' Instead, within the Church Militant, here on earth, 'There are some good and healthy members, who live the human life through union with the Holy Spirit, ... [but] there are others sick, and others [spiritually] dead, because they lack the love and grace of God.' Nevertheless, he concludes, citing Book 7 of Augustine *Against the Donatists*, that 'the bad Christians in the Church are at present stuck [*pegados*] to the good', until Christ comes again, to separate the wheat from the straw and consign the latter to the flames (cf. John the Baptist, in Matthew 3:11–12).[56]

On the question of Scripture, too, Carranza and his friends and allies came down on the conservative side, but in Carranza's case, at least, this was only after considerable experience, both in Spain and abroad. His Catechism is, of course suffused with Scriptural, as well as Patristic, reference and quotation. Indeed, at the end of his edition, Tellechea cites nearly ten pages of references to the Old Testament, Apocrypha and New Testament, in small print and in three columns.[57] Carranza makes the vexed question of the availability of Scripture fundamental to his whole work by discussing it at length in the general preface, addressed to the 'pious reader'. Here, his approach is not just conservative but, in the strictest sense, 'reactionary', in that he uses contemporary experience, including his own on the Continent and in England, to warn of the dangers of making the Bible available in vernacular languages.

---

[55] Luis de Granada, *Guía de Pecadores*, 254.
[56] Carranza, *Comentarios*, i, 370–90, quotations, in order of citation, at 371, 390, 375.
[57] Ibid., 549–58.

The enemies of the Church, he says, have published catechisms, and summaries of Christian doctrine, which use vernacular quotation to mislead the faithful. He admits that the question of translating the Bible into European languages had been debated by the Church, at the highest level, for over 20 years, and that there are valid arguments on both sides. But experience, first in Germany and then elsewhere, has convinced him that the dangers outweigh the benefits, and, as a participant in debates on the subject at Trent, he can evidently speak with authority on the subject. As far as England is concerned, he states that 'when the Catholic Monarchs (*Reyes Catolicos*) Don Felipe and Doña Maria restored the ancient and true religion, one of the first things they did was remove the vernacular Bibles which the heretics had produced'. Carranza goes on to consider, in some detail, the complexity of the various books of the Bible, and distinguishes between their respective contents, aims and styles in a manner that shows the evident influence of Renaissance critical techniques of the more 'advanced' kind. He also summarizes his own pastoral experience, stating, first, that the more straightforward passages of the Bible, 'which contain only counsels, and precepts, and admonitions, and examples of good living, can be read by all, men and women'. In this category he includes, from the Old Testament and Apocrypha (mingled as in the Vulgate), Wisdom books (*libros sapienciales*), such as Proverbs and Ecclesiasticus, and some or all of the Historical books. He was equally selective with the New Testament, including some of the Gospels (unspecified) and those Epistles which are 'clear', as well as the Acts of the Apostles. Even in these cases, though, there should be notes in the margin, 'to water down the strength of the spiritual wine' ('*aguasen la fuerza del vino espiritual*'). The translator should be 'discreet', and provide a kind of paraphrase, rather than a literal translation ('*al pie de la letra*'). It may seem ironical that Carranza should advocate this approach, when Philip and Mary had ordered Erasmus's 'Paraphrases' to be removed from English churches, but the explanation lies, of course, in the type of interpretation of Scripture there included. The Dominican does not suggest that 'the sciences (*ciencias*), that by God's gift have been communicated to men, have no place in Scripture', but he prefers to rely on the Holy Spirit to 'illuminate and help' His disciples (interestingly, in view of earlier religious tensions in Spain itself, involving the so-called *alumbrados* ['illuminated ones'], Carranza's phrase is '*los alumbra y ayuda*'). Thus, in his pastoral experience – which was not inconsiderable, though much less than that of Juan de Ávila and Luis de Granada – individual Christians' respective levels of exposure to the Bible should run the complete gamut, from those, including, as he stresses, some women (Queen Mary for example?), who have profited from reading it all, to those who should be fed only devotional literature, with a basis in Scripture. In the circumstances of mid-sixteenth-century Europe, he thought, it was simply too dangerous to attempt a greater diffusion.[58] Although ambiguity of this kind was certainly a feature of the English Church in Mary's reign, her husband was, notoriously, to adopt the most restrictive of policies on the subject when he finally returned to Spain.

Although none of them produced a complete and systematic scheme for the Roman Catholic Church (as it was just beginning at this time to be called), something approximating to a 'blueprint' for the purpose does emerge from the writings of Carranza and his reforming Spanish contemporaries. What was involved was, of course, a hierarchical Church, in obedience to the Pope, in which the distinction between clergy and laity was rigidly maintained: these writers fully shared the magisterial reformers' loathing of anything that smacked of 'Anabaptism' or antinomianism. Carranza's views on this subject are perfectly encapsulated in a sermon that he preached to Philip and Mary's Court in London, on St Peter's Day (29 June) 1555. Preaching on the text, from the Gospel of the day, 'Tu es Petrus' ('You are Peter, and on this rock I will build my Church' [Matthew 16:18]), his main stress was on Jesus' questions to his disciples, which are recorded slightly earlier in the same chapter. One is 'Who do men say that the Son of Man is?', while the other is 'But who do you say that I am?' (Matthew 16:13, 15). The first, he says, is a question about public opinion, but the second is addressed to those in authority, in Church and state. According to Carranza, Christ demanded of His disciples not only belief, but also open and honest public profession of the Faith. Much of the responsibility for this rested on prelates, who were responsible for their dioceses, just as the Pope, as Peter's successor, was responsible for the whole Church, but it also rested upon the rulers of kingdoms.[59] This preaching could not have been more directly applicable to Philip and Mary's situation in England.

One way in which bishops, and other senior prelates, could begin to fulfil their responsibilities was to live in the place at which they were appointed to work. Carranza and his reforming Spanish contemporaries insisted that, like the rest of the clergy who had pastoral responsibilities, bishops should reside in their dioceses, and take personal charge of the selection and education of parish priests. Such issues had been much discussed at Trent, where the views of Carranza, Juan de Ávila and Pole, among others, had been fully aired and considered. Carranza had

---

[58] Ibid., i, 109–15.
[59] Tellechea, 'Cuatro sermones inéditos de Carranza en Inglaterra, in Tellechea, *Carranza y Pole*, 355–88; the text of the St Peter's Day sermon is at 379–84.

written a major tract on the subject for the Council, the *Controversia de necessaria residentia personali episcoporum et aliorum inferiorum pastorum* ('Controversy on the necessary personal residence of bishops and other lesser pastors') [Venice, 1547]. In it, he is scathing about parish priests who do not carry out their duties:

> Tell me, ecclesiastical pastor, by what law you demand a stipend! By reason of nourishment and necessity? You will naturally answer: 'By divine law' ... [but] why, if I owe you the tithe by divine law, are you not required by that same law to serve the Tabernacle? ... What iniquity is this, that you bind the community with religion on account of your salary, and [yet] you, if you please, are free of religion, if you choose not to act as a soldier [of Christ].[60]

Even after he had left England for the Netherlands, Carranza was still upbraiding his old friend Pole for spending too much time at Court, and not enough in his diocese, though he received an indignant response.[61]

Linked with this hierarchical view of the nature of authority in the Church was the notion, shared by Carranza and his Spanish allies with most reformed leaders, that a better-educated clergy would be a better clergy in every other way. The idea of diocesan seminaries ('*colegios*' in Juan de Ávila's terminology), which was to be adopted generally after 1563, at the end of the Council of Trent, had been discussed by Spanish reformers at least since the 1540s, and was proposed at the English synod of 1555–56. Writing to the Tridentine Fathers in 1551, Juan de Ávila criticized current thinking on Church reformation, on the grounds that it concentrated too much on law-making and punitive enforcement, without regard for the fact that effective teaching involved constant care and the consent of the taught. He gives a vivid illustration from his own experience of teaching children:

> It is obvious that, if a master who teaches children goes away, and tells them: 'Look, I am telling you not to fight, or fool about while I'm away. Keep still and read, and if you don't, you'll have to pay for it when I get back!', he will not be doing his job as a teacher, nor will he get what he wants out of the children.[62]

---

[60] Carranza, *Controversia de necessaria residentia personali episcoporum at aliorum inferiorum pastorum*, facsimile of the Venice 1547 edition, ed. Tellechea (Madrid: Fundación Universitaria Española, 1993), 290–91. See also Homza, *Religious authority*, 126.

[61] Pole's lengthy reply (20 June 1558) is in Tellechea, 'Pole, Carranza y Fresneda. Cara y cruz de una amistad y de una enemistad', in Tellechea, *Carranza y Pole*, 122–97, at 191–6 and is discussed in chapter 6 above, 176–83.

[62] Juan de Ávila, 'Memorial primero al Concilio de Trento (1551)', in *Obras completas del Santo Maestro Juan de Ávila*, ed. Luis Sala Balust and Francisco Martin Fernández, (Madrid: Biblioteca de Autores Cristianos, 1971), vi, 33–68, at 34.

Priests should be much more carefully selected, thoroughly educated in seminaries and tightly controlled by the hierarchy to make sure that they remained conscientious and effective. An important part of this process was preaching, which was to be a priority; although, perhaps naturally as a Dominican, Carranza seems to have regarded it as more important in the English situation than did Pole, according to part of the correspondence between them in 1557, after Carranza had left for the Netherlands.[63]

It is important to note, though, that while these Spaniards had a very high view of the status and role of the clergy, the corollary was that much was demanded of those to whom much was given. Pastors, and cathedral canons, were castigated for their ignorance, greed and idleness, and the general message was clear. It was elaborated with ruthless clarity: if pastors failed their flocks in any of these ways, not only were they threatening the laity with damnation, but they were also heading in that direction themselves. Each parish and church was the scene of a cosmic drama, in which eternal life and death were at issue. Both Maestro Juan and Carranza were clear on this issue, using, in support of their understanding of a priest's responsibility, the passage from the prophecy of Ezekiel [33:7–9], in which the Lord threatens the watchman of Israel with death if he fails to warn those in his charge of the divine retribution which threatens them. As Carranza expresses it: 'we [the clergy] kill as many as die daily from our silence'.[64]

Given the harshness of the discipline to which the clergy were to be subjected, it is hardly surprising that these writers wanted the laity to be kept on a short leash as well. Bishops were to visit their dioceses regularly and thoroughly, while parish priests were to descend almost to 'police-state' tactics to keep their flocks in order. It was a short step from this to the Inquisition, whether in Spain or in England, and this thinking helps to provide a context for the repression of 'heresy' which notoriously took place under Mary. Yet it would be quite wrong to suggest that Carranza and his contemporaries were uniformly pessimistic about human nature, and universally harsh in their treatment of human failings, whether in clergy or laity. An evangelical love of all human beings runs through these writings, even in their many attacks on heresy, which were all made, of course, in the context of what Brad Gregory has aptly characterized as 'the duty of intolerance'.[65] In addition, Carranza and his Spanish colleagues and allies had little,

---

63 Tellechea, 'Pole, Carranza y Fresneda', 188–96.
64 Carranza, *Controversia*, 261.
65 Brad S. Gregory, *Salvation at Stake. Christian Martyrdom in Early Modern Europe* (Cambridge, Mass.: Harvard University Press, 1999), 78–82.

except for the reaffirmation of traditional doctrine, to say about saints and images, did not think that the best place for surplus daughters was necessarily a convent and believed that a Christian's primary duty was to the living rather than the dead. Some puzzles about Marian Catholicism may be solved if these views, widely held among the Spaniards, are borne in mind.

For Philip's Spanish ecclesiastical advisers in England, the opportunity to put such beliefs and policies into practice came to an abrupt end with the death of the queen. For Carranza, the outcome was particularly disastrous. Not only was his Catechism never put into practical use in England, but his return to Spain, as archbishop of Toledo and primate of the Spains, led within a few months to arrest, imprisonment and a notorious trial. He was never to be fully rehabilitated, yet his own chapter in Toledo never abandoned him, and a later archbishop and Inquisitor General, Gaspar de Quiroga, placed his portrait in the chapter house there, in its proper place in the succession to the primatial see.[66] Above all, his Catechism for England had an extraordinary subsequent history, forming a major part of the Tridentine Catechism – a 'Long Reformation' indeed, which could be said to have lasted from Trent to Vatican II.[67]

---

[66] On the 'afterlife' of Carranza, especially in Spain, see Truman, 'Pedro Salazar de Mendoza and the first biography of Carranza', in Edwards and Truman, eds, *Reforming Catholicism*, 177–208.

[67] On Carranza's contribution to the Tridentine catechism, see Pedro Rodriguez, *El Catecismo romano ante Felipe II y la Inquisición española. Las problemas de la introducción en España del Catecismo del Concilio de Trento* (Madrid: Ediciones Rialp, 1998), *passim*.

Part III

The Culture

CHAPTER EIGHT

The Marian Restoration and the Mass

Lucy Wooding

The worthiest thing, most of goodness, In all the world, it is the mass.[1]

So said the *Lay Folks' Mass Book*, that late medieval guide to the meaning of the liturgy, which, like so many other sources, supports the view of the Mass as the linchpin of pre-Reformation belief.[2] Recent work on fifteenth-century devotion has suggested that the Mass was the focal point of communal worship; the rallying point for confraternities; the infallible indication of personal devotion in any individual.[3] The Mass lay at the heart of popular devotion, embodying the central message of salvation through the death of Christ on the cross which it re-enacted, and even for those with little grasp of doctrine it could represent the miraculous power of the divine, bringing ordinary people into real physical proximity with God. The central dramatic moment of the liturgy, when in the prayer of consecration bread and wine was believed to transform into flesh and blood, became the focus of a wide range of popular devotions. People ran to see the moment of elevation, or left instructions in their wills that they should be buried next to the altar, in order that their mortal remains might be as close as possible to the body of Christ, at that magical moment when it appeared in their midst.[4] And just as the Mass was believed to bring together the living

---

[1] *The Lay Folks' Mass Book*, ed. T.F. Simmons, Early English Text Society, first series, 71 (1879), 2–3. The spelling here has been modernized.

[2] See E. Duffy, *The Stripping of the Altars: Traditional Religion in England c.1400–c.1580* (Yale, 1992), especially chapter 3; J. Bossy, 'The Mass as a Social Institution, 1200–1700', *Past and Present*, 100 (1983); M. James, 'Ritual, Drama and the Social Body in the Late Medieval Town', *Past and Present*, 88 (1983); J.J. Scarisbrick, *The Reformation and the English People* (Oxford, 1984); R. Swanson, *Catholic England: Faith, Religion and Observance before the Reformation* (Manchester, 1993);

[3] See M. Rubin, *Corpus Christi: The Eucharist in Late Medieval Culture* (Cambridge, 1991); M.K Jones and M. Underwood, *The King's Mother: Lady Margaret Beaufort, Countess of Richmond and Derby* (Cambridge, 1992).

[4] Duffy, *The Stripping of the Altars*, 96–8.

with the dead and the angels with the saints, so too its function within social groupings was a dynamic one, a means of reconciliation.[5] In the everyday tensions of individual communities, the Mass could provide both a justification and a mechanism for social unity, as congregations were compelled to restore charity between neighbours before being allowed to receive this all-powerful sacrament. It would seem that everything that was most important in pre-Reformation piety was somehow expressed in the liturgy and devotions of the Mass.

In consequence, there is a tendency to take a continued loyalty to the Mass as the most important single indicator of enduring Catholic allegiance in the sixteenth century, and with some justification. What had served as the central expression of popular piety before the Reformation became the central mark of adherence to traditional Catholic belief as the Reformation unfolded, viewed as such by both those who upheld Catholic doctrine and those who attacked it. The beliefs and rituals of the Mass had an immediacy at every level of society, and could command great popular devotion in a way that more abstruse questions of doctrine or ecclesiology might not. It symbolized everything that was important about popular piety: its communal focus, its enduring traditions and its supernatural powers. Reformation Catholic writers said as much in a variety of sermons, homilies and treatises, arguing for a direct correspondence between the inner faith of the individual and its outward demonstration in the Mass. As one sermon explained,

> seinge a sacrifice is an outwarde protestation of our inward faithe and devotion, if we christen men now have no sacrifice private unto us: then be we the moost miserable men that ever were, beinge without any kynde of religion. For take awaye our sacrifice, and take awaye our religion ...[6]

The Mass could serve as the distilled essence of all that was important to the Catholic faith. And it was clearly perceived as such by the opposition. Almost the last recorded words of Archbishop Cranmer were those he called out above the angry commotion in the University Church: 'and as for the sacrament, I believe as I have taught in my book against the Bishop of Winchester'.[7] The Mass was the easiest route to the demarcation of Catholic identity, for those who clung to the old faith and for those who sought to destroy it.

---

[5] S. Brigden, 'Religion and Social Obligation in Early Sixteenth-Century London', *Past and Present*, 103 (1984), 67–112; J. Bossy, *Peace in the Post Reformation* (London, 1998), 73–100.

[6] Thomas Watson, *Twoo Notable Sermons* (1554), RSTC 25115, Sig. B iiii r–v.

[7] D. MacCulloch, *Thomas Cranmer: A Life* (New Haven and London, 1996), 603.

It is no surprise, therefore, to find the Mass at the heart of Mary Tudor's restored Catholic Church. The removal of the English service from the Book of Common Prayer and the return to the Latin Mass was powerfully symbolic of the transition to the new reign, so much so that some congregations signalled their loyalty to Mary by a spontaneous resumption of the Mass even before the official instructions went out.[8] Securing this central aspect of the faith was a pressing concern: an immediate appeal to the security of past sanctities which might serve as a foundation for future restoration. It was therefore the most important focus in the reconstruction of parish worship: visitations emphasized the necessity of parishes replacing the trappings needed for the Mass – the vestments, altar vessels and so on.[9] Meanwhile, the spoken and written word reinforced the message, as sermons and treatises sought to explain and affirm the doctrine behind the rituals. As Bishop Bonner explained in 1555, it was necessary to treat of the subject at length, because on the one hand the Mass, 'bothe in worthynes, and dignitie, doeth greatly surmounte and passe al the other Sacramentes of the Churche', and also because 'of late yeres it hath most of all other, bene assaulted, and impugned, and yet of no good manne, but of the wretched sort alone'.[10]

The Mass therefore became in many ways the centrepiece of the Marian restoration. A ballad from 1555, protesting against heresy, echoed the *Lay Folks' Mass Book* of two centuries before as it explained the sacraments as the foundation of social and ecclesiastical unity, suggesting that the other six sacraments were brought together and consolidated in this most important sacrament of the altar.[11]

> By which all we, membres knitte be
> to Christ, our most chiefe head.
> In unitie, through his Bodie,
> which dyde for quicke and dead:
> Christs Church likewise, doth Sacrifise
> the same, in fourme of bread.
> Very flesh and blood, our daily food,
> in us to byde and dwell,

---

[8] D. Loades, *The Reign of Mary Tudor* (second edition, 1991), 99, 102; J.G. Nichols (ed.), *The Diary of Henry Machyn*, Camden Society, xlii (London, 1848), 42; Charles Wriothesley, *A Chronicle of England during the Reigns of the Tudors*, vol. i, ed. W.D. Hamilton, Camden Society n.s., xx (London, 1877), 101.

[9] See, for example, L.E. Whatmore (ed.), *Archdeacon Harpsfield's Visitation 1557*, together with Visitations of 1556 and 1558, Catholic Record Society, xlv–xlvi (1950–51).

[10] Edmund Bonner, *A profitable and necessarye doctrine* (1554), RSTC 3283.3, Sig. T r.

[11] There is no precise date for the *Lay Folks' Mass Book*, which was probably translated into English from French sometime in the fourteenth century, and which exists in several manuscript versions.

> Bi whom we move, live ever through love,
> in vertew to excell.[12]

Like many other printed works of the time, this ballad was appealing to a well-established understanding that had the sanction of centuries of past belief and practice. Those seeking to provide an explanation and justification of the Mass had plenty of precedents on which to draw.

Yet we should beware of seeing the Marian restoration as no more than a straightforward revival of pre-Reformation attitudes to the Mass. The sermons, treatises, ballads and polemics from the 1550s, as well as the official decrees of Mary I's government, speak a very different language to that of 100, or even 50 years before. In part, this difference was due to the self-consciousness that informed every religious sentiment now that all doctrinal discussions had to be set against a background of confessional division. Yet even this, and the consciousness of the need to respond to Protestant criticism, was only part of the story. Catholicism had also in its own right developed ideas of reform and renewal, and it had acquired a whole new rhetorical dimension in response to the demands and opportunities of a vernacular printing trade. 'Reformation' was a phenomenon that had touched everyone, Catholic and Protestant, traditionalist and evangelical, conservative and radical. The resurrection of past certainties involved a kind of literary nostalgia that only lightly concealed a range of new ideas, anxieties and intentions.

Behind the stark labels of 'Catholic' and 'Protestant', or even behind their more aggressive equivalents of 'papist' and 'heretic', there lay many complex and fluid patterns of religious identity and allegiance. Sixteenth-century religion had become a variegated array of ideas, traditions, community expectations, familial and political loyalties. This is not to imply that the Reformation involved a straightforward transition from a homogeneous pre-Reformation religious harmony to heterogeneous religious conflict. After all, late medieval Catholicism had also been pluralistic, with a range of different emphases and devotions, many of which brought different groups into conflict. In part, the Reformation involved the consolidation of both this pluralism and this conflict. Yet there was more to it than that. The demands of Renaissance scholarship had made churchmen and scholars more self-aware; the influence of humanism had reconfigured notions of religious authority; the development of printing had created a vernacular literary tradition;

---

[12] *An exclamation upon the erroneous and fantasticall spirite of heresy* (1555?), RSTC 10615.

the polemic of the reformers had made believers of every hue both more critical, and more self-critical, and the dynastic ambitions of the Tudors had politicized the faith to an unprecedented extent. In an age where every Church trumpeted with ever-increasing vigour its claims to apostolic succession and continuity with the past, religion was in fact changing as never before. The Catholicism of the 1550s was both creative and defensive, self-consciously nostalgic and urgently prescriptive, an elaborate mixture compounded of scholarship and populism, devotion and polemic, politics and propaganda.[13]

It should therefore be appreciated that one of the reasons why the Mass was such a powerful element within sixteenth-century Catholicism was its enormous versatility as a vehicle for religious meaning. There is a danger that in emphasizing the importance of the Mass we may take that meaning for granted, losing sight of its capacity to embrace a range of different ideas and emphases. Even as it embodied the appeal to antiquity, it could also serve as a vehicle for religious and political reform. During Mary's reign the Mass appeared in a multiplicity of guises, which could be employed to transmit a wide array of messages about the faith, and the changes taking place within that faith. Writers of the time agreed that the essence of the Mass was its ability to bring together many different elements and unify them into one body. One of their favourite metaphors was that of the many grains of wheat that came together to make the communion bread, and the many grapes that were used to produce the wine, 'so of many dystincte persons of Christen men and womenne, aryseth and is made one mystycall bodye and churche of Christ'.[14] It could be argued that this metaphor might work equally well on the historical level, as the theme of the Mass allowed the expression of a variety of ideas about the Catholic faith. This chapter will explore some of the many themes which emerged as representations of the Mass during the reign of Mary Tudor, suggesting that one of the reasons it was such a focus for Catholic loyalism was precisely because it had the ability to synthesize different ideas and bring together manifold layers of meaning.

One powerful attribute the Mass had newly acquired by the reign of Mary Tudor was its political significance, now that the dynastic

---

[13] For a French parallel, see R. Briggs, *Communities of Belief, Cultural and Social Tensions in Early Modern France* (Oxford, 1989), where he remarks that 'there is a danger that in concentrating on the style and structure of popular religion, the great constants, we will underestimate the changes that were possible within them, and their significance for the lives of both communities and individuals' (p. 368).

[14] *A plaine and godlye treatise* (1555), RSTC 17629, Sig. E vii r. The metaphor was used by both St Augustine and St Cyprian, but originated with St Paul.

problems of the Tudors and the invention of the Royal Supremacy had made sacramental doctrine an indicator of political loyalism as never before. Here its significance could be twofold. Its obvious Catholic identity and Mary's own well-known attachment to the Mass made it a vehicle for protestations of support for the queen. Yet its legitimacy as an enduring part of the Henrician religious settlement was also important. For many Catholics, perhaps particularly those like Cardinal Pole who had a more European perspective, Henry VIII's break with Rome remained the start of all England's griefs, the 'cause of the whole disfigurement of the church in this realm, and of all the evils which have arisen in very great numbers in past times', as the decrees of the Lambeth Synod phrased it.[15] Yet despite the apparent vicissitudes of the Henrician era, some contemporary comments show that the reign of Mary's father could also be appealed to as a touchstone of Catholic orthodoxy and a time of political stability. This association with Henry VIII was used to reiterate the important fact of Mary's legitimacy as monarch, but it could also be used to emphasize that Catholicism was the norm, from which the government of Edward VI's reign had so dangerously deviated. The administration of the sacraments was at the heart of this. The Act of Parliament which repealed the Edwardian Acts concerning religion was thought sufficiently good propaganda to be published in 1553 by John Cawood, the printer to the queen. Its intent, it stated, was to restore 'the olde divine service and administration of Sacramentes in suche maner and fourme, as was used in the church of Englande, before the makynge of any of the sayde five (Edwardian) Actes'. In restoring religion to how it was 'in the laste yeare of the raygne of our late Soveraigne Lord, kynge Henry the eight', it made this appeal to continuity clear. The preamble to the Act also stressed that Mary was putting back the religion 'whiche we and our forefathers founde in this Churche of England to us, left by the authoritie of the catholike Churche', and stressed that the Edwardian creeds had been 'such as a feaw of singularitie have of them selves devised'.[16] The appeal to antiquity was of larger scope, but the link to Henry VIII's time was perhaps of more immediate importance. It made Catholic belief and practice appear more permanent, and Protestant encroachment appear less threatening, to date the time of trial from 1549 rather than 1533.

For the Marian regime this could be a valuable advantage. Appeals to Henry VIII's policies facilitated an avoidance of a more partisan

---

[15] G. Bray (ed.), *The Anglican Canons 1529–1947*, Church of England Record Society, 8 (1998), 74–5.

[16] *An Acte for the repeale of certayne Actes made in the tyme of kyng Edwarde the sixt* (1553), RSTC 7852.

Catholic stance, encouraging instead an emphasis on the universality of their creed and tradition. It also established a link between Catholic doctrine and strong kingship, in which the reign of the boy king could be seen as a dangerous aberration. There was a concerted attempt to play down any suggestion that the Marian settlement represented a sharp break with the trusted formulations of the past, and recognizable elements from the previous two reigns, such as the Henrician prayers incorporated into the primers or even the Edwardian homilies reissued as part of the Marian book of homilies, may have been calculated to add to this effect.[17] Such continuities were both political and religious: to secure the succession it was important to emphasize that Mary was 'daughter unto the moost victorious and mooste noble prynce, kinge Henry the viii'; but that such descriptions appeared in religious treatises suggests that dynastic succession was not the only point being emphasized here.[18] Mary herself referred to Henry as 'our father of most pious memory', and many clerical observers followed her lead, choosing to date the times of iniquity from 1547 rather than from the break with Rome.[19] Roger Edgeworth, publishing the accumulated sermons of 40 years, never doubted Henry VIII's Catholicism, but instead depicted him as a scourge of heretics, recalling how Lutheran heresy had infected the realm so that 'the kinges maiestie, and all the catholike clerkes in the realme had muche a do to extinguishe them'.[20] This portrayal of Henry VIII may for some have been a propaganda decision, but for others his maintenance of the Mass would seem to have marked him out as an essentially Catholic monarch, whatever his quarrels with Rome. Here we might see the consequences of much powerful Henrician propaganda.[21]

Be it with confused sincerity or calculated dissimulation, therefore, the Marian regime was capable of perpetuating the notion that the new reign stood in direct line of succession from that of Henry in doctrinal

---

[17] Duffy, *The Stripping of the Altars*, 539–43; Wooding *Rethinking Catholicism in Reformation England* (Oxford, 2000), 161–6.

[18] Thomas Paynell, *Twelve Sermons of Saynt Augustyne* (1553), RSTC 923, Sig. A ii r. See also Cuthbert Tunstall, *Certaine Godly and Devout Prayers* (1558), RSTC 24318, Sig. A ii r.

[19] '*piisimae recordationis patris nostri*': see *Epistolae Reginaldi Poli*, ed A.M Quirini, iv, 121–3; cited in E. Russell, 'Mary Tudor and Mr. Jorkins', *Bulletin of the Institute of Historical Research*, 63 (1990), 272.

[20] Roger Edgeworth, *Sermons very fruitfull, godly and learned* (1557), RSTC 7482, f. ii v.

[21] See, for example, P. Marshall, 'The Rood of Boxley, the Blood of Hailes and the Defence of the Henrician Church', *Journal of Ecclesiastical History*, 46 (1995), which notes how the exposure of clerical abuses was used to defend Henrician policy 'from an essentially conservative standpoint' (693).

as well as dynastic terms. A draft of one of Mary's earliest proclamations concerning religion showed how naturally the rhetoric of her father's proclamations could be re-used, declaring that

> her majesty, being presently by the only goodness of God settled in her just possession of the imperial crown of this realm ... cannot now hide that which God and the world knoweth, how she and her father of famous memory, her grandfather and all her progenitors, kings of this realm, with all their subjects have ever lived like Christian princes.[22]

Within this framework the Mass was the most obvious symbol of religious continuity, and could be used to contribute to the strength of the political regime, helpfully reinforcing Mary's connection with the unambiguous – and unambiguously male – authority of Henry VIII. When Wriothesley recorded in his *Chronicle* the Mass at St Paul's on 10 January 1554, he bore witness to how this continuity was not only driven home by words, but also acted out. 'Procession began in Paules Churche after the olde fashion before highe masse: The Lord Maior and Aldermen goeinge in Procession in their violett gownes and clokes furred, as they used everie Sundaye in King Henry the VIII tyme, afore the sermon began.'[23]

Just as Henry had employed a rhetoric of kingship which brought together his authority and his religion, so too Mary sought to personify the godly prince in whom true faith and true judgement were united. John Proctor wrote how experience had shown his countrymen 'nothing to be more perilous then wicked follye armed with princely authoritee', but how under Mary 'we nowe savour what inestimable good thinge is godly wisedome, coupled with power imperiall'.[24] The imagery of empire, that had served Henry VIII so well, was used by Mary to drive home the same religious and political message. So too was the imagery of Old Testament kingship: where Henry VIII had been David, and Edward VI had been portrayed as King Josiah, Mary was depicted as 'a newe Judith'.[25] This could be given providential overtones: Proctor also wrote how 'nowe last of all he calleth you by a more gentle meane, by his true elect Marye our most noble and godly Quene. Whom his inscrutable providence hathe preserved of a specially purpose no doubt,

---

[22] *Tudor Royal Proclamations*, ed. P.L. Hughes and J.F. Larkin (New Haven and London, 1969), vol. ii, 5n., taken from SP 11/1/14.

[23] Wriothesley, *A Chronicle of England*, 106.

[24] Vincent of Lerins, *The waie home to Christ*, trans. John Proctor (1554), RSTC 24754; Translator's preface addressed to Queen Mary, Sig. A ii r–v.

[25] John Angel, *The agreement of the holye Fathers* (1555), RSTC 634, Sig. A ii r–v. See also Leonard Stokes, *An Ave Maria in Commendation of oure most vertuous Quene*, quoted in Loades, *The Reign of Mary Tudor*, 112.

that by her he might restore his true churche, of late yeres miserably vexed.'[26] Mary was here described as both 'an heavenlye maide, whose integritie of life and constancie of faithe, ought to perswade you al', and as 'a mightie Quene, whose authoritie might compel you all'.[27]

So the Mass became a touchstone of orthodoxy, whether political or religious it was not always easy to tell. From the very start of the reign the celebration of the Mass was used, even whilst it was still technically illegal, to signal strong feelings of loyalty to either the new queen or the old faith. In Yorkshire, Robert Parkyn noted how 'preastes unmariede was veray glade to celebratt and say masse in Lattin ... accordynge for veray ferventt zealle and luffe that thai had unto God and his lawes'.[28] With more overtly political significance, the execution of the Duke of Northumberland, chief instigator of Lady Jane Grey's attempted coup, was an interesting propaganda display for the new regime, with his speech from the scaffold released in printed form. Northumberland's attendance at Mass before his execution was turned into a political display, with an audience of Londoners brought in by the Council to witness this significant mark of repentance.[29] The printed speech, although it admitted his guilt in the usual manner and begged the queen's forgiveness, was far more concerned with religious error than political crime, and sounded the providential note that was to be used to such effect by the new regime. 'Take hede how you enter into straunge opinions or newe doctryne, whiche hath done no smal hurte in this realme, and hath iustlye procured the ire and wrath of god upon us', he was reported to have warned.[30] The speech remained vague as to the details of his errors, or those of the realm, but sounded a strong note of appeal to the sanction of past tradition and the universality of the Catholic faith. In this drama of repentance, it was the duke's attendance at Mass that gave the most unequivocal signal of where true loyalty should lie. In such an amalgam of political conservatism and religious continuity the Mass served to cement a message of permanence and security which on all other doctrinal points could remain non-committal. If the Mass had been a vehicle for the religious theatricality of late medieval piety, it was now proving equally amenable to providing political theatre in a changing world.

---

26 Vincent of Lerins, *The waie home to Christ*, Proctor's preface, Sig. C vi v.
27 Ibid., Sig. C vii v.
28 'Robert Parkyn's Narrative of the Reformation', ed. A.G. Dickens, *English Historical Review*, lxii (1947), 80.
29 Loades, *The Reign of Mary Tudor*, 99.
30 John Dudley, *The sayng of John late Duke of Northumberland uppon the scafolde* (1553), RSTC 7283, f. 2v.

In the same way, the sanction of the Mass might be called upon to reinforce other Marian policies. When Cardinal Pole's legatine synod drew up its constitutions for the reform and restoration of Catholicism in England, it borrowed heavily from the decrees of the Provincial councils that had been held in Germany under Paul III's direction, but the first decree it used was specific to the English situation alone.[31] This decree asserted that the reason for all the ills of recent times was the separation from Rome, and therefore instructed that the reconciliation with the papacy was to be celebrated on its anniversary, every St Andrew's Day (30 November). The decree required that

> a solemn procession shall be held, in which not only the clergy of every place, but also the faithful members of Christ of the secular order, shall gather and renew the memory of so wonderful a blessing received from God ... and that on the same day, in the church from which the procession shall set out, during the solemn rites of the mass, a sermon be preached to the people in which the reason for this solemnity shall be explained.[32]

Here the Mass was to be used in the same way as Accession Day celebrations were used in Elizabeth's reign, to consolidate both religious and political loyalties.

The Mass could serve, therefore, as a mark of continuity with Henry VIII's reign, or as a pledge of renewed friendship with Rome. To see such uses as incompatible is probably to misunderstand the relationship between the queen, the authorities in Rome and the English Church, as well as to underestimate the propaganda value of the Mass, powerful yet malleable. As Elizabeth Russell has shown, Mary's relationship with the papacy was far from being one of slavish obedience: she was clearly capable of self-interested manipulation of Anglo-Papal relations on a level worthy of her father.[33] Her response to Rome when Paul IV was attempting to recall Cardinal Pole was startlingly reminiscent of Henry VIII, and Thomas Mayer has even suggested that with her staunch resistance Mary 'not very subtly threatened another schism'.[34] The pattern is strikingly reminiscent of Henry VIII in his dealings with the papacy, who could produce lavish protestations of obedience when papal decisions seemed likely to benefit Tudor authority, and outright defiance when the royal prerogative was threatened. Papal sanction under Mary was employed when it suited the regime, as in 1554 when

---

[31] Bray, *The Anglican Canons*, xliv–xlv.

[32] Ibid., 74–7.

[33] E. Russell, 'Mary Tudor and Mr. Jorkins', *Bulletin of the Institute of Historical Research*, 63 (1990).

[34] T. Mayer, *Reginald Pole: Prince and Prophet* (Cambridge, 2000), 314.

Cawood published Julius III's bull of indulgence, or when, as with the Lambeth decrees, it seemed likely to reinforce the Catholic restoration. Papal authority might be resisted, or evaded, however, when it offered no immediate advantage to the Marian administration. The merit of the Mass as a symbol was that it might signal different sets of continuities to different audiences. Rome could take it as a badge of obedience, but within England it was perhaps more important as a link to the devotional life of the past, where its associations with social stability and the old patterns of communal life meant more than any institutional authorization.

This understanding of the Mass as a guarantor of an old, familiar way of life, had been most powerfully signalled, perhaps, by the 'Prayer Book Rebellion' of 1549 in the south-west of England. The demands for 'the masse in latten, as was before', was reinforced with no other official justification than 'the lawes of our soverayne lord king Henry the viii concernynge the syxe articles'. Precise specifications as to the details of traditional worship that were to be restored show how important were these familiar elements: the reserved Sacrament hanging over the altar, communion in one kind at Easter, images 'and all other aunciente olde Ceremonyes used heretofore, by our mother the holy church'.[35] The idea of the Church as mother was a powerful one, precisely because it reinforced the familiar and familial nature of Catholic worship in the popular imagination. The theme was picked up and used elsewhere, in reminders of St Augustine's saying, that 'he can not have God for hys father which hath not the churche for hys mother', or as in a Paul's Cross sermon of November 1553, when James Brooks described the Church 'whose spouse, and protectour is our savior Christ himself whose mariage maker and director is the holie Ghost: Whose pappes are the two Testamentes: Whose milke is the true sence of the word of God'.[36] This was a more literary rendering of a popular conception which the Marian regime perceived as a sturdy bedrock of loyalty for the restored Church.

Family relationships, however, exist independently of official control. It does not take a government decree to recognize one's mother, and clearly the Tudor populace felt capable of recognizing the important constituents of traditional religion without waiting for official guidance. This 'mother Church' was one which needed no extensive authorization: Robert Parkyn's narrative makes clear how the Mass was restored at

---

[35] F. Rose-Troup, *The Western Rebellion of 1549* (London, 1913), 220–23.
[36] John Standish, *The triall of the supremacy* (1556), RSTC 23211, Sig. A iii r; John Brooks, *A Sermon very notable, fruictefull and Godlie, made at Paules crosse* (1553), RSTC 3838, Sig. A iii v.

parish level long before Parliament or Pope had been invoked, and he too seemed to think it sufficient when Mary's first parliament established that 'all sacramenttes and ceremonyes of the church sholde be frequenttide and uside in all degrees as thay were in the last yeare of the reign of Kynge Henrie the Eightt her father'.[37] It would seem that the Mass was far more important as a linchpin of the faith than any authority which might seek to command its restoration. The currents of popular religion had a momentum all their own, which undoubtedly strengthened the Marian restoration, but also shaped its direction and rhetoric.

This was a momentum which Mary's regime sought to harness, appreciating that the Mass had a resilience of its own independent of papal sanction. It was portrayed as the keystone of an ancient and lasting consensus, the devotional focus of the community of the faithful throughout all ages, and the chief guarantee of the unity of that community. The Mass was described as the 'mystical bodie of Christe', in which all true believers were brought together, the living with the dead, and in which all conflicts could be resolved. The importance of this in a country which had seen 20 years of religious experimentation, confusion and upheaval was obvious. The development of this theme was linked to the projection of a vision of the Church which did not rest, first and foremost, upon papal headship, but could instead be described in terms of its ubiquity. The advantages of this were also clear, at a time when even committed Catholics might be uncertain as to the precise nature of the papal role. Catholic authority was therefore located within three sources: the scriptures, the early councils and the Church fathers. These could be used to show that the Catholic faith 'is no new invented faythe of late yeares, but hath ben the fayth of the Churche sythe the tyme of the holy Apostles'.[38] The anonymous author of this work on the Mass, argued that 'by these thre, that is to saye, by the holy scriptures, the holy generall counsels, and by the holy auncient writers we are instructed and led in oure faith and Christian maners', and said bluntly that anyone not satisfied with these three authorities was not a Christian.[39] Ratification from Rome was not required.

This is not to say that the Marian authors did not also try to argue for the importance of papal authority. Few works dealt solely with the question of papal headship, but many at least mentioned the importance of the Pope as the head of the Church if unity and true doctrine were to be preserved. In general, it could be argued that references to papal authority were

---

[37] 'Robert Parkyn's Narrative', 81.
[38] *A plaine and godlye treatise*, Sig. A viii r.
[39] Ibid., Sig. A viii v.

included as a necessary but rarely central feature of Marian polemic.[40] Indeed, attempts to reintroduce the notion of obedience to Rome, absent from England for the last 20 years, were often made by trying to link the papacy to another more trusted aspect of Catholic doctrine, such as the Mass. The Pope, sometimes still described in Henrician language as the 'Bishop of Rome', was thus cast in the role of a necessary guarantor of other more unquestionably central aspects of Catholicism.[41] For Watson, for example, the Mass was at the heart of Catholic devotion: 'Al our comfort and ioye is and ought to be in thys Sacrifice and passion of oure Savioure Christe, by whyche onelye we have and may have sure hope of salvation.'[42] Mention of the papacy was unavoidable when it came to an account of that part of the Mass where prayers for the Pope were included, but Watson's description of the 'speciall wordes' used, whilst undeniably upholding papal supremacy, hardly gave it a central position.

> Fyrst generallye for the holle Catholyke Churche of Christe ... and then particularly for the Governers of the Churche, and of common wealthes, as for the Popes holynesse the Successour of Saynt Peter, to whom Christe dydde commytte the cure and charge of hys universall Churche throughoute the worlde; for Byshoppes, for Kinges and Princes, and in especially for suche as the Minister anye waye is bounde to praye, and for them that bee present and communicate wyth the Priest in true faythe and devoute affection.[43]

The Pope was now once more a necessary part of the Catholic Church in England, but the written work of the time did not give him the same centrality it accorded to the Mass. Thus Marian writers described the Mass as having a variety of significations, but they were agreed that above all else the Mass was a sacrifice of the 'whole Church of Chryste, whiche is the misticall body of Chryst, sygnified and represented in the fourmes of breade and wyne'.[44] Time and time again the symbolism was reiterated. This was where they located the Church, first and foremost: not in an institutional form, not by appeals to papacy or hierarchy, but in the constant daily sacrifice of the Mass throughout all ages, 'Whose unitie, by antiquitie/universall is knowne'.[45] The same desire to obtain

---

[40] Wooding, *Rethinking Catholicism*, 127–35. It should be noted that this interpretation has proved contentious. For a very different view, see W.L. Wizeman, SJ, 'Recalled to life: the theology and spirituality of Mary Tutor's Church', unpublished Oxford DPhil thesis, 2002.

[41] See, for example, the two homilies on papal primacy by John Harpsfield in Bonner, *A profitable and necessarye doctrine*.

[42] Watson, *Holsome and catholyke doctryne* (1558), RSTC 25112, f. lxix r.

[43] Ibid, f. lxxvi v–lxxvii r.

[44] *A plaine and godlye treatise*, Sig, A i v.

[45] *An exclamation upon the erroneous and fantasticall spirite of heresy*.

the sanction of the past prompted the anonymous author of *A plaine and godlye treatise, concernynge the Masse*, to begin his work with a rather dubious argument insisting on the ancient Hebrew roots of the word 'Mass'.[46] Given the vagaries of ecclesiastical politics over the preceding two reigns, it was clearly the Mass, hallowed by antiquity, that seemed the most secure manifestation of the Catholic faith. Bonner wrote of the Mass as the central article of faith, 'the veritie of whych Article, the Catholyke Churche, being ruled and governed by the holy ghost, hath always most constantly beleved, and taughte': in the uncertain climate of the 1550s it was perhaps safer to describe the Church as 'governed by the holy ghost' rather than governed by Rome.[47] The Mass was described as the most sure mark of continuance and fidelity. Just as Christ offered himself up, 'so doeth nowe the Churche … in the Sacrament, offer up her self as a lyvely sacrifice in spyrytuall vowe and dedicacyon, promysynge to remayne and contynewe in christ for ever'.[48] The eagerness with which Marian writers attested that the Church could be discovered within the Mass suggests a new resonance for the theme of the 'mystical bodie' at a time when so much uncertainty hovered over the institutional Church.

In this divided age, it was vital that the sacrament be portrayed as including everyone, and everything. Thomas Paynell saw the unity that the Mass promoted prefigured at the Last Supper: 'And note that Chryst at that supper was the gever and the gyft, the feder and the fode, the gest, and the maker of the fest, the offerer and the oblation'.[49] In these sorts of descriptions there hovered the implication that the Mass so totally embraced the central truths of Christianity that it was almost sufficient in itself as the basis of all religion: 'Nothing more setteth forth the benefite of Christ, because in this sacrifice of the masse, we protest to have al thinges by Christ, redemption, remission, sanctification and salvation.'[50] It brought to spiritual men 'swetenes of spirite, peace, and ioye: the hunger of Justice, the thirst of heavenly blesse, the price of their redemption, a pledge of Gods love … humylytye, chastitie, temperaunce, vertue, and to use fewe wordes all kyndes of goodnesse'.[51] Within the Mass

---

[46] *A plaine and godlye treatise*, Sig. A i r.
[47] Bonner, *A profitable and necessarye doctrine*, Sig. T v.
[48] *A plaine and godlye treatise*, Sig A ii r.
[49] *Certaine sermons of Saynt Augustyne*, trans. Thomas Paynell (1557), RSTC 923.5, Sig. P viii r.
[50] Watson, *Twoo notable Sermons*, Sig. T v v.
[51] *A notable Oration made by John Venaeus a Parisien in the defence of the Sacrament of the aultare* (1554), Sig. F viii v–G i r.

> we certenly declare and professe that nothing doth exercise our faythe in the knowledge of God and of oure selves, more then this Sacrifice of the Masse doth, and that nothing dothe more increase oure charitie and hope in the mercye of God ... and so by it we most of al set forth our humilitie, and the glorye of Christe and hys true honour.[52]

Marian writers knew that the Mass was the focus of popular loyalty, and they did all they could to capitalize upon this. This vision of the Mass as a miracle of unity therefore took on a new dimension, as the symbolic victim of the social upheaval that the country had suffered during the reign of Edward VI. Here the imagery of the 'mystical body' became an important vehicle for the language of social protest. The loss of the Mass was described in terms of the loss of all social cohesion, until the country was in a state where 'No man durst trust hys nexte neyghboure'. Here considerations of doctrine were put to one side: it was the more fundamental ties of human kinship and neighbourliness that had been lost. 'Amitie and frendshyp was fled the realme ... and as our mayster Christe saythe: where wyckednesse wexed plentyfull, there charitye wexed colde.'[53] The loss of the Mass was symbolic of the subversion of the natural order of society. A translation of a work by John Venaeus showed how heresy ensured 'that all things are foule disordred, nothing quiete and peasable: that charitie is exiled and banished every where', and again portrayed the tragedy of social inversion, with conflict not only in the state, but in the household where 'the father dissenteth from the sonne, the mother from the doughter'.[54] This appeal to social order was one with universal resonance, and it was used equally emphatically by the Protestants to reinforce their notion of the godly commonwealth.[55]

The power of the Mass to reverse this sorry state of affairs was emphatically expressed by Marian churchmen and writers. Bonner described how the Sacrament 'doeth increase and worke in all them that worthelye doe receaue it, the communion and coniunction in bodye and soule of them to Chryste, and of Chryste to them, with a mutuall coniunction also in loue and charitye, of eche good man in Chryst to other.'[56] In polemical attacks it was a chief grievance, that Protestants were evil livers:

---

52 Watson, *Holsome and Catholyke doctryne*, f. lxiii v.
53 *A plaine and godlye treatise*, Sig A vi r.
54 *A notable Oration made by John Venaeus*, Sig. C ij v.
55 C. Davies, *A Religion of the Word: The Defence of the Reformation in the Reign of Edward VI* (Manchester, 2002), 140–42.
56 Bonner, *A profitable and necessarye doctryne* (1555), f. 74 r.

> it was the very devyse and dryft of the devyl, and the subtilty of great sathan hym seife ... so presumteously and perniciously to abolish the moste holy sacrifice of the masse and most blessed sacrament of the aulter, placyng suche scysmaticali rytes, and plantynge suche detestable bokes of communion thorough the pestilente prachynge and ragyng wythout al reason of a sorte of sottes (nay of Scismaticall and blasphemous heretykes) to spoyle and rob almyghtye God of so greate honour, in thys churche of England ...[57]

It is striking that in this line of attack it was never doubted that the problems stemmed from the reign of Edward VI, and Henry VIII's Catholicism remained unquestioned, thus once more suggesting that within the popular imagination England's identity as a Catholic nation was based first and foremost on the continuance of the Mass.

If the Mass was used as a symbol of virtuous traditionalism by some, yet it could also be used elsewhere as a vehicle for a reforming agenda. The Marian religious authorities, for the most part, even when attacking Protestantism, preferred more straightforward works of religious instruction as more productive than polemic. This served to confirm the impression, which was undoubtedly a genuine conviction for many, that Catholicism was not so much in competition with Protestantism, as manifestly the older and more universally recognized creed, in contrast with which Protestant ideas appeared as unruly or seditious or misguided manifestations of ignorance. Much of the language of the time used this assumption of superiority, antiquity and universality to firmly underline the doctrinal formulations it was explaining. Yet appeals to antiquity could also be appeals for reformation, and there was much within the Marian restoration to indicate that reform was not the sole preserve of the Protestant creed.

In particular, the language used by the Marian restoration seems to suggest that a certain amount of Henrician rhetoric had been absorbed into public opinion to rest alongside the enduring popular devotion to the Mass. The rediscovery of Scripture central to humanism, had been forged into a powerful instrument of church reform by Henry VIII, and Henry's reliance on '*verbum Dei*' had put down roots in popular consciousness. The appeal to the plain words of the Bible had become the best justification available. One treatise gave a characteristic expression of this as it attacked the inconstancy of those who had listened to the Protestant message, lamenting 'the fraile foly and fond madnes of suche beatle blynde people, that so redely and so fondly woulde beleve and credite in so weyghtye matters of the faythe, suche a

---

[57] *A plaine and godlye treatise*, Sig. A v r.

rude raylinge rablemente, agaynste not onely the universal churche, but also agaynst the very manyfest and open scrypture'.[58] This same tract set out to prove the Catholic doctrine with the three authorities of scripture, councils and fathers, but insisted that the first of these was in itself sufficient, namely 'the playn scriptures, whych alone were (or at the leste oughte to be) sufficient to a christen man'.[59] Other sermons emphasized how 'scrypture by playne and manifest wordes, against the whiche hell gates shall never prevayle, dothe testifye and confyrme our fayth in many places, but specially in the wordes of our saviour Christ him selfe in his laste supper'.[60] These Marian Catholics were making their own spirited claim to the scriptural revival which characterized the age.

The threefold use of authorities, with Scripture first and foremost, echoed the Henrician formulations, and demonstrates the influence of the humanists which was working on several levels.[61] The first half of the sixteenth century had confirmed the importance of humanism within English Catholic thought, and for those churchmen who had developed a reformed understanding of the Catholic faith the Marian restoration posed the challenge of reforming as well as restoring the faith. The Mass was able to provide a vehicle for their most fundamental convictions. For those who had been touched by the evangelical enthusiasm of the humanists, the central mystery of the Mass could be confirmed by an appeal to literal exegesis of Scripture, and this was constantly reiterated.[62] It was argued that to deny the Real Presence of Christ in the Sacrament was to deny the truth of the Word of God. This humanist understanding surely lay behind, for example, the 1554 publication of a translation of one of Erasmus's epistles, which vigorously upheld the doctrine of the Real Presence 'speciallye when both the writinges of the Evangelistes, and also of the Apostles do so plainly name the body which is given, and the blode which is shed'.[63] This epistle had Erasmus maintain that in the face of doubt, it was the literal word of the Bible that sustained him: 'yf any of these flying or waveringe thoughtes did once touche my heart, I did easelye avoyde them, considering the inestimable love and charitie of God toward us, and wayinge the wordes of holy scripture'.[64] Equally, the anonymous author of *A plaine and godlye treatise* asked,

---

[58] Ibid., Sig. A v v.
[59] Ibid., Sig. A viii r.
[60] Watson, *Twoo notable Sermons*, Sig. B viii r.
[61] Wooding, *Rethinking Catholicism*, 84–92.
[62] Watson, *Twoo notable Sermons*, Sig. C ii v. 'In man the trueth of hys word dependeth of the trueth of the thyng Contrarye in God the trueth of the thynge dependeth upon the speakng of the woorde, as the Psalme sayeth: Ipse dixit et farta sunt.'
[63] Erasmus, *The epistle ... unto Conradus Pelicanus* (1554), RSTC 10491.
[64] Ibid.

> Who coulde have spoken more playne in so few wordes, to expresse that thynge that we do beleve and intende to prove? that is to saye: That the sacramente whyche he gave wyth hys hande unto hys disciples, was hys very bodye: he sayde not thys is a sygne or fygure of my body. Thys is a signe or figure of my bloud, But most playnly he sayde: Thys is my body, Thys is my bloude.[65]

Humanist influences went beyond biblical literalism, however, to an emphasis on interior faith and spiritual transformation. The reformed emphasis on man's unworthiness and salvation through faith was given expression in various treatments of the Mass, bringing together Catholic loyalism and reformism in a single context, both drawing their emphasis from St Augustine. This was characteristic of the Marian restoration, which used many of the techniques and emphases of the Augustinian understanding to reinforce Catholic doctrine. There was in particular a strong emphasis upon man's degeneracy, and how salvation was brought about entirely by God's initiative, through the free gift of faith and grace, and not in any sense as a response to man's own works. Watson explained how the Mass was a perpetual memory of Christ's sacrifice, but warned 'not that the passion of Christe is unperfytte, or needeth anye woorke of ours to be added to supplye the imperfection of it, but to comforte and relieve our imperfection, that some droppe of grace maye be drawen and broughte unto us oute of the fountayne of all grace'.[66] He urged his readers and listeners 'to call to your remembraunce, the summe and grounde of all our faythe, which is, that we beleve to be saved onelye by the merites of our Saviour Christe', and stressed how Christ's death was 'a sufficient pryce and raunsome for the synnes of al people, from the beginnyng of the worlde to the last ende.'[67] To attend Mass was 'to declare and protest ... that we put oure singular and onely trust of grace and salvation in Christ our Lorde, fore the merytes of his death and passion, and not for the woorthynes of any good woorke that we have done or can doo'.[68]

This was not the only possible emphasis. Richard Smith's work, *A Bouclier of the Catholike Fayth*, where other authors had emphasized how little man was able to earn God's grace, took an opposite view, and when praying for those previously in error, hoped that 'they havyng a whole and a verye perfite fayth, maye observe Gods commaundementes to pourchasse themselfes the glorye and Joyes of Heaven, thorough Christ our Savyour'.[69] This was in clear contradiction of the many

---

[65] *A plaine and godlye treatise*, Sig. B iii v.
[66] Watson, *Holsome and Catholyke doctryne*, f. lxx r.
[67] Ibid., f. lxviii v–lxix r.
[68] Ibid., f. lxxii r.
[69] Richard Smith, *A Bouclier of the Catholike Fayth* (1554), RSTC 22816, Sig B ii r.

authors who went to some lengths to explain how divine grace was not available to be purchased. Yet on the whole the emphasis was more consistently reformed than this, and comments such as this by Smith were the exception that proved the rule. The Mass procured satisfaction for the sins of man, 'whiche remission and delivery no man is able to deserve by any thyng that he can do'.[70]

Another way in which reformed trends were used to reinforce Catholic doctrine was in the use of anti-intellectual language. A key feature of humanism had always been its passionate opposition to the arguments of the scholastics, which, rightly or wrongly, were characterized as pedantic, destructive of a simple and true faith and, in particular, overly dependent on human reason. This kind of rhetoric was put to use in the Marian restoration to reinforce the central mysteries of the Mass, since 'our fayth in this thinge is grounded not in mans reason or sense, but in the almighty power of gods worde'.[71] The sacramental doctrine was portrayed as a divine proof of God's omnipotence, and a trial of faith, particularly in the transformation of bread and wine into Christ's flesh and blood. 'If the word of Helyas was able to bringe fyre from heaven, shall not the worde of Christ be able to chaunge the substaunce of breade? therefore uppon thys grounde of gods almightye power, we submitte our reason to our fayth, and above the reache of reason we beleve Christes worde.'[72]

When Cardinal Pole wrote to Thomas Cranmer, trying to convince him of his errors and reproaching him for his understanding of the Sacrament, he emphasized the point that human reason was not the way to understanding. He told Cranmer that he was misguided to think that he had achieved a higher level of understanding,

> for so yow showe in your letters, persuadeng your selffe to have found a waye in teacheng the doctrine of the Sacrament of the aulter, that other hath nott seene, which is to take awaye the absurditie both to the sence and reason of man, that is in the catholike doctrine.[73]

Pole clearly thought the point of the sacramental doctrine lay in the mystery, and said of Cranmer's view that 'the more probable it is, the more false it is, the greate sophister and father of all lyes, ever deceaveng us by probabilitie of reason, proponyng ever that whiche is more agreable to the sence. But the trew doctrine of Christ is taught by a nother way.'[74] The commonest popular objections to the doctrine of the

---

[70] Watson, *Holsome and Catholyke doctryne*, f. cxl v.
[71] Ibid., f. xxxvii r.
[72] Ibid., f. xliii v–xliiii r.
[73] BL, Harleian MS 417, f. 73v.
[74] Ibid.

Mass were based on the fact that it was contrary to reason: anti-intellectual rhetoric allowed Marian apologists to make this a positive virtue.

For some the 'manifest truth of Scripture' could be set side by side with the inherent mysticism of the doctrine of the Sacrament, and heretics could be reproved with both at once. Cuthbert Tunstall, in a preface to a translation of John Venaeus's work on the Sacrament, argued that although heretics constantly proclaimed their reliance on faith, they in fact pinned their arguments on human reason.

> For yf you laye before them for the veritie of these misteries the wordes of Christ, farre clearer and brighter then the sunne, forthewyth they runne to a perverse sence, cleane voyde of all trueth: They thynke that nothing is so highe, nothing so mystical in the scripture, but they are able to atteyne to it by reason.[75]

For Tunstall, such attempts to rely on reason were liable to take away all true appreciation of God altogether, and Venaeus's own treatise made the same point about the miracle of the Mass: 'For it is a more excellent thinge and higher by much, then that our weake and feble witte shouide attayne to the understanding of it'.[76] He showed a marked disinclination to come too close to an analysis of the sacrament: 'we may honor and embrace it, but to search the misteries of it, we are unable'.[77] And he deplored the common objections to the doctrine of Real Presence: 'As yf you woulde saye, his unmeasurable maiestie shuld be measured with the small measure of thy title witte'.[78]

This in itself could contribute to a reformed outlook. Watson's discussion of the Real Presence showed a certain wariness with the scholastic pedants as much as with the Protestant detractors.

> For our faith in this matter is induced by hys onelye authorytie, and not by our wytte, whose words require necessarily our fayth, and in no wise do admitte our reason, they require a simple beleuer, and reprove a wicked reasoner, so that we must beleue simply, that we can not searche profytablye, wherefore lyke as wee maye not curiouslye serche howe it is done so we maye not Jewishlye doubte whether it be done, but reuerently prepare us to receyue that by faith we are sure is done.[79]

This had overtones of Henry VIII's avoiding both extremes of

---

[75] *A notable Oration made by John Venaeus*, Tunstall's preface, Sig. B iiij v.
[76] Ibid., Sig. D i r.
[77] Ibid., Sig. D ii r.
[78] Ibid., Sig. E v r.
[79] Watson, *Holsome and Catholyke doctryne*, f. xxvii r.

'*sumpsimus*' and '*mumpsimus*'; the language of Catholic reform sought to steer a middle way between scholastic pedantry and heretical error.[80]

All of these emphases revolved around the basic explanation of the doctrine of the Mass, which was twofold: the Mass was both Sacrament and sacrifice. Bonner explained how 'Christ promysed two thynges: the one that he woulde geve a bread that should be his fleshe, and the other is, that he wold geve that fleshe for the lyfe of the worlde'.[81] The Mass therefore consisted of two elements: 'the oblation or offeringe of the said sacrament by the preistes unto almyghtye God, and ... the receavynge of the same'.[82] The oblation to God was the sacrifice of the Mass, the reception of Christ's body was the Sacrament, and both brought about man's salvation, but in different ways. Bonner instructed his audience that 'no one poynt of Christes relygion was more notably prophesied of, and set forthe in the olde testamente ... then was the continuall oblation, that is to saye, this foresayde sacryfice of the Masse'.[83] This sacrifice was the offering of Christ, and his whole Church, to God the Father. The Sacrament which followed, and the reception of Christ's body and blood, was capable of effecting a complete transformation in the worthy receiver.

> For this meate is the strength of our soule, the synewes of our minde, the knot of our trust, the foundation of our hope, our health, our light, our lyfe ... whereby our soules be washed, they be adourned, they be kindled, they are made clearer then the fyre, and brighter than golde.[84]

To provide the underpinning of these doctrines, Marian authors turned first of all to scripture, but their next line of defence was the early Church fathers. The influence of both humanism and Protestantism could also be seen in the use of patristic sources within Marian debate. Since the contemporary understanding of Reformation was of something which looked not forward, but backward in time, to the age of Christ and the Apostles, the beliefs and customs of the early Church became an important source of justification in every kind of religious controversy. When Wriothesley recorded the meeting of the Lambeth Synod, Pole's legatine synod for the reform of the Church, he

---

[80] G. Bernard, 'The making of religious policy, 1533–1546: Henry VIII and the search for the middle way', *Historical Journal*, 41 (1998); P. Marshall, 'Mumpsimus and Sumpsimus: the Intellectual Origins of a Henrician Bon Mot', *Journal of Ecclesiastical History*, 52 (2001).
[81] Bonner, *A profitable and necessarye doctryne*, Sig. T iiii r.
[82] Ibid., Sig. X i v.
[83] Ibid., Sig. X ii r.
[84] Watson, *Holsome and Catholyke doctryne*, f. xlix r.

commented on how 'all the Bishopps with the rest of the cleargie satt twice everie weeke for a reformation of the clergie accordinge to the olde antiquitie of the Churche, which latelye had bene putt downe' (*A Chronicle*, 131–2). Those who sought to reform the Church did so by appealing to the sanction of history and tradition. For both Protestant and Catholic reformers, reformation came by way of antiquity.

In the attempt to establish the certainty of sacramental doctrine, therefore, Catholic writers trained in a humanist tradition knew that their best allies were the early fathers of the Church. When Erasmus argued for the Real Presence, he did it on the basis of 'the auctoritie of common councels, and also by the agreamente of al churches and nations so many ages past'.[85] Bonner pointed out that in addition to the words of the Gospels and the writings of St Paul,

> there are so many and most evidente Authorities and testimonyes of the aunciert holy fathers, aswell of the greke as of the Latyne Churche, concernyng the very true and real presence of Christe hys bodye and bloude, in thys sacrament of the Aultare, that to rehearse them all, it would be a greate and an infinite labour.[86]

This insistence on Greek as well as Latin fathers was testimony to the importance of proving the antiquity and ubiquity of the Mass, as well as to the humanist training of the Marian churchmen and writers. Bonner, having explained that it would be too onerous to cite them all, nevertheless made sure to cite a representative sample, beginning with St John Chrysostom, who, he emphasised, lived 'not foure hundrethe yeare after Christe'.[87] In fact a large proportion of Bonner's defence of the Mass consisted merely of substantial quotations taken from the fathers. John Angel, writing in defence of the Sacrament, cited 36 different authorities, both Greek and Latin, emphasising those who lived in the very earliest years of the Church.[88]

This emphasis on the fathers was not merely a feature of the more learned works of the time: it was also a key feature of the more populist tracts. *A plaine and godlye treatise* was a work which deviated from the otherwise rather lofty tone of many Marian publications to rant at the 'sorte of sottes ... Scismaticall and blasphemous heretykes', who had despoiled the church.[89] In particular it fulminated at the Protestant martyrs of the time, who it described in colourful terms, as those who

---

[85] Erasmus, *The epistle ... unto Conradus Pelicanus*.
[86] Bonner, *A profitable and necessarye doctryne*, Sig. T ii r.
[87] Ibid. Bonner went on in this same passage also to cite Basil, Cyril, Tertullian and Hilary.
[88] John Angel, *The agrement of the holye Fathers*.
[89] *A plaine and godlye treatise*, Sig. A v r.

'never loved chastitie nor purenes of lyfe, but allowed and mayntayned open horedome betwene Priestes and theyr harlottes ... yet they muste have a longe white shirte down to the fote worshipfully to walke to warde the fier, thoughe the soule walke with the devill as blacke as pitche'.[90] It railed against the sort who, through Protestant teaching, were brought 'into such a folish paradice that he thinkes verely him selfe so light, that he shal lepe out of the fyre into gods bosom: wher in very dede dying an obstinat heretyke he lepeth like a flounder out of the fiying pan of temporall death in to the perpetuall and unquenchable fyre of gods iustice'.[91] This work was evidently designed to have popular appeal. Yet it also cited over three dozen of the early fathers, arguing persuasively that since all of them were dead, they 'can now not be iustly suspected to favour specyally any part saving the only syncere truthe'.[92] Here it was possible to see how 'thys our fayth hath continued constantly and fyrmely in the churche syth the Apostles tyme'.[93]

Reforming influences, then, could add new dimensions to traditional doctrine. One of the consequences of this was a move away from the more miraculous emphases of pre-Reformation sermons towards a more internalized spirituality. In the late medieval Church, just the sight of the Sacrament had had the power to save from sudden death, to cure illness, to ensure an array of different and immediate benefits.[94] In the Marian Church, the guaranteed effects were less concrete. The Marian homily of 1558 'Of the effectes of Christes body and bloude in the worthye receiuer', made less immediate promises. The emphasis here was on the spiritual benefits, and indeed the homily advised: 'It is not geven to repayre the ruyne and decayes of this temporall lyfe, whiche lyke a vapour continueth but a whyle, but to repayre the decay of our spirituall lyfe in Chryste.'[95] The bodily effects of worthy reception promised by this homily were disappointingly vague, being only to induce a general disinclination towards sinful living. The daily miracles of the pre-Reformation world had been superseded by a message more exalted, though possibly less broad in its appeal.

Other authors might take a slightly different tack. The treatise by John Venaeus eschewed the more delicate emphases on faithful inner reception that appeared in some of the more humanist works of the

---

[90] Ibid., Sig. G i v.
[91] Ibid., Sig. G i r.
[92] Ibid., Sig. C ii V.
[93] Ibid.
[94] P. Marshall, *The Catholic Priesthood and the English Reformation* (Oxford, 1994), 83n.
[95] Watson, *Holsome and Catholyke doctryne*, f. lxviii v.

time, and discussed the reception of the sacrament in strong and vivid language. 'Thys thynge only is requisite in thee, that thou hunger, that thou open thy greadye Jawes, and swallowe downe Christe: that by thys spirituall meate of a carnall manne, thou mayste be made spirituall.'[96] There was no expectation here of much spiritual sophistication, rather a prosaic acceptance of the limitations of human understanding. By contrast, we might consider Thomas Watson's description of the moment of communion: 'by thys blessed communion thou shalte receive the kynge into thy soule, and when the kynge entreth, there ought to be greate quietnes, silence and peace'.[97] These illustrations of the Mass were not at odds with one another, but they do show the variations that were possible. And where Venaeus required only spiritual hunger, Watson made it a prerequisite that the receiver should be 'in love and perfyt charitie with all menne', and that at the moment of communion he should fix his mind on the Passion, and the doctrine of salvation.[98]

There was also a strong sense that standards needed to be improved. Watson urged his congregations to take communion more frequently, and Bonner too wrote that 'considerynge the moste excellent grace efficacye and vertue of thys sacrament, it were gratelye to be wyshed and prayed for that all chrysten people, had suche devotion thereunto, that they woulde gladly dispose and prepare them selves, to the more often worthy receyuyng of the same'. He also grumbled about those who 'talke, or walke up and downe', and suggested that it would be good for them 'specially in the tyme of masse to behave themselfe reverently, in pure devotion and prayer'.[99] And a comparison was drawn between the lax standards of their own age, and the more ardent piety of the early Church: 'Suche was the fervente charitye of the people in the begynninge of the Churche, that came every daye, or in a maner everye daye to this holy Sacrament, and afterward when devotion decreased, they came everye sondaye, and further as the charitie of the people waxed colde the fewer tymes they prepared themselves to receive this Sacrament'.[100] Clearly there was still some work of reform to be achieved.

But it was not just humanism that had brought its influence to bear. Marian descriptions of the Mass also show the extent to which Protestant rhetoric had served to recalibrate Catholic thought, giving a new consciousness of past errors. The role of the priesthood, in particular, had been refashioned. As Peter Marshall has shown, the

---

[96] *A notable Oration, made by John Venaeus*, Sig. E iij v.
[97] Watson, *Holsome and Catholyke doctryne*, f. lix r.
[98] Ibid., f. lxii v.
[99] Bonner, *A profitable and necessarye doctryne*, f. Aa ii r.
[100] Watson, *Holsome and Catholyke doctryne*, f. lxi v.

understanding of the priestly role in the pre-Reformation Church had been essentially reverential, if many-layered, with perhaps some unease in the encounter between the doctrinal formulations that exalted priestly status, and the popular view, that on the one hand could ascribe to priests almost magical powers, and yet could also be critical of priests who failed to meet popular expectations. In the Marian works that tension seems to have been exacerbated, and there was a tendency to play down the role of the priest, and insist with perhaps greater severity on the necessity of clerical sanctity. 'Your mynde and knowledge,' instructed one homily, 'must be removed, and drawen away from the pryestes that minstreth (for they be but as instrumentes, as for example, the axe is to the wryght, the pen is to the wryter, the knyfe is to hym that cutteth).'[101] And when congregations were warned against improper adoration of the literal Host, it was with a consciousness of the risk of idolatry:

> let every man or woman when he seeth this sacrament in the Priestes handes, direct the eye of his faythe and hyst intent, to honour onely that substaunce of Christ God and man, whiche he seeth not with hys bodelye eyes ... and let him not fyxe his thoughte upon the visible whitenes or roundnesse of the bread ... but let him intend to honour the body and blood of Christ.[102]

Bonner tried to play down the supernatural powers of the priesthood, emphasizing that 'it is not the visible preist, that nowe worketh thys hyghe mysterye, by his owne power or strengthe, but it is Christ hym selfe, the invysible preist, that dothe worke it by the misterye of the vysyble preist'.[103] He said too, that 'we must understand, that betwene the sacrifice which was made upon the crosse, and the sacryfce of the masse, as concernynge the substaunce of the thynge offered, there is no difference, forasmuche as in that respecte, it is one and the same, though the maner of offerynge be diverse'.[104] Here he was replying to the Protestant criticism that the emphasis upon the sacrifice of the Mass rendered Christ's sacrifice on the cross less important.

The Protestants hated the Mass, and with good reason, given the many ways in which it could secure Catholic loyalties at all levels of society. In the previous reign William Turner had argued that it could even serve as a justification for civil disobedience: 'the Mass is contrary unto the Scripture, therefore though the magistrates should command us to believe that it were of God, we are not bound in this case to obey

---

[101] Leonard Pollard, *Fyve Homilies* (1556), Sig. B i v.
[102] Watson, *Holsome and Catholyke doctryne*, ff. lxv v–lxvi r.
[103] Bonner, *A profitable and necessarye doctrine*, Sig. U ii v.
[104] Ibid., Sig. Z i v.

them'.[105] Another Protestant attack upon the Mass, printed in 1556, described it, despairingly, as 'held in such honour and pryce almost of all men ... extemed as the chefe and principall way to honour god in the Christian religion', and argued that 'the more part of men without anye manner of knowledge in matters of Christian religion, not considering the importaunce therof, followe the multitude, Custome and the common sort of men, thinkinge that they offend not but that they do well, and an acceptable worke to god, doinge as other men doo'.[106] Protestants might have sneered at the unquestioning traditionalism of the Catholic laity, but they could also appreciate its strength. Yet Protestant authors had to target not only the ignorance of the populace, but also the intellectual errors of their leaders. The battle over the Mass was one fought on several levels.

Sacramental doctrine was also, of course, the weakest aspect of Protestantism, or so many Catholics maintained, given the division that existed within Protestant ranks concerning the correct understanding of the Eucharist. Many Catholics tried to stress the universality of their own doctrine by pointing out how some Protestants agreed with them about the Real Presence: the epistle of Erasmus reprinted in 1554 noted how the words of Christ at the Last Supper 'did compell, yea Luther him selfe ... to professe the same, which the universal church doth professe, although he is wont gladly to dissent from the same churche'.[107] John Angel pointed out that Luther, Melanchthon and Erasmus had all upheld the Real Presence, dwelling also – and with particular relish – on the testimony of Cranmer's Catechism of 1548 and the first Book of Common Prayer.[108] Equally, such authors also emphasized the extent of disagreement within Protestantism, and its general novelty and inconstancy as a creed. The speech ascribed to the Duke of Northumberland on the scaffold, and printed by the new regime, warned against 'these seditious preachers, and teachers of newe doctryne', characterized by their waywardness, 'who were never able to explicate them selves, they know not to day what they wold have to morowe, there is no stay in theyr teaching and doctryne, they open the boke but they cannot shut it agayne'.[109]

---

[105] William Turner, *A new dialogue, entitled the examination of the Mass* (1548), RSTC 24361.5, Sig. E iij r.

[106] Anthoni de Adamo (Agostino Mainardi), *An anatomi, that is to say a Parting in Peeces of the Mass* (1556), RSTC 17200, Sig. A ij r.

[107] Erasmus, *The epistle ... unto Conradus Pelicanus*, Cawood (1554), STC 10491.

[108] Angel, *The agrement of the holy fathers*, ff. lxxxi r–lxxxii v. For a discussion of the 1548 Catechism which proved such an embarrassment to Cranmer see MacCulloch, *Thomas Cranmer*, 386–41.

[109] Dudley, *The sayng*, f. 2r–v.

In the encounter with Protestantism, the Marian treatment of the Mass showed that while some Protestant notions were defied, others were silently assimilated, and that even in this most contentious area of doctrine there could be similarities in approach, with mutual appeals to Scripture, the early Church or concepts of social order. Yet alongside the niceties of religious debate there was also the dogged pursuit of heresy. In heresy trials the nature of the Sacrament proved perhaps the most infallible indicator of error. In particular, the doctrine of transubstantiation imparted a useful clarity to an area of debate where other Catholic doctrines, such as that of the Real Presence, could be less clearly defined. John Foxe, in his *Acts and Monuments*, gave countless examples of this, such as when the chancellor of Salisbury diocese, examining three heretics in 1556, made it his first enquiry, 'Whether that they did not believe that in the sacrament of the altar [as he termed it], after the words of consecration spoken by the priest at mass, there remained no substance of bread nor wine, but Christ's body, flesh and blood, as he was born of the Virgin Mary?'[110] The tendency of the Marian literature was to dwell far more heavily on the doctrine of the Real Presence, which had far greater reformist credentials, being rooted in Scripture and the early Church, but this was lost in the need for resolution when it came to the heresy trials. The Marian regime tried to use the Mass in many different ways, yet it was as a blunt instrument for the uncovering of heresy that it was destined to be most often remembered.

While Mary was still alive, however, the Mass could be many things to many different people. Yet if the variations within Marian depictions of the Mass were manifold, they were also, for the most part, concealed. Diversity, in propaganda terms, could only be an embarrassment. If the scope of Marian attitudes to the Mass has not always been appreciated, this is in large part because, at the time, it was necessary that it remain unacknowledged by the Marian Catholics who developed these different emphases. Marian propaganda had to stress the homogeneity of its religious message lest it lay itself open to charges of inconstancy, and Tudor Catholics were as sensitive to the accusation of novelty as their Protestant contemporaries. To secure their religious credibility, both Churches had to prove themselves the direct inheritors of an age-old tradition stretching back to the time of Christ, and both relied upon a fair amount of historical distortion to help their case. Yet we are perhaps more strict in examining the dubious accuracy of Protestant claims to historical continuity than we are scrupulous in our treatment of Catholic accounts, which are often equally questionable.

---

[110] John Foxe, *Acts and Monuments*, ed. S.R. Cattley (8 vols, 1836–39), vii, 104.

One of the difficulties here was caused by the rapid development of Elizabethan nostalgia. English Catholics in exile on the Continent or in retreat at home were inclined to idealize the world they had left behind, and wax sentimental about the certainties of pre-Reformation devotional life.[111] They constructed an idea of parish worship which was rooted in a popular understanding characterized by simplicity and devotion, where ignorance was a positive advantage, and they used this as a justification for many aspects of traditional religious practice which reformers, both Catholic and Protestant, had called into question.[112] John Martiall, for example, defending the sign of the cross, argued that 'that which wordes could not print in their heades, the contemplation of this signe doeth so printe in their mindes, that they triumph over the devil'.[113] And Nicholas Sander painted a cosy picture of how images were treated in pre-Reformation times, when you could 'see the Sexten sweeping copwebbes from them, and the Parish Clerke putting the Crosse so homely under his cloke', stressing that the worship accorded to them had been proportionate, or, in other words, that popular religion could be trusted.[114] The 'simple and unlearned' were portrayed as the best safeguard of true doctrine. Most of all, this was true of popular participation in the Mass: Thomas Harding described the value of this pious ignorance, when 'without doubte this godly affection of their myndes, is so acceptable to God, as no understanding of wordes may be compared with it'.[115] Simple popular devotion, which had been viewed with suspicion by reformers in the early part of the century, was now being reconfigured as the most reliable safeguard of true doctrine. Sander urged his reader to 'consider the Christian people as of a good faith' and trust their instincts, and supported this view with citations of God's many promises to be with his people: 'that multitude ... compared to the dust of the earth, and to the sand of the sea (which consisteth of rude and ignorant persons for the most part) must of necessitie continue the people of God ... because the word of God can not faile'.[116] The religion of the ignorant had acquired a new status.

---

[111] See, for example, William Allen, *A defense and declaration ... touching purgatory* (Antwerp, 1565), f. 215 v.

[112] Protestant rhetoric developed an analogous tendency to appeal at times to the purity of popular religion: see Davies, *A Religion of the Word*, 179 and 195, where she cites Robert Crowley's description of how God 'poured out of his spirit upon those little ones that the world taketh for his excrements, revealing unto them those mysteries which he hath hidden from the wise and prudent of this world'.

[113] John Martiall, *A Treatyse of the Crosse* (1564), RSTC 17496, f. 116 v.

[114] Nicholas Sander, *A treatise of the images of Christ* (1567), RSTC 21696, f. 172 v.

[115] Thomas Harding, *An Answere to Maister Iuelles Chalenge* (1564), f. 69 v.

[116] Sander, *A treatise of the images of Christ*, f. 175 r.

This trend had begun during Mary's reign. In part this was a consequence of the notion that Protestantism had made inroads purely because of its ability to seduce and corrupt the ignorant and bewildered: 'an infinite number of innocentes, they have spirituallye poysoned and corrupted within this realme, and caused them to perishe obstinatlye'.[117] Yet Marian propaganda went beyond this, to sketch out an idealized notion of the humble devotion that had been the basis of parish worship in the past. Pole's sermon to the citizens of London deplored the reliance on the printed word, and argued that 'they are most apte to receyve light, that are more obedyent to follow ceremonyes, than to reade'.[118] John Standish described how during the Mass the priest spoke only to God, while the people occupied themselves in private prayer: 'his communication, is to God, and not for the people'. He asked, too, 'What cause is there then why divine service should be in Englishe, except ye thynke that God understandeth no Latine?'[119] He noted the way that key words in the Mass such as '*Alieluya*' or '*Osanna*', '*Amen*' or '*Sabaoth*' had not been translated from the Hebrew, or '*Kyrie eleison*' from the Greek, as an indication that the Mass was *intended* to be unintelligible. 'And that Christ praied in secret and silence alone, the head for the whole bodie, to signifie unto us thereby, that the priestes office is likewise to doe the same.'[120] By contrast, he depicted the English service of Edward's reign as 'an extreme enemie to al godlye prayer and devotion' precisely because 'men phansied so to heare what was readde ... that fervente prayer whyche ought to be, was smally regarded'.[121]

Yet Pole's vision was more an idealized vision of the parish worship of the past than a useful description of an attainable goal in an age of so much printed propaganda. Nor did Standish's account tally with the many attempts of the pre-Reformation Church to encourage lay comprehension during Mass. *The Lay Folks' Mass Book*, for example, had made it clear that the popular experience of the Mass was one embracing many different levels of comprehension, encouraging the congregation to listen to the priest 'if thou of letter kan' – that is if they understood Latin – or to read along in a book, and only in the last resort,

---

[117] John Standish, *A discourse wherin it is debated whether it be expedient that the scripture should be in English for al men to reade that wyll* (1554), RSTC 23207, Sig. A iiii r–v.
[118] J. Strype, *Ecclesiastical Memorials* (1816), vol. III, part ii, 503.
[119] Standish, *A discourse*, Sig. K viii r–v.
[120] Ibid., Sig. L i r.
[121] Ibid., Sig. L ii r–v.

> If thou kan noghte rede ne saye
> Thy paternoster rehers alwaye.[122]

It had always been understood that ignorance of the words spoken at Mass was no barrier to godly participation, but within the Marian and Elizabethan understanding of the Mass there now appeared a shift in emphasis, and an attempt by some to claim that ignorance as a positive good, turning their back on the educational aspirations voiced by humanists in the earlier part of the century. Standish's approach was not characteristic of all Marian tracts; in fact he was at odds with the many who went on seeking to explain the Mass as fully as possible and render it more intelligible to the populace. But he had sounded a note that was to be picked up and used to great effect in the next reign. This helped construct a homogenized picture of popular devotion which concealed a much more complex contemporary reality.

The demands of polemical exchange also meant that the many Catholic voices which had clamoured for reform had to be excised from the collective memory, for they gave too much purchase to the Protestants. Foxe's inclusion of John Colet in his 'Book of Martyrs' is a case in point: Catholic reformers were being claimed for the opposition as crypto-Protestants, and so the picture of late medieval Catholicism had to be redrawn without them. The way in which Erasmus's reputation suffered in Elizabethan times is perhaps the most eloquent example of this.[123] The consequent romanticized vision of pre-Reformation worship involved little recognition of the way in which Catholicism developed new dimensions during the course of Reformation. This has hampered our appreciation of the diversity and individuality to be found at work during Mary's reign.

The English Reformation was an exercise in communication, the demands of which often necessitated some measure of innovation. Whether expounding Protestantism, or defending Catholicism, it was necessary to bridge some of the gaps in understanding and expectation between different layers of society. Reformers of both persuasions were faced with the difficulty of translating intellectual formulations into the language of parish practice. For the Catholics involved in bringing about the Marian restoration, the Mass was the automatic channel to use in order to get their message across. The continuity of the Mass within the Henrician Reformation was used to lay claim to political continuance. The use of bodily imagery was employed in the hope of healing a fractured social body. The doctrines of sacrament and sacrifice could be

---

[122] *The Lay Folks' Mass Book*, 14–16.
[123] Wooding, *Rethinking Catholicism*, 257.

defended by humanist appeals to Scripture. Protestant criticisms could be defied or assimilated. The symbolism of the Mass therefore worked on a multiplicity of different levels. Exploring the different strands of explanation leads us to an understanding of the complexities within Tudor Catholicism and the extent to which it was a developing tradition. The understanding of the Mass which emerged from the Marian restoration was, despite its self-conscious nostalgia for the late medieval Church, a much more intricate and multifaceted construct than its pre-Reformation precursor. Even with regard to this most central element of traditional Catholicism, time could not stand still.

CHAPTER NINE

The Theology and Spirituality of a Marian Bishop: the Pastoral and Polemical Sermons of Thomas Watson

William Wizeman, SJ

'And as younge infantes with great gladnes do suck the breastes of their mothers or nurses, even so with greater gladnes ought we to come to the breast of our Savioure there to suck the grace of the holy gost.'[1] Bishop Thomas Watson used this analogy, perhaps more startling today than in the sixteenth century, to encourage more devout reception of the Eucharist; but the sentiment also illustrated his understanding of Christian life and doctrine in general, as contained in *A Holsome and Catholyke doctryne concerninge the seuen Sacramentes*. This work, together with *Twoo notable Sermons made before the Quenes highnes*, outline Watson's theological vision and its place in the programme for restoring Catholicism in Mary Tudor's reign. In considering Watson's *Catholyke doctryne* and *Twoo Sermons*, readers can discern a coherent theology and spirituality that played an important role in the Marian programme for the renewal of Catholicism in England.

A number of questions must be asked in an examination of Watson's theology and spirituality. How were *A Catholyke doctryne* and *Twoo Sermons* part of the plan for the renewal of Catholic theology and spirituality in the Marian Church? What did Watson perceive as necessary elements of wholesome and Catholic teaching for the instruction and edification of readers and listeners, after 20 years of religious tumult? Finally and most importantly, why is Watson's theology and spirituality significant in the context of the Reformation? Watson's *Catholyke doctryne* and *Twoo Sermons* were two key works that served the Marian Church's attempt to renew Catholic life and

---

[1] Thomas Watson, *Holsome and Catholyke doctrine concerninge the seuen Sacramentes of Chrystes Church, expedient to be knowen to all men, set forth in mauer of shorte Sermons to bee made to the people, by the reuerend father in God Thomas bishop of Lincoln* (London, 1558), RSTC 25112, 58.

doctrine. The *Twoo Sermons* were a polemical tract for an educated audience, expounding views on Christ's corporeal presence in the Eucharist and the sacrificial nature of the Mass, as well as attempting to refute Eucharistic theology that had developed during the reign of Edward VI. *A Catholyke doctryne* was a collection of sermons to be read in parishes as a means of catechesis in Catholic sacramental worship and devotion. These books were the corpus that Watson published in his lifetime, a lifetime spent largely in the service of Catholic belief.

Watson's adult life was dominated by the turmoil of the English Reformation. As England's religious revolution commenced in 1534, he took his first degree and shortly afterwards was elected a fellow of St John's College, Cambridge, when the influence of the traditionally minded humanist, John Fisher, was still very strong.[2] Indeed, Watson was a noted humanist scholar and friend of John Cheke and Roger Ascham.[3] In 1537, Watson became dean of St John's, and then chaplain to Stephen Gardiner in 1545. After being imprisoned with Gardiner following the accession of Edward VI in 1547, he retired from public life, although he found himself in and out of prison until Mary came to the throne in 1553. In that year he became master of St John's and dean of Durham Cathedral. In 1557 he was appointed the Bishop of Lincoln at the age of 44. With the accession of Elizabeth I, Bishop Watson was one of the leaders of those opposed to the restoration of Protestant doctrine. In April 1559 he was arrested immediately after the government-sponsored disputation at Westminster Abbey, and, refusing the oath of supremacy, was deprived of his see. He spent most of his remaining 25 years in various forms of confinement, dying in Wisbech prison in 1584 at the age of 71.[4] Watson had been one of the 'respected and dependable' bishops chosen by Cardinal Pole and Mary for their 'theological and pastoral background', who were called upon to implement the programme for

---

[2] Richard Rex, *The Theology of John Fisher* (Cambridge: Cambridge University Press, 1991), 55–6, 58, 63–4.

[3] Richard Rex, 'The role of English humanists in the Reformation up to 1559', in *The Education of a Christian Society. Humanism and the Reformation in Britain and the Netherlands*. Papers delivered to the Thirteenth Anglo-Dutch Historical Conference, 1997. N. Scott Amos, Andrew Pettegree and Henk Van Nierop, eds (Aldershot: Ashgate, 1999), 29–30; Richard Upsher Smith, 'An Unpublished Translation by Bishop Thomas Watson of a Spurious Sermon of St Cyprian of Carthage: Introduction and Text', *Recusant History*, 21, 4 (1993), 19–20.

[4] For the most extensive biographical treatment of Watson, see T.E. Bridgett and T.F. Knox, *The True Story of the Catholic Hierarchy Deposed by Queen Elizabeth* (London: Burns and Oates, 1889), 120–207.

England's re-Catholicization.[5] He took to heart the strategy outlined by these bishops in Pole's legatine synod of 1555–56, especially the fourth decree's emphasis on the need for preaching and catechesis.[6] 'The Marian church sought to ensure regular parochial preaching and followed Cranmer's precedent on preparing sets of homilies to be used by insufficient preachers', in Eamon Duffy's analysis.[7] The sacraments were among the subjects to be treated in the homilies that the synod proposed, and in fact the bishops remarked that 'the greatest amount of error had arisen on those points which relate to the doctrine of the head of the church and the sacraments'.[8] It was this decree that led to the publishing of Watson's *Catholyke doctryne*, according to Pole's 1558 letter to his friend and fellow primate, Archbishop Bartolomé Carranza of Toledo.[9] In fact it was the only theological work commissioned by the synod to be printed, and so may be regarded as an official statement of the doctrine of the Marian Church.[10] As for Watson's *Twoo Sermons*, which were preached before the queen in Lent 1554 and printed in three known editions later that year, J.W. Blench hypothesized that 'the cogent presentation of reformed doctrine in the Edwardian homilies had to be met with an equally satisfying account of the Catholic position'.[11] It seems that Watson's work was 'satisfying' enough for Protestant Divines like Robert Crowley to respond to it over ten years later.[12] While the role of

---

[5] Rex Pogson, 'The Legacy of Schism: Confusion, Continuity and Change in the Marian Clergy', in *The Mid-Tudor Polity, c. 1540–1560*, Jennifer Loach and Robert Tittler, eds (London: Macmillan, 1980), 123, 125–6.

[6] See Gerald Bray, ed., *The Anglican Canons 1529–1947* (Woodbridge: Boydell, 1998), 100–105, 80–81.

[7] Eamon Duffy, *The Stripping of the Altars: Traditional Religion in England 1400–1580* (New Haven: Yale University Press, 1992), 530.

[8] Philip Hughes, *Rome and the Counter-Reformation in England* (London: Burns and Oates, 1944), 79.

[9] Reginald Pole, *Epistolarum Reginaldi Poli SR. E. Cardinalis Et aliorum ad ipsum*, A.M. Quirini, ed. (Brescia, 1757), vol. V, 74: 'ut de omnibus ad fidem, et religionem pertinentibus, in quibus populi praecipue instruendi, et ad pietatem informandi sunt, de iisque in primus, quae in controversiam hic sunt vocata, Homiliae Anglica lingua scriberentur a quibusdam doctis et piis Viris, ad hoc munus delectis, ex quibus duo, alter Watsonus, qui nunc est Episcopus Lincolniensis.'

[10] There are four known editions printed in 1558: RSTC 25112, 25112.5, 25113–14.

[11] *Twoo notable Sermons, made the thirde and fyfte Fridayes in Lent last past, before the Quenes highnes, concernynge the reall presence of Christes body and bloude in the blessed Sacrament: and also the Masse, which is the sacrifice of the newe Testament* (London, 1554), RSTC 25115, 25115.3, 25115.5; J.W. Blench, *Preaching in England in the Late 15th and 16th Centuries* (Oxford: Blackwell, 1964), 285.

[12] Robert Crowley, *A setting open of the subtyle sophistrie of T. Watson* (London, 1569–70), RSTC 6093.

polemical literature in the Marian Church and the role of preaching in the mind of Cardinal Pole have been debated, it seemed that Watson, by publishing his collections of sermons, viewed both as valuable tools for the renewal of early modern Catholicism in England.[13]

Watson's theology rested upon an erudite, apologetic use of scripture and patristic writings, in accord with the humanist sensibilities of the time. Like his peers, he cited scripture often, but 'chiefly as an arsenal of illustrative texts to illuminate and confirm Catholic doctrine', rather than in exegesis, just as contemporary Jesuits did.[14] The fathers of the Church to whom he chiefly turned were of impeccable pedigree in humanist eyes: Augustine and Chrysostom. But Watson possessed no qualms about drawing proofs from sources that would have been denounced five years earlier. Gregory the Great and Hugh of St Victor found a prominent place among the sources cited in his sermons. However, his references to the scholastics were few; he cited Aquinas only three times.[15] Watson's reluctance to look to the scholastics seems due to his education, rather than disagreement with medieval theology. The scholastics had lost their dominance at St John's before he began his studies in 1529, largely due to the educational reforms of John Fisher, who also cited Aquinas infrequently in his works.[16] Watson therefore stood as a humanist among humanists in his use of theological sources. Although Watson did not employ scholastic theologians as authorities, he nevertheless defended the medieval synthesis of the Church's traditional doctrine of grace, rooted in the Catholic interpretation of Augustine's writings and eventually solidified at Trent. He confirmed that the sacraments, as instruments of God's grace, were God's free gift to sinful humanity and the means to attain its supernatural end of personal union with God. Through the seven sacraments, God 'poureth abundantlye his manyfolde graces into our soules, and by them maketh us people mete to receyue the fruites and benefites of his passion', according to the first sermon in *A Catholyke doctryne*.[17] These 'medicynes,' as

---

[13] For differing considerations of controversial literature see David Loades, *The Reign of Mary Tudor: Politics, Government and Religion in England, 1553–58* (London: Longman, 1991), 110–14, 281–7 and Duffy, *Stripping of the Altars*, 529–31. For views on Pole's estimation of preaching see Rex Pogson, 'Pole and the Priorities of Government in Mary Tudor's Church', *Historical Journal*, XXIII (1975), 13–19; Thomas Mayer, *Reginald Pole: Prince and Prophet* (Cambridge: Cambridge University Press, 2000), 250–51; and Thomas McCoog, 'Ignatius Loyola and Reginald Pole: A Reconsideration', *Journal of Ecclesiastical History*, 47 (1996), 257–73.

[14] Blench, *Preaching in England*, 52; John O'Malley, *The First Jesuits* (Cambridge MA: Harvard University Press, 1993), 260.

[15] Watson, *Twoo Sermons*, X8r–v; *Catholyke doctryne*, 14r, 122r.

[16] Rex, *Theology of Fisher*, 50–64.

[17] Watson, *Catholyke doctryne*, 1r.

vehicles of grace, were to heal human nature bound by sin, and to raise that nature to a participation in the life of Christ. Christians were called, but not compelled, to cooperate with Divine grace that inaugurated these good works. In its transformation of human freedom so that it might heed the commands of Christ, grace worked through human freedom, particularly by the gifts of faith, repentance and conversion, in correspondence to the supernatural goal of human nature.[18] While Christ's sacrificial death on the cross took place for the redemption of all humanity, not all were saved, because of their refusal to participate in the life of grace.[19] Without explicating a theology of grace in explicit terms, Watson nevertheless upheld the Catholic Church's traditional theology of grace in his sermons on the sacraments.

The Church's essential role in the life of believers as sole mediator of Divine grace and arbiter of truths necessary for salvation was foundational for Watson's theological vision. Since Christ had been always with his Church and his Spirit had always guided it, what the Marian Church believed was what the Church had always believed, beginning with the Apostles. The teachings of Protestants were resuscitations of old heresies that had long ago been condemned by the general councils throughout the Church's history. The councils of Nicaea, Constantinople and Ephesus, as well as the medieval councils of Lateran IV, Constance and Florence, had 'determined those thynges, that pertayne to … fayth in Christ, and the purgying of hys churche'. He saw no difference between the determinations of earlier and later general councils; he denied the Protestant position that the Church's doctrinal stances had become corrupt with the passage of time. For example, as the Council of Nicaea had 'inuented' the term 'consubstantial' to end controversy and confusion, so had the word 'transubstantiation' been defined 'in the greatest general counsell that euer was, which was called the counsell Lateranense, where there were present seuenty Archbyshoppes and foure hundred bishops'.[20] Watson furthermore encouraged adherence to the chief of the 'prelates of the uniuersall Church', namely the Pope. Lucy Wooding believed she found a generally ambivalent attitude towards the papacy among Marian religious writers.[21] However, in a group of sermons that need not have touched upon the papacy, Watson referred to it with ardour. He consistently underscored the doctrine of the Pope's unique authority to govern and

---

[18] Ibid., 6r–v, 36r–v.
[19] Watson, *Twoo Sermons*, N7r–v.
[20] Watson, *Catholyke doctryne*, 43r, 1v; Watson, *Twoo Sermons*, L8r, M6r–7v, N1v.
[21] Lucy Wooding, *Rethinking Catholicism in Reformation England* (Oxford: Oxford University Press, 2000), 130.

teach the Church throughout the world, in accord with the mission Christ gave to Peter and those who succeeded him. The Pope is the 'lawfull successour [of St Peter] in the chayre of Christ, gouerning the holle army of Christ's church here on earth'. Mass was offered for members of Christ's body, among whom were 'the Popes holynesse the Successour of Saynt Peter, to whom Christe dydde commytte the cure and charge of hys uniuersall Churche through oute the worlde'.[22] A teaching issued by a Pope in union with a general council bore impressive weight. The doctrine of transubstantiation had been established 'by the greatest aucthoritie that euer Christe lefte in his Churche, ... by the judgement of the successour of saynct Peter in the chayre of Christe, and of the Byshops and pastours of Christes flocke ... in a general counsell'.[23] The apostolic succession of popes and bishops to their own day flowed as a river from the one font of Christ, 'the only supreme head of oure one churche'. No prince could claim that title.[24] The Church, therefore, especially through the authoritative biblical interpretations and teachings of popes, bishops and general councils, presented Christians with the truth of Divine revelation and the means to faithfully adhere to it. Beyond the essential quality of the Church for salvation, Watson presented a positive interpretation of individual and communal Christian existence. The Christian life lay not so much in 'resisting euill, but with good ouercoming euil'. Charity was singled out as the manner of overcoming evil with good, through care and compassion for the poor and forgiveness and reconciliation with others.[25] In addition, 'the iustice of God can not iudge otherwise, but as oure woorkes deserue'.[26] Thus at the beginning of *A Catholyke doctryne*, the bishop reminded readers and potential listeners that the gifts of the Spirit were not only for inward growth and devotion, but also to aid fellow Christians.[27] Whether persons possessed these gifts to a greater or lesser degree, they were not to rely upon personal efforts, riches or works, but on God's gratuitous gift of grace. Through prayer and humble dependence on God, Christians could 'continue stedfaste and immouable from the hope of the Gospell, increasing in good workes' as they grew in holiness.[28] Through the outpouring of grace, the person would be 'inwardelye beautified and enriched and made a happy' Christian.[29]

---

22 Watson, *Catholyke doctryne*, 3v, 77r.
23 Ibid., 47r.
24 Ibid., 155v.
25 Ibid., 31v–33r.
26 Ibid., 95r.
27 Ibid., 2r.
28 Ibid., 33v–34r.
29 Ibid., 30r.

The grace by which Christians were 'enriched' through the power of the Holy Spirit was not beyond the reach of human beings, but, under the guise of the humble elements of sacramental bread, wine, water and oil, they had recourse to that same life-giving Spirit. In partaking of the Church's sacraments, Christians were to recall that they were united to the New Testament or covenant of Christ; the necessary corollary was 'to express in our lyues that we imitate and folow his footsteps, and keepe perpetuall commemoration of him that died for us, and rose againe'.[30] As the sacraments were central to the Catholic spirituality as delineated by Watson, so Christ was at the heart of that sacramental theology and spirituality. Christians received God's grace, and so union with the Divine, most especially through the sacramental life of the Church. This is the core of Watson's theology. His treatment of sacramental theology is thematic, cogent and generally lucid, whether in the didactic format of the *Catholyke doctryne* or in his polemical *Twoo Sermons*. Yet the sacraments are only the centrepiece of a larger spirituality which was part of a Christocentric and incarnational world-view. Working in and through the sacraments, Christ made himself and his saving-power present in the life of individuals and the Church.[31] Watson reiterated that humanity had been saved by Christ's merits alone, when he had innocently died for all sinners.[32] It was Christ

> who loued us so vehemently, that to bring us to life, was content to dye, and for the pryce and ransome of the same lyfe vouchsafed to geue his own body to death: doth styll vouchsafe to nouryshe us so redemed and brought to life with the swete and holsome milke of his owne bloude, and giueth us his fleshe to eate. ...[33]

The Church's sacramental nature had been established when Christ himself was incarnate upon the earth. The incarnation was 'the greatest grace and benefite that god hath geuen man, wherupon mans saluation doth holly depend'.[34] In this way Watson's incarnational spirituality focused on the sacraments, and especially the Eucharist, as a means of union with the incarnate God.

Receiving the Eucharist was the exemplary way in which the incarnate Christ was experienced by redeemed humanity, for Christ became incarnate among them in the Eucharist. It was the same Christ who was crucified whom they beheld or received at Mass under the sign

---

[30] Ibid., 67v.
[31] Watson, *Twoo Sermons*, A3r–4v.
[32] Watson, *Catholyke doctryne*, 68r–v.
[33] Ibid., 36r.
[34] Ibid., 168v.

of bread. Christ's one sacrifice was accomplished on Good Friday. Yet, in the Mass,

> the operation and vertue of this pas[s]ion, is a longe thing, extended to the saluation of man, from the beginning of the worlde to the laste ende ... The effect of it which is man's redemption and satisfaction ceases not ... therefore Christe oure Saviour wylleth that the Sacrifice of thys redemption shoulde neuer cease, but bee alwayes to all men present in grace, and alwayes kept in perpetuall memorye.

The Church lived under the command of Jesus 'to renew hys passion, not by sufferyng of deathe againe, but after an unbloody maner' in the daily celebration of the Eucharist.[35] And by partaking of it, the communicant was 'more inwardly ioined to Christes mistical body, not onely spirituallye by fayth and charytye but also by naturall and corporall participation with Christ and his church'.[36] The concentration on the Eucharist 'as the abiding sacramental presence of Christ in his church' was a defining element of Marian Catholicism, as well as the Counter Reformation in Europe, in the face of the Protestant assault on traditional Catholic teaching on the sacrament.[37] Christ's corporeal presence under the signs of bread and wine, the Mass's sacrificial nature, and other elements of traditional eucharistic doctrine and devotion were passionately explained by Watson. But he also wrote to instil faith in Christ's love and power to effect this sacrament.[38] Christ had not been content in becoming human and in suffering death for his people, but in this sacrament he united himself with his Church 'not onelye by fayth, but also in verye deede'. And Watson called upon people to respond to Christ's 'deede' of love by attending mass and receiving the Eucharist more devoutly.[39]

The act of receiving the Eucharist possessed many benefits, especially those relating to sanctification. Watson informed readers that by taking communion they received medicine for their sinful souls and bodies. It increased their power for virtuous living; interestingly he also commended it as an aid against tyrants and heretics. He stressed that humans did not normally possess these powers. Furthermore, communion effected the body, 'by healynge it, by defendinge, sanctifyinge, strengthening and reducing it to immortalitye'. As baptism

---

[35] Ibid., 69v–70v; also preceding extract.
[36] Ibid., 39r.
[37] H.O. Evennett, *The Spirit of the Counter-Reformation* (Notre Dame: University of Notre Dame Press, 1968), 38.
[38] Watson continued to write on the Eucharist while incarcerated under Elizabeth I. See Smith, 'Unpublished Translation', 419–50.
[39] Watson, *Catholyke doctryne*, 57v.

prepared the soul for eternal life, so the Eucharist prepared the body. Through it the body had greater strength to attend to the movements of the soul, rather than succumbing to its own waywardness.[40] The greatest effect of reception was union with Christ, corporeally as well as spiritually.[41] In communion 'Christes fleshe [is] mingled with our fleshe', Watson declared. He also used Cyril of Alexandria's analogy of two pieces of wax melted together as to become indistinguishable, in his description of receiving the host.[42] The union of Christ and the communicant was 'a true and natural vnitie, and not onely in will and affection by faythe and charitye'. As Christ was in God through his divinity, and Christians are in Christ through the incarnation, so Christ is in Christians through the Eucharist; in other words, 'we are incorporate into hys fleshe, that for our saluation was made our fleshe'.[43] In his stress on the unitive and incarnational aspects of communion, Watson closely followed Fisher.[44] For these theologians, the Eucharist was the means of affectively savouring the intense love of Christ for his people.

One of the most significant changes in traditional religious practice during Mary's reign was the growing call for more frequent communion. The love of Jesus, Watson wrote, poured out in this sacrament, should move Christians to a greater desire to receive it. Frequent communion served as a deterrent to spiritual inconstancy. He related further how the canons of Lateran IV only stipulated the minimum required of people in terms of receiving communion.[45] By regular communion, the Christian could enjoy a closer union with Christ, and so be moved to relinquish that which challenged this union. Furthermore,

> the oftner he cometh the better it is, and the more is he nouryshed to euerlastinge life. And the better the man is, the more desirous is he to be ioyned to god corporally by this Sacrament. For ... Christ by geuing to vs his fleshe and hys bloude declared moste of all his exceadinge loue towardes vs ...[46]

'[L]et vs not defraud our selues of [the benefits of Communion]', Watson wrote, 'by so long absteyning from it ... but as his exceedyng loue towardes vs moued him to geue it to vs, so let it and the benefites we receyue by it increase oure loue towardes him.' He ended his final sermon

---

[40] Ibid., 48r–v, 50r–53v.
[41] Watson, *Catholyke doctryne*, 39r; cf. *Twoo Sermons*, F2v–8r.
[42] Watson, *Twoo Sermons*, F6v–7v; cf. *Catholyke doctryne*, 53v.
[43] Watson, *Catholyke doctryne*, 53v.
[44] Rex, *Theology of Fisher*, 143–4.
[45] Watson, *Catholyke doctryne*, 48r–49v, 61v–62.
[46] Ibid., 61v.

on the eucharist with an exhortation to frequent communion as satisfaction for sin.[47] In his encouragement of more frequent reception, Watson appeared to have been among the early advocates of this key element of Counter-Reformation spirituality.[48] Watson was not, however, an originator of this view in England. The *King's Book* had called for more frequent communion, but not with Watson's insistence.[49] Since 1548, Thomas Cranmer had attempted to encourage more frequent communion in the Edwardine Church.[50] However, the likeliest influence on Watson's position was Fisher, who was an even earlier proponent of frequent reception. Both he and Watson underscored the profound quality of union with Christ in receiving communion.[51] In discussing that union, Watson followed Fisher in citing Cyril of Alexandria and Hilary of Poitiers.[52] They were united in recommending more frequent communion, to intensify that bond between Christ and his people.[53]

Besides defending the Catholic understanding of the Eucharist, Watson also gave great attention to the other sacrament which Protestants had most vilified: penance. In the *Catholyke doctryne*, he presented eleven sermons on the sacrament of penance and on penitence in general, in comparison to seven on the Eucharist. Again, Watson followed Fisher in presenting a spirituality of penitence that included but was not dominated by the sacrament.[54] Of Watson's eleven sermons on penance, only three dealt specifically with the sacrament itself.[55] Examples of his considerations of penitence include a realistic appraisal of the human propensity to sin, and practical means to avoid temptation.[56] Regarding the practice of penitence, he wisely

---

[47] Ibid., 53v–4r, 79r.

[48] Evennett, *Spirit of the Counter-Reformation*, 38–9; for other proponents of frequent Communion see O'Malley, *First Jesuits*, 152–7; Bartolomé Carranza, *Comentarios sobre el Catechismo Cristiano de Bartolomé Carranza*, 2 vols, J.I. Tellechea Idigoras, ed. (Madrid: Editorial Catolica, 1972), II, 217; and Larissa Juliet Taylor, *Heresy and Orthodoxy in Sixteenth-Century Paris: François Le Picart and the Beginnings of the Catholic Reformation* (Leiden: Brill, 1999), 135.

[49] *A Necessary Doctrine and erudition of any Christen man* ... (London, 1543), RSTC 5168, K2°–3'.

[50] Diarmaid MacCulloch, *Thomas Cranmer: A Life* (New Haven: Yale University Press, 1996), 385; Diarmaid MacCulloch, *The Later Reformation in England, 1547–1603*, 2nd edn (Basingstoke: Palgrave, 2001), 12.

[51] Rex, *Theology of Fisher*, 143–4.

[52] Ellen Macek, *The Loyal Opposition: Tudor Traditionalist Polemics, 1535–1558* (New York: Peter-Lang, 1996), 93–4.

[53] Rex, *Theology of Fisher*, 142–3.

[54] Ibid., 34–7, 48.

[55] Watson, *Catholyke doctryne*, 114v–31v.

[56] Ibid., 147r–50r.

recommended a tripartite approach. Christians should unite fasting, or any other difficult spiritual exercise, with prayer and doing good works in their lives. Otherwise they ran the risk of a compartmentalized spiritual life: for example, giving to the poor while remaining a glutton.[57] Through such careful explication of the sacrament and concentration on a spirituality of penitence in this collection of sermons, Watson may have been following the lead of the legatine synod, the fourth decree of which stipulated that preachers firstly 'exhort the people to repentance, which is so much the more necessary' due to England having fallen into heresy.[58] Besides such considerations of repentance in general, Watson viewed catechesis regarding the sacrament as essential. He described the three traditional elements of penance – contrition, confession, satisfaction – and continually stressed both the gratuity of God's forgiveness and grace in order to participate in it, and the need for human cooperation with grace. For example, he presented a balanced view of contrition as being rooted in the person's faith-filled relationship with God, rather than dread of infamy or fear of Divine punishment, which nevertheless could be an introduction to contrition. Watson followed Fisher in remarking that contrition came about through human cooperation with the promptings of grace.[59] People could also be moved to compunction by recalling God's generosity in numerous natural and supernatural gifts. Humility was the key to contrition; the greater the affective understanding of dependence on God, the deeper the remorse.[60] Repentant sinners must not despair of forgiveness, for God the Father loves gratuitously, like the father of the Prodigal Son, and Christ never rejected a contrite heart.[61] Contrite Christians must confess their sins, but even before confessing to a priest, Watson encouraged people to first privately confess themselves to God; not because God did not know their sins, but so that they might know God's mercy and so grow in their relationship to God.[62] Therefore Watson offered a format for examination of conscience that, rather than a method of cataloguing sins, allowed for a positive reflection on the Christian's relationship with God. Penitents commenced this exercise with gratitude for God's manifold kindnesses; sin was described in terms of unkindness in response to God's personal kindness. God's 'kindness' was featured and repeated throughout this sermon, so that penitence was a way of

---

[57] Ibid., 144r–5v.
[58] Bray, *Anglican Canons*, 104–5.
[59] Watson, *Catholyke doctryne*, 102v, 104r; Rex, *Theology of Fisher*, 39.
[60] Watson, *Catholyke doctryne*, 101v–103r, 106r, 97v–8r.
[61] Ibid., 86r–v, 88r–v, 90v–91r, 100r, 105r–v.
[62] Ibid., 108r–10v.

renewing the relationship with a kindly God.[63] Watson nevertheless reminded readers that they must humble themselves before God like the publican in the Temple, for '[c]onfession is the fruite of humilitie, whyche is also the mother of grace'. People should practise such a daily examination of conscience before retiring, praying for the grace to make amends for sins. Such practice could aid in the avoidance of future sin.[64]

Christians needed to not only elude sin but be reconciled with each other, and Watson offered a sermon on confession to, and reconciliation among, neighbours. God loved reconciliation before any sacrifice, and Christians must make peace and amends before they exert themselves in prayer and almsgiving for the sake of reconciliation with God.[65] For Watson, penance was a matter of restoring charity among Christians, as well as an affair between a repentant sinner and God. In this emphasis he demonstrated a more complex picture of Reformation and Counter-Reformation penitence than John Bossy's view. Communal reconciliation as practised among late-medieval Christians did not give way to reconciliation as a private matter between early-modern individuals and God.[66]

Watson insisted that the Church required confession to a priest in order for him to judge the sins of penitents and absolve them, so they were no longer bound to the punishment due to sin, which in the case of mortal sin was damnation. After preparing for confession by self-examination, the penitent should go to a priest, concentrating on the power of the sacrament to grant peace and reconciliation, not the manner of the priest's life.[67] Complete confession should help inculcate greater humility, and prepare the person to receive God's grace more readily; it would also move the merciful God to forget the person's sins completely.[68]

After confession, penitents must also make satisfaction for their sins. In the sacrament, penitents confessed their sins and remorse, and were forgiven the punishment for mortal sins in hell, so that they were restored to grace. Watson again stressed God's gratuitous mercy shown in penance, which applied the satisfaction made for sin by Christ's

---

63 Ibid., 126v–31v.
64 Ibid., 112r–13v.
65 Ibid., 132r–132r [recte 137r], 138r–v.
66 John Bossy, 'The Social History of Confession in the Age of Reformation', *Transactions of the Royal Historical Society*, Fifth Series, vol. 25 (1975), 21–38. For recent challenges to Bossy's analysis, see Katherine Jackson Lualdi and Anne T. Thayer, eds, *Penitence in the Age of Reformations* (Aldershot: Ashgate, 2000), 4, 88, 99, 103, 118, 137, 248–9.
67 Watson, *Catholyke doctryne*, 119r–20v.
68 Ibid., 122r–5v.

death. But sins were still punished for the 'correction' of sinners and because of the requirements of God's justice; he illustrated this point with the 40 years of punishment God imposed on Israel, although God had forgiven their ingratitude.[69] The satisfaction may be the penance given by the priest in confession, or good works, or sorrow for sin such as Peter and Mary Magdalen had undergone.[70]

Throughout his sermons on penance and penitence, Watson underlined the gratuity of divine grace in the quest for reconciliation with God and neighbour, and the necessity of human beings' free cooperation with God's grace in order for these relationships to be renewed. In her recent monograph, however, Lucy Wooding asserts that Marian theologians acceded to belief in justification by faith – for humans and their works were 'degenerate', and were incapable of freely responding to divine grace.[71] Dr Wooding notes that Trent's sixth session – its decree on justification – will define Catholic dogma very differently in the 1560s. She fails to note that in Watson's *Catholyke doctryne*, which she also describes as an authorized declaration of the Marian Church's beliefs, the bishop translated an excerpt from the fourteenth chapter of the sixth session of that decree regarding the need to do good works in satisfaction for sin.[72] But Watson's unique translation is more remarkable because the decree had no force until its promulgation with the other Tridentine decrees in 1564. Watson doubtless saw his teaching on penance as united with the stance of the rest of the contemporary Catholic Church.[73]

Watson was also apparently unique in his discussion of the sacrament of confirmation. As baptism was the Church's bulwark against original sin, so confirmation was a weapon against sin. For Watson, the Christian was 'made stronge in that grace which he receyued before' in baptism. It increased the grace that Christians possessed in order to be 'bold to fight' against the temptations that confronted them in the years

---

[69] Ibid., 139v–41v.

[70] Ibid., 143r–47v [recte 145v].

[71] Wooding, *Rethinking Catholicism*, 154–64.

[72] Ibid., 153, 159; Watson, *Catholyke doctryne*, 143r; 'the penaunce of a christen man sinning deadly after baptisme, conteyneth satisfaction by fastinge, almes, prayer, and other godly exercises of spiritual life, not for the eternal paine of hel, which with the synne is remitted to the vsing of the sacrament of penance, or els if the sacrament can not be had, in the desire of ful purpose to vse it, when it may be had, but for temporal payne which (as the scriptures teache), is not holly always remitted to theim that take the grace of God in vayne.' Margin: 'Concilium Tridentinum Sess.v.[sic] cap.xiiii.'; cf. Sixth Session, Chapter XIV, *The Canons and Decrees of the Council of Trent*, trans. H.J. Schroeder (Rockford, IL: Tan Books, 1978), 39.

[73] On the status of the Tridentine decrees before their promulgation see Hubert Jedin, *Crisis and Closure of the Council of Trent* (London: Sheed and Ward, 1967), 15–17.

of discretion. As the disciples had courageously proclaimed the Gospel after Pentecost, after hiding in the Upper Room, so Christians received the same militant inspiration in confirmation.[74] Through this sacrament, moreover, Watson intended to heal England's heretical past. He advised priests and people to ensure that children baptized during the schism be confirmed, for they had not received the grace of baptism; they could receive it in confirmation.[75] T.E. Bridgett found this to be an extraordinary view, and not that of the Council of Trent, which had considered both sacraments in 1547–49. Nor, he claimed, was it the opinion of the Latin and Greek fathers, Aquinas or Suarez.[76] There is no repetition of Watson's view in the legatine synod or in the treatment of the sacraments in Bishop Edmund Bonner's *Profitable doctryne*, the most important and comprehensive catechetical work of Marian Catholicism.[77] Bridgett ascribed Watson's opinion to his reading of a text falsely attributed to Augustine. Like his fellow theologians, he had great regard for Augustine, who 'seems to deny over and over again, in the most emphatic way, that grace can be conferred by the baptism of heretics'.[78]

We may possess a clue to Watson's thinking in Richard Smith's 1547 *Brief treatyse settynge forth truthes left to the church by the apostles*. Smith, who became Marian vice-chancellor of the University of Oxford and went into exile under Elizabeth, had defended the traditional teaching of the validity of baptism as administered by heretics and schismatics. But he quoted Augustine in *De Baptismo contra Donatistas*, II, 7: '[t]he churche kepeth a custome most holsome in these schismatickes, and heretickes, (that is to saye, in theyr christenynge or baptising) to amend that which was yll, not to gyue it againe that, which was gyuen, to heale that, which was wounded, not to cure the thing hole or sound.' He also remarked that '[w]herfore Austen iudged wel that is a tradition of the holy apostles not wrytten in the scripture, that who soeuer was ones baptised of a heretique or schismatike shulde not be baptised againe, but onely that amended which was yl done of them'.[79]

---

74 Watson, *Catholyke doctryne*, 24v–7r.

75 Ibid., 28v.

76 *Canons and Decrees of Trent*, 53–5; see Bridgett's discussion in Thomas Watson, *Sermons on the Sacraments by Thomas Watson*, T.E. Bridgett, ed. (London: Burns and Oates, 1876), 356–8.

77 Hughes, *Rome and England*, 72–84; *Anglican Canons*, 85; see Edmund Bonner, *A profitable and necessarye doctryne, with certayne homelies adioyned* (London, 1555), M3r–P2v.

78 Watson, *Catholyke doctryne*, 28r. Margin: 'Aug. de eccle. dogmat. cap. Iii.'; see Bridgett in Watson, *Sermons*, 356–8.

79 Richard Smith, *A brief treatyse settynge forth diuers truthes necessary both to be*

Infuriatingly, Augustine – and Smith – did not delve into what kind of 'yl' might be 'amended'. But it may be that Watson followed Tertullian and Pope Hippolytus and Pope Stephen I in stressing the rite of anointing with chrism at baptism as the means of receiving the grace. In a tract contemporaneous with these patristic authors, entitled *De rebaptismate*, baptism itself was associated only with the cleansing from sin, and anointing with the gift of the Spirit.[80] Perhaps Watson, widely read in the fathers, had taken this view to heart. Chrism for baptism had been one of the 'vnwryten verytyes' defended by Smith.[81] In his catechism written for the Marian Church – and which was being translated into English in 1558 – Bartolomé Carranza gave particular attention to chrism in his discussion of confirmation, insisting on its necessity.[82] The Tridentine or Roman catechism, which was largely based on Carranza's catechism, states that, while water is all that is necessary for administering emergency baptism, 'yet when baptism is administered in public with solemn ceremonies, the Catholic Church, guided by Apostolic tradition, has uniformly observed the practice of adding holy chrism which, as is clear, more fully signifies the effect of baptism'.[83] The 1552 Prayer Book had omitted the rite of anointing, and Christians had been traditionally required to ensure that their parish priest supply the other elements of the baptismal rite which had been omitted in an emergency baptism.[84] This requirement probably explains a complaint made in the 1530s against a priest in Devon who had allowed a child to die 'unchristened except that the midwife did to it'.[85] It would appear

---

beleued of chrysten people, and kept also, which are not espressed in the scripture but left to the church by the apostles tradition (London, 1547), M3r–5r.

[80] J.N.D. Kelly, *Early Christian Doctrines* (New York: Harper and Row, 1978), 208–10.

[81] Smith, *Brief treatyse*, 12v–H4r [*recte* 14r].

[82] Carranza, *Catechismo* II, 196–7; for Carranza's intention that the *Catechismo* be used in England, see Carranza, *Catechismo* I, 107: 'Lo mismo pienso publicar presto en latin … por aprovechar a todas naciones con lo que Dios me ha dado a entender; y particularmente a Inglaterra, donde sé por experiencia que es necessary …' For its translation into English, see Pole's letter to Carranza, *Epistolarum* V, 74; 'ac te quoque Dei providentia voluit, in hoc Anglicanam nostram Ecclesiam adjuvare tuo illo docto et pio Catechismo, quem, dum hic esses, Hispanice scripsisti, qui nunc in nostram linguam vertitur.'

[83] *Catechism of the Council of Trent for Parish Priests, Issued by the order of Pope Pius V*, trans. J.A. McHugh, C.J. Callan, eds (London: Herder, 1956), 166; for the Roman Catechism's dependence on Carranza's *Catechismo*, see Tellechea's introduction, Carranza, *Catechismo* 1, 88–9: 'El muestrario de paralelismos que aduce entre et Catechismo de Carranza y et tridentino es suficiemente probativo para monstrar la soprendente dependencia del segundo respecto al primero.'

[84] Adrian Fortescue, *The Ceremonies of the Roman Rite Described*, J. O'Connell, ed. (London: Burns and Oates, 1951), 382–3.

[85] Peter Marshall, *The Catholic Priesthood and the English Reformation* (Oxford: Clarendon Press, 1994), 182.

that Watson hoped to remedy the lack of anointing for those baptized according to the 1552 Prayer Book, as any Catholic would be bound to do after an emergency baptism. His opinion, while unique, was not as heterodox as Bridgett believed.

As well as distinctive views on confirmation, '[a] few Marian writers, notably Thomas Watson, attempted a more reasoned and persuasive justification of Catholic priesthood than had often been heard in England', in the opinion of Peter Marshall.[86] Priestly ministry was indeed a great concern of Watson's, for it was essential to the sacramental life of the Church, but the Catholic teaching on it had been viscerally attacked by Edwardine theologians and polemicists.[87] His two sermons on order were filled with implicit allusions to the revolution that had dismantled the Catholic priesthood; but as with all of Watson's theology and spirituality, Christ stood at the centre of these sermons, rather than polemic. Through the sacrament of order, Christ became present in the Church's ministers, 'to whom by the imposition of handes of Priesthoode, he hath geuen authorite and commaundement to instruct his soldiours', to aid and console the dying, and to order the Church 'by unitie of fayth, charitie and obedience'. Watson reiterated that those ordained must be authorized visibly by Christ's Church through the laying on of hands, to ensure the Church's good order and the true preaching of God's Word.[88] He followed Fisher in holding that the grace of the sacrament of ordination was conferred through the laying on of hands. The question regarding the essence of the sacrament had been debated by medieval theologians, and William Tyndale had mocked Catholic theologians in their inability to determine what constituted the sacrament; indeed, Trent would decide otherwise than Fisher's and Watson's views.[89]

Interestingly, Watson stressed the role of priest as minister of the Word of God rather than as presider at Mass. It is 'by regeneration, and also by the ministrie of Gods woorde, sacraments, and discipline' that the priest cared for his people. In baptism the infant signed with the cross on his ears, for 'the priest in the person of Christe doth open the eares ... that he shoulde nowe begynne to heare the voyce and woorde of GOD, ... and to receyue the swete sauour of Gods knowledge'.[90] The

---

[86] Ibid., 233, 235.
[87] Ibid., 211–32.
[88] Watson, *Catholyke doctryne*, 3r–v, 153v–6r.
[89] John Fisher, *The Defence of the Priesthood*, trans. Philip Haller (London: Burns and Oates, 1935), 58–63; Rex, *Theology of Fisher*, 134–5, 146; for Tyndale's comments, see Marshall, *Catholic Priesthood*, 139–40; *Catechism of Trent*, 322–3, 330–31.
[90] Watson, *Catholyke doctryne*, 20r–v.

first benefit of traditional Church order was the inculcation of virtue among the people through preaching.[91] The people were to obey what their priests preached, for the sake of ecclesial order and unity. In what may be a rather chilling reference to the burning of Protestants, Watson wrote that clerics were not only to be obeyed when they preached and administered the sacraments, 'but also when as good Surgeanes they bynde the parties that refuse to be cured, and by the censures of the churche and the strayte discipline doe cut and serche their uncurable woundes, executynge the offyce of almyghty GOD'.[92]

Yet whether preaching, administering sacraments or employed in 'exercisyng of discipline and jurisdiction', the priest was to labour 'for the edifienge and buildyng of the same churche in grace and vertue, and for the weedinge out and banyshing of all … ungodly liuing'. Watson stressed this notion of 'edifienge' throughout his two sermons on order in his *Catholyke doctryne*. By their efforts, bishops and priests served God by bringing people to the Church's true life and doctrine, for which God had given them authority 'onelye to builde, and not to destroye'.[93] So Watson implored those who heard his sermons to put their trust in the priests of the Church, because they were

> teachinge holesome and Catholyke doctryne, and the imitation of the lyfe of our Sauiour, and also concerninge the kepinge and fulyllynge of the auncyent and godlye constitutions ordeyned by the Prelates of the uniuersall Church of Chryste for good order and conformitie of good lyuynge to be kept in the same.[94]

Watson's exposition of the sacrament of order closely linked priests to Christ, and the 'enormously high doctrine of priesthood', inherited from the medieval Church and propounded at Trent, found its place in the Marian Church.[95] As priests brought an increase of grace to the Church, so matrimony brought an increase in the number of Christians to share in it. And as with the sacrament of order, Watson stressed the Christocentric quality of the sacrament of marriage, as well as advanced traditional doctrine relating to it. The bishops of Pole's synod, referring to Ephesians 5:32, also presented the union of Christ and the Church as the foremost significance of matrimony.[96] Watson, too, closely associated this sacrament with Christ's incarnation: the union between men and women embodied the love of God who had been united with human

---

[91] Ibid., 153v.
[92] Ibid., 163v.
[93] Ibid., 161r, 158v.
[94] Ibid., 162v.
[95] Duffy, *Stripping of the Altars*, 110; *Canons and Decrees of Trent*, 160–64, 172–3.
[96] Bray, *Anglican Canons*, 90–91.

flesh in the person of Jesus.⁹⁷ While Christine Peters possesses 'doubts about the centrality of the Ephesians analogy to late medieval perceptions of marriage as a sacrament' in England, Watson and the other Marian bishops insisted that marriage made present Christ's union with his Church. Nevertheless, the views of Watson display a continuation of the process by which marriage was 'integrated into the shifting, and increasingly christocentric, focus of later medieval devotion'.⁹⁸ Even though consent between the husband and wife was the essence of the sacrament, Watson reminded Christians that the presence of a priest during the exchange of vows was valuable. At the wedding at church the priest reminded the couple that they can only live happily together with God's help. They also gained further aid from the prayers of the church and the blessing of the priest, which is God's blessing, and freedom from any doubt regarding the marriage's validity. Even though he did not explicitly raise the issue of clandestine marriage, Watson underscored the role of the priest, and so joined the growing chorus in that regard in Counter-Reformation Europe.⁹⁹ Nevertheless, following Aquinas and the Council of Florence, he insisted, along with Pole's synod, Trent and Carranza, that consent was the 'form' or essence of the sacrament; if Peters is correct that Scotus's unique division of the validity and sacramentality of marriage influenced the nuptial liturgy and the understanding of marriage in England, that influence cannot be perceived in the theology of Watson.¹⁰⁰

In administering the sacrament of matrimony to each other by their consent, the couple made the loving union between Christ and all Christians present through the 'mutuall loue which [God] poureth into their hartes'. If 'they haue together faythful lou[ing] kyndenesse, and ioye, one of another, and godly and comfortable agrement', then they have received the grace of the sacrament.¹⁰¹ Watson's interpretation that grace made marriage possible does not correspond with Peters's view

---

⁹⁷ Watson, *Catholyke doctryne*, 167r–8r.

⁹⁸ Christine Peters, 'Gender, sacrament and ritual: the making and meaning of marriage in late medieval and early modern England', *Past and Present*, 169 (2000), 71, 64.

⁹⁹ Watson, *Catholyke doctryne*, 177v–8r; John Bossy, *Christianity in the West, 1400–1700* (Oxford: Oxford University Press, 1985), 22–5; Carranza, *Catechismo* II, 341; Jedin, *Crisis and Closure of Trent*, 141–5.

¹⁰⁰ *Anglican Canons*, 90–91; *Catechism of Trent*, 339–42; Carranza, *Catechismo* II, 323; James Brundage, *Law, Sex and Christian Society in Medieval Europe* (Chicago: University of Chicago Press, 1987), 433; Peters, 'Gender, Sacrament and Ritual', 65–71. For an overview of medieval and early modern views on marriage, see E.J. Carlson, *Marriage and the English Reformation* (Oxford: Blackwell, 1994), 9–33.

¹⁰¹ Watson, *Catholyke doctryne*, 169r–v, 181v.

that the sacrament was perceived 'as a channel of grace which was dependent on the ability of the spouses to live well and keep the order of matrimony'.[102] But Watson was unique among Catholic and Protestant theologians in listing the comfort and help of men and women in this life as the first virtue of this sacrament.[103] As there was no greater love on earth than that found among married couples, there was no greater love in heaven than the love of Christ for his Church.[104] Watson's exposition concluded with practical wisdom of how to chose a partner and how to live as husband and wife.[105] But ultimately, spouses should cherish each other as they would wish themselves to be loved, not only in the first days of marriage, but particularly in sickness and other troubles.[106]

In his sermons, Watson not only expounded upon the sacraments, he also discussed other elements of Catholic doctrine and devotion that were associated with them. Among these are prayers to the saints and for the dead, which were found in the Eucharistic prayer or canon of the Mass. These doctrines had also been maligned for longer than any other element of Catholic belief in Reformation England, with the exception of the papacy. While historians such as Ronald Hutton assert that these doctrines in the Marian Church were '[t]he abiding casualties of the preceding reformations', and Lucy Wooding describes Marian interest in purgatory and the cult of the saints as 'peripheral', Watson described the communion of saints and purgatory and prayer for the dead in the context of the Eucharist and the Mass, the greatest sacrament and the one of chief concern to the Marian Church, and therefore in pivotal sections of his sermons.[107] It was a perspicacious strategy on his part to link these most-vilified beliefs to the Mass, the part of Catholic belief which had been most central to late-medieval piety and most swiftly restored upon the accession of Mary.[108]

---

[102] Peters, 'Gender, Sacrament and Ritual', 76.

[103] Watson, *Catholyke doctryne*, 166v; cf. Carranza, *Catechismo* II, 328–9, 351, 324. '[M]utual societie' is the third virtue of marriage given in the 1549 and 1552 Prayer Books; see *The First and Second Prayer Books of Edward VI*, (London: Prayer Book Society, 1999), 252, 410; MacCulloch, *Cranmer*, 420–21; Carlson, *Marriage and Reformation*, 37–49.

[104] Watson, *Catholyke doctryne*, 168r–v.

[105] Ibid., 179r–85r.

[106] Ibid., 185r, 193r [*recte* 183r].

[107] Hutton, 'The Local Impact of the Tudor Reformations', in *The English Reformation Revised*, Christopher Haigh, ed. (Cambridge: Cambridge University Press, 1987), 131; Wooding, *Rethinking Catholicism*, 177.

[108] Duffy, *Stripping of the Altars*, 91–5. For the popular restoration of the Mass at the beginning of Mary's reign, see Christopher Haigh, *English Reformations: Religion, Politics, and Society under the Tudors* (Oxford: Clarendon Press, 1993), 206–8.

In the Eucharistic prayer and some of the collects of the Sarum rite, the priest sought the intercession and companionship of the saints for the Church on earth and in purgatory.[109] Due to their holiness and therefore proximity to God, saints served as powerful intercessors. Watson described the saints as 'careful for vs' and who 'cease not to communicate with vs in prayer'. Christians sought the aid of their prayers to gain the grace of God's protection and Christ's merits. He also noted that the Christian begs the intercession of the angels and saints in the general confession at the beginning of Mass, and they 'praye for hys pardone and amendement'.[110] He discussed the distinction between *latria* — worship given to God alone — and *dulia* — honour given to the saints. Despite this differentiation he linked the saints closely to Christ their redeemer, for the honour given to the saints redounded to Christ. The bishop reminded Christians that altars were dedicated to God and not to Mary and the saints, and the worship offered there was of the highest kind, and thus offered to God alone.[111] Furthermore Watson stated that believers recalled the saints in thanksgiving to God for their deeds and to follow 'theyr footesteppes' in conquering 'our ghostly enemies'; thus he presented the saints as exemplars of living virtuously and conquering vice, which was a chief component of the Christian vocation.[112] He also portrayed the saints as friends and companions in Christian living: they are 'oure brethren ... beyng knyt to vs in one communion by the bande of perfite charitie'.[113] He, like the Council of Trent and the robust spirituality of the Counter Reformation, worked to refocus devotion to the saints in order 'to end the abuses associated with their veneration while reasserting their intercessory power and emphasizing their roles as models of Christian life'.[114] He also wished to ensure that the Church's 'meditative practices were largely focused on the life and passion of Christ'.[115] In his close association of the saints with Christ, Watson not only anticipated the Tridentine decree on invoking the saints, but also revealed his sermons' continuity with efforts by the official Church to redirect devotion from the saints to the person of Christ since the fourteenth century.[116]

---

[109] *The Sarum Missal Done into English and Abridged* (London: Alban Press, 1989), 14–15, 17, 30.
[110] Watson, *Catholyke doctryne*, 77v, 76v, K7v.
[111] Ibid., 73v–4r, K6v.
[112] Ibid., 74r, 77v.
[113] Ibid., 77v.
[114] Robert Bireley, *The Refashioning of Catholicism, 1450–1700* (London: Macmillan, 1999), 113.
[115] Evennett, *Spirit of the Counter-Reformation*, 41; cf. Duffy, *Stripping of the Altars*, 364.
[116] *Canons and Decrees of Trent*, 215–16; Ronald Finucane, *Miracles and Pilgrims: Popular Beliefs in Medieval England* (New York: St Martin's Press, 1995), 195–202.

Christians were not only 'knyt' to the saints in heaven, but also to the dead in purgatory, for whom they prayed in the canon of the Mass.[117] After succinctly explaining how Mass was offered for the living, Watson described at some length how the Church offered Mass for 'the absolution and perfection of them that be deade, that they being for a tyme deteyned in the temporall afflictions and purgacions, might the sooner by the vertue of thys blessed sacrifice be deliuered and brought to light and eternall peace, where nothyng entreth that is spotted and unperfite'. Having received grace in this life, Masses could further 'helpe and relieue theym after theyr deathe' in their progression to heaven.[118] In his *Twoo Sermons*, he underlined the concurrence of this doctrine with patristic interpretations of scripture.[119] Watson also discussed prayer for the dead in the context of the Eucharistic liturgy in his *Catholyke doctryne*.[120] In so doing he treated it in key passages of his texts, in contrast to the Henrician doctrinal works, the *Bishops' Book* and *King's Book*, where prayer for the dead and purgatory had been relegated to the end.[121] Through good works and prayer, especially celebrating the Eucharist, Watson wrote, Christians could assist the entry of the dead into eternal life.[122] Release from purgatory was an 'inestymable effecte, and fruyte' of the Mass, and he focused on this point.[123] However, the liturgy could be offered only for the peace of the dead who had shown 'the sygnes of faythe, whyche be the holye sacramentes and good workes'.[124] As with his discussion of the cult of the saints, Watson's short, clear and uncompromising exposition of the doctrine of purgatory also prefigured Trent's decree on the same subject:

> the holy council commands ... that the sound doctrine of purgatory ... be everywhere taught and preached. The more difficult and subtle questions, however, and those that do not make for edification and from which there is for the most part no increase in piety, are to be excluded from popular instructions to uneducated people.[125]

For Watson, the dead, like the saints, was not an 'abiding casualty' of the previous reformations.

---

[117] *Sarum Missal*, 16–17.
[118] Watson, *Catholyke doctryne*, 77r–v.
[119] Watson, *Twoo Sermons*, B2v–3r, X1v–5v.
[120] Watson, *Catholyke doctryne*, K6v, K8v, 77r–v, 79r.
[121] *Institution of a Christen man* ... (London, 1537), RSTC 5163, Aa3v–4r; *Necessary doctrine*, 1v–2v.
[122] Watson, *Catholyke doctryne*, 77r.
[123] Watson, *Twoo Sermons*, B2v–3r, U4r, X1v–5v.
[124] Watson, *Catholyke doctryne*, 77r.
[125] *Canons and Decrees of Trent*, 214.

Bishop Thomas Watson's theology and spirituality, as revealed in his published sermons, demonstrated a way of contemplating and practising Catholicism that focused on the incarnation and passion of Christ. Christ had left to members of his body, the Catholic Church, a variety of means of approaching him and being united with him. Dependent upon God's mercy and Christ's redemption, Christians enacted the Church's traditional forms of prayer, penitence, charity and good works, and most especially participated in the seven sacraments, in order to live holy lives and so respond to that redemption. The sacraments offered to participants concrete modes of Christ's presence at key points in their lives, modes that not only recalled them to Christ's saving incarnation, passion, death and resurrection, but enabled them to share in a personal union with Christ. In this union with the Divine, Christians were to make Christ present in the world, in practices of communal charity for the sake of Christ who was in heaven and among them on earth, in the person of the neighbour. These works of Christian love and this union with Christ through sacramental signs could only occur in the one Catholic Church, led and sustained by the Spirit of Christ through the ministries of its Pope, bishops and priests. Moreover, while the sacraments were at the heart of Marian Catholicism, Watson shrewdly linked the cult of the saints and prayers for the dead to the greatest sacrament, the Eucharist, in order to aid the renewal of these doctrines after 20 years of Tudor-sponsored assault.

Although Watson's presentation of Catholic theology and spirituality was influenced by the Reformation in England in terms of choosing to closely connect the cult of the saints and prayer for the dead to the Mass, and go out of his way to discuss papal primacy, his theology and spirituality were significant because they were nothing new. His expositions of Catholic doctrine were largely similar to those of Fisher, Carranza and his fellow religious authors in Marian England.[126] Moreover, Watson's Christian vision was very much in line with that of Counter-Reformation Catholicism. Watson's use of scripture and the fathers, his Christology, soteriology, sacramental theology and ecclesiology virtually duplicated the doctrine propounded in the canons and decrees of the Council of Trent, including advocacy of frequent Communion.[127] The spirituality of his works coincided with the 'certain powerful and distinctive traits' of Counter-Reformation spirituality; it too, in the words of H.O. Evennett,

---

126 See my 2002 Oxford DPhil thesis, 'Recalled to Life: the Theology and Spirituality of Mary Tudor's Church'.

127 *Canons and Decrees of Trent*, 78.

> was highly sacramental; ... its great masters were all highly impregnated with the Bible, and its meditative practices were largely focused on the life and passion of Christ; .... practical, in that it closely linked active good works and self-improvement, and assumed the placing of a high value on the former in the sight of God for Justification. ...[128]

Finally, Watson might have seen himself and his labours reflected in the decree for reform in Trent's twenty-fourth session, which stated:

> that the faithful may approach the sacraments with greater reverence and devotion of mind, the holy council commands all bishops that not only when they are themselves about to administer them to the people, they shall first, ... explain their efficacy and use, but also they shall see to it that the same is done piously and prudently by every parish priest ...[129]

Bishop Watson was very much in unison with the spirit of the Counter Reformation, although he was confined in the Tower of London when Trent's decrees were promulgated in 1564.[130]

Through the *Twoo Sermons* and *A Catholyke doctryne*, Thomas Watson presented and attempted to inculcate Catholic theology and spirituality among his fellow Christians to further the renewal of the Marian Church. But Watson desired that priests and people should possess not only a knowledge of Christian fundamentals, but also an affective devotion, so that the members of the English Church might approach their redeemer more closely in their minds, hearts and lives, and thus be drawn into closer union with him. Watson desired that they should receive Christ, truly present in his Church and in his sacraments, 'with greater gladnes' than even an infant would receive milk from her mother's breast.

---

[128] Evennett, *Spirit of the Counter-Reformation*, 41.
[129] *Canons and Decrees of Trent*, 197.
[130] See Bridgett and Knox, *True Story of the Catholic Hierarchy*, 167.

CHAPTER TEN

Marking the Days: Henry Machyn's Manuscript and the Mid-Tudor Era[1]

Gary G. Gibbs

Henry Machyn's manuscript offers a familiar but neglected source for historians of the mid-Tudor period. A lengthy document, rich in evidence and unique for its time, it has long been recognized as providing a sympathetic portrayal of the regime of Mary I. The English-speaking world had ready access to this text after 1848 when the Camden Society published a version edited by John Gough Nichols. For more than a century after that publication, in the era of meta-narratives such as Marxism and both Whiggish and Weberian interpretations of history and religion, the text and its author seemed rather out of place. Machyn, an urban businessman, sympathized with the old religion, which went against the historical paradigms of the late Victorian era and early twentieth century. Contrary to ideological expectations of modern historians, Machyn's sympathies seemed to put him in opposition with the larger forces Protestantizing sixteenth-century England. Machyn's text apparently failed to capture the correct tone for a man living in the horrendous times of Bloody Mary. As a result of this dichotomy between modern expectations and a divergent historical voice, historians dealt with Machyn's worldview largely through judgements of 'exceptionalism'. The 1848 published edition of Machyn's manuscript mislabelled it as a 'diary,' rendering the document a private and personal text. Subsequently, early twentieth-century scholars constructed a

---

[1] Some of the ideas expressed in this chapter were presented previously in two papers: 'Mary I, Henry Machyn, and the Return of a 'Goodly' Sermon', delivered at the Medieval and Tudor London Seminar, Institute of Historical Research, University of London, 27 May 1999 and 'Processions, Belief, and National Identity in London during the Reign of Mary I', delivered to the American Society of Church History Conference, Tallahassee, FL, 2–4 April 1998 (available from the Theological Research Exchange Network, Portland, OR). I wish to thank Caroline M. Barron and Vanessa Harding for inviting me to the London Seminar, and also James S. Amelang, John P.D. Cooper, Whitney A.M. Leeson, Jennifer Berenson Maclean, Ian Mortimer, James M. Ogier, Florinda Ruiz (for help with Latin) and Suzanne Schadl for their advice and comments at various stages of this project.

fictionalized biography for Machyn that further marginalized him as representative of a London voice.

For historians influenced by postmodernism, an engagement with the text is a natural part of academic discourse, and a new approach to Machyn is in order. Henry Machyn's descriptions of London life during the reign of Mary I provide a useful field for testing the ways in which alternative readings can expose new meanings to long familiar texts. The last bastion of an attempted Catholic regime in what would become a Protestant culture, Mary's reign has never enjoyed positive presentations by later historians. From Machyn's perspective, however, the regime seemed different; his text describes a religious culture with its own unique political structures, and it provides valuable insight into the nature not just of Mary's rule, but mid-Tudor culture in general. At the centre of this religious and political system resided numerous rituals and pageants that created a direct tie between Henry Machyn, his queen and his God. This relationship forms a major subtext of Machyn's accounts of London life in the reign of Mary I.

The key to understanding Machyn's descriptions of his world begins with reconstructing, as much as possible, the relationship between the author and text, and the exact manner in which the text became misidentified as a diary. To begin with the author, Henry Machyn was born about 1497[2] and died in early November 1563 (buried on 11 November),[3] probably of the plague.[4] He was a citizen of London, a member of the Merchant Taylors' guild, a renter of funeral trappings and a parishioner of 'Holy Trinity the Little, Queenhithe, not far from the Tower of London',[5] where he served as a parish clerk for a time. He

---

[2] Machyn contradicted himself when writing about his birthday, stating that he was 56 on 16 May 1554, and 66 on 20 May 1562. That would imply his birth year as either 1496 or 1498, so I split the difference for about 1497. See, *The Diary of Henry Machyn, citizen and Merchant-Taylor of London, from A.D. 1550 to A.D. 1563*, ed. John Gough Nichols, printed for the Camden Society (London, 1848; London and New York: reprinted with the permission of the Royal Historical Society, AMS Press, 1968), pp. 63 and 283; and *DNB*, 12, 552–3. Ian Mortimer points out that both birth dates given by Machyn fell on the Wednesday after Whitsun in their respective years, meaning that Machyn probably associated his birthday more with the liturgical year than the calendar. See Ian Mortimer, 'Tudor Chronicler or Sixteenth-Century Diarist? Henry Machyn and the Nature of his Manuscript', *Sixteenth Century Journal*, 33/4 (Winter 2002), 981–98.

[3] From the parish register of Holy Trinity the Less, November 1563: 'The 11th daie Henrye Macham tayler and Clarck of the parishe churche of Trinitie the Lesse was buried.' As cited by Mortimer, 987ff.

[4] R.M. Wilson, 'The Orthography and Provenance of Henry Machyn', in *Early English and Norse Studies*, eds Arthur Brown and Peter Foote (London: Methuen, 1963), p. 202; James S. Amelang, *The Flight of Icarus: Artisan Autobiography in Early Modern Europe* (Stanford CA: Stanford University Press, 1998), 312.

[5] *English Diaries*, ed. Elizabeth D'Oyley (London: Edward Arnold, 1930), 31.

had a brother named Christopher, a first wife named Jone who died in childbirth,[6] a second wife named Dorothy, two sons named John[7] and William, the latter of whom predeceased his father, and four daughters: Jane, Mary, Katherine (who was christened in September 1557)[8] and Awdrey,[9] of whom only Jane survived her father. He also had a niece named Kynborow.[10] A family man, Henry Machyn was also a watcher of people, an observer of his culture, a witness to important events and a writer. Machyn composed a manuscript that has been referred to as his 'diary' ever since its transcription and publication under that designation in 1848; but that was an unfortunate editorial decision.

Machyn's manuscript consists of 162 leaves octavo, and contains entries in largely chronological order from 1550 to 1563.[11] It is now housed at the British Library (Cotton Vitellius F. v.), but its early history from Machyn's death to the end of the sixteenth century is unknown. Robert Cotton acquired the manuscript for his collection by 1631.[12] In the early eighteenth century, John Strype drew several passages from the manuscript for inclusion in his *Ecclesiastical Memorials, Relating Chiefly to Religion, and the Reformation of it, and the Emergencies of the Church of England under King Henry VIII, King Edward VI, and Queen Mary I, with the large appendices, containing original papers, records &c.* (London, 1721). Later scholarship showed that Strype often misread Machyn's original handwriting, but Strype's very use of the document gained great importance in subsequent years.[13] The manuscript, housed with the Cottonian Library, suffered damage in the fire at Ashburnham House in 1731; that fire destroyed or blackened the tops and upper edges of many pages, obscuring one or two lines at the top of those pages, as well as the initial lettering of some sentences.[14] The initial pages are the hardest to read. This damage lessens as the text proceeds but words, phrases and whole sentences are obliterated here

---

[6] Mortimer, 990.

[7] Guildhall Library, London: Register Copy of the Will of Henry Machyn. Archdeaconry of London, register n. 3 ff. 49v and 50r, found and transcribed by Ian Mortimer, who kindly shared his work with me for the purpose of this chapter; for surviving his father, see Mortimer, 990.

[8] Nichols, *Diary*, p. 153; and *ODNB*.

[9] D'Oyley, 31; and *ODNB*.

[10] Nichols uses 'Kynlure'; Ian Mortimer uses 'Kynborowe'. See Mortimer, 985; Nichols, *Diary*, 287; and *ODNB*.

[11] Axel Wijk, *The Orthography and Pronunciation of Henry Machyn, the London Diarist: a Study of the South-East Yorkshire Dialect in the Early 16th Century* (Uppsala: Appelbergs Boktryckeriaktiebolag, 1937), 1.

[12] Mortimer, 987.

[13] Nichols, *Diary*, viff.

[14] Wilson, 202–3.

and there throughout the manuscript. 'For nearly a hundred years after the fire the leaves were kept loose in a case and seemed to frustrate all attempts to arrange them in their proper order.'[15] In 1829, Sir Frederick Madden used the Strype citations as a guide for reassembling the pages in the correct order.[16] The manuscript seems internally consistent now, and at most one page has been lost in the near century between fire and restoration.[17] Frederick Madden described his work in a memorandum on the flyleaf:

> The fragments forming the present Volume were formerly kept in a case, without any regard to order, and are thus described by Dr. Smith in his Catalogue:
>
> Cod. Chartac. In fol. constans foliis solutis circiter 150. in pixide asservatis, quae ritè disponere frustra tentavimus.
>
> By the aid of Strype, who made use of the MS. when perfect, and who quotes largely from it, the leaves have been restored to their proper order; the chronology marked on each folio, and references given to the pages of Strype, who often uses the lacunæ here visible. The curiosity and value of these fragments seemed a sufficient warrant for the labour and time consumed in arranging them in their present form. – F.M. 1829[18]

As stated before, John Gough Nichols published his edition of the manuscript with the Camden Society in 1848. Faced with a damaged manuscript, Nichols sought to restore the original narrative by looking to Strype or, in fact, by his own conjecture.[19] As was first pointed out in the 1930s by Axel Wijk, mistakes can be found on almost every page.[20]

Wijk's research was part of a linguistic study that sought to localize Machyn's dialect through an analysis of spelling and a study of 'stressed vowels and Diphthongs'. Wijk compared Machyn's orthography with examples of transcriptions of English dialects, concluding that Machyn's English showed little evidence of London speech patterns, but rather those from the north of England: 'from the western part of se. Yks, from the marshland between Holderness and the Ouse.'[21] Wijk's source for his comparative analysis was a nineteenth-century text by R.J. Ellis, entitled

---

[15] Nichols, *Diary*, xii–xiii; and (quote) Wijk, 1.
[16] Wijk, 1.
[17] Mortimer, 987.
[18] British Library, Cotton Vitellius, F.v: codex chartaceus, in folio constans ...; and cited in Nichols (who capitalized the 'c' in 'constans' and italicized the underlined passages), xiii. Latin translates roughly: Containing around 150 disordered pages, kept in tar [pitch?], which we tried unsuccessfully to order according to custom.
[19] Nichols, *Diary*, xiii.
[20] Wijk, 2–3.
[21] Ibid., 15.

On Early English Pronunciation. Part V (1889).[22] Ellis, separated from Henry Machyn by 300 years, transcribed Victorian speech patterns as part of a study of nineteenth-century dialects. R.N. Wilson presented this and many more points dismantling Wijk's methodology in his 1963 study.

So, was Henry Machyn from south-east Yorkshire or anywhere else besides London? In some ways it hardly matters. In his writing, Machyn never longed for the countryside. Indeed, his text reveals a thoroughly urban focus and concern that comes from either his own civic identity or from a desire to project a civic identity. He was about 50 years old at the time the surviving manuscript begins and he recorded no indication of his origin. By that time – as proved by evidence in the records of the Merchant Taylors' Company which places Machyn in London by the age of 30 – he had lived in London for about two decades.[23] Ian Mortimer offers good evidence of the family's ties to Hoby, in the north-east part of Leicestershire, but Henry had probably started his apprenticeship in London by the age of 14.[24] His was a London life, and he gave attention to urban events and many London affairs. He appears to have been fascinated by the culture of London regardless of his place of birth and manifested diphthongs.

This entire linguistic debate has made little impression on the historiography of Tudor studies except to re-enforce the paradigm of Machyn as simply an exception to the mid-Tudor London worldview. Historians have employed the text as a source of anecdotal evidence for urban and cultural studies of Tudor London, but in a minor fashion. Nichols's preface presented an explanation of Machyn that marginalized his importance and qualified his ability to represent topics in a sophisticated manner. The Victorian explanation for Machyn conformed to a class-conscious, progressive, Protestant nationalist interpretation of the mid-Tudor century. Nichols introduces us to Machyn with the following passage:

> The writer was a citizen of London, of no great scholarship or attainments, as his language and cacography plainly testify, sufficiently prejudiced no doubt, and not capable of any deep views either of religious doctrine or temporal policy; but the matters of fact which he records would be such as he either witnessed himself, or had learned immediately after their occurrence: and the opinions and sentiments which he expresses would be shared by a large proportion of his fellow-citizens.[25]

---

[22] Wilson, 204ff; Mortimer, 989.
[23] Mortimer, 990.
[24] Ibid., 989.
[25] Nichols, *Diary*, v.

The 'old' *Dictionary of National Biography* (*DNB*) told us

> He was a devout catholic and welcomed Mary's accession and the restoration of the old religion. On 30 July 1557 he attended an oyster feast at a friend's house in Anchor Lane. On 23 Nov. 1561 he did penance at St. Paul's Cross for having circulated a libellous story respecting M. Vernon, the French Protestant preacher.[26]

And in a recent study of artisan autobiography in early modern Europe, James S. Amelang described Machyn as a 'Catholic craftsman' and states (via a quotation from the study of *English Dairies* [1923] by A. Ponsonby) that 'the diary is as impersonal as a diary may be'.[27]

Impersonal indeed, but the conviction that the author was a devout Catholic seems rather personal knowledge to draw from such an impersonal 'diary'. Machyn referred to himself in his manuscript on few occasions and usually in the third person. The majority of circa 162 folios contain no explicit mention of either the author (and sparse expression of his feelings) or family life. Relying on Strype, Nichols dated the manuscript's first entry 4 August 1550, although the date on the manuscript is now missing. The second entry is 27 August 1550, but the year is based on external evidence. The topics of both of these entries are funerals; the former records the funeral of Sir Thomas Wriothesley, earl of Southampton, Knight of the Garter; the latter that of Sir William Locke (also no longer readable in the manuscript), knight, alderman and former sheriff of London (buried at St Thomas Acons).[28] The theme – funerals of important national and civic individuals – sets the tone for the initial entries, and many subsequent ones as well. This fact has prompted many to view the manuscript as originating out of Machyn's business interests, and in fact he does record some minute details of the funerals, including banners, mourners, outfits, order, emblematic representations and so on. The tenth entry records the death of Henry Machyn's brother Christopher,

> **M:** The ... xxx day of November was bered Crystoffer Mac ... marchand tayllor in the **parryche** of saynt James **and** brodur ... Henry Machyn the company of marchand tayllers behy ... at ys berehyng **and the** compeny of **the** clarkes syngyng an[29] ... Maydwell dyd pryche for hym **the** iiij yer of K.E.VIth[30]
>
> **N:** The xxx day of November was bered Crystoffer Machyn,

---

[26] *DNB*, 143, 272; Strype, *Annals*, i, 237.
[27] Amelang, 312.
[28] Nichols, *Diary*, 1.
[29] Words in bold are abbreviated in the manuscript and ellipses in the main represent damaged parts.
[30] BL, Cotton Vitellius, 1v.

Marchand-tayllor, in the parryche of saynt James, and brodur [of] Henry Machyn: the compeny of Marchand-tayllers behyng at ys berehyng, and the compeny of Clarkes syngyng, and ... Maydwell dyd pryche for him, – the iiij yer of K.E.vj^t.[31]

This is the first entry that clearly represents something different from the original theme, a greater personalization of the record and even an inclusion of the author himself. It may in fact be the second such entry, because among the great national and civic personages that precede mention of Christopher Machyn's burial, there appears the entry of one M. Heys, buried at the altar of St Peter Cornhill 'with the ffeyleshyp of the clarkes of London.'[32] That funeral entry preceded Christopher Machyn's funeral account by several days and the deceased could possibly have been a friend and was certainly a colleague since Machyn was also a parish clerk; M. Heys stands apart with Christopher from the more important individuals that make up the rest of the initial entries.

Following the account of Christopher Machyn's burial comes another entry that represents a new interest: the deprivation of Stephen Gardiner from the bishopric of Winchester and his subsequent transportation to the Tower. The diary then returns to burials of important people for two entries. Then comes another innovative entry:

> M: The ix day of marche was a proclamasyon that no ... woman shuld nott ett no ffleshe in lent nor fryday nor ... thrught the yere nor ymbering days nor no days that ys ... by the chryche apone payne of forfyt.[33]

This is a useful bit of information to record in a document that thus far seems to have served memorial purposes. Following this entry, the entire tone of the diary changes. Funeral entries are an ever-present concern, but Henry Machyn begins to record all sorts of items. These entries bear evidence of the emergence of Machyn's writing style, a transformation that moves him beyond his funerary focus to an examination of the world around him. He records examples of civic punishment such as the executions of murderers on 14 March 1551, the trial and imprisonment of a Scottish pirate on the same day, the April 1552 punishment of a young lady for 'her shameful ded dohyng,' the hanging of nine women and two men for reasons not stated on 12 September 1552, the attempted execution on 3 January 1553 of a murderer who escaped with his life when two different ropes burst in attempts to hang him, and many more. These include a very curious entry from 25 February 1553, when a wizard and the wife of the parson of St Alphege, and 'a nodur

---

[31] Nichols, *Diary*, 3.
[32] BL, Vit. F.v., f. 1v; Nichols, *Diary*, 2: 'with the fellowship of the Clarkes of London'.
[33] BL, Vit. F.v., f. 2r; Nichols, *Diary*, 4.

... [b?]owdry' were carted around town for shameful deeds. In 1554, on 21 February and again on 7 March, two different butchers had to ride around London sitting backwards on a horse apparently for maintaining poor standards.[34]

Odd events captured Machyn's attention, such as this entry from 1552:

> M: ... e xxj day of marche dyd ryd thrugh Lo ... ke ij yonge feylles boyth of on horse and o ... arehyng a spytt up right and a duke rostyd ... nugatt and ther they dyd a lyth of ther horse ... and the duke at nugatt and so was led with the begers thrugh fflet lane with many pepull wo[n?] ... to the rosse at the fflet bryge that tavarn wher ... to have hetten that there and I left them ther and the ... [? odd writing] ... one of them dewlt at the sun. ...[35]

> N: The xxj day of Marche dyd ryd through Lo[ndon on horseb]ake ij yonge feylles both of on horse and on [of them] carehyng a spytt up ryght and a duke rostyd, and ... Nugatt, and ther they alyth of ther horse and ... the duke at Nugatt, and so was led with the ... begers thrugh Flet lane with many pepull won ... to the Rose at the Flet bryge, the taverne wher ... to have hetten yt there, and I left them ther, and [came to] the court to dener; one of them dweltt at the Sun. ...[36]

On 10 September 1552, Machyn described a commotion in the Thames. The original manuscript is destroyed in a crucial part of the entry, but Nichols informs us that three great fish were attracting lots of attention and boatmen with nets.[37]

Occasionally economic proclamations made their way into his manuscript, such as this entry from 1552:

> M: The v day of September was a proclamasyon that the bochers of london shuld sell beyffe and mutun and vell the best for 1^d fardyng the lb and nekes and legs at iij fardyngs the lb and the best lam the qut viij^d and yff thay wyll nott thay to loysse ther ffredom for ever and ever.[38]

Machyn also noted important national events such as the removal of Edward VI from Westminster to Hampton Court on 10 July 1551 after an outbreak of plague in London.[39] That entry was followed by

---

[34] BL, Vit. F.v., ff. 2r, 8r, 12v, 15v, 16v, 29r, & 29v; Nichols, *Diary*, 4, 17, 25, 30, 32, 56 and 57.
[35] BL, Vit. F.v., f. 8r.
[36] Nichols, *Diary*, 16.
[37] BL, Vit. F.v., f. 12v; Nichols, *Diary*, 25.
[38] BL, Vit. F.v., f. 12r; Nichols, *Diary*, 24.
[39] BL, Vit. F.v., f. 3v; Nichols, *Diary*, 7.

> M: The xxiiij day august the kings grace went f ... amton court unto wyndsore and ther was stallyd ... the ffrenche kyng of the nobull order of the grat[te?] ... with a grett baner of armes iij bordered w^t flowr[s?] ... delussys of gold bosted the mantylls of tysshuw and the elmett clene gylt and his sword and the goodly gere was.[40]

King Edward described only his own installation in the French Order of St Michael, not the induction of Henry II as a Knight of the Garter.[41] Machyn and the boy king wrote about the same event on other occasions as well, such as these entries from 1552,

> M: The xiiij day of october was depossyd of ys bysshope pryke the good bysshope of duram and whent unto the towre a gayn and so remanyth styll.[42]
>
> EdVI: The Bishop Tunstall of Durham was deprived of his bishopric.'[43]

About 14 months earlier, in the summer of 1551, Henry Machyn had written,

> M: ...e viij day of July was a plage and a proclamasyon the ... d be but ix^d and a grot iij^d and a nodns proclamasyon cam ... xviij day of august that testerns cryd at vi^d a pese a g ... jd but j^d ob and a alpeny a fardyng.[44]
>
> M: he x day of July the kings grace removyd from west ... nto Hamtun courte for ther ded serten besyd the court ... syd the kynges grace to be gone so sune for ther ded in ... mony marchants and grett ryche men and women and yonge men ... of the nuw swett the v of k e vi^th.[45]

The king's journal also mentions these events:

> EdVI: [9th July]: Proclamation made that a teston should go at 9d., and a groat at 3d. in all places of the realm at once.
>
> At this time came the sweat into London, which was more vehement than the old sweat. For if one took cold, he died within three hours, and if he escaped, it held him but nine hours, or ten at the most. Also, if he slept the first six hours, as he should be very desirous to do, then he raved and should die raving.

---

[40] BL, Vit. F.v., f. 4r; Nichols, *Diary*, 9.
[41] *The Chronicle and Political Papers of King Edward VI*, ed. W.K. Jordan (Ithaca, NY: published for the Folger Shakespeare Library, Cornell University Press, 1966), 71–3.
[42] BL, Vit. F.v., f. 13r; Nichols, *Diary*, 26.
[43] Jordan, 150.
[44] BL, Vit. F.v., f. 3v; Nichols, *Diary*, 7.
[45] Ibid.

> 11. It grew so much—for London the tenth day there died seventy in the liberties, and this day 120, (that I did remove *crossed out*) and also one of my gentlemen, and another of my grooms fell sick and died—that I removed to Hampton Court with very few with me.[46]

Lastly, pageants and spectacle attracted Machyn's attention, especially the civic entries of members of the royal family; the 1551 visit of Mary of Guise, the Dowager Queen of Scotland; the January 1553 arrival at the Tower of the King's Lord of Misrule; and accounts of the Lord Mayor's procession.

If every text is in fact a tactic, to paraphrase Walter Benjamin, it remains to explore the 'tactic' expressed by Henry Machyn.[47] Machyn's text is not really a diary – a genre of great importance to Victorians like Nichols. Nor is Machyn's manuscript an example of autobiographical writing in the sense that the writer explored his own inner thoughts and experiences as in the fashion of the seventeenth-century Ralph Josselin or Nehemiah Wallington.[48] It might be considered autobiographical in nature if we accept James Amelang's broader definition of a 'literary work that expresses lived experience from a first-person point of view'.[49] However, even that definition is ill-suited since Machyn's narrative voice is typically that of the detached observer, sometimes omniscient – as when he described royal events which he could not have viewed in person. While his manuscript does not easily conform to the typologies of autobiographical writing, the entire text resulted from numerous authorial decisions that still make the identity of the writer a central theme. John Gough Nichols was wrong in his assessment of the author. Henry Machyn was neither simple nor incapable; he had no passive relationship with either words or people, especially those who exercised authority over him.[50] He looked for meaning and significance in the world around him, keeping a record of what occurred in a Renaissance, humanist style. He noticed worthy issues and created a testament of the events he wished to remember in a culturally specific fashion. As a witness, he was empowered to look for order in his culture. But what criteria did Machyn use to judge certain events as worthy enough to record?

---

[46] Jordan, 71.

[47] Amelang paraphrases Walter Benjamin in this fashion on p. 115, citing Susan Sontag, *Under the Sign of Saturn* (New York: Farrar, Straus, Giroux, 1980), 122 as his source.

[48] Alan Macfarlane, *The Family Life of Ralph Josselin* (New York: Norton, 1977); and Paul Seaver, *Wallington's World* (Stanford CA: Stanford University Press, 1985).

[49] Amelang, 47.

[50] Amelang wrote (57) that 'Early Modern artisan autobiographical writing represented the conversion of the craftsman's seemingly passive relationship with the written word – as reader of the works of others – into the more active role of author.'

In his will Machyn leaves to 'master Clapenans all my skochyns [escutcheons, funeral ornaments] and my Cronacle the rest of my goodes Cattelles Debtes plate Jewelles Readie money after my Debtes paid ...'[51] Was the chronicle his manuscript, or did he own a copy of a published one such as *Hall's Chronicle* (1548) which would have been a prized possession for a man like Machyn? *Hall's Chronicle* presents information in a retrospective fashion, in contrast to Machyn's approach, but other Tudor chronicles contained entries of topics similar to those found in the main body of Machyn's manuscript, often begun with the identification of the pertinent day and month.[52] The possibility of Machyn owning a Tudor-era chronicle is an intriguing idea, but of course it is only speculation without further evidence. The fact that a printed edition of *Hall's Chronicle* would have possessed a monetary value – that is it would have been worth something in the culture at large – while his own manuscript would have had only sentimental or personal value provides some suggestion that his will refers to a published book.[53] But even if this were not in fact the case, the chronicles of the Tudor era would have been a literary model to a man educated enough to write as Machyn did. The implications of this fact become fundamental to our understanding of his manuscript, exposing the uncritical fashion in which the contents have been anecdotally employed.

Machyn's tone is informational and largely celebratory of the royal rulers, themes especially important to other Tudor chronicles.[54] Much of the celebratory tone applied to events in the reign of Mary I, but since the diary only pre-dates and postdates Mary's reign by a few years, that apparent celebration of Mary's regime may be partly coincidental. Machyn described at least one sermon in the latter and very Protestant

---

[51] Found and transcribed by Ian Mortimer from the original. Archdeaconry of London, will register no. 3, ff. 49–50.

[52] The *Chronicle of the Grey Friars of London* was not published until the Victorian period and therefore could not have been possessed by Machyn, but it contains numerous entries from the reign of Henry VIII that record daily information, just like Machyn did. See, *Chronicle of the Grey Friars of London*, ed. John Gough Nichols (London: J.B. Nichols and Sons, printed for the Camden Society, 1852).

[53] Ian Mortimer has done a splendid bit of archival detective work offering a theory that Machyn might actually have left his chronicle to William Hervy, Clarenceux King of Arms, which may have been twisted into 'master Clapenans', a name that did not exist. Then, instead of 'skochyns', Machyn left his 'escutcheons' to Hervy. If this is true, then Henry Machyn had social ties of much greater importance than most have recognized, and it bolsters my argument that Machyn cannot be marginalized. There is logic to Machyn leaving his manuscript to Hervy, but proof still lacks. See Mortimer, 996–7.

[54] Alison Taufer, *Holinshed's Chronicles* (New York: Twayne Publishers, 1999), chap. 1.

years of Edward's reign with the adjective 'godly'.⁵⁵ Appropriate deference and emphasis informs his descriptions of Edward's deeds and all of Elizabeth's London visits prior to her accession; as heir presumptive, Mary did not elicit any more admiration than Elizabeth. Machyn's style alone does not establish his partisanship since the style is derivative of that genre [1551]:

> M: The vi day July **the** kyngs grace rod through grewyche parke unto blake heth **and** my lord of darbe **and** my lord of Warwyk **and** my lord admerall clyntun **and** sr wyllm harbard **and** odur lords **and** knights **and gentyllmen and** trumpeters playhyng **and** alle the gardes in ther dobletts **and** ther hosse **with** bowes **and** arowes **and** halbards ij **and** ij to gether **and** the kings grace in the mids on horsse bake **and** ther the kings grace ran at **the** ryng on blake heth **with** lords **and** knyghts ... [the entry continues on the next page, but the manuscript is badly damaged here and so I will refer to the reconstruction by Nichols].⁵⁶

> N: The vj day of July the Kynges grace rod through Grenwyche parke unto Blake heth, and my lord of Darby, and my lord of Warwyke, and my lord admerall Clyntun, and sir William Harbard, and odur lorde and knyghts and gentyllmen and trumpeters playhyng, and alle the gardes in ther dobelets and ther hosse, with bowes and arowes and halbards ij and ij to-gether, and the Kynges grace in the myds on horsse-bake, and ther the Kynges grace ran at the ryng on Blake heth with lordes and knyghts. [The earl of Warwick met the king there with 100 men of arms, and great horses, and gentlemen] in clothe, and brodered the alffe, and the same night the Kyng suppyd at Depforth in a shype with my lord Admiral, [and the lords] of the conselle, and with many gentlemen.⁵⁷

Machyn certainly knew of the chronicle genre, for in his diary we find this entry from 1557:

> M: The xix day of June was bered in **the parryche** of ... benett sheyroge old masteres Hall, the mother of **master** Edw ... Hall of gray in **the** whyche he sett for the **the** cronn ... **the** whyche hes callyd **master** Hall cronnacull **and** she dyd ... sserton good gownes boyth for **men and** women a x ... [damaged, a partial 'x' seems indicated] ... **and** ij ffyre whytt branchs **and** x staygfes torches **and master** Garrett **and** my lade behyng sectors **and** my lade War ... **and master** Mossear **and** ys wyff **and** dyver odur had blake gownes.⁵⁸

---

⁵⁵ A Dr Bartelett. The entry is damaged in the manuscript, but Machyn was clearly writing a positive account although the 'godly' is missing. BL, Vit. F.v., f. 6v; Nichols, *Diary*, p. 13.

⁵⁶ BL, Vit. F.v., f. 3r–v.

⁵⁷ Nichols, *Diary*, 6–7.

⁵⁸ BL, Vit. F.v., f. 73v; Nichols, *Diary*, 139.

Machyn knew of Hall's work, and he admired it, which also proves his general awareness of the literary model of the chronicle. No proof exists that he possessed a copy of *Hall's Chronicle*. However, if he did, given that *Hall's Chronicle* stops in 1548, his motivation to write might have revealed a desire to keep the work up to date for his own private enjoyment, or for his friends and loved ones. This motivation, of course, is conjecture. Other possible personal motivations to write could have included an attempt to define the problems of identity and belief arising from the changes manifested in London's society and culture. Given the largely civic focus of the text, he might have been exploring the boundaries of one part of his identity, that of citizen of London. Given the focus on the monarchs and others in authority, perhaps he explored the role of a good subject. With the religious theme, perhaps he tested the requirements for a faithful son of the Church. The written record could have helped him order his thoughts concerning all of these and more.

What if the 'cronacle' mentioned in Machyn's will refers not to Hall or any other printed book, but rather to his own manuscript? What better proof do we need that the author himself understood his work to be in the genre of the chronicles? His motivation to write and his intended audience remain an issue, nevertheless. Ian Mortimer's theory is that Henry Machyn, already one of the parish clerks of Holy Trinity the Little, might have kept the parish register in the 1550s, and the scribbling that became his own manuscript represents extra-parochial deaths and other concerns that struck him as important.[59] Unfortunately Holy Trinity's registers that survive from 1547 onwards are later Elizabethan or even Jacobean copies, not the originals, and so no handwriting comparison is possible. However, the parish registers of Holy Trinity the Little do contain some interesting and chatty entries from the same period.

The comparison with burial registers only goes so far. As already demonstrated, the numerous entries of court activities, episcopal proclamations, civic events and so on have nothing in common with even the chattiest burial register. Machyn's emergence as a writer rested on prior experiences, including perhaps keeping the registers for his parish and certainly the sorts of records connected to his occupation as a renter of funerary trappings, but neither of these authorial experiences explain the bulk of the entries that deal with pageantry and national themes. Machyn's manuscript may best be explained as having been influenced by many approaches to writing. As a literate man of solid standing, Machyn would

---

[59] Mortimer, 993.

have been familiar with many types of texts. When something transformed him from a reader to a writer, he emerged as a new participant in the negotiations of his culture.[60] The creation of a written record empowered Machyn to establish a meaning and significance for current events. The term 'diary' (given all of the modern connotations of that word) was misapplied in the Victorian era and has continued to be misapplied ever since. A 'diary' defined the document as more eccentrically personal to Machyn than to the wider urban experience of his day. This construction paralleled the later projection of Machyn himself as an anachronistic traditionalist interloper from Yorkshire. These facile conclusions are understandable but false. Machyn's manuscript fits into a larger literary movement of his day, a movement mentioned by Charles Lethbridge Kingsford in his introduction to the *Chronicles of London*: 'From the beginning at least of the fifteenth century aldermen and citizens of London had shown their interest in civic and general history by compiling, or encouraging others to compile, English Chronicles arranged under the years of the municipality.'[61] Kingsford does not mention Machyn, of course, but a perusal of chapter 3, the MS Vitellius A XVI (dating 1440–1516) shows that Machyn differs only in his lack of municipal dating – but even Vitellius A XVI includes regnal dating. The last three entries transcribed by Kingsford and dated to 1516 are as follows.

> **Vitellius A XVI:** This yere died Ric. Grey, scheref, for whom was chosen William Bailley, Alderman, for that yere. Item this yere was brought to London the Cardynalles hatte for the Cardynall of York, the wich rially receyved by the Duke of Suffolk w^t dyuers other grett astates, the Meire and his brethren, w^t all the craftes in their lyueres.
>
> This yere was grett ponyshement of puriurye by the seid Cardynall, being in gret auctorite vnder the kynge; for he was chaunceller of England made the day of of in the vijth yere, for because the archbishop of Canterbury was aged, and desired to take his yeres in his diosies, the whiche hadde byn Chaunceler before ix yeres, and right nobully behaued hym, in asmuche he was praised of all men for his wisdom and gentilness.
>
> This yere the kynges sister, queen of Schottes, and the yerle of Angwyshe, her husbonde, cam into England for socur for fere of the Duke of Albayn, that hadde take her to sonnes; but after that her husbonde, the seid yerle, lyke vnto the nature of his Cuntre, went howme ayen in to Schotlande, taking no love; wherefore the kynge sende for her to London, wher sche was rially receyved, and logged at Baynardes Castell.[62]

---

[60] Amelang (57) presents this point in general; I have made it specific for Machyn.

[61] *Chronicles of London*, ed. Charles Lethbridge Kingsford (Oxford: Oxford University Press, 1905; Dursley: Alan Sutton, 1977), v.

[62] Kingsford, 263.

Styles differ, of course, but here again are the same themes and issues expressed in Machyn's manuscript. Even Machyn's creative spelling resonates in these passages. The *Chronicle of the Grey Friars of London* also records events on a daily basis, and it too might offer a clue to Machyn's purpose in writing.[63] Could Machyn have been engaged in some endeavour to create a chronicle for an association such as the clerks' company? If so the endeavour failed to achieve success, and the project has vanished from the historic record. Regardless of his motivation, however, Henry Machyn's voice was very much part of a larger sixteenth-century literary moment in London.

Historians have been slow to appreciate this point, either ignoring the evidence of Machyn's manuscript or intertwining the political implications of Machyn's commentary within negative judgements of Mary I's regime. Mary and Machyn both ended up being depicted as anachronisms in their own time, and not really like everybody else – Machyn a conservative voice from Yorkshire and Mary as 'The Spanish Tudor'.[64] Thus the historical judgements of England's first queen *regnant* became an influence in the defining of Machyn and his manuscript. Mary I has been depicted as a middle-aged, hysterical woman who could not handle power, and as a fanatically religious bigot who was so psychologically damaged by her personal history that she could barely function without the strong and constant support of the people she trusted; and, alas, these trusted few tended to be not the men trained and schooled in the intricacies of English government, but foreigners and Roman clerics serving hidden and foreign agendas.[65] These seductively simplistic explanations have framed the scholarship of Mary's reign for two main reasons. First, the fact that English culture does become a Protestant culture by the end of the sixteenth century renders Mary's attempt to return her people to the Church of Rome a futile and tortuous endeavour. Second, the symbolically central role of Mary's successor, Elizabeth I, in the creation of an English Protestant national identity has encouraged comparative approaches that result in explanations of Mary defined more or less explicitly in comparison with other members of her family, especially her sister – a method in which Mary can only look deficient. H.F.M. Prescott, author of the mid-

---

[63] Nichols, *Chronicle of the Grey Friars of London*.

[64] H.F.M. Prescott, *The Spanish Tudor: the life of 'Bloody Mary'* (New York: Columbia University Press, 1940).

[65] Mary Tudor's most recent biography is by David Loades, *Mary Tudor: A Life* (London: Blackwell, 1989). Prior to Loades, the best studies were Carolly Erickson, *Bloody Mary* (New York: Doubleday, 1978) and H.F.M. Prescott, *Mary Tudor* (New York: Macmillan, 1954).

twentieth-century standard biography, stressed Mary's love of children and female attendants and deprived the queen of adult sensibilities: 'She was indeed cut out by nature and inclination for the intimate personal relationships of a private life. In such a life she might have been happy. As it was, her women loved her and respected her, and yet they sometimes treated her as one who needed instruction in the ways of the world.'[66] Carolly Erickson's late 1970s study depicts Mary as a woman who possessed many natural talents but whose education disempowered her, undermining her agency and ability to rule.[67] G.R. Elton wrote 'The evidence of her [Mary I] ... recorded words and actions ... shows her ... to have been arrogant, assertive, bigoted, stubborn, suspicious, and (not to put too fine a point upon it) rather stupid. Her portraits show her a bitter and narrow-minded woman, curiously unlike her father, brother, and sister.'[68] Penry Williams observed, 'Portraits of Mary Tudor convey very little of the majesty of Kingship: in spite of her fine costumes and splendid jewellery she appears in the paintings by Antonio Mor and Hans Eworth as sour, inhibited, and drab: there is no reflection here of God's image on earth.'[69]

Given the historical judgements of Mary, Machyn's frequently positive and celebratory representations of the regime appear incongruous. The image of a sullen populace enduring the policies of Mary is minimized, but Machyn did not ignore the issue of government-sanctioned violence. The larger London culture looms violent and bloody in the text, not just the Marian persecutions but all of the punishments: public hangings, burnings, nailing people to the pillory, rituals of shame and disgrace, and so on. Such is the case for all of the years that Machyn wrote, from 1550 to 1563. Beyond the official punishments, human suffering was an everyday experience and Henry himself had to bury five of his own children. His entire life was surrounded by death and suffering; they infuse his writing. Yet pathos does not dominate his manuscript. Machyn did express a subtle sense of danger and death even while he marvelled at life's serendipity.

Likewise, religion also infuses the text, although Machyn never makes an explicitly dogmatic or doctrinal statement. He expressed pleasure at the return of old practices under Mary, but positive statements regarding religious practices and events were made about religious events under Edward and Elizabeth that were anything but

---

[66] Prescott, 185.
[67] Erickson, 44–5 and 303.
[68] G.R. Elton, *Reform & Reformation; England, 1509–1558* (Cambridge MA: Harvard University Press, 1977), 376.
[69] Penry Williams, *The Tudor Regime* (Oxford: Clarendon Press, 1979), 362.

Catholic. His admiration for pageantry and deference to status might account for some of those positive assessments. Why else would the 'Catholic' Machyn write this entry from 1558: 'The xx day of November dyd pryche at powlls crosse doctor byll quen **Elisabeth** chaplain **and** mad a godly sermon.'[70] Interestingly for all of the positive word choice he employed, there is no real oppositional or explicitly critical commentary in the text. Machyn did employ a discursive succinctness that provides a subtle counterpoint to his usual tone, a writing strategy found especially in accounts dealing with two particular subjects: the return to Protestantism in the reign of Elizabeth and the persecutions under Mary. These topics he succinctly reports and offers no commentary. Regarding the burnings, Machyn wrote,

> **M:** The vi day of Feybruary doctor tayller w ... sent in to ssuffoke **and** to be brentt.[71]

> **M:** The xvi day of marche was a veyver bornyd in Smyth ffeld dwelling in sordyche for herese by viij of **the** cloke in **the** morning ys nam was.[72]

> **M:** The x day of juin was **delevered** owt of nuegatt ... men to be cared in to essex and ssuffoke to borne.[73]

Regarding the changes under Elizabeth, we find,

> **M:** The xij day of June **the** ffrers of grenwiche whent aw ... [damaged].[74]

> **M:** The x day of July whent **the** ffrers blake in Smyth feld ... went a way.[75]

> **M:** The iiij day of July **the** thursday **the** preste and nuns of Syon whent a way **and the** charter howsse.[76]

> **M:** The abbott of Westmynster **and the** monkes was reprevyd.[77]

These were followed by an entry that was more in the style of Machyn's writing,

> **M:** The day of July kyng phelype was mared unto **the** ffrenche kyng dowthur **and** grett justes mad ther **and the** ffrenche kyng

---

[70] BL, Vit. F.v., f. 94v; Nichols, *Diary*, 178.
[71] BL, Vit. F.v., f. 42v; Nichols, *Diary*, 82.
[72] BL, Vit. F.v., f. 43r; Nichols, *Diary*, 83.
[73] BL, Vit. F.v., f. 46v; Nichols, *Diary*, 89.
[74] BL, Vit. F.v., f. 107r; Nichols, *Diary*, 204.
[75] The date is obscure on the manuscript. Nichols produced 'xiij' but noted that it might be 'xvj'. I see only an 'x' clearly, and the dates for this section are not consistent. Machyn may have been 'catching up' entries. BL, Vit. F.v., p. 107 r; Nichols, *Diary*, 204.
[76] BL, Vit. F.v., f. 107r; Nichols, *Diary*, 204.
[77] Ibid.

> dyd just **and** ther he had on of ys ees stryken owtt **with** a spyld of a spayre **that** he ded of **the** stroke by ...[78]

Given the lack of either negative judgements or fuller exposition, the discursive succinctness becomes noteworthy in a narrative that is largely positive in tone. Machyn's strategy of succinctness allowed him to describe distasteful events while remaining within the manners of his own deferential culture and maintaining the style of the chronicles. Indeed, Machyn's discursive strategy becomes the key to recognizing the main importance of the text.

Machyn described a religious culture, illustrating issues of cultural coherence and governance quite different from the operations of our own post-Enlightenment, secular cultures. The evidence from Machyn's manuscript describes the religiously political world of Marian England, revealing the spiritual and political relationship between subject and prince. There was a direct tie between Machyn and Mary, centred particularly in pageantry, ritual and spectacle. James Amelang has written that 'Ceremonies – the most visible intersection of local identity, political power, and spiritual life – are perhaps the public theme most frequently evoked in artisan diaries'.[79] Once again, Machyn's literary vision has a solid cultural context, although his own personality, and that of his queen, helped define political and spiritual meaning. That tie had a history too. Many traditional religious rituals became controversial or even suspect in the reign of Henry VIII, illegal and forbidden under Edward VI, reintroduced during the reign of Mary I, and largely forbidden or uneasily tolerated under Elizabeth. Most historians have assumed that such religious rituals were simply part and parcel of Mary's religious programme, which originated ultimately from the personality and religious beliefs of the monarch herself. While the personality and character of Mary define the major focus of many studies of her regime, when it comes to religious issues the analysis is usually dominated by circa 300 martyrs or the Protestant exiles, not everybody else.[80]

The traditional definition of Mary I's policies as an aberration in the more fundamental trends evidenced in the reigns of Edward VI and Elizabeth I fails to approach both Mary and her regime on their own terms. Mary survived several dynastic/political crises in her youth,

---

[78] Ibid.

[79] Amelang, 32.

[80] Eamon Duffy has observed that a proper study of Mary's reign has never been produced, especially in regards to her religious policies. See, Eamon Duffy, *The Stripping of the Altars: Traditional Religion in England, 1400–1580* (New Haven CT: Yale University Press, 1992), 524.

rallied forces and fought against an attempt to deny her the throne on the death of her brother Edward VI, put down a rebellion against her government in 1554, and led the government and ruling classes of England to an acceptance of every policy she devised during her reign, including marriage to a foreign prince and the restoration of Roman Catholicism as the official state religion. Some historians have argued that Mary could occasionally rise above her limitations to act in ways that seemed more like the other members of her family.[81] Thus, now we have a hysterical, emotional and bipolar Mary. To make Mary's actions fit into the traditional paradigm requires an inconsistent person who acts in bafflingly incongruous ways. Sometimes historians have grasped for the cultural categories to analyse Mary. Prescott, when faced with Mary's 'stout courage' in the face of Wyatt's rebellion, her obstinate pursuit of the Spanish marriage and her role in religious persecutions, reflected on her life as follows: 'For, mistaken often, almost always misguided in her public office, with much blindness, some rancour, some jealousy, some stupid cruelty to answer for, she had yet trodden, lifelong and manfully, the way that other sinners know.'[82]

Even if we accept these judgements, it is amazing that she survived on the throne as long as she did, dying in her bed of natural causes in November 1558. A female ruler of a patriarchal society who consistently made political blunders and who was on the losing side of a religious and cultural realignment needed some sort of political support if she was to last for long. Mary pursued policies that were truly unpopular with large groups of politically important people, and therefore she needed some negotiating leverage. The emperor and the rest of her Spanish relatives had never been really successful in aiding their English cousin, but she clung to them. The Pope was in no position to aid Mary in domestic politics, and indeed a contentious war divided much of the international arena during Mary's reign – a divide that allied England, Spain and the empire against France, Scotland and the Holy See. Edward, his council and the bishops had supported another claimant to the throne in 1553. And even Elizabeth, who conformed to Mary's religious policies when she had to, was troublesomely 'ill' and absent whenever a crisis arose. If historians search among this contingent of players for Mary's political base, they find none, and the queen does appear to be isolated and out of step. If the scope of analysis were widened to include conservative and loyal people who held Mary in high esteem regardless of who they were or where they lived, then a

---

[81] An assessment made by David Loades while describing Mary's reaction to Wyatt's rebellion. See Loades, 214.

[82] Prescott, 248 and 390.

different image might appear, even in London. What would four years of Mary's Catholic rule do to such a populace, especially when in very short order she married the Prince of Spain and joined in a war with Spain against France – a war which cost English money, lives and energy? Machyn tells us about an event on 15 August 1557:

> M: after evynysong all chyrchys in lo ... was Te deum laudamus songe **and** Ryngyng solemn ... t nyght bone ffyres **and** drynkyng in evers strett in l ... thankyng be to god almighty **that** gyffs the victore.[83]

This night of celebration and thanksgiving occurred in response to the French defeat at the Battle of San Quentin. By this time, all of the policies traditionally associated with Mary's government were in full force, but Machyn's account describes a rousing celebration of success. In the following months religion, rituals and national politics continued their association.

> M: The xix day of September cam a commond ... downe to all paryrche in london **that** they shuld go in prossessyon to powlles **and** Te deum laudamus to synge **and** rynge for wynnyng of perro in ffransse and odur plasses.[84]

> M: The vi day of October cam a comdemen ... in to london **that** evere paryche shuld make bon ... ffyrers **and** ryngyng **that the** pope **and the** emperowr be frynds **and** lovers **and the** ware ended be twy ... them.[85]

In these three passages Machyn provides evidence of the government's call for support, and the manner in which it represented policies to the inhabitants of the City. Machyn occasionally gives insight into popular reactions to these orders, but even when he simply records them he provides proof that the message was getting through to those who would hear it. Machyn's 'exceptionalism' follows easy logic: if the queen is out of step with the fundamental cultural developments of her society, and Machyn wrote approvingly of her policies, then he must be an anachronism as well. Such a position fits nicely with a traditional historiographical approach to both the Reformation and the reign of Queen Mary, and the Victorian labelling of Machyn's manuscript as a 'diary' emphasized the personal nature of his musing. But were the queen and this merchant-citizen really such exceptions in their own culture?

---

[83] BL, Vit. F.v., f. 77v; Nichols, *Diary*, 147.
[84] The ink in the manuscript is very faint here. BL, Vit. F.v., f. 79v; Nichols, *Diary*, 152.
[85] BL, Vit. F.v., f. 80v; Nichols, *Diary*, 154.

Machyn tells us, in one passage from 1555,

> M: The xv day of May was a generall ... ffrom powles and unto leydynhall and downe gr ... Strett and tornyd done estchepe and so to powlls ... ffor whent ij c pore men with beds in ther han ... and iij c power women of evere paryche ij men and ij women ... ij and ij to gether and after all the men chylderyn of the hospetall and after the chylderyne of sant antonys and then all the chyltheryn of powlls and all ther masturs and ther husshers and then all the prestes and clarkes and the bysshope and my lord mare and the althermen and all the crafts of London in ther leveray. The sam tym as thay whera gohyng a prosessyon in chepe ther cam a ffrantyke man and hangyd a bowt a prest ij podyngs and after he was browth to the bysshope and after to my lord mayre and to the contur for ys ffolyssnes.[86]

> N: The xv day of May was a generall prossessyon from Powlles and unto Leydynhall and downe Gracious-strett, and tornyd done Estchepe, and so to Powlles a-gayn; for [there] whent ij C. pore men with bedes in ther handes, and iij C. powre women of evere parryche, ij men and ij women, ij and ij together, and after all the men-chylderyn of the hospetall, and after the chylderne of sant Antonys, and then all of the chyltheryn of Powlles and all of ther masters and husshers, and then all of the prestes and clerkes, and the bysshope, and my lord mare and the althermen, and all of the crafftes of London in ther leveray. The same tym as thay wher a-gohyng a-prossessyon in Chepe ther cam a frantyke man and hangyd a-bowt a prest ij podynges, and after he was browth to the bysshope, and after to my lord mayre, and after to the contur for ys folyssnes.[87]

Many people, it seems, had joined the processions. Seeking the exact number and then raising issues of majorities is not that important in this instance, neither is focusing on the one individual who protested while ignoring the hundreds of people processing the best analysis of this event. More important was the potential personal experience for those individuals who identified themselves as good subjects of Mary and who embraced her restoration of traditional religion. For those not coerced into processing, as surely some were, the rituals allowed the monarch to connect with sympathizers throughout her capital city in a religiously and politically profound manner. It is not outside the realm of possibility that the rituals might have enticed some back to the practices of their youth. The wisdom of this approach was solid. Mary I, faced with a ruling class that had attempted to keep her off the throne, reached out

---

[86] BL, Vit. F.v., f. 45r.
[87] Nichols, *Diary*, 87.

to those who would form a power base and help consolidate her rule. Two groups represented potential help: her own internationally important family, and those English men and women who would support a traditional regime. She had a large and powerful block of such folks – not just in the back of beyond but even in her capital city. Her conservative and traditionalist subjects crossed all categories of status, gender and region. Her regime reached those people, claimed their allegiance and marshalled their support for royal policies. Rituals both spiritual and political allowed the queen and her ministers to use narrative and symbol to call people to their duty. An analysis of the ceremonies and processions which took place in her capital city reveals a regime that operated within a religious culture and which communicated issues of national and international policy to her own people and to the world at large, even to one Henry Machyn who had a fondness for writing. The use of spectacle and ritual was not a revolutionary change in Tudor government and culture because London's religious and secular ceremonies had always sent messages to domestic and foreign observers.[88] While many such observances were ordered from above, it was still up to the local community to complete the tasks. Certainly, Londoners understood the ritual actions and those symbolic messages. During Mary's reign, the universal aspects of Christianity challenged the citizens of London to bring their own private opinions into line with the larger congregation. The queen's international dynastic ties and international Church allegiance played against the nationalist themes of early English Protestantism, but they offered Mary's regime a political and ideological foundation.

Whatever deficiencies defined Mary Tudor, whatever limitations her personality knew, she was still a highly educated royal princess. Far from being an anachronism, disconnected from her own people, Mary knew her own culture well enough to use symbols and rituals not only to communicate with her subjects but also to help establish a political base. This approach pre-dated her accession. On 15 March 1551, Mary rode to London with a large retinue: over 50 knights and gentlemen in velvet coats preceding her and over 80 ladies and gentlemen behind her.[89] Machyn's description is as follows:

> N: [The xv day the Lady Mary rode through London unto St. John's, her place, with fifty knight and gentlemen in velvet coats and chains of gold afore] her, and after her iiij [score gentlemen and ladies, every] one having a peyre of bedes [of

---

[88] Sidney Anglo, *Spectacle, Pageantry, and early Tudor Policy*, 2nd edn (Oxford: Clarendon Press, 1997).

[89] Erickson, 271.

black. She rode through] Chepe-syde and thrugh Smythfeld, – v.K.E.vj.⁹⁰

This entry occurred at the height of Mary's conflict with Edward's government over her observance of the outlawed Roman Mass in her chapel. Imperial representative Jehan Scheyve wrote to the emperor on 6 April 1551, 'I had had it from a good source that they [Edward's council] ... had resolved to treat her roughly.'⁹¹ Here, Mary came to the capital clearly in the style of the heir to the throne, the wealthiest woman in the land, a daughter of two royal houses, and she and each of the participants in this royal procession wore a rosary (an old fashion in England). Machyn's account indicates that people from the city of London ran 5 or 6 miles out of town to greet her.⁹² Carolly Erickson wrote that Londoners saw miracles and visions surrounding this procession but failed to provide evidence.⁹³ Even accounting for hyperbole, the evidence indicates a phenomenal public reaction to Mary's arrival. Most historians have interpreted these accounts as valid enough. Like Erickson, David Loades mentions this procession into London, but neither biographer explored the politics of symbolism fully; the posthumously published biography of Edward VI by Jennifer Loach does not mention Mary's entry, although there is a discussion of the subsequent meetings between council and princess.⁹⁴ In another study of Edward VI's reign, Hester Chapman wrote: 'It was characteristic of Mary to lend herself to an unnecessary and tactless demonstration, bound to irritate the Lords and upset her brother.'⁹⁵ Why this display was tactless implies more about Chapman's sensibilities than the politics of mid-Tudor London. For those devout Catholics forced into Protestantism, however small their number, Mary's display must have seemed courageous and a source of hope to sincere people outlawed from practising their beliefs. Mary's entry was also an exercise in political intimidation prior to the meeting between Mary and her brother's council. Faced with meeting men who had changed the religion of the land during a minority rule, Mary was rallying forces as a first step in the tense negotiations with her brother's Protestant government.

---

⁹⁰ What is left of this passage comes early in the manuscript, and is almost completely obliterated. I have used Nichols's reconstruction. See, BL, Vit. F.v., f. 2v; Nichols, *Diary*, 4–5.
⁹¹ *Cal. Span.*, 10:251.
⁹² Nichols, *Diary*, 4–5.
⁹³ Erickson, 271.
⁹⁴ Jennifer Loach, *Edward VI* (New Haven and London: Yale University Press, 1999).
⁹⁵ Hester W. Chapman, *The Last Tudor King: a Study of Edward VI [12 October 1537–6 July 1553]* (New York: Macmillan Company, 1959), 200.

In this action we see illustrated a paradigm for her political *modus operandi* and a skill typically overlooked. Once she became queen, Mary's use of traditional religious symbols, rituals and pageants not only revitalized them for her people, but also allowed the regime to incorporate her supporters – whatever their status, gender and location – into the political and religious debates of her day.[96]

Throughout Mary's five-year reign, Machyn records about 60 religious processions held in London which existed amidst numerous other ceremonies such as royal entries, mayoral inaugurations, funeral processions, visits of important people and the early December visitations of several St Nicholases. Those circa 60 religious processions often combined religious ceremony with political motivations. Other rituals did as well. About three years after Mary's 1551 entry to London, in the aftermath of the failed rebellion led by Sir Thomas Wyatt, the now Queen Mary continued to acknowledge and exploit ritual action to communicate and rally support. Machyn tells us that,

> M: The viij day of Feybruary was **commondyd** by **the** queen **and the** byshope of London **that** powlls **and** evere **parryche** that they shuld syng te deum laudamus **and** ryngyng ffor **the** good victory **that the** quen grace had a ganst Wyatt **and the** rebellious of Kent **the** wyche wher over come thankes be unto god **with** lytyll blud shed **and** the reseduw taken **and** had to presun **and** after wher dyvers of them putt to deth in dyvers places in londun **and** Kent **and prossessyon** ever wher that day for joy.[97]

This imprisoned group was released in a public ceremony about two weeks later, on 22 February, when,

> M: ... alle **the** kent men whent to **the** cowrt **with** halters a bowt ther nekes **and** bone **with** cordes ij **and** ij to gether through london to Westmynster **and** be twyn **the** ij tilts **the** power presonars knelyd downe in **the** myre **and the the** quen grace lokyd owt over **the** gatt **and** gayff them all pardon **and** thay cryd owt god save quen mare **and** so to Westmynster hall **and** ther thay cast they alters a bowt the hall **and** capes **and** in **the** stretes **and** cryd owt god save quen mare as thay whent.[98]

While each of these passages suggests that the Marian regime 'connected' with some part of the city's population through symbols and

---

[96] The idea of 'revitalization' of rituals is discussed in Peter Arnade, *Realms of Ritual: Burgundian Ceremony and Civic Life in Late Medieval Ghent* (Ithaca NY: Cornell University Press, 1996).

[97] BL, Vit. F.v., f. 28r; Nichols, *Diary*, 55.

[98] The word 'lokyd' is inserted above the line. BL, Vit. F.v., f. 29r; Nichols, *Diary*, 56.

rituals, proving either the depth of popular comprehension of these messages or the effectiveness of using ritual to build, rouse and expand popular support becomes very difficult. The point is not that everyone consented, but rather that Machyn and other Londoners engaged with most of the issues of Mary's reign through this manner and were brought into those policies via their participation in ritual action. Even Philip of Spain, whom historians have long told us was highly unpopular with Londoners, received no irreverent comment when associated with royal and religious ceremonies, as on St George's Day (23 April) 1554 when, Machyn tells us,

> M: ... he xxiij of aprell was sant gorge day ... grace whent unto the chapel and whent a pro ... all the knyghtes of the garter that was ther pres ... mes in the feld ther wher creatyd the sam day k ... rter prynsse of spain one and the yerle of ssussex.[99]

And by these actions, the court set examples of religious and political importance for both the City and nation, as in Rogation Week in 1554:

> M: The iij day of May at the cowrt of sant Jam ... the quen grace whent a prossessyon with in san ... with harolds and siantes of armes and iiij bysshopes m ... and all iij days thay whent her chapell a bowt ... ffeldes first day to sant Gylles and ther song masse ... the next day tuwseday to sant Martens in the ffel ... a sermon and song masse and so thay dronke ther and the iij day to Westmynster and ther a sermon and then masse and mad good chere and aft a bowt the Parke and so to sant James cowrt ther.[100]

The same week, several precincts from around the Tower observed Rogationtide by processions of priests, clerks, the officials of the Tower and the local inhabitants, 'a-bowt the feldes of sant Katheryns and the prevelegys'.[101] The methodology of ritual display worked as a part of government, and presented a cultural model for others to emulate.

The impetus for the use of traditional ceremonies and rituals remained tied to Mary herself. Perhaps she consciously knew what she was doing, or perhaps the method emerged coincidentally from her stubborn sense of the ways things should be, but the tie went straight from Machyn to the queen. The essential element in Mary's use of ritual was the incorporation of the trappings of the old religion, which neither

---

[99] BL, Vit. F.v., f. 31v; Nichols, *Diary*, 60.

[100] The word 'siantes' is very difficult to discern, and has an abbreviation mark on the initial letter, so Nichols was probably correct in transcribing it as 'serjants' since 'at armes' follows. BL, Vit. F.v., f. 31v; Nichols, *Diary*, 61.

[101] The entry in the manuscript is badly damaged, so I cite the reconstruction by Nichols, *Diary*, 61.

Edward's nor Elizabeth's government would have ever employed. Given the use of sermons to define the reforming kingship of Edward, Mary's use of traditional symbols and rituals to establish her Catholic queenship becomes an obvious strategy.[102] However, the cultural meanings of rosaries, images and processions had transformed since the 1530s, and they engendered a new range of responses in the 1550s – from nostalgic comfort to xenophobic hatred and fear of idolatry. These cultural responses rendered the trappings of the old religion much more politically powerful for Mary's government, and they made use of them. The processions were not spread evenly throughout Mary's reign, but come in key moments, especially in the crucial period of 1553 and 1554 when the regime was still defining itself. In fact, the last recorded procession in Machyn's diary comes in spring 1558, implying the slow evaporation of the regime's strength as the queen went into her final decline before her death in November 1558. But in the nation's capital before 1558, these rituals spoke to a religious culture – what remained of the Catholic and traditional English-speaking world – and helped to integrate those subjects so inclined not into a body politic but into a spiritual communion. Symbolic meaning and ritual action conveyed and defined national and dynastic policies for the whole nation, and thus became a part of government. In the famous episode of Mary's false pregnancy, we find,

> M: The xxix day of november was **commondyd** by ... f london thrughe ys dyosesse **that** thay shuld say ... **the** holygost **possessyon and** to syng te deum **and** ryngyng ... pray to God to gyffe hym thankes of owr ... quen of her qwyckenyng **with** chyld **and** to pray.[103]

And, when in the springtime a false report of the arrival of a prince and heir spread throughout the City, spontaneous celebrations resulted in many London parishes. The City's reaction to this false rumour provides our best evidence that the Marian regime had succeeded in integrating large numbers of Londoners into a religious and political culture. Again, Machyn tells us,

> M: The xxx day of a prell **and the** last day of a prell thydy ... cam to london **that the** quen grace was **delevered** of a p ... **and** so ther was grett ryngyng thrugh london **and** dyv ... plases te deum laudamus songe **and the** morow aft yt w ... tornyd odur ways to **the** plesur of god but yt shall be when yt plesse god

---

[102] For a study of Edward's kingship and sermons, see Stephen Alford, *Kingship and Politics in the Reign of Edward VI* (Cambridge: Cambridge University Press, 2002).

[103] BL, Vit. F.v., f. 40r; Nichols, *Diary*, 76–7.

for I trust god that he wyll remembur ys tru servands that putt ther trust in hym when that they calle on hym.[104]

The churchwardens' account of the parish of St Benet Gracechurch Street contains an entry of their reaction to the false news: 'Item paid upon May even last to a priest and six clerks for singing of *Te Deum* and playing upon the organs for the birth of our prince which was then thought to be.'[105] Neither the heir nor the queen's religious and dynastic vision of the future would arrive. Mary's death in 1558 brought her half-sister to the throne, and by the end of the century the nationalized Church had successfully nurtured a Protestant culture in the realm. To the descendants of that Protestant, national culture, Mary and her government have appeared bloody, baffling and backwards. However, measured in the more valid terms of her own reign, a different image of Mary I develops – one that has at least some realistic political grounding. When seen through the writings of a London artisan who liked to write, the queen and her regime exploited the power of ceremony to form an alliance with those members of her society who would accept a restoration of the old ways and serve as her loyal subjects, while bypassing those members of the aristocracy and gentry classes who had embraced Protestantism. Mary Tudor's reign demonstrates the importance of spectacle to an early modern government operating within a religious culture. Machyn's manuscript demonstrates how those rituals could bring a loyal and sympathetic subject into a common purpose with the queen and her government.

This chapter does not remove the interpretation of Machyn's manuscript from the context of Mary Tudor's London, rather it offers a paradigmatic shift and reading. By looking for the models of literature that influenced the author, it becomes possible to understand Machyn's work more astutely. An approach that does not carry a predisposition to dismiss the doomed sensibilities of a traditionalist in the era of reform allows the author's own vision greater clarity. As a result Henry Machyn stands in a different light. He lived in a hierarchical, authoritative and deferential culture; he understood and found comfort in the cultural forms he knew, and he recognized his allegiance to three Tudor monarchs whose policies would force him to face some major reconstructions of his sense of truth, justice and righteousness. His writing probably became a method for dealing with these changes. He looked for meaning and significance; he noticed and testified to significant events and kept a record of what occurred. His observations,

---

[104] BL, Vit. F.v., f. 44v; Nichols, *Diary*, 86.
[105] GL, MS 1568.

for years called a diary, are not easily explained; the complex author refuses to be defined by simplistic models. While expressing an autobiographical aspect, the text also expressed a subtle political commentary. Henry Machyn was a loyal Englishman imbued with a fascination for his city; a sincere Christian with Catholic tastes; a discerning participant in the cultural negotiations of his day; a family man; a lover of good times with a self-deprecating sense of humour; an incredibly curious watcher of people and their manners, he ultimately empathized with his fellow citizens and their plight. Mid-Tudor London, in the throes of social and cultural transformation, was full of colour, smells and sounds; it also possessed a Merchant Taylor of no great social significance who marked the days with scribbled notes firmly engaged with the great issues of his day.

CHAPTER ELEVEN

The Persecution in Kent[1]

Patrick Collinson

No doubt the Protestant martyrs should have their place in a book on Marian Catholicism. It will not do to shove them into an embarrassed corner, as J.J. Scarisbrick did in *The Reformation and the English People* with just seven words: 'We today are horrified by the burnings.'[2] (Actually the current scholarly fixation on John Foxe and his 'Book of Martyrs', more properly *Actes and Monuments*,[3] suggests an almost voyeuristic fascination rather than horror.) Whatever we read out of the Foxeian narratives (and without Foxe we should know no more about the bulk of the martyrs than we know about most ordinary people at most times, which is precious little) they are an essential source of our empathy for these events.

---

[1] Tom Freeman has contributed a great deal to this chapter. I am no less indebted to Joy Lloyd of the John Foxe Project (Humanities Research Institute, University of Sheffield) who has helped me to navigate the shoals of the successive editions of the *Acts and Monuments*.

[2] J.J. Scarisbrick, *The Reformation and the English People* (Oxford, 1984), 136.

[3] Following the Latin text published at Basle in 1559, *Rerum in ecclesia gestarum commentarii*, four editions of *Actes and Monuments* appeared in Foxe's lifetime, in 1563 *Actes and monuments of these latter and perillous dayes, touching matters of the church*, 1570 (greatly enlarged and substantially altered in scope and purpose), 1576 and, in 1583, *Actes and monuments of matters most special in the church*. Historians have for the most part used and cited the nineteenth-century edition in eight volumes, *The Acts and Monuments of John Foxe*, ed. S.R. Cattley (London, 1837–41). For a compelling case against this practice, see Thomas Freeman, 'Texts, Lies, and Microfilm: Reading and Misreading Foxe's "Book of Martyrs"', *Sixteenth Century Journal*, xxx (1999), 23–46. The British Academy John Foxe Project, based at the University of Sheffield and directed by David Loades, is dedicated to the (electronic) publication of a collated and critical text of the four editions of 1563, 1570, 1576 and 1583. A first fruit of the project is a CD-ROM facsimile, *John Foxe's Book of Martyrs 1583*, presented by David G. Newcombe with Michael Pidd and published by the Oxford University Press for the British Academy (2001). Much of the Foxe research generated by the project can be sampled in the published proceedings of three related colloquia: *John Foxe and the English Reformation*, ed. David Loades (Aldershot and Brookfield, VT, 1997), *John Foxe An Historical Perspective*, ed. David Loades (Aldershot and VT, 1999), *John Foxe and his World*, ed. Christopher Highley and John N. King (Aldershot and Burlington, VT, 2002). All references to *AM* in this chapter are to the 1583 edition, with cross-references to the earlier editions where they have proved of relevance.

What can we know about the scenarios, the 'public sphere', in which the executions, a piece of theatre for both the persecutors and the persecuted, took place? The historian must weigh in his right hand and his left evidence on the one hand of what in Scotland is called 'a braw divert', a spectacle (like any other execution), the holiday crowds for whom the burning of the young Dartford linen draper Christopher Wade was a day out, the 'braynesicke foles' caricatured by Miles Huggarde, 'flockyng together on heapes' ('if there be any vayne syghtes to be seen, or any folishe matters to be heerd, lorde howe they runne and sweate in their busines');[4] on the other, Foxe's description of the dignified and moving scene at the last burnings in Smithfield: 'the godly multitude and Congregation', making 'a generall sway toward the prisoners, ... meetyng and embracing, and kissing them'. Huggarde's brilliant Catholic journalism in *The displayinge of the protestantes* tells us more than anything in the pages of Foxe about what it may have looked and sounded like, reconciling godliness and 'brainsickness'. He quotes 'the fonde wordes of the simple and rude people, exclamed to the heretikes passing to death': 'What crueltie is this, to put to death the brethren in Christ? ... It is mere tyrannie thus to persecute the litle flocke, the chosen and elect vessels of God.' 'Be constant dere brethren, be constant in the faith, sticke to it ... Your brekefast is sharpe, your supper shalbe merye.'[5]

But why Kent? More heretics were burned in Kent in the course of Mary's reign than in any other part of England, London (narrowly) excepted, the majority in Canterbury. The burnings happened at the place of public executions in Wincheap, to the south of the city, marked since the nineteenth century by a martyrs' memorial which today is hidden in suburban streets but deserves to be as well known as the more famous monument in Oxford. In London the largest number burned in any one year of the Marian persecution appears to have been 16, and many of those executed in the capital had been brought there from Colchester and other places in Essex. But in 1555 18 heretics were burned in Canterbury and within the six months from July 1555 to January 1556 the tally was 23, half the total burned at Smithfield in the entire reign. In all, 41 people were burned at Canterbury, one in seven of all the Marian martyrs. The last five victims in England died at Canterbury only a week before Mary's death, when, according to Foxe, relying on hearsay ('some there be that say'), Archdeacon Nicholas

---

[4] *AM*, 1679–80; Miles Huggarde (or Hogarde), *The displayinge of the protestantes* (1556), 49; *AM*, 2074.

[5] Huggarde, *The displayinge*, fol. 43. Foxe himself quotes the slogan about a sharp breakfast and a merry supper (*AM*, 2005)

Harpsfield, who was in London at the time, knew very well that she was dying.⁶ They made a grand total for Kent of 61, give or take one or two, 67 if we count as martyrs those who died in prison and were denied Christian burial.⁷ The spectacle must have lost the novelty value which it had had at Dartford in June 1555. Yet, as A.G. Dickens observed, in a place like Kent the persecution will have seemed more dramatic and severe than the national totals suggest to a detached modern observer.⁸

Beyond the bare statistics, we shall find that the Kentish martyrs possessed identities, and opinions, which raise important questions about the character of 'Protestant' dissent in the extreme south-east of England in the mid-sixteenth century. Many, perhaps half, of the victims came from the villages and cloth towns of the Kentish Weald (five from Tenterden, three from Biddenden, two from Cranbrook, two from Staplehurst, two from Frittenden), and six from Maidstone. None can be shown to have belonged to Canterbury itself. All but two were laypeople, the vast majority from the lower orders of society. Eighteen of the Kentish martyrs were women, or almost one in three, whereas the proportion of female martyrs nationally was 17 per cent.⁹ Trial records once in Foxe's possession, which must have been an embarrassment to him – not least because they were generated in a court presided over by the man who was later to become his most effective critic, Nicholas Harpsfield¹⁰ – prove that several of the Wealden martyrs were not

---

⁶ *AM*, 2053. Foxe had already included this allegation in the 1563 edition, 1672–3.

⁷ Various figures have been offered by various historians for the total of martyrs both nationally and in Kent. David Loades (*The Reign of Mary Tudor* (London, 1979), 158, n. 7) has the very conservative figure of 49 for the diocese of Canterbury. A.G Dickens (*The English Reformation* (2nd edn, London, 1988, 295) put the Kentish total at 58, 'all except six of them executed at Canterbury'. This too was an underestimate, while of those whose place of execution is known, 41 were burned in Canterbury and 18 in other places (7 in Maidstone, 3 at Rochester, 2 at Ashford, 2 at Wye, 1 each at Dartford and Tonbridge and 2 outside the county). I arrive at my figure by conflating the Foxeian record with the list in William Cecil's papers (the Lansdowne MSS) printed by John Strype (*Ecclesiastical Memorials*, iii (2) (Oxford, 1822), 554–6), adding two names supplied by *significavit* certificates of relaxation to the secular arm (PRO, C 85/27/20, 85/144/33–6). For details of those who died in prison, see *AM*, 1970. See also J.W. Martin, 'Side lights on Foxe's Account of the Marian Martyrs', in his *Religious Radicals in Tudor England* (London and Roncoverte, WV, 1989), 171–8, where use is made of Thomas Price's *A compendious register in metre containing the names and sufferings of the members of Jesus Christ* (London, 1559), and Robert Crowley's edition of the *Epitome of chronicles* (1559).

⁸ Dickens, *The English Reformation*, 297.

⁹ Christopher Haigh, *English Reformations: Religion, Politics and Society under the Tudors* (Oxford, 1993), 230; Philip Hughes, *The Reformation in England*, ii (London, 1961), 259.

¹⁰ In the sixth of his *Dialogi sex contra ... pseudomartyres* (Antwerp, 1566). No doubt because he wrote in Latin, Harpsfield's criticism (of which Foxe took account in his

orthodox Protestants but held extremely heterodox opinions, not least on the doctrine of the Trinity. This is some of the most important evidence we have, for or against the theory of a continuity of radical dissent, 'from Lollards to Levellers'.[11]

It would be a mistake to suppose that the social profile of the Kentish martyrs offers us as it were on a plate a cross-section of Protestantism in the county. We must never forget that most Protestants by one means or another avoided martyrdom, and that for those with the means to take it there was the option of moving away from home, not necessarily into the 'Marian Exile' as it has been most commonly understood, the Swiss and German diaspora, but as part of a less well-documented internal exile. Calais, still an English town, and only 20 miles away, was where many of those from Kent who chose to shift went. That is why this chapter will have little to say about such prominent Kentish gospellers as Mrs Joyce Hales, daughter-in-law of the judge and Privy Counsellor Sir James Hales, whose response to the predicament of the Marian reaction was to drown himself in the River Stour above Canterbury. Joyce Hales corresponded with John Bradford up to the time of his martyrdom, but then withdrew to Calais, where she formed a link between the prisons in England and her fellow exiles.[12]

How 'Protestant' was Kent in the mid-sixteenth century? Traditionally the county has been presented as an example of Protestant precocity. Dickens asserted that, within the south-east of England, 'London, Kent and Essex were, by any criteria foremost in the movement', while Eamon Duffy believes that 'Kent almost certainly had a greater proportion of committed Protestants than any other part of

---

1570 edition) has received less attention than Robert Persons's *A treatise of three conversions of England* (St Omer, 1603), which itself is not as well known as it might be. (See Ceri Sullivan, '"Oppressed by the Force of Truth": Robert Persons Edits John Foxe', in Loades, *John Foxe: An Historical Perspective*, 154–66.) But Tom Freeman will put this right in a work which is forthcoming.

[11] Christopher Hill, 'From Lollards to Levellers', in his *Collected Essays*, ii (Brighton, 1986), 89–116; *The World of Rural Dissenters, 1520–1725*, ed. Margaret Spufford (Cambridge, 1995). The case 'against' is touched on in my 'Critical conclusion' included in Spufford, 388–96.

[12] Tom Freeman has helped with Joyce Hales, pointing me to letters written to her in BL, MS Add. 19400, fols 351–60r, 76r-7v, 80r–81v; and Emmanuel College, Cambridge Library, MS 260, ff. 79r–81v, 233r–4v. In Canterbury Cathedral there is a remarkable monument to Sir James Hales and his son, who was buried at sea (in the Portuguese expedition of 1589), incorporating a painted landscape scene of Hales's suicide, which was intended to commemorate the lawsuit which led to Hales's property being released to his heirs. (Katherine Eustace, 'The Post-Reformation Monuments', in *A History of Canterbury Cathedral*, ed. Patrick Collinson, Nigel Ramsay and Margaret Sparks (Oxford, 1995), 515–17.)

England.'¹³ Historians have pointed to the evidence of a significant Lollard presence, uncovered in the major drive against heresy mounted on behalf of Archbishop Warham by some of his ablest lieutenants in 1511, which found that the heretical virus had been active, especially in the Weald, since at least the days of Edward IV.¹⁴ Foxe, for reasons which are not in the least mysterious, was anxious to link the old heresy with the new.¹⁵ A perfect case for his purposes was the story of the Brownes, father and son. John Browne had been burned at Ashford in 1511, when someone had suggested that his children too should be thrown into the fire, 'for they would spring ... of his ashes', a story 'often' told by Browne's widow. Richard Browne, the son, was in Canterbury Castle, awaiting execution, on the day that Queen Mary died.¹⁶

The other side of this coin was the religious conservatism of much of the ruling establishment of the county, including Christ Church Canterbury in its last days as a monastery and first as a new cathedral foundation. Peter Clark has demonstrated the strength of evangelical dissent in the towns, and not least in Canterbury itself, with its centuries-old tradition of animosity between the city and the great church towering over it.¹⁷ Entrenched conservatism was offset by the potent influence of Archbishop Cranmer, whose extensive enquiries into the plot to unseat him in 1543 yielded evidence of heated pulpit controversies (at Lenham the vicar and curate took it in turns to preach against each other), the presence of actively prosyletizing Protestants in some parishes and of heretical cells in Canterbury and some other places, as well as bringing to light much (dubious?) evidence of preaching that was downright eccentric.¹⁸ (But Hugh Cooper of

---

¹³ Dickens, *The English Reformation*, 326; Eamon Duffy, *The Stripping of the Altars: Traditional Religion in England c.1400–c.1580* (New Haven and London, 1992), 555.

¹⁴ *Kent Heresy Proceedings, 1511–12*, ed. Norman Tanner, Kent Records (Maidstone, 1997).

¹⁵ Margaret Aston, 'Lollardy and the Reformation: Survival or Revival?', and 'John Wycliffe's Reformation Reputation', in her *Lollards and Reformers: Images and Literacy in late Medieval Religion* (London, 1994), 219–71; Anne Hudson, ' "No Newe Thyng": The Printing of Medieval Texts in the Reformation Period', in her *Lollards and Their Books* (London and Roncoverte, WV, 1985), 227–48.

¹⁶ *AM*, 1292–3.

¹⁷ Peter Clark, *English Provincial Society from the Reformation to the Revolution: Religion, Politics and Society in Kent 1500–1610* (Hassocks, 1977), 38–44; Peter Clark, 'Reformation and Radicalism in Kentish Towns c.1500–1553', in *The Urban Classes, the Nobility and the Reformation: Studies on the Social History of the Reformation in England and Germany*, ed. W. Mommsen et al. (Stuttgart, 1979).

¹⁸ Corpus Christi College, Cambridge, MS 12.8, extensively calendared in the oddly entitled 'Cranmer and the Heretics of Kent', *Letters and Papers, Foreign and Domestic of*

Tenterden proved himself an orthodox and card-carrying Protestant when he preached that 'neither almes deedes fasting neither prayer dothe help the soule of manne but faith allonly'.[19] Such 'godly learned ministers', as the Elizabethans would call them, were in short supply, and very few would be prepared to face the Marian music when it came. The exceptions were Richard Turner, vicar of Chartham – a particularly controversial figure in the early 1540s[20] – and John Bland, the dynamic vicar of Adisham, placed there by Cranmer's commissary and nephew-in-law Christopher Nevinson, a more advanced Protestant than his master. The core of Bland's teaching seems to have been denunciation of auricular confession: 'It was sufficient to say that I am a synner and have offended in thought wourde and dede.'[21]

Cranmer had a justified reputation among conservative clerics of being soft on some of the most radical elements in his own metropolitan city, and in particular of tolerating 'so ranke an heretique' as Joan Bocher, of whom more anon.[22] Members of the Toftes household of Northgate parish were known to be supporters and harbourers of 'suspect persons', including Bocher, and Bland and Turner. Margaret Toftes, who had declared 'that her daughter could piss as good holy water as the priest could make any', boasted to her enemies that 'when my lord of Canterbury's Grace comethe down to Canterbury we trust to have a day against you'.[23] One small incident of perhaps 1538 suggests how the wind had been blowing. In a letter from Cranmer to Thomas Cromwell we learn that 'certen men of Smarden and Pluckley' had been indicted for holding 'unlawfull assembles', and on no other ground than that they were accounted favourers of the new doctrine. Cromwell was urged to ensure that the charges were dropped, 'For if the kingys subiectes within this realme which favour goodes wourde shalbe uniustly vexed at sessions, it wolbe no marvaile though moche sedition be dayly engendered within this realme.'[24] Were these the blameless

---

the Reign of Henry VIII, xviii (2). Some of the detail reported here will only be found in the MS. See also Brian M. Hogben, 'Preaching and the Reformation in Henrician Kent', *Archaeologia Cantiana*, ci (1984), 169–85.

[19] Corpus Christi College, Cambridge, MS 128, 36.

[20] *Letters and Papers*, xviii (2), 301, 311–12; Clark, *English Provincial Society*, 60, 64–5; Diarmaid MacCulloch, *Thomas Cranmer: A Life* (New Haven and London, 1996), 302–5.

[21] Corpus Christi College, Cambridge, MS 128, 68. See Tom Freeman's article on Bland in the *Oxford Dictionary of National Biography* (2004).

[22] Ibid., 78–80; *Letters and Papers*, xviii (2), 291, 313–14, 331. Miles Huggarde reported (*The displayinge of the protestantes*, fol. 75) that Bocher 'in the beginnyng of our newfound opinions was greatly mainteyned by Cranmer in Canterbury and other places of Kent.'

[23] *Letters and Papers*, xviii (2), 300, 307.

[24] Cranmer to Cromwell, 29 April n.y., PRO, S.P. 1/131, 239.

evangelicals the archbishop took them for? Among those indicted from Pluckley was Henry Hart, to whom we shall come in a moment, soon to be a thorn in the archbishop's side.

Against what we may call the Dickensian view of the Kentish scene there is contrary evidence to suggest that here, as much as anywhere in England, Protestants were a minority sect until well into Elizabeth's reign, with the 1570s forming a watershed. It was in that decade that 'the preachers of Kent' came to the fore and that 'minister of the word of God' in this or that place became the common style for many clergy.[25] In a passage which is admittedly patient of more than one construction, an Essex minister born in Sandwich reported of his native county: 'Myself, as young as I am [he was probably born at about the time of Elizabeth's accession, since he matriculated in Cambridge in 1573], did know the time not long sithence the happy reign of her Majesty when we in Kent was most accounted, and also was indeed, the most popish place of all that country.' It was only when preaching spread more widely in the county that popery 'vanished as the mist before the sun', so that Kent [if 'that country' and 'place' meant Kent] was now 'less noted for popery than any other place'.[26] Of course this was not dispassionate observation. Thomas Stoughton was making a strong case for the indispensability of the preaching ministry, like the Kentish puritan Josias Nicholls, who contrasted the well-informed parishioners from places 'where there hath been diligent teaching' with the woeful ignorance of people who had not been exposed to Protestant indoctrination.[27]

Yet in our approach to the Marian persecution in Kent we have to rid our minds of the unhelpful assumption that Protestantism was already socially as well as legally the established religion of this part of the kingdom before 1553, and due for restoration six years later, after a brief reactive aberration. If the Marian authorities in Kent, Archdeacon Harpsfield prominently included, had said what a Suffolk justice

---

[25] Patrick Collinson, 'Cranbrook and the Fletchers Popular and Unpopular Religion in the Kentish Weald', in his *Godly People. Essays on English Protestantism and Puritanism* (London, 1983), 415.

[26] Thomas Stoughton, *A general treatise against poperie* (Cambridge, 1598), 4–5. A biographical account of Stoughton will be found in *Conferences and Combination Lectures in the Elizabethan Church: Dedham and Bury St Edmunds, 1582–1590*, ed. Patrick Collinson, John Craig and Brett Usher, Church of England Record Society, x (Woodbridge, 2003).

[27] Josias Nicholls, *The plea of the innocent* (London, 1602), 218–20. See the helpful analysis of Nicholls in John Craig, *Reformation, Politics and Polemics: The Growth of Protestantism in East Anglian Market Towns, 1500–1610* (Aldershot and Burlington, VT, 2001), 12–14.

reportedly said of the heretics of his own county, 'it is time to weed out such fellows as you be indeed',[28] that would have been a realistic assessment of what the repression of heresy might have been expected to achieve. The heretics were not yet a field of wheat but the cockles growing here and there among the corn. This is not to deny that there were already strong pockets of Protestantism before Mary's reign. One such was Maidstone, and another Herne, between Canterbury and the north coast. In 1556 ten Herne parishioners were prosecuted for words and flagrant gestures of contempt against the sacrament of the altar. They were not the stuff of which martyrs are made, for all appear to have conformed when brought into court.[29] This may be evidence of the influence of the most potent of Protestant evangelists in this part of Kent, John Bland of Adisham.

So far we have skirted around the question, what do we mean by Protestantism? Diarmaid MacCulloch has warned us that it is anachronistic to use the term with definitional precision before the reign of Edward VI, and we are looking at the religious scene in Kent within the same decade.[30] With Lollard roots, more than one heretical and dissenting tendency may have coexisted, and it was only from a Protestant establishment perspective that some of these 'sects' were labelled 'Anabaptist'. There is actually no evidence of Anabaptism in a literal sense in Kent, although the heresy was present, and perhaps endemic, which denied the humanity of Christ, alleging that he took 'heavenly flesh', the Virgin being but a 'saffron bag' through which he passed with none of the normal processes of gestation, a doctrine associated on the Continent with the Anabaptist Melchior Hoffmann.[31] It was held and propagated by the alarmingly militant Joan Bocher, who seems to have come from near Colchester but was living in the early 1540s in the Wealden village of Frittenden, before joining herself to the

---

[28] The magistrate was Sir Clement Higham, father of the staunchly puritan Sir John Higham; quoted, J.F. Mozley, *John Foxe and His Book* (London, 1940), 199.

[29] BL, MS Harley 421, fols 97–8.

[30] Diarmaid MacCulloch, *Tudor Church Militant: Edward VI and the Protestant Reformation* (London, 1999), 2–3.

[31] John Davis, 'Joan of Kent, Lollardy and the English Reformation', *Journal of Ecclesiastical History*, xxxiii (1982), 225–33. Humphrey Cotton, a chantry priest at Tenterden, was accused of denouncing from the pulpit those preachers who were supposedly 'beating into the people's heads that some had called Our Lady a saffron bag, and that they would Our Lady to have no honor.' (*Letters and Papers*, xviii (2), 294.) Richard Turner of Chartham was reported to have taught the children of Northgate parish, Canterbury, that when they said the Ave Maria they should add, under their breath: 'a due and god be with you'. (Corpus Christi College, Cambridge, MS 128, 75.) This suggests that the 'saffron bag' image did not necessarily have Melchiorite implications, but implied some demotion of the Virgin in popular devotion.

radical sectarian group gathered by the Tofteses in Canterbury. All attempts by Archbishop Cranmer and the other Edwardian authorities to avoid the cruel embarrassment of burning 'Joan of Kent' at the stake failed, she having a strong will for martyrdom. That was one less heresiarch for the Marian authorities to have to deal with. But her death in Smithfield in May 1550 was a moment of high drama for the fledgling Protestant regime, thanks to Joan herself, who, far from dying the death of a patient martyr, screamed abuse at the preacher, John Scory, soon to be bishop of Rochester, and continually made the sign of the gallows in his direction. If Cranmer was embarrassed, Foxe was scandalized by an act which left the regime with blood and ashes on its hands, and his disapproval was only thinly disguised in *Actes and Monuments*, not least in the somewhat ambivalent obit he gave to the man Henry VIII had called, jocularly, the greatest heretic in Kent, Thomas Cranmer.[32]

Joan of Kent had been a busy proselytizer at court, and claimed to have a thousand disciples in London. But an altogether more serious threat to the integrity of the Protestant cause was posed by the Freewillers, whose territory seems to have spanned the Thames estuary, from north Kent to Essex, especially since, unlike Joan, they could not stand accused of any whopping great heresies, but only of denying predestination and asserting the contrary doctrine of human free will, with which went a no-nonsense moralism which suggests a Lollard inheritance. From the point of view of Cranmer, these were separatist sectarians, who advocated a severe strategy of shunning any of whom they morally disapproved. But from where one of their leaders and publicists Henry Hart was standing, it was the predestinarians who were the dividers and sheep-stealers, distracting the faithful brethren in their conventicles with over-academic and literally demoralizing doctrine. Hart told a conventicle meeting in Faversham that learned men were the cause of great errors (it was said to be a 'generall affirmation' in these circles that predestination was 'a dampnable doctryne'), and said more of the same in a book which he managed to get published, *A godly newe short treatise instructyng euery parson, hove they shulde trade theyr lyues* (1548). Cranmer was alarmed that the first master of Maidstone Grammar School, Thomas Cole, was of this persuasion, and Cole was

---

[32] Davis, 'Joan of Kent'; *Letters and Papers*, xviii (2), 291, 312–14, 331; Huggarde, *The displayinge of the protestantes*, f. 45; MacCulloch, *Thomas Cranmer*, 424, 474–8. Foxe's frank criticism of Cranmer for the execution of Bocher and the other Edwardian radical to be burned at the stake, George van Parris, first appeared in the *Rerum gestarum* of 1559 but was subsequently softened. (MacCulloch, *Thomas Cranmer*, 475–6.) In later editions, Foxe reported, in a manner with which readers of this chapter will become familiar, that Bocher and Parris 'died for certain articles not necessary here to be rehearsed.' (MacCulloch, *Tudor Church Militant*, 197.)

leant on to repudiate the Freewilling doctrine and divisive separatism, which he duly did in *A godly and frutefull sermon, made at Maydstone ... against the opinions of the anabaptistes and others* (1553).³³ Tom Freeman suggests that by the end of Edward VI's reign, Freewilling gatherings 'had evidently blossomed into congregations comparable to their "orthodox" Protestant rivals in size, geographical distribution and cohesion'.³⁴

Such was the distinctly confused religious scene on which the Marian regime and its local functionaries, clerics like Nicholas Harpsfield and justices like Sir John Baker of Cranbrook, launched their indiscriminate drive against heresy, any heresy. Finally, the story of the Kentish martyrs is worth retailing because of what it tells us about how Foxe obtained his information, how he was able to put some flesh on the bare bones of the official record and, when necessary, to massage and manipulate the evidence. To discover what Foxe was told, when and by whom, and what he chose to do or not do with the material supplied is another valuable avenue for the exploration of the religious tensions in this part of England in the Marian episode and its aftermath.

Prolegomena aside, let us get on with the story. It was the high summer of 1555 and the Kentish proto-martyr was young Christopher Wade of Dartford. To interrogate his story, as told to Foxe and by Foxe, takes us at once into this labyrinth which was the Kentish religious scene in the mid-sixteenth century. It is one of the most circumstantially vivid narratives in the whole of the *Actes and Monuments*. Wade was transported out of Dartford town to 'the common place of the execution of felons' in a cart which also carried the stake and many bundles of reeds, while 'broom-faggots' and larger timber were also assembled; 'unto which place resorted the people of the country in great numbers, and there tarried his coming, insomuch that thither came divers fruiterers with horse-loads of cherries, and sold them.' Soon the sheriff and other gentlemen arrived, escorting both Wade and Margery Polley of Tonbridge, singing psalms. Margery was to be burned at Pembury the next day. She shouted across to Wade: 'You maye reioice, Waide, to see suche a companie gathered to celebrate youre marriage this day.' This was to be a spiritual marriage, for Wade already had a wife who had

---

³³ Thomas Freeman, 'Dissenters from a dissenting Church: the challenge of the Freewillers, 1550–1558', in *The Beginnings of English Protestantism*, ed. Peter Marshall and Alec Ryrie (Cambridge, 2002), 129–56. See also D. Andrew Penny, *Freewill or Predestination: The Battle Over Saving Grace in Mid-Tudor England* (Woodbridge, 1990). Champlin Burrage printed some of the documentation from which I quote in *The Early English Dissenters* (Cambridge, 1912), ii, 1–8. I owe the notion of 'sheep-stealing' to C.J. Clement, *Religious Radicalism in England, 1535–1565* (Carlisle, 1997).

³⁴ Freeman, 'Dissenters from a dissenting Church', 132.

made him a new shirt for the occasion. Wade came to the stake, kissed and embraced it, and stepped into a barrel of pitch fetched from the local beacon. A smith fastened him to the stake with an iron hoop and staples. A friar appeared in an improvised pulpit and began to preach. Wade exhorted the people to Beware the Whore of Babylon, and when the sheriff told him to shut up and die patiently, he retorted 'I am, I thanke God, quiet Maister Sheriffe! and so trust to die.' The friar withdrew 'and went away down to the town'. As the reeds began to burn, and the fire was 'throughly kindled', Wade continued to testify even when he could no longer speak, 'holding hys bandes up over his head together towards heauen, even when he was dead and altogether rosted'.[35]

What is important is what Wade was reported to have said while he could still utter, and how we happen to have a record of his words. He admonished the crowd not only to flee Babylon but 'to imbrace the doctrine of the gospel preached in king Edward his daies'. Foxe knew none of this, even as late as 1576 when he published the third Elizabethan edition of *Acts and Monuments*. (The full story appeared only in 1583.) Thanks to internal evidence we can be more precise. The account of Wade's martyrdom reached Foxe between 1576 and 1581. His informants were eyewitnesses of the event, Richard Fletcher, vicar of Cranbrook, and his son Richard, who would end his days as bishop of London, but when Foxe was supplied with the Wade narrative was minister of Rye in Sussex. The younger Fletcher, who was probably the author of the account, was nine years of age when he saw Wade burn. At the age of 41, as dean of Peterborough, he would see the head of Mary Queen of Scots struck from her shoulders at Fotheringhay. In between, Fletcher had buried hundreds of his parishioners, victims of two onslaughts of the plague in Rye: an expert, we might say, in ways of dying in the sixteenth century. He had a speedy and merciful end himself. Sitting in his chair, taking tobacco, he told his favourite servant: 'Oh boy, I die.'[36]

Why were the Fletchers anxious that their version of Wade's

---

[35] *AM*, 1679–80. Until 1583, this was the entirety of Foxe's information about Wade: 'As touching Christopher Waide, albeit I have no full certeintie where he suffred, yet most it is [*sic*] that hys martyrdom was at Dartford, about the said xix of July.' (*AM* (1570), 1859.) In 1583 Foxe placed the executions of Wade and the bricklayer Nicholas Hall no more precisely than 'in the month of July'. The signification of the relaxation of Wade, Hall and Margery Polley to the secular arm is dated 7 July. (PRO, C/85/144.33.) Were these then the first Kentish executions (carried out, of course, in the diocese of Rochester), preceding by a day or two those of John Bland, John Frankesh, Nicholas Sheterden and Humfrey Middleton on 12 July?

[36] Collinson, 'Cranbrook and the Fletchers', 420–22.

martyrdom should appear in *Acts and Monuments*, and why so late in the piece, when we know that the vicar of Cranbrook had supplied Foxe with other material before 1570?[37] In the 1570s there was a religious storm in the Cranbrook teacup. Fletcher was opposed by the radical Puritan preacher and printer John Strowd and his supporters, who would later bring to Cranbrook the intellectual hope of Elizabethan Puritanism, Dudley Fenner. Fletcher was a conformist, a client of Archbishop Parker who wore the surplice and ministered the sacrament to kneeling communicants. Strowd, who arrived in Cranbrook in 1575, was a renegade and a provocation by his mere presence, and soon his anti-establishment preaching stirred up a hornet's nest. When Fletcher attempted to defend conformity from the pulpit he was shouted down. People said: 'The vicar of Cranbrook proposeth but God disposeth.' The younger Fletcher was brought in from Rye to shore up his father's crumbling credibility, and he got into a hot dispute with Strowd's lieutenant, the schoolmaster Thomas Good. This was why the Fletchers decided to tell Foxe the Christopher Wade story. Their (supportive) presence at the execution was proof of their Protestant credentials in the dangerous days of Queen Mary. Moreover their testimony alleged that Wade had died affirming the religion of the Edwardian Prayer Book which was under attack in Cranbrook in the late 1570s.[38]

This tells us how far we have travelled in our appreciation of Foxe. In the nineteenth century he was accused of making it all up. In the mid-twentieth century he was rehabilitated as a dependable, archivally based historian. Now we know much more about how his history was accumulated and shaped, both by his informants and by the author himself. The Kentish persecution appears to have consisted of two main phases, separated by nine months of remission through much of 1556. There were 29 victims between June 1555 and April 1556, 25 between January and June 1557 and, after a second pause in the repressive process, 5 on 10 November 1558. Many of the earlier batch, like Christopher Wade, appear to have had 'orthodox' Edwardian Protestant credentials, while some of the later martyrs were located to the left (as we would say) of mainstream Protestantism, perhaps because the inquisitory process was only then digging into the endemically heretical subsoil of the Kentish Weald. Foxe relates the second wave of burnings to what he calls a 'terrible proclamation', or 'Bloudy Commission', issued by Philip and Mary on 8 February 1557, which he prints in full.[39]

---

[37] Thomas Freeman, 'Notes on a Source for John Foxe's Account of the Marian Persecution in Kent and Sussex', *Historical Research*, lxvii (1994), 204.

[38] Collinson, 'Cranbrook and the Fletchers', 416–22.

[39] *AM*, 1970. In 1563 (1561–63), Foxe was more specific about the proclamation

However, he wants us to know that while the 'inquisitors'[40] were thus armed with new authority, Richard Thornden (in Foxe 'Thornton'), the suffragan bishop of Dover, and Nicholas Harpsfield, archdeacon of Canterbury, hardly needed such a proclamation 'to stir up the coles of their burning crueltie ... who of their owne nature were so furious and fierye against the harmles flocke of Christ'.[41]

This requires us to determine, if we can, who was responsible for the Kentish holocaust, almost unique in England for the scale of the persecution. The embarrassing fact is that nobody seems to know. The latest biographer of the Cardinal Archbishop of Canterbury, Reginald Pole, encounters many problems in his exploration of the personal role of someone who had been on both ends of the inquisitorial process, but he seems to concur with Foxe, who let Pole off lightly.[42] But the symbolism of so many *autos da fe* in Pole's metropolis leaves us with a few questions. Foxe utterly incriminates Thornden and Harpsfield, and he puts Harpsfield on the same point on the Richter Scale of evilly motivated repression as Bloody Bishop Bonner.[43] Harpsfield has been rescued from this vilification by several historians, including Bishop Mandell Creighton.[44] David Loades remarks that the scrupulously detailed account of the visitation of his archdeaconry in 1557 (a scribal gem) 'makes scarcely a mention of heresy, but picks up every missing chalice and altar cloth, every leaking roof and missing patronal saint.'[45] The editor of the visitation, L.E. Whatmore, and Eamon Duffy, both note that this document contains no evidence of an anti-heretical vendetta, rather of a process the object of which was to achieve compliance and conformity without violence.[46]

But on many occasions suspected heretics were referred by Harpsfield to the royal commission dealing with such cases at Canterbury, of which

---

(which does not appear in Hughes and Larkin's *Tudor Royal Proclamations*), supplying the date. Those addressed in the document were all lay magistrates/commissioners. While primarily directed against seditious and heretical publications, it required the recipients 'to enquyre and search out all such persons as obstinately do refuse to receiue the blessed sacrament of the aultar, to heare masse, or come to their parish churches'.

[40] A term justified by John Edwards, 'A Spanish Inquisition? The Repression of Protestantism Under Mary Tudor', *Reformation and Renaissance Review*, no. 4 (2000), 62–74: 'It was certainly an Inquisition, but it was not particularly Spanish.'
[41] *AM*, 1978.
[42] Thomas F. Mayer, *Reginald Pole, Prince and Prophet* (Cambridge, 2000), 272–83.
[43] *AM*.
[44] In the (old) *Dictionary of National Biography*.
[45] Loades, *The Reign of Mary Tudor*, 343–4.
[46] *Archdeacon Harpsfield's Visitation, 1557*, ed. L.E. Whatmore, Catholic Record Society, xlv (1950), 1, 77, 118, 145, 208, 209, 244, 250; Duffy, *The Stripping of the Altars*, 560.

he was also a member, wearing another hat, and, occasionally, to Cranbrook, the seat of the most active and powerful of the lay justiciary in Kent with an interest in repression, Sir John Baker, who kept his own gaol in the room above the church porch.[47] We do not know how active Harpsfield may have been on the commission, and Foxe may not have totally misrepresented his role. Foxe told a good story about the death of Bishop Thornden. He was watching his servants playing bowls when he had a stroke. Carried to bed, he was asked whether he believed in God. 'Yea, so I doe ... and my Lord Cardinall to[o].'[48] How Foxe would have enjoyed being able to tell a similar story about Harpsfield. But the archdeacon lived on until 1575, making use of the Fleet Prison to publish some devastating criticism of Foxe, of which the martyrologist was obliged to take account in his later editions.[49]

Harpsfield's *Visitation*, and other sources, do tell us how heretics were exposed and identified. Those at risk of detection included any who did not wear beads, those who refused holy bread, or failed to kiss the pax, singing men who had withdrawn their services from the parish choir, and those who were absentees from church, or who failed to behave with suitable devotion while in church, especially at the moment of the elevation of the consecrated elements, or who sat in their seats when they ought to have been joining in procession.[50] Such was Thomasine Asshenton of Westgate, Canterbury, who, when she failed to join the procession which preceded Mass was told by a certain Richard Baker: 'Well, Asshendens wife, thow was an heretique before that thow camest hither, and will be an heretike still ... You would have been burnt for your heresye vii yeres agoon.' It says something for Mrs Asshenton's civil courage, or for her desperation, that she took Baker to court for his slanderous words.[51] Perhaps she was merely suffering from arthritis.

The best of all Foxe's good stories concerned a Kentish justice called Drainer, whom in 1563 he named 'Justice Nine Holes' (as he was known in his own cabbage patch), since he had allegedly bored nine holes in the

---

[47] *Archdeacon Harpsfield's Visitation*, 77, 120, 123, 127, 129, 177, 183, 186, 229. For 'Baker's Jail', see William Tarbutt, *Annals of Cranbrook Church*, i (Cranbrook, 1870), 11–14.

[48] *AM*, 2099.

[49] See above, n. 10.

[50] *Archdeacon Harpsfield's Visitation*, 25, 27, 53, 68, 77, 118, 129, 135, 185, 201, 203, 206, 227, 247, 250; C.E. Woodruff, 'Extracts from Original Documents Illustrating the Progress of the Reformation in Kent', *Archaeologia Cantiana*, xxxi (1915), 106–7. Ways of indicating a lack of reverence for the elevated Host included holding down the head and hiding behind a pillar.

[51] Kent Archives Office, Canterbury, Archdeaconry of Canterbury Acta, X.10.6., fols 122v–6r.

rood loft through which, while Mass was proceeding, he could spot those who failed to hold up their hands at the elevation. When this appeared in print, Drainer stormed into the printing shop of Foxe's publisher John Day, demanding to speak to Foxe, and, finding only Day at home, said: 'You have printed me false in your broke.' He had made only five holes and the parson had made the rest. Day was able to tell him that it was all over London that at supper in Cheapside Drainer had boasted that he made his holes 'rather to looke upon fayre wenches than otherwise'. Naturally Foxe printed this too, in his next edition.[52] What this evidence, most of what we have, cannot tell us is whether the dog was wagging its tail, or the tail the dog. Were the martyrs grassroots martyrs, betrayed in one way or another by their neighbours, neighbours like Richard Baker of Westgate? Or were their prosecutions and convictions motivated and promoted from above, a true inquisition?

Those detected as being of a heretical disposition by some such means would be asked, before the commission, why they were absent from church, or whether they believed with the Church in the real presence of Christ's body and blood in the consecrated elements of the Mass. The likelihood is that most, at this point, submitted and conformed, swelling the numbers of those John Calvin called Nicodemites.[53] Our Kentish martyrs were the products of a winnowing process. The repression had begun high-profile, with a long process involving John Bland of Adisham, an impeccably orthodox Edwardian and a Cambridge man, a northerner from Sedbergh and an ex-religious who had been tutor to the future Archbishop Edwin Sandys at St John's College and perhaps to Archbishop Edmund Grindal too.[54] The trial lasted from Bland's first appearance before Archdeacon Harpsfield in May 1554 until his execution, over a year later. It was a sensational case with on one occasion standing room only in the Canterbury chapter house. As a foreigner (some took him to be a Scot), Bland had had the kind of impact which a trueborn Man of Kent could perhaps not have made, but he also had many enemies, who included one of his own churchwardens. With Bland were burned John Frankesh, vicar of Rolvenden, the only other clerical victim of the persecution in Kent, and two laymen, Nicholas Sheterden and Humfrey Middleton: 'two stakes, but all in one

---

[52] AM, 2111–12. The original story had appeared in 1563 (1703) as 'A note of a cruell iustice in Kent'.

[53] Andrew Petregree, *Marian Protestantism: Six studies* (Aldershot, 1996).

[54] The nature and likely duration of Bland's tutorial relationship to Sandys and Grindal is clarified in my articles on the two archbishops in the *Oxford Dictionary of National Biography* (2004). And see Tom Freeman on Bland in the *ODNB*.

fire together'.⁵⁵ We shall never know whether those in charge were aware of the irony of this scene, enacted on 12 July 1555, a week or two after Wade's execution at Dartford. For Sheterden and Middleton were two of the most prominent Freewillers, with whom the likes of Bland had been in fierce contention.⁵⁶ Since all four had denied the Real Presence in the sacrament, they may have been lumped together in the official mind. But if it could be shown that Bland and Sheterden were tied to one stake, Frankesh and Middleton to the other, that would have made an intentionally symbolical point.

Another of the 1555 victims, John Newman – a pewterer of Maidstone who was unlucky to be picked up and burned at Saffron Walden in Essex on 31 August – recorded a confession of faith of impeccable orthodoxy, specifically sound on the Trinity. Attempts to implicate him in the Melchiorite heresy that Christ did not take flesh of his mother were a failure. In an affirmation submitted to Bishop Thornden of Dover, Newman wrote that 'for the space of all the tyme of kyng Edwards raigne, we were diligently instructed with continuall Sermons, made by suche men, whose fayth, wisdome, learning, and vertuous liuyng, was commended unto all men under the kyngs hand and seale, and under the handes of the whole Counsaile.' All this we should more or less expect, since John had had the ways and means to make himself scarce, and was the brother of Roger Newman, a leading man in Maidstone who was one of those who chose to spend Mary's reign in Calais.⁵⁷

'About the latter end of August' were burned, the first holocaust in Canterbury, six men who were apparently part of the spin-off of the Bland case. All that Foxe tells us of these six suggests unexceptionally Protestant opinions. William Stere of Ashford said that he still considered Thomas Cranmer, then in prison in Oxford, to be his diocesan, denying that the bishop of Dover had any jurisdiction in the case.⁵⁸ Much the same seems to have been true of the next three Canterbury victims, burned in about November 1555, 'three other stout

---

⁵⁵ *AM*, 1665–73. The whole story had originally appeared in 1563 (1217–30) but in 1570 and subsequent editions the date of the execution was corrected from 12 June to 12 July.

⁵⁶ Freeman, 'Dissenters from a dissenting Church'. Dr Freeman's forthcoming edition for the Church of England Record Society, of the 'Letters of the Martyrs' (from the MSS in Emmanuel College Cambridge) will include letters to Sheterden from such prominent predestinarians as John Bradford and John Careless.

⁵⁷ *AM*, 1686. Tom Freeman wishes to emphasize the importance of Roger Newman, as revealed in the networking of the 'Letters of the Martyrs' (Emmanuel College Cambridge, MSS 260, 261) which he is editing.

⁵⁸ *AM*, 1688–9.

and bold souldiours', including the only gentleman martyr burned in Kent, John Webbe; and a certain George Roper (could he have belonged to Sir Thomas More's family-in-law?), a young man of a fresh colour, courage and complexion (the others were 'somewhat more elderly'), who made quite a splash as he came to the stake, fetching 'a great leap'. 'So soone as the flame was about hym, the said Roper put out both hys armes from hys bodye lyke a Rood, and so stood stedfast, continuyng in that maner, not pluckyng his armes in, tyll the fire had consumed them, and burnt them of.'[59] This is a good example of the true courage, or *apatheia*, with which the martyrs were reported to have faced their extinction.[60]

One of Foxe's stars was the Frittenden miller, Edmund Allin, burned at Maidstone on 18 June 1557, part of the next and noticeably more heterodox Wealden batch, but so far as we can tell not himself a radical in that sense. The bulk of Foxe's information about Allin came to him between the 1563 and 1570 editions and was supplied by Richard Fletcher of Cranbrook and John Webbe of Frittenden. It makes one of the most idealized and misty-eyed of Foxe's stories. Godly, even honest, millers are rare enough in English cultural memory, but Allin sold his corn to his neighbours at half price during a time of scarcity and 'also fedde them wyth the foode of life, reading to them the scriptures and interpreting them'. Asked by the fiercely orthodox magistrate, Sir John Baker, by what authority he preached and interpreted ('let me see thy licence'), Allin's response was memorable: 'I am persuaded that God hath geven me this authority, as he hath geven to all other Christians. Why are we called Christians, if we do not folow Christ, if we do not read his Law, if we do not interpret it to others that have not so much understanding.' We are, said Allin, 'liuely stones to give light to other. For as out of flint stones coometh foorth that that is able to set al the world on fire, so out of Christians shoulde springe the beames of the Gospell, which should inflame; al the world.' Allin and his wife had escaped from prison thanks to a negligent (or sympathetic) jailer who had taken them to the pub and had forgotten to bring them back, and

---

[59] Ibid., 1794. Some of these details had been lacking in 1563 (1386–7), which suggests that Foxe's usual Kentish informants had again been prompted to supply further material.

[60] Patrick Collinson, 'Truth and Legend: The Veracity of John Foxe's Book of Martyrs', in his *Elizabethan Essays* (London and Rio Grande, Ohio, 1994), 174–5; Patrick Collinson, '"A Magazine of Religious Patterns": An Erasmian Topic Transposed in English Protestantism', in his *Godly People*, 511–13; Patrick Collinson, 'Truth, lies, and fiction in sixteenth-century Protestant historiography', in *The Historical Imagination in Early Modern Britain*, ed. Donald R. Kelley and David Harris Sacks (Cambridge, 1997), 65–6.

with John Webbe they had made their way to the cave of Adullam of Calais. But, troubled in conscience, Allin had returned to Kent to face the music. Foxe learned some of the details of this story too late to integrate them into the main narrative.[61]

Foxe's late informant was a Maidstone man, Roger Hall. Hall's sister, Alice Benden of Staplehurst, had been burned at Canterbury on 19 June 1557, one of seven consumed by the same fire. In 1563 Foxe had known nothing beyond her name and the date of the execution. But by 1570 he was able to publish one of the most affecting of his stories, the 'imprisonment and tragical handling' of Alice. It was a story with, as historians now have to say, a gender dimension, for it was Alice's conforming husband who betrayed her to the authorities, who imprisoned her in appalling conditions in Canterbury, and it was her father who sent her to prison with a shilling of Philip and Mary, a bent shilling, perhaps to denote that she was no longer any daughter of his. (Anne Askew, Joan Bocher, Alice Benden: these martyrs are surely trying to tell us something about the status and experience of daughters and wives in early modern England.[62]) At the stake Alice took off a piece of white lace from around her middle and asked that it be given to her brother Roger (no keepsake for her husband), and that the shilling be returned to her father.[63] Hall sent this material to Foxe some time between 1563 and 1570.[64]

We know nothing about Alice Benden's religious beliefs: only that she obstinately refused to attend church 'because there was much idolatry committed against the glory of God'. But since she had good family connections, and a husband who was, we are told, one of 'the welthy men of Stapleherst', we may suspect that she was, like the Allins, an 'orthodox' Protestant in the Edwardian sense. We know a little more about the martyrs who had been incinerated on the King's Meadow at Maidstone the day before, 18 June 1557, whom we may call the Maidstone Seven. They included the Frittenden miller Edmund Allin and his wife, Walter Appleby of Maidstone, and four women, including a 'vertuous maiden', Joan Bradbridge,[65] and 'a blind maiden', Elizabeth

---

[61] *AM*, 1979–80. For how, between 1563 and 1570, Foxe was supplied with such further details of the Allin story as his escape from custody to Calais, and his return, see Freeman, 'Notes on a Source', 204–5, 211.

[62] See my 'What Are the Women Doing in Foxe's "Book of Martyrs"?', in *Women of the Atlantic World*, ed. Emily Clark and Mary Laven (forthcoming).

[63] *AM*, 1980–82. In 1570 the story occurs at 2167–9. Only the barest facts were available to Foxe in 1563 (1571).

[64] Freeman, 'Notes on a Source', 205–6.

[65] Bradbridge was probably the widow either of George Bradbridge, who had been burned at Canterbury on 6 September 1555, or of Matthew Bradbridge of Tenterden,

Lewes, whom everyone knew as 'Blinde Besse'. Roger Hall sent Foxe a vivid detail of what had happened at the King's Meadow. Joan Bradbridge and Elizabeth Lewes must have been friends. Joan asked the onlookers what the time was and, when told that it was ten o'clock cried: 'Thanks be to God! Bye eleven we shalbe [with] our God.' Turning to Elizabeth she said: 'Now sister Besse be of goodcher. Thou dyd never see, but soone yow shalt see Lord Jesus Cryst.' Poor Bess left the world with her only recorded utterance: 'I trust so.'[66]

Why did Foxe make no use of this story, nor of the other side of the same piece of paper which we find in his files, carrying a letter from Roger Hall's brother John, a local Maidstone worthy of some distinction, a surgeon, a founder of Maidstone Grammar School and a religious poet?[67] Our suspicions are aroused by what Foxe tells us about the schedule of heresies for which the Maidstone Seven were condemned: 'It differeth not much from the usuall maner expressed before, page 1585, neither did their aunsweares in effect much differ from the other that suffered 'under the same Ordinarie in the foresaid dioces of Canterburie.'[68] When Foxe says something like that we are entitled to suspect that he has something to hide, and so it appears from John Hall's letter, of which Foxe made no use in *Acts and Monuments*.

Hall had written to complain about a certain John Day, a vicar of Bray who had been curate of Maidstone at the time of the 1557 holocaust and was still curate of Maidstone when Hall wrote to Foxe in 1566 – and on into the 1570s, when Richard Fletcher of Cranbrook was one of his outspoken critics.[69] Day had attempted to preach a sermon on that fatal day in the King's Meadow, and when the martyrs shouted him down he had turned to the people to say: 'Good people, ye ouyght not in any wyse to pray for these obstinat heretykes, for loke how ye shall se ther bodyes burne here with materiall fyre, so shall ther damnable

---

burned in January 1557; most probably of the latter, since she was said to have been pregnant. (*AM*, 1980–81, 1708, 1970.) Tom Freeman tells me that George Bradbridge (or Brodebridge) of Bromfield probably lived and died a Freewiller.

[66] BL, MS Harley 416, fols 123–41v; Freeman, 'Notes on a Source', 210. Foxe's files contain the original sentence against the Maidstone Seven, pronounced on 14 June 1557 by Bishop Thornden of Dover, in the presence of Archdeacon Harpsfield, Francis Baker, notary public, Thomas Royden, Thomas Handley and George Clarke. (BL, MS Harley 590, fols 78v–9r.)

[67] John W. Bridge, 'John Hall of Maidstone: A Famous Surgeon of the Sixteenth Century', *Archaeologia Cantiana*, lxiii (1951), 119–21.

[68] *AM*, 1979. Foxe intended to refer the reader to the articles administered to John Bland 'and likewise to the rest folowyng after him'. The reference is in fact incorrect and should be to 1672. In 1570 (2165) Foxe had correctly cross-referenced to the Bland articles at 1852.

[69] Collinson, 'Cranbrook and the Fletchers', 405.

soules burne in the unquenchabel fyre of hell everlastynge.' He repeated his denunciation of the Seven in his sermon the following Sunday. But Day's pigeons came home to roost when Maidstone's Protestant elite, including the Halls and Roger Newman, returned from internal and external exile. Forced to clear himself from the pulpit, Day confessed that he could hardly remember what he had said on that terrible day, 'by meanes of the flame of the fyre and the great smoke that the wynde browght so violently towardes me'. 'But this I know,' he went on, 'that some of them did deny the humanity of Christe and the equalitie of the Trinitie and no man dowbteth but such ar heretykes.' Now as Day and all reasonably educated people knew, whether or not it was heresy to deny the real presence in the sacrament of the altar, and to be absent from church on account of that denial (the ostensible reason why most Marian martyrs perished), it was certainly heresy to deny the Trinity and the nature of Christ as defined by the Council of Chalcedon. That had been heresy for a thousand years.

But the Halls were not having this. As Day made his habitual exit from the church in the direction of the alehouse, they intercepted him. Which of the Maidstone Seven had denied the humanity of Christ, or the equality of the Trinity? The intimidated Day 'stode still and paused as one astonied', but at last confessed that none of them had held such opinions. '"Dyd yow", quod he, "never lye in yowr lyves? Ar ye not men? Ye seme", sayd he, "to be justyfiers of yowr selves and hipokrytes."' And having to his own satisfaction categorized the Halls as hypocritical Puritans, Day proceeded to the pub, 'whych he so much frequentyth that he veray often goyth home dronke, scant able to speak or stande on his legs'. The Halls intended to formalize their complaints to Archbishop Parker. They also besought God 'in his mercie to delyver us' from Day, and hoped that Foxe would come to their rescue.[70]

Foxe made no use of John Hall's letter, and it is not hard to see why. Even the suspicion that any of the Maidstone Seven might have been radical anti-trinitarian heretics was too hot a potato to handle. For Foxe had in his possession evidence that several of the later victims of the persecution in Kent did indeed hold opinions which the Council of Chalcedon would have declared to be anathema. These were not transcripts from Archdeacon Harpsfield's register. They are the originals, torn out of the register, and, since the foliation is not continuous, we have to suspect that there were pages still more incriminating which Foxe chose to destroy, expunging them altogether from the historical record.[71]

---

[70] BL, MS Harley 416, fols 123–4v; Freeman, 'Notes on a Source, 209–10.
[71] BL, MS Harley 421, fols 92r–3r (Philpot), 94r (Prowtyng), 94v (Symmes), 94v–5r (Kynge), 101–3 (Fishcocke).

These are grave charges. On what do they rest? We need to pay close attention to Foxe's cross-references. In summarizing the opinions of these martyrs, he refers us to an earlier page where we find the articles objected to by John Bland of Adisham. There were only seven of these, relating to standard Protestant positions on the service said in Latin, on transubstantiation and on communion in one kind. But Foxe tells us that the Canterbury Ten were charged not with seven but with twenty articles, 'conteining such like matter as served to the mainteinaunce of the Romish See'.[72] This should alert us to what was going on.

Of the martyrs condemned and executed between January 1557 and November 1558, some affirmed in their trials orthodox Protestant convictions: among them John Philpot of Tenterden, who was burned at Canterbury on 10 January 1557.[73] Philpot believed 'Christ to be God, and the holly gost to be god and god the father'. But William Prowtyng, a sawyer of Thornham who was able to sign his name, and who died on the same occasion after confessing to his judges that he had stayed away from church because he objected to the service in a foreign tongue and the doctrine of transubstantiation, went on to affirm

> that yt ys no artycle of our fayth that there ys one God and three persons but one god almyghty in whom he belevyth ... he belevyth and sayth that christe ys not allmyghty of hym selfe but receyved all poowre of hys father and ys made god over all things unto us. And sayth that a was not god of the sayd substance of god fro the beginnynge. And as for the holly ghoste, he sayth that he belevyth he ys the spyryt of god the father only gevyn to the sonne, and not god of hyme selfe.

John Symmes of Brenchley (not, so far as we know, a martyr) denied that Christ was consubstantial, 'God fro the begynnynge ... He belevyth the father the wurde and the holly ghost ys one god but not three persons.' Robert Kynge of East Peckam (who also seems to have saved his skin) said that he would believe that Christ was consubstantial if anyone could show him the word consubstantial in the Bible, 'or els not'. And if anyone could show him in scripture that there are three persons and one God he would believe it, 'Or else not ... Item he sayth he doubtyth whether yt can be provyd be scripture that the holleghost ys god or no.'

The evidence relating to John Fishcocke of Headcorn (another signer) is confused, but of particular interest. Fishcocke professed the radically separatist views associated with the Freewillers, of whom he was perhaps one: 'He saith he will not communicate with an advouterer [adulterer] nor a covetous parson that first was a brother in crist nether will he pray

---

[72] *AM*, 1970.
[73] Ibid.

with him nether salute him.' He 'thought not to eate nor drincke' with adulterers, fornicators and worshippers of images. Fishcocke seems to have been a radically alienated person. Back in the reign of Henry VIII as a 16-year-old, he had refused to kiss the pax at Mass and had shaken his fist at the children who brought it to him.[74] Yet he told his judges that he had 'a good iudgment of the Trynytie and for any man to have any yvill opynyon therein it [sic] thincketh it yvill and ungodly.' And he endorsed the royal supremacy and condemned unauthorized preaching by laymen. At a subsequent appearance in court, Fishcocke even hedged his bets on the doctrine of the real presence:

> He doth desire to be respectuated bicause he humblye desirethe to be assertyned what my lorde cardynalles graces conscyence and ['opynyon' erased] fayth ys in the said blessed sacrament, sayings that he doth beleeve assuredlye that his grace knowethe the trewthe. And therapon did faythfullye promyse to receyve my lordes graces iudgemente in good parte and that be will beleve itt accordinglye as his grace by his letters or writinges shall advise him, in this part.

Yet this did not save his life. Fishcocke shared the same fire with Alice Benden, on 19 June 1557.[75] What did Foxe do with this evidence? 'It were too tedious exactly and particularly to prosecute the severall storie of every one of these godly Martyrs.' Let us rather concentrate on 'the cruel and unchristian handling of Alice Benden' – which was to privilege Roger Hall's anecdotes (and the story of one of the 'better sort' of martyrs) over the embarrassment of Harpsfield's register. And of the Canterbury Ten, who included Philpot and Prowtyng:

> To these articles what theyr answeres were likewise, needed no great rehearsall, seeing they all agreed together, though not in the same fourme of woordes, yet in much like effecte of purposes ... And though they did al answere uniformly in some smaller things, as theyr learning serued them, yet in the most principall and chiefest matters they did not greatly discord, etc.[76]

---

[74] *Letters and Papers*, xviii (2), 311.

[75] Ibid., 1980–81. In Harpsfield's visitation of Headcorn 'Agnes Fiscock' was one of three persons detected and ordered to be sent to Cranbrook. The other two submitted to the court, but Agnes made herself scarce, 'abiit'. (*Archdeacon Harpsfield's Visitation*, 127.) The little that we know about the Fishcockes, including the fact that Agnes could afford to leave the area, suggests that they were prominent (we might say conspicuous) parishioners. Note that no occupation was given for John Fishcocke.

[76] *AM*, 1970. Foxe cross-references to 1672 and to the articles objected 'to them of Canterbury Dioces', namely the articles administered to Bland. An acute critic, Father Robert Parsons SJ, noted Foxe's silences in handling such evidence, including his failure to document the trials of the Maidstone Seven; 'their causes, examinations, answers or condemnations'. *The third part of a treatise intituled of three conversions of England* (Douai, 1604), 509.

There can be little doubt that here Foxe is pulling the wool over our eyes, or attempting to do so. These Wealden artisans were not talking off the record about the Trinity and Christology. Were they responding to some of those 15 articles (15 more than were offered to Bland) which Foxe has chosen not to tell us about? Probably not. The numbering of the articles put to them suggest a quite different schedule. There had been attempts as early as 1543 to implicate John Bland in anti-Trinitarian heresy.[77] For some reason Harpsfield was choosing, in 1557, to go for the jugular in the trials of people who, in comparison with the vicar of Adisham, were nameless and insignificant. What might have been the motive? Genuine concern about what, even in the reign of Edward VI, had been called 'Anabaptism'? Or the need to nail copper-bottomed heresy on the Kentish dissidents?

At this point the essayist looks for a punchline, an effective way of coming to a tidy conclusion. He might be tempted to end with another of Roger Hall's good stories. Widow Bradbridge, who was one of the Canterbury Seven burned in June 1557, had two daughters, Patience and Charity. She said to the bishop (presumably Thornden of Dover) that she hoped that he would 'take and keepe Patience and Charity'. ' "Nay", quoth the Bishop, "by the faith of my bodye, I will meddle with neither of them both".'[78]

But that sounds too good to be true, and even to repeat the tale may be to collude in the hagiographical agenda of Hall and Foxe. In truth our story lacks what is nowadays called closure. Rather it is arbitrarily cut off by the death of Mary. Historians, like those they study, are the passive victims of contingency. We will never know whether the persecution in Kent would have continued if Mary had lived and had had progeny, or what might have been the character of a continuing underground Protestant Church, except that there would certainly have been one. Everything was now smothered in the blanket of the Elizabethan Settlement. 'Papists' who objected to the newly restored new religion – complaining about the removal of the rood loft and imagery, denouncing married clergy, walking out of the church in protest against an anti-Catholic sermon – these came to the attention of the ecclesiastical authorities, especially in the early days of the new dispensation.[79] But other kinds of religious dissidence disappear from the

---

[77] Bland was charged with having preached 'that the image of the Trinity is not to be suffered and he cannot find *Trinitas* throughout Scripture; but that Athanasius put it in his *Symbolum*.' (*Letters and Papers*, xviii (2), 312.)

[78] AM, 1981–2.

[79] Kent Archives Office, Canterbury, Visitation of the Archdeaconry of Canterbury 1560, MS X.1.2.

record. The Freewillers simply vanish,[80] and so too the 'Anabaptists' who were such a problem in the reign of Edward VI, and who were perhaps the same people we have found denying the Trinity and having to explain themselves on the subject of Christ's humanity. (And how had these two groups related to each other? We shall never know.) Were the awkward squad now all dead, at the stake or, like old Henry Hart, in their beds? Or were they absorbed by some sort of osmosis into a more regular Protestantism? Or like streams in limestone country did they and their beliefs flow underground, to resurface two or three generations later when, in the mid-seventeenth century, all manner of sects flourished and Cranbrook was full of Baptists?[81] We cannot say.

There is a tradition among Protestant historians, not entirely unfounded, that the persecution was counterproductive, in that for the first time it made Protestantism a popular religion. Protestants were a small minority in Colchester before Mary's reign, but the burnings in that town went down very badly, and in Elizabeth's reign it proved hard to live with the reputation of someone who had participated actively in the repression.[82] Bishop John Christopherson, writing in 1554, actually anticipated the burnings when he repudiated what was evidently already a common saying: 'twenty-thowsand wil rise of his asshes.'[83] Of our Kentish victims, John Symmes of Brenchley affirmed 'that those of late were burned be saved', and that 'yt ys agaynst scripture to burn heretykes', citing the parable of the tares; while Robert Kynge of East Peckham said that 'yt ys not lawfull to put a man, to death for hys conscience sake'.[84]

But if there had been no Foxe, no *Actes and Monuments*, would the martyrs have lived on in folk memory, as they seem to have done in Sussex, where the Pope is still burned in effigy in Lewes every 5 November? One side of our brain answers 'probably not'; the other remembers that it was the men of Kent – the Fletchers of Cranbrook, the Halls of Maidstone, Webbe of Frittenden – who supplied Foxe with most of his copy, and were determined that these stories should not be forgotten. At an early Elizabethan visitation of the archdeaconry of Canterbury, the churchwardens were asked whether any in their parish had suffered in the recent persecution. At Cranbrook, supposedly a

---

[80] Freeman, 'Dissent from a dissenting Church', 129, 146–7, 154.

[81] Collinson, 'Cranbrook and the Fletchers', 427–8.

[82] Mark Byford, 'The Birth of a Protestant Town: the Process of Reformation in Tudor Colchester, 1530–80', in *The Reformation in English Towns, 1500–1640*, ed. Patrick Collinson and John Craig (Basingstoke, 1998), 23–47.

[83] John Christopherson, *A exhortation to all menne to take hede and beware of rebellion* (London, 1554), Sig. Jiii.

[84] BL, MS Harley 421, fols 94v, 95r.

Protestant hotspot and the home of the actively zealous Sir John Baker, the wardens could only remember that 'one Hopper' had been burned (his name was William Hopper), and 'dyvers other imprisoned whose names we know not.' (We know, thanks to Foxe, that they included one John Archer, who had died in prison in Canterbury.) They seem to have forgotten about William Lowick, the other Cranbrook martyr.[85] But the chapter of Canterbury Cathedral had longer memories. Twenty years on, they awarded five shillings to John Bland 'whose father was brent, to help him withall'.[86] But by and large I think that we have to conclude that the Kentish martyrs would not have existed, in a manner of speaking, but for Foxe and those who read 'themselves both into and out of his book'.[87]

---

[85] Collinson, 'Cranbrook and the Fletchers', 403, 405; *AM*, 1970. From Elmstead it was reported 'that one John Pardeus was burnt at Canterbury.' (Kent Archives Office, MS X.1.2; fol. 23.) It is more likely that this was a mistake for Nicholas Pardue, one of the Canterbury seven burned on 19 June 1517 (*AM*, 1980–81) than that it was a new name, otherwise unknown to Foxe, or to us.

[86] Patrick Collinson, 'The Protestant Cathedral', in *A History of Canterbury Cathedral*, ed. Collinson, N. Ramsay and M. Sparks (Oxford, 1995), 165.

[87] Patrick Collinson, 'John Fox and National Consciousness', in Highley and King, *John Foxe and his World*, 10–34.

Index

Abbes, James 137
Accession Day (17 November) 236
Acworth, Thomas 63
Adamo, Anthoni de 252
Adewold, (Adthelwolde) William 84, 106
Adisham, Kent 314
Adthelstone, Thomas 106
Aguilar, Alonso de 211
Aguirre, a royal chaplain 212
Aldrich, Robert, bishop of Carlisle 37, 40
All Saints, Thornton le Moor 168
Allen, Thomas 63
Allen, William 75, 254
Allin, Edmund 325, 326
Alms giving 191
Alumbrados 5
Ampleforth Abbey 77
Anabaptism 221, 316, 331, 332
Anderson(e), Anthony 86, 106
Angel, John 248, 252
Anglican church xxiv, 232
  canons 232
Angus, Archibald Douglas, Earl of 294
Anne of Cleves 90, 96
Anti-intellectualism 245
Apatheia 325
Apostolic poverty 2
Appeals 151
Appleby, Walter 326
Archer, John 333
Arches, Court of 151, 152, 153, 155, 156, 157, 159, 160, 163, 173
Ark of the Covenant 192
Arms, College of, 96
Arthur, Prince 3
Ascham, Roger 259
Ashcombe, Devon 170
Askew, Anne 326
Askew, family 168
Askew, Sir Francis 168
Asshenton, Thomasine 322

Athee, Arthur 86, 87, 107
Atkinson, Dr Richard 64, 65
Atkyns, John 140
Attleborough, Norfolk 126
Augsburg 163
Aulton, Thomas 107
Austin, Walter 63
Aveling, Dom Hugh 78, 87, 106
Avila, Juan de 215, 216, 218, 220, 221, 222, 223
Ayala, Martin Perez de 145

Bacon, John 141
Bailey, Thomas 75
Bailly, William 294
Baker, Philip 75
Baker, Richard 322, 323
Baker, Sir John 318, 322, 325, 333
Bale, Dorothy 142
Bangor, diocese 154
Banks, John 63
Banks, Robert 61
Barlow, William, bishop of Bath and Wells 35, 41
Barnard, Thomas 61
Barnes, Thomas 59
Barret, John 125, 127, 128, 131, 133, 138, 139, 143, 145, 146
Barwyk, Robert 134
Basford, George 99
Bath and Wells, diocese 152, 154
Bautista, Juan de 215
Bayle, Pierre ix
Baylie, Stephen 107
Baynes, Ralph, bishop of Coventry and Lichfield 43, 52
Beamonde, Thomas 127
Beaufort, Lady Margaret, Countess of Richmond 3
Beaumont, Robert 63
Becerra, Cristobal 208, 211, 212
Bellin, Nicholas 96
Belysyre 74
Bemond, Thomas 130

Benden, Alice 326, 330
Benden, Roger 326
Benet Hulme, Abbey 38
Bentham, Thomas 63
Berkeley (Bartley), Gilbert 126, 128
Bernher, Augustine 61
Bible xvii, 5, 217, 238, 247, 273
    English 6, 21, 52, 219, 220, 243
    literalism 244
Bickley, Thomas 63
Biddenden, Kent 311
Bill, William 64, 75, 297
Bilney, Thomas 71
Birch, William 63
Bird, Henry 129, 136, 137
Bird, John, bishop of Chester 35, 42
Bishops Book (1537) 278
Bizzani, Peter 62
Bland, John 314, 316, 323, 329, 331, 333
Bocher, Joan 314, 316, 317, 326
Bocking, Deanery 171
Boleyn, Anne, Queen 9, 10, 11, 26, 58
Bologna 43, 191
Bonner, Edmund, bishop of London 33, 35, 39, 40, 41, 42, 48, 49, 69, 182, 185, 190, 212, 217, 229, 240, 241, 248, 250, 251, 321
    Certain Homilies 50
Bonvisi, Antonio 193, 194, 199
Bourne, Gilbert, bishop of Bath and Wells 40, 48
Bourne, Sir John 41
Bowcer, Thomas 108
Bowes, Sir Martin 190
Bowland, Humphrey 101
Boxall, John 183
Boy bishop 94
Bradbridge, Joan 326, 327, 331
Bradford, John 66, 312
Brampston, Thomas 86, 87, 90, 108
Brenchely, Kent 329, 332
Brenz, Johannes 209
Brethren of the Common Life 5
Briges (Briggs), Thomas 138
Brisley, Richard 170, 171, 174
Bristol, diocese 152, 153, 154, 171, 172
Broadbridge, Augustine 63
Bromsgrove, John 109

Brooks, James, bishop of Gloucester 40, 42, 49, 53, 68, 70, 172, 237
Browne, John 313
Browne, Richard 313
Bruerne, Richard 210
Brussels 161
Bucer, Martin 60, 68, 71, 132, 139, 211
Bucknall, Francis 89, 109
Bulkley, Arthur, bishop of Bangor 33
Bullinger, Heinrich 64, 74, 139
Bullock, George 75
Bush, Paul, bishop of Bristol 35

Caius, Dr John 72, 75
Calais xix, 312, 324, 326
Calvin, John 68, 138, 139, 218
Campion, Edmund 76
Campion, Robert 75
Campo, Almodovar del 215
Canon Law 58
Canterbury
    archdeaconry 155
    Capilla Real 201
    Christ Church 313
    diocese 152, 153, 154, 157, 158, 179, 180, 212, 310, 313, 317
Carafa, Carlo 163
Cardiff 35
Carew, Mathew 63
Carman, William 135, 136
Carr, Richard 75
Carranza, Bartolomé xvii, xx, 26, 73, 177, 178, 179, 181, 182, 183, 186, 187, 189, 195, 199, 200, 201, 203, 204, 205, 207, 208, 209, 210, 211, 212, 213, 214, 215, 216, 218, 219, 220, 221, 222, 223, 224, 260, 272, 275
    Comentarios sobre el Catechismo christiano 203, 217, 272
Carvell, Nicholas 63
Carvell, Robert 134
Castro, Alfonso de 26, 145, 201, 207, 214
Castro, Pedro de 201
Castro, Rodrigo de 204
Cathedral chapters 54
    Henrician 80
Catherine of Aragon, Queen 3, 5, 6, 7, 8, 10, 11, 18, 24, 29, 58, 206

Catherine Howard, Queen 12
Catherine Parr, Queen 12, 13, 15, 27
  Lamentations of a Sinner 13
  Prayers and Meditations 13
Catholic(s) ix, xv, xxiii, 18, 131, 146, 230, 299
  'Black Legend' xxiii
  ceremonies 198, 298, 301
  Church restored xi, xiv, 51, 57, 233, 258, 279
  finances 189
  cults 4
  English 202, 298, 302
  faith 1, 231, 235
  of Henry VIII xx, 17
  'old church' xiii, xv, xxi, 51, 253, 281, 296
  recusants xxiii, xxv
  Roman xix, xx, xxv
  triumphalism 188
  unity 186
  worship 94, 308
Cawood, John 232, 237
Cervantes, Miguel de 206
Chambers, John, bishop of Peterborough 35, 38, 40
Chancery 156, 161
Chantry Commissions (1548) 190
Chapel Royal 213
Chapman, Edmund 63
Chapuys, Eustace, Imperial ambassador 9, 10, 11, 12
Charles V, Holy Roman Emperor 11, 14, 16, 17, 46, 67, 73, 97, 208, 209, 214, 299
Chartham, Kent 314
Chedsey, William 60, 65, 74
Cheke, Sir John 63, 259
Chester, diocese 154
Chichester, diocese 152, 169, 170
Christopherson, John, bishop of Chichester 47, 48, 49, 64, 71, 131, 139, 152, 332
Chrysostom, John 248, 261
Church *passim*
  discipline 180
  fathers 238
  Militant 219
  nature 264
  Primitive 217
  'under the cross' xviii

Clement VII, Pope 166
Clergy 1, 2, 3, 25, 124, 191, 223, 251, 273
  authority 27, 28, 191
  celibacy of 2, 25
  education 55, 58
  married 19
  pluralism 164, 166, 167, 168, 170
  residence 185, 222
  selection 221
  Spanish 206
  supernatural powers 250, 251
Clerke, Thomas 86, 88, 109
Cley (al. Freestone), Peter 109
Clinton, Edward Fiennes, Lord 292
Cockrofte, Henry 63
Codde, Thomas 141, 144
Colby, Andrew 125, 128, 129
Colchester 310
Cole, Henry, Dr 65, 69, 70, 80, 194
Cole, Robert 63
Cole, Thomas 317
Cole, William 63, 75
Colet, John 2, 256
Commendone, Francesco 19
Commission, Episcopal 53
  Cromwell's 58
Common Prayer, Book of 37, 228
Conge d'elire 52
Coniers, Thomas 125
Consueta, bull 165, 166
Contarini, Gasparo 46
Convocations 51
Coo, Roger 138
Cook, Anthony 75
Cooke, Thomas 89, 109
Cooke, William 171
Cooper, Elizabeth 135, 138, 141
Cooper, Hugh 313
Copynger, William 90, 110
Corbet, John 142
Cordell, Sir William 93
Corpus Christi (1555) 211, 212
Cosyn, Edmund 64, 75
Cotes, George, bishop of Chester 42
Cotton, Robert 283
Council
  of Chalcedon 328
  of Constance 262
  of Constantinople 262
  early 238

of Ephesus 262
Fourth Lateran (1215) 164, 262, 266
of Florence 185, 262
of Nicea 262
of Trent xvii, 1, 46, 165, 177, 179, 185, 208, 215, 220, 221, 222, 261, 270, 271, 275, 277, 278
Council in the Marches of Wales 38
Counter Reformation xvi, xviii, xx, xxiv, 40, 78, 176, 177, 202, 265, 267, 275, 277, 279
Courtenay, family 21
Courts
  of audience, Canterbury 150
  church 140, 190
  of delegates 156
  deposition books 153
  prerogative, Canterbury 159
Coventri, Thomas 110
Coventry and Lichfield, diocese 156
Coverdale, Miles, bishop of Exeter 33, 35
Cox, Richard 59, 60, 61, 63, 65, 98
Cranbrook, Kent 311, 319, 322, 333
Cranmer, Thomas, Archbishop of Canterbury 10, 14, 15, 29, 34, 35, 40, 41, 42, 45, 47, 48, 50, 59, 65, 66, 67, 69, 71, 73, 81, 166, 194, 202, 209, 210, 228, 245, 260, 267, 313, 314, 317, 324
  Catechism 252
Crashfield, Richard 135, 138
Croarienis, Andrew 61
Crome, Edward 66
Cromwell, Thomas, Lord Privy Seal 11, 12, 38, 59, 142, 314
Crowley, Robert 254, 260
Croydon, Deanery 171
Cum ex eo, bull 166
Curtop, James 61
Cyril of Alexandria 266, 267

Dacre, Lord 21
Dakyn, John 157, 173
Dalbie, William 171, 172, 173, 174
Dannett, Thomas 63
Dawkes, Anthony 75
Dawkes, Robert 75

Day, George, bishop of Chichester 33, 35
Day, John, printer 323, 327, 328
Delft, Francois Van der, Imperial ambassador 15, 16
Devotio Moderna 218
'diary', of Henry Machyn 281, 286, 290, 294
Diaz, Juan Bernal de Luca 215
Dickens, A.G., xii
Dillingen, Bavaria 209
Disputation, at Oxford (1554) 41
  formal (1549) 60
Dodd, Charles xii
Douai 75
Drainer, 'Mr Justice Nine-Holes' 322, 323
Dubois, Jehan 16
Dulia 277
Dunning, Michael, Chancellor of Norwich 43, 130, 132, 134, 135, 137, 173, 174
Durham cathedral, 259
  statutes 79
Durham, diocese 33

East Peckham 329
Easte, William 85
Ebden 86, 87
Eden, Richard 89, 92, 110, 111
Edward IV 44, 313
Edward VI xiii, xiv, xxi, 12, 14, 27, 38, 41, 53, 61, 74, 77, 96, 97, 103, 126, 132, 144, 206, 232, 234, 288, 289, 292, 296, 298, 299, 303
  Church xx
  conscience 17
  funeral 18
Edgeworth, Roger 233
Egers, John 86, 87, 111
Elect, The 219
Elizabeth, later Queen xi, xiii, xv, xvi, xx, xxi, xxiii, 10, 24, 42, 47, 48, 51, 56, 73, 76, 97, 101, 127, 143, 292, 295, 296, 299
  accession 185
  Church of xiv, xix, xxiv, 43, 50, 51, 145, 331
Elles, John 83
Ely, diocese 154

Emden 132
Epidemic disease xix
Episcopate xxiv
　estates 23
　residence 184
Erasmus, Desiderius 3, 6, 52, 248, 252, 256
　Paraphrases 13, 220
Este, William 111, 112
Eternal life 278
Eton College 37
Evangelicals 12
Evesham 90
Eworth, Hans 296
Execrabilis, bull 165
Exeter, diocese 153, 154, 179
Exiles, for religion 312

Faculty Office (1534) 165, 166
Fagius, Paul 60, 62, 71
Fairchilde (Farechilde), William 87, 112
Farnese, Cardinal 161
Farrer, Robert, bishop of St Davids 34, 35, 44, 66, 194
Fasts 22
Faversham, Kent 317
Featherstone, Richard 7, 8, 9, 10
Feckenham, John xxii, 65, 77, 80, 82, 84, 87, 89, 90, 94, 95, 97, 98, 99, 100, 101, 102, 112, 113, 188
Feckenham, William 86, 87, 113
Fenner, Dudley 320
Ferdinand I, King of Aragon 208
Ferre, John 86, 87, 113
Figge, Thomas 88, 89, 113, 114
Figueroa, Don Gomex Suarez de, Count of Feria 99, 176
Filde (al. Hyde), Thomas 114
First Fruits 53
Fish, the great 288
Fishcocke, John 329, 330
Fisher, John, bishop of Rochester 3, 9, 10, 69, 72, 145, 192, 193, 194, 197, 199, 206, 259, 261, 266, 267, 268, 273
Flanders 100
Fletcher, Richard, senior 319, 332
Fletcher, Richard, junior 319, 320, 325, 327, 332
Flower, Thomas 208

Forty-two Articles 126
Foster, John 114
Fotheringay 319
Fountenay, Laurence 86, 87
Fountenay, Martin 115
Foxe, John xi, xxiii, xxiv, 28, 29, 39, 40, 46, 98, 124, 132, 135, 136, 137, 138, 140, 141, 143, 171, 172, 173, 207, 253, 256, 309, 310, 311, 313, 317, 318, 319, 320, 321, 323, 324, 325, 326, 329, 330, 331, 332
　Acts and Monuments xi, xxiv, 52, 124, 253, 309, 317, 318, 319, 320, 327, 332
France, war with (1557) 300
Francis I, King of France 11
Frankesh, John 323
Free will 5
Freewillers 317, 318, 324, 329, 332
Frensham, Edward 63
Fresnada, Bernado de 201
Frevell, George 115
Friars, 2, 23
　Carthusians 24
　Dominican xxi, 23, 24, 205, 297
　Franciscan, third order 7
　　Greyfriars 190
　Observants 24, 85, 190, 297
Frias, Martin de 215
Frittenden, Kent 311, 316, 325
Froschover, Christopher 61
Froude, J.A. xii
Fulham 212
Fuller, John 126
Fyscher (Fysher), Richard 86, 88, 116

Gage, Sir John 84
Garcina, Juan de *see* Villagarcia
Gardiner, Stephen, bishop of Winchester xx, xxi, 13, 15, 19, 27, 28, 33, 35, 36, 37, 39, 40, 41, 42, 48, 49, 53, 54, 59, 62, 64, 67, 69, 70, 80, 127, 128, 205, 217, 259, 287
　De vera obedientia 49
Gardyner 86
Gascoigne, Edward 75
Geffrey, William 172, 173, 174
George (Plantagenet) Duke of Clarence 44

Germany xxi
Gervaise, George 89
Gibson, Richard 196
Gilby, Anthony 63
Gilby, Thomas 168
Glastonbury, Abbey 84, 85
Gloucester, diocese 152, 154, 173
Glyn, William, bishop of Bangor 45, 46, 64, 65
Godly New Short Treatise, A 317
Goldwell, Thomas, bishop of St Asaph 45, 46, 52
Good, Thomas 320
Goodlooke (al. Allen), John 116
Goodman, Christopher 61, 63
Goodrich, Thomas, bishop of Ely 35, 37, 38, 39, 40, 48, 53
Grace of God 197, 269
   theology of 262
Grafton, Richard, printer 190
Granada, Luis de 215, 216, 218, 220
Greek, language 3
Green, Walter 158
Greenwich 23, 24, 85
Gregory XIII, Pope 205
Gregory the great, Pope 261
Grey (Dudley), Lady Jane 37, 57, 61
Grey, Richard 129, 294
Greyfriars Chronicle 295
Griffin, Maurice, bishop of Rochester 43
Grindal, Edmund 60, 63, 75, 323
Gropper, Johann 145
Grundge, Roger 116
Grundye 86
Gualter, Rudolph 61
Gustinian, Marian 10

Habsburg, family xxi
Haddon, Walter 65
Hales, John 19
Hales, Joyce 312
Hales, Sir James 312
Hall, Edward, his *Chronicle* 291, 293
Hall, family 328, 332
Hall, John 327, 328
Hall, Roger 326, 327, 330, 331
Hallybred, John 126
Hammon(d), William 136, 138, 141
Hampton Court 208, 288
Harband, Sir William 292

Harcocke, Edmund 140
Harding, Thomas 254
Harley, John, bishop of Hereford 35, 39
Harpesfield, John, Archdeacon of London 171, 185
Harpesfield, Nicholas, Archdeacon of Canterbury xi, xii, 65, 153, 157, 173, 194, 196, 310, 311, 315, 318, 321, 322, 323, 330, 331
   visitation 322
Hart, Henry 315, 317, 332
Hartfield, Sussex 46
Harvey, Henry 75, 171
Hastings, Sir Edward 84
Hawes, John 190
Hawford, Edward 75
Head, Mr 141
Headcorn 329
Heath, Nicholas, archbishop of York 34, 35, 36, 40, 54
Hemming, John 75
Henry II, King of France 289
Henry VII 103
Henry VIII 1, 3, 7, 8, 11, 14, 21, 24, 38, 44, 46, 53, 58, 59, 61, 74, 77, 80, 96, 101, 132, 193, 194, 202, 206, 233, 234, 242, 298, 330
   schism 192, 232
   will 15
Henshaw 74
Hereford, diocese 152, 154, 163, 171, 172
Heresy 20, 27, 28, 191, 247
   Lutheran 207, 233
Herne, Kent 316
Herniman, John 75
Heylin, Peter 91
Heys, Mr 287
Hilary of Poitiers 267
Hill, Elizabeth 131
Hingham, Norfolk 135
Hippolytus, Pope 272
Hoby, Lincolnshire 284
Hoffman, Melchior 316
Holbeach, Henry 59
Holgate, Robert 34, 35
Holyman, John, bishop of Bristol 41, 172

Homilies
    of Bonner 249
    of Cranmer 233
Hontiveros, Alonso de 205
Hooper, John, bishop of Gloucester 33, 34, 35, 37, 40, 43, 51, 53, 55, 61, 66, 207
Hopper, William 333
Hopton, John, bishop of Norwich 42, 48, 52, 130, 132, 134, 137, 173
Horn(e), Robert 75, 87
Horribilis, bull 166
Horton, Thomas 63
Hosius, Stanislaus 145
Hospitallers 161
Hovius, Mathew 177
Hoyos, Pedro de 211
Huggarde (Hogarde), Miles xviii, 199, 310
Hugh of St Victor 261
Hughes, Philip xii, xxiii
Huick, Thomas 63
Hullier, John 69
Hulme, Basil, archbishop of Westminster 77
Hulme Cultram, Abbey, Cumberland 66
Humanists 3, 72, 216, 243, 244, 248, 261, 290
Humphrey, Laurence 63, 74
Hunt(e), Ralph 86, 88, 117
Hutton, Robert 63
Hutton le Moor, Lincolnshire 168
Hyde, David de la 75

Images 13
Inhibitions 158
Innocent III, Pope 164
Innocent VIII, Pope 204
Inquisition, Spanish 203, 204, 209, 216, 223
    Roman 203
Intercession 4
Interim, Imperial 59
Ireland, William 63

Jeffrey, John 63
Jeffreys, Thomas 63
Jesuits xxii, xxiii, 55, 73, 76, 81, 176, 177, 178
Jewel, John 61, 63, 74, 172

John XXII, Pope 165
Johnson, Robert 117
Johnson, Thomas 86, 126, 127, 130
Joseph, Robert 90, 91
Josselin, Ralph 290
Julius II, Pope 166
Julius III, Pope 163, 166, 177, 209, 237
Justification
    double 218
    by Faith alone 25, 217, 219, 314

Kelke, Roger 63, 75
Kempe, John 145
Kenninghall, Norfolk 16, 138
Kent xxiii, 309, 310, 311, 312, 315, 316, 326
    martyrs of 318, 320, 321
Kentwyne, William 84, 89, 117
Kett, Robert 125, 126
    his rebellion 144
Kimbolton 11
King, Henry 125, 128, 130
King, Robert, bishop of Oxford 35, 38, 40
Kings Book, The (1543) 267, 278
Kingston on Thames 211, 212
Kirk, Hugh 63
Kitchin, Anthony, bishop of Landaff 35, 39, 40
Kling, Conrad 145
Kynborow 283
Kynge, Robert 329, 332
Kyngeswoode 117

Lakin, Thomas 63
Lambert, John 14
Lambert, Mark 89
Langham, Simon, archbishop of Canterbury 165
Langton, Cardinal 105
Latimer, Hugh 41, 48, 65, 66, 67, 71, 194, 210
Latria 277
Lay education xvi, 1
Layton, Richard 58
Legge 118
Lenham, Kent 313
Leo X, Pope 5
Letters Patent 34
Lever, John 63
Lever, Ralph 63

Lever, Thomas 63, 64
Lewkenor, Sir Richard 169
Lewes, Elizabeth 327
Lewes, Sussex 155, 170, 332
Linacre, Thomas 6
Lincoln, diocese 153, 154
   archdeaconry 155
   bishop of 259
Lindamus, Wilhem 145
Lingard, John xii
Locke, Sir William 286
Lollards 312, 313, 316, 317
Lombard, Peter, the *Sentences* 58, 210
London xvii, xxii, xxiii, 40, 54, 150, 152, 180, 181, 184, 186, 187, 193, 195, 196, 199, 205, 208, 221, 300, 304, 305, 310, 317
   aldermen 188
   Baynards Castle 294
   Bridewell 190
   Charterhouse 195
   Cheapside 195
   Christ's Hospital 190
   Chronicles 294
   civic punishments 287
   culture 282, 284, 293
   diocese 79, 85, 154, 159, 160
      Commissary Court 162
      Consistory Court 171
   Holy Trinity the Less, church 282, 293
   Newgate 288, 297
   Pauls Cross 182, 186
   Plague ('new sweat') 288, 289
   poor relief 190
   Protestant congregation xv, 295
   St Bartholomew's Hospital 190
   St Benet's Gracechurch Street 307
   St James's 188
   St Paul's 188
   St Peter's Cornhill 287
   St Thomas's Hospital 190
   Smithfield xv, 67, 196, 310
   The Tower 287, 305
London, Dr 58
Long Melford, Suffolk 138
Longden, Thomas 117, 118
Lord of Misrule 290
Louvain 194
Lowell, Thomas 118
Lowick, William 333

Loyola, Ignatius xxi, 176
Lucie 118
Ludlow, Shropshire 6
Luther, Martin 4, 68, 139, 213, 216, 218, 219, 252
Lynage, Peter 141

Machyn, Christopher 283, 286, 287
Machyn family 283
Machyn, Henry xiv, xv, 82, 95, 196, 281, 282, 285, 286, 287, 288, 290, 291, 292, 293, 294, 295, 296, 298, 300, 301, 302, 303, 304, 305, 306, 308
   London 'artisan' 307
   Merchant Taylor 308
Madden, Sir Frederick 284
Maidstone, Kent 311, 316
Maitland, S.R. xii
Maldon, Reginald 88, 118
Man, Henry, bishop of Sodor and Man 35, 39, 40
Manchester College 23
Mapstyd, Laurence 64
Margaret, Queen of Scots 294
Marriage, clandestine 275
Marillac, Francois, French Ambassador 12
Marshall, George 119
Marshall, John 254
Marshall, Richard 62, 63, 65, 74
Marsham, Thomas 141, 144
Martin, Anthony 89
Martyn, Justin 133
Mary, Blessed Virgin 1, 4, 21,
Mary of Guise, Queen of Scots 290
Mary of Hungary 12
Mary Magdalene 270
Mary, Queen xi, xiii, xiv, xv, xix, xxi, xxiv, 1, 5, 6, 7, 9, 10, 11, 12, 13, 14, 15, 16, 19, 20, 22, 23, 26, 27, 28, 29, 33, 35, 36, 39, 43, 44, 47, 48, 49, 53, 55, 56, 57, 58, 61, 76, 77, 96, 97, 103, 104, 156, 157, 169, 176, 177, 180, 183, 184, 194, 206, 207, 208, 217, 220, 221, 223, 229, 231, 232, 234, 235, 253, 258, 281, 282, 291, 292, 295, 297, 298, 300, 301, 302, 304, 305, 320, 331

conflict with Edward 303
death 307
faith xvi
legitimacy 8
portraits 296
pregnancy ('the prince') 26, 306
private chapel 20
proclamation of 18 August 1553 18
the Spanish Tudor 295
supreme head 34
wedding 20, 21
will xxii, 24
Mary Stewart, Queen of Scots 319
Mason, Sir John 62, 69, 70, 80
Mason, William 129
Mass xix, xxiv, 15, 17, 19, 22, 62, 127, 129, 134, 188, 192, 198, 212, 214, 227, 228, 229, 230, 231, 233, 235, 236, 238, 239, 240, 241, 242, 243, 244, 245, 246, 247, 250, 251, 252, 253, 255, 256, 257, 265, 273, 276, 277, 278, 279, 303, 323, 330
  clandestine xix
  elevation 227
  Latin rite 19, 255
  The Lay Folks' Mass Book 227, 229, 255
  social unity 228, 241, 252
  transubstantiation 14, 28, 55, 60, 131, 133, 140, 213, 262, 329
Mather, Alexander 140
Mathew, Thomas 119
Matilda, Queen 134
Mayhew, Anthony 63
Melanchthon, Philip 139, 252
Melchiorites 324
Memmo, Dominic 6
Mere, John 70
Mervin, John 89
Mey, John 75
Mey, Dr William 64, 75
Michieli, Giovanni, Venetian Ambassador 22, 23, 82, 83, 209
Middleton, Humphrey 135, 323, 324
Mid-Tudor culture 282
Milan 191
Mildmay, Sir Walter 100

Miller, Simon 135
Mingay, William 140
Modena 96
Monasteries xxii, 13, 23, 99, 189
  Benedictine 77
  lands 80, 189
  Monte Cassino xxii, 81
  revenues 91
  surrender (1559) 99
Mor, Antonio 296
More family 194
More, 'father' 136
More, John 193
More, Sir Thomas xvi, 1, 3, 9, 10, 24, 72, 193, 194, 196, 197, 199, 206
  Works 192
Morgan, Henry, bishop of St Davids 43,48, 53
Morison, John 158
Morley, Henry Parker, Lord 13
Morrant, Alice 136
Morwin, Peter 63, 65, 70
Moulton, John 81, 92, 93, 101
Mowse, Dr William 64, 75
Mullins, John 63
Muscovy, Grand Duke of 95
Musculus 139
Mynyvere, Thomas 86, 88, 119

Naples 46
Navarre 208
Neott, (Newte) John 84, 119
Nevinson, Christopher 314
New Learning 8
Newcastle upon Tyne, diocese of 33
Newman, John 324
Newman, Roger 324, 328
Newton, Theodore 63
Nicholls, Josias 315
Nichols, J.G. 281, 284, 286, 290
Nicodemism xviii, 143, 145, 323
Norfolk, Thomas Howard, 3rd Duke of 127, 128, 142
Northumberland, John Dudley, Duke of 18, 25, 29, 35, 61, 62, 65, 67, 194, 235, 252
Norwich xviii, 124, 150
  diocese 154, 163, 173, 174
  Mayor's court 124
  'novelty' in teaching 253

Protestants 130
St Andrews Church 126, 127, 144
St Martins at Place 129
St Mary in the Fields 137
St Peter Mancroft 126, 130
St Stephens 130
Nuns, at Kings Langley 23, 24
    at Syon 297
Nykke, Richard, bishop of Norwich 137

Obedience, canonical 197, 198, 236, 239
Ochino, Bernard 178
Oecolampadius 68
Oglethorpe, Owen, bishop of Carlisle 47, 65, 98
Opus dei 3
Order of the Garter 289
Order of St Michael 289
Ormanetto (Ormanet), Nicholas 70, 71, 73, 82, 165
Ormes, Cecily 135, 137, 138, 142
Orphinstrange, John 63
Osbourne, Peter 100
Osney, Abbey 38
Otto, Cardinal 164
Ottobono, Cardinal 164
Ottomans 11
Owersby, Lincolnshire 168, 169
Oxford, diocese 41
    Martyrs Memorial 310

Pagham, Deanery 171
Pageants xiv, 297
Palmer, Helen 158
Papacy, office x, xxiv, 8, 18, 185, 221, 237, 238, 239, 262, 263, 299
    Commissary 41
    settlement with 22
Parfew, Robert, bishop of Hereford 35, 39, 40, 45
Parish churches 189
Parker, Mathew 60, 64, 75, 126, 187, 320, 328
Parker, Thomas 146
Parkhurst, John 61, 63, 137
Parkyn, Robert 234, 237
Parliament xix, 9, 14, 16
    1553 (autumn) 34

1554 67
1559 xiii, 99
Act of Repeal (1555) 45, 103
Act in Restraint of Appeals (1533) 156
Act of Six Articles (1539) 37, 39
Act of Supremacy (1536) 33
Act of Supremacy (1559) 104
Act of Uniformity (1549) 38, 62, 74
Parry, Sir Thomas 93
Parsons, Robert xii, xxiii
Pate, Richard, bishop of Worcester 45, 48, 52
Paul III, Pope 46, 163, 167, 236
Paul IV, Pope xxi, 25, 45, 77, 80, 105, 161, 167, 204, 236
Paynell, Thomas 49, 240
Peacock, Mr 71
Peckham, John, archbishop of Canterbury 165
Pedagogium in Christum 197
Pedder, John 63
Pelham, John 63
Pembury, Kent 318
Penning, Henry 12
Pentecost 271
Percy family 21
Perne, Andrew 64, 75
Peterborough, diocese 35, 153
Petre, Sir John 75
Peto, William 25, 45, 190
Phagan, John 84, 120
Philistines 192
Philip, King of England xx, 22, 25, 26, 27, 28, 29, 46, 67, 99, 161, 176, 177, 179, 201, 202, 203, 206, 212, 213, 214, 220, 221, 224, 297, 300, 305, 320
    courtiers xxi
Phillips, Dom Hugh 97, 120
Philpot, John 42, 55, 329, 330
Physicians, College of 72
Pie, Dr 65
Piety
    popular 228, 332
    traditional 228, 230
Pilgrimages 3
Pilgrimage of Grace 12
Pilkington, James 63, 75
Pilkington, Leonard 63

Pius V, Pope xi
Plaine and Godlye Treatise, A 240, 243, 248
Plowden, Edmund 93
Pluckley, Kent 314, 315
Pole, David, bishop of Peterborough 47, 48, 52
Pole, Margaret, Countess of Salisbury 7, 8, 44
Pole, Reginald, Cardinal archbishop of Canterbury xiv, xvi, xx, xxi, xxiii, xxiv, 12, 20, 21, 24, 25, 27, 29, 36, 37, 41, 42, 44, 45, 46, 48, 49, 50, 52, 54, 55, 67, 69, 70, 72, 73, 76, 79, 104, 149, 150, 151, 154, 155, 156, 157, 159, 160, 161, 162, 163, 164, 165, 167, 169, 171, 172, 174, 176, 177, 179, 180, 181, 183, 188, 190, 191, 192, 196, 209, 212, 214, 217, 221, 222, 223, 232, 245, 255, 259, 261, 321
   Legatine Court of Appeals 159
   Legatine Court of Audience 150, 151, 153, 156, 157, 159, 160, 163
   Legatine Register 104, 151
   Legatine Synod xvi, xx, 21, 83, 164, 170, 182, 185, 232, 236, 247, 260, 268, 274, 275
   Pro ecclesiasticae defensione 193
   St Andew's day sermon xxii, 184, 187, 198, 200
   A Treatise on Justification 50
Pollard, A.F. xii
Polley, Margery 318
Ponet, John, bishop of Winchester 33, 35, 43
Poor relief 199
Pope, Sir Thomas 72
Pory, John 138
Postmodernism 282
Poullain, John 63
Praeclara charissimi, bull 77, 80, 103, 104
Prayer 263
Preaching xvi, xvii, 20, 51, 177, 178, 181, 182, 184, 185
Presse, Thomas 86, 87, 121

Prince, Edward 86, 87, 121
Printing Press 50
Priuli 22
Privy Council 16, 17, 26, 29, 40, 42, 43, 54, 97, 126, 127
Processions xiv, 300, 306
Proctor, John 234
Property, ecclesiastical xxiv, 22, 180, 199
Protectorate (1547-49) 14
Protestants xi, xv, xvi, xviii, xix, xxi, xxiii, 19, 27, 37, 49, 53, 55, 57, 59, 61, 65, 73, 126, 128, 144, 177, 192, 195, 219, 230, 242, 251, 262, 302, 303, 307, 316, 332
   dissent 311
   Gospel 199
   orthodox xiii, xxiii, 312
   persecution xii, xiii, xxiii, 43, 309, 315
   polemic xxiv, 186, 242
   policies 15, 249
   Prayer Book 15, 16, 60
   youth movement 195
Prowtyng 329, 330
Purefoy, Luke 63
Purgatory 13, 24, 68, 278
Pye, William 170
Pykeringe, William 134

Quiroga, Gaspar de 224

Ramirez, Diego 204
Randolph, Thomas 63
Rebels in Devon and Norfolk 17
Rebuffi, Pierre 167
Reconciliation 269
Redbourne, John 121
Redman, George 136
Redman, John 75
Reformation ix
Religious instruction 7, 242
Renaissance scholarship 230
Renard, Simon, Imperial Ambassador 20, 207
Reniger, Michael 63
Rescius, Anthony 73
Rewley, Abbey 38
Reynolds 74
Rhodes, Knights of 188

INDEX

Ribadeniera, Pedro 176
Richards, Thomas 158
Richmond, Surrey 180
Ridley, Nicholas, bishop of London
    33, 35, 41, 42, 43, 48, 53, 54,
    60, 64, 65, 66, 67, 71, 190,
    194, 210
Ringwoode, Austin 89
Risborough, Deanery 171
Ritual 282, 305
Rokeby, John 157
Rogers, John 40, 43, 66, 67, 207
Rogers, Richard 63
Rolvenden, Kent 323
Rome 191
    Church of 295
Roper, George 325
Rose, Thomas 125, 128, 132, 133,
    139, 141, 143
Rowle, Henry 6
Royal Commissions 33
Royal Injunctions 128
Royal Supremacy 17, 19, 37, 51, 232
Royal Visitations 34, 55
Rugge, William, bishop of Norwich
    125, 142
Rye, Sussex 319, 320

Sacraments xvii, 2, 5, 185, 186, 191,
    192, 250, 261, 276, 279
    of the altar 1, 25, 28, 29, 59, 65,
        68, 135, 136, 185, 211, 213
    baptism 265, 270, 272
    A Brief treatise 271
    confession 269
    confirmation 270
    corporeal presence 259
    De Baptismo 271
    Eucharist xvii, 59, 133, 214, 252,
        258, 264, 265, 266, 276,
        277, 278
    frequent communion 266, 267
    marriage 275, 276
    orders 274
    penance 188, 267, 268, 270
    A profitable doctrine 271
    real presence 139, 213, 243, 246,
        248, 252, 253, 323, 324
    Reformed 131, 214
    Rock of the Church 169
Sacramentals xvii, 264

Sackville, Sir Richard 100
Saffron Walden, Essex 324
Saints 4, 277
St Asaph, diocese 154
St Augustine 4, 237, 244, 261, 271,
    272
    Against the Donatists 219
St Cuthbert 21
St David's, diocese 154
St Edward the Confessor 21
    shrine of 77, 95
St Frideswide 211
St Jerome 134
St John, Austin 89
St John, Order of 23, 188
Santa Maria sopra Minerva 204
St Mary the Great, Cambridge 71
St Mary's church, Oxford 68, 69, 70
St Michael in Caslany 140
St Paul 4, 248
St Peter 263, 270
St Thomas Aquinas 8, 261, 271, 275
St Thomas of Canterbury 21
Salcot, John, bishop of Salisbury 35,
    36, 38, 39, 40
Salisbury, diocese 154, 155, 172, 173
Salisbury, John 125, 128, 131
Saltfleet, Lincolnshire 168, 169
Sampson, Richard 38, 40, 48
Sampson, Thomas 63, 74
San Quentin, battle (1557) 300
Sanders, Laurence 207
Sanders, Nicholas 74, 169, 210, 254
Sandwich, Kent 315
Sandys, Edwin 60, 61, 62, 63, 323
Sarum rite 277
Saule, Arthur 63
Saunderson, John 75
Savoy Hospital 23, 24
Say, Mr 66
Sayer, Gregory 89
Scheyfve, Jehan, Imperial ambassador
    303
Schmutz, Alexander 61
Scholasticism 245, 247
Scory, John, bishop of Chichester 33,
    35, 43, 317
Scott, Cuthbert, bishop of Chester 64
Scott, Maurice 89
Seaberte 86, 87
Seaton, (Seton) Dr John 65, 75

Sebante, Robert 121
Sebastian of Portugal 10
Second Coming, the ix
Sedbergh, Yorkshire 323
Sedgewick, Dr 65
Sedon, William 129
Selbe 122
Seminaries, diocesan 222
Seymour, Jane, Queen 12
Shelton, Sir John 142
Shene 23, 24
Sherbourne, Robert, bishop of Chichester 170
Sheterden, Nicholas 323, 324
Shorham, Deanery 171
Show trials (1554) 65
Sidall, Henry 61, 68, 69
Silva, Ruy Gomez da 211
Sin 4
Slythurst 74
Smarden, Kent 314
Smith, Dr Richard 59, 65, 68, 244, 271, 272
Somerset, Edward Seymour, Duke of 15, 59
Soranzo, Giacomo, Venetian Ambassador 21, 26
Sotherton, Richard 128
Sotherton, Thomas 141, 142, 145
Soto, Pedro de xx, 73, 201, 202, 204, 205, 208, 209, 210, 211
South Kelsey, Lincolnshire 168
South Petherwyn, Cornwall 66
Southame, Christopher 63
Southampton 23, 201
Spaniards xix, 183
　influence xx
　language 10
Sparchforde, Richard 171
Spencer, Thomas 63
Spenser, Miles 137
Spirituali 178
Spirituality, international 249
Sprowston, Norfolk 142
Stampe, William 125, 128
Standish, John 52, 255, 256
Staplehurst, Kent 311
Stapleton, Thomas 74, 169
Stephen I, Pope 272
Stere, William 324
Steventon, Berkshire 102

Stoke by Nayland, Suffolk 137
Stoughton, Thomas 315
Stow, John 190
Stratforde, John 122
Strowd, John 320
Strype, John xii, 283, 284, 286
　Ecclesiastical Memorials 283
Stumphius, John Rudolf 61
Style, Henry 88, 90, 122
Stywarde, Augustine 146
Suarez 271
Succession crisis (1553) 18
Sussex, Henry Radcliffe, Earl of 142
Sutterton, John 130
Swift, Robert 63
Swinburn, Rowland 60
Switzerland xxi
Sydnor, Richard 7
Symons, John 329, 332
Syon 23, 24, 195
Syston, Leicestershire 66

Talbot, Robert 145
Tapper, Ruard 145
Taylor, James 63
Taylor, John, bishop of Lincoln 34, 35, 40, 43
Taylor, Rowland 66, 142, 297
Taylor, William 75
Tedman, Thomas 139
Tenterden, Kent 311, 314, 329
Terenziano, Guilio 62
Tertullian 272
Theatines xxii, 46
'Theatre of faith' 310
Theddlethorpes 168
Theological training 3
Theology, Pauline 181
　patristic 247
　scholastic 210
Thirlby, Thomas, bishop of Ely 35, 36, 38, 39, 40, 47, 48, 69, 126, 130
Thomism xxi
Thornbury, Herefordshire 7
Thornden, Richard, bishop of Dover 168, 321, 322, 324, 331
Thornton 169
Toftes, Margaret 314
Toftes family 314, 317
Toledo, Archbishop of 178, 183, 203, 224; *see also* Carranza

Tomlinson 71
Torquemada, Tomas 204
Torreleguna 204
Torres, Bartolome 201
Tremayne, Richard 63
Tremelius, John Immanuel 62
Tresham, Sir Thomas 188
Tresham, Dr William 65, 75
Trinity, doctrine of 312
Tunstall, Cuthbert, bishop of Durham 34, 35, 39, 40, 48, 49, 50, 53, 54, 246, 289
Turberville, James, bishop of Exeter 45, 46
Turner, Richard 314
Turner, William 251
Twysden, Thomas 89, 90
Tyndale, William 273

Udall, Nicholas 13
Ulborne 122
Ulmis, John ab 61
Universities xvi, xxi, 57
   Alcala de Henares 204, 215
   Baeza 216
   Cambridge 3, 57, 58, 62, 207, 209
      Gonville and Caius College 72, 88
      King's College 71
      St John's College 259, 323
      Trinity College 25, 67, 71, 88
   legatine visitations 73
   Oxford 3, 25, 57, 58, 62, 67, 207, 209, 210
      Chair of Hebrew 210
      Christ Church 65, 69
      Corpus Christi 65, 75
      Durham College 72
      Magdalen 65, 210
      St John's College 72
      Trinity College 72
   Padua 72
   Salamanca 215
Uplyme, Dorset 170
Urban V, Pope 166
Utterby, Lincolnshire 169

Valdes, Fernando de 201, 204, 218
   index 216
Valensem, Peter 127

Valladolid 204
   San Gregorio 208
Valtanas, Diego de 215, 216
Venaeus, John 241, 246, 249, 250
Vermigli, Peter Martyr 49, 59, 60, 62, 64, 178
   wife 70, 211
Veysey, John, bishop of Exeter 33, 35, 39, 40, 45, 48
Vigilantius 134
Villagarcia (Garcina) Juan de xx, 69, 73, 201, 202, 205, 208, 209, 210, 211
Visitation, process of 184
Vives, Juan Luis 5, 6, 7, 19
   De Institutione Foeminae Christianae 5
Vowell, William 122

Wade, Christopher 310, 318, 319, 320, 324
Waldburg, Otto Truches von 163
Wallington, Nehemiah 290
Warham, William, Archbishop of Canterbury 313
Warwick, John Dudley, Earl of 292
Watson, Thomas, bishop of Lincoln xvi, xvii, 47, 48, 49, 50, 54, 64, 65, 66, 71, 125, 127, 130, 131, 132, 139, 142, 144, 182, 239, 244, 246, 250, 258, 261, 263, 264, 265, 266, 267, 268, 269, 270, 271, 272, 273, 274, 275, 276, 278, 279, 280
   Aetiologia Roberti Watson 124, 132
   A Bouclier of the Catholike Fayth 244
   A Holsome and Catholyke doctrine 258, 259, 260, 261, 263, 264, 267, 270, 274, 275, 278, 280
   Catechetical and polemical writings xvii
   Twoo sermons 259, 260, 264, 278, 280
Wattes, Peter 126, 129, 134, 142
Wattes, Thomas 63
Wayte, Richard 86, 123
Weald, of Kent 311
Webbe, John 325, 326, 332

Wentworth, Lord 95
Westgate, Canterbury 322
Westminster Abbey xxii, 21, 23, 24, 77, 78, 79, 101, 104, 188, 205, 288
   abbot of 297
   accounts 92
   franchise 102
   leases 93
   The names of the brethren 83
   patent of endowment 82, 102
   pensions to Chapter 92
   sanctuary 83, 102
   titles to orders 88
Westminster cathedral 103
   Dean and Chapter 103
Westminster, diocese 95, 104, 205
   St Margaret's Church 208
Weston, Hugh 65
White, John 42, 49, 66, 88
White, Sir Thomas 72
White, Thomas 123, 190
Whitehall 187, 188
Whittingham, William 61, 63
'Whore of Babylon' 319
Wiburne, Percival 63
Wilkes, Richard 64
Williams, John, Lord of Thame 68, 69
Williams, John 172, 173, 174
Willoughby, Margaret 129
Wilson, Thomas 63
Wincheap, Canterbury 310
Winchester, diocese 152, 154, 206
Winterton 126, 130

Wisbech prison 259
Wollman, Richard 9
Wolman, Thomas 136, 138
Wolsey, Thomas, Cardinal Archbishop of York 8, 38, 58, 72, 163, 294
   Legatine Court 8, 9
Woodhouse, Sir William 143
Wooster 123
Worcester, diocese 152, 154
Word, the 5, 181
Works, good 270
Wright, Dr 70, 74
Wriothesley, Charles 82, 247
   Chronicle 234
Wriothesley, Sir Thomas 13, 286
Writer, a 294
Wyatt, Sir Thomas xv, 25, 67
   rebellion xix, 129, 304
Wycliffe, John 6
Wymondham, Norfolk 135

Xenophobia 306

York, diocese 70, 150, 152, 154, 156, 157, 159, 163
   Court of Appeal 160
York, Exchequer 155
Yorkshire 294, 295
   South East 284, 285
Young, Dr John 61, 64, 65, 75, 132

Zurich 74
   English church 64
Zwingli, Ulrich 68